*Major Problems*
*in the History*
*of American Workers*

*MAJOR PROBLEMS IN AMERICAN HISTORY SERIES*

GENERAL EDITOR

THOMAS G. PATERSON

# *Major Problems in the History of American Workers*

DOCUMENTS AND ESSAYS

SECOND EDITION

EDITED BY
## EILEEN BORIS
UNIVERSITY OF CALIFORNIA, SANTA BARBARA

## NELSON LICHTENSTEIN
UNIVERSITY OF CALIFORNIA, SANTA BARBARA

HOUGHTON MIFFLIN COMPANY
Boston     New York

*To Daniel*

Editor in Chief: Jean L. Woy
Senior Associate Editor: Frances Gay
Project Editor: Jane Lee
Editorial Assistant: Talia Kingsbury
Associate Production/Design Coordinator: Christine Gervais
Senior Manufacturing Coordinator: Priscilla Bailey
Senior Marketing Manager: Sandra McGuire

Cover image: San Francisco Mural by Diego Rivera, courtesy of City College of San Francisco.

Printed in the U.S.A.

Library of Congress Control Number: 00-133896

ISBN: 0-618-04254-7

123456789-CRS-06 05 04 03 02

# Contents

# C H A P T E R   4
## *Slavery and the Transition to Free Labor*
### *Page 90*

# C H A P T E R   5
## *The Age of Industrial Conflict*
### *Page 124*

C H A P T E R   6
*From Peasant to Proletarian*
Page 163

C H A P T E R   7
*Cultures of the Workplace*
Page 200

P H O T O G R A P H   E S S A Y
*Americans at Work in the Industrial Era*
Page 237

C H A P T E R   8
*Labor in the Progressive Era*
Page 248

C H A P T E R   9
*Industrial Unionism During the Great Depression*
Page 282

C H A P T E R   1 5
*New Labor, New Century*
Page 521

A P P E N D I X
*American Labor: A Statistical Portrait*
Page 560

# Preface

When the first edition of *Major Problems in the History of American Workers* appeared in 1991 scholars and students made a sharp distinction between the study of the working class and the fate of organized labor in the United States. The latter seemed a rather dull subject at the start of the 1990s. Although the history of strikes, organizing, and unionism had once been full of drama and excitement, the cautious and conservative leadership of most American unions seemed to have made all that ancient history.

But much has changed in the last dozen years. A new generation of energetic labor leaders are attempting to revitalize trade unions and recast the American labor movement, making it the voice of a new working class that is far more immigrant, female, and multiracial than that of just a few years before. In this process, the new labor movement is reaching out to students, intellectuals, and immigrant organizations. Thousands of young people at hundreds of colleges have gained first-hand experience working with the unions and with the living wage and anti-sweatshop campaigns that have flourished in the new century. In the process they have discovered that universities and colleges are also contested workplaces.

This new edition of *Major Problems in the History of American Workers* reflects this excitement, as well as the ever-changing character of labor scholarship. We have added dozens of new documents and essays and completely recast almost every chapter. These changes will enable students and their teachers to discuss the social and cultural meaning of low-wage work in Chapter 1, to debate the impact of working-class "whiteness" on the fate of the nineteenth-century labor movement in Chapter 3, and to explore the differential impact of the state on male craftsmen and female operatives in Chapter 8. In the twentieth-century chapters, new essays and documents enable students to discuss the impact of the civil rights movement on American workers in Chapters 10 and 12, to chart the growth of white collar and public employee unionism in Chapter 12, to see the way in which gender identities shape the labor impulse in Chapters 7 and 13, to explore the meaning of globalization in Chapter 14, and to debate the strategic choices confronting the new leadership of the labor movement in Chapter 15.

New selections include classic essays by Howard Lamar and David Roediger and engaging journalism by Barbara Ehrenreich, Harvey Swados, Harold Myerson, and Kim Moody. There are also new pieces by labor studies educators James Green, Dorothy Sue Cobble, Joshua Freeman and Gordon Lafer; feminists Nan Enstad, Alice Kessler-Harris, Eileen Boris, and Grace Chang; and activist scholars Jeremy Brecher, Joseph A. McCartin, Ellen Schrecker, Majorie Murphy, Michael Honey, Andrew Ross, and Robin D.G. Kelley. Also new to this edition are thirty-seven documents, ranging from descriptions of household production in early California and the night shift in 1970s New Jersey to Woodrow Wilson on industrial democracy,

Betty Friedan on trade union feminism, and John Sweeney on labor's future. The voices of emancipated African American washerwomen, Memphis sanitation men, Thai immigrant sweatshop sewers, Los Angeles janitors, and Harvard clerical employees are present as well.

Indeed, the history of labor and the life experience of working Americans stand close to what many scholars think of as the central issues that have shaped the United States. What we usually consider the traditional subject matter of American history—politics and elections, business innovation and trade, diplomacy and war, and slavery and conquest—can no longer be investigated without reference to the popular moods and shifting class relations of the workplace and working-class neighborhood. Thus our understanding of the colonial economy, the American Revolution, the Civil War and Reconstruction, the rise of the railroads and the birth of the automobile industry, and the changing fortunes of the political parties and their leading politicians, not to mention the civil rights movement and the great surges of immigration that have periodically reshaped the American social landscape, have all been enriched, and in some cases transformed, by the last few decades of labor history scholarship.

This renaissance in the study of the history of American workers has been accompanied by a vast redefinition and elaboration of the subject. Today one cannot study the history of labor without exploring the changing structure of the family, the character of race relations, the history of American culture and social ideas, the technology of work, the organization of business enterprise, and the legal and political history of reform and reaction. In short, the lines dividing labor history from the general study of U.S. society and politics are fading.

In this book of readings, we have selected documents and essays exemplifying an expanded sense of what constitutes a history of the American working class. We include accounts of strikes, trade unions, and collective bargaining, but also studies of rural farm life, women's work culture, slavery, emancipation, management theory, and labor law. The chapters are arranged in a general chronological order, but we have tried to offer documents throughout the text that demonstrate the way in which particular themes flow from one generation to the next. Labor history is a contentious field, and the documents and readings in this anthology, like those that appear in other volumes in the *Major Problems in American History* series, are intended to introduce students to a broad range of arguments and interpretations.

Each chapter in this collection opens with a brief introduction to its topic followed by a selection of relevant documents and essays by experts in the field. The documents offer authentic voices from each era, sometimes descriptive and sometimes engaged in passionate debate. Historical documents can yield different meanings, depending on the politics and interpretative framework of the historian who reads and evaluates them. The essays sometimes reveal a set of counterpoised viewpoints; in other cases we have chosen selections to demonstrate how historians and other scholars complement each other's work to build a rounded sense of the past. Headnotes, setting the readings in historical and interpretive perspective, introduce each chapter's documents and essays sections. For those who wish to explore topics in more depth, a list of books and articles for further reading appears at the end of each chapter. A photographic essay portraying Americans at work and an appendix of labor statistics are also featured.

For this second edition we would like to thank the following reviewers who provided detailed and constructive written comments: Eric Arnesen, University of Illinois at Chicago; Joshua B. Freeman, Queens College, City University of New York; Julie Greene, University of Colorado, Boulder; Meg Jacobs, Massachusetts Institute of Technology; Jennifer Klein, Yale University; David A. Zonderman, North Carolina State University.

We would also like to thank Floyd Cheung, Jennifer Klein, Leslie Rowland, and Laurel Thatcher Ulrich for their aid in identifying documents and Brooke Patricia Weddle for research assistance. Steve Babson, Pete Daniels, Thomas Featherstone, Barbara Pepper, Harry Rubinstein, and Jim West assisted us in preparing the photographic section, and April Haynes helped update the statistical portrait. Finally, we are grateful to Thomas G. Paterson, general editor of the Major Problems in American History series, who got us started and helped us shape the volume; to Houghton Mifflin editor-in-chief Jean Woy and development editor Fran Gay, who nurtured the second edition of this work; and to production editor Jane Lee and permissions editor Shirley Webster.

E. B
N.L.

CHAPTER

1

# *The Meaning of Work*
# *and the History of Labor*

*What constitutes the history of American workers? To answer this question is to
confront a series of intensively political choices about how a society functions, who
is powerful and powerless, and what are the hopes and aspirations of ordinary
people. The very notion that we might gain insight from studying the history of
labor implies that workers and their employers may not have identical interests
and that class is a category of analysis that remains exceptionally potent. These
ideas seem to contradict much of the dominant American ethos. Moreover, most
labor historians believe that there is something unique and important about how
people act in the workplace and what they think about their everyday work. They
believe that the hours spent at labor—whether in the home, the field, the office, the
factory, or behind a counter—somehow shape people in a way uniquely different
from, but not unrelated to, the ways in which their gender, region, religion, family
status, and ethnic and racial background do. Obviously, these are contentious
propositions, far too important to be left to historians alone. Today the study of
American workers is a subject to which sociologists, economists, political scientists,
journalists, and novelists turn their special talents and unique perspectives.*

## ⚓ *ESSAYS*

The following essays are meditations on the meaning of work, offered by two of
America's most imaginative writers, who chose to immerse themselves, if only briefly,
in the world of routine employment. The author of the first essay, Harvey Swados, who
died in 1971, was a novelist and short story writer. He grew up in the Great Depression,
took part in some of the radical union struggles of the 1930s and 1940s, and then set
out to write the great American novel. But he ran out of money, so in 1956 and 1957 he
spent almost a year working on a Ford assembly line. Afterwards he wrote "The Myth
of the Happy Worker." Although published almost fifty years ago, Swados's essay
raises questions about class and work that remain unresolved and controversial. Why
do Americans find the idea of class such an uncomfortable subject? Does the working
class vanish when its members live lives otherwise indistinguishable from that of their

1

middle-class neighbors? Are occupations once considered middle class, like those of teachers and physicians, becoming proletarianized?

Barbara Ehrenreich, author of the second essay, grew up a generation after Swados. Although trained as a biologist, her formative political experiences were the sixties and the feminist renaissance that followed. In her contemporary essay "Nickel-and-Dimed," she explores a work-a-day world that was almost invisible when Swados made the plight of the male factory worker the focus of his moral imagination. In contrast, Ehrenreich puts women service workers—such as hotel maids and restaurant waitresses—at the heart of America's new working class. And whereas Swados assumed that productivity and prosperity were boosting working-class living standards, Ehrenreich pays scrupulous attention to the minimum wage pay that makes life so unpredictable for these women.

Why is service work so pervasive in twenty-first-century America? What are the differences, if any, between factory work and service work? Does unionization offer much hope for liberation, or should people place their faith in the passage of laws against racial and gender discrimination? What do these two essays say about what historians of labor should properly study?

## The Myth of the Happy Worker

### HARVEY SWADOS

*"From where we sit in the company," says one of the best personnel men in the country, "we have to look at only the aspects of work that cut across all sorts of jobs—administration and human relations. Now these are aspects of work, abstractions, but it's easy for personnel people to get so hipped on their importance that they look on the specific tasks of making things and selling them as secondary. . . ."*

—THE ORGANIZATION MAN
WILLIAM H. WHYTE JR.

The personnel man who made this remark to Mr. Whyte differed from his brothers only in that he had a moment of insight. Actually, "the specific tasks of making things" are now not only regarded by his white-collar fellows as "secondary," but as irrelevant to the vaguer but more "challenging" tasks of the man at the desk. This is true not just of the personnel man, who places workers, replaces them, displaces them—in brief, manipulates them. The union leader also, who represents workers and sometimes manipulates them, seems increasingly to regard what his worker do as merely subsidiary to the job he himself is doing in the larger community. This job may be building the Red Cross or the Community Chest, or it may sometimes be— as [recent] Senate hearings suggest—participating in such communal endeavors as gambling, prostitution and improving the breed. In any case, the impression is left that the problems of the workers in the background (or underground) have been stabilized, if not permanently solved.

With the personnel man and the union leader, both of whom presumably see the worker from day to day, growing so far away from him, it is hardly to be wondered at that the middle-class in general, and articulate middle-class intellectuals in particular, see the worker vaguely, as through a cloud. One gets the impression that

From Harvey Swados, *On the Line* (Urbana: University of Illinois Press, 1990), pp. 235–247. "The Myth of the Happy Worker." This essay first appeared in *The Nation,* August 17, 1957. Reprinted with permission from the August 17, 1957 issue of *The Nation.*

when they do consider him, they operate from one of two unspoken assumptions: (1) The worker has died out like the passenger pigeon, or is dying out, or becoming accultured, like the Navajo; (2) If he *is* still around he is just like the rest of us—fat, satisfied, smug, a little restless, but hardly distinguishable from his fellow TV-viewers of the middle-class.

Lest it be thought that (1) is somewhat exaggerated, I hasten to quote from a recently-published article apparently dedicated to the laudable task of urging sloth-ful middle-class intellectuals to wake up and live: "The old-style sweatshop crippled mainly the working people. Now there are no workers left in America; we are almost all middle-class as to income and expectations." I do not believe the writer meant to state—although he comes perilously close to it—that nobody works anymore. If I understand him correctly, he is referring to the fact that the worker's rise in real income over the last decade, plus the diffusion of middle-class tastes and values throughout a large part of the underlying population, has made it increasingly diffi-cult to tell blue-collar from white-collar worker without a program. In short, if the worker earns like the middle-class, votes like the the middle-class, dresses like the middle-class, dreams like the middle-class, then he ceases to exist as a worker.

But there is one thing that the worker doesn't do like the middle-class: he works like a worker. The steel-mill puddler does not yet sort memos, the coal miner does not yet sit in conferences, the cotton millhand does not yet sip martinis from his lunchbox. The worker's attitude toward his work is generally compounded of hatred, shame and resignation.

Before I spell out what I think this means, I should like first to examine some of the implications of the widely-held belief that "we are almost all middle-class as to income and expectations." I am neither economist, sociologist nor politician, and I hold in my hand no doctored statistics to be haggled over. I am by profession a writer who has had occasion to work in factories at various times during the Thirties, Forties and Fifties. The following observations are simply impressions based on my last period of factory servitude, in 1956.

The average automobile worker gets a little better than two dollars an hour. As such he is one of the best-paid factory workers in the country. After twenty years of militant struggle led by the union that I believe to be still the finest and most democratic labor organization in the United States, he is earning less than the starting salaries offered to inexperienced and often semi-literate college grad-uates without dependents. After compulsory deductions for taxes, social security, old-age insurance and union dues, and optional deductions for hospitalization and assorted charities, his paycheck for forty hours of work is going to be closer to seventy than to eighty dollars a week. Does this make him middle-class as to in-come? Does it rate with the weekly take of a dentist, an accountant, a salesman, a draftsman, a journalist? Surely it would be more to the point to ask how a family man can get by in the Fifties on that kind of income. I know how he does it, and I should think the answers would be a little disconcerting to those who wax glib on the satisfactory status of the "formerly" underprivileged.

For one thing, he works a lot longer than forty hours a week—when he can. Since no automobile company is as yet in a position to guarantee its workers any-thing like fifty weeks of steady forty-hour paychecks, the auto worker knows he has to make it while he can. During peak production periods he therefore puts in nine, ten, eleven and often twelve hours a day on the assembly line for weeks on end. And that's not all. If he has dependents, as like as not he also holds down a "spare time" job. I have worked on the line with men who doubled as mechanics, repair-men, salesmen, contractors, builders, farmers, cab-drivers, lumberyard workers, countermen. I would guess that there are many more of these than show up in the official statistics: often a man will work for less if he can be paid under the counter with tax-free dollars.

Nor is that all. The factory worker with dependents cannot carry the debt load he now shoulders—the middle-class debt load, if you like, of nagging payments on car, washer, dryer, TV, clothing, house itself—without family help. Even if he puts in fifty, sixty or seventy hours a week at one or two jobs, he has to count on his wife's paycheck, or his son's, his daughter's, his brother-in-law's; or on his mother's social security, or his father's veteran's pension. The working-class family today is not typically held together by the male wage-earner, but by multiple wage-earners often of several generations who club together to get the things they want and need—or are pressured into believing they must have. It is at best a precarious arrangement; as for its toll on the physical organism and the psyche, that is a ques-tion perhaps worthy of further investigation by those who currently pronounce themselves bored with Utopia Unlimited in the Fat Fifties.

But what of the worker's middle-class expectations? I had been under the im-pression that this was the rock on which Socialist agitation had foundered for generations: it proved useless to tell the proletarian that he had a world to win when he was reasonably certain that with a few breaks he could have his own gas station. If these expectations have changed at all in recent years, they would seem to have narrowed rather than expanded, leaving a psychological increment of resig-nation rather than of unbounded optimism (except among the very young—and even among them the optimism focuses more often on better-paying opportunities elsewhere in the labor market than on illusory hopes of swift status advancement). The worker's expectations are for better pay, more humane working conditions, more job security. As long as he feels that he is going to achieve them through an extension of existing conditions, for that long he is going to continue to be a middle-class conservative in temper. But only for that long.

I suspect that what middle-class writers mean by the worker's middle-class expectations are his cravings for commodities—his determination to have not only fin-tailed cars and single-unit washer-dryers, but butterfly chairs in the rumpus room, African masks on the wall and power boats in the garage. Before the middle-class intellectuals condemn these expectations too harshly, let them consider, first, who has been utilizing every known technique of suasion and propaganda to con-vert luxuries into necessities, and second, at what cost these new necessities are acquired by the American working-class family.

Now I should like to return to the second image of the American worker: satis-fied, doped by TV, essentially middle-class in outlook. This is an image bred not of communication with workers (except as mediated by hired interviewers sent "into the field" like anthropologists or entomologists), but of contempt for people, based perhaps on self-contempt and on a feeling among intellectuals that the worker has let them down. In order to see this clearly, we have to place it against the intellec-tual's changing attitudes toward the worker since the Thirties.

At the time of the organization of the C.I.O. [Congress of Industrial Organizations], the middle-class intellectual saw the proletarian as society's figure of virtue—heroic, magnanimous, bearing in his loins the seeds of a better future; he would have found ludicrous the suggestion that a sit-down striker might harbor anti-Semitic feelings. After Pearl Harbor, the glamorization of the worker was taken over as a function of government. Then, however, he was no longer the builder of the future good society; instead he was second only to the fighting man as the vital winner of the war. Many intellectuals, as government employees, found themselves helping to create this new portrait of the worker as patriot.

But in the decade following the war intellectuals have discovered that workers are no longer either building socialism or forging the tools of victory. All they are doing is making the things that other people buy. That, and participating in the great commodity scramble. The disillusionment, it would seem, is almost too terrible to bear. Word has gotten around among the highbrows that the worker is not heroic or idealistic; public-opinion polls prove that he wants barbecue pits more than foreign aid and air-conditioning more than desegregation, that he doesn't particularly want to go on strike, that he is reluctant to form a Labor Party, that he votes for Stevenson and often even for Eisenhower and Nixon—that he is, in short, animated by the same aspirations as drive the middle-class onward and upward in suburbia.

There is of course a certain admixture of self-delusion in the middle-class attitude that workers are now the same as everybody else. For me it was expressed most precisely last year in the dismay and sympathy with which middle-class friends greeted the news that I had gone back to work in a factory. If workers are now full-fledged members of the middle-class, why the dismay? What difference whether one sits in an office or stands in a shop? The answer is so obvious that one feels shame at laboring the point. But I have news for my friends among the intellectuals. The answer is obvious to workers, too.

They know that there is a difference between working with your back and working with your behind (I do not make the distinction between hand-work and brain-work, since we are all learning that white-collar work is becoming less and less brain-work). They know that they work harder than the middle-class for less money. Nor is it simply a question of status, that magic word so dear to the hearts of the sociologues, the new anatomizers of the American corpus. It is not simply status-hunger that makes a man hate work which pays *less* than other work he knows about, if *more* than any other work he has been trained for (the only reason my fellow-workers stayed on the assembly line, they told me again and again). It is not simply status-hunger that makes a man hate work that is mindless, endless, stupefying, sweaty, filthy, noisy, exhausting, insecure in its prospects and practically without hope of advancement.

The plain truth is that factory work is degrading. It is degrading to any man who ever dreams of doing something worthwhile with his life; and it is about time we faced the fact. The more a man is exposed to middle-class values, the more sophisticated he becomes and the more production-line work is degrading to him. The immigrant who slaved in the poorly-lighted, foul, vermin-ridden sweatshop found his work less degrading than the native-born high school graduate who reads Judge Parker, Rex Morgan, M.D., and Judd Saxon, Business Executive, in the funnies, and works in a fluorescent factory with ticker-tape production-control machines. For the immigrant laborer, even the one who did not dream of socialism, his long hours were going to buy him freedom. For the factory worker of the Fifties, his long hours are going to buy him commodities . . . and maybe reduce a few of his debts.

Almost without exception, the men with whom I worked on the assembly line last year felt like trapped animals. Depending on their age and personal circumstances, they were either resigned to their fate, furiously angry at *themselves* for what they were doing, or desperately hunting other work that would pay as well and in addition offer some variety, some prospect of change and betterment. They were sick of being pushed around by harried foremen (themselves more pitied than hated), sick of working like blinkered donkeys, sick of being dependent for their livelihood on a maniacal production-merchandising setup, sick of working in a place where there was no spot to relax during the twelve-minute rest period. (Someday—let us hope—we will marvel that production was still so worshipped in the Fifties that new factories could be built with every splendid facility for the storage and movement of essential parts, but with no place for a resting worker to sit down for a moment but on a fire plug, the edge of a packing case, or the sputum- and oil-stained stairway of a toilet.)

The older men stay put and wait for their vacations. But since the assembly line demands young blood (you will have a hard time getting hired if you are over thirty-five), the factory in which I worked was aswarm with new faces every day; labor turnover was so fantastic and absenteeism so rampant, with the young men knocking off a day of two every week to hunt up other jobs, that the company was forced to over-hire in order to have sufficient workers on hand at the starting siren.

To those who will object—fortified by their readings in C. Wright Mills and A. C. Spectorsky—that the white-collar commuter, too, dislikes his work, accepts it only because it buys his family commodities, and is constantly on the prowl for other work, I can only reply that for me at any rate this is proof not of the disappearance of the working-class but of the proletarianization of the middle-class. Perhaps it is not taking place quite in the way that Marx envisaged it, but the alienation of the white-collar man (like that of the laborer) from both his tools and whatever he produces, the slavery that chains the exurbanite to the commuting timetable (as the worker is still chained to the time-clock), the anxiety that sends the white-collar man home with his briefcase for an evening's work (as it degrades the workingman into pleading for long hours of overtime), the displacement of the white-collar slum from the wrong side of the tracks to the suburbs (just as the working-class slum is moved from old-law tenements to skyscraper barracks)—all these mean to me that the white-collar man is entering (though his arms may be loaded with commodities) the grey world of the working man.

Three quotations from men with whom I worked may help to bring my view into focus:

Before starting work: "Come on, suckers, they say the Foundation wants to give away *more* than half a billion this year. Let's do and die for the old Foundation."

During rest period: "Ever stop to think how we crawl here bumper to bumper, and crawl home bumper to bumper, and we've got to turn out more every minute to keep our jobs, when there isn't even any room for them on the highways?"

At quitting time (this from older foremen, whose job is not only to keep things moving, but by extension to serve as company spokesmen): "You're smart to get out of here. . . . I curse the day I ever started, now I'm stuck: any man with brains that stays here ought to have his head examined. This is no place for an intelligent human being."

Such is the attitude towards the work. And towards the product? On the one hand it is admired and desired as a symbol of freedom, almost a substitute for freedom, not because the worker participated in making it, but because our whole culture is dedicated to the proposition that the automobile is both necessary and beautiful. On the other hand it is hated and despised—so much that if your new car smells bad it may be due to a banana peel crammed down its gullet and sealed up thereafter, so much so that if your dealer can't locate the rattle in your new car you might ask him to open the welds on one of those tailfins and vacuum out the nuts and bolts thrown in by workers sabotaging their own product.

Sooner or later, if we want a decent society—by which I do not mean a society glutted with commodities or one maintained in precarious equilibrium by over-buying and forced premature obsolescence—we are going to have to come face to face with problem of work. Apparently the Russians have committed themselves to the replenishment of their labor force through automatic recruitment of those intellectually incapable of keeping up with severe scholastic requirements in the public educational system. Apparently we, too, are heading in the same direction: although our economy is not directed, and although college education is as yet far from free, we seem to be operating in this capitalist economy on the totalitarian assumption that we can funnel the underprivileged, undereducated, or just plain underequipped, into the factory, where we can proceed to forget about them once we have posted the minimum fair labor standards on the factory wall.

If this is what we want, let's be honest enough to say so. If we conclude that there is nothing noble about repetitive work, but that it is nevertheless good enough for the lower orders, let's say that, too, so we will at least know where we stand. But if we cling to the belief that other men are our brothers, not just Egyptians, or Israelis, or Hungarians, but *all* men, including millions of Americans who grind their lives away on an insane treadmill, then we will have to start thinking about how their work and their lives can be made meaningful. That is what I assume the Hungarians, both workers and intellectuals, have been thinking about [during their revolt against the Soviets in 1956]. Since no one has been ordering us what to think, since no one has been forbidding our intellectuals to fraternize with our workers, shouldn't it be a little easier for us to admit, first, that our problems exist, then to state them, and then to see if we can resolve them?

## Working Poor Blues

### BARBARA EHRENREICH

At the beginning of June 1998 I leave behind everything that normally soothes the ego and sustains the body—home, career, companion, reputation, ATM card—for a plunge into the low-wage workforce. There, I become another, occupationally much diminished "Barbara Ehrenreich"—depicted on job-application forms as a divorced homemaker whose sole work experience consists of housekeeping in a few private homes. I am terrified, at the beginning, of being unmasked for what I am: a middle-class journalist setting out to explore the world that welfare mothers are entering, at the rate of approximately 50,000 a month, as welfare reform kicks in. Happily, though, my fears turn out to be entirely unwarranted: during a month of poverty and toil, my name goes unnoticed and for the most part unuttered. In this parallel universe where my father never got out of the mines and I never got through college, I am "baby," "honey," "blondie," and, most commonly, "girl." . . .

On the morning of my first full day of job searching, I take a red pen to the want ads, which are auspiciously numerous. Everyone in Key West's booming "hospitality industry" seems to be looking for someone like me—trainable, flexible, and with suitably humble expectations as to pay. I know I possess certain traits that might be advantageous—I'm white and, I like to think, well-spoken and poised—but I decide on two rules: One, I cannot use any skills derived from my education or usual work—not that there are a lot of want ads for satirical essayists anyway. Two, I have to take the best-paid job that is offered me and of course do my best to hold it; no Marxist rants or sneaking off to read novels in the ladies' room. In addition, I rule out various occupations for one reason or another: Hotel front-desk clerk, for example, which to my surprise is regraded as unskilled and pays around $7 an hour, gets eliminated because it involves standing in one spot for eight hours a day. Waitressing is similarly something I'd like to avoid, because I remember it leaving me bone tired when I was eighteen, and I'm decades of varicosities and back pain beyond that now. Telemarketing, one of the first refuges of the suddenly indigent, can be dismissed on grounds of personality. This leaves certain supermarket jobs, such as deli clerk, or housekeeping in Key West's thousands of hotel and guest rooms. Housekeeping is especially appealing, for reasons both atavistic and practical: it's what my mother did before I came along, and it can't be too different from what I've been doing part-time, in my own home, all my life.

So I put on what I take to be a respectful-looking outfit of ironed Bermuda shorts and scooped-neck T-shirt and set out for a tour of the local hotels and supermarkets. Best Western, Econo Lodge, and HoJo's all let me fill out application forms, and these are, to my relief, interested in little more than whether I am a legal resident of the United States and have committed any felonies. My next stop is Winn-Dixie, the supermarket, which turns out to have a particularly onerous application process, featuring a fifteen-minute "interview" by computer since, apparently, no human on the premises is deemed capable of representing the corporate point of view. I am conducted to a large room decorated with posters illustrating how to look "professional" (it helps to be white and, if female, permed) and warning of the slick promises that union organizers might try to tempt me with. The interview is multiple choice: Do I have anything, such as child-care problems, that might make it hard for me to get to work on time? Do I think safety on the job is the responsibility of management? Then, popping up cunningly out of the blue: How many dollars' worth of stolen goods have I purchased in the last year? Would I turn in a fellow employee if I caught him stealing? Finally, "Are you an honest person?"

Apparently, I ace the interview, because I am told that all I have to do is show up in some doctor's office tomorrow for a urine test. This seems to be a fairly general rule: if you want to stack Cheerio boxes or vacuum hotel rooms in chemically fascist America, you have to be willing to squat down and pee in front of some health worker (who has no doubt had to do the same thing herself). The wages

Winn-Dixie is offering—$6 and a couple of dimes to start with—are not enough, I decide, to compensate for this indignity. . . .

Three days go by like this, and, to my chagrin, no one out of the approximately twenty places I've applied calls me for an interview. I had been vain enough to worry about coming across as too educated for the jobs I sought, but no one even seems interested in finding out how overqualified I am. Only later will I realize that the want ads are not a reliable measure of the actual jobs available at any particular time. They are . . . the employers' insurance policy against the relentless turnover of the low-wage workforce. Most of the big hotels run ads almost continually, just to build a supply of applicants to replace the current workers as they drift away or are fired, so finding a job is just a matter of being at the right place at the right time and flexible enough to take whatever is being offered that day. This finally happens to me at one of the big discount hotel chains, where I go, as usual, for housekeeping and am sent, instead, to try out as a waitress at the attached "family restaurant," a dismal spot with a counter and about thirty tables that looks out on a parking garage and features such tempting fare as "Pollish [sic] sausage and BBQ sauce" on 95-degree days. Phillip, the dapper young West Indian who introduces himself as the manager, interviews me with about as much enthusiasm as if he were a clerk processing me for Medicare, the principal questions being what shifts can I work and when can I start. I mutter something about being woefully out of practice as a waitress, but he's already on to the uniform: I'm to show up tomorrow wearing black slacks and black shoes; he'll provide the rust-colored polo shirt with HEARTHSIDE embroidered on it, though I might want to wear my own shirt to get to work, ha ha. At the word "tomorrow," something between fear and indignation rises in my chest. I want to say, "Thank you for your time, sir, but this is just an experiment, you know, not my actual life."

So begins my career at the Hearthside, I shall call it, one small profit center within a global discount hotel chain, where for two weeks I work from 2:00 till 10:00 P.M. for $2.43 an hour plus tips. In some futile bid for gentility, the management has barred employees from using the front door, so my first day I enter through the kitchen, where a red-faced man with shoulder-length blond hair is throwing frozen steaks against the wall and yelling, "Fuck this shit!" "That's just Jack," explains Gail, the wiry middle-aged waitress who is assigned to train me. "He's on the rag again"—a condition occasioned, in this instance, by the fact that the cook on the morning shift had forgotten to thaw out the steaks. For the next eight hours, I run after the agile Gail, absorbing bits of instruction along with fragments of personal tragedy. All food must be trayed, and the reason she's so tired today is that she woke up in a cold sweat thinking of her boyfriend, who killed himself recently in an upstate prison. No refills on lemonade. And the reason he was in prison is that a few DUIs caught up with him, that's all, could have happened to anyone. Carry the creamers to the table in a monkey bowl, never in your hand. And after he was gone she spent several months living in her truck, peeing in a plastic pee bottle and reading by candlelight at night, but you can't live in a truck in the summer, since you need to have the windows down, which means anything can get in, from mosquitoes on up.

At least Gail puts to rest any fears I had of appearing overqualified. From the first day on, I find that of all the things I have left behind, such as home and identity, what I miss the most is competence. Not that I have ever felt utterly competent in the writing business, in which one day's success augurs nothing at all for the next. But in my writing life, I at least have some notion of procedure: do the research, make the outline, rough out a draft, etc. As a server, though, I am beset by requests like bees: more iced tea here, ketchup over there, a to-go box for table fourteen, and where are the high chairs, anyway? Of the twenty-seven tables, up to six are usually mine at any time, though on slow afternoons or if Gail is off, I sometimes have the whole place to myself. There is the touch-screen computer-ordering system to master, which is, I suppose, meant to minimize server-cook contact, but in practice requires constant verbal fine-tuning: "That's gravy on the mashed, okay? None on the meatloaf," and so forth—while the cook scowls as if I were inventing these refinements just to torment him. Plus, something I had forgotten in the years since I was eighteen: about a third of a server's job is "side work" that's invisible to customers—sweeping, scrubbing, slicing, refilling, and restocking. If it isn't all done, every little bit of it, you're going to face the 6:00 P.M. dinner rush defenseless and probably go down in flames. I screw up dozens of times at the beginning, sustained in my shame entirely by Gail's support—"It's okay, baby, everyone does that sometime"—because, to my total surprise and despite the scientific detachment I am doing my best to maintain, I care.

The whole thing would be a lot easier if I could just skate through it as Lily Tomlin in one of her waitress skits, but I was raised by the absurd Booker T. Washingtonian precept that says: If you're going to do something, do it well. In fact, "well" isn't good enough by half. Do it better than anyone has ever done it before. Or so said my father, who must have known what he was talking about because he managed to pull himself, and us with him, up from the mile-deep copper mines of Butte to the leafy suburbs of the Northeast, ascending from boilermakers to martinis before booze beat out ambition. As in most endeavors I have encountered in my life, doing it "better than anyone" is not a reasonable goal. Still, when I wake up at 4:00 A.M. in my own cold sweat, I am not thinking about the writing deadlines I'm neglecting; I'm thinking about the table whose order I screwed up so that one of the boys didn't get his kiddie meal until the rest of the family had moved on to their Key Lime pies. That's the other powerful motivation I hadn't expected—the customers, or "patients," as I can't help thinking of them on account of the mysterious vulnerability that seems to have left them temporarily unable to feed themselves. After a few days at the Hearthside, I feel the service ethic kick in like a shot of oxytocin, the nurturance hormone. The plurality of my customers are hard-working locals—truck drivers, construction workers, even housekeepers from the attached hotel—and I want them to have the closest to a "fine dining" experience that the grubby circumstances will allow. No "you guys" for me; everyone over twelve is "sir" or "ma'am." I ply them with iced tea and coffee refills; I return, mid-meal, to inquire how everything is; I doll up their salads with chopped raw mushrooms, summer squash slices, or whatever bits of produce I can find that have survived their sojourn in the cold-storage room mold-free. . . .

Sometimes I play with the fantasy that I am a princess who, in penance for some tiny transgression, has undertaken to feed each of her subjects by hand. But the non-princesses working with me are just as indulgent, even when this means flouting management rules—concerning, for example, the number of croutons that can go on a salad (six). "Put on all you want," Gail whispers, "as long as Stu isn't looking." She dips into her own tip money to buy biscuits and gravy for an out-of-work mechanic who's used up all his money on dental surgery, inspiring me to pick up the tab for his milk and pie. Maybe the same high levels of agape can be found throughout the "hospitality industry." I remember the poster decorating one of the apartments I looked at, which said "If you seek happiness for yourself you will never find it. Only when you seek happiness for others will it come to you," or words to that effect—an odd sentiment, it seemed to me at the time, to find in the dank one-room basement apartment of a bellhop at the Best Western. At the Hearthside, we utilize whatever bits of autonomy we have to ply our customers with the illicit calories that signal our love. It is our job as servers to assemble the salads and desserts, pouring the dressing and squirting the whipped cream. We also control the number of butter patties our customers get and the amount of sour cream on their baked potatoes. So if you wonder why Americans are so obese, consider the fact that waitresses both express their humanity and earn their tips through the covert distribution of fats.

Ten days into it, this is beginning to look like a livable lifestyle. I like Gail, who is "looking at fifty" but moves so fast she can alight in one place and then another without apparently being anywhere between them. I clown around with Lionel, the teenage Haitian busboy, and catch a few fragments of conversion with Joan, the svelte fortyish hostess and militant feminist who is the only one of us who dares to tell Jack to shut the fuck up. I even warm up to Jack when, on a slow night and to make up for a particularly unwarranted attack on my abilities, or so I imagine, he tells me about his glory days as a young man at "coronary school"—or do you say "culinary"?—in Brooklyn, where he dated a knock-out Puerto Rican chick and learned everything there is to know about food. I finish up at 10:00 or 10:30, depending on how much side work I've been able to get done during the shift, and cruise home to the tapes I snatched up at random when I left my real home—Marianne Faithfull, Tracy Chapman, Enigma, King Sunny Ade, the Violent Femmes—just drained enough for the music to set my cranium resonating but hardly dead. Midnight snack is Wheat Thins and Monterey Jack, accompanied by cheap white wine on ice and whatever AMC has to offer. To bed by 1:30 or 2:00, up at 9:00 or 10:00, read for an hour while my uniform whirls around in the landlord's washing machine, and then it's another eight hours spent following Mao's central instruction, as laid out in the Little Red Book, which was: Serve the people.

I could drift along like this, in some dreamy proletarian idyll, except for two things. One is management. If I have kept this subject on the margins thus far it is because I still flinch to think that I spent all those weeks under the surveillance of men (and later women) whose job it was to monitor my behavior for signs of sloth, theft, drug abuse, or worse. Not that managers and especially "assistant managers" in low-wage settings like this are exactly the class enemy. In the restaurant business, they are mostly former cooks or servers, still capable of pinch-hitting in the kitchen or on the floor, just as in hotels they are likely to be former clerks, and paid a salary of only about $400 a week. But everyone knows they have crossed over to the other side, which is, crudely put, corporate as opposed to human. Cooks want to prepare tasty meals; servers want to serve them graciously; but managers are there for only one reason—to make sure that money is made for some theoretical entity that exists far away in Chicago or New York, if a corporation can be said to have a physical existence at all. Reflecting on her career, Gail tells me ruefully that she had sworn, years ago, never to work for a corporation again. "They don't cut you no slack. You give and you give, and they take."

Managers can sit—for hours at a time if they want—but it's their job to see that no one else ever does, even when there's nothing to do, and this is why, for servers, slow times can be as exhausting as rushes. You start dragging out each little chore, because if the manager on duty catches you in an idle moment, he will give you something far nastier to do. So I wipe, I clean, I consolidate ketchup bottles and recheck the cheesecake supply, even tour the tables to make sure the customer evaluation forms are all standing perkily in their places—wondering all the time how many calories I burn in these strictly theatrical exercises. When, on a particularly dead afternoon, Stu finds me glancing at a *USA Today* a customer has left behind, he assigns me to vacuum the entire floor with the broken vacuum cleaner that has a handle only two feet long, and the only way to do that without incurring orthopedic damage is to proceed from spot to spot on your knees.

On my first Friday at the Hearthside there is a "mandatory meeting for all restaurant employees," which I attend, eager for insight into our overall marketing strategy and the niche (your basic Ohio cuisine with a tropical twist?) we aim to inhabit. But there is no "we" at this meeting. Phillip, our top manager except for an occasional "consultant" sent out by corporate headquarters, opens it with a sneer: "The break room—it's disgusting. Butts in the ashtrays, newspapers lying around, crumbs." This windowless little room, which also houses the time clock for the entire hotel, is where we stash our bags and civilian clothes and take our half-hour meal breaks. But a break room is not a right, he tells us. It can be taken away. We should also know that the lockers in the break room and whatever is in them can be searched at any time. Then comes gossip; there has been gossip; gossip (which seems to mean employees talking among themselves) must stop. Off-duty employees are henceforth barred from eating at the restaurant, because "other servers gather around them and gossip." When Phillip has exhausted his agenda of rebukes, Joan complains about the condition of the ladies' room and I throw in my two bits about the vacuum cleaner. But I don't see any backup coming from my fellow servers, each of whom has subsided into her own personal funk; Gail, my role model, stares sorrowfully at a point six inches from her nose. The meeting ends when Andy, one of the cooks, gets up, muttering about breaking up his day off for this almighty bullshit.

Just four days later we are suddenly summoned into the kitchen at 3:30 P.M., even though there are live tables on the floor. We all—about ten of us—stand around Phillip, who announces grimly that there has been a report of some "drug activity" on the night shift and that, as a result, we are now to be a "drug-free" workplace, meaning that all new hires will be tested, as will possible current employees on a random basis. I am glad that this part of the kitchen is so dark, because I find myself blushing as hard as if I had been caught toking up in the ladies' room myself: I haven't been treated this way—lined up in the corridor, threatened with locker searches, peppered with carelessly aimed accusations—since junior high school. Back on the floor, Joan cracks, "Next they'll be telling us we can't have sex on the job." When I ask Stu what happened to inspire the crackdown, he just mutters about "management decisions" and takes the opportunity to upbraid Gail and me for being too generous with the rolls. From now on there's to be only one per customer, and it goes out with the dinner, not with the salad. He's also been riding the cooks, prompting Andy to come out of the kitchen and observe—with the serenity of a man whose customary implement is a butcher knife—that "Stu has a death wish today."

Later in the evening, the gossip crystallizes around the theory that Stu is himself the drug culprit, that he uses the restaurant phone to order up marijuana and sends one of the late servers out to fetch it for him. The server was caught, and she may have ratted Stu out or at least said enough to cast some suspicion on him, thus accounting for his pissy behavior. Who knows? Lionel, the busboy, entertains us for the rest of the shift by standing just behind Stu's back and sucking deliriously on an imaginary joint.

The other problem, in addition to the less-than-nurturing management style, is that this job shows no sign of being financially viable. You might imagine, from a comfortable distance, that people who live, year in and year out, on $6 to $10 an hour have discovered some survival stratagems unknown to the middle class. But no. It's not hard to get my co-workers to talk about their living situations, because housing, in almost every case, is the principal source of disruption in their lives, the first thing they fill you in on when they arrive for their shifts. After a week, I have compiled the following survey:

• Gail is sharing a room in a well-known downtown flophouse for which she and a roommate pay about $250 a week. Her roommate, a male friend, has begun hitting on her, driving her nuts, but the rent would be impossible alone.

• Claude, the Haitian cook, is desperate to get out of the two-room apartment he shares with his girlfriend and two other, unrelated, people. As ar as I can determine, the other Haitian men (most of whom only speak Creole) live in similarly crowed situations.

• Annette, a twenty-year-old server who is six months pregnant and has been abandoned by her boyfriend, lives with her mother, a postal clerk.

• Marianne and her boyfriend are paying $170 a week for a one-person trailer.

• Jack, who is, at $10 an hour, the wealthiest of us, lives in the trailer he owns, paying only the $400-a month lot fee.

• The other white cook, Andy, lives on his dry-docked boat, which, as far as I can tell from his loving descriptions, can't be more than twenty feet long. He offers to take me out on it, once it's repaired, but the offer comes with inquiries as to my marital status, so I do not follow up on it.

• Tina and her husband are paying $60 a night for a double room in a Days Inn. This is because they have no car and the Days Inn is within walking distance of the Hearthside. When Marianne, one of the breakfast servers, is tossed out of her trailer for subletting (which is against the trailer-park rules), she leaves her boyfriend and moves in with Tina and her husband.

• Joan, who had fooled me with her numerous and tasteful outfits (hostesses wear their own clothes), lives in a van she parks behind a shopping center at night and showers in Tina's motel room. The clothes are from thrift shops.

It strikes me, in my middle-class solipsism, that there is gross improvidence in some of these arrangements. When Gail and I are wrapping silverware in napkins—the only task for which we are permitted to sit—she tells me she is thinking of escaping from her roommate by moving into the Days Inn herself. I am astounded: How can she even think of paying between $40 and $60 a day? But if I was afraid of sounding like a social worker, I come out just sounding like a fool. She squints at me in disbelief, "And where am I supposed to get a month's rent and a month's deposit for an apartment?" I'd been feeling pretty smug about my $500 efficiency, but of course it was made possible only by the $1,300 I had allotted myself for start-up costs when I began my low-wage life: $1,000 for the first month's rent and deposit, $100 for initial groceries and cash in my pocket, $200 stuffed away for emergencies. In poverty, as in certain propositions in physics, starting conditions are everything.

There are no secret economies that nourish the poor; on the contrary, there are a host of special costs. If you can't put up the two months' rent you need to secure an apartment, you end up paying through the nose for a room by the week. If you have only a room, with a hot plate at best, you can't save by cooking up huge lentil stews that can be frozen for the week ahead. You eat fast food, or the hot dogs and styrofoam cups of soup that can be microwaved in a convenience store. If you have no money for health insurance—and the Hearthside's niggardly plan kicks in only after three months—you go without routine care or prescription drugs and end up paying the price. Gail, for example, was fine until she ran out of money for estrogen pills. She is supposed to be on the company plan by now, but they claim to have lost her application form and need to begin the paperwork all over again. So she spends $9 per migraine pill to control the headaches she wouldn't have, she insists, if her estrogen supplements were covered. Similarly, Marianne's boyfriend lost his job as a roofer because he missed so much time after getting a cut on his foot for which he couldn't afford the prescribed antibiotic.

My own situation, when I sit down to assess it after two weeks of work, would not be much better if this were my actual life. The seductive thing about waitressing is that you don't have to wait for payday to feel a few bills in your pocket, and my tips usually cover meals and gas, plus something left over to stuff into the kitchen drawer I use as a bank. But as the tourist business slows in the summer heat, I sometimes leave work with only $20 in tips (the gross is higher, but servers share about 15 percent of their tips with the busboys and bartenders). With wages included, this amounts to about the minimum wage of $5.15 an hour. Although the sum in the drawer is piling up, at the present rate of accumulation it will be more than a hundred dollars short of my rent when the end of the month comes around. Nor can I see any expenses to cut. True, I haven't gone the lentil-stew route yet, but that's because I don't have a large cooking pot, pot holders, or a ladle to stir with (which cost about $30 at Kmart, less at thrift stores), not to mention onions, carrots, and the indispensable bay leaf. I do make my lunch almost every day—usually some slow-burning, high-protein combo like frozen chicken patties with melted cheese on top and canned pinto beans on the side. Dinner is at the Hearthside, which offers its employees a choice of BLT, fish sandwich, or hamburger for only $2. The burger lasts longest, especially if it's heaped with gut-puckering jalapeños, but by midnight my stomach is growling again.

So unless I want to start using my car as a residence, I have to find a second, or alternative, job. I call all the hotels where I filled out housekeeping applications weeks ago—the Hyatt, Holiday Inn, Econo Lodge, HoJo's, Best Western, plus a half dozen or so locally run guesthouses. Nothing. Then I start making the rounds again, wasting whole mornings waiting for some assistant manager to show up, even dipping into places so creepy that the front-desk clerk greets you from behind bulletproof glass and sells pints of liquor over the counter. But either someone has exposed my real-life housekeeping habits—which are, shall we say, mellow—or I am at the wrong end of some infallible ethnic equation: most, but by no means all, of the working housekeepers I see on my job searches are African Americans, Spanish-speaking, or immigrants from the Central European post-Communist world, whereas servers are almost invariably white and monolingually English-speaking. When I finally get a positive response, I have been identified once again as server material. Jerry's, which is part of a well-known national family restaurant chain and physically attached here to another budget hotel chain, is ready to use me at once. The prospect is both exciting and terrifying, because, with about the same number of tables and counter seats, Jerry's attracts three or four times the volume of customers as the gloomy old Hearthside.

Picture a fat person's hell, and I don't mean a place with no food. Instead there is everything you might eat if eating had no bodily consequences—cheese fries, chicken-fried steaks, fudge-laden desserts—only here every bit must be paid for, one way or another, in human discomfort. The kitchen is a cavern, a stomach leading to the lower intestine that is the garbage and dishwashing area, from which issue bizarre smells combining the edible and the offal: creamy carrion, pizza barf, and that unique and enigmatic Jerry's scent—citrus fart. The floor is slick with spills, forcing us to walk through the kitchen with tiny steps, like Susan McDougal in leg irons. Sinks everywhere are clogged with scraps of lettuce, decomposing lemon wedges, waterlogged toast crusts. Put your hand down on any counter and you risk being stuck to it by the film of ancient syrup spills, and this is unfortunate, because hands are utensils here, used for scooping up lettuce onto salad plates, lifting out pie slices, and even moving hash browns from one plate to another. The regulation poster in the single unisex restroom admonishes us to wash our hands thoroughly and even offers instructions for doing so, but there is always some vital substance missing— soap, paper towels, toilet paper—and I never find all three at once. You learn to stuff your pockets with napkins before going in there, and too bad about the customers, who must eat, though they don't realize this, almost literally out of our hands.

The break room typifies the whole situation: there is none, because there are no breaks at Jerry's. For six to eight hours in a row, you never sit except to pee. Actually, there are three folding chairs at a table immediately adjacent to the bathroom, but hardly anyone ever sits here, in the very rectum of the gastro-architectural system. Rather, the function of the peritoilet area is to house the ashtrays in which servers and dishwashers leave their cigarettes burning at all times, like votive candles, so that they don't have to waste time lighting up again when they dash back for a puff. Almost everyone smokes as if his or her pulmonary well-being depended on it—the multinational mélange of cooks, the Czech dishwashers, the servers, who are all American natives—creating an atmosphere in which oxygen is only an occasional pollutant. My first morning at Jerry's, when the hypoglycemic shakes set in, I complain to one of my fellow servers that I don't understand how she can go so long without food. "Well, I don't understand how you can go so long without a cigarette," she responds in a tone of reproach—because work is what you do for others;

smoking is what you do for yourself. I don't know why the antismoking crusaders have never grasped the element of defiant self-nurturance that makes the habit so endearing to its victims—as if, in the American workplace, the only thing people have to call their own is the tumors they are nourishing and the spare moments they devote to feeding them.

Now, the Industrial Revolution is not an easy transition, especially when you have to zip through it in just a couple of days. I have gone from craft work straight into the factory, from the air-conditioned morgue of the Hearthside directly into the flames. Customers arrive in human waves, sometimes disgorged fifty at a time from their tour buses, peckish and whiny. Instead of two "girls" on the floor at once, there can be as many a six of us running around in our brilliant pink-and-orange Hawaiian shirts. Conversations, either with customers or fellow employees, seldom last more than twenty seconds at a time. On my first day, in fact, I am hurt by my sister servers' coldness. My mentor for the day is an emotionally uninflected twenty-three-year-old, and the others, who gossip a little among themselves about the real reason someone is out sick today and the size of the bail bond someone else has had to pay, ignore me completely. On my second day, I find out why. "Well, it's good to see you again," one of them says in greeting. "Hardly anyone comes back after the first day." I feel powerfully vindicated—a survivor—but it would take a long time, probably months, before I could hope to be accepted into this sorority.

I start out with the beautiful, heroic idea of handling the two jobs at once, and for two days I almost do it: the breakfast/lunch shift at Jerry's, which goes till 2:00, arriving at the Hearthside at 2:10, and attempting to hold out until 10:00. In the ten minutes between jobs, I pick up a spicy chicken sandwich at the Wendy's drive-through window, gobble it down in the car, and change from khaki slacks to black, from Hawaiian to rust polo. There is a problem, though. When during the 3:00 to 4:00 P.M. dead time I finally sit down to wrap silver, my flesh seems to bond to the seat. I try to refuel with a purloined cup of soup, as I've seen Gail and Joan do dozens of times, but a manager catches me and hisses "No eating!" though there's not a customer around to be offended by the sight of food making contact with a server's lips. So I tell Gail I'm going to quit, and she hugs me and says she might just follow me to Jerry's herself.

But the chances of this are minuscule. She has left the flophouse and her annoying roommate and is back to living in her beat-up old truck. But guess what? she reports to me excitedly later that evening: Phillip has given her permission to park overnight in the hotel parking lot, as long as she keeps out of sight, and the parking lot should be totally safe, since it's patrolled by a hotel security guard! With the Hearthside offering benefits like that, how could anyone think of leaving?

Gail would have triumphed at Jerry's, I'm sure, but for me it's a crash course in exhaustion management. Years ago, the kindly fry cook who trained me to waitress at a Los Angeles truck stop used to say: Never make an unnecessary trip; if you don't have to walk fast, walk slow; if you don't have to walk, stand. But at Jerry's the effort of distinguishing necessary from unnecessary and urgent from whenever would itself be too much of an energy drain. The only thing to do is to treat each shift as a one-time-only emergency: you've got fifty starving people out there, lying scattered on the battlefield, so get out there and feed them! Forget that you will have to do this again tomorrow, forget that you will have to be alert enough to dodge the drunks on the drive home tonight—just burn, burn, burn! Ideally, at some point you enter what servers call "a rhythm" and psychologists term a "flow state," in which signals pass from the sense organs directly to the muscles, bypassing the cerebral cortex, and a Zen-like emptiness sets in. A male server from the Hearthside's morning shift tells me about the time he "pulled a triple"—three shifts in a row, all the way around the clock—and then got off and had a drink and met this girl, and maybe he shouldn't tell me this, but they had sex right then and there, and it was like, beautiful.

But there's another capacity of the neuromuscular system, which is pain. I start tossing back drugstore-brand ibuprofen pills as if they were vitamin C, four before each shift, because an old mouse-related repetitive-stress injury in my upper back has come back to full-spasm strength, thanks to the tray carrying. In my ordinary life, this level of disability might justify a day of ice packs and stretching. Here I comfort myself with the Aleve commercial in which the cute blue-collar guy asks: If you quit after working four hours, what would your boss say? And the not-so-cute blue-collar guy, who's lugging a metal beam on his back, answers: He'd fire me, that's what. But fortunately, the commercial tells us, we workers can exert the same kind of authority over our painkillers that our bosses exert over us. If Tylenol doesn't want to work for more than four hours, you just fire its ass and switch to Aleve.

True, I take occasional breaks from this life, going home now and then to catch up on e-mail and for conjugal visits (though I am careful to "pay" for anything I eat there), seeing *The Truman Show* with friends and letting them buy my ticket. And I still have those what-am-I-doing-here moments at work, when I get so homesick for the printed word that I obsessively reread the six-page menu. But a the days go by, my old life is beginning to look exceedingly strange. The e-mails and phone messages addressed to my former self come from a distant race of people with exotic concerns and far too much time on their hands. The neighborly market I used to cruise for produce now looks forbiddingly like a Manhattan yuppie emporium. And when I sit down one morning in my real home to pay bills from my past life, I am dazzled at the two-and three-figure sums owed to outfits like club BodyTech and Amazon.com.

## ⚜ *F U R T H E R     R E A D I N G*

Amott, Teresa, and Julie Matthaei. *Race, Gender and Work: A Multi-Cultural Economic History of Women in the United States* (1996).

Arnesen, Eric, Julie Greene, and Bruce Laurie, eds. *Labor Histories: Class, Politics, and the Working Class Experience* (1998).

Asher, Robert, and Charles Stephenson, eds. *Labor Divided: Race and Ethnicity in United States Labor Struggles* (1990).

Babson, Steve. *The Unfinished Struggle: Turning Points in American Labor, 1877–Present* (1999).

Baron, Ava, ed. *Work Engendered: Toward a New History of American Labor* (1991).

Baxandall, Rosalyn, and Linda Gordon, eds. *America's Working Women: A Documentary History, 1960 to the Present,* 2nd ed. (1995).

Blackwelder, Julia Kirk. *Now Hiring: The Feminization of Work in the United States, 1900–1995* (1997).

Bowe, John, ed. *Gig: Americans Talk About Their Jobs at the Turn of the Millennium* (2000).

Braverman, Harry. *Labor and Monopoly Capitalism: The Degradation of Work in the Twentieth Century* (1974, 1998).

Buhle, Paul, and Alan Dawley, eds. *Working for Democracy: American Workers from the Revolution to the Present* (1985).

Cantor, Milton, and Bruce Laurie, eds. *Class, Sex, and the Woman Worker* (1977).

Clark, Christopher, et al. *Who Built America? Working People and the Nation's Economy, Politics, Culture, and Society,* vols. 1 and 2 (2000).

Commons, John R., et al., eds. *A History of Labor in the United States,* 4 vols. (1918–1935).

Davis, Mike. *Prisons of the American Dream* (1986).

Dubofsky, Melvyn, and Warren Van Tine, eds. *Labor Leaders in America* (1987).

Dulles, Foster Rhea, and Melvyn Dubofsky. *Labor in America* (1984).

Ehrenreich, Barbara. *Nickel and Dimed: On (Not) Getting By in America* (2001).

———. *The Snarling Citizen* (1995).

Foner, Philip. *History of the Labor Movement in the United States,* 5 vols. (1947–1983).

Freeman, Richard, and Joel Rogers. *What Workers Want* (1999).

Frisch, Michael, and Daniel Walkowitz, eds. *Working-Class America* (1983).

Gerstel, Naomi, and Harriet Engel Gross, eds. *Families and Work* (1987).

Goldin, Claudia. *Understanding the Gender Gap: An Economic History of American Women* (1990).

Gordon, Robert, Richard Edwards, and Michael Reich. *Segmented Work, Divided Workers* (1982).

Green, James. *Taking History to Heart: The Power of the Past in Building Social Movements Today* (2000).

Green, James, ed. *Worker's Struggles, Past and Present* (1983).

Groneman, Carol, and Mary Beth Norton, eds. *"To Toil the Live-Long Day": America's Women at Work* (1987).

Harris, William H. *The Harder We Run: Black Workers Since the Civil War* (1982).

Jacobson, Julius, ed. *The Negro and the American Labor Movement* (1968).

Jones, Jacqueline. *American Work: Four Centuries of Black and White Labor* (1998).

———. *A Social History of the Laboring Classes: From Colonial Times to the Present* (1999).

Kessler-Harris, Alice. *Out to Work: A History of Wage-Earning Women in the United States* (1982).

Lichtenstein, Nelson. *State of the Union: A Century of American Labor* (2002).

Murray, R. Emmett. *Lexicon of Labor: More than 500 Key Terms, Biographical Sketches, and Historical Insights Concerning Labor in America* (1998).

Perlman, Selig. *A Theory of the Labor Movement* (1928).

Sacks, Karen Brodkin, and Dorothy Remey, eds. *My Troubles Are Going to Have Trouble with Me: Everyday Trials and Triumphs of Women Workers* (1984).

Schlosser, Eric. *Fast Food Nation: The Dark Side of the All-American Meal* (2001).

Stephenson, Charles, and Robert Asher, eds. *Life and Labor* (1986).

Swados, Harvey. *On the Line* (1957, 1990).

———. *A Radical's America* (1963).

Thompson, E. P. *The Making of the English Working Class* (1963).

Vanneman, Reeve, and Lynn Weber Cannon. *The American Perception of Class* (1987).

Weiner, Lynn Y. *From Working Girl to Working Mother* (1985).

Yates, Michael. *Why Unions Matter* (1998).

Zieger, Robert. *American Workers, American Unions* (1995).

# The Labor Systems
# of Early America

When European settlers reached North American shores early in the seventeenth century, they brought along a whole set of values, customs, and laws that reflected an Old World poised halfway between its feudal past and bourgeois future. Feudalism no longer reigned in Western Europe, but almost all economic activity was heavily regulated so that it might conform to a world of hierarchy and deference. This was particularly true in the mercantile economies of Spain, the Netherlands, and France. But it also distinguished economic relations in England. For example, the Tudor Industrial Code, enacted late in the sixteenth century, mandated compulsory labor for all able-bodied persons. Those who refused to work at the rates set by local authorities were considered petty criminals and were subjected to whippings and forced labor in houses of correction.

Thus free labor in our modern sense was unknown when the English and Spanish colonists of America established their first farms, fisheries, missions, and workshops in the seventeenth century. Workers were in short supply throughout the colonies, but instead of bidding wages higher, plantation owners, merchants, missionaries, and sea captains sought to secure their laborers through various systems of coercion and servitude. In the Southwest, Franciscan friars and Spanish military authorities levied tributes and workdays on the Pueblos, while also trafficking in Indian slaves. In the Chesapeake region, a decreased supply of white servants and fear of rebellion among them led to the wholesale importation of enslaved Africans. Farther north, indentured servants, who were bound to their masters for a set term of years, became an important source of colonial labor. In Pennsylvania, nearly two-thirds of all eighteenth-century immigrants had come as such servants.

In New England, the Pilgrim and Puritan settlements were more often based on subsistence farms and the artisan's workshop. Slavery and indentured servitude were less prevalent in New England than in regions of commercial agriculture or extractive land use, like the hunting and mining economies of the Southwest. But even here production was bound up in a set of relationships that made the free exchange of goods and labor difficult.

Historians have been interested particularly in the nature of the household economy, both in New England and farther south. Were domestic-production units *largely self-sufficient, or did the sale and purchase of crops and manufactured goods shape daily life even in these early years?*

*Historians have also probed the extent to which uniquely American conditions transformed the status of labor on this continent. Did the existence of a large expanse of free land undermine traditional hierarchies? Did American abundance advance, in equal proportion, the status of indentured servants, women members of the household, Indian hunters, and the enslaved? And to what extent did the changing aspirations and beliefs of colonial workers in British North America mesh with the larger movement for independence that became so powerful in the late eighteenth century?*

## ⚓ D O C U M E N T S

Documents 1–4 reveal the conditions under which servants and slaves labored in the New World. Writing to his parents in London, an indentured servant of the Virginia Company captures in Document 1 the unrewarded toil of men struggling to survive in a land where freewheeling speculation became a hallmark of the booming tobacco economy. Document 2, lyrics sung to a popular mid-seventeenth-century tune, chronicles the tasks of female servants in Virginia. Not only were women from the British Isles responsible for the traditionally female work of cooking, sewing, and child rearing, but they were also put to the "plow and cart" to such an extent that they sometimes saw their lives little distinguished from those of enslaved Africans. Swedish botanist Peter Kalm compares different types of servitude in Document 3, which he composed during travels through the British colonies between 1741 and 1751. Finally, the African experience of enslavement finds graphic expression in Document 4, an account of the Middle Passage written by African Olaudah Equiano in 1791, twenty-six years after his childhood capture. Given this wide range of unfree labor in the American colonies, one might well ask, what conditions distinguish slavery from lesser forms of servitude?

Documents 5 and 6 offer a comparative glimpse of household labor in British New England and in early Spanish California. Document 5 humorously views the world of the New England village from the perspective of a country parson's wife who lacked a maid for domestic chores. It should be compared with Document 6, an excerpt from the memoirs of Eulalia Pérez, who recounts her housekeeping tasks at the San Gabriel mission in the early nineteenth century. How did law, culture, and regional environment shape household production in early America? Pérez relied on Indian help. Document 7, a report on the Indian village of San Diego County to the U.S. Commissioner of Indian Affairs in 1873, suggests the tension between native economies and European settlement that persisted with the transfer of California to the United States.

## 1. An Indentured Servant Writes Home, 1623

Loving and kind father and mother:

My most humble duty remembered to you, hoping in God of your good health, as I myself am at the making hereof. This is to let you understand that I your child am in a most heavy case by reason of the nature of the country, [which] is such that it causeth much sickness, [such] as the scurvy and the bloody flux and diverse

From Susan M. Kingsbury, ed., *The Records of the Virginia Company of London,* vol. 4 (Washington, D.C.: U.S. Government Printing Office 1935), 58–62.

other diseases, which maketh the body very poor and weak. And when we are sick there is nothing to comfort us; for since I came out of the ship I never ate anything but peas, and loblollie (that is, water gruel). As for deer or vension I never saw any since I came into this land. There is indeed some fowl, but we are not allowed to go and get it, but must work hard both early and late for a mess of water gruel and a mouthful of bread and beef. A mouthful of bread for a penny loaf must serve for four men which is most pitiful. [You would be grieved] if you did know as much as I [do], when people cry out day and night—Oh! that they were in England without their limbs—and would not care to lose any limb to be in England again, yea, though they beg from door to door. For we live in fear of the enemy [Powhatan Indians] every hour, yet we have had a combat with them on the Sunday before Shrovetide [Monday before Ash Wednesday], and we took two alive and made slaves of them. But it was by policy, for we are in great danger; for our plantation is very weak by reason of the death and sickness of our company. For we came but twenty for the merchants, and they are half dead just; and we look every hour when two more should go. Yet there came some four other men yet to live with us, of which there is but one alive; and our Lieutenant is dead, and [also] his father and his brother. And there was some five or six of the last year's twenty, of which there is but three left, so that we are fain to get other men to plant with us; and yet we are but 32 to fight against 3000 if they should come. And the nighest help that we have is ten miles of us, and when the rogues overcame this place [the] last [time] they slew 80 persons. How then shall we do, for we lie even in their teeth? . . .

And I have nothing to comfort me, nor there is nothing to be gotten here but sickness and death, except [in the event] that one had money to lay out in some things for profit. But I have nothing at all—no, not a shirt to my back but two rags (2), nor no clothes but one poor suit, nor but one pair of shoes, but one pair of stockings, but one cap, [and] but two bands. My cloak is stolen by one of my own fellows, and to his dying hour [he] would not tell me what he did with it; but some of my fellows saw him have butter and beef out of a ship, which my cloak, I doubt [not], paid for. So that I have not a penny, nor a penny worth, to help me to either spice or sugar or strong waters, without the which one cannot live here. For as strong beer in England doth fatten and strengthen them, so water here doth wash and weaken these here [and] only keeps [their] life and soul together. But I am not half [of] a quarter so strong as I was in England, and all is for want of victuals; for I do protest unto you that I have eaten more in [one] day at home than I have allowed me here for a week. You have given more than my day's allowance to a beggar at the door; and if Mr. Jackson had not relieved me, I should be in a poor case. But he like a father and she like a loving mother doth still help me.

For when we go up to Jamestown (that is 10 miles of us) there lie all the ships that come to land, and there they must deliver their goods. And when we went up to town [we would go], as it may be, on Monday at noon, and come there by night, [and] then load the next day by noon, and go home in the afternoon, and unload, and then away again in the night, and [we would] be up about midnight. Then if it rained or blowed never so hard, we must lie in the boat on the water and have nothing but a little bread. For when we go into the boat we [would] have a loaf allowed to two men, and it is all [we would get] if we stayed there two days, which is hard; and [we] must lie all that while in the boat. But that Goodman Jackson pitied me and made me a cabin to lie in always when I [would] come up, and he would give me some poor jacks [to take] home with me, which comforted me more than peas or water gruel. Oh, they be very godly folks, and love me very well, and will do anything for me. And he much marvelled that you would send me a servant to the Company; he saith I had been better knocked on the head. And indeed so I find it now, to my great grief and misery; and [I] saith that if you love me you will redeem me suddenly, for which I do entreat and beg. And if you cannot get the merchants to redeem me for some little money, then for God's sake get a gathering or entreat some good folks to lay out some little sum of money in meal and cheese and butter and beef. Any eating meat will yield great profit. Oil and vinegar is very good; but, father, there is great loss in leaking. But for God's sake send beef and cheese and butter, or the more of one sort and none of another. But if you send cheese, it must be very old cheese; and at the cheesemonger's you may buy very good cheese for twopence farthing or half-penny, that will be liked very well. But if you send cheese, you must have a care how you pack it in barrels; and you must put cooper's chips between every cheese, or else the heat of the hold will rot them. And look whatsoever you send me—be it never so much— look, what[ever] I make of it, I will deal truly with you. I will send it over and beg the profit to redeem me; and if I die before it come, I have entreated Good-man Jackson to send you the worth of it, who hath promised he will. If you send, you must direct your letters to Goodman Jackson, at Jamestown, a gunsmith. (You must set down his freight, because there be more of his name there.) Good father, do not forget me, but have mercy and pity my miserable case. I know if you did but see me, you would weep to see me; for I have but one suit. (But [though] it is a strange one, it is very well guarded.) Wherefore, for God's sake, pity me. I pray you to remember my love to all my friends and kindred. I hope all my brothers and sisters are in good health, and as for my part I have set down my resolution that certainly will be; that is, that the answer of this letter will be life or death to me. Therefore, good father, send a soon as you can; and if you send me any thing let this be the mark.

ROT                                                                    Richard Frethorne,
                                                                       Martin's Hundred

## 2. "The Trappan'd Maiden: Or the Distressed Damsel," (Popular Song, mid-1600s)

*This Girl was cunningly Trappan'd, sent to Virginny from England,*
    *Where she doth Hardship undergo, there is no Cure it must be so:*
*But if she lives to cross the Main, she vows she'll ne'r go there again.*

> *Tune of Virginny, or, When that I was weary, weary, O.*

> Give ear unto a Maid, that lately was betray'd,
>     And sent into Virginny, O:
> In brief I shall declare, what I have suffer'd there,
>     *When that I was weary, weary, weary, weary, O.*

---

From C. H. Firth, ed., *An American Garland, Being a Collection of Ballads to America, 1563–1764* (Oxford: B. H. Backwell, 1915), 51–53.

[Since] that first I came to this Land of Fame,
    Which is called Virginny, O,
The Axe and the Hoe have wrought my overthrow,
    *When that I was weary, weary weary, weary O.*

Five years served I, under Master Guy,
    In the land of Virginny, O,
Which made me for to know sorrow, grief and woe.
    *When that I was weary, weary, weary, weary, O.*

When my Dame says "Go" then I must do so.
    In the land of Virginny, O.
When she sits at Meat, then I have none to eat,
    *When that I am weary, weary, weary, weary, O.*

The Cloath[e]s that I brought in, they are worn very thin,
    In the land of Virginny, O,
Which makes me for to say, "Alas, and Well-a-day!"
    *When that I am weary, weary, weary, weary, O.*

Instead of Beds of Ease, to lye down when I please,
    In the Land of Virginny, O;
Upon a bed of straw, I lye down full of woe,
    *When that I am weary, weary, weary, weary, O. . . .*

So soon as it is day, to work I must away,
    In the Land of Virginny, O;
Then my Dame she knocks, with her tinder-box,
    *When that I am weary, weary, weary, weary, O. . . .*

If my Dame says "Go!" I dare not say no,
    In the Land of Virginny, O;
The Water from the Srping, upon my head I bring,
    *When that I am weary, weary, weary, O.*

When the Mill doth stand, I'm ready at command,
    In the Land of Virginny, O;
The Morter for to make, which makes my heart to ake,
    *When that I am weary, weary, weary, weary, O.*

When the Child doth cry, I must sing "By-a-by!"
    In the Land of Virginny, O;
No rest that I can have, whilst I am here a Slave,
    *When that I am weary, weary, weary, weary, O. . . .*

Then let Maids beware, all by my ill-fare,
    In the Land of Virginny, O;
Be sure to stay at home, for if you do here come,
    *You all will be weary, weary, weary, weary, O.*

> But if it be my chance, Homewards to advance,
>> From the Land of Virginny, O;
> If that I, once more, land on English Shore,
>> *I'll no more be weary, weary, weary, weary, O.*

## 3. Traveler Peter Kalm on Unfree Labor in Pennsylvania, 1753

*Servants.* The servants which are employed in the English-American colonies are either free persons or slaves, and the former, again, are of two different classes.

1. Those who are entirely free serve by the year. They are not only allowed to leave their service at the expiration of their year, but may leave it at any time when they do not agree with their masters. However, in that case they are in danger of losing their wages, which are very considerable. A man servant who has some ability gets between sixteen and twenty pounds in Pennsylvania currency, but those in the country do not get so much. A maidservant gets eight or ten pounds a year. These servants have their food besides their wages, but they must buy their own clothes, and whatever they get of these as gifts they must thank their master's generosity for.

*Indenture.* 2. The second kind of free servants consists of such persons as annually come from Germany, England and other countries, in order to settle here. These newcomers are very numerous every year: there are old and young of both sexes. Some of them have fled from oppression, under which they have labored. Others have been driven from their country by religious persecution, but most of them are poor and have not money enough to pay their passage, which is between six and eight pounds sterling for each person. Therefore, they agree with the captain that they will suffer themselves to be sold for a few years on their arrival. In that case the person who buys them pays the freight for them; but frequently very old people come over who cannot pay their passage, they therefore sell their children for several years, so that they serve both for themselves and for their parents. There are likewise some who pay part of their passage, and they are sold only for a short time. From these circumstances it appears that the price on the poor foreigners who come over to North America varies considerably, and that some of them have to serve longer than others. When their time has expired, they get a new suit of clothes from their master and some other things. He is likewise obliged to feed and clothe them during the years of their servitude. Many of the Germans who come hither bring money enough with them to pay their passage, but prefer to be sold, hoping that during their servitude they may get a knowledge of the language and character of the country and the life, that they may the better be able to consider what they shall do when they have gotten their liberty. Such servants are preferable to all others, because they are not so expensive. To buy a negro or black slave requires too much money at one time; and men or maids who get yearly wages are likewise too costly. But this kind of servant may be gotten for half the money, and even for

From Adolf B. Benson, ed., *Peter Kalm's Travels in North America*, vol. 1 (New York: Wilson-Erickson, 1937), 204–210.

less; for they commonly pay fourteen pounds, Pennsylvania currency, for a person who is to serve for years, and so on in proportion. Their wages therefore are not above three pounds Pennsylvania currency per annum. . . . When a person has bought such a servant for a certain number of years, and has an intention to sell him again, he is at liberty to do so, but is obliged, at the expiration of the term of servitude, to provide the usual suit of clothes for the servant, unless he has made that part of the bargain with the purchaser. . . .

3. The *negroes* or blacks constitute the third kind. They are in a manner slaves; for when a negro is once bought, he is the purchaser's servant as long as he lives, unless he gives him to another, or sets him free. However, it is not in the power of the master to kill his negro for a fault, but he must leave it to the magistrates to proceed according to the laws. Formerly the negroes were brought over from Africa, and bought by almost everyone who could afford it, the Quakers alone being an exception. But these are no longer so particular and now they have as many negroes as other people. However, many people cannot conquer the idea of its being contrary to the laws of Christianity to keep slaves. There are likewise several free negroes in town, who have been lucky enough to get a very zealous Quaker for their master, and who gave them their liberty after they had faithfully served him for a time.

At present they seldom bring over any negroes to the English colonies for those which were formerly brought thither have multiplied rapidly. In regard to their marriage they proceed as follows: in case you have not only male but likewise female negroes, they may intermarry, and then the children are all your slaves. But if you possess a male negro only and he has an inclination to marry a female belonging to a different master, you do not hinder your negro in so delicate a point, but it is of no advantage to you, for the children belong to the master of the female. It is therefore practically advantageous to have negro women. . . .

## 4. African Prince Olaudah Equiano Survives the Middle Passage, 1791

The first object which saluted my eyes when I arrived on the coast, was the sea, and a slave ship, which was then riding at anchor, and waiting for its cargo. These filled me with astonishment, which was soon converted into terror, when I was carried on board. I was immediately handled, and tossed up to see if I were sound, by some of the crew; and I was now persuaded that I had gotten into a world of bad spirits, and that they were going to kill me. Their complexions, too, differing so much from ours, their long hair, and the language they spoke, (which was very different from any I had ever heard) united to confirm me in this belief. Indeed, such were the horrors of my views and fears at the moment, that, if ten thousand worlds had been my own, I would have freely parted with them all to have exchanged my condition with that of the meanest slave in my own country. When I looked round the ship too, and saw a large furnace of copper boiling, and a multitude of black people of every description chained together, every one of their countenances expressing

---

From *The Life of Olaudah Equiano, or Gustavus Vassa, The African. Written by Himself* (Boston: Isaac Knapp, 1837), 43–49.

dejection and sorrow, I no longer doubted of my fate; and, quite overpowered with horror and anguish, I fell motionless on the deck and fainted. . . .

I now saw myself deprived of all chance of returning to my native country, or even the least glimpse of hope of gaining the shore, which I now considered as friendly; and I even wished for my former slavery in preference to my present situation, which was filled with horrors of every kind still heightened by my ignorance of what I was to undergo. I was not long suffered to indulge my grief; I was soon put down under the decks, and there I received such a salutation in my nostrils as I had never experienced in my life: so that, with the loathsomeness of the stench, and crying together, I became so sick and low that I was not able to eat, nor had I the least desire to taste any thing. I now wished for the last friend, death, to relieve me; but soon, to my grief, two of the white men offered me eatables; and, on my refusing to eat, one of them held me fast by the hands, and laid me across, I think the windlass, and tied my feet, while the other flogged me severely. I had never experienced any thing of this kind before, and although not being used to the water, I naturally feared that element the first time I saw it, yet, nevertheless, could I have got over the nettings, I would have jumped over the side, but I could not; and besides, the crew used to watch us very closely who were not chained down to the decks, lest we should leap into the water; and I have seen some of these poor African prisoners most severely cut, for attempting to do so, and hourly whipped for not eating. This indeed was often the case with myself. In a little time after, amongst the poor chained men, I found some of my own nation, which in a small degree gave ease to my mind. I inquired of these what was to be done with us? [T]hey gave me to understand, we were to be carried to these white people's country to work for them. I then was a little revived, and thought, if it were no worse than working, my situation was not so desperate; but still I feared I should be put to death, the white people looked and acted, as I thought, in so savage a manner; for I had never seen among any people such instances of brutal cruelty; and this not only shown towards us blacks, but also to some of the whites themselves. One white man in particular I saw, when were permitted to be on deck, flogged so unmercifully with a large rope near the foremast, that he died in consequence of it; and they tossed him over the side as they would have done a brute. This made me fear these people the more; and I expected nothing less than to be treated in the same manner. I could not help expressing my fears and apprehensions to some of my countrymen; I asked them if these people had no country, but lived in this hollow place? (the ship) they told me they did not, but came from a distant one. "Then," said I, "how comes it in all our country we never heard of them?" They told me because they lived so very far off. I then asked where were their women? had they any like themselves? I was told they had. "And why," said I, "do we not see them?" They answered, because they were left behind. I asked how the vessel could go? [T]hey told me they could not tell; but that there was cloth put upon the masts by the help of the ropes I saw, and then the vessel went on; and the white men had some spell or magic they put in the water when they liked, in order to stop the vessel. I was exceedingly amazed at this account, and really thought they were spirits. I therefore wished much to be from amongst them, for I expected they would sacrifice me; but my wishes were vain—for we were so quartered that it was impossible for any of us to make our escape. . . .

At last, when the ship we were in, had got in all her cargo, they made ready with many fearful noises, and we were all put under deck, so that we could not see how they managed the vessel. But this disappointment was the least of my sorrow. The stench of the hold while we were on the coast was so intolerably loathsome, that it was dangerous to remain there for any time, and some of us had been permitted to stay on the deck for the fresh air; but now that the whole ship's cargo were confined together, it became absolutely pestilential. . . . The shrieks of the women, and the groans of the dying, rendered the whole a scene of horror almost inconceivable. Happily perhaps, for myself, I was soon reduced so low here that it was thought necessary to keep me almost always on deck; and from my extreme youth I was not put in fetters. . . .

. . . One day, when we had a smooth sea and moderate wind, two of my wearied countrymen who were chained together, (I was near them at the time,) preferring death to such a life of misery, somehow made through the nettings and jumped into the sea: immediately, another quite dejected fellow, who, on account of his illness, was suffered to be out of irons, also followed their example; and I believe many more would very soon have done the same, if they had not been prevented by the ship's crew, who were instantly alarmed. Those of us that were the most active, were in a moment put down under the deck, and there was such a noise and confusion amongst the people of the ship as I never heard before, to stop her, and get the boat out to go after the slaves. However, two of the wretches were crowned, but they got the other, and afterwards flogged him unmercifully, for thus attempting to prefer death to slavery.

## 5. Ruth Belknap, a Country Parson's Wife, on "The Pleasures of a Country Life," c. 1782

Up in the morning I must rise
Before I've time to rub my eyes.
With half-pin'd gown, unbuckled shoe,
I haste to milk my lowing cow.
But, Oh! it makes my heart to ake,
I have no bread till I can bake,
And then, alas! it makes me sputter,
For I must churn or have no butter.
The hogs with swill too I must serve;
For hogs must eat or men will starve.
Besides, my spouse can get no cloaths
Unless I much offend my nose.
For all that try it know it's true
There is no smell like colouring blue.
Then round the parish I must ride
And make enquiry far and wide

From Ruth Belknap, "The Pleasures of a Country Life," c. 1782 in *Collections of the Massachusetts Historical Society* 6th series, vol 4 (Boston: Massachusetts Historical Society: 1891), 228–229.

To find some girl that is a spinner,
Then hurry home to get my dinner.

If with romantic steps I stray
Around the fields and meadows gay,
The grass, besprinkled with the dews,
Will wet my feet and rot my shoes.

If on a mossy bank I sleep
Pismires and crickets o'er me creep,
Or near the purling rill am seen
There dire mosquitos peirce my skin.
Yet such delights I seldom see
Confined to house and family.

All summer long I toil & sweat,
Blister my hands, and scold & fret.
And when the summer's work is o'er,
New toils arise from Autumn's store.
Corn must be husk'd, and pork be kill'd,
The house with all confusion fill'd.
O could you see the grand display
Upon our annual butchering day,—
See me look like ten thousand sluts,
My kitchen spread with grease & guts,— . . .

Yet starch'd up folks that live in town,
That lounge upon your beds till noon,
That never tire yourselves with work,
Unless with handling knife & fork,
Come, see the sweets of country life,
Display'd in Parson B—'s wife.'

## 6. Eulalia Pérez Remembers Early California, 1823

When I came to San Gabriel the last time, there were only two women in this part of California who knew how to cook [well]. One was María Luisa Cota, wife of Claudio López, superintendent of the mission; the other was María Ignacia Amador, wife of Francisco Javier Alvarado. She knew how to cook, sew, read and write and take care of the sick. She was a good healer. She did needlework and took care of the church vestments. She taught a few children to read and write in her home, but did not conduct a formal school. . . .

---

From Carlos N. Hijar, Eulalia Pérez and Agustín Escobar, *Three Memoirs of Mexican California,* 1877, from the Friends of the Bancroft Library, University of California at Berkeley, 1988. Reprinted by permission.

The priests wanted to help me out because I was a widow burdened with a family. They looked for some way to give me work without offending the other women. Fathers Sánchez and [José María] Zalvidea conferred and decided that they would have first one woman, then the other and finally me, do the cooking, in order to determine who did it best, with the aim of putting the one who surpassed the others in charge of the Indian cooks so as to teach them how to cook. . . .

. . . No one told me anything regarding what it was all about, until one day Father Sánchez called me and said, "Look, Eulalia, tomorrow it is your turn to prepare dinner—because María Ignacia and Luisa have already done so. We shall see what kind of a dinner you will give us tomorrow."

The next day I went to prepare the food. I made several kinds of soup, a variety of meat dishes and whatever else happened to pop into my head that I knew how to prepare. . . .

Because of all this, employment was provided for me at the mission. At first they assigned me two Indians so that I could show them how to cook, the one named Tomás and the other called "The Gentile." . . .

The missionaries were very satisfied; this made them think more highly of me. I spent about a year teaching those two Indians. I did not have to do the work, only direct them, because they already had learned a few of the fundamentals.

After this, the missionaries conferred among themselves and agreed to hand over the mission keys to me. This was in 1821, if I remember correctly. . . .

The duties of the housekeeper were many. In the first place, every day she handed out the rations for the mess hut. To do this she had to count the unmarried women, bachelors, day-laborers, vaqueros. . . . Besides that, she had to hand out daily rations to the heads of households. In short, she was responsible for the distribution of supplies to the Indian population and to the missionaries' kitchen. She was in charge of the key to the clothing storehouse where materials were given out for dresses for the unmarried and married women and children. Then she also had to take care of cutting and making clothes for the men.

Furthermore, she was in charge of cutting and making the vaqueros' outfits, from head to foot—that is, for the vaqueros who rode in saddles. Those who rode bareback received nothing more than their cotton blanket and loin-cloth, while those who rode in saddles were dressed the same way as the Spanish-speaking inhabitants; that is, they were given shirt, vest, jacket, trousers, hat, cowboy boots, shoes and spurs; and a saddle, bridle and lariat for the horse. Besides, each vaquero was given a big silk or cotton handkerchief, and a sash of Chinese silk or canton crepe, or whatever there happened to be in the storehouse.

They put under my charge everything having to do with clothing. I cut and fitted, and my five daughters sewed up the pieces. When they could not handle everything, the father was told, and then women from the town of Los Angeles were employed, and the father paid them.

Besides this, I had to attend to the soap-house, . . . to the wine-presses, and to the olive-crushers that produced oil, which I worked in myself. . . .

I handled the distribution of leather, calf-skin, chamois, sheepskin, Morocco leather, fine scarlet cloth, nails, thread, silk, etc.—everything having to do with the making of saddles, shoes and what was needed for the belt- and shoe-making shops.

# 7. Report on the Indian Villages of San Diego County, 1873

LOS ANGELES, CAL.,
July 31, 1873

DEAR SIR: I have the honor to submit the following report of my visit to the Indian villages of San Pasqual, Santa Ysabel, and Agua Caliente, in the county of San Diego, State of California. . . .

The villagers began to assemble early. At the appointed hour the captain rose, and in a short speech in the Indian language, which seemed to be both eloquent and well appreciated, gave his hearers to understand the errand upon which I visited them. A lively interest was manifested by every one. They complained of the encroachments of their American neighbors upon their land, and pointed to a house near by, built by one of the more adventurous of his class, who claimed to have pre-empted the land upon which the largest part of the village lies. On calling upon the man afterward, I found that such was really the case, and that he had actually paid the price of the land to the register of the land-office of this district, and was daily expecting the patent from Washington. He owned it was hard to wrest from these well-disposed and industrious creatures the homes they had built up. "But," said he, "if I had not done it somebody else would, for all agree that the Indian has no right to public lands." These Indians further complain that settlers take advantage of them in every way possible; employ them to work and insist on paying them in trifles that are of no account to them; "dock" them for imaginary neglect, or fail entirely to pay them; take up their stock on the slightest pretext and make exorbitant charges for damages and detention of the stock seized. They are in many cases unable to redeem it. They have therefore little encouragement to work or to raise stock. Nor do they care to plant fruit trees or grape-vines as long as land thus improved may be taken from them, as has been the case in very many instances. Among the little homes included in the pre-emption claim above referred to are those adorned with trees and vines. Instead of feeling secure and happy in the possession of what little is left to them, they are continually filled with anxiety. They claim that they ought to be allowed to remain where their forefathers have lived for so long, and that they should be protected by law in the peaceful possession of the homes that have been handed down to them.

I asked them how they would like for their children to go to school, learn to speak the English language, and to live more like white people. It would be very nice, they replied, but it would do them little good if they could not have their homes protected.

I asked them how they would like to be moved to some place where they could be better protected, have ground of their own secured to them, and more comfortable homes. The answer was, "Our fathers lived and died here, and we would rather live here than at any other place."

In conclusion I assumed them that I should report what I had learned about them, and that I had little doubt but that the Government at Washington would be able to

From "Letter from Luther E. Sleigh, July 31, 1873," in *Report of the Commissioner of Indian Affairs for 1873,* Appendix A (Washington, D.C.: U.S. Government Printing Office, 1874), 29–40.

do something to better their condition, charging them at the same time to strive, as I felt they had been doing, to keep the peace among themselves and with the whites.

I proceeded thence by the most direct route to Santa Ysabel rancheria. On reaching that place, I found the captain, Augustine, absent; sent a messenger for him, and also one for the chief of the Diegenes, Pablo Pene, who lives in a neighboring rancheria. There are about one hundred and twenty-five souls at Santa Ysabel. They occupy the finest valley of the ranch of the same name, on one side of which are about twenty adobe houses for winter-quarters, while on the other side, near their fields of grain, are as many brush-houses, now occupied. At the time that I reached the village, men, women, and children were scattered over the fields harvesting their grain. Some were reaping, some thrashing, some grinding, while near the houses women were making it into bread for immediate use. It was altogether an interesting picture to look upon.

The chief and captain arrived during the night, and as soon as possible in the morning I sought a conference with them in relation to the condition and wants of their people. I was glad to find them exempt from many of the annoyances of which the Indians of San Pasqual complain. The land which they occupy is claimed under a grant from the Mexican government by private parties, who have hesitated to undertake to eject the Indians for fear of violence on their part in resisting, as they (the Indians) dispute any ownership more sacred than their own, and insist that they should not be disturbed in their possession. . . .

At San Pasqual and Agua Caliente I was called upon by white settlers, the majority of whom had no good word for their dusky neighbors. "They are thieves; they are treacherous; they are vagabonds." It was urged that they should be taken to some one of the Territories and surrounded by soldiers to keep them at home, or to some island in the sea. I found, however, little in my journey to confirm such opinions, but was glad to note many indications of thrift. I could but wonder, indeed, that they are as reliable, honest, and peaceable as I found them to be. The sentiments entertained by very many white men in Southern California toward the Indians are well illustrated in the conclusion to which the proprietor of a small ranch near Temecula came in presenting the subject to me from his stand-point. It is well to mention that a family of Indians has occupied one corner of his ranch "from time immemorial." His wise and humane(?) conclusions was that the owners of large ranches should not drive "their Indians" away, but should keep them to work for them, and set apart certain portions of the ranch for them. "There is worthless land enough upon every ranch," he said, "for Indians to live on." . . .

LUTHER E. SLEIGH

✥ *E  S  S  A  Y  S*

In the first essay, Richard S. Dunn, director of the McNeil Center for Early American Studies at the University of Pennsylvania, divides colonial British America into four regional labor systems: the Caribbean and the southern mainland, both with various forms of slavery; the mid-Atlantic, with its mixture of wage labor and servitude; and New England, with its reliance on free labor. Dunn contends that the sale and purchase of crops and goods in a market economy quickly supplanted self-sufficient agriculture, even in New England, where household production proved so versatile and valuable. In the second essay, Howard R. Lamar of Yale University surveys the various forms of unfree labor—including slavery, tribute, contracts, and debt peonage—in the American West from Spanish conquest to the mid-nineteenth century. He charts the impact of bondage on Apaches and Aleuts, Siberians and Kanakas, Chinese and Italians. Were there any similarities among these different systems of labor in early America? How does region matter in the development of a distinctive labor system? To what extend did economic necessity rather than racism lead to bondage?

# Servants and Slaves in the East

### RICHARD S. DUNN

The history of labor in colonial America is a large subject because it embraces more than half the colonial population during a 170-year span, as well as labor practices in seventeenth- and eighteenth-century England, West Africa, Ireland, Wales, Scotland, and Germany, the chief catchment areas for immigrant colonial laborers. It is a complex subject because each region of British America evolved a distinctive labor system: in the Caribbean sugar colonies, a quick dependence on African slave labor; in the southern mainland colonies, a slow conversion from white servants to black slaves, with heavy use also of white family labor; in the mid-Atlantic colonies, a mix of family and wage labor with immigrant servants and slaves; and in New England, a prime reliance upon native-born family and wage labor. Finally, it is a difficult subject because it treats the history of the inarticulate—laboring men and women who left few records or artifacts and who must be studied chiefly through the observations of their employers. It is much harder to reconstruct the bygone experiences and work habits of obscure servants and slaves than those of prominent planters and merchants, yet the effort must be made if we are to comprehend the labor systems of colonial America. . . .

I will define a colonial laborer as any person who performed manual labor, with or without wages, for a head of household: a slave, a servant, an apprentice, a wage laborer, or a dependent family worker. This definition *excludes* a great many colonial manual workers: self-employed small farmers and craftsmen, because they were independent producers; tenant farmers, because they were semi-independent producers; and members of the armed forces, because they were employed by the state rather than by individual entrepreneurs. . . .

By the mid-eighteenth century the American colonists had developed four strikingly different labor systems in the Caribbean, the southern mainland, the mid-Atlantic colonies, and New England. Let us briefly consider the functional aspects of each system and compare some of their social and economic characteristics.

In the Caribbean, ever since the days of Hawkins and Drake the English had pursued economic exploitation more than full-scale settlement. The sugar boom of the 1640s legitimized this tendency. Not only did the sugar planters convert from white to black workers but they became totally dependent upon massive slave

From Richard S. Dunn, "Servants and Slaves: The Recruitment and Employment of Labor," in *Colonial British America,* edited by Jack Greene and J. R. Pole (Baltimore: Johns Hopkins University Press, 1984), 157–158, 172–188. Reprinted with permission of Johns Hopkins University Press.

imports. Between 1640 and 1780 the islands bought about 1,225,000 Africans to stock their slave gangs, keeping just enough white overseers, doctors, and clerical workers on hand to maintain control. This social mode, a small cadre of white masters driving an army of black slaves, was totally without precedent in English experience. Already by 1680 in Barbados the gulf between the privileged gentry and the unprivileged laborers was much greater than at home. At this date the Barbados slaves outnumbered their masters by only two to one. By 1750 the Barbados ratio had climbed to four to one. In the Leeward Islands the ratio was seven to one: in the parish of St. Mary, in Antigua, as of 1767 only 65 white paid taxes, and they held an average of 86 slaves apiece. Jamaica was the chief English sugar island by 1750, and it had a slave ratio of ten to one. A few hundred big entrepreneurs owned all of the best acreage and farmed on a very large scale. They raised cattle, cut timber, and cultivated indigo, cocoa, pimento, ginger, coffee, and cotton, but sugar was by far the most important crop. Surveys of the island taken in 1739, 1768, and 1832 disclose that half or more of the Jamaican slaves were attached to sugar estates, living and working in village-sized compounds. By 1814 in Westmoreland Parish, Jamaica, half of the slaves lived in gangs of 200 or more, and only 10 percent were placed in gangs of less than 30. While the black laborers were thus congregated into factorylike units, many of their employers had retired to England as absentees, leaving their estates in the hands of attorneys and overseers. . . .

To illustrate what can be learned by close study of Caribbean plantation records, let us consider the slave labor system in the Westmoreland sugar district of western Jamaica, as documented by the estate records of Mesopotamia plantation and by the diary of a Westmoreland estate manager, Thomas Thistlewood. The Mesopotamia records provide the fullest documentation yet found for any Caribbean slave community; they include eighty-five inventories of the slave force taken between 1736 and 1832. By correlating these inventories, we can reconstruct the careers of eleven hundred individual slaves, often from birth (or purchase) to death. Thistlewood's diary is the most minutely detailed day-by-day record yet discovered for the activities of any colonial planter. He kept this diary for thirty-six years, from his arrival in Jamaica in 1750 to his final illness in 1786, and he discloses almost more than the reader can bear about the underside of slave management.

Reading through Thistlewood's diary, one wonders how the slaves he dealt with could possibly endure such a regime and why they did not rebel far more frequently and violently. Thistlewood's first job in Jamaica was to manage a cattle pen in a remote mountain district. During the twelve months he held this job, in 1750–51, Thistlewood lived alone with forty-two slaves most of whom were African-born. In the first few days Thistlewood was there, the owner of the pen inspected the place and showed him how to manage the slaves: he ordered that the head slave, driver Mulatto Dick, be tied to an orange tree in the garden and given nearly three hundred lashes "for his many crimes and negligencies." It was nine days before Dick emerged from his cabin to go back to work. Thistlewood got the message: in the next twelve months he had 35 slaves whipped a total of 52 times. The punishment ranged from 50 to 150 lashes per whipping. In his diary Thistlewood recorded that he kept a slave mistress, with whom he had intercourse almost nightly. He also had sex with nine of the other fifteen females who lived at the pen. Thistlewood frequently reported that the slaves were shirking their work. Nine of them ran away at least once and two of them disappeared repeatedly. All of them complained of hunger and kept stealing food. Several became violent: one man hacked a woman with a machete, and two men pulled knives when they were cornered. Yet Thistlewood was never personally threatened. He quit the job because he quarreled with the owner, not the slaves. Indeed, he went on lengthy hunting and fishing trips with some of the men whom he had flogged and whose wives he had raped, and he distributed rum, food, and other presents all round on leaving.

Turning to the Mesopotamia records, one begins to understand why these Jamaican slaves were not more rebellious: they were trapped into a labor routine that kept them exhausted, enervated, sickly, and dull. Mesopotamia was a fairly typical Jamaican sugar production unit, staffed by a labor gang that fluctuated in size between 250 and 350 during the last century of Jamaican slavery. Between 1762 and 1832, when the Mesopotamia records are most complete, nearly twice as many slaves died as were born on this estate, and the work force was sustained by introducing 147 new Africans—mostly male teenagers—and 278 "seasoned" slaves, bought from neighboring estates. During this seventy-year span only 4 slaves were sold, 12 were manumitted, and 9 escaped. Slaves born at Mesopotamia had a definite occupational advantage over slaves purchased from the slave ships or from other estates: they held the lion's share of the supervisory, craft, and domestic jobs. To some extent craftworkers and domestics secured preferential employment for their children, but the key factor was color. By 1832, 10 percent of the Mesopotamia slaves were mulattoes and quadroons, and these people were always assigned domestic or semiskilled jobs.

The majority of the Mesopotamia laborers were field workers, kept busy six days a week, year round, with twelve hours of monotonous drudge labor: digging cane trenches, weeding and dunging the young cane, tending the cattle, and harvesting the mature cane. The slaves were given simple hand tools and no labor-saving devices. Much of their work would have been performed by draft animals in English or North American agriculture. Sugar was then, as it is now, a seasonal crop, but the overseers stretched out the tasks to keep the slaves fully occupied at all times. The Mesopotamia records show a clear correlation between slave occupation and longevity: field workers broke down in health more quickly, and died younger, than craftworkers. Furthermore, females survived this labor routine better than males. During this seventy-year span 105 more males than females died at Mesopotamia, so that female workers considerably outnumbered male workers on this estate by 1832. A large majority of the field workers were women, even on the First Gang, which performed the heaviest field labor.

The Mesopotamia women who worked so hard produced few living children. Between 1762 and 1832 about half of the female slaves aged eighteen to forty-five were childless, and those who did raise children had small families. The disease environment, dietary deficiencies, and the debilitating labor regimen were probably the most important factors in explaining this infertility. It cannot be a pure coincidence that the Jamaican population began to increase naturally almost immediately after emancipation; when many women withdrew from field labor. According to the Mesopotamia records, about 20 percent of the slave deaths on this estate were attributable to diet and bad hygiene. The absentee owners of Mesopotamia were upset by the high mortality and the low fertility; they attempted to encourage motherhood by excusing from labor women with five or more children. The owners were bothered a good deal more, however, by the fact that so many of their slaves were elderly or invalids. A surprisingly large number of Mesopotamia slaves lived into their sixties and seventies. Although the owners kept adding young male workers, most of the labor was performed by women, and at any one time about 20 percent of the adult slaves were too sick or old for productive labor. Thus at Mesopotamia the Caribbean slave labor system proved to be inefficient as well as inhumane.

Turning to the southern mainland colonies, we find not one labor system but several. At one extreme, the South Carolina low-country rice planters employed slave labor practices reminiscent of those in the West Indies. In a parish like St. James Goose Creek, adjacent to Charleston, blacks outnumbered whites by four to one as early as the 1720s. The slaves were congregated into large work gangs, as in Jamaica, and compelled to plant, hoe, harvest, thresh, and husk the rice by hand. In the 1760s about half of the slaves in the low country were African-born; adult male slaves heavily outnumbered adult female slaves; and 40 percent of the blacks lived and worked in large gangs of at least fifty. At the opposite extreme, in the North Carolina piedmont, an entirely different labor system was in operation. Orange County, one of the few piedmont counties with surviving pre-revolutionary tax records, was a district of corn, wheat, and livestock agriculture. The taxpayers were small farmers of English, Scotch-Irish, or German stock who had migrated south from the Chesapeake or the mid-Atlantic colonies. In 1755 only 10 percent of the Orange County householders owned any slaves, and no planter in the county possessed as many as ten.

A third southern labor system, in many respects a median system combining features of the South Carolina low country and the North Carolina piedmont, was to be found in the Chesapeake, especially in the oldest settled tidewater counties of Virginia and Maryland. Here the tobacco planters, while just as interested as their South Carolina or Jamaica counterparts in making money through the exploitation of cheap labor, were also trying to shape a society in which both rich and poor whites had status and could feel comfortably at home. Between the 1680s and the 1750s they created an elaborately tiered social and economic hierarchy with slave laborers at the base, convict and indentured servants ranked next, then tenant farmers, then small landholders, then middling planters, and a handful of large planters—one to five [in] each county—at the top. By mid-century, slaveholding was very widely distributed throughout Virginia and Maryland. No Chesapeake county was so heavily tilted towards slave labor as the South Carolina rice parishes, but only the remote western frontier counties were without significant slave holdings. In 1755 the population in fourteen of the sixty-three Chesapeake counties was more than half black; all of these counties were in Virginia, served by the James, York, and Rappahannock rivers, where the African slave traders principally brought their cargoes. Maryland had noticeably fewer slaves at this date, which helps to explain why the planters from the upper Chesapeake were especially eager for convict servants. Even in the Virginia counties with the largest black populations slaveholding was far from universal. . . .[I]t appears that fewer than half of the small planters and tenant farmers in the Chesapeake were slaveholders in the 1760s and 1770s. . . .

While Chesapeake slavery was certainly not as brutal or repressive as in the Caribbean, the slaveholders seem to me to have stymied black resistance pretty effectively and to have thwarted most forms of black achievement.

In order to set up a meaningful comparison with Jamaican slavery as documented by the Mesopotamia estate records and Thomas Thistlewood's diary, let us consider parallel collections of evidence concerning the slave labor system in the northern neck of tidewater Virginia: the papers of the Tayloe family of Mount Airy, overlooking the Rappahannock, and the diary of Landon Carter, who lived next-door to the Tayloes at Sabine Hall. The Tayloes and the Carters were far from being representative Chesapeake slaveholders. They were among the largest entrepreneurs in the Chesapeake: the slave communities at Mount Airy and at Sabine Hall were equivalent in size to the slave community at Mesopotamia, Jamaica. John Tayloe I held 167 slaves at Mount Airy in 1747; his grandson held 383 slaves at Mount Airy in 1809, as well as hundreds of other slaves elsewhere in the Chesapeake. . . . How does Virginia slavery, as documented by the Tayloes and Landon Carter, chiefly differ from Jamaican slavery?

In the first place, the Tayloes and Carters saw themselves as patriarchs, in the fullest sense of the term, and this impelled them to manipulate their black workers' private lives and not simply to exploit their labor. In Jamaica, Thomas Thistlewood kept a diary in order to preserve his sanity, but in Virginia, Landon Carter kept a diary in order to nurture his self-image of father/ruler over his white family and black slaves. Through this diary, the reader can follow Carter's efforts to supervise the work of his slaves, and manage their lives, for his own profit and their moral betterment. Carter moved constantly among the Sabine Hall field workers as well as the domestics, badgering them to work and doctoring them when sick. He would stay for hours in the threshing house in order to make the threshers work faster and more carefully. He knew his slaves as individuals, identifying some 150 blacks in his diary by name. His comments on slave behavior were almost invariably negative, for despite his wealth and status, Carter suffered acutely from paranoia. His diary in the 1760s and 1770s was a dumping ground, filled with diatribes against the people who betrayed him: his children and grandchildren and his slaves. In Carter's view, the Sabine Hall slaves, through "villinous lazyness," were constantly frustrating his best-laid plans. Thus carpenter Jimmy, who should have been building a corn house, was too lame to work, his legs swollen from wearing tight shoes. Far from feeling sorry for Jimmy, Carter punished this "splay footed rascal" by prohibiting him from going home at night to his wife, who lived on another quarter. Carpenter Tony, who should have been building Carter's garden fence, "goes on pretending with his scheme of old age creeping and whindling about often pretending to be sick." Plowman Manuel also had a scheme: to kill off Carter's oxen and horses by miring them in the mud. Body servant Nassau's strategy was to be constantly drunk.

. . . Carter played his role of patriarch ineptly, and his slaves knew how to out-maneuver and humiliate him. But they did so at great physical and psychic cost. Some of them escaped, at least briefly: Carter reports about forty runaway (mainly short-term) over a twenty-year span. Some of them were flogged: Carter reports twenty whippings in the year 1770 alone. Worse than the whippings must have been the endless intrusion, inspection, and harassment by this crabbed, obnoxious master. The slaves who knew Carter best, such as his body servant Nassau, were the ones most likely to run away. When Lord Dunmore called upon the Virginia slaves to revolt against their masters in 1775, fourteen of Carter's people fled to the British governor. This upset the proud old man very much. He dreamed one night that the runaways, looking "most wretchedly meager and wan," came back and begged for his help. But in truth, Carter's slaves had had quite enough of his help.

Landon Carter can be dismissed, and perhaps he should be, as an aberrant mental case. But the slaves who lived next-door at the Tayloes' Mount Airy plantation were also manipulated and intruded upon to a high degree. Admittedly, they worked less hard and lived much better than the slaves at Mesopotamia, Jamaica. Over a sixty-year span the Mount Airy records show that nearly twice as many slaves were born as died on this plantation. The labor pattern was designed to achieve total self-sufficiency: the field workers raised corn and pork in addition to tobacco, and they tended their gardens in off-hours; slave spinners and weavers made cloth from local cotton and wool; slave shoemakers tanned and dressed local leather; the smiths and joiners made wagons, ploughs, and hoes and shod horses; and the carpenters, masons, and jobbers erected and repaired buildings. Work logs kept by the overseers show a definite seasonal rhythm, with the harvest frenzy in midsummer and a long slack period in the winter. A third of the Mount Airy black workers were domestics or craftworkers, and women did much less of the heavy field labor than at Mesopotamia.

On the other hand, the lives of the Mount Airy slaves were continually disrupted by the Tayloes' practice of moving workers from one quarter to another or from one plantation to another and by their frequent sale of surplus slaves. . . . In 1792 John Tayloe III advertised: "For Sale 200 Virginia born, men, women and children, all ages and descriptions." At least 50 Mount Airy slaves were among those sold that year. Between 1809 and 1828 John Tayloe III sold 52 Mount Airy slaves, mainly teenage girls. Between 1828 and 1860 his sons moved 364 Mount Airy slaves to other Tayloe properties, about half of them to distant cotton plantations in Alabama. By this method the Tayloes kept the Mount Airy work force well organized for maximum productivity, with a high percentage of prime-aged male laborers. They clearly played favorites, keeping the domestics and craftworkers they liked best, together with their children, at Mount Airy. But among the field workers, husbands and wives generally lived at separate work quarters, and children were customarily taken from their parents at an early age. Thus the Tayloes' constant shuffling of the slave population, while sensible from a business viewpoint, was destructive of black family life.

To turn from the plantation slavery of tidewater Virginia to the farm, shop, and household environment of the mid-Atlantic colonies is to enter a different world. It was, to be sure, a variegated world, incorporating such laborers as the Yankee tenants, who staffed many of the baronial estates in the Hudson Valley; the Scottish tenants, who preserved their peculiar "farmtoun" style of husbandry in East Jersey; the African slaves, who labored on Quaker farms in West Jersey; the German redemptioners, who worked in rural Pennsylvania; and the Ulster servants, who bound themselves to masters in Philadelphia. But throughout this region the labor pattern differed in three important respects from the labor patterns of the Chesapeake and the Caribbean. First, the mid-Atlantic employers relied overwhelmingly on white labor, not black; and on apprentices, servants, and wage workers, not slaves. Second, they made heavy use of non-English imported white labor, especially Scotch-Irish and German immigrants. Third, the mid-Atlantic employment pattern more closely resembled the pattern in Britain or Europe than that in the plantation colonies. Agricultural laborers raised small grain crops and tended livestock, urban laborers were trained for crafts or tended shops, and female laborers were engaged for domestic service—all much as in the Old World.

Towns were more central work places in the mid-Atlantic economy than in the southern plantation economies; and since we will be focusing upon farm labor when discussing New England, it is appropriate to focus upon urban labor in the mid-Atlantic region. The premier town in this region during the eighteenth century was Philadelphia, which grew from around two thousand inhabitants in 1690 to nine thousand in 1740 and twenty-five thousand in 1776. By the Revolution, Philadelphia was the largest town and employment center in British America. Unhappily, many of the Philadelphia laborers—apprentices, servants, slaves, journeymen, and other wage workers (most particularly the female workers)—are impossible to find in the existing records. Some of them surface in the Philadelphia tax records for 1693, 1709, 1756, 1767, 1769, 1772, 1774, and 1775, in the twenty-four hundred inventories of estates filed between 1682 and 1780, in the newspapers, or in business records kept by merchants, shopkeepers, and artisans. But in many respects the Philadelphia servant or wage laborer remains a more shadowy figure than the Jamaica or Virginia slave.

Our understanding of labor practices in pre-revolutionary Philadelphia has been strongly colored by the example and the writings of Benjamin Franklin. He started out as a bound apprentice, became a wage-earning journeyman, and quickly rose through skill and hard work to be a self-employed printer, bookseller, and newspaper editor. And though he retired from the printing business at age forty-two, he was tremendously proud of his workingman's roots and of his craft as a printer, which enabled him to work with his hands and exercise his brain simultaneously. Franklin's *Autobiography* devotes considerable space to a description of the labor climate in Philadelphia from 1723, when he arrived as a runaway apprentice, to the 1730s, when he established himself as a successful printer. But the *Autobiography* was written for propaganda purposes; it is far more selective and less candid than the private diaries of Thomas Thistlewood and Landon Carter. Looking back as an old man upon his youth, Franklin was more concerned with character building than with the work practices in his printing shop. He encourages the reader to believe that any laborer, through industry, sobriety, and frugality, can rise up in the world. He introduces vignettes of lazy, drunken apprentices and journeymen as exemplars of behavior to avoid. He also contrasts the openness of the Philadelphia labor market with the proletarian restrictiveness of opportunity in London, where he also labored as a journeyman printer. Thanks to Franklin, we have tended to assume that Philadelphia provided an ideal environment for the struggling workingman and that most, if not all, of its inhabitants enjoyed expanding opportunities and a rising standard of living.

Recently this rosy picture has been challenged. A group of historians more influenced by E. P. Thompson's *The Making of the English Working Class* than by Franklin's *Autobiography* has been investigating servitude and slavery in Philadelphia, as well as job opportunities, wages, prices, and the distribution of wealth.

Their findings suggest that while laborers in this town enjoyed generally favorable working and living conditions into the 1740s, their circumstances deteriorated badly in the next thirty years. Initially, as elsewhere in seventeenth-century America, the pioneers who founded Philadelphia relied heavily upon bound labor. The early inhabitants brought with them numerous indentured servants, and they purchased a shipload of 150 African slaves in 1684. . . . Philadelphians who died in the 1680s, during the first decade of settlement, held more slaves and servants per capita than at any later date. During the next forty years, from 1690 to 1730, servant imports were low, and slave imports were also fairly low. During this period Philadelphians did not abandon bound labor. Rather, they recruited apprentices and journeymen locally in the urban English fashion or hired migrant laborers from other colonies, such as seventeen-year-old Benjamin Franklin from Boston in 1723. And as the town grew rapidly and the local labor market expanded, Philadelphians bought many of the African slaves and the Irish and German servants who were shipped into the city between 1729 and 1775. These immigrant laborers came in overlapping waves: slave shipments in 1729–41, followed by shipments of German and Irish servants in 1732–56, then slave shipments in 1759–65 (at a time when it was impractical to import servants because the British enrolled large numbers of them into the army during the Seven Years' War), and Irish servants again from 1763 to 1775.

Despite this large-scale infusion of bound labor the proportion of slaves and immigrant servants in the total Philadelphia labor force was probably not rising during the years 1729–62, and it was certainly declining during the years 1763–75. Immigrant servants had to be constantly replaced, since they soon earned their freedom, and slaves had to be replaced also, since they had little chance to develop family life in Philadelphia and were not reproducing themselves. When offered a choice, Philadelphia employers preferred servants to slaves; they bought Africans mainly when immigrant whites were unavailable. And probably Philadelphia employers preferred native-born to immigrant workers. If African slaves and Irish servants had been especially sought-after, one would expect that the rich merchants and professionals, who could pay top prices, would have snapped up most of them. But instead we find that Philadelphia artisans of modest means bought much of the immigrant bound labor. In 1745, two-thirds of the 253 servants imported into the city were bound to artisans, and in 1767 about half of the 905 slaves in Philadelphia were held by artisans.

During and after the Seven Years' War there was a decisive shift away from bound to free wage labor. From 1754 onward the Philadelphia Quakers campaigned actively against slave ownership. Meanwhile, many free white laborers were drawn to the city because the wartime business boom of 1754–63 drove wages up in Philadelphia for mariners, shipwrights, and other semiskilled workers. In the peacetime depression that followed, there was a labor glut, wages fell, and Philadelphia employers discovered that wage labor was cheaper than bound labor. . . . [T]he 1760s and 1770s saw a great constriction in job opportunities for mariners and unskilled laborers and a great increase in the number of underemployed and unemployed workers. . . . [T]he wages of unskilled and semiskilled workers were now no longer adequate to cover the minimum cost of food, rent, fuel, and clothing. The wives and children of the laboring poor had to find marginal employment if families were to survive. The city fathers had to devise new measures of poor relief for the destitute.

Had young Benjamin Franklin wandered into Philadelphia in 1763 instead of 1723, according to this interpretation, he would have had much more difficulty in picking himself up from the bottom. The pre-revolutionary labor surplus in Philadelphia among unskilled and semiskilled workers was a new phenomenon in America, for labor had always been scarce in the colonies. We will encounter a parallel labor surplus—which might be better described as a population surplus—in the farm villages of eastern Massachusetts during the generation before the Revolution. There was also a population surplus in the Chesapeake, but it developed thirty or forty years later, after the Revolution, when tidewater planters sold their superfluous slaves or moved them to new work places in the piedmont or further west and south. But if all the oldest settled parts of America were becoming overstocked with laborers during the late eighteenth century, there was a marked difference between the southern and northern methods of coping with this situation. In Virginia the use of slave labor became more widespread among all white householders, rich and poor; consequently, the institution of slavery became more deeply entrenched in the years between 1750 and 1800. In Philadelphia the opposite occurred: slavery was abolished after the Revolution, indentured servitude sharply declined, and both immigrant and native-born unskilled and semiskilled workers were thrown onto the free wage market.

. . . The Virginia slaveholders may have been patriarchal and pre-capitalistic, but as we have seen, the masters of Mount Airy continually sold their slaves or transferred them to new job assignments not of their choice in order to maintain an effective labor force. The businessmen of Philadelphia likewise manipulated their proletarian employees, but the unskilled workers who flocked to this town came out of free choice, and if they were underpaid they had the further option (which many exercised) of moving on to other places in America where labor was still scarce. I do not wish to minimize the plight of Philadelphia's laboring poor, but they did have an ultimate freedom that was not available to their counterparts in England (where unskilled labor was in permanent surplus) nor to the Afro-American slaves in the Chesapeake and the Caribbean.

In New England, the chief singularity of the labor system was that during the eighteenth century nearly all work was performed by native-born whites. After the great Puritan migration of the 1630s had ended, the New England colonists imported few white servants or black slaves from abroad. . . . The few blacks were employed chiefly in the coastal towns, especially Newport and Boston. In addition to this slave labor, the New Englanders got the local Indians to do some of their dirty work. In 1774 a third of the Indians living in Rhode Island were boarding with white families, employed as servants. On the island of Nantucket the merchants who organized the whaling industry maneuvered the local Indians into manning the whaling boats. But Indians were no longer numerous in New England, having been nearly annihilated in the wars of the seventeenth century. Censuses of the four New England colonies taken during the 1760s and 1770s indicate that the Indians and Negroes together formed a tiny nonwhite minority—only a little over 3 percent of the regional population. The descendants of the Puritans, with their well-established reputation for clannish hostility to strangers and aliens, thus performed most of the labor assigned elsewhere in America to immigrant servants and slaves.

The New Englanders were the only American colonists to develop a homogeneous society, closely resembling in ethnic composition the society their ancestors had known in England. But the New Englanders did not perpetuate the mother country's sharp social division between the propertied, privileged upper and middling orders and the propertyless, unprivileged wage laborers. On the contrary, New England was the most egalitarian sector of colonial America, far less stratified than the Caribbean or Chesapeake colonies and somewhat less stratified than the mid-Atlantic colonies.

To be sure, New England had a growing poverty problem in the mid-eighteenth century. In Boston, more pronouncedly than in Philadelphia, unskilled wage workers began to resemble the permanently depressed laboring poor of England. A very large number of mariners were congregated in the coastal towns. In 1740 it was calculated that 74 percent of the fishing, coasting, and long-distance merchant ships in the American colonies sailed from New England ports. During the war years, wages on naval, privateering, and merchant ships were high; when shipping declined and wages plummeted during peacetime, some seamen quit, but many others became trapped in careers of unattractive, irregular, low-paying wage work. The wages of Boston seamen did not keep pace with commodity prices, and their probated estates declined significantly in value between 1685 and 1775. Sailors ranked below shoemakers and tailors as the most depressed occupational group in Boston. But the plight of the mariners was not indicative of the New England labor systems as a whole. Most of the unskilled and semiskilled work in this region was performed on farms and not at sea. To get a sense of farming conditions, we must turn to the country villages, where the majority of New Englanders lived and worked.

Eighteenth-century New England farmers seem to have used formally bound labor—indentured servants or wage workers hired by the year—less than did Pennsylvania or Virginia farmers. For example, in Bristol, Rhode Island, two-thirds of the householders in 1689 had no live-in servants. Every one of these Bristol households included at least one adult woman—a wife, a grown daughter, or a female live-in servant—because men could not or would not do the cooking, needlework, cleaning, and processing of raw farm produce that every household required. Furthermore, nine out of ten Bristol households in 1689 included children, and overall there were 3.2 children per household. While this census does not tell which of these children were old enough to work, a later Bristol census, taken in 1774, divides the population between males and females over sixteen (hence old enough for full-scale work) and boys and girls up to sixteen (too young for work). On average there were three white workers per household. More than a third of these Bristol "adults" were listed as singles: . . . as unmarried sons and daughters. The same pattern reappears in a colonywide census of Massachusetts taken in 1764, which shows 3.4 nonworking children per household and 3.6 "adults." The mean Massachusetts household size of 7.0 white persons in 1764 is very much larger than the mean household size of 4.8 persons found in mid-eighteenth-century England and larger also than the white households of small planters in the Caribbean or the Chesapeake.

. . . [T]hese large Massachusetts households generated a great deal of family labor. . . .

Clearly the labor systems in the several regions of colonial America diverged remarkably from each other by 1775. And clearly these divergences held consequences for the future. The New England method, with its prime reliance upon family labor and supplementary help from hired hands and neighbors, was cumbersome and inefficient, but it was a functional method, and one that the New Englanders would carry westward with them after the Revolution as they set up new family farms in Ohio and beyond. The Philadelphia method, with its increasing reliance upon underpaid wage labor supplied by a pool of unskilled and semiskilled workers, was exploitive and inhumane, but it too was a functional method that capitalistic entrepreneurs would utilize as they built new western cities and recruited factory workers after the Revolution. The Chesapeake method, with its prime reliance upon unpaid labor by chattel slaves; appears to me to have been rather more exploitive and inhumane than labor practices further north, but here again was a functional method that cotton planters would carry westward after the Revolution as they set up new plantations in Alabama and elsewhere in the Deep South. But the Caribbean method of slave labor, in my view, was becoming truly dysfunctional by 1775. The sugar planters could sustained their work force only through continuous recourse to the African slave trade, and their labor management was so patently inhumane that the abolitionists in England were able to mount an effective parliamentary attack upon them. When Parliament voted to close the slave trade in 1806, the Caribbean labor system was placed in jeopardy, pointing the way towards emancipation of the West Indian blacks and the near paralysis of the West Indian sugar industry. There are of course other reasons for the collapse of the sugar planters. But they were the only colonists in British America whose labor system went bankrupt, in both a moral and a business sense.

## Bonded and Contract Labor in the Southwest

### HOWARD LAMAR

One of the most arresting images in American historiography has been that of America as a virgin land. Frederick Jacson Turner's famous essay "The Significance of the Frontier in American History" suggests that white pioneers penetrated an empty—and therefore innocent—preindustrial continent in which the absence of laws and organized society reduced Europeans to a more simple, open, free, and democratic status. . . . This ideal of preindustrial innocence was projected into the settlement period by Thomas Jefferson when he pictured the yeoman farmer as a self-sufficient person beholden to one and therefore truly free and independent.

These various images—as arresting and as useful as they sometimes are—create more problems than they solve. The frontier, for example, is associated with freedom and democracy, and the American West with rugged individualism. The mountain men of the fur-trade era are associated with freedom amounting to anarchy. Even the obviously fraudulent concept of "manifest destiny" has been accepted as an ex post facto rationalization for extending the area of political freedom. Such approaches do not allow for the fact that precontact Indian societies not only flourished in North America, they had a large variety of labor systems that persisted into the contact

---

From Howard Lamar, "From Bondage to Contract: Ethnic Labor in the American West, 1600–1890," in Steven Hahn and Jonathan Prude, eds., *The Countryside in the Age of Capitalist Transformation* (Chapel Hill: University of North Carolina Press, 1985), pp. 293–317. Reprinted by permission of the University of North Carolina Press.

period and were frequently adjusted to fit the economic demands of the European intruders. Indians working for or in alliance with whites constituted the first ethnic laborforce in colonial America. Very early on the Europeans developed trading and mercantile systems, one of which was the fur-trading company, which reached far beyond the frontiers of settlement to affect all native societies in North America.

It is also incontrovertible that many persons in the colonial economies of both North and South America were not free when it came to a definition of their status as laborers. Instead, they were slaves in slave societies (as was the case of Indian societies in the Pacific Northwest) or slaves in slaveowning societies (as was the case in Mexico and the America South), or they had the status of indentured servants (as in the British colonies) or were the victims of debt-peonage or harsh labor contracts (as was the case in Mexican New Mexico, Mexican California, and Russian Alaska). These conditions were so common in regions west of the Mississippi River that the question must be asked: Was the American West and the Western frontier more properly a symbol of bondage than of freedom when it comes to labor systems? A second related question has emerged from this study: How much so-called frontier or western violence has stemmed from economic conditions in which labor was abused, rather than from race hatred between Indians and whites, or between ethnic groups, or from the excesses of rugged individualism—although all three of these factors were very much in evidence? . . .

. . . [T]he labor history of the American West has yet to be meshed with the history of American slavery or with the history of labor generally. Those who do discuss Western labor tend to write about it regionally or in terms of craft or race; they treat, for example, the Chinese laborer, the Mexican worker, the Basque sheepherder, the cowboy, the hardrock miner, and the Anglo and Chicano migratory worker. There is nothing wrong with these specific approaches, and they do stress ethnicity, but they lack a national or comparative perspective.

In various ways the Trans-Mississippi West presented the same problem that had occurred at Jamestown after 1607: where to find an adequate labor supply. In Virginia, the first answer was indentured servants who, because of the availability of free lands, could not be fully controlled. The second solution was to import African bondsmen. . . .

In the long run, Indian labor, though a mainstay of the Atlantic colonial fur trade, was not used as generally as it was in the early Spanish, Russian, and British systems in the Trans-Mississippi West. Moreover, the hunting of furs was an occupation that fitted the life-style of the Indians while drawing on the seemingly boundless animal resources of their forested environment. No sooner had they adjusted to this new economy, however, than Europeans began to come in such numbers that they were able to supply their own labor and could, indeed, reproduce a European economy based on agriculture and commerce rather than on hunting and trading. It was also the case that disease had so decimated the Indian populations of eastern America by the eighteenth century that they could not be counted on as a realistic source of labor.

In southern Africa the resistance of the native populations to smallpox, the limited resources of the environment, and the reverse ratio of white and black created a very different situation. Unlike the European experience in Mexico or southern Africa or elsewhere, by the nineteenth century native labor had no practical meaning for Americans, and so Indian-Americans were placed on small reservations and their few remaining lands were taken from them. In an ironic way Frederick Jackson Turner was right when he argued that it was a virgin land into which the white settler could move, but it was a virginity achieved by the cauterizing surgery of epidemic, abuse, and removal.

# I

The first European observer of the American Southwest was Alvar Nuñez Cabeza de Vaca, who was a member of a Spanish exploring party shipwrecked on the coast of Texas in 1528 after the group had experienced a disastrous sojourn in Florida. During the eight years that Cabeza, a few companions, and a Moorish slave Estevanito worked their way westward in the hope of reaching the northern borders of New Spain, they were captured and enslaved by local Indian tribes. Later they worked as indentured servants for other Indians, and finally secured a freedom of sorts by becoming successful medicine men with a large following. Thus Cabeza ran a gamut of native labor systems in his memorable but miserable trek across the American Southwest. He described it as a world of cruelty in which his few surviving companions had become so fearful that some refused to flee with him when the opportunity arose. They preferred bondage to danger and possible death. Ironically, Cabeza learned that he had reached civilization when, near Culiacán in Sinaloa, he encountered terrified and wounded Indians fleeing from Spanish slave-hunting parties from central Mexico. He recalled that "we gave many thanks to God our Lord. Having almost despaired of finding Christians again, we could hardly restrain our excitement." It is instructive to learn that after Cabeza returned to his job as a crown official he worked for the remainder of his life as an opponent of slavery.

When Francisco Vasquez de Coronado came to New Mexico in 1540–41 in search of the golden cities of Cibola, he found slaves from the Caddoan villages of Kansas living in the Pueblo towns along the Rio Grande. Soon after the Spanish settled in New Mexico in 1598, the governor of that province began trafficking in Indian slaves taken from the Navaho tribes, and sent them south to work in the mines of New Spain. In essence the Spanish allied themselves to an already existing trade and raid system that had been carried on between the Pueblos and the Plains Indians for generations.

Although Spain tried to prevent the exploitation of Indians by detailed legislation dealing with tribute and labor, France V. Scholes has found that "almost without exception the governors of New Mexico were interested in using the Indians for their own profit, and instead of curbing abuses, were often the worst offenders." The efforts to supply mining labor to New Spain occurred in the seventeenth century, but they bore some resemblance to the sale of Indian captives from the Yamasee War (1715) by South Carolina officials. In the latter case captured Indians were sent to the Caribbean Islands as a labor supply.

After the Spanish brought the sedentary Pueblo Indians of the Rio Grande Valley under tribute, they forced them to manufacture *mantas* (cloth), deliver salt, travel to the Plains to bargain with Apaches for hides and slaves, collect piñon nuts for the Mexico City market, and serve as carpenters and artisans for the Spanish settlers. Indians were also shanghaied to serve as muleteers and cartmen for the supply trains that periodically went from Santa Fe to Chihuahua. At the end of the trip many did not receive pay and, indeed, were often abandoned in Chihuahua. When Governor Mendizabal of New Mexico had his accounts reviewed by the Crown in 1661, he was found to "owe 2,400 pesos to Indians for various services, or an equivalent of 19,000 days of labor at the rate of one real a day."

The actual enslavement of adult Pueblo Indians in Spanish New Mexico was rare; if it occurred it was as a punishment for certain crimes. On the other hand, soldiers could seize Pueblo orphans as house servants. It was more common for Spanish settlers to use captive Apache boys and girls as house servants, however, and, as Scholes has noted, "the governors received their share of these spoils of frontier warfare." Apache children were estimated to be worth 30–40 pesos, or the value of a good mule. An adult Apache slave was worth four oxen. . . . Apaches for their part often captured Spanish children as well as the off-spring of other Indian tribes to use as their own laborforce or to sell.

With the Pueblos paying multiple tribute in the form of corn to mission fathers, blankets and labor to the governor, and work days to Spanish settlers, it is no wonder that the Revolt of 1680 took place. In that upheaval the Pueblos and their allies killed 400 Spaniards and drove out some 1,900 more. The point I would like to argue here is that this revolt was not an Indian—white frontier war or a race war in the usual sense of such terms, but a revolt of slave or bonded labor.

It took the Spanish fourteen years to reestablish their authority in the Rio Grande Valley, but this time they gave the Pueblos better treatment. Even so, trafficking in captives continued in the border towns of Pecos and Taos where annual trade fairs were held. There Plains Indians sold captives for horses. By 1720, Ute Indians were selling Jicarilla Apache women and children at Taos and some Pawnee captives were still coming in from Kansas. By this time, however, the captives went to local citizens rather than to the mining towns of New Spain. . . .

Eventually the eastern Apaches suffered such a decline in strength and numbers that between the 1780s and the Mexican War it was the Comanches who carried on the trade in captives. In April 1849, a party of gold seekers crossing Texas on the southern trail to California caught a glimpse of this situation when they ran into fifteen Comanche Indians accompanied by five or six Mexican boys herding about 500 Mexican horses and mules to Torrey's Station, a trading post near present-day Waco, Texas. The post was owned by two Connecticut Yankees who, it is said, had Sam Houston as a silent partner. At first the Indians and the whites were sociable and actually participated in a joint dancing contest in the evening. But the gold seekers soon learned that the boy herders and the horses had both been captured in a devastating raid on a Mexican village a few days before. Infuriated by this news, the overlanders wanted to ambush the Comanches, but one of the Torrey brothers argued against this plan, saying that such an act would start a war. Instead the Torreys appear to have purchased the boys from the Indians and probably some of the horses as well.

By concentrating on black slavery in the United States, historians have tended to ignore the practice in the Southwest of older, more classic forms of bondage that had existed in Greece and Rome, and in parts of Africa and Asia. And, as had been the case in the Old World, it was a system in which captives were often incorporated into the households and even became citizens of the tribes or province that had captured them.

## II

While Spanish-Mexicans were busy capturing Indians and Indians were capturing Spanish-Mexican children, another form of bondage appeared in New Mexico during the eighteenth and nineteenth centuries, especially before 1848. In this system of debt-peonage, a *patron* or head of a family with a flock of sheep lent cash and some of the herd to a young man, often a relative. The recipient had to pay an annual rent of so many ewes for the sheep and for supplies. In most cases the recipient never quite paid off his debt. By this so-called *partidaro* system the *patron* became the head of an enormous extended family. Some observers have noted that by 1800 this system had concentrated the economic and political power of New Mexico into the hands of some twenty prominent families. In 1821 William Becknell, father of the Santa Fe trade, said that New Mexico society was character- ized by "the rich keeping the poor in dependency and subjugation." As late as 1900 one such *patron,* Pedro Perea, controlled 27,000 sheep through a variation of the *partidaro* system. . . .

Tribute systems between whites and Indians in the late eighteenth and early nineteenth centuries could also be found in Spanish California, where intruding Europeans in this instance Franciscan missionaries—resorted to coercion in order to maintain both a congregation and a labor supply. For purposes of efficient Chris- tianization, Indians were congregated around the California coastal missions and, along with religious instruction, were taught to ranch and farm. The records reveal that they were whipped if they neglected their duties, and soldiers were stationed nearby to insure obedience. Such treatment seems all the more tragic because re- cent studies of the Indians of California assert that they were so peaceful they could be called "Red Quakers." Not only were they pacifists by and large, they also possessed such a strong sense of territoriality that they were able to prevent con- flict by a careful avoidance of trespass on the land of another tribelet.

Yet, if the Spanish mission system seemed coercive, what followed during the period of secularization after 1833, when the mission laborforce—as well as its lands—were taken over by private individuals, was worse. As David J. Weber has observed:

> Without the protections of the Franciscans, many former mission Indians fell easily into a system whereby Californios advanced them goods, money, or liquor, then required them to repay their debts. Father Narciso Durán described the condition of two or three hundred Indians living in debt peonage on the edge of Los Angeles in 1833: "All in reality are slaves, or servants of white men who know well the manner of securing their services by binding them for a whole year for an advanced trifle. An Indian who tried to flee," Durán said, "experiences the full rigor of the law."

Despite the consequences, Indians did begin to flee to the foothills of the Sierras to escape forced labor. They also began to form fighting bands to resist local au- thorities sent out to recapture them or to recruit fresh labor from inland *rancherias.* At the same time the crowded conditions of the native quarters of the missions had increased the frequency of endemic diseases which, when combined with white epidemic diseases and the atmosphere of abuse and despair, reduced the native population from 275,000 during the Spanish-Mexican years to less than 150,000 by the time the Americans arrived on the scene in the 1840s.

After 1848 California Indians were quick to see that gold could be used to purchase white luxuries and joined in the gold rush as miners. American miners regarded them as a nuisance and quickly reduced their numbers still further by shootings, small wars, and arbitrary removals—this despite the perceptive comment of John Marsh, the California rancher, who wrote in 1846, "The Indians are the principal laborers: without them the business of the country could hardly be carried on." Indeed, Albert L. Hurtado has found that between 1846 and 1860 Hispanic and Anglo farmers, ranchers and townspeople in California—as opposed to miners—continued to use Indian labor, particularly in the southern and central coast areas. As Major John Bidwell noted, there was "hardly a farm house—a kitchen without them." Bidwell himself depended on Indians for his grain farming. Although many California Indians seemed willing to work for whites voluntarily, they were also forced to do so by state laws which provided for the "arrest and indenture of loitering and intoxicated Indians."

Hurtado has also found that Anglo ranchers and farmers in certain areas, whether they employed the more numerous male Indians as workers or the less numerous females, tended to segregate the sexes in living arrangements so that Indians could not reproduce at a normal rate. This situation, combined with the continued toll of white diseases on the California tribes had, by 1860, reduced the native population to 35,000.

## III

The labor system in Russian Alaska for the period 1780 to 1867 furnishes still other examples of bondage that ranged from the extremes of forced labor to the more moderate forms of written contracts and even symbiotic trade relations between Indians and whites.

In the Russian expansion across Siberia in the sixteenth and seventeenth centuries, Cossack parties and semimilitary fur-hunting groups brought the natives under a system of fur tribute known as the *yasak,* which lasted until 1788 when it was replaced by a compulsory labor tribute. By the time the Russians had penetrated Alaska, the possibility of a mobile labor supply from Russia itself had been reduced by the institution of serfdom: Russian serf owners understandably objected to an exodus of their labor. The landed nobility also argued on the grounds of social class that they could not let mere merchants have serfs. Faced with this situation, the Russian American Company sought labor from at least six alternative sources.

First, they recruited workers from an idle population that could be found in Siberian villages from Irkutsk to Okhotsk. Arthur Okun noted in his study of the Russian American Company that they were "runaway peasants, small merchants and artisans who had lost everything," and who had gone "east" to escape the authorities. Mixed in with them was a floating population of ex-soldiers and sailors. . . . They were in effect shanghaied; once on board, if the ship was not at sea, their clothes were taken away and the newly contracted workers wrapped in sacks. In somewhat similar fashion agents in London and Bristol enticed men, women, and children to the English colonies as indentured servants. Meanwhile, in Europe, "Newlanders" sought out Rhinelanders who would be willing to accept indentured status in return for their passage to America. . . .

The ways in which these workers were defrauded almost compels admiration. Prices at the company store were twice those at Okhotsk. Workers recruited from the Siberian mainland were often told not to lay in food because the company would feed them; in fact the company charged them for the food they got from the company store. They were also forbidden to manufacture homebrew vodka, but if they bought vodka at the store, they could be fined for drunkenness. In a revealing letter from Alexander Baranov, the local company director, to Baroness Shelikov, the widow of the head of the firm, he reassured her that the labor supply would be forthcoming for "liquor will always get them into debt."

In the half-share division one finds again a form of sharecropping or a variation of the *partidaro* system. In Alaska, however, the working conditions and abuses proved to be so brutal that labor shortages occurred, and in 1815 the Russian American Company was forced to pay the men with wages, although the currency of such wages appears to have been stamps, good only at the company store. Moreover, the wages were so low that the workers continued to fall into debt, which meant that they could not leave the colony. "The longer a man worked," Okun writes, "the more debts he accumulated," as a laborer made only 350 rubles a year while it took 728 to live. "To all intents and purposes," concludes Okun, "it was a condition of slavery."

The second source of labor for the company was the native population of the Aleutian Islands. Some 20,000 persons lived on this attenuated chain when the Russians first appeared in Alaska during the 1740s. The use of Aleut labor was necessitated by the fact that although the Russians were excellent hunters on land, they had neither the skills nor the patience to hunt the sea otter, the most valuable fur-bearing animal in the northern Pacific. The Aleuts, on the other hand, could sit for hours in their small bobbing kayaks or *bidarkas* waiting with their harpoons for the sea otter to surface. To persuade the Aleuts to do the hunting, the Russians used brute force or held women and children hostage until the Aleut males brought in a catch. Once the system was stabilized Aleut men were expected to serve the company from age eighteen to fifty. In season the Russians went to a village and drafted one-half of the men for service. When the furs had been taken, the Aleuts had to sell theirs to the firm at the company price and accept company stamps in payment. The company also acted to control the use among the Aleuts of such luxury items as bread, tea, and other European foodstuffs.

As the more northern sea otter heards declined, the Aleut hunters were moved to the Alaskan Panhandle and eventually down to California to exploit the herds found there. Meanwhile, the company had learned to secure its labor supply by manipulating the chiefs or *toyons*. "Do not forget," wrote one official, "to send over for the toyons twenty of the best suits of clothes with flashy trimmings; . . . we must attach them to us." Writing in 1800, Alexander Baranov instructed a subordinate in the handling of Aleuts. Treat them kindly, he said, and help them with food in bad weather. "The more eminent are to be singled out whenever possible and should sometimes be seated with the Russians at table during the holidays, for instance the Kalmai toion Gavril, [and] toion . . . Charnov."

At the same time Baranov observed that the Aleuts were naturally lazy, rough, and ignorant.

> We must hope that time will improve their opinion of us and order will tame them because these people being used to natural freedom since the creation of the world have

never thought of nor know how to submit to the will of others and can bear no slight without retaliating. . . . It is important that you bear this in mind as well as their uncontrollable greed, covetousness and ingratitude. Therefore, do not accept a single item from them without bargaining, and forbid anyone else to take anything without payment or by force.

Baranov's letter bears comparison with that of a Southern slave owner writing directions to his overseer. The *toyons* or elders gave orders to the Aleut workers and became, in effect, drivers. . . .

The Aleut population declined during the period of Russian control from an estimated 20,000 at the beginning of white contact to 4,000 or less in 1859. Here as elsewhere in North America epidemics took a fearful toll of the population, but forced labor also helps account for the shrinking numbers. The tragedy was the greater because the Aleuts appear to have enjoyed the work of hunting and went at their task with zeal. On the eve of the transfer of Alaska to the United States, a member of the governing board of the Russian American Company concluded that "neither the Negro of Guinea, nor the Chinese Coolie, nor the European worker can take the place of the Aleut in the art and practice of hunting."

As a third source of labor the Russians sought to subdue the Tlingit Indians of the Alaska Panhandle. The latter, however, not only resisted becoming workers, but sometimes attacked the Russians at their posts and occasionally drove them out. Nevertheless, after years of open hostility, the Tlingits began to supply the Russians with food. By the 1820s these Indians annually filled from 160 to 250 boats with potatoes, wild mutton, and berries to sell to the Russians at New Archangel. As the Tlingits had slaves of their own, perhaps they understood all to well the disadvantages of working for the Russians.

The fourth source of labor was provided by the offspring of Russian men and native women. They became the mainstay of the clerical bureaucracy or entered the workforce as sailors and artisans. But as Okun has noted, "they, too, were in a state of servile dependency upon the Company."

When the Russians established Fort Ross in California in 1812 in the hope of raising grain and cattle to supply Alaskan workers, they imported Aleut hunters to farm and herd cattle. The Aleuts were unsuccessful at the first task and hated dealing with cattle. The Russians then tried to persuade the local Pomo Indians to farm and milk cows, but as James R. Gibson has reported in his *Imperial Russia in Frontier America,* this experiment also failed: "Indians hired to do harvest became bored and left. If the harvest failed the Indian laborers were held responsible and made to remain to redeem the lost crop with other work. So they became understandably reluctant to toil for the company. At first they worked voluntarily for the Russians, but eventually they had to be recruited by force." By 1835 the California Indians living near the Russians had become so hostile they began to steal wheat from company fields and in 1838 tried to rustle Russian cattle at Fort Ross.

Faced with perennial labor shortages, the handful of Russians in Alaska and California grew so desperate for help that in the 1830s they sent agents to Hawaii to recruit Kanakas, the sixth source of labor. Perhaps as many as 1,000 came to serve as sailors or workers, an arrangement that allowed half of the Aleuts in California to return to their home islands to carry on sea otter hunts there. Certainly the Russian American Company is a classic example of a mercantile monopoly manipulating the factors of isolation, distance, debt, and force for their own advantage. Although the ways in which they recruited and held a laborforce together were not unusual, there were marked excesses in terms of exploitation and cruelty.

## IV

Some 2,000 miles east of the Russian American Company, the Hudson's Bay Company, founded in 1670 to exploit the fur-bearing lands of the northern reaches of the present Canadian provinces of Ontario, Quebec, and Manitoba, brought a vast territory into dependence on British goods and firearms. They achieved this by turning Canadian Indians with whom they came into contract into professional hunters. In the short run, the Indians may not have viewed the change as particularly great; but as Arthur Ray has observed, the shift for many was not only significant culturally but eventually catastrophic, for the tribesmen now hunted animals for furs to sell rather than food or clothing. And when they traded these furs for guns, sugar, coffee, rum, or other luxuries, the benefits often went to the male hunter rather than to his tribe or his family, who were then obliged to seek food as best they could. In this way the Hudson's Bay Company succeeded in achieving a voluntary form of labor tribute to the company. . . .

In the mobile fur brigades could be found Englishmen, Scots, French Canadians, Iroquois Indians from the St. Lawrence Valley, local tribesmen, and even Hawaiian Kanakas. Despite killings and ambushed of one party of trappers by another, and many abuses, the trappers and traders appear to have signed contracts for a given wage for a set number of years of service. They also appear to have had far more freedom than did laborers for the Russian American Company, if we can believe the comments of an old voyageur to Alexander Ross in 1825. "There is no life as happy as a voyageur's life; none so independent; no place where a man enjoys so much variety and freedom as in the Indian country." The point to be stressed, however, is that whether the Indian hunted for furs on his own to trade at the factories, or became a member of a fur brigade, he was crucial to the success of a vast European mercantile operation that stretched over a large part of North America for more than two centuries.

Considering the whole range of labor systems employed in the Trans-Mississippi Rocky Mountain fur trade between 1822 to 1850, however, some curious contrasts and contradictions become evident. In 1822 the federal government ended its efforts to control the fur trade through designated official trading posts and licensed traders—although it was still necessary to get a license to enter Indian country. This government withdrawal allowed fur companies to create their own posts and to downplay the role of Indians in the trade by sending brigades of American white trappers into the wilderness. It was a period of intense rivalry between firms and equally intense exploitation of the animal resources of the Great Plains and Rockies. Thus workers could choose between outfits. Moreover, the use of decentralized brigades consisting largely of white trappers stressed efficiency through freedom rather than by control.

In short, no American fur firm, whether it was William Ashley's Rocky Mountain outfit or John Jacob Astor's more centrally controlled and hierarchical American Fur Company, had the authority of the Russian American Company or the Hudson's

Bay Company over its laborforce or over the territory and its peoples. And although blacks and Indians were occasionally to be found in a brigade, the sense of ethnic difference usually centered on the fact that perhaps a third of the trappers were of French or French-Canadian origin, although outfits operating out of Taos, New Mexico, or Bent's Fort in present-day Colorado, may have been largely Spanish-Mexican. In any case it did not mean that one ethnic group dominated or exploited another. Although French-Canadians often occupied the more menial positions as keelboatmen or camp tenders and were referred to as the "cheerful slaves of the fur trade," the fact was that many of the most successful fur-trade entrepreneurs in St. Louis were of French descent.

American trappers voluntarily signed contracts to hunt and/or trade for one or more years. They were charged high prices at the trading posts or at the annual rendezvous on the Green River. It is true they frequently drank or gambled away their earnings, and were forced to return to the mountains in order to pay off the new debts. But it should be understood that the contractual arrangements and the degree of control were far less coercive than they were in Russian Alaska.

Finally, it should be noted that American fur trappers exhibited two characteristics that protected them from exploitation. First, they were exceptionally mobile. Not only did they move over much of the inland West, they also moved from company to company or became independent trappers. Many returned to Missouri after years in the mountains, while others migrated to California and Oregon or New Mexico. Still others allied themselves with an Indian tribe or opened a trading post at some spot on the overland trails. Second, and equally significant, they often moved into new occupations. Jim Bridger, for example, began as a trapper, then became a post trader on the California–Oregon Trail during the 1840s, and later served as a guide for the U.S. army and for railroad survey parties. Rather than ordinary laborers, they were small entrepreneurs or incipient capitalists prepared to work at whatever job or trade promised a good living. For these reasons it appears that the 3,000 or more persons engaged in the Rocky Mountain fur trade did enjoy some of the freedom and excitement that has so often been associated with that trade.


## V

In the early 1820s Dr. O. Hotchkiss, a kindly Yale professor, found a Hawaiian youth named Obookiah weeping on the steps of the Yale College Library. Obookiah was what seafaring men called a Kanaka sailor. He had been brought to Connecticut by one Captain Brintnall. Natives from Hawaii and other Pacific islands often shipped as sailors on the vessels of all nations from the eighteenth century onward, but they were usually found on Yankee whaling vessels or British, Russian, and American ships engaged in the seal and sea otter fur trade of the Pacific. Obookiah was taken in, educated, and cared for in New Haven until he died at an early age.

Kanakas laboring under three-year contracts first appeared on the Pacific coast of North America in 1788, long before they were recruited by Russians for work in Alaska. As was the case with the Aleuts, native governors served as the labor factors who supplied sailors for ships and workers for the fur trade, for which they received a percentage of the wages paid. John Meares, one of the earliest British traders in the Pacific Northwest, established a colony of Chinese laborers on Nootka Sound and gave them Hawaiian wives, possibly, writes George V. Blue, with the idea that the less conversation between married folk, the more the harmony. . . .

By the 1830s some 300 to 400 Kanakas could be found working at the British port of Fort Vancouver under a three-year contract paying $10 a month. In addition to collecting furs, the Kanakas served as herders for the sheep and cattle of the Hudson's Bay Agricultural Company located in Puget Sound. When the North West Company established Fort Walla Walla in 1818, the operation included 25 Canadians, 32 Kanakas, and 38 Iroquois workers. Nathaniel Wyeth, the Boston ice merchant who went into the Western fur trade in 1834, sent 20 Kanakas to work at Fort Hall, his outpost in Idaho. Narcissa Whitman, wife of Dr. Marcus Whitman of the Walla Walla Mission, employed a Kanaka servant. . . .

But as with other nonwhite ethnic groups, the impact of white diseases and labor demands devastated the aboriginal population of Hawaii. At the time of first contact Hawaii's population appears to have been about 300,000. By 1823 smallpox had reduced the number to 134,750. At this time probably as many as 1,000 males a year were leaving the islands, and by 1848 the number of departing Kanakas had risen to 3,500 from a population base that was now only 82,000. By 1860, as Janice Duncan has found, 12 percent of the population over the age of eighteen had left the islands. The crucial role Kanakas played in the first laborforces assembled in the Pacific Northwest cannot be exaggerated; yet when white American settlers came to Oregon, they declared that the Kanakas should be viewed as Indians—that is, as noncitizens—and should be fired from their jobs or deported. After they had petitioned unsuccessfully for citizenship in Oregon, many Kanakas moved to California.

The Kanaka experience once again demonstrated that white Americans, having become accustomed to a plentiful labor supply by virtue of immigration, saw other ethnic groups either as competitors or as having no useful function in their economy or their society. In gold-rush California, this took the form of relegating local Indians to a nonproductive role in mining, and of seeing Californios, Sonorans, Chileans, and indeed all foreigners as competitors.

## VI

Undoubtedly the supremely ironic twist to the convoluted history of ethnic labor in the West can be found in the story of the first black migration to California. When the news of gold discoveries reached the East in 1848–49, Frederick Douglass and other leading abolitionists urged free blacks to go West for a new start. Nearly 3,000 black Americans had reached California by 1850 in what was one of the most intriguing invisible migrations in American history. Not all of them were free, for some came with Southern masters, but the fact is that for most it was a voluntary trip—the first large voluntary migration of blacks to take place in the United States. . . .

At first, Americans in California also resisted the presence of Chinese immigrants whom they saw as competitors. But the Chinese arrived at a crucial moment in the industrialization of the American Far West. First, the prospect of making millions by large-scale investments in quartz mining, and especially the deep shaft mines of Nevada's Comstock Lode, left placer mining and even the tailings of quartz mines available to Chinese workers who moved into this less attractive side of the mining business. They were so patient and so thorough at the task of recycling that they not only managed to make a living, they constituted the majority of the population in some mining areas. Second, when the urgent need for labor to build the Central Pacific Railroad developed in the 1860s, Chinese labor proved essential. The result was a blending of the older mercantile system of contract labor—in this instance the Chinese workers were supplied by labor factors from the Pearl River delta in China—for a new industrial system that sought cheap labor wherever it might secure it.

It is not the purpose of this essay to recount the well-known history of Chinese workers in America, but simply to observe that they, like the Kanakas, came as temporary laborers. In this instance it was on a "credit ticket" system requiring them to work in order to pay their fare over and back. That arrangement, writes Gunther Barth, left them the slaves of their own countrymen. Understandably, they obeyed the "invisible control" of the labor agents as they were not only in debt to these men, but also dependent on them for the pay needed by families back home. Of the 200,000 Chinese who came to America in the nineteenth century some 100,000 returned to China. Despite the fact that only 50 percent remained, American labor's fear of competition led to the Chinese Exclusion Act of 1882, to the violent anti-Chinese outbursts in the Pacific Northwest in 1884, and to the killing of twenty-eight Chinese at Rock Springs, Wyoming, a year later.

Chinese laborers working as railway laborers, small-scale shopkeepers, domestics, or in the canneries of the Pacific Northwest, have received ample coverage by historians. Less well documented are the 80,523 Chinese who served in American merchant shipping between 1876 and 1896. Indeed, by 1900 some 80 percent of this nation's seamen were foreign-born, and of these many were Chinese. The LaFollette Seamen's Act of 1915, sometimes hailed as the first piece of progressive legislation under Woodrow Wilson, was also a device to get rid of Asians in the merchant marine.

In the case of California, it is interesting to see the oldest and newest labor systems existing side by side. On 2 October 1854, the *Alta California* reported that people were stealing Indian children in the north and selling them to *rancheros* in the southern part of the state. Later it was estimated that between 3,000 and 4,000 children had been stolen in the fifteen-year period from 1852 to 1867. Meanwhile, in the gold camps. individual Anglo-Americans feared that Sonoran peons or Southern capitalists with gangs of slaves would exploit the gold fields in such an efficient way that free labor would be driven out. When Thomas Jefferson Green of Texas appeared at Rose Bar on the Yuba River with his slaves to work the placers, the miners unceremoniously tossed him out and put into effect a local code prohibiting all master–servant teams in mining operations no matter what their relationship. The ordinance was originally directed at Mexican and Chilean mining *patrons* and their workers, but it was also applied to Mr. Green of Texas. . . .

## VII

. . . Examples of ethnic contract labor in the American West since 1860 are seemingly endless. Italian laborers operating under a contract system came to California in large numbers after 1865 to work either in construction or in vineyards or agriculture. By 1900 a large part of the laborforce for the maintenance of Western railroads consisted of Mexican-Americans living away from home. During the 1920s, as Julian Nava has observed, "American recruiters actually ranged over Mexico hiring people to fill labor ranks in the United States," and "immigration officials looked the other way as thousands crossed the border." In the depressed 1930s, however, there was a reversal of policy and Mexican immigrants were urged to return or were deported. Even today Mexican nationals continue to operate under conditions that are far from ideal, as the career of Cesar Chavez has so eloquently reminded us.

On the surface the early labor history of Mormon Utah seems at odds with all the foregoing accounts, for the Latter-Day Saints initially came to the Great Basin in such numbers that there was no labor shortage. Moreover, the converts they recruited from Europe came largely from Great Britain and Scandinavia, so that ethnic distinctions in the laborforce were absent. Nor did the Mormons coopt the labor of local Indian groups although they did befriend them. The Mormon church also used a system of labor tithes, but the evidence does not suggest that specific groups, ethnic or otherwise, were exploited.

On the other hand, the historian of labor in twentieth-century Utah can point to disturbing parallels to Aleut *toyons* or Hawaiian contract governors in the chronicle of Leonidas Skliris, a powerful and demanding labor *padrone,* who pushed the number of his Greek countrymen in the state from 3 in 1900 to 4,000 in 1910. Although the Greek immigrants worked as regular laborers, some were used as strike breakers in the Bingham Canyon area, said by observers to have been one of the most miserable mining camps in the United States. Here again one finds the blending of the old and the new: a traditional form of labor recruitment to supply a modern industrial operation.

This confrontation between a traditional labor system and the new industrial order brings us back to the questions posed at the outset of this essay. First, was the American West and the Western frontier more properly a symbol of bondage than freedom when it came to labor systems? And second, how much so-called frontier or Western violence has stemmed from the economic conditions in which labor has been abused rather than from race hatred or other factors?

To the first, the answer must be that it was indeed an area of bondage exemplified by captive Indians in New Mexico, cowed mission neophytes in California, and Aleutian forced labor in Alaska; but it was also a place where capitalist competition in the fur trade and flood migration of white labor into the mining industry either used traditional systems of native labor without unduly abusing the workers, or, in the case of mining, ignored the presence of a potential native laborforce. In short, varying conditions of bondage and freedom existed side by side.

Thus it is nearly impossible to say when these earlier conditions of slavery and/or debt-peonage were replaced by a system of job contracts and cash wages. Certainly the ratification of the Thirteenth Amendment in 1865 outlawing slavery and involuntary servitude was a symbolic turning point, for although it was directed at the South, the amendment applied to the entire nation. And Congress, not unmindful of the fact that debt and Indian peonage had long existed in New Mexico, passed *An Act to Abolish . . . The System of Peonage* on 2 March 1867 and had it proclaimed in New Mexico a month later. The law was not really enforced, however, until 1868, and even then master and servant relations did not change significantly. As every student of Reconstruction knows, Southern black workers continued to live in conditions of debt-peonage after 1865 in the South and else-where. The persistence of debt-peonage led the Supreme Court to declare in 1911 that all forms of peonage were unconstitutional. Perhaps the best evidence that we have passed from a tolerance of involuntary labor is the public's reaction of shock when it hears, for example, that an entire village in India is burdened by debt-peonage or that Mexican laborers in Arizona have been held in chains by an employer on an isolated Arizona ranch. . . .

## VIII

As a way of placing the discussion of bonded and contract labor in the American West in some larger perspective, the observations of M. I. Finley are instructive.

> Throughout most of human history labor for others has been performed in large part under conditions of dependence or bondage; that is to say the relations between the man who works and his master or employer rested neither on ties of kinship nor on a volun-tary revocable contract of employment, but rather on a birth into a class of dependents or debtors or some other precondition, which by custom and law automatically removed from the dependent, usually for a long term, some measure of choice or action.

From Finley's point of view labor in the early American West seems more tradi-tional than unique. Thus it appears even more remarkable that there have been so few comparisons of the age-old ethnic labor systems of the West with those of the South, or with African, Asian, or European systems. By neglecting the story of labor, Western historians have missed an opportunity to explain Western race rela-tions more fully, the nature of the Western economy, Western violence, and the remarkable continuity between the bonded labor system of the past and the contract labor systems of the nineteenth and twentieth centuries. . . .

This brief and selective survey should suggest that economic expectations rather than racism sometimes account for slavery or bondage in an abundant land, although racism can easily become a rationalization for slavery or abuse. At the same time, this essay may also suggest why bondage did not flourish on other American frontiers. A comparative approach to the history of bonded and contract labor within the whole of the United States cannot help but place slavery in the ante-bellum South in a new perspective. And finally it may be hoped that such a study also helps to explain the possibly ironic and yet profound meaning of Turner's be-lief that free land meant free people and a democratic society. For Turner, like Jefferson, insisted on talking about an ideal West rather than a real West. We may celebrate the names of both men one day, not for their presentation of the grim facts, but for this vision of what the West and America itself could mean.

## ⚓ F U R T H E R   R E A D I N G

Berlin, Ira. *Many Thousands Gone: The First Two Centuries of Slavery in North America* (1998).

Bolster, W. Jeffrey. *Black Jacks: African American Seamen in the Age of Sail* (1997).

Brown, Kathleen M. *Good Wives, Nasty Wenches, and Anxious Patriarchs: Gender, Race, and Power in Colonial Virginia* (1996).

Clark, Christopher. *The Roots of Rural Capitalism: Western Massachusetts, 1780–1960* (1990).

Donald, Leland. *Aboriginal Slavery on the Northwest Coast of North America* (1997).

Dunn, Richard S. *Sugar and Slaves: The Rise of the Planter Class in the English West Indies, 1624–1713* (1972).

Hahn, Steven, and Jonathan Prude, eds. *The Countryside in the Age of Capitalist Transformation* (1985).

Henretta, James, ed. *The Origins of American Capitalism: Collected Essays* (1991).

Hurtado, Albert L. *Indian Survival on the California Frontier* (1988).

Innes, Stephen, ed. *Work and Labor in Early America* (1988).

———. *Creating the Commonwealth: The Economic Culture of Puritan New England* (1995).

Jensen, Joan. *Loosening the Bonds: Mid-Atlantic Farm Women, 1750–1850* (1986).

Klein, Herbert S. *The Atlantic Slave Trade* (1999).

Kulikoff, Alan. *The Agrarian Origins of American Capitalism* (1992).

Linebaugh, Peter, and Marcus Rediker. *The Many-Headed Hydra: Sailors, Slaves, Commoners, and the Hidden History of the Revolutionary Atlantic* (2000).

Martin, Calvin. *Keepers of the Game: Indians, Animals, and the Fur Trade* (1978).

Morgan, Edmund. *American Slavery, American Freedom: The Ordeal of Colonial Virginia* (1975).

Morgan, Kenneth. *Slavery and Servitude in Colonial North America* (2001).

Morgan, Philip D. *Slave Counterpoint: Black Culture in the Eighteenth-Century Chesapeake and Lowcountry* (1998).

Nash, Gary. *Race, Class, and Politics: Essays on American Colonial and Revolutionary Society* (1986).

Rediker, Marcus. *Between the Devil and the Deep Blue Sea: Merchant Seamen, Pirates, and the Anglo-American Maritime World, 1700–1750* (1987).

Salinger, Sharon V. *"To Serve Well and Faithfully": Labor and Indentured Servants in Pennsylvania, 1862–1800* (1987).

Smith, Billy. *The "Lower Sort": Philadelphia's Laboring People, 1750–1800* (1990).

Steffen, Charles G. *The Mechanics of Baltimore: Workers and Politics in the Age of Revolution, 1763–1812* (1984).

Ulrich, Laurel Thatcher. *The Age of Homespun: Objects and Stories in the Creation of an American Myth* (2001).

———. *Good Wives: Image and Reality in the Lives of Women in Northern New England, 1650–1750* (1980).

———. *A Midwife's Tale: The Life of Martha Ballard, Based on Her Diary, 1785–1812* (1990).

Vickers, Daniel. *Farmers and Fishermen: Two Centuries of Work in Essex County, Massachusetts, 1630–1830* (1994).

Weber, David J. *The Spanish Frontier in North America* (1992).

White, Richard. *The Roots of Dependency: Subsistence, Environment and Social Change Among the Choctaws, Pawnees, and Navajos* (1983).

White, Shane. *Somewhat More Independent: The End of Slavery in New York City, 1770–1810* (1991).

Wood, Betty. *Women's Work, Men's Work: The Informal Slave Economies of Lowcountry Georgia* (1995).

CHAPTER
3

# *From the Artisan's Republic to the Factory System*

*When Philadelphians celebrated the newly ratified U.S. Constitution in 1791, masters, journeymen, and apprentices marched through the streets under banners that announced the unity reigning within each craft; only seventy years later, in the era when northern men rallied in support of the Union, urban workmen no longer felt it possible to march in the same ranks with merchants and manufacturers, who now employed them. In 1865 most Americans were farmers, and artisans working in traditional ways still produced most manufactured goods. But the egalitarianism of the early-nineteenth-century workshop had been replaced by a gaping social chasm that divided wage laborers in almost every trade from the factory owners and great merchants of the Civil War era.*

*The artisanal world had been characterized by small-scale production, local markets, skilled craftsmanship, and a self-reliant sense of community and citizenship. Early-nineteenth-century workmen thought of themselves as masters both in their household and in their trade, the upholders of an equal-rights tradition whose roots stretched back to the American Revolution. Historians have found in republicanism, the ideology that links civil virtue and personal independence to self-government, a powerful standard by which nineteenth-century workers judged and rejected the new men of wealth and power, who seemed to rise so quickly and to challenge so dramatically the values and livelihood of America's producing classes.*

*White women, blacks, and unskilled immigrants would obviously have an ambiguous relationship to this tradition. When white male workers denounced "wage slavery" in antebellum America, they may also have been separating themselves from all those whose standing, by virtue of their citizenship, gender, or race, was less autonomous and secure than their own. The republican tradition disdained all those whose work lives generated dependence and poverty; therefore, many white men came to define their own freedom and dignity in terms of the social, economic, and cultural distance they maintained from white women and African Americans, as well as the Asians and Mexicans with whom they would come in conflict in the years after the Civil War.*

*Factories, banks, railroads, and mines did not appear overnight. In nineteenth-century America, as in many underdeveloped nations today, large, mechanized enterprises existed alongside extensive systems of home production and the craft-based trades.*

*In fact, the process of industrialization had a patchwork quality that deskilled and depressed some trades and skipped others entirely. In New York and Philadelphia, a process of "metropolitan industrialization" created a marvelously heterogenous working class divided by skill, race, sex, and nationality. In contrast, the textile industry, which put its mills on isolated sites along the New England rivers, generated a more homogeneous class of workers. At the famous Lowell, Massachusetts, mills, Boston capitalists recruited thousands of young farm women and housed them in dormitory-like boarding houses. The textile factories of Rhode Island and Pennsylvania more typically employed whole families, relying heavily on a brutal system of child labor.*

*To what extent did unskilled textile operatives share the same outlook as the more skilled artisans? Could women share with their menfolk the equal-rights ideology that sustained antebellum workingmen? Or was the republicanism of these artisans an obstacle to gender equality and class consciousness? Could former slaves and other free people of color find a place within republicanism?*

## ✥ D O C U M E N T S

The rise of the factory system revolutionized the shoemaking trade in the pre–Civil War era. Documents 1–3 offer a glimpse of the work culture and protest traditions of workers in the Lynn, Massachusetts, shoe industry. In sketching apprenticeship life during the days of the old-time shoe workshop, David Johnson, a Lynn resident, re-creates in Document 1 the masculine work culture that members of the Mutual Benefit Society of Journeymen Cordwainers celebrated in the 1844 "Cordwainer's Song," reprinted here as Document 2. Document 3, a reporter's account of a mass meeting of Lynn women during the Great Strike of 1860, demonstrates that both men and women drew on the equal-rights tradition to attack wage slavery, but it also exposes persistent and deep gender divisions within the shoemaking work force. Document 4, a voice from the Lowell Female Labor Reform Association, demonstrates how women in another industry also made an ideologically charged attack on wage slavery. Document 5, an 1836 New York City handbill, shaped like a coffin, demonstrates the way in which journeymen tailors drew on the language of slavery and freedom to attack judges who jailed workers for forming a trade union. Document 6 is a selection from the autobiography of Frederick Douglass, the famed African American abolitionist, who encountered abuse, both physical and verbal, from the white apprentices and laborers when he worked in a Baltimore shipyard.

Why might workers have chosen to turn to the state rather than to their own organizations to fight the factory system? What roles did the increasing division of labor and employer hiring practices play in the inability of so many workers to find common ground? What is the interpretation that Frederick Douglass gives to the white hostility he encountered in Baltimore?

## 1. David Johnson Remembers Apprenticeship Life in the Artisan Shoe Shop, 1830

A boy while learning his trade was called a "seamster"; that is, he sewed the shoes for his master, or employer, or to use one of the technicalities of the "craft," he "worked on the seam." Sometimes the genius of one of these boys would outrun all limits. One of this kind, who may be called Alphonzo, worked on the seam for a

From David N. Johnson, *Sketches of Lynn or The Changes of Fifty Years* (Lynn, Mass.: Thomas P. Nichols, 1880), 30, 32–35, 59–62.

stipulated sum. He seemed to regard his work as an incidental circumstance. When he left the shop at night he might be expected back the next morning: but there were no special grounds for the expectation. He might drop in the next morning, or the next week. He left one Saturday night and did not make his appearance again until the following Thursday morning. On entering the shop he proceeded to take off his jacket as though there had been no hiatus in his labor. His master watched him with an amused countenance to see whether he would recognize the lapse of time. At length he said, "Where have you been, Alphonzo?" Alphonzo turned his head in an instant, as if struck with the preposterousness of the inquiry, and exclaimed, "Me? I? O, I've been down to Nahant." The case was closed. . . .

In almost every one of these shops there was one whose mechanical genius outran that of all the rest. He could "temper wax," "cut shoulders," sharpen scrapers and cut hair. The making of wax was an important circumstance in the olden time. To temper it just right so that it would not be too brittle and "fly" from the thread, or too soft and stick to the fingers, was an art within the reach of but few, or if within reach, was attained only by those who aspired to scale the heights of fame, and who, "while their companions slept, were toiling upward in the night." Such a one eyed his skillet of melted rosin as the alchemist of old viewed his crucible wherein he was to transmute the baser metals into gold. When the rosin was thoroughly melted, oil or grease was added until the right consistency was supposed to be nearly reached, the compound being thoroughly stirred in the meantime. Then the one having the matter in charge would first dip his finger in cold water and then into the melted mass, and taking the portion that adhered to his finger, would test its temper by pulling it, biting it, and rolling it in his hands. If found to be too hard, more oil or grease would be added, but very cautiously, as the critical moment was being reached. Then the test would be again applied. When the right result was supposed to be nearly gained, a piece of wax would be passed around among the crew for a confirmatory verdict. If the judgment of the master of ceremonies was indorsed, the experiment ended, and the mixture was poured into a vessel of cold water—usually the "shop-tub"—to cool sufficiently to be "worked." . . .

The shop-tub was an indispensable article in every shop. In early times, before the manufactures of wooden ware had become plenty and cheap, some rudely-constructed wooden vessel of home manufacture served the purpose. Afterwards a paint-keg or a firkin with the top sawed off, and still later a second-hand water-pail, was made to do service.

The theory was that the water of the shop-tub was to be changed every day. As this water was used for *wetting* the "stock"—which meant all the sole leather put into the shoe—and also often used for washing hands, it was somewhat necessary that it should be changed occasionally. The shifting of the "tub" often devolved upon the boy of the shop, except when he was too bright. In that case he "shirked" with the rest of the crew. This was the sort of boy that looked out of the attic window of the dormitory where he slept, to see if the smoke was gracefully curling from the shop's chimney, in the gray of the morning as he stretched himself for a supplementary snooze.

The man who had an "eye" for cutting "shoulders" occupied a niche of distinction among his fellow-craftsmen. If it was not necessary that he should have a "microscopic eye"—which Mr. Pope [the eighteenth-century English poet] tells us man does not need because he "is not a fly,"—it was needful that he should have a "geometric eye" when called upon to adjust the "shoulder" to "convex" and "concave" edges. To do this successfully required little less than a stroke of genius. Two cents was the usual price for cutting a "shoulder," and an experienced cutter would gather in each week quite a pile of the larger-size coppers of those days, whose purchasing power of many things was twice as great as at present. . . .

Perhaps one of the sorest experiences a boy had in old times in learning the "craft," was that which came from *breaking awls.* In order to fully appreciate the situation, the reader must take a survey of the whole field. It was a period of low wages. Awls were the most expensive "kit" used by the shoemaker. . . .

The awls were of two kinds, diamond and round, so called from the shape of their points. The diamond-shaped were usually preferred, as they were thought to be less liable to become dulled by use; but the so-called round awls—these were rather flatted at their points—were often used by "don" workmen, as they were less liable to "cut" the "upper." The awls first in use in this country were of English manufacture. The name of the manufacturer was stamped upon each awl, and there were three kinds, more or less in use, some fifty or more years ago when those of American make began to take their place. These were known as the Allerton, Wilson, and Titus awls, respectively. After the introduction of the American awl, the English article was not held in very high esteem by workmen employed upon ladies' shoes. They were badly shaped, and the points were left unfinished. The Allerton and Wilson had usually too long a crook, while the Titus was faulty in the opposite direction, being too straight, especially for certain kinds of work. They had, however, two important recommendations—they were better tempered, and therefore less liable to break, and their cost was only one-half, or less, that of the American awl.

Before the English awl was used, it was necessary to finish the points. This was sometimes done by grinding, sometimes by filing, and sometimes by sandpaper; and the points were smoothed off on a "whet-board," or by rubbing them on the pine floor. The man who could do this job skillfully was considered something of a genius. As already intimated, a boy could spoil a day's wages by breaking a few awls. If he was working on the seam on "long reds," and had a lot of extra hard soles on hand—some *hemlock tanned leather* for instance,—he had gloomy forebodings of the peril of the situation. If the master was a "hard" one, and the boy somewhat careless, there would most likely be an appeal to the "stirrup," whenever accidents of this kind rose above the average in frequency. . . .

## 2. Jessie Hutchinson, "Cordwainers' Rallying Song," 1844

(Tune—"My Bible Leads to Glory")

The cause of labor's gaining,
The cause of labor's gaining,
The cause of labor's gaining,

Throughout the town of Lynn.

---

From Jessie Hutchinson, "Cordwainers' Rally Song," *Awl,* February 22, 1845.

*Chorus*
Onward! onward! ye noble-hearted working men;
Onward! onward! and victory is yours.

Arouse the working classes, &c.
Unite the free cordwainers, &c.
Let JUSTICE be our motto, &c,
Come, join us, all true hearted, &c.
Our prices are advancing, &c.
The WOMEN, too, are *rising,* &c.
New members daily join us, &c.
Our victory is certain, &c.
We'll *stitch* our SOLES still closer, &c.
Let all protect free labor, &c.
There'll soon be joy and gladness, &c.

## 3. A Reporter's Account of Lynn Women's Mass Meeting During the Great Strike, 1860

About noon, the procession from Lynn, consisting of about 3,500 men, preceded by a brass band, entered the village green, escorted by 500 Marbleheaders. The sight from the hotel steps was a very interesting one. Four thousand men, without work, poor, depending partially upon the charities of their neighbors and partially upon the generosity of the tradesmen of their town, giving up a certainty for an uncertainty, and involving in trouble with themselves many hundreds of women and children, while to a certain extent the wheels of trade are completely blocked, and no immediate prospect of relief appears. Their banners flaunted bravely. Their inscriptions of "Down with tyranny," "We are not slaves," "No sympathy with the rich," "Our bosses grind us," "We work and they ride," "No foreign police," and many others of like import, read very well and look very pretty, but they don't buy dinners or clothing, or keep the men at work or the women at home about their business. By this strike $25,000 *weekly is kept from circulation in Lynn alone,* and who can say what the effect will be on the storekeepers, dealers in articles of home consumption, if such a state of drainage is kept up for any great length of time? . . .

The most interesting part of the whole movement took place last evening, and will be continued tonight. I refer to the mass meeting of the binders and stitchers held by the female strikers at Liberty Hall. . . .

There are two classes of workers—those who work in the shops and those who work at home—the former use the machines and materials of the bosses, while the latter work on their own machines, or work by hand, furnishing their own materials. It is evident that the latter should receive higher pay than the former, and the report not having considered this fact, was subjected to severe handling. The discussion which followed was rich beyond description—the jealousies, piques and cliques of the various circles being apparent as it proceeded. One opposed the adoption of the

---

From Howard, "The Bay State Strike," *New York Times,* February 29, 1860, 3.

report because, "the prices set were so high that the bosses wouldn't pay them." Cries of "Put her out," "Shut up," "Scabby," and "Shame" arose on all sides; but, while the reporters were alarmed, the lady took it all in good part, and made up faces at the crowd. The Chairman stated that, hereafter, Pickleeomoonia boots were to be made for three cents a pair less, which announcement was received with expressions of dismay, whereupon he corrected himself, and said they were to be three cents higher; and this announcement drew forth shouts and screams of applause. "There, didn't I *say* so?" said an old lady behind me. "You shut up," was the response of her neighbor; "you think because you've got a couple of machines you're some; but you ain't so more than anybody else." At this point some men peeped in at the window—"Scat, scat, and put 'em out," soon drove them away, and the meeting went into a Committee of the Whole, and had a grand chabbering for five minutes. Two ladies, one representing the machine interest, and the other the shop girls, became very much excited, and were devoting themselves to an *exposé* of each other's habits, when the Chairman, with the perspiration starting from every pore, said in a loud and authoritative tone of voice: "Ladies! look at me; stop this wranglin'. Do you care for your noble cause? Are you descendants of old Molly Stark or not? Did you ever hear of the spirit of '76? [Yes, yes, we've got it.] Well, then, do behave yourselves. There ain't nobody nowhere who will aid you if you don't show 'em that you're regular built Molly Starks over agin." [Cheers, clappings, &c.] . . .

A proposition to march in the procession was the next topic which drew forth discussion. Some thought that proper minded women would better stay at home than be gadding about the streets following banners and music. To this there was some assent, but when a younger girl asked the last speaker what she meant by talking that way, when everybody in Lynn knew that she had been tagging around on the sidewalk after the men's processions the last week. . . .

Some of the statements were quite interesting. A Mrs. Miller said that she hired a machine on which she was able to make $6 per week—out of that she paid—for the machine, $1; for the materials, $1.50; for her board, $2; for bastings, $1;—making $5.50 in all, which left her a clear profit of only fifty cents a week. One of the bosses says, however, that if a woman is at all smart she can make $10 per week with her machine, which would be clear $3, sure. In fact, from remarks which were dropped around I judge that Mrs. Miller's estimate is rather low. The leading spirit of the meeting, Miss Clara Brown, a very bright, pretty girl, said that she called at a shop that day and found a friend of hers hard at work on a lot of linings. She asked what she was getting for them, and was told *eight cents for sixty*. "Girls of Lynn," said Clara, "*Girls* of Lynn, do you hear that and will you stand it? Never, Never, NEVER. Strike, then—strike at once; demand 8½ cents for your work when the binding isn't closed and you'll get it. Don't let them make niggers of you; [Shame, there are colored persons here.] I meant Southern niggers:—keep still; don't work your machines; let 'em lie still till we get all we ask, and then go at it, as did our Mothers in the Revolution."

This speech was a good one; it seemed to suit all parties, and they proposed to adjourn to Tuesday night, when they would have speeches and be more orderly. Canvassing Committees were appointed to look up female strikers and to report female "scabs." And with a vote of thanks to the Chairman, the meeting adjourned to meet in Lyceum Hall. . . .

## 4. Amelia, a Woman Worker, Protests Lowell Wage Slavery, 1845

For the purpose of illustration, let us go with that light-hearted, joyous young girl who is about for the first time to leave the home of her childhood, that home around which clusters so many beautiful and holy associations, pleasant memories, and quiet joys; to leave, too, a mother's cheerful smile, a father's care and protection; and wend her way toward this far famed "city of spindles," this promised land of the imagination, in whose praise she has doubtless heard so much.

Let us trace her progress during her first year's residence, and see whether she indeed realizes those golden prospects which have been held out to her. Follow her now as she enters that large gloomy looking building—she is in search of employment, and has been told that she might here obtain an eligible situation. She is sadly wearied with her journey, and withal somewhat annoyed by the noise, confusion, and strange faces all around her. So, after a brief conversation with the overseer, she concludes to accept the first situation which offers; and reserving to herself a sufficient portion of time in which to obtain the necessary rest after her unwonted exertions, and the gratification of a stranger's curiosity regarding the place in which she is now to make her future home, she retires to her boarding house, to arrange matters as much to her mind as may be.

The intervening time passes rapidly away, and she soon finds herself once more within the confines of that close noisy apartment, and is forthwith installed in her new situation—first, however, premising that she has been sent to the Counting-room, and receives therefrom a Regulation paper, containing the rules by which she must be governed while in their employ; and lo! here is the beginning of mischief; for in addition to the tyrannous and oppressive rules which meet her astonished eyes, she finds herself compelled to remain for the space of twelve months in the very place she then occupies, however reasonable and just cause of complaint might be hers, or however strong the wish for dismission; thus, in fact, constituting herself a slave, a very slave to the caprices of him for whom she labors. Several incidents coming to the knowledge of the writer, might be somewhat interesting in this connection, as tending to show the prejudical influence exerted upon the interests of the operative by this unjust requisition. The first is of a lady who has been engaged as an operative for a number of years, and recently entered a weaving room on the Massachusetts Corporation: the overseers having assured her previous to her entrance, that she should realize the sum of $2.25 per week, exclusive of board; which she finding it impossible to do, appealed to the Counting-room for a line enabling her to engage elsewhere but it was peremptorily refused. . . .

But to return to our toiling Maiden,—the next beautiful feature which she discovers in this *glorious* system is, the long number of hours which she is obliged to spend in the above names close, unwholesome apartment. It is not enough, that like the poor peasant of Ireland, or the Russian serf who labors from sun to sun, but during one half of the year, she must still continue to toil on, long after Nature's

---

From "Voices from Lowell, 1845," in Philip Foner, ed., *The Factory Girls,* 1977, pp. 135–138 (Urbana: University of Illinois Press, 1977).

lamp has ceased to lend its aid—nor will even this suffice to satisfy the grasping avarice of her employer; for she is also through the winter months required to rise, partake of her morning meal, and be at her station in the mill, while the sun is yet sleeping behind the eastern hills; thus working on an average, at least twelve hours and three fourths per day, exclusive of the time allotted for her hasty meals, which is in winter simply one half hour at noon,—in the spring is allowed the same at morn, and during the summer is added 15 minutes to the half hour at noon. Then too, when she is at last released from her wearisome day's toil, still may she not depart in peace. No! her footsteps must be dogged to see that they do not stray beyond the corporation limits, and she *must,* whether she will or no, be subjected to the manifold inconveniences of a large crowded boarding-house, where too, the price paid for her accommodation is so utterly insignificant, that it will not ensure to her the common comforts of life; she is obliged to sleep in a small comfortless, half ventilated apartment containing some half a dozen occupants each; but no matter, *she is an operative*—it is all well enough for her; there is no "abuse" about it; no, indeed; so think our employers,—but do we think so? time will show. . . .

Reader will you pronounce this a mere fancy sketch, written for the sake of effect? It is not so. It is a real picture of "Factory life"; nor is it one half so bad as might truthfully and justly have been drawn. But is has been asked, and doubtless will be again, why, if these evils are so aggravating, have they been so long and so peacefully borne? Ah! and why have they? It is a question well worthy of our consideration, and we would call upon every operative in *our* city, aye, throughout the length and breadth of the land, to awake from the lethargy which has fallen upon them, and assert and maintain their rights. We call upon you for action—*united and immediate action.* But, says one, let us wait till we are stronger. In the language of one of old, we ask, when shall we be stronger? Will it be the next week, or the next year? Will it be when we are reduced to the service conditions of the poor operatives of England? for verily we shall be and that right soon, if matters be suffered to remain as they are. Says another, how shall we act? we are but one amongst a thousand, what shall we do that our influence may be felt in this vast multitude? We answer there is in this city an Association called the Female Labor Reform Association, having for its professed object, the amelioration of the condition of the operative. Enrolled upon its records are the names of five hundred members—come then, and add thereto five hundred or rather five thousand more, and in the strength of our united influence we will soon show these *drivelling* cotton lords, this mushroom aristocracy of New England, who so arrogantly aspire to lord it over God's heritage, that our rights cannot be trampled upon with impunity; that we will no longer submit to that arbitrary power which has for the last ten years been so abundantly exercised over us.

One word ere we close, to the hardy independent yeomanry and mechanics, among the Granite Hills of New Hamsphire, the woody forests of Maine, the cloud capped mountains of Vermont, and the busy, bustling towns of the old Bay State— ye! who have daughters and sisters toiling in these sickly prison-houses which are scattered far and wide over each of these States, we appeal to you for aid in this matter. Do you ask how that aid can be administered? We answer through the Ballot Box. Yes! if you have one spark of sympathy for our condition, carry it there, and see to it that you send to preside in the Councils of each Commonwealth, men who have hearts as well as heads, souls as well as bodies; men who will watch zealously over the interests of the laborer in every department; who will protect him by the strong arm of the law from the encroachments of arbitrary power; who will see that he is not deprived of those rights and privileges which God and Nature have bestowed upon him—yes,

> From every rolling river,
> > From mountain, vale and plain.
> We call on you to deliver
> > Us, from the tyrant's chain:

And shall we call in vain? We trust not. More anon.

## 5. Journeymen Tailors Protest Wage Slavery, 1836

The Rich against the Poor! Judge Edwards, the tool of the Aristocracy, against the People! Mechanics and workingmen! a deadly blow has been struck at your Liberty! The prize for which your fathers fought has been robbed from you! The Freemen of the North are now on a level with the slaves of the South! with no other privileges than laboring that drones may fatten on your life-blood! Twenty of your brethren have been found guilty for presuming to resist a reduction of their wages! and Judge Edwards has charged an American jury, and agreeably to that charge, they have established the precedent, that workingmen have no right to regulate the price of labor! or, in other words, the Rich are the only judges of the wants of the Poor Man! On Monday, June 6, 1836, these Freemen are to receive their sentence, to gratify the hellish appetites of the Aristocracy! On Monday, the Liberty of the Workingmen will be interred! Judge Edwards is to chant the Requiem! Go! Go! Go! every Freeman, every Workingman, and hear the hollow and the melancholy sound of the earth on the Coffin of Equality! Let the Court-room, the City-hall— yea, the whole Park, be filled with Mourners! But, remember, offer no violence to Judge Edwards! Bend meekly, and receive the chains wherewith you are to bound! Keep the peace! Above all things keep the peace!

## 6. Frederick Douglass Confronts Working-Class Racism, 1836

Very soon after I went to Baltimore to live, Master Hugh succeeded in getting me hired to Mr. William Gardiner, an extensive ship-builder on Fell's Point. I was placed there to learn to calk, a trade of which I already had some knowledge, gained while in Mr. Hugh Auld's ship-yard. Gardiner's, however, proved a very unfavorable place for the accomplishment of the desired object. Mr. Gardiner was that season engaged in building two large man-of-war vessels, professedly for the Mexican government. These vessels were to be launched in the month of July of that year, and in failure

From John R. Commons et al., *A Documentary History of American Industrial Society,* vol. 5 (Cleveland: Arthur H. Clark, 1910), 317–318.

From *Life and Times of Frederick Douglass: The Complete Autobiography* (Hartford, Conn.: Park Publishing, 1881), 178–187.

thereof Mr. Gardiner would forfeit a very considerable sum of money. So, when I entered the ship-yard, all was hurry and driving. There were in the yard about one hundred men; of these, seventy or eighty were regular carpenters—privileged men. There was no time for a raw hand to learn anything. Every man had to do that which he knew how to do, and in entering the yard Mr. Gardiner had directed me to do whatever the carpenters told me to do. This was placing me at the beck and call of about seventy-five men. I was to regard all these as my masters. Their word was to be my law. My situation was a trying one. I was called a dozen ways in the space of a single minute. I needed a dozen pairs of hands. Three or four voices would strike my ear at the same moment. It was "Fred, come help me to cant this timber here,"—"Fred, come carry this timber yonder,"—"Fred, bring that roller here,"—"Fred, go get a fresh can of water,"—"Fred, come help saw off the end of this timber,"—"Fred, go quick and get the crow-bar,"—"Fred, hold on the end of this fall,"—"Fred, go to the blacksmith's shop and get a new punch,"—"Halloo, Fred! run and bring me a cold-chisel,"—"I say, Fred, bear a hand, and get up a fire under the steam-box as quick as lightning,"—"Hullo, nigger! come turn this grindstone,"—"Come, come; move, move! and *bowse* this timber forward,"—"I say, darkey, blast your eyes! why don't you heat up some pitch?"—"Halloo! halloo! halloo! (three voices at the same time)"—"Come here; go there; hold on where you are. D—n you, if you move I'll knock your brains out!" Such, my dear reader, is a glance at the school which was mine during the first eight months of my stay at Gardiner's ship-yard. At the end of eight months Master Hugh refused longer to allow me to remain with Gardiner. The circumstance which led to this refusal was the committing of an outrage upon me, by the white apprentices of the ship-yard. The fight was a desperate one, and I came out of it shockingly mangled. I was cut and bruised in sundry place, and my left eye was nearly knocked out of its socket. The facts which led to this brutal outrage upon me illustrate a phase of slavery which was destined to become an important element in the overthrow of the slave system, and I may therefore state them with some minuteness. That phase was this—the conflict of slavery with the interests of white mechanics and laborers. In the country this conflict was not so apparent; but in cities, such as Baltimore, Richmond, New Orleans, Mobile, etc., it was seen pretty clearly. The slaveholders, with a craftiness peculiar to themselves, by encouraging the enmity of the poor laboring white man against the blacks, succeeded in making the said white man almost as much a slave as the black slave himself. . . .

Until a very little while before I went there, white and black carpenters worked side by side in the ship-yards of Mr. Gardiner, Mr. Duncan, Mr. Walter Price and Mr. Robb. Nobody seemed to see any impropriety in it. Some of the blacks were first-rate workmen and were given jobs requiring the highest skill. All at once, however, the white carpenters swore that they would no longer work on the same stage with negroes. Taking advantage of the heavy contract resting upon Mr. Gardiner to have the vessels for Mexico ready to launch in July, and of the difficulty of getting other hands at that season of the year, they swore that they would not strike another blow for him unless he would discharge his free colored workmen. Now, although this movement did not extend to me in *form*, it did reach me in *fact*. The spirit which it awakened was one of malice and bitterness toward colored people *generally,* and I suffered with the rest, and suffered severely. My fellow-apprentices very soon began to feel it to be degrading to work with me. They began to put on high looks and to talk contemptuously and maliciously of "the niggers," saying that they would take the "country," and that they "ought to be killed." Encouraged by workmen who, knowing me to be a slave, made no issue with Mr. Gardiner about my being there, these young men did their utmost to make it impossible for me to stay. They seldom called me to do anything without coupling the call with a curse, and Edward North, the biggest in everything, rascality included, ventured to strike me, whereupon I picked him up and threw him into the dock. Whenever any of them struck me I struck back again, regardless of consequences. I could manage any of them *singly,* and so long as I could keep them from combining I got on very well. In the conflict which ended my stay at Mr. Gardiner's I was beset by four of them at once—Ned North, Ned Hayes, Bill Stewart, and Tom Humphreys. Two of them were as large as myself, and they came near killing me, in broad daylight. One came in front, armed with a brick; there was one at each side and one behind, and they closed up all around me. I was struck on all sides; and while I was attending to those in front I received a blow on my head from behind, dealt with a heavy hand-spike. I was completely stunned by the blow, and fell heavily on the ground among the timbers. Taking advantage of my fall they rushed upon me and began to pound me with their fists. With a view of gaining strength, I let them lay on for awhile after I came to myself. They had done me little damage, so far; but finally getting tired of that sport I gave a sudden surge, and despite their weight I rose to my hands and knees. Just as I did this one of their number planted a blow with his boots in my left eye, which for a time seemed to have burst my eye-ball. When they saw my eye completely closed, my face covered with blood, and I staggering under the stunning blows they had given me, they left me. As soon as I gathered strength I picked up the hand-spike and madly enough attempted to pursue them; but here the carpenters interfered and compelled me to give up my pursuit. It was impossible to stand against so many.

Dear reader, you can hardly believe the statement, but it is true and therefore I write it down; that no fewer than fifty white men stood by and saw this brutal and shameful outrage committed, and not a man of them all interposed a single word of mercy. There were four against one, and that one's face was beaten and battered most horribly, and no one said, "that is enough"; but some cried out, "Kill him! kill him! kill the d—n nigger! knock his brains out! he struck a white person!" I mention this inhuman outcry to show the character of the men and the spirit of the times at Gardiner's ship-yard; and, indeed, in Baltimore generally, in 1836. As I look back to this period, I am almost amazed that I was not murdered outright, so murderous was the spirit which prevailed there. On two other occasions while there I came near losing my life. On one of these, I was driving bolts in the hold through the keelson, with Hayes. In its course the bolt bent. Hayes cursed me and said that it was my blow which bent the bolt. I denied this and charged it upon him. In a fit of rage he seized an adze and darted toward me. I met him with a maul and parried his blow, or I should have lost my life.

After the united attack of North, Stewart, Hayes, and Humphreys, finding that the carpenters were as bitter toward me as the apprentices, and that the latter were probably set on by the former, I found my only chance for life was in flight. I succeeded in getting away without an additional blow. To strike a white man was death by lynch law, in Gardiner's ship-yard; nor was there much of any other law toward the colored people at that time in any other part of Maryland. . . .

After learning to calk, I sought my own employment, made my own contracts, and collected my own earnings—giving Master Hugh no trouble in any part of the transactions to which I was a party. . . .

I was living among *freemen,* and was in all respects equal to them by nature and attainments. *Why should I be a slave?* There was *no* reason why I should be the thrall of any man. Besides, I was now getting . . . a dollar and fifty cents per day. I contracted for it, worked for it, collected it; it was paid to me, and it was *rightfully* my own; and yet upon every returning Saturday night, this money—my own hard earnings, every cent of it,—was demanded of me and taken from me by Master Hugh. He did not earn it; he had no hand in earning it; why, then should he have it? I owed him nothing. He had given me no schooling, and I had received from him only my food and raiment; and for these, my services were supposed to pay from the first. The right to take my earnings was the right of the robber. He had the power to compel me to give him the fruits of my labor, and this *power* was his only right in the case. . . .

## ✤ E S S A Y S

Because it provided such a classic example of the replacement of artisan labor by the factory system, the evolution of the shoemaking industry in its American capital, Lynn, Massachusetts, had long captured historians' interest. In the first essay, Alan Dawley of Trenton State College finds that the mechanization of shoe manufacture enhanced the power of Lynn's entrepreneurial class while it robbed artisan producers of their authority and independence. Dawley argues that women's presence in the Great Strike of 1860 offers a notable example of the inclusive character of the equal-rights doctrine. In contrast, in the second essay, David Roediger of the University of Illinois, Urbana, makes the case for the power of "whiteness" as an essential element in the ideological self-definition of Northern workers. Fearful that the factory system would reduce them to mere "hirelings" or even "white slaves" on a par with enslaved blacks, some antebellum workers conflated and denounced both the institution of slavery and those African Americans ensnared within its bonds.

How did the rise of the factory system change the character of the shoemaking work force? What accounts for the different views of Dawley and Roediger toward the labor rhetoric employed by the Lynn strikers? Why was the striker of 1860 defeated?

## Lynn Shoemakers and the Solidarity of Class

### ALAN DAWLEY

For two centuries after the initial white settlement of New England, profit hungry investors and frustrated fortune hunters encountered powerful restraints on economic development. They were impeded by Puritan strictures against profiteering, by mercantilist regulations of the economy, and by environmental backwardness. But they persevered, and by the second quarter of the nineteenth century their

Reprinted by permission of the publishers from *Class and Community: The Industrial Revolution in Lynn* by Alan Dawley, Cambridge, Mass.: Harvard University Press. Copyright ©1976, 2000 by the President and Fellows of Harvard College.

boundless ambition for gain had achieved significant breakthroughs in extending the principles and practices of [the] marketplace directly into the sphere of production.

Leading the way were shoes and textiles, which stood first and second in the industrial statistics of New England from the first statistical surveys in the 1830s through the Civil War. Together these industries carved great basins of industrialization out of the hilly, rock-ribbed countryside that straddled the Merrimack and Connecticut River valleys and ran inland from the shores of Rhode Island and eastern Massachusetts. Lynn lay in one of these basins stretching from Boston to the White Mountains and including the major manufacturing cities of Lowell, Lawrence, Haverhill, Salem, Manchester, and Newburyport, plus several other smaller cities in Massachusetts, New Hamsphire, and Maine. Furthermore, dozens of additional villages in the country imitated the enterprise of the more renowned urban centers, and in some of these hamlets outworkers for the shoe industry labored in the shadow of a local textile mill. Everywhere central shops, factories, and warehouses were shouldering their way in among the artisan shops, hay barns, livery stables, and grist mills that represented the vanishing era of economic restraint.

Lynn manufacturers joined the headlong rush toward unimpeded economic development. Between 1830 and 1836 they increased production by two-thirds, making this a time of "feverish excitement" when the character of the town changed "more rapidly and more essentially than at any previous period in her history." The number of streets and buildings nearly doubled in these years, and the physical strain on the community was compounded by social dislocation. The only thing that held back the rapacity of the entrepreneurs was the fearsome grip of panic, which took hold in 1837 and stopped them in their tracks. For the next seven years, they chafed at the restraints of the prolonged depression in the industry and organized through the Whig party to improve their prospects by increasing the tariff on imported shoes. But foreign competition was no longer a major factor in the industry, and when the domestic market finally responded to the proddings of the manufacturers in the mid-1840s, those who had survived congratulated themselves on being sounder and stronger than their fallen competitors and rushed ahead with renewed vigor. Another period of feverish expansion ensued between 1845 and 1850; boosted by the rapidly lengthening railroad network, shoe production came close to doubling. . . . Freed from the restraints of the past, the marketplace did not produce Adam Smith's version of stable, self-regulating progress, but manic cycles of expansion and contraction.

The main resource for expansion was labor. Increased output in the prefactory era was directly proportional to an increase in the number of shoemakers, and employers calculated profits in these terms: so many hands, so many dollars. During business upturns, they hired hand over fist; for every three employees of a Lynn firm in 1845, there were five in 1850. . . . Like the declining dominions of the Old South which were sending slave laborers to the more profitable cotton lands of the West, rural New England yielded up its laborers to employers who mined the area as if it were filled with gold. Making the transfer from farming to shoemaking was not difficult for the rural inhabitants, who had worked with their hands from childhood. What teenage girl did not know how to stitch and sew? What man who mended harnesses and repaired saddles could not learn the gentle craft of shoemaking, especially now that cutting was done by specialists? So for a quarter of a century the land readily gave up its people.

But no resource, however abundant, is inexhaustible. Employers quickly depleted the areas close to the cities, and they had to range ever further afield. Driven by gold fever, shoe manufacturers ventured into northern New Hampshire and Vermont, while textile employers prospected as far away as upstate New York and Canada in search of young female operatives. Competition among the employers was compounded by the migration of labor out of the region; enough Massachusetts natives moved to New York to make the number living there in 1850 almost equal to the total number of people employed by the entire Massachusetts boot and shoe industry. The shoe industry felt these pressures in the form of a diminishing marginal product in the branch where competition for labor was most keen—binding. In the 1830s each binder stitched an average of 934 pairs a year, but by 1850 the number had fallen below 700. . . .

Because textile recruiters sent most of the ready women without children to the factories, the boot and shoe firms had difficulty finding full-time binders and, instead, had to rely on new recruits who bound shoes intermittently between their other chores at home. "Women's nimble fingers," wrote one observer, "were found inadequate to the demand."

The geographical outreach of the outwork system heightened the manufacturers' dilemma by making production most sluggish at the frontiers of expansion. Transportation of raw materials to the fringes of the system 150 miles from Lynn consumed two or three weeks, and the return trip doubled the time lost in transit. When this delay was added to the easy going work pace logged by farmer shoemakers, the result was a waiting time that ranged as high as six to nine months before a pair of shoes was finished. The further the system expanded without changing its technological base the more difficult it encountered reaching its objectives. As the distance and time between the various steps in the manufacturing process increased and as it became harder to get binding done quickly, the method of sending work out of town, originally designed as a means of raising peak seasonal output, was beginning to have just the opposite result. The gold rush was coming to a close.

### Deus ex Machina

The manufacturers' problem was resolved by a deus ex machina in the form of a sewing machine. Minor modifications of the original invention enabled an operator to bind the uppers in a fraction of the time it took by hand. Therefore the manufacturer no longer had to expand the geographical frontiers of his labor force and instead could cut back the total number of female employees and hire a greater proportion from among residents of Lynn. The importance of the machine was emphasized by a newspaper closely identified with the manufacturers: "The introduction of sewing machines for stitching and binding of shoes was the result of an absolute necessity."

Since the uppers were made of cloth or light leather, the same machine could be used for binding uppers and mending a dress. Initially, the cost of the machines restricted their use to people with substantial savings, but their price steadily declined from the $75 to 100 range of the early 1850s to a level around $20 in the early 1860s, before Civil War inflation drove the price up again. Newspaper ads were frequently addressed to "the lady operator and the shoe manufacturer" and strained to make the point that they were for family use, as well as for manufacturing. The ads were effective, and soon "almost every house" in Lynn sported a sewing machine; the number of sewing machines per capita was more than the number of hogs had ever been in preindustrial Lynn.

However, the trend in manufacturing was unmistakably away from the household and toward the factory. The first machines were tried out and proved in the shops of three of the larger manufacturers in 1852. Because they employed two to three times as many people as the average firm, these manufacturers were more deeply entangled in the contradictions of the outwork system than the smaller employers and were especially eager for a way out. Their initiative spread, and by 1855 most of the leading manufacturers had begun to use sewing machines. Sometimes smaller contractors set up independent stitching shops, but usually manufacturers outfitted rooms of their own. From this point on through 1880 the trend in female employment was downward, even as total output rose: between 1850 and 1860 the number of women employed declined 40 percent, while their output doubled. Both speed and quality were enhanced by bringing operators and machines together under one roof, so that only one-fifth of the women employed in 1875 were left working at home.

From the outset, the stitching shops looked strikingly like factories. The gathering of as many as three or four dozen women in one room and the clatter of their machines were such a contrast to the picture of a woman quietly at work in her own kitchen that everyone agreed a fundamental change had taken place.

The invention of the sewing machine opened a new frontier, which "soon transformed the old fashioned 'shoe-binders' into a new and more expansive class of 'machine girls' whose capacity for labor was only limited by the capabilities of the machines over which they presided. Iron and steel came to the aid of wearied fingers and weakened eyes. This was the beginning of a new era, which is destined to produce results big with lasting benefit to our flourishing city."

Glowing enthusiasm for the factory system appeared in an 1860 federal census report on the boot and shoe industry. Describing the sewing machine as a "crowning invention," the article said that along with a sole-cutting machine it was bringing about "a silent revolution" in manufacturing. The report sensed the shoe industry was "assuming the characteristics of a factory system, being conducted in large establishments of several stories, each floor devoted to a separate part of the work, with the aid of steam-power, and all the labor-saving contrivances known to the trade. It is safe to predict that this change will go on until the little 'workshop' of the shoemaker, with its 'bench' and 'kit,' shall become a thing of the past, as the 'hand-card' and the great and little 'spinning wheel' have disappeared from other branches of the clothing manufacture." This report jumped the gun by a few years, but because the major forms of factory organization were fully represented in machine stitching, and because the model of textile industry was so compelling, it is not surprising that the report assumed the inevitability of a full-scale factory system.

## The Great Strike

The manufacturers' enthusiasm for machines and factories did not spread to the shoemakers. Binders and journeymen looked back over a quarter century of social dislocation, and now in the 1850s they feared that once again the manufacturers were up to no good. The first sewing machines introduced into the city "aroused the ire" of the binders, who saw them as another incursion on their household independence. A delegation of binders tried to block the spread of the new devices by visiting a central shop where one had been installed and requesting the operator to cease her work on the grounds that the machine "would ultimately be the ruin of the poor workingwomen." These early machines, which cost a third to a half of a binder's annual income, were clearly implements designed to benefit only capitalists; both the binders who went into the stitching shops and the shrinking group of those who worked at home continued to regard the new methods of production with extreme distrust. Each binder knew that the labor the new devices saved could well be her own, and what good, she wondered, could possibly come of something that eliminated hundreds of jobs each season.

The binders' ire was mollified for a time by the declining price of the sewing machine (making it more accessible for family use) and by the persistence of high levels of employment in the shoe industry. But when the Panic of 1857 brought the shoe business to a standstill, and workers all over the city were given the sack, the twin pressures of depression and displacement converged on shoemaker families to force discontent to the surface again, as in the 1830s and 1840s. The tensions between shoemakers and their bosses were apparent at two mass meetings held on the edge of winter in the depression's first year. As journeymen shoemakers and other laboring men of the community filed into Lynn's rustic Lyceum Hall, the chill November air reminded them of the blankets, overcoats, cordwood, and provisions they would need in the coming months, and of the long winter layover looming ahead when they would have little or no income. They listened with growing indignation while businessmen and politicians proposed emergency public relief, as if the honest workingmen of Lynn were nothing but paupers. Were they not able-bodied men willing to work?

At a second community meeting the following week, these sentiments buried the proposals for public relief. "Would it not be better," asked one opponent of charity, "for the show manufacturers to give full price—to say to the workman we will give you a little something to do until business is better?" And he added, "Let the rich come forward and say we will give you ten per cent of the profits we have made." The idea was radical enough to prompt a quick rejoinder from a shoe manufacturer and leather dealer named John B. Alley that the purpose of the meeting was not to degrade business for the benefit of labor. Alley was an up-and-coming politician on his way to the House of Representatives polishing the techniques of rhetorical compromise; he endorsed the work ethic but argued present circumstances made public relief a practical necessity.

Despite Alley's compromise, this debate set a tone of hostility for encounters between shoemakers and shoe manufacturers during the next three years. Eight months later several hundred journeymen sweltered through a July meeting in the Lyceum to consider a strike to raise wages. No action was taken immediately, but economic distress kept up a steady pressure, and by the spring of 1859 journeymen had established the Lynn Mechanics Association and had begun publishing the *New England Mechanic*. The Association and the *Mechanic* continued operation for the remainder of the year, becoming a solid core of organizational strength among the journeymen. Finally, in the winter of 1860 all the years of anxiety over the effects of machine stitching combined with the years of depression to produce a mounting frustration that bursts forth in the Great Shoemakers Strike.

The biggest strike the United States had ever experienced hit the whole upper New England basin like a driving "Nor'easter." The shoe centers along the North Shore bore the full brunt of the storm, where a clear majority of shoemakers joined the strike, and it also swept inland to secondary towns and outwork villages. All in all, probably a minimum of 20,000 people quit work, somewhat more than half the employees living in this region and a third of the 60,000 employees of all Massachusetts firms. The progress of the strike was given large play in most of the region's major newspapers, and national journals sent illustrators and reporters to the scene. The experience left an indelible mark on folk memory, and for a generation it was recalled with the frequency and vividness people usually reserved for earthquakes or hurricanes. . . .

Lynn was at the center of the storm. The strike began on Washington's Birthday, a date the journeymen picked to demonstrate they were acting in the best traditions of the Republic. They believed the producers were the bone and sinew of society, and in a community of interdependent households the producers should be able to unite and carry everyone along with them. The dimensions of their success were revealed in the scope and style of demonstrations and parades held in support of the strike. In six weeks, five processions passed through the streets of Lynn, each with 1,000 or more people in the line of march, plus hundreds of sympathizers in the sidelines. The largest demonstration occurred on March 16; besides strikers from Lynn marching in ward units, the 6,000 people who crowded into the procession included companies of militia and firemen, brass bands, and several out-of-town strike delegations. . . .

The strikers immersed themselves in the pageantry of waving banners and brightly festooned uniforms to show that their strike had the support and expressed the will of the general community. The presence of the militia companies and firemen—themselves mostly laboring men in special uniforms—emphasized the interdependence among the householders of an artisan community. The organization of the strikers into ward units bespoke the ties of neighborhood fraternity and sorority. The joint participation of men and women expressed the solidarity of all who labored in the craft. The strike processions, therefore, emerged from the customs and traditions of preindustrial society. They were festivals of the old artisan way of life presented in the context of the new system of industrial capitalism. Influences from the past and forces leading to the future simultaneously fashioned the present event.

The presence of women was a noteworthy feature of the processions. Without the action of women, it is questionable whether the strike would have occurred at all, and certainly without them it would have been far less massive in its impact. Women's grievances helped cause it; their demands shaped its objectives; their support ratified it as a community undertaking. Whether they worked at home or in the manufacturers' shops, all women employees earned piece wages, and both home and shop workers focused their demands on an increase in wages. They held their own strike meetings, did their own canvassing in Lynn and nearby towns to win support, and turned out in strength for the big street demonstrations. The laborer, they contended, was worthy of her hire.

The demonstration on March 7 was held in their honor. Escorted by a detach-ment of musket-bearing militia, 800 women strikers started at Lynn Common and marched in the falling snow for several hours past the central shops on Lynn's major thoroughfares. Their action was a bold violation of the cultural code that stipulated women should not venture beyond kitchen hearth and church pew. The keepers of this code of True Womanhood were middle-class families in retreat from the dis-order of urban life into their parlors, sewing circles, and church clubs. But working-women were bound to no such cult of domesticity. For several generations their labor had mingled with that of other producers, just as their protests had blended with the journeymen, and they were not about to renounce their own heritage of Equal Rights.

At the head of their procession they carried a banner with an inscription taken from the Equal Rights philosophy: "AMERICAN LADIES WILL NOT BE SLAVES: GIVE US A FAIR COMPENSATION AND WE LABOUR CHEERFULLY." Slavery had long been the measure of the ultimate degradation of labor, the point to which the shoe bosses seemed to be driving their employees. With the execution of John Brown only three months before the strike, artisans felt the immediacy of the conflict between slavery and Free Soil, and analogies linking manufacturers to slavemasters flowed freely. One speaker at a mass meeting declared it was not necessary to go to "bleeding Kansas" to find oppressors of labor; there were plenty who had been "drawing the chains of slavery, and riveting them closer and closer around the limbs of free laboring men at home." . . . The Equal Rights tradition contenanced a limited version of feminism: women who worked should be accorded a place of honor among the ranks of toilers, should be paid a fair and equal compensation, and should take an active role in defending the rights of labor. But this was the ex-tent of labor feminism: when it came to critical strike strategy, to political affairs, and to final arbitration in domestic matters, men ought to be in charge. Thus the cultural environment of the strike was filled with symbols of manhood which could hardly appeal to women strikers. The call to "stand for your rights like men!" must have left women seated in their chairs.

The "Cordwainers' Song" rallied shoemakers to the defense of the Tree of Liberty. Striking a classic Jeffersonian pose, the brave shoemakers prepared to shed their blood, should tyrants order their soldiers to fire. The tyrants of the song were the big shoe bosses of Lynn, especially those who practiced "dishonest com-petition" and affected an air of superiority in their dealings with the masses. But some of the manufacturers held the trust of the shoemaker, and four bosses re-ceived "Hurrahs!" when the Washington's Birthday marchers passed their central shops. One of the four reciprocated the holiday spirit by decorating his building with flags and bunting for the occasion. This was the kind of harmony between labor and capital many strike leaders hoped for. The week before Washington's Birthday, officers in the Mechanics Association had carried a bill of wages around to the manufacturers asking for voluntary agreement to pay the advanced rates. The committee even solicited contributions from the bosses to the strike fund! Shoe-makers were not surprised when several manufacturers actually subscribed to pay; leading the list was a boss who "agreed to be taxed $300." Believing they repre-sented the general will of their community, shoemakers found nothing strange in their plan to "tax" their neighbors.

Shoemakers prepared for the strike as members of the "producing classes." As producers they felt they were entitled to a fair reward for their toil, which they defined as an exchange of the goods they made for an equivalent value of food, clothing, shelter, and enjoyments. Anything less was cheating. Thus "monopolists" and "grinders" who cut their prices or cheapened their wares to increase their sales practiced "dishonest competition." In their train followed a host of unfortunate laborers forced to toil for a pittance on cheap goods until their existence approached the pauper labor of Europe. The dire result was the degradation of the earnings and reputations of "honest labor." When artisans divided their employers into "good bosses" and "bad bosses," they were not indulging in meaningless moralizing; they expressed a view of reality that conformed to the heritage of a community of householders.

Yet reality itself went well beyond this view. The central shop was no simple producer's household. The marketplace compelled manufacturers to adhere to the laws of competition, opposing the interest of those who bought labor to the interest of those who sold it. Moreover, shoemakers did not control the instruments of public authority. In the course of the strike, shoemakers were forced to face these disturbing facets of reality. The image of the artisan seemed to dissolve before their eyes, and in its place they saw an image of the industrial worker taking shape.

Shoemakers had to come to terms with the fact that manufacturers did not behave like fellow household producers. Only one came through on his pledge to the strike fund; the rest either reneged completely or paid only a trifling sum, such as a $20 contribution from the man who had agreed to be taxed $300. Worse than that, the manufacturers connived to break the back of the strike by hiring scab labor. They sent agents to ransack the surrounding states for workmen and hired "everything in the shape of a shoemaker." To the manufacturer, business was business, and the laws of the marketplace were more compelling than the will of the majority. With debts to pay, orders to fill, and customers to keep, manufacturers were not about to suspend the quest for profits just because the shoemakers desired it. But to the shoemakers, the manufacturers' effort to keep up production, after promising "to help us through, if we would strike and stick for a few weeks," was an outrageous betrayal. In a retrospective article fuming with indignation, two strike leaders snarled that the manufacturer, virtually without exception, tried to "defeat and disgrace us." One of the leaders told a group of binders in early April that the events of the past few weeks proved "the interest of capital is to get as much labor for as little money as possible."

Shoemakers had interests and compulsions of their own. Money wages were the staff of life; no one could survive any longer on home-grown pork and greens. Because shoemakers were wholly dependent on their industrial income, the wages of industrial unemployment were debt and destitution. Going into debt during the winter layover was a normal experience for shoemakers, but every year since the Panic of 1857 getting out of debt in the spring had been unusually difficult. The manufacturers were "grinding us down so low that men with large families could not live within their own means." Neither could young men with little experience (who were given low-paid tasks) nor women of any age and skill (whose wages were the lowest in the industry). Wage earners of all types concluded that the degradation of free labor was at hand.

In a mood of bitter determination shoemakers vowed that if the manufacturers would not willingly raise their wages, then they must be compelled to do so through a complete cessation of labor. This feeling motivated some strikers to use force to win their objectives, a marked contrast to the holiday atmosphere of the strike processions. On the morning of the day after Washington's Birthday a crowd of strikers gathered in front of the Central Square railroad depot. It was apparent that most manufacturers intended to maintain business as usual, because they continued to send cases of shoe stock to the depot for shipment to outworkers. A considerable portion of the crowd was in favor of preventing all such cases from leaving Lynn. Many who assembled that morning were piqued by a hoax played on them the previous afternoon, when they had carried what appeared to be a case of shoe stock back to its owner, only to discover it was filled with leather scraps and floor sweepings. This provocation was heightened by the local city marshal who addressed the crowd in insulting terms that "only served to increase irritation and excitement among the strikers who heard them."

The marshal got another crack at the shoemakers the same afternoon. With a few deputies in tow he fell upon a handful of men who were dumping cases destined for scab outworkers off an express wagon. The marshal's force succeeded in replacing the cases on the wagon, but in the eyes of the strikers, the marshal was now firmly identified with the shoe bosses, and his office lost whatever majesty it might have had. Pursuing their own justice, the strikers attempted to cast down the cases once again, and when the marshall stood in their way, they pummeled him and his men with their fists. It was reported that one of the strikers drew a knife. Overpowered in this fracas, the marshal refrained from further adventures that afternoon, and several more cases were taken from the train depot and returned to the central shops. In addition, the pugnacious expressman who tried to defend his cargo was "badly hurt," and strikers roughed up at least one journeyman on his way home with fresh materials.

In the eyes of the manufacturers the interference with the flow of trade and the attack on the city marshal constituted a vile threat to the social order bordering on insurrection. Through friends in city government, they prevailed upon the mayor to call out the militia. In his letter to the commander of the Lynn Light Infantry, Co. D, Eighth Regiment of the Massachusetts Volunteers, the mayor took note that "bodies of men have tumultuously assembled in [Lynn], and have offered violence to persons and property, and have, by force and violence resisted and broken the laws of the Commonwealth; and that military force is necessary to aid the civil authority in suppressing the same." The men were called to appear at their armory the next morning "armed, equipped with ammunition." Then while the mayor went off to counsel moderation before a mass meeting of shoemakers, other city officials got in touch with the state attorney general, the sheriff of Essex County, a major general in the state militia, and the city officials and police chiefs of Boston and South Danvers. The manufacturers were taking no chances with unruly employees.

The next day, February 24, shoemakers arose with dawning amazement to find their community occupied by outside police and armed militia. In the morning a detachment of deputies from South Danvers stood guard at the train station to see that there was no more interference with the shipment of shoe materials, and at 1:00

o'clock a posse of twenty uniformed Boston policemen arrived at the depot. These professional law officers joined the militia at an inn named the Sagamore House, which had been converted into command headquarters for the day. Decisions were in the hands of the attorney general, the major general, the city marshal, and several aldermen; conspicuously absent from the Sagamore were the mayor, who had fallen ill, and the city councilors. Apparently with the aim of arresting those who were disorderly the day before, the Boston regulars were sent back into the streets. Led by the hated city marshal, they roved through town for two hours, stimulating near riots where ever they went. Hounded by hoots and hisses, pelted by stones and brickbats, they ran the gauntlet of a hostile crowd, participated in a "general melee in which several of the crowd were knocked down," and finally ended their tumultuous trek through town at the railroad depot in Central Square where it had begun.

Most residents of the community were outraged at this incursion on their right of self-government. . . .Widespread indignation apparently blocked the prosecution of the five men arrested that day. Though they were spirited away to Salem for safekeeping and arraigned and bound over to the grand jury in Lynn a few days later, there is no record that the grand jury was ever convened or that any of the men were ever convicted by riotous conduct. The five benefited from community opposition to the odious actions of manufacturers and public officials, even though only one of the men arrested was a long-standing, propertied resident of Lynn. The others were newcomers, immigrants living in poverty, including the Irishman reported to have pulled a knife.

The turmoil of the first three days of the strike was the worst fury of the storm. On the evening of the third day the outside police and state officials left town, and the temporary soldiers dismantled their rifles and went home. That was the end of violence. But the passions stirred up in these days imparted a force and momentum to the strike that carried it through six weeks of mass organizing on a scale never before seen in American industry. While manufacturers hunted for scabs, teams of strike canvassers combed the neighborhoods of Lynn and visited a score of other shoe towns to mobilize support. Thousands of people were organized into strike processions, with thousands more watching. On the days of the processions, dozens of kitchens kept up a steady outpouring of food to provide refreshment to those who marched. In addition, there were rallies in Central Square, mass meetings in Lyceum Hall, and frequent meetings of the strike leadership in the Mechanics Association and the Ladies' Association of Binders and Stitchers.

Support of nonshoemakers was also mobilized. Besides other laboring men who marched in the fire and militia companies (with the conspicuous absence of the infamous Lynn Light Infantry), the city's retail businessmen were called upon to aid the strikers. Most grocers and provisions dealers were compelled to defer collection of shoemakers' bills, regardless of their opinion of the strike, but because of neighborhood ties and revulsion against the military invasion of their community, many retailers actively sympathized with the strikers. One lumber dealer, for example, gave shoemakers free access to a stand of trees he owned so they would not have to purchase cordwood. Several politicians also came forth, though their effort to curry favor with the voters led them into some strange political contortions. Congressman John B. Alley sent a donation of $100 to the strike fund, but after bending over backwards to be identified as a friend of labor he spun around and lectured the shoemakers on the foolishness and futility of their strike, intoning the perpetual murmur of the manufacturers, "the interests of the manufacturer and the journeymen are identical."

The strike was carried through March on high spirits, but by the beginning of April it was fast losing momentum, and within another two weeks it had subsided. Though a substantial number of manufacturers were paying higher wages by the end of the strike, the shoemakers were completely frustrated in their other goal of getting their employers to sign the bill of wages and thereby accede to the principle that shoemakers collectively had a voice in determining their wages. In this regard, the strikers were defeated partly by the decentralized character of bottoming (enabling manufacturers to get shoes bottomed by outworkers with less organization and militancy than Lynn artisans) and partly by the very economic factors that had caused the strike in the first place. To someone with no means of support except his labor, even low wages are better than no wages. Finally, the manufacturers' ability to lay their hands on the instruments of institutionalized violence (even though the effectiveness of the local police force on their behalf was nullified by the shoemakers) put the coercive power of the state on their side and tipped the balance of power their way. Coming after several decades of social dislocation caused by the growth of industrial capitalism, the Great Strike exposed the class fears and hatreds generated by the rising order. In the expanding marketplace, the manufacturer was both the hunter and the hunted, predator and prey. He sharpened his weapons, knowing that creditors and competitors did the same. Thus when a committee of his employees politely asked that he disarm, he politely refused, and when disorderly bands of employees broke his weapons in the street, he gave them a taste of martial law. For their part, the workers knew that the weapons of competition, though they be aimed at business competitors, struck them first. When it came to businessmen buying cheap and selling dear, employees' livelihoods could only suffer. And unless they could act collectively and affectively in their own cause, each would stand alone, the hunted and the prey.

## White Artisans and the Solidarity of Race

### DAVID R. ROEDIGER

In 1836, supporters of New York City's journeymen tailors papered the city with handbills featuring a coffin. The tailors had just lost a conspiracy case and with it their right to organize. The handbill encouraged protest and demanded redress in strong republican language familiar since the Revolution. It appealed to "Freemen" and to the power of "Mechanics and workingmen." But confidence that the cause of independence would prevail was at an ebb. The coffin signified that the "Liberty of the workingmen [would] be interred!" at the sentencing of the tailors. "Tyrant *masters*" had the upper hand, and the handbill's authors made a direct comparison

From David R. Roediger, *The Wages of Whiteness: Race and the Making of the American Working Class* (New York: Verso, 1991), pp. 65–92. Reprinted by permission of Verso.

that had been unthinkable even a decade before: "Freemen of the North are now on a level with the slaves of the South."

The "coffin handbill" shows both the new ease and the continuing hesitancy with which white workers in Jacksonian America began to describe themselves as slaves. Its unqualified North-South comparison is most striking, but the document also suggests some of the ways in which white workers remained beyond comparison with slaves. The whites, if slaves, were also simultaneously "freemen." If "tyrant *masters*" had prevailed, according to one line of the handbill, another line settled for invoking the fear of "would-be masters." Nor was it clear that the "slavery" of the tailors was "wage slavery." They were cast as slaves not because they were "hirelings" but because the state had deprived them of the freedoms necessary for defending their rights. The emphasis on the "slavery" of the tailors in fact proved rather short-lived. After hearing of a more favorable court decision in another conspiracy case upstate, "the journeymen's fury abated."

Other instances of comparison between wage labor and chattel slavery between 1830 and 1860 were likewise both insistent and embarrassed. They could not have been otherwise. Labor republicanism inherited the idea that designing men perpetually sought to undermine liberty and to "enslave" the people. Chattel slavery stood as the ultimate expression of the denial of liberty. But republicanism also suggested that long acceptance of slavery betokened weakness, degradation and an unfitness for freedom. The Black population symbolized that degradation. Racism, slavery and republicanism thus combined to require comparisons of hirelings and slaves, but the combination also required white workers to distance themselves from Blacks even as the comparisons were being made.

Chattel slavery provided white workers with a touchstone against which to weigh their fears and a yardstick to measure their reassurance. An understanding of both the stunning process by which some white workers came to call themselves slaves and the tendency for metaphors concerning white slavery to collapse thus takes us to the heart of the process by which the white worker was made. . . .

## The Winding Road to *White Slavery*

. . . By the Age of Jackson, several changes had created the setting in which white workers would begin to make and press, as well as deny and repress, comparisons between themselves and slaves. The rise, after 1829, of a highly visible movement to abolish slavery evoked reexamination of the line between slavery and freedom. Since free Blacks and slave rebels played so central a role in the Black freedom movement, the tendency to equate blackness and servility was likewise called into question. If abolitionism did not recruit more than a minority of white workers, it did make clear that equations between race and fitness for liberty were not eternal truths but objects of political debate.

Meanwhile, the experiences of the white artisans themselves encouraged the consideration of white slavery as a possible social category. In a nation agonizing over the fate of the Republic as the last of its revolutionary generation passed from the scene, urban craftsmen fought monumental struggles, concentrated between 1825 and 1835, for a ten-hour working day. Linking these struggles to time for self-education and full citizenship, the growing labor movement advocated the ten-hour system as the key to workers' independence and to the nation's. Seeking the immediate freedom of being less bossed by increasingly profit-driven masters—and ultimately to be free from having a boss—artisans who undertook concerted actions contrasted the fetters they felt and the liberty they longed for at every possible turn. The workers who gained the ten-hour day in the great 1835 Philadelphia general strike, for example, massed in Independence Square, marched to fife and drum and carried ten-hour banners alongside others proclaiming "LIBERTY, EQUALITY AND THE RIGHTS OF MAN."

The responses of employers tended to sharpen the artisans' sense that a great contest between freedom and its opposite was unfolding and encouraged them to raise the issue in terms of white slavery. In some cases, employers made the initial comparison of free US labor with British "slaves" and with Black slaves. They insisted that the ten-hour system could not function in the United States because the nation had to compete with Britain. The response of the *Working Man's Advocate* to this argument in 1832 reflected labor's view of the British system as utterly degrading. "Are we to slave thirteen or fourteen hours a day," the *Advocate* asked, "because the Manchester spinner or the Birmingham blacksmith so slaves?" As ten-hour struggles continued, US workers learned more about British resistance to long hours and answered employers' objections that British competition must be met in new ways that challenged the idea that only British workplaces encouraged servility. The *New England Artisan* wondered in 1834, "If the poor and oppressed but gallant working men of Great Britain have the daring hardihood to declare that they will work but eight hours . . . , how should the comparatively free . . . American working citizen feel?" In the midst of the shorter hours campaigns of the 1830s, some immigrant US workers also came to maintain that work in America was harder than it had been in Britain. When it was later argued that the ten-hour system could not prevail in Northern states because workplaces on that schedule could not match the production of Southern slave labor, the extent of the republican freedom of the white worker was still more sharply called into question.

Opposed to these substantial reasons for white workers to at least entertain comparisons of themselves and slaves was the continuing desire *not* to be considered anything like an African-American. Not only was the verb *slave* used, as we have seen, to indicate the performance of work in ways unbecoming to whites, but new and negative phrases such as *white nigger* (that is, "drudge") and *work like a nigger* (that is, "to do hard drudging work") came into American English in the 1830s, at roughly the same time that the term *white slavery* became prominent. Richard Henry Dana's searing indictment of the oppression of antebellum sailors in *Two Years Before the Mast* took care to quote an irate captain screaming at his crew: "You've got a driver over you! Yes, a *slave-driver,*—a *nigger driver!* I'll see who'll tell me he isn't a NIGGER slave!"

Such usages, which should give considerable pause to those who believe race and class are easily disentangled, remind us that comparing oneself to a slave or to any Black American could not be lightly undertaken in the antebellum United States. Moreover, it should be obvious that for all but a handful of committed abolitionists/labor reformers, use of a term like *white slavery* was not an act of solidarity with the slave but rather a call to arms to end the inappropriate oppression of whites. Critiques of white slavery took form, after all, alongside race riots, racially exclusive trade unions, continuing use of terms like *boss* and *help* to deny comparison with slaves, the rise of minstrel shows, and popular campaigns to attack further the meager civil rights of free Blacks.

In such a situation, it is not surprising that labor activists rather cautiously backed into making comparisons between white workers and slaves. Many of the earliest comparisons emphasized not that whites were enslaved but rather that they were threatened with slavery. In Dover, New Hampshire in 1828, leaders of four hundred striking women textile workers both connected and disconnected themselves to chattel slavery by asking who among them could "ever bear the shocking fate of slaves to share?" In 1833, male and female members of the Manayunk (Pennsylvania) Working People's Committee refused a wage cut because it would, as they put it, "rivet out chains still closer" and, over time, "terminate, if not resisted, in slavery." In 1834 Lowell's female strikers permitted themselves considerable ambiguity. In a single paragraph they cast themselves as virtually in "bondage," as threatened with *future* slavery by the "oppressing hand of avarice" and as the "daughters of freemen" still. Two years later protesting Lowell women sang:

> Oh! I cannot be a slave;
> I will not be a slave.
> For I'm so fond of liberty
> That I cannot be a slave.

For male artisans, who led the first labor movement, the rise of a small sector of full-fledged factory production both symbolized threats to independence and offered the possibility to experiment with application of the slavery metaphor to white (often child and female) factory workers without necessarily applying it to *themselves*. The factory system tended to confine and discipline workers to an unprecedented extent, at least by the 1840s. Moreover, it was identified with the degrading, antirepublican labor said to be required in Europe, a comparison that gave force to labor leaders' branding of it as a "gaol" or a "Bastille."

That US textile factories employing large workforces of single women (and smaller ones employing whole families) justified their management practices as paternalistic ones only sharpened suspicions of them. Blacklists and the whipping of workers in some small mills likewise provoked outrage. In the 1834 textile strike in Dover, one complaint of the women workers was that management called them "their *slaves*." Perhaps the managers meant to refer to their own paternal responsibilities in adopting this usage, or perhaps to their dictatorial powers. In any case, they hit just the wrong note. Quitting and other forms of informal protest far outdistanced strikes among early mill workers, but for male artisans contemplating the new industrial system the issue of permanent "factory slavery" was a fearsome one.

Many early references to white slavery thus focused on so identifying British manufacturing workers and on adding that women and children in the United States were, or were about to be, so enslaved. "The Factory Girl," an abominable piece of British verse that was in the US perhaps the most widely reprinted of the early treatments of white slavery, combined the ideas that British workers, and women workers in textiles, were in bondage. It portrayed the sad end of a female British worker:

> That night a chariot passed her
> While on the ground she lay;

> The daughters of her master
> An evening visit pay—
> Their tender hearts were sighing,
> As negroes' wrongs were told;
> While the white slave was dying,
> Who gained their fathers' gold.

This highly sentimental pressing of the comparison with chattel slavery ran through much antebellum writing on white female and child workers by male activists. Seth Luther's stirring 1832 *Address to the Workingmen of New England,* for example, does not refer to American male journeymen as slaves, but it does find factory women in bondage and does quote sentimental verse describing child laborers as "little sinless slaves."

Once made, comparisons to slaves could of course be extended, and artisans sometimes did come to be included in them. By 1835, for example, Luther was helping to write the "Ten-Hour Circular," which bitterly castigated "slavery among [white] mechanics." Stephen Simpson, intellectual leader and first Congressional candidate of the Philadelphia Working Men's party, began his 1831 *Working Man's Manual* by arguing that factory slavery had taken root in Britain where a "serf class" worked in manufacturing but that it could never grow in the US, which had disconnected the age-old links among "slavery, labor [and] degradation" and had made work the province of a "community of FREEMEN." Simpson then proceeded to take virtually all other possible positions. He noted the presence of huge numbers of slaves in the South, where he admitted that "labour shares in . . . disgrace, because it is a part of the slave." Within a few lines the US was characterized as a society sustained by a "mixture of slavery and labor." White women and children suffered special exploitation because "custom . . . classed them with slaves and servants." And, for that matter, Simpson argued, all Northern workers faced a situation in which "capital [was] the Master" and in which employers calculated wages in a manner like that of the "lords of the South [who oppress] sable herds of brutalized humanity."

Some workers, usually in factories, did describe themselves and their peers as already and fully enslaved. As early as 1831, Vermont operatives protested that they were "slaves in every sense of the word," while Lynn shoemakers of the 1840s saw themselves as having "masters—aye, masters" and as being "slaves in the strictest sense of the word." Lowell textile women echoed the Vermont millhands, describing themselves as slaves to long hours, as slaves to the "powers that be" and as "slaves in every sense of the word."

However, radical artisans remained more comfortable discussing the "slavery" of others than that of themselves. George Henry Evans, the printer, labor leader and land reformer who probably did more than anyone else to popularize the terms *white slavery* and *slavery of wages,* could be direct and sweeping in describing even male artisans as, if landless, then unequivocally enslaved. "Stealing the man away from his land, or his land away from the man," he argued, "alike produces slavery." Even Evans's individual writings did not tend to discuss the "slavery" of artisans but instead to concentrate on that of tenant farmers, the unskilled, women workers and child laborers. Though eloquent and expressive of the real fears of white workers, comparisons with slaves did not automatically lead to sustained self-examination among those groups of "hirelings" who were most active in organized labor in the antebellum years.

## White Slavery and Wage Slavery

. . . [A] closer look at the labor and radical Democratic press of the 1840s shows that *white slavery* was the most common phrasing of metaphors regarding white workers' oppression with *slavery of wages* second and *wage slavery* a very distant third. Indeed, the term *white slavery* was at times used even in articles speculating about the fate of free *Blacks* if abolition prevailed! Probably because *wage slavery* survived the Civil War in much wider currency and continued to be a phrase used by Marxist writers (and soapboxers) into the twentieth century, it was read back into antebellum history as the most common way for white workers to press comparisons with slavery. *White slavery* meanwhile came to be much more narrowly associated with female prostitution, and its use in accounts of the earlier period declined.

. . . If some labor writers did at times freely substitute *white slavery* and *slavery of wages* for each other, that pattern needs to be explained, for the terms carry quite different implications.

*Slavery of wages* came to be used alongside *white slavery* by land reformers and utopian socialists in the last half of the 1840s, often in dialogue with abolitionists. Its wording raised the old issue of whether hireling labor and republican independence could coexist. But its very precision and directness raised problems. Many of those being described as slaves were not wage-earners. Thus, tenant farmers and those imprisoned for debt were frequently discussed, but the problem of the latter was precisely that they could not enter the wage labor market. Most early labor activists remained tied to one of the major political parties, usually the Democrats, and sought unity among the "producing classes," including small employers. To refer to such employers as "masters, aye masters," made sense in terms of fleshing out the metaphor of slavery of wages, but it did not make political sense. Moreover, many masters were simply self-employed workers or men who sporadically employed others while depending mainly on their own labor. Many failed and again became wage-earners. Some evidence suggests that small employers paid better than manufacturers with larger workshops, and clearly merchant capitalists often pressured masters to maintain tough labor policies. Journeymen *aspired* to run a small shop of their own. "Men must be masters," Whitman wrote, "under themselves."

Metaphors regarding the slavery of wages thus confronted the problem that, if the worker could be called a *slave,* the wage-paying master could not, except in the heat of labor conflict, really be regarded as a *slavemaster.* One stopgap solution was to hold that the master himself was a "slave." Boston's "Ten-Hour Circular" thus argued:

> We would not be too severe on our employers [for] they are slaves to the Capitalists, as we are to them. . . . But we cannot bear to be the servant of servants and slaves to oppression, let the source be where it may.

Evans, in keeping with his emphasis on land and rent, similarly maintained that small manufacturers in Lynn were mastered by landlords who owned their shops, while the New York *Mechanic* complained of the "capitalists . . . bossing all the mechanical trades."

The advantages of the phrase *white slavery* over *wage slavery* or *slavery of wages* lay in the former term's vagueness and in its whiteness, in its invocation of *herrenvolk* republicanism. *White slavery* was particularly favored by radical Democratic politicians for a time because it could unite various elements of their coalition—wage workers, debtors, small employers and even slaveholders—without necessarily raising the issue of whether the spread of wage labor was always and everywhere anti-republican. Abolitionists, free Blacks, bankers, factory owners and prison labor could, in sundry combinations, be cast as villains in a loose plot to enslave white workers. Moreover, *white slavery* did not necessarily require a structural solution—arrest of the spread of hireling labor. Although some who employed the term did go on to argue that all long-term wage dependency was bondage, *white slavery* itself admitted solutions short of an attack on the wage system. White workers could be *treated* better—reforms could occur, as they did in the "coffin handbill" case—and the comparison with slavery could be exorcised.

*White slavery* also served well because it did not call into question chattel slavery itself, an issue that sharply divided the labor movement, the Jacksonians and the nation. . . .

Attacking white slavery did not, however, necessarily mean accepting Black slavery. The very title of the New York Society for the Abolition of All Slavery, an organization active in the 1840s, signalled that some militants favored attacks on both chattel slavery and the wage system. Some artisans, heirs to the radical democratic and antislavery traditions of Tom Paine, Benjamin Franklin and Robert Owen, did attempt to apply the principles of liberty and equality to both races. Craft workers and native-born women textile workers were important supporters of the abolitionist movement in the 1830s and 1840s. On a few occasions labor organizations took abolitionist positions and labor papers more often did so. It was even possible, in theory at least, to hold that white slavery was more oppressive than Black slavery, but that both deserved to be abolished. In practice, however, the "Down with all slavery!" position proved exceedingly hard to maintain, and its supporters were inconsistent in advocating emancipation. . . .

### Free Labor, White Slavery and the Fate of Labor Abolitionism

. . . Amidst new peaks in the numbers of wage workers and amidst what Robert Fogel has described as a protracted, severe decline in the living standards of native-born workers, the metaphor *white slavery* dramatically gave way. Horace Greeley's trajectory was not atypical, moving as he did from a utopian socialist conviction that Northern workers were "slaves" to the wage system in the 1840s to a Republican defense of Northern *free labor* by 1860. Republicans continued to spill tremendous amounts of ink over the threat of white slavery, but it was seen as just that—a threat and not a reality. And the threat was increasingly seen as coming, not from capital, but from a conspiracy of slaveholders against the Republic. . . .

One overlooked reason for the hesitancy of many workers to call themselves slaves was that a significant minority of the Northern working class was abolitionist. . . . [A]rtisans and workers in shoe and textile factories formed a significant part of the abolitionist rank-and-file, probably out of proportion to their share of the population. And we have long known that Black workers provided much of the energy of the abolitionist movement. It was, of course, possible to support abolitionism and to attack "wage slavery" at the same time. Whites like John A. Collins, William West, Sarah Bagley, Horace Greeley, Nathaniel P. Rogers and Evans sought to attack "all slavery," and some free Blacks even referred to themselves as slaves. However, especially before the alliance of Evans and Gerrit Smith around a program of abolition and land reform in the late 1840s, a consistent lesson taught by abolitionism was that chattel slavery was a category of oppression much harsher than any other.

Escaped slaves made this point especially vividly. . . . Black abolitionists recounted telling stories about informing "white slaves" that their former position on the plantation was open after their escape but never finding anyone eager to take the job. The escaped slave and abolitionist William Wells Brown squarely confronted the chattel slavery/white slavery debate by reminding audiences that even in relatively antirepublican Britain, white workers were free to change employers, free to educate their children and free to make use of the judicial system. White abolitionists echoed these distinctions.

And they were heard. Even labor papers making the case for the existence of white slavery printed arguments sharply calling the metaphor into question. The letter of "A Factory Girl" to the *Voice of Industry* in 1845 came at the height of class struggle in the textile industry. It encouraged workers to listen to the "eloquent appeals" of Frederick Douglass and to realize that there "is a depth in *slavery* beyond the reach of any, but those who have been made the recipients of its horrors." . . . Similarly, during the militant Lynn shoe strike in 1860, women workers carried banners promising that they would not be "SLAVES." But at the same time a worker wrote, "You know we are not a quarter as bad off as the slaves of the South, though we are by our foolishness ten times as bad off as we ought to be. They can't vote, nor complain and we can." . . . A *New England Offering* editorial in 1848 began by allowing that the "Northern laborer has not its rightful privileges [that] in some things he suffers what a slave may never be called upon to endure [and] that poverty and dependence are thraldom." But it added immediately that "every freeman should repel with indignation" the white slavery metaphor. The editorial argued that this was necessary out of "self respect" and was required for the white worker to do "justice to himself" as well as to do justice to the slave. To call the white workers a slave, according to the *Offering*, not only "obliterate[d] nice distinctions" but "detract[ed] from the dignity of the laborer." . . .

It was . . . when the debate moved away from stacking the material grievances of the slave against those of the white worker—that the white slavery metaphor collapsed. . . .

The grounds for defending the white slavery metaphor were typically quite ill-connected to republican traditions. In one 1846 National Reform debate on slavery, for example, a speaker raised sharp objections to the phrase *slavery of wages,* pointing out that white workers could not be sold. True enough, came the reply, but the Black slave has "attendance in sickness" not enjoyed by whites. A third speaker then added that such differences were as inconsequential as those "twixt dweedledum and tweedledee." The exchange illustrates the tendency of those attacking "all slavery" to liquidate the republican critique of hireling labor, to lose focus on the question of dependency, and to suggest, amidst fierce rhetoric, that liberal, even paternal, reforms could save the day. "AMERICAN LADIES WILL NOT BE SLAVES" ran the motto of Lynn's striking shoe workers before concluding "GIVE US A FAIR COMPENSATION AND WE LABOUR CHEERFULLY." . . .

That proslavery Southerners were also using the term *white slavery* highlighted the fact that the term could not lastingly justify itself in terms of the very *herrenvolk* republicanism that had initially given it life. Some white workers might ally themselves with Southerners like Calhoun for specific reasons, stressing common enemies. But the proslavery South was, not surprisingly, a very inconsistent ally, ultimately more ready and able to forge alliances with Northern merchant capital, especially in the labor movement center of New York City, than with workers. Suggestions that the United States embrace a *herrenvolk* labor system shunting all undesirable work onto Black slaves and "freeing" whites for higher tasks were only episodically made. In such a situation, to be called "slaves" by lordly Southerners came to be seen as a considerable affront. That some Southerners argued that slavery was a superior way to organize society, and that ideally white workers should also be chattel, did not help matters. As some Southern writers on white slavery confessed, "Free society! We sicken of the name." The entire metaphor itself became disgraced. When proslavery Southerners characterized Northern workers as "greasy mechanics" or "menials" as well as white slaves, it became clearer that these were words of contempt, not of sympathy. . . .

As a badge of degradation, shorn of the possibility of quick dramatic change, the term *white slavery* could not survive as a phrase embraced by Northern white workers. Antislavery poets, especially James Russell Lowell, searingly mocked the politicians—North and South—who called workers "witewashed [sic] slaves." Labor reformers, some of whom had used and were using *white slavery,* by the late 1840s began inching toward a defense of the free labor North and pointing to the particular degradation of white Southerners. The latter group was said to obey "like bondmen" and to live in a society that, because it did not recognize that the mechanic's "capital is his ingenuity and his sinews," attacked the workers' "dignity as citizens, and their manhood as freemen." . . .[T]he main appeals of the Republican party to workers in the 1856 election consisted of publicizing degrading comments made about Northern wage-earners by Southern proslavery figures.

Bernard Mandel . . . has pointed out that, from the 1830s on, some white workers became angry when *others* called them slaves. He cited several examples of what he called early "I can say it about myself but you can't" rejections of metaphors using slavery to describe white labor. The process by which the term *white slave* came to be rejected by Northern workers when it came from Southerners suggests something of the same logic. But a deeper explanation—and one more able to account for the language and practice of Northern white workers all the way from the attacks on the word *servant* to the embrace of the term *free white labor*—would run: "You can't say it and I can say it about myself only with great hesitation and trepidation."

That is, the term *white slavery* always fought an uphill battle in a nation in which racism, slavery and republicanism conspired to make it exceedingly hard to cast oneself as in bondage. To be a slave, even a white slave, was to be associated with degradation. Genteel factory women who rejected the term knew this, and knew that slavery implied sexual exploitation as well. To be a slave also implied connection with blackness. Northern workers became angry not only when called *white slaves* by Southerners but also, and undoubtedly more so, when called *white niggers.* The proponents of the term *white slavery,* Republican advocates of free white labor cleverly charged in 1857, made the white "the counterpart of the negro."

Both white slavery metaphors and working class abolitionism served to locate the position of hired labor within a *slaveholding* republic. Both failed because they could not do so unproblematically. Comparisons of white workers with slaves, which are too often considered as simply *class* expressions, were shot through with resonances regarding America's racial realities. To ask workers to *sustain* comparisons of themselves and Black slaves violated at once their republican pride and their sense of whiteness. Since justifications for the metaphors tended to focus on the *treatment* of white workers, the republican critique of hireling labor as a threat to personal and political independence was generally not sharpened or advanced by comparisons to chattel slavery. . . .

We know that many abolitionists were evangelical Christians who claimed control over their own moral and economic destiny. We know that mechanics and other workers were important parts of the mass base of abolitionism. We know that many mechanics joined the revivals and the temperance movement. In such a situation it is likely that only some of the mechanics supporting abolition were rebels also inclined toward trade unionism. In arguing for the importance of workers in early abolitionism, the antislavery leader Thomas Wentworth Higginson referred, for example, not to freethinkers but to those afire with "the Second Advent delusion." Many were workers who, whatever their doubts and whatever their chances, sought to achieve independence through moral reform and steady habits. They worried about being "slaves to drink" or "slaves to sin" but claimed the ability to change individually and to prosper. In many ways, this worldview salvaged as much as the republican vision as the critique of white slavery did. But in a nation in which whiteness was so important and emancipation so hard to imagine, abolition was bound to be a minority movement within the working class as in the larger society. If the rhetorical framework of white slavery was limited because it asked white workers to liken themselves to Black slaves, working class abolitionism was limited because it asked white workers to organize energetically on the Black slaves' behalf.

The defense of free white labor, around which the Republican party gained ground in the 1850s and to which opposing parties also sought to appeal, succeeded among white workers because it better appealed to the values of *herrenvolk* republicanism than did either the languages of white slavery or of abolitionism. It did not ask white workers to consider themselves slaves nor devote themselves to slaves. But a broader similarity among the various languages of labor should also be noted. All of the three approaches liquidated the question of hireling labor. The abolitionist and free labor analyses tended to regard the wage bargain as freely arrived at, and perhaps temporary. The white slavery position had to force the comparison it sought to make through hyperbole by chronicling the ill-treatment of white workers and often retreated from its criticisms at the first sign of liberalization.

. . . [I]n looking at US working class history, it is clear that the existence of *slavery,* not just of antislavery, stalled the development of a telling critique of hireling labor—a critique that might have built on and transcended the republican heritage. It was not just the abolitionists and Republicans who failed to produce such a critique. Also failing were the often proslavery laborites who argued that workers were white slaves. As long as slavery thrived, any attempt to come to grips with wage labor tended to lapse into exaggerated metaphors or frantic denials of those metaphors. Only with Black emancipation could a more straightforward critique of wage slavery, and a fierce battle over the meaning of *free labor,* develop. By that time, the importance of a sense of whiteness to the white US worker was a long-established fact, not only politically but culturally as well.

## ✣ F U R T H E R    R E A D I N G

Blewett, Mary H. *Men, Women, and Work: Class, Gender, and Protest in the New England Shoe Industry, 1780–1910* (1988).

Boydston, Jeanne. *Home and Work: Housework, Wages, and Ideology in the Early Republic* (1990).

Clark, Christopher. *The Roots of Rural Capitalism: Western Massachusetts, 1780–1860* (1990).

Dawley, Alan. *Class and Community: The Industrial Revolution in Lynn* (1976).

Dublin, Thomas. *Transforming Women's Work: New England Lives in the Industrial Revolution* (1994).

———. *Women and Work: The Transformation of Work and Community in Lowell, Massachusetts, 1826–1860* (1979).

Eisler, Benita. *The Lowell Offering: Writings by New England Mill Women, 1840–1845* (1997).

Fahler, Paul G. *Mechanics and Manufacturers in the Early Industrial Revolution: Lynn, Massachusetts, 1780–1860* (1981).

Foner, Philip S., ed. *The Factory Girls* (1977).

Gilje, Paul, and Howard B. Rock, eds. *Keepers of the Revolution: New Yorkers at Work in the Early Republic* (1992).

Gillespie, Michele. *Free Labor in an Unfree World: White Artisans in Slaveholding Georgia, 1789–1960* (2000).

Glickstein, Jonathan. *Concepts of Free Labor in Antebellum America* (1991).

Greenberg, Brian. *Worker and Community: Response to Industrialization in a Nineteenth-Century American City, Albany, New York, 1850–1884* (1985).

Hirsch, Susan. *Roots of the American Working Class: The Industrialization of Crafts in Newark, 1800–1860* (1978).

Jacobson, Matthew Frye. *Whiteness of a Different Color: European Immigrants and the Alchemy of Race* (1998).

Katznelson, Ira, and Aristide Zolberg, eds. *Working-Class Formation* (1886).

Laurie, Bruce. *Artisans into Workers: Labor in Nineteenth-Century America* (1989).

———. *Working People of Philadelphia, 1800–1850* (1980).

Levine, Bruce. *The Spirit of 1848: German Immigrants, Labor Conflict, and the Coming of the Civil War* (1992).

Montgomery, David. *Beyond Equality: Labor and the Radical Republicans, 1862–1872* (1967).

———. *Citizen Worker: The Experience of Workers in the Union States with Democracy and the Free Market During the Nineteenth Century* (1994).

Murphy, Teresa Anne. *Ten Hours' Labor: Religion, Reform, and Gender in Early New England* (1992).

Osterud, Nancy Grey. *Bonds of Community: The Lives of Farm Women in Nineteenth-Century New York* (1991).

Prude, Jonathan. *The Coming of the Industrial Order: Town and Factory Life in Rural Massachusetts, 1810–1860* (1993).

Rock, Howard. *Artisans of the New Republic: The Tradesmen of New York City in the Age of Jefferson* (1979).

Rock, Howard B., Paul A. Gilje, and Robert Asher, eds. *American Artisans: Crafting Social Identity, 1750–1850* (1995).

Roediger, David. *The Wages of Whiteness: Race and the Making of the American Working Class* (1991).

Roediger, David, and Martin H. Blatt, eds. *The Meaning of Slavery in the North* (1998).

Ross, Stephen J. *Workers on the Edge: Work, Leisure, and Politics in Industrializing Cincinnati, 1878–1890* (1985).

Saxton, Alexander. *The Rise and Fall of the White Republic: Class Politics and Mass Culture in Nineteenth-Century America* (1990).

Stanley, Amy Dru. *From Bondage to Contract: Wage Labor, Marriage, and the Market in the Age of Slave Emancipation* (1999).

Stansell, Christine. *City of Women: Sex and Class in New York: 1789–1860* (1986).

Tomlins, Christopher. *Law, Labor, and Ideology in the Early Republic* (1993).

Turbin, Carole. *Working Women of Collar City: Gender, Class, and Community in Troy, New York, 1864–1886* (1992).

Walkowitz, Daniel J. *Worker City, Company Town: Iron and Cotton-Worker Protest in Troy and Cohoes, New York, 1855–1884* (1978).

Wallace, Anthony F. C. *Rockdale: The Growth of an American Village in the Early Industrial Revolution* (1978).

Ware, Caroline. *The Early New England Cotton Manufacture* (1931).

Ware, Norman. *The Industrial Worker, 1840–1860* (1924).

Way, Peter. *Common Labour: Workers and the Digging of North American Canals, 1780–1850* (1993).

Wilentz, Sean. *Chants Democratic: New York City and the Rise of the American Working Class, 1788–1850* (1984).

CHAPTER
4

# Slavery and the Transition
# to Free Labor

*Artisans' struggle against the factory system proved to be a central theme in Northern industrial society, while slavery and emancipation defined Southern economic and social life. Historians now recognize that cotton pickers, cane cutters, household servants, and slave carpenters were also part of working-class America. So too were the tenant farmers, sharecroppers, and farm laborers who emerged from the Southern agricultural economy after the Civil War. Black labor had built the antebellum Southern economy, and its cotton exports generated the single greatest source of capital that industrialized America.*

*But was the slave system of the American South merely a more exploitative form of Northern "wage slavery"? Were plantation owners simply agricultural capitalists who availed themselves of a particularly low-cost class of laborers? And what did the slaves think of their own servitude? How did they resist, and how did they accommodate the will of their masters? Historians have debated these issues for years. Many now think of the antebellum South as a society quite different from that of the North, and one characterized by its own peculiar set of social relations. Some masters did hire out their slave by the month or year to mines, docks, and workshops, but most considered plantation agriculture the highest and best use of their human property because it insured their political and social dominance in a society fundamentally at odds with that of the bourgeois, capitalist North.*

*The plantation ruling class could hardly be expected to relinquish its power voluntarily, and it took a war of revolutionary proportions to abolish slavery in the American South once and for all. Although the Union armies freed the slaves, the labor question formed the heart of Reconstruction politics in the years immediately after the war. A bitter conflict over the character and control of agricultural labor became central to the meaning of blacks' freedom and eman- cipation. Would the former slaves become peasant proprietors cultivating their own land, or rural wage laborers supervised by old-regime slavemasters? Would women be forced to work in the fields, as they had under slavery, or would their labor be of a more domestic sort? And finally, would the former slaves have access to education, the franchise, and political organizations that represented their own interests? The outcome of this intensely fought struggle, in which Northern capital and the federal government had a significant stake, would prove decisive in shaping the class structure and the political life of the Southern states for generations afterward.*

## ⚜ D O C U M E N T S

Plantation management was a complicated task, involving the coordination of many types of labor. Planters often kept detailed operational records in diary and account books. A page from such a log, listing slaves and the amount of cotton they picked, appears as Document 1. In Document 2, Solomon Northup, a free black kidnapped into slavery, describes cotton planting and harvesting on the Bayou Boeuf in Avoyelles Parish, Louisiana. Document 3, a planter's advice on rearing slave children, sustains abolitionists' charges that masters bred slaves for the market in the Old South.

Documents 4 and 5 illustrate the difficulty of creating a class of free wage laborers in the postwar South. Document 4 records one way in which Northern unionists sought to instill the virtues of "free labor" among the former slaves. Here Captain Charles Soule addressed the recently freed population of Orangeburg District, South Carolina, on their responsibilities as wage laborers. But his advice on the rewards of hard work contrasts sharply with the sentiments expressed in Document 5, a petition to the president of the United States from the freedmen of Edisto Island, South Carolina. In Documents 6 and 7, Reconstruction-era washerwomen also resist a free labor system that consigned them to the mercy of the unfettered labor market. Finally, the poverty and inequality endemic to the sharecropping system are recounted in Document 8, Nate Shaw's account of his life working on shares in the second decade of the twentieth century.

# 1. Slave Production at Pleasant Hill Plantation, 1850

**Daily Records of Cotton Picked on *Pleasant Hill* Plantation During the Week Commencing on *21st Day of Octr., 1850, Jones* Overseer**

| NAME | NO. | MONDAY | TUESDAY | WEDNESDAY | THURSDAY | FRIDAY | SATURDAY | WEEK'S PICKING BROUGHT FORWARD |
|---|---|---|---|---|---|---|---|---|
| Sandy | 1 | Ginning | Pressing | Ginning | Ginning | Ginning | Ginning | |
| Scott | 2 | Clearing | Pressing | Clearing | Clearing | Hauling corn | | 64 |
| Solomon | 3 | Clearing | Hauling rails | Clearing | Gone to Clinton | Hauling | | 54 |
| Bill | 4 | Clearing | Do | Clearing | Clearing | Hauling | | 30 |
| Jerry | 5 | Clearing | Clearing | Clearing | Clearing | Do Do | | 90 |
| Isaac | 6 | Clearing | Clearing | Clearing | Clearing | Do Do | | 70 |
| Jim | 7 | Sick | Sick | Sick | Sick | Sick | | Sick |
| Dotson | 8 | Gone after shoes | Clearing | Clearing | Clearing | Ho corn | | 60 |

**The Planter's Annual Report of his Negroes upon *Pleasant Hill* Plantation, During the year 1850, *E. J. Capell* Overseer**

MALES

| NAME | AGE | VALUE AT COMMENCEMENT OF THE YEAR | VALUE AT END OF THE YEAR |
| --- | --- | --- | --- |
| John | 70 | $50.00 | 75.00 |
| Tom | 49 | 1000.00 | 1200.00 |
| Sandy | 38 | 600.00 | 800.00 |
| Edmund | 35 | 1000.00 | 1300.00 |
| Jerry | 40 | 700.00 | 950.00 |
| Solomon | 38 | 700.00 | 950.00 |
| William | 24 | 1000.00 | 1100.00 |
| Charles | 10 | 500.00 | 650.00 |
| Tom | 5 | 250.00 | 275. |
| Monroe | 4 | 200.00 | 225. |
| Aaron | 3 | 175.00 | 200 |
| Jerry | 1 | 75.00 | 100 |

FEMALES

| NAME | AGE | VALUE AT COMMENCEMENT OF THE YEAR | VALUE AT END OF THE YEAR |
| --- | --- | --- | --- |
| Hannah | 60 | $100.00 | 125.00 |
| Mary | 34 | 800.00 | 900.00 |
| Fanny | 23 | 800.00 | 900.00 |
| Rachel Sen. | 32 | 675.00 | 750.00 |
| Lucy | 28 | 600.00 | 750.00 |
| Azaline | 13 | 600.00 | 700.00 |
| Sarah | 9 | 350.00 | 450.00 |
| Harriet | 8 | 300.00 | 400.00 |
| Melissa | 3 | 100.00 | 125.00 |
| Carolina | 3 | 150.00 | 150.00 |
| Laura | 1 | 100.00 | 125.00 |

## 2. Slave Solomon Northup's View of Cotton Planting and Harvesting, 1854

The ground is prepared by throwing up beds or ridges, with the plough—back-furrowing, it is called. Oxen and mules, the latter almost exclusively, are used in ploughing. The women as frequently as the men perform this labor, feeding, curry-ing, and taking care of their teams, and in all respects doing the field and stable work, precisely as do the ploughboys of the North.

The beds, or ridges, are six feet wide, that is, from water furrow to water fur-row. A plough drawn by one mule is then run along the top of the ridge or center of the bed, making the drill, into which a girl usually drops the seed, which she carries in a bag hung round her neck. Behind her comes a mule and harrow, covering up the seed, so that two mules, three slaves, a plough and harrow, are employed in planting a row of cotton. This is done in the months of March and April. Corn is planted in February. When there are no cold rains, the cotton usually makes its appearance in a week. In the course of eight or ten days afterwards the first hoeing is commenced. This is performed in part, also, by the aid of the plough and mule. The plough passes as near as possible to the cotton on both sides, throwing the furrow from it. Slaves follow with their hoes, cutting up the grass and cotton, leaving hills two feet and a half apart. This is called scraping cotton. In two weeks more commences the second hoeing. This time the furrow is thrown towards the cotton. Only one stalk, the largest, is now left standing in each hill. In another fortnight it is hoed the third time, throwing the furrow towards the cotton in the same manner as before, and killing all the grass between the rows. About the first of July, when it is a foot high or there-abouts, it is hoed the fourth and last time. Now the whole space between the rows is ploughed, leaving a deep water furrow in the center. During all these hoeings the overseer or driver follows the slaves on horseback with a whip. . . The fastest hoer takes the lead row. He is usually about a rod in advance of his companions. If one of them passes him, he is whipped. If one falls behind or is a moment idle, he is whipped. In fact, the lash is flying from morning until night, the whole day long. The hoeing season thus continues from April until July, a field having no sooner been finished once, than it is commenced again.

In the latter part of August begins the cotton picking season. At this time each slave is presented with a sack. A strap is fastened to it, which goes over the neck, holding the mouth of the sack breast high, while the bottom reaches nearly to the ground. Each one is also presented with a large basket that will hold about two barrels. This is to put the cotton in when the sack is filled. The baskets are carried to the field and placed at the beginning of the rows.

When a new hand, one unaccustomed to the business, is sent for the first time into the field, he is whipped up smartly, and made for that day to pick as fast as he can possibly. At night it is weighed, so that his capability in cotton picking is known. He must bring in the same weight each night following. If it falls short, it

---

From *Twelve Years a Slave: Narrative of Solomon Northup* (Auburn, N.Y. : Derby and Miller, 1853), 163–175, 208–212.

is considered evidence that he has been laggard, and a greater or less number of lashes is the penalty.

An ordinary day's work is two hundred pounds. A slave who is accustomed to picking, is punished, if he or she brings in a less quantity than that. There is a great difference among them as regards this kind of labor. Some of them seem to have a natural knack, or quickness, which enables them to pick with great celerity, and with both hands, while others, with whatever practice or industry, are utterly unable to come up to the ordinary standard. Such hands are taken from the cotton field and employed in other business. Patsey, of whom I shall have more to say, was known as the most remarkable cotton picker on Bayou Bœuf. She picked with both hands and with such surprising rapidity, that five hundred pounds a day was not unusual for her.

Each one is tasked, therefore, according to his picking abilities, none, however, to come short of two hundred weight. I, being unskillful always in that business, would have satisfied my master by bringing in the latter quantity, while on the other hand, Patsey would surely have been beaten if she failed to produce twice as much. . . .

The hands are required to be in the cotton field as soon as it is light in the morning, and, with the exception of ten or fifteen minutes, which is given them at noon to swallow their allowance of cold bacon, they are not permitted to be a moment idle until it is too dark to see, and when the moon is full, they often times labor till the middle of the night. They do not dare to stop even at dinner time, nor return to the quarters, however late it be, until the order to halt is given by the driver.

The day's work over in the field, the baskets are "toted," or in other words, carried to the gin-house, where the cotton is weighed. No matter how fatigued and weary he may be—no matter how much he longs for sleep and rest—a slave never approaches the gin-house with his basket of cotton but with fear. If it falls short in weight—if he has not performed the full task appointed him, he knows that he must suffer. And if he has exceeded it by ten or twenty pounds, in all probability his master will measure the next day's task accordingly. So, whether he has too little or too much, his approach to the gin-house is always with fear and trembling. Most frequently they have too little, and therefore it is they are not anxious to leave the field. After weighing, follow the whippings; and then the baskets are carried to the cotton house, and their contents stored away like hay, all hands being sent in to tramp it down. If the cotton is not dry, instead of taking it to the gin-house at once, it is laid upon platforms, two feet high, and some three times as wide, covered with boards or plank, with narrow walks running between them.

This done, the labor of the day is not yet ended, by any means. Each one must then attend to his respective chores. One feeds the mules, another the swine—another cuts the wood, and so forth; besides, the packing is all done by candle light. Finally, at a late hour, they reach the quarters, sleepy and overcome with the long day's toil. Then a fire must be kindled in the cabin, the corn ground in the small hand-mill, and supper, and dinner for the next day in the field, prepared. All that is allowed them is corn and bacon, which is given out at the corncrib and smoke-house every Sunday morning. Each one receives, as his weekly allowance, three and a half pounds of bacon, and corn enough to make a peck of meal. That is all—no tea, coffee, sugar, and with the exception of a very scanty sprinkling now and then, no salt.

## 3.  A Planter on Child Rearing, 1836

I have a nurse appointed to superintend all my little negroes, and a nursery built for them. If they are left to be protected by their parents, they will most assuredly be neglected. I have known parents take out an allowance for their children and actually steal it from them, to purchase articles at some shop. Besides, when they would be honest to their offspring, from their other occupations, they have not the time to attend to them properly. The children get their food irregularly, and when they do get it, it is only half done. They are suffered, by not having one to attend to them, to expose themselves; and hence many of the deaths which occur on our plantations.

I have just stated that I have a nursery for my little negroes, with an old woman or nurse to superintend and cook for them, and to see that their clothes and bedding are well attended to. She makes the little ones, generally speaking, both girls and boys, mend and wash their own clothes, and do many other little matters, such as collecting litter for manure, &c. In this they take great pleasure, and it has the tendency to bring them up to industrious habits. The nurse also cooks for them three times a day; and she always has some little meat to dress for them, or the clabber or sour milk from the diary to mix their food. In *sickness* she sees that they are well attended to; and from having many of them together, one is taught to wait upon the other. My little negroes are consequently very healthy; and from pursuing the plan I have laid down, I am confident that I raise more of them, than where a different system is followed.

## 4.  A Northern Unionist Lectures Ex-Slaves on the Work Ethic, 1865

*To the Freed People of Orangeburg District.*

You have heard many stories about your condition as freemen. You do not know what to believe: you are talking too much; waiting too much; asking for too much. If you can find out the truth about this matter, you will settle down quietly to your work. Listen, then, and try to understand just how you are situated.

You are not free, but you must know that the only difference you can feel yet, between slavery and freedom, is that neither you nor your children can be bought or sold. You may have a harder time this year than you have ever had before; it will be the price you pay for your freedom. You will have to work hard, and get very little to eat, and very few clothes to wear. If you get through this year alive and well, you should be thankful. Do not expect to save up anything, or to have much corn or provisions ahead at the end of the year. You must not ask for more pay than free people get at the North. There, a field hand is paid in money, but has to spend all his pay every week, in buying food and clothes for his family and in paying rent

---

From "Notions on the Management of Negroes," *Farmer's Register* 4 (December 1836): 495.

From Captain Charles Soule to General Oliver Otis Howard, Freedman's Bureau, June 12, 1865, in S-17, 1865, Letters Received (Series 15), Washington Headquarters, Records of the Bureau of Refugees, Freedmen & Abandoned Lands, Record Group 105, National Archives.

for his house. You cannot be paid in money,—for there is no good money in the District,—nothing but Confederate paper. Then, what can you be paid with? Why, with food, with clothes, with the free use of your little houses and lots. You do not own a cent's worth except yourselves. The plantation you live on is not yours, nor the houses, nor the cattle, mules and horses; the seed you planted with was not yours, and the ploughs and hoes do not belong to you. Now you must get something to eat and something to wear, and houses to live in. How can you get these things? By hard work—and nothing else, and it will be a good thing for you if you get them until next year, for yourselves and for your families. You must remember that your children, your old people, and the cripples, belong to you to support now, and all that is given to them is so much pay to you for your work. If you ask for anything more; if you ask for a half of the crop, or even a third, you ask too much; you wish to get more than you could get if you had been free all your lives. Do not ask for Saturday either: free people everywhere else work Saturday, and you have no more right to the day than they have. If your employer is willing to give you part of the day, or to set a task that you can finish early, be thankful for the kindness, but do not think it is something you must have. When you work, work hard. Begin early at sunrise, and do not take more than two hours at noon. Do not think, because you are free you can choose your own kind of work. Every man must work under orders. The soldiers, who are free, work under officers, the officers under the general, and the general under the president. There must be a head man everywhere, and on a plantation the head man, who gives all the orders, is the owner of the place. Whatever he tells you to do you must do at once, and cheerfully. Never give him a cross word or an impudent answer. If the work is hard, do not stop to talk about it, but do it first and rest afterwards. If you are told to go into the field and hoe, see who can go first and lead the row. If you are told to build a fence, build it better than any fence you know of. If you are told to drive the carriage Sunday, or to mind the cattle, do it, for necessary work must be done even on the Sabbath. Whatever the order is, try and obey it without a word.

Captain Charles Soule

## 5. "We Demand Land": Petition by Southern Freedmen, 1865

Edisto Island S. C. Oct 28th, 1865.

To the President of these United States. We the freedmen of Edisto Island South Carolina have learned From you through Major General O O Howard commissioner of the Freedman's Bureau. with deep sorrow and Painful hearts of the possibility of government restoring These lands to the former owners. We are well aware Of the

---

From Freedman of Edisto Island to General Howard and to President Johnson, October 28, 1865, in Henry Bram et al. to Major General O. O. Howard [October 28, 1865], and Henry Bram et al. to the President of the United States, October 28, 1865, B-53, 1865 and P-27, 1865, Letters Received (Series 15), Washington Headquarters, Records of the Bureau of Refugees, Freedmen & Abandoned Lands, National Archives.

many perplexing and trying questions that burden Your mind. and do therefore pray to god (the preserver of all. and who has through our Late and beloved President [Lincoln] proclamation and the war made Us A free people) that he may guide you in making Your decisions. and give you that wisdom that Cometh from above to settle these great and Important Questions for the best interests of the country and the Colored race: Here is where secession was born and Nurtured Here is were we have toiled nearly all Our lives as slaves and were treated like dumb Driven cattle. This is our home, we have made These lands what they are. we were the only true and Loyal people that were found in possession of these Lands. we have been always ready to strike for Liberty and humanity yea to fight if needs be To preserve this glorious union. Shall not we who Are freedman and have been always true to this Union have the same rights as are enjoyed by Others? Have we broken any Law of these United States? have we forfeited our rights of property in Land?— If not then! are not our rights as A free people and good citizens of these United States To be considered before the rights of those who were Found in rebellion against this good and just Government (and now being conquered) come (as they Seem) with penitent hearts and beg forgiveness For past offences and also ask if their lands Cannot be restored to them are these rebellious Spirits to be reinstated in their *possessions* And we who have been abused and oppressed For many long years not to be allowed the Privilige of purchasing land But be subject To the will of these large Land owners? God forbid. Land monopoly is injurious to the advancement of the course of freedom, and if Government Does not make some provision by which we as Freedmen can obtain A Homestead, we have Not bettered our condition.

We have been encouraged by Government to take Up these lands in small tracts, receiving Certificates of the same—we have thus far Taken Sixteen thousand (16000) acres of Land here on This Island. We are ready to pay for this land When Government calls for it. and now after What has been done will the good and just government take from us all this right and make us Subject to the will of those who have cheated and Oppressed us for many years God Forbid!

We the freedmen of this Island and of the State of South Carolina—Do therefore petition to you as the President of these United States, that some provisions be made by which Every colored man can purchase land. and Hold it as his own. We wish to have A home if It be but A few acres. without some provision is Made our future is sad to look upon. yess our Situation is dangerous. we therefore look to you In this trying hour as A true friend of the poor and Neglected race. for protection and Equal Rights. with the privilege of purchasing A Homestead— A Homestead right here in the Heart of South Carolina.

We pray that God will direct your heart in Making such provision for us as freedmen which Will tend to united these states together stronger Than ever before—May God bless you in the Administration of your duties as the President Of these United States is the humble prayer Of us all.–

In behalf of the Freedmen
Henry Bram
Committee    Ishmael. Moultrie.
yates. Sampson

## 6. African-American Washerwomen Demand Higher Wages, 1866

Mayor Barrows

Jackson, Mississippi, June 20, 1866

Dear Sir:

At a meeting of the colored Washerwomen of this city, on the evening of the 18th of June, the subject of raising the wages was considered, and the following preamble and resolution were unanimously adopted:

Whereas, under the influence of the present high prices of all the necessaries of life, and the attendant high rates of rent, we, the washerwomen of the city of Jackson, State of Mississippi, thinking it impossible to live uprightly and honestly in laboring for the present daily and monthly recompense, and hoping to meet with the support of all good citizens, join in adopting unanimously the following resolution:

Be it resolved by the washerwomen of this city and county, That on and after the foregoing date, we join in charging a uniform rate for our labor, and any one belonging to the class of washerwomen, violating this, shall be liable to a fine regulated by the class. We do not wish in the least to charge exorbitant prices, but desire to be able to live comfortably if possible from the fruits of our labor. We present the matter to your Honor, and hope you will not reject it. The prices charged are:

$1.50 per day for washing

$15.00 per month for family washing

$10.00 per month for single individuals

We ask you to consider the matter in our behalf, and should you deem it just and right, your sanction of the movement will be gratefully received.

Yours, very truly,
THE WASHERWOMEN OF JACKSON

## 7. "Colored" vs. Chinese in Galveston, 1877

Monday night colored women, emboldened by the liberties allowed their fathers, husbands and brothers decided to have a public hurrah of their own, and as the men had demanded two dollars for a day's labor they would ask $1.50 or $9 per week. As women are generally considered cleansers of dirty linen, their first move was against the steam laundry, corner of Avenue A and Tenth Street, owned by J. N. Harding.

About 6:30 A.M. colored women began collecting around his house, until they numbered about twenty-five. The laundry women were soon seen coming to work. When met and told that they should not work for less than $1.50 per day, four turned back; but, one, a Miss Murphy went into the house and began working. Seeing this,

---

From *Jackson Daily Clarion*, June 24, 1866.

From *Galveston News*, August 1, 1877.

the women rushed in, caught her and carried her into the street, and by threats forced her to leave.

This success emboldened the women to further demonstrations. The cry was raised, "Let's lock them out for good; here's nails I brought especially." An axe lying in the wood pile was grabbed, and the laundry house doors and windows secured. Then off they started for the heathen Chinese, who "washed Mellican man clothes so cheapee." Down Market street they went, led by a portly colored lady, whose avoir-dupois is not less than 250.

Each California laundry was visited in turn, beginning at Slam Sing's and ending at Wau Loong's corner of Bath Avenue and Post-office Street. At these laundries all the women talked at once, telling Slam Sing, Wau Loong and the rest that "they must close up and leave this city within fifteen days or they would be driven away," each Chinaman responding "Yees, yees," "Me go, yees," and closed their shops. The women scattered after avowing they would meet again at 4 o'clock and visit each place where women are fired, and if they receive less than $1.50 per day or $9 per week they would force them to quit.

## 8. Sharecropper Nate Shaw Makes His Crop, 1913

I've made a crop more or less every year, come too much rain or too much sun. I've had my cotton grow so fast as to grow to a weed. I've picked from many a stalk of cotton that growed so high until it was just a stalk, not many bolls I'd get for it. On the other hand, when the seasons just hit right, I've had stalks of cotton weren't no more than three foot high, just laying down with bolls. It don't take the tallest cotton to make a big crop.

In the year 1912, second crop I ever made on Miss Hattie Lu Reeve's place, good God it come a snap—and my cotton should have been thinned out, by right, but I weren't done chopin it out. And it come a cold day and and it sleeted on my crop. Done that again the next year, sleeted on that cotton in May, 1912, and 1913, too. And that cotton turned yellow as a fox and shedded off every leaf on it, but left the buds. I examined it and it looked terrible—in a day or two when the weather moderated, I examined my little old cotton and seed it was still alive, and them buds, after the sun hit em good, turnin hot after the snap of weather, little old cotton buds just kept livin and commenced a puttin out, flourishin. I just chopped it regular when I seed all that. And when I laid that cotton by, plowed it and put the dirt to it, it still looked weak and yellow. But it wouldn't die, it just kept a comin, kept a comin until it come out and made me that year eight good bales of cotton—1913. That was a high production for a one-horse farm. In them days people didn't make a bale to the acre. I had about eleven or twelve acres under cultivation and it weren't no first class land. But it was smooth land, easy to work. . . .

We hand-picked that cotton, all of it. Five years old, that's big enough to pick many a little handful, and my daddy had me out in the field pickin cotton before that. And I picked until I picked many a hundred pounds for my boy Vernon, for

From Theodore Rosengarten, *All God's Dangers: The Life of Nate Shaw,* copyright © 1974 by Theodore Rosengarten. (New York: Alfred A. Knopf, 1975), pp. 182–190. Used by permission by Alfred A. Knopf, a division of Random House, Inc.

four years after I quit foolin with it myself. When I quit off pickin for Vernon I was able to pick as much as a hundred pounds a day—that was a little help to him. Pickin regular on my own farm, to pick up to three hundred pounds a day. The Bible says, once a man and twice a child—well, it's that way pickin cotton. I picked at the end of my cotton pickin days how much I picked at the start. . . .

Gathered that cotton from when it first opened up, around the latter part of August or the first week in September, and right through till it was all gathered. White man get out there and raise a big crop of cotton—when I was a boy and after I was grown, every little Negro chap in the whole country around, as far as he had time to go get em, go get em and put em in his field pickin cotton. And his little crowd, maybe, if he had any chaps, they'd be pickin some on off-hours of school. Come home and go to pickin cotton. But mainly it was nigger children gathered the white man's crop when I come along. And if a chap had in mind that he didn't want to pick this man's cotton—chaps knowed whose cotton it was—mama and papa was sufficient to make him pick it. Carry that child out, some of em, in a white man's field, they'd work his little butt off with a switch if he didn't gather that cotton. You'd find some industrious white people that would work like colored; they was poor people, they'd get out there and pick. But ones that didn't care so much about stoopin down and pickin cotton, their cotton got ready—the little nigger chaps wasn't goin to school; scoop em up like flies and put em in the field.

Picked cotton in a sack—that's how we done it in this country, and other cotton countries I've heard spoke of. Put a sack on, long sack, sometimes the sack would be draggin behind you far enough that a little chap could walk up on the end of it. You'd have a strap to that sack, cross your chest and over your shoulder, resemblin to a harness, and the mouth of that sack right under your arm; you'd pick cotton and just drop it in there. That sack'd hold a full hundred pounds.

Take that sack and empty it in a big basket, cotton basket. White man would set it in his field, or a Negro, if it was his field and he had baskets. I used my own baskets, I made cotton baskets. Didn't pick my crops no other way but empty the cotton out of the sack and into the basket, and that relieved my sack, the weight of it on me, that would take it off, any amount of cotton I had picked in my sack.

I'd take my wagon to the field after me and my children done picked several baskets of cotton, stand it there and go the emptyin that cotton in the wagon. Set them baskets out there to keep a gatherin. I could nicely weigh my cotton in a basket then throw it on the wagon. Weighed my cotton right there, as I loaded it. My wife had good book learnin, she'd take the figures to the house—I could make figures but I didn't know enough to add em up: give her the book with the cotton figures on it, she'd add it up and tell me when I got a bale. That wagon had to move out of the field then. . . .

From my first startin off farmin after I married, even workin on halves, I had to carry my cotton to the gin. And when I got to where I rented, I'd gin at any gin I wanted to. I had mules able to do it; hitch them mules to my wagon, take em to the field; take em from the field to the barn; pull out from the barn to the gin. Drive up under a suction pipe; that suction would pull that lint cotton off the wagon and into them gins and the gins would gin it out—separate the lint from the seed and the seed would fall in a box. Another pipe carried the seed overhead from that box to a seed house out yonder. Didn't have nothin to do but go out there and open up that seed-house box and catch all my seed. Cotton went from the gin machines to a press—all them seeds and whatever trash was picked with that cotton done been ginned out. And a man at the press would work a lever and the press would press the cotton down into a box the shape of a bale so he could bale it off. He'd already have a underbaggin under it and he'd pull the top baggin down and wrap that cotton up, faster them hooks, and bale it. . . .

Right there and then, and aint aimin to sell that cotton, you take that cotton back home and dump it off your wagon. It's used, startin at home—my mother, after the cotton come back from the gin, seed removed and leave the pure lint. I've seen her take a pair of cards, two cards each about as wide as my four fingers, and its made in the resemblance and in the manner and in the style of a mule brush. And she'd take one in one hand and lay a handful of that cotton on it, take the other card and comb it—that's called cardin batts—then change cards and comb it the other way until she got a nice clear batt of cotton in them brushes. And she'd have a quilt linin stretched out in the house and she'd take that batt of cotton, nice wad of cotton, and lay them batts all over that quilt; she could lay em as thick or thin as she wanted, then spread the next layer of cloth over it and sew the top layer and the bottom layer together around the edge—sewin that cotton in there and pullin it just tight enough to make it flat like she wanted a quilt. And when she sewed as far as she could reach, then she'd roll that quilt, take it loose from the corners of her frames, pull out them nails or small spikes and roll that quilt under, roll it under, just get it far enough, close enough, far as she could reach with her hand sewin. She'd do all around that quilt thataway, from one corner to the other. Had a bed quilt then, warm quilt, plied through with cotton. . . .

. . . If you want to sell your cotton at once, you take it to the market, carry it to the Apafalya cotton market and they'll sample it. Cotton buyin man cuts a slug in the side of your bale, reaches in there and pulls the first of it out the way and get him a handful, just clawin in there. He'll look over that sample, grade that cotton—that's his job. What kind of grade do it make? You don't know until he tells you. If it's short staple, the devil, your price is cut on that cotton. Color matters too, and the way it was ginned—some gins cuts up the cotton, ruins the staple. . . .

And so, I'd have my cotton weighed and I'd go up and down the street with my sample. Meet a white man, farmin man like myself, on the street; he'd see what I been offered for my sample—the buyer's marks would be on the wrapper—or I'd tell him. And he'd take that sample, unwrap it, look at it; he'd say, "Nate, I can beat you with your own cotton, I can get more for it than that."

Aint that enough to put your boots on! The same sample. He'd say, "Let me take your sample and go around in your place. I can beat what they offered you."

Take that cotton and go right to the man that had his bid on it and he'd raise it; right behind where I was, had been, and get a better bid on it. I've gived a white man my sample right there on the streets of Apafalya; he'd go off and come back. Sometimes he'd say, "Well, Nate, I helped you a little on it but I couldn't help you much."

And sometime he'd get a good raise on it with another fellow out yonder. He'd bring my sample back to me with a bid on it. "Well, Nate, I knowed I could help you on that cotton."

That was happenin all through my farmin years: from the time I stayed on the Curtis place, and when I moved to the Ames place, and when I lived with Mr. Reeve, and when I moved down on Sitimachas Creek with Mr. Tucker, and when I lived up there at Two Forks on the Stark place, and when I moved down on the Pollard place and stayed there nine years. Colored man's cotton weren't worth as much as white man's cotton less'n it come to the buyer in the white man's hands. But the colored man's labor—that was worth more to the white man than the labor of his own color because it cost him less and he got just as much for his money.

## ✢ E S S A Y S

In the first essay, Eugene Genovese of Atlanta University compares the work rhythms of plantation slaves with those of other preindustrial peoples and explores the ways in which the slaves' African inheritance and plantation experience together forged a black work ethic that accommodated the otherwise harsh requirements of the slave system. Genovese contends that neither the planter class nor their slaves embraced bourgeois notions of time and work discipline. Most masters had to accommodate the slaves' preference for collective patterns of labor. After emancipation, blacks and whites, Northerners and Southerners waged a protracted struggle over the structure and content of the labor the former slaves would perform, as Columbia University historian Eric Foner shows in the second essay. Whereas the freedmen and freedwomen sought their own homesteads, on which only the adult males would be expected to labor regularly in the fields, Northern officials wanted all the former slaves, men and women, to enter the labor market as wage workers.

How fundamentally did emancipation change the everyday work of black Southerners? Does Foner find the same combination of collectivism and individualism among black laborers that Genovese claims to be a characteristic of slave culture itself?

## The Plantation Work Ethic

### EUGENE GENOVESE

The slaveholders presided over a plantation system that constituted a halfway house between peasant and factory cultures. The tobacco and cotton plantations, which dominated the slave economy in the United States, ranged closer to the peasant than the factory model, in contradistinction to the great sugar plantations of the Caribbean, which in some respects resembled factories in the field; but even the small holders pushed their laborers toward modern work discipline. The planter's problem came to this: How could they themselves preserve as much as possible of that older way of life to which they aspired and yet convince their slaves to repudiate it? How could they instill factorylike discipline into a working population engaged in a rural system that, for all its tendencies toward modern discipline, remained bound to the rhythms of nature and to traditional ideas of work, time, and leisure?

They succeeded in overcoming this contradiction only to the extent that they got enough work out of their slaves to make the system pay at a level necessary to

From *Roll, Jordan, Roll: The World the Slaves Made* by Eugene D. Genovese. Copyright © 1972, 1974 by Eugene D. Genovese. Reprinted by permission of Pantheon Books, a division of Random House, Inc.

their survival as a slaveholding class in a capitalist world market. But they failed in deeper ways that cast a shadow over the long-range prospects for that very survival and over the future of both blacks and whites in American society. Too often they fell back on the whip and thereby taught and learned little. When they went to other incentives, as fortunately most tried to do, they did get satisfactory economic results, but at the same time they reinforced traditional attitudes and values instead of replacing them with more advanced ones.

The black work ethic grew up within a wider Protestant Euro-American community with a work ethic of its own. The black ethic represented at once a defense against an enforced system of economic exploitation and an autonomous assertion of values generally associated with preindustrial peoples. As such, if formed part of a more general southern work ethic, which developed in antagonism to that of the wider American society. A Euro-American, basically Anglo-Saxon work ethic helped shape that of southerners in general and slaves in particular and yet, simultaneously, generated a profound antithesis.

In the medieval Catholic formulation the necessity to work both derived from the Fall of Man and served as an expression of humility and submission. . . . To this stern doctrine of work as duty the slave opposed a religion of joy in life that echoed traditional Africa and, surprising as it may seem, even more firmly echoed the spirit of the plantation community itself. To speak of a "calling" or vocation for slaves would be absurd; but more to the point, worldly asceticism neither corresponded to the sensibilities shaped by the historical development from Africa to the New World nor could take root among a people who had no material stake in its flowering. . . .

The slaves' attitude toward time and work arose primarily from their own experience on the plantations of the South. Comparisons with Africa suggest some important cultural continuities. Traditional African time-reckoning focuses on present and past, not future. Time, being two-dimensional, moves, as it were, backward into a long past; the future, not having been experienced, appears senseless. This idea of time, which inhibited the appearance of an indigenous millennialism prior to Islamic and Christian penetrations, encouraged economic attitudes not readily assimilable to early bourgeois demands for saving, thrift, and accumulation. But, however, strong the specifically African influence, even more important are those tendencies which characterize preindustrial agricultural peoples in general, for whom the Africans provided a variant or, rather, a series of variants. . . .

Traditional society measured its time by calendars based on agricultural and seasonal patterns, which themselves formed part of an integrated religious worldview. The year proceeded according to a certain rhythm, not according to equal units of time; appropriate festivals and rites broke its continuity and marked the points at which the human spirit celebrated the rhythm of the natural order. Not pure quantities of time obtained, but such flexible units as the beginning of planting and of the harvest. Time became subordinated to the natural order of work and leisure, as their servant rather than their master.

Whereas in peasant farming the work tasks and such natural conditions as the amount of daylight determine the length of the workday, the acceptable number and duration of breaks, and the amount and type of leisure, in factory work "the arbitrarily fixed time schedule determines the beginning and the end of the work periods." In peasant societies work tasks such as planting and harvesting, which appear to conform to the demands of nature, have oriented the notation of time. E. P. Thompson argues convincingly that this "task orientation" has rendered work more humanly comprehensible: "The peasant or labourer appears to attend upon what is an observed necessity." For the preindustrial English community as a whole the distinction between "work" and "life" was much less clear than it was to become; the working day itself lengthened and contracted according to necessary tasks, and no great conflict appeared between the demands of work and those of leisure. One need not idealize the undoubtedly harsh physical conditions of preindustrial rural life to appreciate the force of Thompson's argument, especially since those who passed under industrial work discipline probably were themselves the ones who came most to idealize their previous existence and, thereby to heighten either their resistance or their despair. . . .

The advent of clock time represented more than a marking of regular work units—of minutes and hours—and of arbitrary schedules, for it supported the increasing division of labor and transformed that division of labor into a division of time itself. Capitalism production had to be measured in units of labor-time, and those units themselves took on the mysterious and apparently self-determining properties of commodities. When Benjamin Franklin said that time is money, he said much more than is generally understood. E. P. Thompson comments: "In a mature capitalist society all time must be consumed, marketed, put to *use;* it is offensive for the labour force merely to pass the time." Natural rhythms of work and leisure gave place to arbitrary schedules, which were, however, arbitrary only from the point of view of the laborers. The capitalists and those ideologues who were developing a new idea of rationality based on the demands of a rapidly developing economy saw the matter differently. The process of cultural transformation had to rest on economic and extra-economic compulsion and ultimately on violence. It served as the industrial equivalent of that which the West Indian slaveholders, with fewer inhibitions, called "seasoning." . . .

The slaves could not reckon time either according to preindustrial peasant models or according to industrial factory models. The plantations, especially the sugar plantations, that dominated most of the slaveholding regions of the New World, although not of the United States, did resemble factories in the field, but even if we take them as our norm we cannot escape the implications of their preindustrial side. However much their economic organization required and tried to compel quasi-industrial discipline, they also threw up countervailing pressures and embodied inescapable internal contradictions.

The setting remained rural, and the rhythm of work followed seasonal fluctuations. Nature remained the temporal reference point for the slaves. However much the slaveholders might have wished to transform their slaves into clock-punchers, they could not, for in a variety of sense both literal and metaphoric, there were no clocks to punch. The planters, especially the resident planters of the United States and Brazil but even the typical West Indian agents of absentee owners, hardly lived in a factory world themselves and at best could only preach what the most docile or stupid slave knew very well they did not and could not practice. Since the plantation economy required extraordinary exertion at critical points of the year, notably the harvest, it required measures to capitalize on the slaves' willingness to work in spurts rather than steadily. The slaveholders turned the inclinations of the slaves to their own advantage, but simultaneously they made far greater concessions to the value system and collective sensibility of the quarters than they intended.

The slaveholders, as usual, had their way but paid a price. The slaves, as usual, fell victim to the demands of their exploiters but had some success in pressing their own advantage. Thus, the plantation system served as a halfway house for Africans between their agricultural past and their imposed industrial future. But, it froze them into a position that allowed for their exploitation on the margins of industrial society. The advantage of this compromise, from the black point of view, lay in the protection it provided for their rich community life and its cultural consolidation. The disadvantage lay in its encouragement of a way of life that, however admirable intrinsically, ill prepared black people to compete in the economic world into which they would be catapulted by emancipation. . . .

The black view of time, conditioned by the plantation slave experience, has provided a great source of strength for a people at bay, as one of Bishop A. G. Dunston's sermons makes clear:

> You know, that's the way God does it. Same as you can't hurry God—so why don't you wait, just wait. Everybody's ripping and racing and rushing. And God is taking his time. Because he knows that it isn't hurtin' nearly so bad as you and I think it's hurtin'—and that is the way he wants us to go. But by and by he brings relief. . . .

Black people, in short, learned to take the blow and to parry it as best they could. They found themselves shut out by white racism from part of the dominant culture's value system, and they simultaneously resisted that system both by historically developed sensibility and by necessity. Accordingly, they developed their own values as a force for community cohesion and survival, but in so doing they widened the cultural gap and exposed themselves to even harder blows from a white nation that could neither understand their behavior nor respect its moral foundations.

. . . The African tradition, like the European peasant tradition, stressed hard work and condemned and derided laziness in any form. Not hard work but steady, routinized work as moral duty was discounted. In this attitude African agriculturalists resembled preindustrial peoples in general, including urban peoples. The familiar assertion that certain people would work only long enough to earn the money they needed to live was leveled not only against day laborers but against the finest and most prestigious artisans in early modern Europe. . . .

The slaves' willingness to work extraordinarily hard and yet to resist the discipline of regularity accompanied certain desires and expectations. During Reconstruction the blacks sought their own land; worked it conscientiously when they could get it; resisted being forced back into anything resembling gang labor for the white man; and had to be terrorized, swindled, and murdered to prevent their working for themselves. This story was prefigured in antebellum times when slaves were often allowed garden plots for their families and willingly worked them late at night or on Sundays in order to provide extra food or clothing. The men did not generally let their families subsist on the usual allotments of pork and corn. In addition to working with their wives in the gardens, they fished and hunted and trapped animals. In these and other ways they demonstrated considerable concern for the welfare of their families and a strong desire to take care of them. But in such instances they were working for themselves and at their own pace. Less frequently, slaves received permission to hire out their own time after having completed the week's assigned tasks. They were lured, not by some internal pressure to work steadily, but by the opportunity to work for themselves and their families in their own way.

Many slaves voluntarily worked for their masters on Sundays or holidays in return for money or goods. This arrangement demonstrated how far the notion of the slaves' "right" to a certain amount of time had been accepted by the masters; how readily the slaves would work for themselves; and how far the notion of reciprocity had entered the thinking of both masters and slaves.

The slaves responded to moral as well as economic incentives. They often took pride in their work, but not necessarily in the ways most important to their masters. Solomon Northup designed a better way to transport lumber only to find himself ridiculed by the overseer. In this case it was in the master's interest to intervene, and he did. He praised Northup and adopted the plan. Northup comments: "I was not insensible to the praise bestowed upon me, and enjoyed especially, my triumph over Taydem [the overseer], whose half-malicious ridicule had stung my pride."

From colonial days onward plantation slaves, as well as those in industry, mining, and town services, received payments in money and goods as part of a wider system of social control. These payments served either as incentive bonuses designated to stimulate productivity, or more frequently, as a return for work done during the time recognized as the slaves' own. Many planters, including those who most clearly got the best results, used such incentives. Bennett H. Barrow of Louisiana provides a noteworthy illustration, for he was not a man to spare the whip. Yet his system of rewards included frequent holidays and dinners, as well as cash bonuses and presents for outstanding work. In Hinds County, Mississippi, Thomas Dabney gave small cash prizes—a few cents, really—to his best pickers and then smaller prizes to others who worked diligently even if they could not match the output of the leaders. In Perry County, Alabama, Hugh Davis divided his workers into rival teams and had them compete for prizes. He supplemented this collective competition with individual contests. In North Carolina at the end of the eighteenth century Charles Pettigrew, like many others before and after him, paid slaves for superior or extra work.

The amounts sometimes reached substantial proportions. Captain Frederick Marryat complained that in Lexington, Kentucky, during the late 1830s a gentleman could not rent a carriage on Sundays because slaves with ready money invariably rented them first for their own pleasure. Occasionally, plantation records reported surprising figures. One slave in Georgia earned fifty to sixty dollars per year by attending to pine trees in his off hours. Others earned money by applying particular skills or by doing jobs that had to be done individually and carefully without supervision. Amounts in the tens and even hundreds of dollars, although not common, caused no astonishment.

The more significant feature of these practices, for the society as a whole if not for the economy in particular, was the regularity—almost the institutionalization—of payments for work on Sundays or holidays. Apart from occasional assignments of Sunday or holiday work as punishment and apart from self-defeating greed, not to say stupidity, which led a few masters to violate the social norm, Sunday was the slaves' day by custom as well as law. The collective agreement of the slaveholders on these measures had its origin in a concern for social peace and reflected a sensible attitude toward economic efficiency. But once the practice took root, with or without legal sanction, the slaves transformed it into a "right." So successfully did they do so that the Supreme Court of Louisiana ruled in 1836: "According to . . . law, slaves are entitled to the produce of their labor on Sunday; even the master is bound to remunerate them, if he employs them." Here again the slaves turned the paternalist doctrine of reciprocity to advantage while demonstrating the extent to which that doctrine dominated the lives of both masters and slaves. . . .

Underlying black resistance to prevailing white values, then, has been a set of particular ideas concerning individual and community responsibility. It is often asserted that blacks spend rather than save as someone else thinks they should. But the considerable evidence for this assertion must be qualified by the no less considerable evidence of the heartbreaking scraping together of nickels and dimes to pay for such things as the education of the children, which will generally draw Anglo-Saxon applause, and the provision of elaborate funerals, which generally will not but which for many peoples besides blacks constitutes a necessary measure of respect for the living as well as the dead.

The slaves could, when they chose, astonish the whites by their work-time élan and expenditure of energy. The demands of corn shucking, hog killing, logrolling, cotton picking, and especially sugar grinding confronted the slaves with particularly heavy burdens and yet drew from them particularly positive responses.

With the exception of the Christmas holiday—and not always that—former slaves recalled having looked forward to corn shucking most of all. . . .

Certainly, the slaves had some material incentives. The best shuckers would get a dollar or a suit of clothes, as might those who found a red ear. But these incentives do not look impressive and do not loom large in the testimony. Those plantations on which the prize for finding a red ear consisted of a dollar do not seem to have done any better than those on which the prize consisted of an extra swig of whiskey or a chance to kiss the prettiest girl. The shucking was generally night work—overtime, as it were—and one might have expected the slaves to resent it and to consider the modest material incentives, which came to a special dinner and dance and a lot of whiskey, to be inadequate.

The most important feature of these occasions and the most important incentive to these long hours of work was the community life they called forth. They were gala affairs. The jug passed freely, although drunkenness was discouraged; the work went on amidst singing and dancing; friends and acquaintances congregated from several plantations and farms; the house slaves joined the field slaves in common labor; and the work was followed by an all-night dinner and ball at which inhibitions, especially those of class and race, were lowered as far as anyone dared.

Slavery, a particularly savage system of oppression and exploitation, made its slaves victims. But the human beings it made victims did not consent to be just that; they struggled to make life bearable and to find as much joy in it as they could. Up to a point even the harshest of masters had to help them do so. The logic of slavery pushed the masters to try to break their slaves' spirit and to reconstruct it as an unthinking and unfeeling extension of their own will, but the slaves' own resistance to dehumanization compelled the masters to compromise in order to get an adequate level of work out of them.

The combination of festive spirit and joint effort appears to have engaged the attention of the slaves more than anything else. Gus Brown, an ex-slave from Alabama, said simply, "On those occasions as we all got together and had a regular good time." The heightened sense of fellowship with their masters also drew much comment. Even big slaveholders would join in the work, as well as in the festivities and the drinking albeit not without the customary patriarchal qualifications. They would demand that the slaves sing, and the slaves would respond boisterously. Visitors expressed wonder at the spontaneity and improvisation the slaves displayed. The songs, often made up on the spot, bristled with sharp wit, both malicious and gentle. The slaves sang of their courtships and their lovers' quarrels; sometimes the songs got bawdy, and the children had to be hustled off to bed. . . .

But the songs also turned to satire. White participation in these festivals was always condescending and self-serving, and the slaves' acceptance of it displayed something other than childlike gratitude for small favors. They turned their wit and incredible talent for improvisation into social criticism. Occasionally they risked a direct, if muted, thrust in their "corn songs," as they came to be called.

> Massa in the great house, counting out his money,
> Massa in the great house, counting out his money,
> Oh, shuck that corn and throw it in the barn.
> Mistis in the parlor, eating bread and honey,
> Oh, shuck that corn and throw it in the barn.

More often, they used a simpler and safer technique. Ole Massa was always God's gift to humanity, the salt of the earth, de bestest massa in de whole wide worl'. But somehow, one or more of his neighbors was might bad buckra. . . . Blacks—any blacks—were not supposed to sass whites—any whites; slaves—any slaves—were not supposed to sit in judgment on masters—any masters. By the device of a little flattery and by talking advantage of the looseness of the occasion, they asserted their personalities and made their judgments.

A curious sexual division of labor marked the corn shuckings. Only occasionally did women participate in the shucking. The reason for the exclusion is by no means clear. Field women matched the men in hard work, not only in picking cotton but in rolling logs, chopping wood, and plowing. Yet at corn shuckings they divided their time between preparing an elaborate spread for the dinner and taking part in quilting bees and the like. As a result, the corn shuckings took on a peculiarly male tone, replete with raucous songs and jokes not normally told in front of women, as well as those manifestations of boyish prancing associated with what is called—as if by some delightful Freudian slip—a "man's man."

The vigor with which the men worked and the insistence on a rigid sexual separation raise the central question of the slaves' attitude toward work in its relationship to their sense of family and community. The sense of community established by bringing together house and field slaves and especially slaves from several plantations undoubtedly underlay much of the slaves' positive response, and recalled the festivities, ceremonials, and rituals of traditional societies in a way no office

Christmas party in an industrial firm has ever done. And corn shucking, like hog killing, had a special meaning, for at these times the slaves were literally working for themselves. The corn and pork fed them and their families; completion of these tasks carried a special satisfaction.

From this point of view the sexual division of labor, whatever its origin, takes on new meaning. In a limited way it strengthened that role of direct provider to which the men laid claim by hunting and fishing to supplement the family diet. Even the less attractive features of the evening in effect reinforced this male self-image. Nor did the women show signs of resentment. On the contrary, they seem to have grasped the opportunity to underscore a division of labor and authority in the family and to support the pretensions of their men. Slavery represented a terrible onslaught on the personalities and spirit of the slaves, and whatever unfairness manifested itself in this sexual bias, the efforts of male and female slaves to create and support their separate roles provided a weapon for joint resistance to dehumanization. . . .

The evidence from the sugar plantations is especially instructive. Louisiana's sugar planters reputedly drove their slaves harder than any others in the slave states. Such reputations are by no means to be accepted at face value, but they certainly drove them hard during the grinding season. Yet, slaves took to the woods as limited and local runaways more often during the spring and summer months than during the autumn grinding season, when the work reached a peak of intensity and when the time for rest and sleep contracted sharply. Once again, the small material incentives cannot account for the slaves' behavior.

The slaves brought to their labor a gaiety and élan that perplexed observers, who saw them work at night with hardly a moment to catch their breath. Many, perhaps most, found themselves with special tasks to perform and special demands upon them; by all accounts they strained to rise to the occasion. The planters, knowing that the season lasted too long to sustain a fever pitch of effort, tried to break it up with parties and barbecues and at the very least promised and delivered a gala dinner and ball at the end. Ellen Betts, an ex-slave from Texas, recalled: "Massa sho' good to dem gals and bucks what cuttin' de cane. When dey git done makin' sugar, he give a drink called 'Peach 'n' Honey' to de women folk and whiskey and brandy to de men." Another ex-slave, William Stone of Alabama, said that the slaves were "happy" to work during the sugar harvest "'cause we knowed it mean us have plenty 'lasses in winter."

Still, the demands of the sugar crop meant the sacrifice of some Sundays and even the Christmas holiday. The slaves showed no resentment at the postponement of the holiday. It would come in due time, usually in mid-January, and the greater their sacrifices, the longer and fuller the holiday would likely be. For the slaves on the sugar plantations Christmas did not mean December 25; it meant the great holiday that honored the Lord's birth, brought joy to His children, and properly fell at the end of the productive seasons.

Cotton picking was another matter. One ex-slave recalled cotton-picking parties along with corn-shucking parties but added, "Dere wasn't so much foolishness at cotton pickin' time." The slaves missed, in particular, the fellowship of slaves from other plantations. An exchange of labor forces on a crash basis sometimes occurred, and ex-slaves remembered precisely those times warmly. The planters had to have their cotton picked at about the same time and could not easily exchange labor forces. But the neighborly tradition was too strong to be denied entirely, and when a planter fell dangerously behind, others would come to his aid. Unable to take time away from their own work unless well ahead of schedule, friendly planters had to send their slaves after hours to pick by moonlight. The slaves, instead of becoming indignant over the imposition, responded with enthusiasm and extra effort. Many of them later recalled this grueling all-night work as "big times," for they were helping their own friends and combining the work with festivity. Bonuses, parties, and relaxed discipline rewarded their cooperation. Scattered evidence suggests less whipping and harsh driving during the cotton-picking season on some plantations but the opposite on others.

Some planters congratulated themselves on their succession in getting a good response during the critical cotton harvest. Virginia Clay visited Governor Hammond's noteworthy plantation in South Carolina and enthusiastically reported on the magnificent singing and general spirit of the slaves, and Kate Stone was sure that "the Negroes really seemed to like the cotton picking best of all." Henry William Ravenel, in his private journal, made an interesting observation that provides a better clue to the slaves' attitude. Writing in 1865, immediately after their emancipation, he declared that the slaves had always disliked planting and cultivating cotton and would now prefer almost any alternative labor. The picking season must have struck the slaves as a mixed affair. It meant hard and distasteful work and sometimes punishment for failure to meet quotas, but also the end of a tough season, prizes for good performances, and the prelude to relaxation and a big celebration. Yet, the special spirit of the season was not strong enough to carry the slaves through the rigors of labor; the whip remained the indispensable spur. . . .

Whatever the origins of the slaves' strong preference for collective work, it drew the attention of their masters, who knew that they would have to come to terms with it. Edmund Ruffin, the South's great soil chemist and authority on plantation agriculture, complained that the pinewoods of North Carolina were set afire every spring by inconsiderate poor whites who cared nothing for the damage they did in order to provide grazing land for their few cows. He added that the slaves also set many fires because they intensely disliked collecting turpentine from the trees. This work was light and easy in Ruffin's estimation, but the slaves resisted it anyway because it had to be performed in isolation. "A negro," Ruffin explained from long experience, "cannot abide being along and will prefer work of much exposure and severe toil, in company, to any lighter work, without any company." . . .

The powerful community spirit and preference for collective patterns of working and living had their antithesis in an equally powerful individualism, manifested most attractively during and after Reconstruction in an attempt to transform themselves into peasant proprietors. This particular kind of individualism has also had less attractive manifestations, from the creation of the ghetto hustler and the devil-take-the-hindmost predator to the creation of a set attitudes that many blacks hold responsible for a chronic lack of political unity. Certainly, the old collective spirit remains powerful, as the very notion of a black "brotherhood" demonstrates, but it does rest on a contradictory historical base. The work ethic of the slaves provided a firm defense against the excesses of an oppressive labor system, but like the religious tradition on which it rested, it did not easily lend itself to counterattack. Once the worst features of the old regime fell away, the ethic itself began to dissolve into its component parts. Even today we witness the depressing effects of this dissolution in a futile and pathetic caricature of bourgeois individualism, manifested both in the frustrated aspirations so angrily depicted in E. Franklin Frazier's *Black Bourgeoisie* and in violent, antisocial nihilism. But we also witness the continued power of a collective sensibility regarded by some as "race pride" and by others as a developing black national consciousness.

# Emancipation and the Reconstruction of Southern Labor

### ERIC FONER

Of the many questions raised by emancipation, none was more crucial for the future of both blacks and whites in Southern society than the organization of the region's economy. Slavery had been first and foremost a system of labor. And while all Republicans agreed that "free labor" must replace slavery, few were certain how the transition should be accomplished. "If the [Emancipation] Proclamation makes the slaves actually free," declared the *New York Times* in January 1863, "there will come the further duty of making them work. . . . All this opens a vast and most difficult subject." . . .

. . . Beginning in 1865, and for years thereafter, Southern whites throughout the South complained of the difficulty of obtaining female field laborers. Planters, Freedmen's Bureau officials, and Northern visitors all ridiculed the black "female aristocracy" for "acting the *lady*" or mimicking the family patterns of middle-class whites. White employers also resented their inability to force black children to labor in the fields, especially after the spread of schools in rural areas. Contemporaries appeared uncertain whether black women, black men, or both were responsible for the withdrawal of females from agricultural labor. There is no question that many black men considered it manly to have their wives work at home and believed that, as head of the family, the male should decide how its labor was organized. But many black women desired to devote more time than under slavery to caring for their children and to domestic responsibilities like cooking, sewing, and laundering.

The shift of black female labor from the fields to the home proved a temporary phenomenon. The rise of renting and sharecropping, which made each family responsible for its own plot of land, placed a premium on the labor of all family members. The dire poverty of many black families, deepened by the depression of the 1870s, made it essential for both women and men to contribute to the family's income. Throughout this period, a far higher percentage of black than white women and children worked for wages outside their homes. Where women continued to concentrate on domestic tasks, and children attended school, they frequently engaged in seasonal field labor. Thus, emancipation did not eliminate labor outside the home by black women and children, but it fundamentally altered control over their labor. Now blacks themselves, rather than a white owner or overseer, decided where and when black women and children worked. . . .

Nowhere were blacks' efforts to define their freedom more explosive for the entire society than in the economy. Freedmen brought out of slavery a conception of themselves as a "Working Class of People" who had been unjustly deprived of the fruits of their labor. To white predictions that they would not work, blacks responded that if any class could be characterized as lazy, it was the planters, who had "lived in idleness all their lives on stolen labor." It is certainly true that many blacks expected to labor less as free men and women than they had as slaves, an understandable aim considering the conditions they had previously known. "Whence comes the assertion that the 'nigger won't work'?" asked an Alabama freedman. "It comes from this fact: . . . the freedman refuses to be driven out into the field two hours before a day, and work until 9 or 10 o'clock in the night, as was the case in the days of slavery."

Yet freedom meant more than shorter hours and payment of wages. Freedmen sought to control the conditions under which they labored, end their subordination to white authority, and carve out the greatest measure of economic autonomy. These aims led them to prefer tenancy to wage labor, and leasing land for a fixed rent to sharecropping. Above all, they inspired the quest for land. Owning land, the freedmen believed, would "complete their independence."

To those familiar with the experience of other postemancipation societies, blacks' "mania for owning a small piece of land" did not appear surprising. Freedmen in Haiti, the British and Spanish Caribbean, and Brazil all saw ownership of land as crucial to economic independence, and everywhere former slaves sought to avoid returning to plantation labor. Unlike freedmen in other countries, however, American blacks emerged from slavery convinced that the federal government had committed itself to land distribution. Belief in an imminent division of land was most pervasive in the South Carolina and Georgia lowcountry, but the idea was shared in other parts of the South as well, including counties that had never been occupied by federal troops. Blacks insisted that their past labor entitled them to at least a portion of their owners' estates. As an Alabama black convention put it: "The property which they hold was nearly all earned by the sweat of *our* brows."

In some parts of the South, blacks in 1865 did more than argue the merits of their case. Hundreds of freedmen refused either to sign labor contracts or to leave the plantations, insisting that the land belonged to them. On the property of a Tennessee planter, former slaves not only claimed to be "joint heirs," to the estate but, the owner complained, abandoned the slaves quarters and took up residence "in the rooms of my house." Few freedmen were able to maintain control of land seized in this manner. A small number did, however, obtain property through other means, squatting on unoccupied land in sparsely populated states like Florida and Texas, buying tiny city plots, or cooperatively purchasing farms and plantations. Most blacks, however, emerged from slavery unable to purchase land even at the depressed prices of early Reconstruction and confronted by a white community unwilling to advance credit to sell them property. Thus, they entered the world of free labor as wage or share workers on land owned by whites. The adjustment to a new social order in which their persons were removed from the market but their labor was bought and sold like any other commodity proved in many respects difficult.

For it required them to adapt to the logic of the economic market, where the impersonal laws of supply and demand and the balance of power between employer and employee determine a laborer's material circumstances.

Most freedmen welcomed the demise of the paternalism and mutual obligations of slavery and embraced many aspects of the free market. They patronized the stores that sprang up throughout the rural South, purchasing "luxuries" ranging from sardines, cheese, and sugar to new clothing. They saved money to build and support churches and educate their children. And they quickly learned to use and influence the market for their own ends. The early years of Reconstruction witnessed strikes or petitions for higher wages by black urban laborers including Richmond factory workers, Jackson washerwomen, New Orleans and Savannah stevedores, and mechanics in Columbus, Georgia. In rural areas, too, plantation freedmen sometimes bargained collectively over contract terms, organized strikes and occasionally even attempted to establish wage schedules for an entire area. Blacks exploited competition between planters and nonagricultural employers, seeking work on railroad construction crews and at turpentine mills and other enterprises offering pay far higher than on the plantations.

Slavery, however, did not produce workers fully socialized to the virtues of economic accumulation. Despite the profits possible in early postwar cotton farming, many freedmen strongly resisted growing the "slave crop." "If ole massa went to grow cotton," said one Georgia freedman, "let him plant it himself." Many freedmen preferred to concentrate on food crops and only secondarily on cotton or other staples to obtain ready cash. Rather than choose irrevocably between self-sufficiency and market farming, they hoped to avoid a complete dependence on either while taking advantage of the opportunities each could offer. . . .

Historical experience and modern scholarship suggest that acquiring small plots of land would hardly, by itself, have solved the economic plight of black families. Without control of credit and assess to markets, land reform can often be a hollow victory. And where political power rests in hostile hands, small landowners often find themselves subjected to oppressive taxation and other state policies that severely limit their economic prospects. In such circumstances, the autonomy offered by land ownership tends to be defensive, rather than the springboard for sustained economic advancement. Yet while hardly an economic panacea, land redistribution would have had profound consequences for Southern society, weakening the land-based economic and political power of the old ruling class, offering blacks a measure of choice as to whether, when, and under what circumstances to enter the labor market, and affecting the former slaves' conception of themselves.

Blacks' quest for economic independence not only threatened the foundations of the Southern political economy, it put the freedmen at odds with both former owners seeking to restore plantation labor discipline and Northerners committed to reinvigorating staple crop production. But as part of the broad quest for individual and collective autonomy, it remained central to the black community's effort to define the meaning of freedom. Indeed, the fulfillment of other aspirations, from family autonomy to the creation of schools and churches, all greatly depended on success in winning control of their working lives and gaining access to the economic resources of the South. . . .

For the majority of planters, as for their former slaves, the Confederacy's defeat and the end of slavery ushered in a difficult adjustment to new race and class relations and new ways of organizing labor. The first casualty of this transformation was the paternalist ethos of prewar planters. A sense of obligation based on mastership over an inferior, paternalism had no place in a social order in which labor relations were mediated by the impersonal market and blacks aggressively pressed claims to autonomy and equality. "The Law which freed the negro," a Southern editor wrote in 1865, "at the same time freed the master, all obligations springing out of the relations of master and slave, except those of kindness, cease mutually to exist." And kindness proved all too rare in the aftermath of war and emancipation. Numerous planters evicted from their plantations those blacks too old, or infirm to labor, and transformed "rights" enjoyed by slaves—clothing, housing, access to garden plots—into commodities for which payment was due. . . .

Carl Schurz and other Northerners who toured the South in 1865 concluded that white Southerners "do not know what free labor is." To which many planters replied that Northerners "do not understand the character of the negro." Free labor assumptions—economic rationality, internal self-discipline, responsiveness to the incentives of the market—could never, planters insisted, be applied to blacks. "They are improvident and reckless of the future," complained a Georgia newspaper. Nor was another free labor axiom, opportunity for social mobility, applicable in the South. A Natchez newspaper informed its readers: "The true station of the negro is that of a servant. The wants and state of our country demand that he should remain a servant."

The conviction that preindustrial lower classes share an aversion to regular, disciplined toil had a long history in both Europe and America. In the Reconstruction South, this ideology took a racial form, and although racism was endemic throughout nineteenth-century America, the requirements of the plantation economy shaped its specific content in the aftermath of emancipation. Charges of "indolence" were often directed not against blacks unwilling to work, but at those who preferred to labor for themselves. "Want of ambition will be the devil of the race, I think," wrote Kemp P. Battle, a North Carolina planter and political leader, in 1866. "Some of my most sensible men say they have no other desire than to cultivate their own land in grain and raise bacon." On the face of it, such an aspiration appears ambitious enough, and hardly unusual in the nineteenth-century South. But in a plantation society, a black man seeking to work his way up the agricultural ladder to the status of self-sufficient farmer seemed not an admirable example of industriousness, but a demoralized freedman unwilling to work—work, that is, under white supervision on a plantation.

The questions of land and labor were intimately related. Planters quickly concluded that their control of black labor rested upon maintaining their own privileged access to the productive land of the plantation belt. Even if relatively few freedmen established themselves as independent farmers, plantation discipline would dissolve since, as William H. Trescot explained, "it will be utterly impossible for the owner to find laborers that will work contentedly for wages alongside of these free colonies." At public meetings in 1865, and in their private correspondence, planters resolved never to rent or sell land to freedmen. In effect, they sought to impose upon blacks their own definition, of freedom, one that repudiated the former slaves' equation of liberty and autonomy. "They have an idea that a hireling is not a freed-man," Mississippi planter Samuel Agnew noted in his diary. . . .

Between the planters' need for a disciplined labor force and the freedmen's quest for autonomy, conflict was inevitable. Planters attempted through written contracts to reestablish their authority over every aspect of their laborers' lives. "Let everything proceed as formerly," one advised, "the contractual relation being substituted for that of master and slave." These early contracts prescribed not only labor in gangs from sunup to sundown as in antebellum days, but complete sub-servience to the planter's will. One South Carolina planter required freedmen to obey the employer "and go by his direction the same as in slavery time." Many contracts not only specified modes of work and payment, but prohibited blacks from leaving plantations, entertaining visitors, or holding meetings without per-mission of the employer.

Such provisions proved easier to compose than to enforce. Planters quickly learned that labor contracts could not by themselves create a submissive labor force. On the aptly named Vexation plantation in Texas, blacks in September 1865 were said to be "insolent and refusing to work." The employees of Louisiana's former Confederate governor, Thomas O. Moore, set their own pace of work, refused to plow when the ground was hard, and answered his complaints in a "disrespectful and annoying" manner. Conflict was endemic on plantations throughout the South. Some blacks refused to weed cotton fields in the rain. Others would not perform the essential but hated "mud work" of a rice plantation—dredging canals and repairing dikes—forcing some rice planters "to hire Irishmen to do the ditching." House ser-vants, too, had their own ideas of where their obligations began and ended. Butlers refused to cook or polish brass, domestics would not black the boots of plantation guests, chambermaids declared that it was not their duty to answer the front door, serving girls insisted on the right to entertain male visitors in their rooms.

Southern whites were not the only ones to encounter difficulty disciplining for-mer slaves. During and immediately after the war, a new element joined the South's planter class: Northerners who purchased land, leased plantations, or formed part-nerships with Southern planters. These newcomers were a varied, ambitious group, mostly former soldiers anxious to invest their savings in this promising new frontier and civilians lured South by press reports of "the fabulous sums of money to be made in the South in raising cotton." Joined with the quest for profit, however, was a reforming spirit, a vision of themselves as agents of sectional reconciliation and the South's "economic regeneration." As an Illinois man farming in Texas wrote: "I am going to introduce new ideas here in the farming line and show the beauties of free over slave labor."

Southern planters predicted that the newcomers would soon complain about the character of black labor, and they were not far wrong. The very "scientific" methods Northerners hoped to introduce, involving closely supervised work and changes in customary plantation routines, challenged the more irregular pace of work preferred by blacks and their desire to direct their own labor. As time passed, the Northern planters sounded and acted more and more like Southern. Some sought to restore corporal punishment, only to find that the freedmen would not stand for it. Perhaps the problem arose from the fact that, like Southern whites, most of the newcomers did not believe recently emancipated blacks capable of "self-directed labor." If the freedmen were to become productive free laborers, said the *New York Times* with unintended irony, "it must be done by giving them new masters." Blacks, however, wanted to be their own masters. And, against employers both Southern and Northern, they used whatever weapons they could find in the chaotic economic conditions of the postwar South to influence the conditions of their labor.

Blacks did, indeed, enjoy considerable bargaining power because of the "labor shortage" that followed the end of slavery. Particularly acute in sparsely populated Florida and the expanding cotton empire of the Southwest, competition for labor affected planters throughout the South. "The struggle seems to be who will get the negro at any price," lamented Texas planter Frank B. Conner. Planters, he concluded, must band together to "establish some maximum figure," stop "enticing" one another's workers, and agree that anyone, "breaking the established custom should be driven from the community."

The scarcity of labor was no mirage. Measured in hours worked per capita, the supply of black labor dropped by about one-third after the Civil War, largely because all former slaves were determined to work fewer hours than under slavery, and many women and children withdrew altogether from the fields. But the "labor shortage" was a question not only of numbers, but of power. It arose from black families' determination to use the rights resulting from emancipation to establish the conditions, rhythms, and compensation of their work. . . .

Despite the intensity of their conflict, neither former master nor former slave possessed the power to define the South's new system of labor. A third protagonist, the victorious North, also attempted to shape the transition from slavery to freedom. To the Freedmen's Bureau, more than any other institution, fell the task of assisting at the birth of a free labor society. The Bureau's commissioner was Gen. Oliver Otis Howard, whose close ties to the freedmen's aid societies had earned him the sobriquet "Christian General." Although temporary, Howard's agency was an experiment in social policy that, a modern scholar writes, "did not belong to the America of its day." Its responsibilities can only be described as daunting; they included introducing a workable system of free labor in the South, establishing schools for freedmen, providing aid to the destitute, aged, ill, and insane, adjudicating disputes among blacks and between the races, and attempting to secure for blacks and white Unionists equal justice from the state and local governments established during Presidential Reconstruction. The local Bureau agent was expected to win the confidence of blacks and whites alike in a situation where race and labor relations had been poisoned by mutual distrust and conflicting interests. Moreover, the Bureau employed, at its peak, not more than 900 agents in the entire South. Only a dozen served in Mississippi in 1866, and the largest contingent in Alabama at any time comprised twenty. "It is not . . . in your power to fulfill one tenth of the expectations of those who framed the Bureau," Gen. William T. Sherman advised Howard. "I fear you have Hercules' task."

At first glance, the Bureau's activities appear as a welter of contradictions, reflecting differences among individual agents in interpreting general policies laid down in Washington. But unifying the Bureau's activities was the endeavor to lay the foundation for a free labor society. To the extent that this meant putting freedmen back to work on plantations, the Bureau's policies coincided with the interests of the planters. To the extent that it prohibited coercive labor discipline, took up the burden of black education, sought to protect blacks against violence, and promoted the removal of legal barriers to blacks' advancement, the Bureau reinforced the freedmen's aspirations. In the end, the Bureau's career exposed the ambiguities and inadequacies of the free labor ideology itself. But simultaneously, the former slaves seized the opportunity offered by the Bureau's imperfect efforts on their behalf to bolster their own quest for self-improvement and autonomy. . . .

In the war's immediate aftermath, federal policy regarding black labor was established by the army. And the army seemed to many freedmen to have only one object in view—to compel them to return to work on the plantations. . . . [T]he assumption underpinning military policy, that the interests of all Americans would be best served by blacks' return to plantation labor, remained intact as the Freedmen's Bureau assumed command of the transition to free labor. . . .

. . . The free labor ideology rested on a theory of universal economic rationality and the conviction that all classes in a free labor society shared the same interests. In reality, former masters and former slaves inherited from slavery work habits and attitudes at odds with free labor assumptions, and both recognized, more clearly than the Bureau, the irreconcilability of their respective interests and aspirations. The free labor social order, moreover, ostensibly guaranteed the ambitious worker the opportunity for economic mobility, the ability to move from wage labor to independence through the acquisition of productive property. Yet what became of this axiom in an impoverished society where even the highest agricultural wages remained pitiably low, and whose white population was determined to employ every means at its disposal to prevent blacks from acquiring land or any other means of economic independence?

Establishing themselves in the South in the summer and fall of 1865, Bureau agents hoped to induce Southerners to "give the system a fair and honest trial." To planters' desire for a disciplined labor force governed by the lash, agents responded that "*bodily coercion* fell as an incident of slavery." To the contention that blacks would never work voluntary or respond to market incentives, they replied that the problem of economic readjustment should be viewed through the prism of labor, rather than race. . . .

The "two evils" against which the Bureau had to contend, an army officer observed in July 1865, were "cruelty on the part of the employer and shirking on the part of the negroes." Yet the Bureau, like the army, seemed to consider black reluctance to labor the greater threat to its economic mission. In some areas agents continued the military's urban pass systems and vagrancy patrols, as well as the practice of rounding up unemployed laborers for shipment to plantations. Bureau courts in Memphis dispatched improvised blacks convicted of crimes to labor for whites who would pay their fines. "What a mockery to call those 'Freedmen' who are still subjected to such things," commented a local minister.

United as to the glories of free labor, Bureau officials, like Northerners generally, differed among themselves about the ultimate social implications of the free labor ideology. Some believed the freedmen would remain a permanent plantation labor force; others insisted they should enjoy the same opportunity to make their way up the social ladder to independent proprietorship as Northern workers; still others hoped the federal government would assist at least some blacks in acquiring their own farms. Howard believed most freedmen must return to plantation labor, but under conditions that allowed them the opportunity to work their way out of the wage-earning class. At the same time, he took seriously the provision in the act establishing his agency that authorized it to settle freedmen on confiscated and abandoned lands. In 1865, Howard and a group of sympathetic Bureau officials attempted to breathe life into this alternative vision of a free-labor South.

. . . [T]he Bureau controlled over 850,000 acres of abandoned land in 1865, hardly enough to accommodate all the former slaves but sufficient to make a start toward creating a black yeomanry. Howard's subordinates included men sincerely committed to settling freedmen on farms of their own and protecting the rights of those who already occupied land. . . .

Initially, Howard himself shared the radical aims of [his subordinates]. At the end of July 1865 he issued Circular 13, which instructed Bureau agents to "set aside" forty-acre tracts for the freedmen as rapidly as possible. But [President] Andrew Johnson, who had been pardoning former Confederates, soon directed Howard to rescind his order. A new policy, drafted in the White House and issued in September as Howard's Circular 15, ordered the restoration to pardoned owners of all land except the small amount that had already been sold under a court decree. Once growing crops had been harvested, virtually all the land in Bureau hands would revert to its former owners. . . .

The restoration of land required the displacement of tens of thousands of freedmen throughout the South. The army evicted most of the 20,000 blacks settled on confiscated and abandoned property in southeastern Virginia. The 62,000 acres farmed by Louisiana blacks were restored to their former owners. . . .

Nowhere, however, was the restoration process so disruptive as in the Georgia and South Carolina lowcountry. On more than one occasion freedmen armed themselves, barricaded plantations, and drove off owners attempting to dispossess them. Black squatters told one party of Edisto Island landlords in February 1866, "you have better go back to Charleston, and go to work there, and if you can do nothing else, you can pick oysters and earn your living as the loyal people have done—by the sweat of their brows." Bureau agents, black and white, made every effort to induce lowcountry freedmen to sign contracts with their former owners, while federal troops forcibly evicted those who refused. In the end, only about 2,000 South Carolina and Georgia freedmen actually received the land they had been promised in 1865.

The events of 1865 and 1866 kindled a deep sense of betrayal among freedmen throughout the South. Land enough existed, wrote former Mississippi slave Merrimon Howard, for every "man and woman to have as much as they could work." Yet blacks had been left with

> no *land,* no *house,* not so much as [a] place to lay our head. . . . Despised by the world, hated by the country that gives us birth, denied of all our writs as a people, we were friends on the march, . . . brothers on the battlefield, but in the peaceful pursuits of life it seems that we are strangers.

Thus, by 1866 the Bureau found itself with no alternative but to encourage virtually all freedmen to sign annual contracts to work on the plantations. Its hopes for long-term black advancement and Southern economic prosperity now came to focus exclusively on the labor contract itself. By voluntarily signing and adhering to contracts, both planters and freedmen would develop the habits of a free labor economy and come to understand their fundamental harmony of interests. Agents found themselves required to perform a nearly impossible balancing act. Disabusing blacks of the idea that they would soon obtain land from the government, and threatening to arrest those who refused to sign a contract or leave the plantations, agents simultaneously insisted on blacks' right to bargain freely for employment and attempted to secure more advantageous contracts than had prevailed in 1865. Some Bureau officers approved agreements in which the laborer would receive nothing at all if the crop failed and could incur fines for such vaguely defined offenses as failure to do satisfactory work or "impudent, profane or indecent language." More conscientious agents revoked contract provisions regulating blacks' day-to-day lives and insisted that laborers who left plantations before the harvest must be paid for their work up to the date of departure. And virtually all agents insisted that planters acknowledge that their power to employ physical coercion had come to an end.

The Bureau's role in supervising labor relations reached its peak in 1866 and 1867; thereafter, federal authorities intervened less and less frequently to oversee contracts or settle plantation disputes. To the extent that the contract system had been intended to promote stability in labor relations in the chaotic aftermath of war and allow commercial agriculture to resume, it could be deemed a success. But in other ways, the system failed. For the entire contract system in some ways violated the principles of free labor. Agreements, Howard announced soon after assuming office, "should be free, *bona fide* acts." Yet how voluntary were labor contracts signed by blacks when they were denied access to land, coerced by troops and Bureau agents if they refused to sign, and fined or imprisoned if they struck for higher wages? Propertyless individuals in the North, to be sure, were compelled to labor for wages, but the compulsion was supplied by necessity, not by public officials, and contracts did not prevent them from leaving work whenever they chose. Why, asked the New Orleans *Tribune* again and again, did the Bureau require blacks to sign year-long labor contracts when "laborers throughout the civilized world"—including agricultural laborers in the North—could leave their employment at any time? To which one may add that even the most sympathetic Bureau officials assumed that blacks would constitute the rural labor force, at least until the natural working of the market divided the great plantations into small farms. "Idle white men" were never required to sign labor contracts or ordered to leave Southern cities for the countryside, a fact that made a mockery of the Bureau's professed goal of equal treatment for the freedmen.

Howard always believed that the Bureau's policies, viewed as a whole, benefited the freedmen more than their employers, especially since civil authorities offered blacks no protection against violence or fraud and the courts provided no justice to those seeking legal redress. He viewed the system of annual labor contracts as a temporary expedient, which would disappear once free labor obtained a "permanent foothold" in the South "under its necessary protection of equal and just laws properly executed." Eventually, as in the North, the market would regulate employment. Yet in the early years of Reconstruction, operating within the constraints of the free labor ideology, adverse crop and market conditions, the desire to restore production of the South's staple crops, and presidential policy, Bureau decisions conceived as temporary exerted a powerful influence on the emergence of new economic and social relations, closing off some options for blacks, shifting the balance of power in favor of employers, and helping to stabilize the beleaguered planter class. . . .

In 1866 and 1867, the freedmen's demand for an improvement in their economic condition and greater independence in their working lives set in motion a train of events that fundamentally transformed the plantation labor system. Blacks' desire for greater autonomy in the day-to-day organization of work produced a trend toward the subdivision of the labor force. Gang labor for wages persisted where planters had access to outside capital and could offer high monthly wages, promptly paid. Thanks to an influx of Northern investment, this was the case on sugar plantations that managed to resume production. On many sugar plantations in 1866 and 1867, however, squads of a dozen or fewer freedmen replaced the gangs so reminiscent of slavery. Generally organized by the blacks themselves, these squads sometimes consisted entirely of members of a single family, but more often included unrelated men. By 1867 the gang system was disappearing from the cotton fields.

The final stage in the decentralization of plantation agriculture was the emergence of sharecropping. Unlike the earlier share-wage system, with which it is often confused, in sharecropping individual families (instead of large groups of freedmen) signed contracts with the landowner and became responsible for a specified piece of land (rather than working in gangs). Generally, sharecroppers retained one-third of the year's crop if the planter provided implements, fertilizer, work animals, and seed, and half if they supplied their own. The transition to sharecropping occurred at different rates on different plantations and continued well into the 1870s, but the arrangement appeared in some areas soon after the Civil War.

To blacks, sharecropping offered an escape from gang labor and day-to-day white supervision. For planters, the system provided a way to reduce the cost and difficulty of labor supervision, share risk with tenants, and circumvent the chronic shortage of cash and credit. Most important of all, it stabilized the work force, for sharecroppers utilized the labor of all members of the family and had a vested interest in remaining until the crop had been gathered. Yet whatever its economic rational, many planters resisted sharecropping as a threat to their overall authority and inefficient besides (since they believed blacks would not work without direct white supervision). A compromise not fully satisfactory to either party, the system's precise outlines remained a point of conflict. Planters insisted sharecroppers were wage laborers who must obey the orders of their employer and who possessed no property right in the crop until they received their share at the end of the year. But sharecroppers, a planter complained in 1866, considered themselves "partners in the crop," who insisted on farming according to their own dictates and would not brook white supervision. Only a system of wages, payable at the end of the year, he concluded, would allow whites to "work in accordance with our former management." But precisely because it seemed so far removed from "our former management," blacks came to prefer the sharecropping system.

If freedmen in the cotton fields rejected the gang labor associated with bondage, those in the rice swamps insisted on strengthening the familiar task system, the foundation of the partial autonomy they had enjoyed as slaves. "We want to work just as we have always worked," declared a group of freedmen in South Carolina's rice region, and to attract labor, rice planters found themselves obliged to let the blacks "work . . . as they choose without any overseer." Out of the wreck of the rice economy and blacks' insistence on autonomy emerged an unusual set of labor relations. Some planters simply rented their plantations to blacks for a share of the crop or divided the land among groups of freedmen to cultivate as they saw fit. Others agreed to a system of labor sharing in which freedmen worked for two days on the plantation in exchange for an allotment of land on which to grow their own crops.

Thus, the struggles of early Reconstruction planted the seeds of new labor systems in the rural South. The precise manner in which these seeds matured would be worked out not only on Southern farms and plantations, but also on the Reconstruction battlefields of local, state, and national politics.

## *FURTHER READING*

Berlin, Ira. *Slaves Without Masters: The Free Negro in the Antebellum South* (1974).
Berlin, Ira, and Philip D. Morgan, eds. *Cultivation and Culture: Labor and the Shaping of Slave Life in the Americas* (1993).
———. *The Slaves' Economy: Independent Production by Slaves in the Americas* (1995).
——— et al., eds. *Freedom: A Documentary History of Emancipation, 1861–1867,* series 1, vol. 1: *The Destruction of Slavery* (1985); series 1, vol. 2: *The War Time Genesis of Free Labor: The Upper South* (1990): series 1, vol. 3: *The War Time Genesis of Free Labor: The Lower South* (1990).
Clark-Lewis, Elizabeth. *Living In, Living Out: African American Domestics in Washington, D.C.: 1910–1940* (1994).
Daniel, Pete. *Breaking the Land: The Transformation of Cotton, Tobacco, and Rice Cultures Since 1880* (1985).
Dew, Charles. *Bond of Iron: Master and Slave at Buffalo Forge* (1994).
Du Bois, W. E. B. *Black Reconstruction in America, 1860–1880* (1935).
Fields, Barbara Jeanne. *Slavery and Freedom on the Middle Ground: Maryland During the Nineteenth Century* (1985).
Fogel, Robert W., and Stanley L. Engerman. *Time on the Cross: The Economics of American Negro Slavery* (1974).
Foner, Eric. *Nothing But Freedom: Emancipation and Its Legacy* (1983).
———. *Politics and Ideology in the Age of the Civil War* (1980).
———. *Reconstruction: America's Unfinished Revolution* (1988).
Frankel, Noralee. *Freedom's Women: Black Women and Families in Civil War Era Mississippi* (1999).
Genovese, Eugene. *The Political Economy of Slavery* (1965).
———. *Roll, Jordan, Roll: The World the Slaves Made* (1974).
Gutman, Herbert. *Slavery and the Numbers Game: A Critique of "Time on the Cross"* (1975).
Hudson, Larry E., Jr. *To Have and to Hold: Slave Work and Family Life in Antebellum South Carolina* (1997).
Hunter, Tera. *To 'Joy My Freedom: Southern Black Women's Lives and Labors After the Civil War* (1998).
Johnson, Walter. *Soul by Soul: Life Inside the Antebellum Slave Market* (2000).
Jones, Jacqueline. *Labor of Love, Labor of Sorrow: Black Women, Work, and the Family from Slavery to the Present* (1985).

Kolchin, Peter. *Unfree Labor: American Slavery and Russian Serfdom* (1987).

Lichtenstein, Alex. *Twice the Work of Free Labor: The Political Economy of Convict Labor in the New South* (1997).

Mohr, Clarence L. *On the Threshold of Freedom: Masters and Slaves in Civil War Georgia* (2001).

Morton, Patricia, ed. *Discovering the Women in Slavery: Emancipating Perspectives on the American Past* (1996).

Ransom, Roger L., and Richard Sutch. *One Kind of Freedom: The Economic Consequences of Emancipation* (1977).

Reidy, Joseph. *From Slavery to Agrarian Capitalism in the Cotton Plantation South* (1992).

Ripley, C. Peter, et al., eds. *Witness for Freedom: African American Voices on Race, Slavery, and Emancipation* (1993).

Rodrigue, John C. *Reconstruction in the Cane Fields: From Slavery to Free Labor in Louisiana's Sugar Parishes, 1862–1880* (2001).

Rose, Willie Lee. *Rehearsal for Reconstruction: The Port Royal Experiment* (1964).

Saville, Julie. *The Work of Reconstruction: From Slave to Wage Laborer in South Carolina, 1869–1870 (1994).*

Schwalm, Leslie A. *A Hard Fight for We: Women's Transition from Slavery to Freedom in South Carolina* (1997).

Stanley, Amy Dru. *From Bondage to Contract: Wage Labor, Marriage, and the Market in the Age of Slave Emancipation* (1998).

Starobin, Robert S. *Industrial Slavery in the Old South* (1970).

Stevenson, Brenda. *Life in Black and White: Family and Community in the Slave South* (1996).

Takagi, Midori. *Rearing Wolves to Our Own Destruction: Slavery in Richmond, Virginia, 1782–1865* (1999).

Wayne, Michael. *Death of an Overseer: Reopening a Murder Investigation from the Plantation South* (2001).

White, Deborah Gray. *Ar'n't I a Woman? Female Slaves in the Plantation South* (1986)

Wiener, Jonathan M. *Social Origins of the New South: Alabama: 1860–1885* (1978).

Wood, Betty. *Women's Work, Men's Work: The Informal Slave Economies of Lowcountry Georgia* (1995).

Wright, Gavin. *The Political Economy of the Cotton South* (1978).

# C H A P T E R
## 5

# *The Age of*
# *Industrial Conflict*

*The last quarter of the nineteenth century is often labeled the Gilded Age after an 1885 novel by Mark Twain and Charles Dudley Warner that satirized the inequitable, excessive, corrupting wealth of those years. These years were indeed an era of rapid industrialization and great fortunes, during which the national railroad grid was finished and in which manufacturing cities like Pittsburgh, Chicago, St. Louis, and Cleveland doubled and tripled in size. But that era might be more aptly described as an age of industrial conflict, because this was a time of bitter, violent industrial clashes that startled the nation and frightened elites in politics and business.*

*From the first national railroad strike of 1877 (the Great Upheaval) through the massive eight-hour workday movement of the mid-1880s and the bloody confrontations in the next decade at Homestead, Coeur d'Alene, Cripple Creek, and all across the railroad network during the Pullman Boycott of 1894, labor and capital seemed to draw a line that increasingly divided the society into foe and friend. Unable to contain or accommodate these working-class insurrections, employers turned first to private police forces, like the Pinkertons, and then called on courts, the state militias, and the U.S. Army to quell such disturbances. After a clash between workers and police at Chicago's Haymarket Square in 1886 left several dead on both sides, a wave of political repression, including the trial and hanging of four working-class anarchists, seemed to confirm the brutal nature of labor-capital conflict in this industrial era. The fortress armories that still stand in the center of so many northern cities serve as brick and mortar reminders of the fear that swept through elite circles.*

*Working people experimented with a wide variety of ideas, movements, and organizational structures to meet the challenge of industrial transformation. This was an era in which socialism and anarchism flourished among German and Italian immigrants; an era in which the struggle for the liberation of Ireland and of Irish working people in North America seemed one and the same; an era in which, in the 1880s, the Knights of Labor, and in the first decade of the twentieth century, the Industrial Workers of the World, sought to organize workers into unions that paid little respect to craft, trade, or occupation. It was an era in which demonstrations, marches, and strikes might engage an entire city. When the railroad workers struck in 1877, they were often supported by the entire working population of the towns in which the rail lines had their switching yards and warehouses; and when an economic depression sent joblessness soaring in the early 1890s, many joined Jacob Coxey's "industrial army" of the unemployed to march on Washington for jobs and relief.*

*But the working class fought in a more private, covert fashion as well. Immigrant workers, especially the Irish and the Germans, formed secret societies and clubs that preached a radical overthrow of the wage system. Given the bare legality of most working-class activity in this era of conflict, it is remarkable that some unions managed to grow. The new craft unions, pioneered by Samuel Gompers and Adolph Strasser in the cigar making trade, were cautious institutions that avoided strikes whenever possible and usually limited their membership to men with a valuable, clearly defined skill. By the 1890s such unions, now organized into the American Federation of Labor, had established themselves in trades like carpentry, printing, masonry, cigar making and among railroad engineers, firemen, and conductors. The craft unions sought to monopolize the labor market in a particular occupation, so they restricted entry into their unions, frequently at the expense of white women, African Americans, and Asians. In contrast, the industrywide industrial unions of that era, including the United Mine Workers, The International Ladies Garment Workers Union, and the short-lived American Railway Union, were far more inclusive and politically radical.*

*In this age of industrial conflict, why did so many single-firm disputes turn into citywide popular revolts? Was the violence of the employers, the workers, or the government ever justified? Why do metaphors of war and militarism so dominate our memory of this industrial era?*

## ✤ D O C U M E N T S

Documents 1 and 2 capture the critique of capitalism embraced by the "Haymarket martyrs." In Document 1, before the Chicago court that would convict him in 1886, Michel Schwab explains the principles of anarchism, defending their reasoned appeal against the violence inherent in class society. His comrade Albert Parsons began his defense in the same trial by reading the poem "Freedom," reprinted here as Document 2. Document 3, a description of a Labor Day parade in 1889 by a *Boston Herald* reporter, reflects the degree to which unionists took pride in their movement and saw it as a cornerstone of all society.

Documents 4 and 5 represent contrasting labor views on the relationship between capital and labor. In Document 4, Samuel Gompers, a founder of the American Federation of Labor, defends the right to strike, comparing the use of this weapon to the struggle waged by the House of Commons to make the English Crown accountable to the people. In contrast, Document 5, the 1905 preamble to the constitution of the Industrial Workers of the World, holds that "the working class and the employing class have nothing in common."

During this era of industrial conflict, antiunion elites were also certain of their cause. In Document 6, Fitz John Porter, a former army officer, justifies the most extreme use of force when authorities confront strikers. In Document 7, George Pullman defends managerial paternalism in the aftermath of the 1894 walkout at the Pullman Palace Car works, which led to a national railway strike.

To what extent did these bitterly antagonistic individuals share a similar view of capitalist society? To what extend did they all agree that class conflict was inevitable and violence useful? Why are military metaphors so pervasive?

# 1. Haymarket Anarchist Michael Schwab
## Fights for Freedom, 1886

Talk about a gigantic conspiracy! A movement is not a conspiracy. All we did

WAS DONE IN OPEN DAYLIGHT.

There were no secrets. We prophesied in word and writing the coming of a great revolution, a change in the system of production in all industrial countries of the globe. And the change will come, and must come. Is it not absurd, as the State's Attorney and his associates have done, to suppose that this social revolution—a change of such immense proportions—was to be inaugurated on or about the first of May in the city of Chicago by making war on the police! The organizer Furthman searched hundreds of numbers of the *Arbeiter-Zeitung* and the *Alarm,* and so the prosecution must have known very well what we understood when we talked about the coming revolution. But the prosecuting attorneys preferred to ignore these explanatory articles.

The articles in evidence were carefully selected and paraded as samples of violent language, but the language used in them was just the same as newspapers used in general against us and their enemies. Even against the police and their practices they used words

OF THE SAME KIND AS WE DID.

The president of the Citizens' Association. Edwin Lee Brown, after the last election of Mayor Harrison, made a speech in North Side Turner Hall in which he called on all good citizens to take possession of the courthouse by force, even if they had to wade in blood. It seems to me that the most violent speakers are not to be found in the ranks of the Anarchists.

It is not violence in word or action the attorneys of the State and their urgers-on are waging war against; it is our doctrine—Anarchy.

We contend for communism and Anarchy—why? If we had kept silent, stones would have cried out. Murder was committed day by day. Children were slain, women worked to death, men killed inch by inch, and these crimes are never punished by law. The great principle underlying the present system is

UNPAID LABOR.

Those who amass fortunes, build palaces, and live in luxury, are doing that by virtue of unpaid labor. Being directly or indirectly the possessors of land and machinery, they dictate their terms to the workingman. He is compelled to sell his labor cheap, or to starve. The price paid him is always far below the real value. He acts under compulsion, and they call it a free contract. This infernal state of affairs keeps him poor and ignorant; an easy prey for exploitation. . . .

. . . When I came to the United States, I found that there were classes of workingmen who were better paid than the European workmen, but I perceived that the state

From *The Accused and the Accusers: The Famous Speeches of the Eight Chicago Anarchists in Court* (New York: Arno, 1969), 24–28.

of things in a great number of industries was even worse, and that the so-called better paid skilled laborers were degrading rapidly into mere automatic parts of machinery. I found that the proletariat of the great industrial cities was in a condition that could not be worse. Thousands of laborers in the city of Chicago live in rooms without sufficient protection from the weather, without proper ventilation, where never a stream of sunlight flows in. There are hovels where two, three and four families live in one room. How these conditions influence the health and the morals of these unfortunate sufferers, it is needless to say. And how *do* they live? From the ash-barrels

### THEY GATHER HALF-ROTTEN VEGETABLES,

in the butcher shops they buy for some cents offal of meat, and these precious morsels they carry home to prepare from them their meals. The delapidated houses in which this class of laborers live need repairs very badly, but the greedy landlord waits in most cases till he is compelled by the city to have them done. Is it a wonder that disease of all kinds kill men, women and children in such places by wholesale, especially children? Is this not horrible in a so-called civilized land where there is plenty of food and riches? Some years ago a committee of the Citizen's Association, or League, made an investigation of these matters, and I was one of the reporters that went with them. What these common laborers are today,

### THE SKILLED LABORERS WILL BE TOMORROW.

Improved machinery that ought to be a blessing for the workingman, under the existing conditions turns for him to a curse. Machinery multiplies the army of unskilled laborers, makes the laborer more dependent upon the men who own the land and the machines. And that is the reason that Socialism and Communism got a foothold in this country. The outcry that Socialism, Communism and Anarchism are the creed of foreigners, is a big mistake. There are more Socialists of American birth in this country than foreigners, and that is much, if we consider that nearly half of all industrial workingmen are not native Americans. There are Socialistic papers in a great many States edited by Americans for Americans. The capitalistic newspapers conceal that fact very carefully.

Socialism, as we understand it, means that land and machinery shall be held in common by the people. The production of goods shall be carried on by producing groups which shall supply the demands of the people. Under such a system every human being would have an opportunity to do useful work, and no doubt would work. Some hours' work every day would suffice to produce all that, according to statistics, is necessary for a comfortable living. Time would be left

### TO CULTIVATE THE MIND,

and to further science and art.

That is what the Socialist propose. Some say it is un-American! Well, then, is it American to let people starve and die in ignorance? Is exploitation and robbery of the poor, American? What have the great political parties done for the poor? Promised much; done nothing, except corrupting them by buying their votes on election day. A poverty-stricken man has no interest in the welfare of the community. It is only natural that in a society where women are driven to sell their honor, men should sell their votes.

But we "were not only Socialists and Communists: we were Anarchists."

What is Anarchy? . . . Anarchy is a dream, but only in the present. It will be realized.

### REASON WILL GROW

in spite of all obstacles. Who is the man that has the cheek to tell us that human development has already reached its culminating point? I know that our ideal will not be accomplished, this or next year, but I know that it will be accomplished as near as possible, some day, in the future. It is entirely wrong to use the word Anarchy as synonymous with violence. Violence is one thing and Anarchy another. In the present state of society violence is used on all sides, and, therefore, we advocated the use of violence against violence, but against violence only, as a necessary means of defense.

## 2. "Freedom," Poem by Haymarket Anarchist Albert R. Parsons, 1886

Toil and pray! The world cries cold;
Speed thy prayer, for time is gold
At thy door Need's subtle tread:
Pray in haste! for time is bread.

And thou plow'st and thou hew'st,
And thou rivet'st and sewest,
And thou harvestest in vain;
Speak! O, man; what is thy gain?

Fly'st the shuttle day and night.
Heav'st the ores of earth to light.
Fill'st with treasures plenty's horn;
Brim'st it o'er with wine and corn.

But who hath thy meal prepared,
Festive garments with thee shared;
And where is thy cheerful hearth,
Thy good shield in battle dearth?

Thy creations round thee see
All thy work, but naught for thee!
Yea, of all the chains alone thy hand forged,
These are thine own.

Chains that round the body cling.
Chains that lame the spirits wing.

From *The Accused and the Accusers: The Famous Speeches of the Eight Chicago Anarchists in Court* (New York: Arno, 1969), 90–91.

Chains that infants' feet, indeed
Clog! O, workman! Lo! Thy meed.

What you rear and bring to light.
Profits by the idle wight,
What ye weave of diverse hue,
'Tis a curse—your only due.

What ye build, no room insures,
Not a sheltering roof to yours,
And by haughty ones are trod—
Ye, whose toil their feet hath shod.

Human bees! Has nature's thrift
Given thee naught but honey's gift?
See! the drones are on the wing.
Have you lost the will to sting?

Man of labor, up, arise!
Know the might that in thee lies,
Wheel and shaft are set at rest
At thy powerful arm's behest.

Thine oppressor's hand recoils
When thou, weary of thy toil.
Shun'st thy plough thy task begun.
When thou speak'st: Enough is done!

Break this two-fold yoke in twain;
Break thy want's enslaving chain;
Break thy slavery's want and dread;
Bread is freedom, freedom bread.

## 3. "Labor's Great Army," 1889

An army, with banners flying and music sounding, on its march to the battlefield, is a grand and inspiring spectacle. . . . An army in days of peace, with its pomp of ordered motion and its glowing colors and glitter of weapons, is always an attractive sight, charming the gazers, young and old, for a little while, away from the commonplaces of the everyday struggle for bread and wealth. . . . But an industrial army, such as Boston witnessed yesterday parading its historic streets, with a record of invincible patience, an ever widening purpose of righteous achievement, is a sight more attractive, a spectacle more impressive. It means more for the future than all the battlefields that have been drenched with human blood. It is a celebration of the partial reign of the common people.

So excellent were the exhibitions of all the different crafts that it would be almost invidious to particularize any as the chief ornaments. Yet, perhaps to most

From *The Boston Herald,* September 3, 1889.

people, the "floats" of the carpenters, by their striking contrast of the old log cabin of the fathers with a modern building caused the greatest impression and suggested, in addition, the immense strides in quality of work made by the workers in the last few years, just as the procession suggests in a larger way the immense strides made by the workers themselves in securing the recognition of their important position in the body politic. The industrial army of yesterday seemed to feel that the workers are the base of the heaven-seeking pyramid of civilization, and that, if that is not well founded and secure, the top must topple. . . .

Union 33 of Boston was most profuse in its exhibition of mottoes. . . . One was a huge saw made of wood and painted quite realistically. On one side was the inscription, "We are organized to elevate," and on the reverse, "Set on eight hours." Another device was a carpenter's square enlarged to a fairly heroic size. The inscription was: "We are all square union men; non-union men are not square."

Other mottoes which attracted especial attention were these: "Honest labor never rusts: up with wages, down with trusts." "Nine hours a day has paved the way: eight hours a day has come to stay." "Less work, more recreation." "We build the cities." "Those who build palaces should not dwell in hovels."

The Operative Tailors' Union gave some very sharp raps. They were accompanied by two large open wagons, trimmed and decorated, one drawn by four horses, and bearing a representation of a tailor shop in active operation with men engaged in cutting, sewing and pressing. The other wagon was fitted to resemble the interior of a room in a tenement house, with all its squalor and misery. The first wagon bore a large sign inscribed: "Away with the filthy scab tenement house labor. We will investigate a few tenement houses for $20." The second bore simply the pregnant remark: "Twenty coats a day's work."

## 4. Samuel Gompers Defends the Right to Strike, 1899

The working people find that improvements in the methods of production and distribution are constantly being made, and unless they occasionally strike, or have the power to enter upon a strike, the improvements will all go to the employer and all the injuries to the employees. A strike is an effort on the part of the workers to obtain some of the improvements that have occurred resultant from bygone and present genius of our intelligence, of our mental progress. We are producing wealth today at a greater ratio than ever in the history of mankind, and a strike on the part of workers is, first, against deterioration in their condition, and, second, to be participants in some of the improvements. Strikes are caused from various reasons. The employer desires to reduce wages and lengthen hours of labor, while the desire on the part of employees is to obtain shorter hours of labor and better wages, and better surroundings. Strikes establish or maintain the rights of unionism; that is, to establish and maintain the organization by which the rights of the workers can be the better protected and advanced against the little forms of oppression,

From testimony of Samuel Gompers, November 20, 1899, U.S. Congress, House of Representatives, *Report of the Industrial Commission on the Relations and Conditions of Capital and Labor,* 56th Congress, 2d Session, House Document 495, Part 7, 605–606.

sometimes economical, sometimes political—the effort on the part of employers to influence and intimidate workmen's political preferences; strikes against victimization; activity in the cause of the workers against the blacklist. . . .

It required 40,000 people in the city of New York in my own trade in 1877 to demonstrate to the employers that we had a right to be heard in our own defense of our trade, and an opportunity to be heard in our own interests. It cost the miners of the country, in 1897, sixteen weeks of suffering to secure a national conference and a national agreement. It cost the railroad brotherhoods long months of suffering, many of them sacrificing their positions, in the railroad strike of 1877, and in the Chicago, Burlington, and Quincy strike, of the same year, to secure from the employers the right to be heard through committees, their representatives. . . . Workmen have had to stand the brunt of the suffering. The American Republic was not established without some suffering, without some sacrifice, and no tangible right has yet been achieved in the interest of the people unless it has been secured by sacrifices and persistency. After a while we become a little more tolerant to each other and recognize all have rights; get around the table and chaff each other; all recognize that they were not so reasonable in the beginning. Now we propose to meet and discuss our interests, and if we can not agree we propose in a more reasonable way to conduct our contests, each to decide how to hold out and bring the other one to terms. A strike, too, is to industry as the right that the British people contended for in placing in the House of Commons the power to close the purse strings to the Government. The rights of the British people were secured in two centuries— between 1500 and 1700—more than ever before, by the securing of that power to withhold the supplies; tied up the purse strings and compelled the Crown to yield. A strike on the part of workmen is to close production and compel better terms and more rights to be acceded to the producers. The economic results of strikes to workers have been advantageous. Without strikes their rights would not have been considered. It is not that workmen or organized labor desires the strike, but it will tenaciously hold to the right to strike. We recognize that peaceful industry is necessary to successful civilized life, but the right to strike and the preparation to strike is the greatest preventive to strikes. If the workmen were to make up their minds tomorrow that they would under no circumstances strike, the employers would do all the striking for them in the way of lesser wagers and longer hours of labor.

## 5. Preamble of the Industrial Workers of the World, 1905

The working class and the employing class have nothing in common. There can be no peace so long as hunger and want are found among millions of working people and the few, who make up the employing class, have all the good things of life.

Between these two classes a struggle must go on until the workers of the world organize as a class, take possession of the earth and the machinery of production, and abolish the wage system.

From Industrial Workers of the World, *Preamble and Constitution of the Industrial Workers of the World, Organized July 7, 1905* (Chicago: Industrial Workers of the World, 1916).

We find that the centering of management of the industries into fewer and fewer hands makes the trade unions unable to cope with the ever growing power of the employing class. The trade unions foster a state of affairs which allows one set of workers to be pitted against another set of workers in the same industry, thereby helping defeat one another in wage wars. Moreover, the trade unions aid the employing class to mislead the workers into the belief that the working class have interests in common with their employers.

These conditions can be changed and the interest of the working class upheld only by an organization formed in such a way that all its members in any one industry, or in all industries if necessary, cease work whenever a strike or lockout is on in any department thereof, thus making an injury to one an injury to all.

Instead of the conservative motto, "A fair day's wage for a fair day's work," we must inscribe on our banner the revolutionary watchword, "Abolition of the wage system."

It is the historic mission of the working class to do away with capitalism. The army of production must be organized, not only for the every day struggle with capitalists, but also to carry on production when capitalism shall have been over-thrown. By organizing industrially we are forming the structure of the new society within the shell of the old.

## 6. Fitz John Porter Explains How to Quell Mobs, 1885

Riots generally originate in crowded cities or in districts where the population is principally composed of operatives. They are due to two causes. First: the restless-ness or peevish discontent of the working-classes, who imagine that others are reaping large gains from their labor. Second: the plotting of demagogues and designing men, too indolent to earn their bread by their own exertions, who hope to receive power and profit, or perhaps notoriety. A third cause may be mentioned: the desire of honest but misguided men to obtain a better position for themselves and their families, who, brooding over real or fancied wrongs, finally resort to unlawful measures for redress.

The actors in the first movements which finally lead to a riot rarely, if ever, imagine that they are inaugurating one of these ebullitions of popular fury.

A combination of workmen, who have banded together presumably for proper purposes, believing themselves to be imposed upon by their employers, take mea-sures to secure what they consider their rights. Sometimes one, sometimes another method is adopted, either one of which finally leads to a breach between employers and employed. Then comes a strike. Perhaps the strikers are in the employ of a rail-road company, which, with its connections, reaches across the continent: all opera-tions are suspended upon the railroad; passenger and freight cars are stopped upon the tracks; each individual striker has a little circle which he influences; the circum-ferences of these circles touch each other, and thus commotion is spread through the land. Human sympathy always goes out to the oppressed; the strikers represent

From Fitz John Porter, "How to Quell Mobs," *North American Review* 141 (October 1885): 351–360.

themselves as oppressed by the monopolizing corporations, and the sympathy of the community for the weaker unites with its natural prejudices against the stronger in the contest; disorder begins; confusion becomes worse confounded. Now appear the baser elements of society—the tramp, the thief, the rogue, the burglar—and these elements, which before were the outcasts of society, now become the rulers of the hour. The quarrel, before confined to the railroad and its employés, now enlarges its field, and the bad is arrayed against the general good. Pillagers at first despoil the railroad company, and then seek the property of others, no matter whom, to satisfy their greed. The community awakes to the danger of the situation, but it is too late; anarchy has the upper hand, and vice and lawlessness reign supreme. . . .

"How shall the future riot be suppressed? Upon whom lies the duty of suppression—upon the general government, the State, or the municipality?"

These are the practical questions to be discussed.

The general government has no power, except such as is derived by cession from the States. It is the creature of the State governments, and in its relations with the States is governed by organic law, beyond which it cannot step. Like all general rules, there is an exception to this rule; for there is a law, not to be found in any written constitution, which must from necessity control the general government, and that is the law of self-preservation. While it cannot interfere in any of the municipal regulations of the States, still there may be an exigency when it is not only its right, but its duty to interfere. Whenever the property of the government is endangered by an unlawful assemblage of persons, the government should protect its property, even with the sacrifice of life. It can make no difference where that property is situated. It is not subject to the laws of the States; no taxes are paid to the State for its protection. . . .

It is very difficult to draw the line where forbearance shall cease to be a virtue, and where stern duty compels the authorities to use coercion. All this must be left to their good sense, alert judgment, and proper appreciation of each individual case. There should be no dallying with a mob. It is hydra-headed, many-sided, and, at the outset, undecided as to its future movements; but if, without the use of decided measures for prevention, it be suffered to take its own way, a leader will soon be found of sufficient capacity to direct and control these movements. Let this period once be passed, and let a master-mind be placed in command, with subservience on the part of his followers, and the control of the mob in the right direction is forever lost. . . .

The qualities most needed, in those who are charged with the duty of preventing riots, are coolness, decision, alertness, and courage. Let the mob once ascertain that any of these qualities are wanting in those who seek to suppress, and the opportunity for suppression is lost. It would have been more merciful in the end to those composing many mobs, certainly to those who suffered from their excesses, if instead of firing blank cartridges a few bullets had found their way into the muskets. One determined man, with fearless front and undaunted courage, has been of more service in preventing a riot than scores of dilly-dallying mayors and governors who read the riot act and begged and besought the rioters to disperse, and called them by endearing names.

In 1877 riots broke out all over the land. The history of these riots reveals strange inconsistencies and many shameful derelictions of duty. In the city of Pittsburg, with the police of the city at his back, and a large number of State troops at his command, the mayor of that great town, with an indecision which was indefensible and unaccountable (except upon the supposition that by so doing he hoped to preserve his popularity), suffered anarchy and pillage and murder to rule for days. He strove to stem a torrent of turbulence and violence with soft speeches, by reading the riot act, by kind words. But it was too late. The time for such formalities had passed. The sacrifice of a few lives by charges of fixed bayonets, or by salvos of musketry charged with bullets, would have scattered the howling, demoniac mob back to the holes and dreary retreats from which so many of them had come.

At Harrisburg, the same policy at first placed the troops of the great State of Pennsylvania, sent to relieve its capital from the depredations of the mob, prisoners in the hands of that very mob that they were sent to suppress. The militiamen were marched up and down the streets amid the jeers and howls of the rioters. But a different state of affairs was soon inaugurated, through the exertions of one determined man, the mayor of the city. He selected some of the best citizens, and with the sheriff of the county marched at their head, and almost in an instant dispelled the mob while in the very act of pillaging.

All along the line of the railroads extending west from Buffalo the employés were in commotion. Mobs of several thousand people had gathered at different points, but only at one place was the mob beyond the control of the authorities. This was at the city of Buffalo. At East Buffalo, where a mob which was estimated at more than three thousand persons was hooting, howling, and threatening vengeance, a captain of police, with the aid of the baton forcibly brought in contact with the heads of the rioters, in a very few moments dispelled the mob, so that, in the words of the historian who records this incident, "the East Buffalo grounds were as clear and quiet as a country field on a Sunday afternoon." . . .

Mobs are cowards at first. Crime always enervates. They only gain courage as they find that those whose duty it is to suppress them are themselves cowards. A mob is not to be feared when it is first aroused. It is only as its passion for carnage is whetted by the taste of blood, or its greed for pillage is gratified, that it becomes dangerous.

Upon whomsoever devolves the duty of suppression, let this be his first effort: check at the very beginning; allow no tumultuous gatherings; permit no delay; a few stern, resolute words; if these be not heeded, then strike resolutely, boldly; let there be no hesitation; if necessary, take life at the outset. It will be more merciful to take one life then than to suffer the mob to take the lives of many, or to be compelled to sacrifice the innocent with the guilty at the point of the bayonet, or in the discharge of musketry or cannon. But the necessity to take life will not arise unless there be inactivity and indecision at the outset on the part of the authorities.

Before the time shall come when it will be necessary to use musket-ball or bayonet, the opportunity will be afforded to suppress the riot; perhaps at the sacrifice of a few broken heads, or by the imprisonment of some of its leaders.

In every large city, in fact in every city where a police force is employed, a perfect drill should prepare policemen to meet the exigencies arising from any tumultuous assemblage of the people; so that, at a moment's warning, these conservators of the peace will be ready to act, and to act understandingly and promptly. It will be found that a few determined policemen, placed in the field at a moment's notice, will prove one of the best and most direct methods of quelling a mob. These, by skillful maneuvers, can take a mob in flank, or in rear, or in front, if necessary, and so employ themselves and their clubs that almost before the mob would know what was impelling them they would be driven from the field of action. . . .

The most fertile cause of all riots is the peevish discontent of wage-workers—too often ignorant of the true relations between themselves and their employers. This peevish discontent may perhaps be confined to a few, but those few will be able to avail themselves of the restlessness which may pervade the whole body of operatives. This discontent arises not so much from any real oppression, or from any wrong, but simply from the natural jealousy which every man feels, more or less, when he sees others living more luxuriously than himself, and especially when that luxury appears to be the result of his labor. Now this discontent may be dispelled, perhaps not in the present generation, though it may be greatly moderated; but, certainly, means can be taken to prevent it in the future. The employer and employé may surely be brought together in more intimate relations than those they at present sustain. Where lies the fault in the present system? Who is justly chargeable with the origin of this discontent? That question cannot be settled in this discussion. But so much may be said: the working-classes can be educated up to a higher tone of feeling, a better appreciation of their duty to their employers, a higher standard of morals, and a nobler level of thought and action. May not the employers find something in the present condition of things for which they are responsible; and which they, in the exercise of the duty they owe to common humanity, may be able to better?

There is a factory, in one of the large manufacturing towns of the country, where one of the employers, imbued with true Christian philanthropy, brings himself, in a measure, down to a level with his hundreds of employés. He mingles with their families; finds out the social status and wants of all; gives a word of advice to one; imparts counsel to another; sympathizes with the mourner; puts his strong arm round the weak; and employs all of his ability to raise his workingmen in the scale of human existence. He provides a reading-room for them, furnishes them with reading matter, and gives them lectures. Let this example be emulated by every employer in the land, and riots would be impossible.

## 7. George Pullman Defends Managerial Paternalism, 1894

The object in building Pullman was the establishment of a great manufacturing business on the most substantial basis possible, recognizing as we did, and do now, that the working people are the most important element which enters into the successful operation of any manufacturing enterprise.

We decided to build, in close proximity to the shops. homes for workingmen, of such character and surroundings as would prove so attractive as to cause the best class of mechanics to seek that place for employment in the preference to others.

From "Mr. Pullman Talks Freely," *New York Sun*, July 5, 1894, reprinted in *The Strike at Pullman: Statement of Geo. M. Pullman and T. H. Wickes, Before the U.S. Strike Commission* (1894).

We also desired to establish the place on such a basis as would exclude all baneful influences, believing that such a policy would result in the greatest measure of success, both from a commercial point of view, and also, what was equally important, or perhaps of greater importance in a tendency toward continued elevation and improvement of the condition not only of the working people themselves but of their children growing up about them.

Accordingly, the present location of Pullman was selected. That region of the country was the very sparsely populated, a very few hundred people, mostly farmers, living within a radius of perhaps a mile and a half of the site selected, where there are now living some 25,000.

It was not the intention to sell workmen homes in Pullman, but to so limit the area of the town that they could buy homes, at convenient distances from the works, if they chose to do so. If any lots had been sold in Pullman it would have permitted the introduction of the very baneful elements which it was the chief purpose to exclude from the immediate neighborhood of the shops and from the homes to be erected about them.

The plan was to provide homes in the first place for all people who should desire to work in the shops, at reasonable rentals, with the exception that as they became able, and should desire to do so, they would purchase lots and erect homes for themselves within convenient distances, or avail themselves of the opportunity to rent homes from other people who should build in that vicinity. . . . The company neither planned nor could it exercise any municipal powers in Pullman. It was in fact within the boundaries of what was legally called the village of Hyde Park. . . . The relations of those employed in the shops are, as to the shops, the relations of employees to employer, and as to those of them and others living in the homes, the relations are simply and only the relations of tenant to landlord. The company has not now and never has had any interest whatever in the business of any of the stores or shops in the town; they are rented to and managed by outside parties free of any control by the company. The people living in the town are entirely free to buy where they choose, and as a matter of fact the large disbursements in wages at Pullman, amounting to an average of $2,360,000 a year from September 1880, to July 1894, has created a great competition for the trade of Pullman in the small surrounding towns, as well as in Chicago, the natural result of which would be to bring the prices of all merchandise down to a minimum.

In carrying out this general plan, every care was taken in making perfectly sanitary conditions by a water supply and an extensive and scientific system of sewerage, paved and well lighted streets and open places properly ornamented with trees and shrubbery, all of which are kept in perfect repair and cleanliness by the company, and at its expense. Due attention was paid to the convenience and general well being of the residents by the erection of stores and markets, a church, public schools, a library and public halls for lectures and amusements; also a hotel and boarding houses. The basis on which rents were fixed was to make a return of 6 percent on the actual investment, which at that time (1881) was a reasonable return to be expected from such an investment: and in calculating what, for such a purpose, was the actual investment in the dwellings on the one hand and the other buildings on the other, an allowance was made for the cost of the streets and other public improvements, just as it has to be considered in the valuation of any property for renting anywhere, all public improvements having to be paid for by the owner of a lot, either directly or by special taxation, and by him considered in the valuation.

The actual operations have never shown a net return of 6 percent, the amount originally contemplated. The investment for several years returned a new revenue of about 4½ percent, but during the last two years additional taxes and heavier repairs have brought the net revenue down to 3.82 percent.

Of course there are matters which are proper subjects of arbitration. A matter of opinion may often be a proper subject of arbitration, for instance, a question of title. What settlement shall be made as to a transaction which has come to an end, may be a proper subject of arbitration, and the affair be put at rest by it, but as to whether a fact which I know to be true, is true or not, I could not agree to submit to arbitration.

If asked about the application to the case in hand, what I would say is this: That the question as to whether the shops at Pullman should be continuously operated at a loss or not, is one which it was impossible for the company, as a matter of principle, to submit to the opinion of any third party, and as to whether they were running at a loss upon contract work in general, as explained to the committee of the men in my interview with them, that was a simple fact which I knew to be true, and which could not be made otherwise by the opinion of any third party. . . .

The surplus of the company has been accumulated through a period of twenty-seven years, in conformity with a policy of conservation adopted to keep the company at all times financially strong, so that its owners would be assured a regular and permanent income, and confidence in the intrinsic value of the company's securities would be so established as to make them at all times negotiable in the market, and furthermore to enable the company to meet just such conditions as exist at this time.

# ✣ E S S A Y S

The railroads were by far the biggest and most important enterprise in late-nineteenth-century America. When tens of thousands of railroad workers struck in 1877, in the country's first nationwide walkout, they inaugurated a new kind of civil war, as hopeful to some as it was frightening to others. In the first essay, an independent author and screenwriter, Jeremy Brecher, reconstructs the dramatic events of July 1877 and assays their significance to all American history. In the immediate aftermath, of the great upheaval of 1877, few memorialized those killed, but after the Haymarket "riot" of 1886, memory and memorial proved a potent weapon for those who sought to build an anticapitalist movement in the United States. This is the theme of labor educator James Green of the University of Massachusetts at Boston, who in the second essay describes both the eight-hour-workday protest that gave rise to Chicago's bloody Haymarket conflict and the uses to which the dramatic events of May 4, 1886, have since been put. Green raises important questions about the function of memory in the contest for control of usable working-class history.

Why did violence erupt so often in industrial disputes? Were there alternative institutional means to resolve conflicts between capital and labor at the time? How do film, television, and other media represent working-class protests today?

# The Great Upheaval

### JEREMY BRECHER

In the centers of many American cities are positioned huge armories, grim nineteenth-century edifices of brick or stone. They are fortresses, complete with massive walls and loopholes for guns. You may have wondered why they are there, but it has probably never occurred to you that they were built to protect America not against invasion from abroad but against popular revolt at home. Their erection was a monument to the Great Upheaval of 1877.

July 1877 does not appear in many history books as a memorable date, yet it marks the first great American mass strike, a movement that was viewed at the time as a violent rebellion. Strikers seized and closed the nation's most important industry, the railroads, and crowds defeated or won over first the police, then the state militias, and in some cases even the federal troops. General strikes brought work to a standstill in a dozen major cities and strikers took over authority in communities across the nation.

It all began on Monday, July 16, 1877, in the little railroad town of Martinsburg, West Virginia. On that day, the Baltimore and Ohio Railroad cut wages 10 percent, the second cut in eight months. Men gathered around the Martinsburg railroad yards, talking, waiting through the day. Toward evening the crew of a cattle train, fed up, abandoned the train, and other workers refused to replace them.

As a crowd gathered, the strikers uncoupled the engines, ran them into the roundhouse, and announced to B&O officials that no trains would leave Martinsburg until the pay cut was rescinded. The mayor arrived and conferred with railroad officials. He tried to soothe the crowd and was booed. When he ordered the arrest of the strike leaders they just laughed at him, backed up in their resistance by the angry crowd. The mayor's police were helpless against the population of the town. No railroad workers could be found willing to take out a train, so the police withdrew and by midnight the yard was occupied only by a guard of strikers left to enforce the blockade.

That night, B&O officials in Wheeling went to see Governor Henry Matthews, took him to their company telegraph office, and waited while he wired Col. Charles Faulkner, Jr., at Martinsburg. Matthews instructed Faulkner to have his Berkeley Light Guards "prevent any interference by rioters with the men at work, and also prevent the obstruction of the trains."

The next morning, when the Martinsburg master of transportation ordered the cattle train out again, the strikers' guard swooped down on it and ordered the engineer to stop or to be killed. He stopped. By now, hundreds of strikers and townspeople had gathered, and the next train out hardly moved before it was boarded, uncoupled, and run into the roundhouse.

About 9 a.m., the Berkeley Light Guards arrived to the sound of a fife and drum; the crowd cheered them. Most of the militiamen were themselves railroaders. Now the cattle train came out once more, this time covered with militiamen, their rifles

---

Jeremy Brecher, "The Great Upheaval," in *Strike!* (Boston: South End Press, 1997), pp. 13–37. Reprinted by permission of South End Press.

loaded with ball cartridges. As the train pulled through the yelling crowd, a striker named William Vandergriff turned a switch to derail the train and guarded it with a pistol. A soldier jumped off the train to reset the switch. Vandergriff shot him and in turn was fatally shot himself.

At this, the attempt to break the blockade at Martinsburg was abandoned. The strikebreaking engineer and fireman climbed down from the engine and departed. Col. Faulkner called in vain for volunteers to run the train, announced that the governor's orders had been fulfilled, dismissed his men, and telegraphed the governor that he was helpless to control the situation.

With this confrontation began the Great Upheaval of 1877, a spontaneous, nationwide, virtually general strike. The pattern of Martinsburg—a railroad strike in response to a pay cut, an attempt by the companies to run trains with the support of military forces, and the defeat or dissolution of those forces by amassed crowds representing general popular support—became the pattern for the nation.

With news of success at Martinsburg, the strike spread to all divisions of the B&O, with engineers, brakemen, and conductors joining with the firemen who provided the initial impetus. Freight traffic was stopped all along the line, while the workers continued to run passenger and mail cars without interference. Seventy engines and six hundred freight cars were soon piled up in the Martinsburg yards.

Governor Matthews, resolved to break the strike, promised to send a company "in which there are no men unwilling to suppress the riots and execute the law." He sent his only available military force, sixty Light Guards from Wheeling. But the Guards were hardly reliable, for the sentiment in Wheeling was strongly in favor of the strike.

The Guards marched out of town surrounded by an excited crowd, who, a reporter noted, "all expressed sympathy with the strikers." Box-makers and can-makers in Wheeling were already on strike and soon people were discussing a general strike of all labor. When the Guards' train arrived in Martinsburg, it was met by a large, orderly crowd. The militia's commander conferred with railroad and town officials, but dared not use the troops, lest they "further exasperate the strikers." Instead, he marched the Guards away to the courthouse. . . .

This "insurrection" was spontaneous and unplanned, but it grew out of the social conditions of the time and the recent experience of railway workers. The tactics of the railroad strikers had been developed in a series of local strikes, mostly without trade union support, that occurred in 1873 and 1874. In December 1873, for example, engineers and firemen on the Pennsylvania Railroad system struck in Chicago, Pittsburgh, Cincinnati, Louisville, Columbus, Indianapolis, and various smaller towns, in what Ohio's *Portsmouth Tribune* called "the greatest railroad strike" in the nation's history.

Huge crowds gathered in depot yards and supported the strikers against attempts to run the trains. State troops were sent into Dennison, Ohio, and Logansport, Indiana, to break strike strongholds. At Susquehanna Depot, Pennsylvania, three months later, shop and repair workers struck. After electing a "Workingmen's Committee," they seized control of the repair shops; within twenty minutes the entire works was "under complete control of the men." The strike was finally broken when 1,800 Philadelphia soldiers with thirty pieces of cannon established martial law in the town of 8,000.

The railroad strikes of 1873 and 1874 were generally unsuccessful; but, as historian Herbert Gutman wrote, they "revealed the power of the railroad workers to disrupt traffic on many roads." The employers learned that "they had a rather tenuous hold on the loyalties of their men. Something was radically wrong if workers could successfully stop trains for from two or three days to as much as a week, destroy property, and even 'manage' it as if it were their own." . . .

The more immediate background of the 1877 railroad strike also helps explain why it took the form of virtual insurrection, for this struggle grew out of the failure of other, less violent forms of action. The wage cut on the B&O was part of a pattern initiated June 1 by the Pennsylvania Railroad. When the leaders of the Brotherhoods of Engineers, Conductors, and Firemen made no effort to combat the cut, railroad workers on the Pennsylvania system took action themselves. A week before the cut went into effect, the Newark, New Jersey, division of the Engineers held an angry protest meeting against the cut. The Jersey City lodge met the next day, voted for a strike, and contacted other workers; by the day the cut took effect, engineers' and firemen's locals throughout the Pennsylvania system had chosen delegates to a joint grievance committee, ignoring the leadership of their national unions.

The wage cut was not the workers' only concern; the committee proposed what amounted to a complete reorganization of work. They opposed the system of assigning trains in which the first crew into town was the first crew out, leaving them no time to rest or see their families; they wanted regular runs to stabilize pay and work schedules; they wanted passes home in case of long layovers; and they wanted the system of "classification" of workers by length of service and efficiency—used to keep wages down—abolished.

But the grievance committee delegates were easily intimated and cajoled by Tom Scott, the masterful ruler of the Pennsylvania Railroad, who talked them into accepting the cut without consulting those who elected them. A majority of brakemen, many conductors, and some engineers wanted to repudiate the committee's action; but, their unit broken, the locals decided not to strike.

Since the railroad brotherhoods had clearly failed, the workers' next step was to create a new, secret organization, the Trainmen's Union. It was started by workers on the Pittsburgh, Fort Wayne and Chicago line. Within three weeks, lodges had sprung up from Baltimore to Chicago, with thousands of members on many different lines. The Trainmen's Union recognized that the privileged engineers "generally patched things up for themselves," so it included conductors, firemen, brakemen, switchmen, and others as well as engineers. The union also realized that the various railroad managements were cooperating against the workers, one railroad after another imitating the Pennsylvania with a 10 percent wage cut. The union's strategy was to organize at least three-quarters of the trainmen on each trunk line, then strike against the cuts and other grievances. When a strike came, firemen would not take engineers' jobs and workers on nonstriking roads would not handle struck equipment.

But the union was full of spies. On one railroad the firing of members began only four days after the union was formed, and other railroads followed suit. "Determined to stamp it out," as one railroad official put it, the company issued orders to discharge all men belonging to "the Brotherhood or Union." Nonetheless, on June 24 forty men fanned out over the railroads to call a general railroad strike for the following week. The railroads learned about the strike through their spies, fired the strike committee in a body, and thus panicked part of the leadership into spreading false word that the strike was off. Local lodges, unprepared to act on their own, flooded the union headquarters with telegrams asking what to do. Union officials were denied use of railroad telegraphs to reply, the companies ran their trains, and the strike failed utterly.

Thus the Martinsburg strike broke out because the B&O workers had discovered that they had no alternative but to act on their own initiative. Not only were their wages being cut, but, as one newspaper reported, the men felt they were "treated just as the rolling stock or locomotives"—squeezed for every drop of profit. Reduced crews were forced to handle extra cars, with lowered pay classifications and no extra pay for overtime. . . .

On July 19, four days into the strike, 300 federal troops arrived in Martinsburg to quell the "insurrection" and bivouacked in the roundhouse. With militiamen and U.S. soldiers guarding the yards, the company was able to move a few trains loaded with U.S. regulars through the town. When 100 armed strikers tried to stop a train, the sheriff and the militia marched to the scene and arrested the leader. No one in Martinsburg would take out another train, but with the military in control, strikebreakers from Baltimore were able to run freights unimpeded. The strike seemed broken.

But the population of the surrounding area also now rallied behind the railroad workers. Hundreds of unemployed and striking boatmen on the Chesapeake and Ohio Canal lay in ambush at Sir John's Run, where they stoned the freight train that had broken the Martinsburg blockade, forced it to stop, and then hid when the U.S. regulars attacked. The movement soon spread into Maryland, where a crowd of boatmen, railroaders, and others swarmed around the train at Cumberland and uncoupled the cars. When the train finally got away, a mob at Keyser, West Virginia, ran it onto a side track and took the crew off by force—while the U.S. troops stood by helplessly. Just before midnight, the miners of the area met at Piedmont, four miles from Keyser, and resolved to go to Keyser in the morning and help stop trains. Coal miners and others—"a motley crowd, white and black"—halted a train guarded by fifty U.S. regulars after it pulled out of Martinsburg. At Piedmont a handbill was printed warning the B&O that 15,000 miners, the united citizenry of local communities, and "the working classes of every state in the Union" would support the strikers. "Therefore let the clashing of arms be heard . . . in view of the rights and in the defense of our families we shall conquer, or we shall die." . . .

Faced with the spread of the strike through Maryland, the president of the B&O now persuaded Governor John Carroll of Maryland to call up the National Guard in Baltimore and send it to Cumberland. They did not expect, however, the reaction of Baltimore to the strike. "The working people everywhere are with us," said a leader of the railroad strikers in Baltimore. "They know what it is to bring up a family on ninety cents a day, to live on beans and corn meal week in and week out, to run in debt at the stores until you cannot get trusted any longer, to see the wife breaking down under privation and distress, and the children growing up sharp and fierce like wolves day after day because they don't get enough to eat."

The bells rang in Baltimore for the militia to assemble just as the factories were letting out for the evening, and a vast crowd assembled as well. At first they cheered the troops, but then severely stoned them as they started to march. The crowd was described as "a rough element eager for disturbance; a proportion of mechanics [workers] either out of work or upon inadequate pay, whose sullen hearts rankled; and muttering and murmuring gangs of boys, almost outlaws, and ripe for any sort of disturbance." As the 250 men of the first regiment marched out, 25 of them were injured by the stoning of the crowd, but this was only a love-tap. The second regiment was unable even to leave its own armory for a time. Then, when the order was given to march anyway, the crowd stoned them so severely that the troops panicked and opened fire. In the bloody march that followed, the militia killed ten and seriously wounded more than twenty of the crowd, but the crowd continued to resist, and one by one the troops dropped out, went home, and changed into civilian clothing. By the time they reached the Baltimore train station, only 59 of the original 120 men remained in line. Even after they reached the depot, the remaining troops were unable to leave for Cumberland, for a crowd of about 200 drove away the engineer and firemen of the waiting train and beat back a squad of policemen who tried to restore control.

The militia charged the growing crowd, but were driven back by brickbats and pistol fire. It was at that stage that Governor Carroll, himself bottled up in the depot by the crowd of 15,000 desperately wired President Hayes to send the U.S. Army.

Like the railroad workers, others joined the "insurrection" out of frustration with other means of struggle. Over the previous years they had experimented with one means of resistance after another, each more radical than the last.

The first to prove their failure had been the trade unions. Craft unions had grown rapidly during and after the Civil War and had organized nationally. The number of national unions grew from six in 1864 to about thirty-three in 1870, enrolling perhaps 5 percent of nonfarm workers. Railroad workers formed the Brotherhoods of Locomotive Engineers, Railway Conductors, and Firemen. But the depression devastated the unions. By 1877 only about nine of these unions survived. Total membership plummeted from 300,000 in 1870 to 50,000 in 1876.

Under depression conditions, the unions were simply unable to withstand the organized attack levied by lockouts and blacklisting. Unemployment demonstrations in New York had been ruthlessly broken up by police. Then the first major industrial union in the United States, the Workingmen's Benevolent Association of the anthracite miners, led a strike that was finally broken by the companies, one of which claimed the conflict had cost it $4 million. Next the Molly Maguires—a secret organization Irish miners developed to fight the coal operators through terrorist methods—were infiltrated and destroyed by agents from the Pinkerton Detective Agency, which specialized in providing spies, agents provocateurs, and private armed forces for employers combating labor organizations. Thus, by the summer of 1877 it had become clear that no single group of workers—whether through peaceful demonstration, tightly-knit trade unions, armed terrorism, or surprise strikes—could stand against the power of the companies, their armed guards, the Pinkertons, and the armed forces of the government.

Indeed, the Great Upheaval had been preceded by a seeming quiescence on the part of workers. The general manager of one railroad wrote on June 21: "The experiment of reducing the salaries has been successfully carried out by all the Roads that have tried it of late, and I have no fear of any trouble with our employees if it is done with a proper show of firmness on our part and they see that they must accept it cheerfully or leave." The very day the strike was breaking out at Martinsburg, Governor John Hartranft of Pennsylvania was agreeing with his adjutant general that the state was enjoying a calm it had not known for several years. In less than a week, it would be the center of the insurrection.

Three days after Governor Hartranft's assessment, the Pennsylvania Railroad ordered that all freights eastward from Pittsburgh be run as "double-headers"—with two engines and twice as many cars. This meant in effect a speed-up—more work and increased danger of accidents and layoffs. Pennsylvania trainmen were sitting in the Pittsburgh roundhouse listening to a fireman read them news of the strike elsewhere when the order came to take out a "double-header." At the last minute a flagman named Augustus Harris, acting on his own initiative, refused to obey the order. The conductor appealed to the rest of the crew, but they too said no. When the company sent for replacements, twenty-five brakemen and conductors refused to take out the train and were fired on the spot. When the dispatcher finally found three yard brakemen to take out the train, a crowd of twenty angry strikers would not let the train go through. One of them threw a link at a strikebreaker, whereupon the volunteer yardmen gave up and went away. Said flagman Andrew Hice, "It's a question of bread or blood, and we're going to resist."

Freight crews joined the strike as their trains came in and were stopped, and a crowd of mill workers, tramps, and boys began to gather at the crossings, preventing freight trains from running while letting passenger trains go through. The company asked the mayor for police, but since the city was nearly bankrupt the force had been cut in half, and only eight men were available. Further, the mayor had been elected by the strong working-class vote of the city, and shared with the city's upper crust a hatred for the Pennsylvania Railroad and its rate discrimination against Pittsburgh. The railroad was given no more than seventeen police, whom it had to pay itself.

As elsewhere, the Trainmen's Union had nothing to do with the start of the strike. Its top leader, Robert Ammon, had left Pittsburgh to take a job elsewhere, and the president of the Pittsburgh Division didn't even know that trouble was at hand; he slept late that morning, didn't hear about the strike until nearly noon—his first comment was "Impossible!"—and then busied himself persuading his colleagues to go home and keep out of trouble.

The Trainmen's Union did, however, provide a nucleus for a meeting of the strikers and representatives of such groups as the rolling-mill workers. "We're with you," said one rolling-mill man, pledging the railroaders support from the rest of Pittsburgh labor. "We're in the same boat. I heard a reduction of ten percent hinted at in our mill this morning. I won't call employers despots, I won't call them tyrants, but the term capitalists is sort of synonymous and will do as well." The meeting called on "all workingmen to make common cause with their brethren on the railroad."

In Pittsburgh, railroad officials picked up the ailing sheriff, waited while he gave the crowd a *pro forma* order to disperse, and then persuaded him to appeal for state troops. That night state officials ordered the militia to be called up in Pittsburgh, but only some of the troops arrived. Some were held up by the strikers, while others simply failed to show up. Two-thirds of one regiment made it; in another regiment not one man appeared. Nor were the troops reliable. As one officer reported to his superior, "You can place little dependence on the troops of your division; some have thrown down their arms, and others have left, and I fear the situation very much."

Another officer explained why the troops were unreliable.

> Meeting an enemy on the field of battle, you go there to kill. The more you kill, and the quicker you do it, the better. But here you had men with fathers and brothers and relatives mingled in the crowd of rioters. The sympathy of the people, the sympathy of the troops, my own sympathy, was with the strikers proper. We all felt that those men were not receiving enough wages.

Indeed, by Saturday morning the militiamen had stacked their arms and were chatting with the crowd, eating hardtack with them, and walking up and down the streets with them, behaving, as a regular army lieutenant put it, "as though they were going to have a party." "You may be called upon to clear the tracks down there," said a lawyer to a soldier. "They may call on me," the soldier replied, "and they may call pretty damn loud before they will clear the tracks." . . .

All day Friday, the crowds controlled the switches, and the officer commanding the Pittsburgh militia refused to clear the crossing with artillery because of the slaughter that would result. People swarmed aboard passenger trains and rode through the city free of charge. The sheriff warned the woman and children to leave lest they be hurt when the army came, but the women replied that they were there to urge the men on. "Why are you acting this way, and why is this crowd here?" the sheriff asked one young man who had come to Pittsburgh from Eastern Pennsylvania for the strike. "The Pennsylvania [Road] has two ends," he replied, "one in Philadelphia and one in Pittsburgh. In Philadelphia they have a strong police force, and they're with the railroad. But in Pittsburgh they have a weak force, and it's a mining and manufacturing district, and we can get all the help we want from the laboring elements, and we've determined to make the strike here."

"Are you a railroader?" the sheriff asked.

"No, I'm a laboring man," he replied.

Railroad and National Guard officials, realizing that the local Pittsburgh militia units were completely unreliable, sent for 600 fresh troops from its commercial rival, Philadelphia. A Pittsburgh steel manufacturer came to warn railroad officials not to send the troops out until workingmen were back in their factories. "I think I know the temper of our men pretty well, and you would be wise not to do anything until Monday. . . . If there's going to be firing, you ought to have at least ten thousand men, and I doubt if even that many could quell the mob that would be brought down on us."

These words were prophetic. But, remembering the 2,000 freight cars and locomotives lying idle in the yards, and the still effective blockade, the railroad official replied, "We must have our property." He looked at his watch and said,

"We have now lost an hour and a half's time." He had confidently predicted that "the Philadelphia regiment won't fire over the heads of the mob." Now the massacre he counted on—and the city's retaliation—was at hand.

As the imported troops marched toward the 28th Street railroad crossing, a crowd of 6,000 gathered, mostly spectators. The troops began clearing the tracks with fixed bayonets and the crowd replied with a furious barrage of stones, bricks, coal, and possibly revolver fire. Without orders, the Philadelphia militia began firing as fast as it could, killing twenty people in five minutes as the crowd scattered. Meanwhile, the local Pittsburgh militia members stood on the hillside and ran for cover when they saw the Philadelphia regiment's Gatling gun come forward. Soon most militia members went home or joined the mob.

With the crossing cleared, the railroad fired up a dozen doubleheaders, but even trainmen who had previously declined to join the strike now refused to run the trains, and the strike remained unbroken. Their efforts in vain, the remaining members of the Philadelphia militia retired to the roundhouse.

Meanwhile, the entire city mobilized in a fury against the troops who had conducted the massacre and against the Pennsylvania Railroad. Workers rushed home from their factories for pistols, muskets, and butcher knives. A delegation of 600 workingmen from nearby Temperanceville marched in with a full band and colors. In some cases the crowd organized itself into crude armed military units, marching together with drums. Civil authority collapsed in the face of the crowd; they mayor refused to send police or even to try to quiet the crowd himself.

The crowd peppered the troops in the roundhouse with pistol and musket fire, but finally decided, as one member put it, "We'll have them out if we have to roast them out." Oil, coke, and whiskey cars were set alight and pushed downhill toward the roundhouse. A few men began systematically to burn the yards, despite rifle fire from the soldiers, while the crowd held off fire trucks at gunpoint. The roundhouse caught fire and the Philadelphia militia was forced to evacuate. As it marched along the street it was peppered with fire by the crowd and, according to the troops' own testimony, by Pittsburgh policemen as well. Most of the troops were marched out of town and found refuge a dozen miles away. The few left to guard ammunition found civilian clothes, sneaked away, and hid until the crisis was over. By Saturday night, the last remaining regiment of the Pittsburgh militia was disbanded. The crowd had completely routed the army.

On Sunday morning, hundreds of people broke into the freight cars in the yards and distributed goods they contained to the crowds below—on occasion with assistance from police. Burning of cars continued. (According to first U.S. Commissioner of Labor Carroll D. Wright, "A great many old freight cars which must soon have been replaced by new, were pushed into the fire by agents of the railroad company," to be added to the damages they hoped to collect from Allegheny County.) The crowd prevented firemen from saving a grain elevator, though it was not owned by the railroad, saying, "It's a monopoly, and we're tired of it," but workers pitched in to prevent the spread of the fire to nearby tenements. By Monday, 104 locomotives, more than 2,000 cars, and all of the railroad buildings had been destroyed.

Across the river from Pittsburgh, in the railroad town of Allegheny, a remarkable transfer of authority took place. Using the pretext that the governor was out of the state, the strikers maintained that the state militia was without legal authority, and therefore proposed to treat them as no more than a mob. According to the mayor, the strikers armed themselves by breaking into the local armory, dug rifle pits and trenches outside the Allegheny depot, set up patrols, and warned civilians away from the probable line of fire. The strikers took possession of the telegraph and sent messages up and down the railway. They took over management of the railroad, running passenger trains smoothly, moving the freight cars out of the yards, and posting regular armed guards to watch over them. Economic management and political power had in effect been taken over by the strikers. Of course, this kind of transfer of power was not universally understood or supported, even by those who approved of the strike. For example, a meeting of rolling-mill workers in Columbus, Ohio, endorsed the railroad strikers, urged labor to combine politically and legislate justice, but rejected "mobbism" as apt to destroy "the best form of republican government."

The strike spread almost as fast as word of it, and with it came conflict with the military. In the Pennsylvania towns of Columbia, Meadville, and Chenago, strikers seized the railroads, occupied the roundhouses, and stopped troop trains. In Buffalo, New York, the militia was stoned on Sunday but scattered the crowd by threatening to shoot. The next morning a crowd armed with knives and cudgels stormed into the railroad shops, brushed aside militia guards, and forced shopmen to quit work. They seized the Erie roundhouse and barricaded it. When a militia company marched out to recapture the property, a thousand people blocked it and drove it back. By Monday evening, all the major railroads had given up trying to move anything but local passenger trains out of Buffalo. . . .

. . . [T]he movement was no longer simply a railroad strike. With the battles between soldiers and crowds drawn from all sectors of the working population, it was increasingly perceived as a struggle between workers as a whole and employers as a whole. This was now reflected in the rapid development of general strikes. After the burning of the railroad yards in Pittsburgh, a general strike movement swept through the area. At nearby McKeesport, workers of the National Tube Works gathered and marched all over town to martial music, calling fellow workers from their houses. From the tube works the strike spread first to a rolling mill, then a car works, and then a planing mill. In mid-morning, 1,000 McKeesport strikers marched with a brass band to Andrew Carnegie's great steel works, calling out planing-mill and tin-mill workers as they went. By mid-afternoon, the Carnegie workers and the Braddocks car workers joined the strike. At Castle Shannon, 500 miners struck. On the South Side, laborers struck at Jones and Laughlin and at the Evans, Dalzell and Co. pipe works. . . .

In San Francisco, 7,000 attended a rally called by the Workingmen's Party, a national organization that had been formed the year before by predominantly immigrant followers of Karl Marx and Ferdinand Lassalle. The speakers demanded the eight-hour day and government operation of the struck railroads. But the movement soon was swamped by burgeoning hostility to the 50,000 Chinese workers who had been brought to California to build the railroads, many of whom had then been abandoned by the railroad companies and were finding their way into other occupations. At the Workingmen's Party rally someone in the crowd proposed the appointment of a committee to demand the discharge of Chinese workers from the

Central Pacific, but the chair refused to entertain the motion. The rally ended peacefully, but in its wake gangs began attacking Chinese laundries and residences. Several nights of anti-Chinese rioting were finally brought to an end by police and a Committee of Safety.

In Chicago, the Workingmen's Party called a series of mass rallies. At the same time, forty switchmen struck on the Michigan Central Railroad. The switchmen roamed through the railroad property with a crowd of 500 others, including strikers from the East who had ridden in to spread the strike, calling out other workers and closing down those railroads that were still running. Next the crowd called out the workers at the stockyards and several packinghouses. Smaller crowds spread out to broaden the strike; one group, for example, called out 500 planing-mill workers, and with them marched down Canal Street and Blue Island Avenue closing down factories. Crews on several lake vessels struck. With transportation dead, the North Chicago rolling mill and many other industries closed for lack of coke and other supplies.

The next day the strike spread still further: streetcars, wagons, and buggies were stopped; tanneries, stoneworks, clothing factories, lumberyards, brickyards, furniture factories, and a large distillery were closed in response to roving crowds. A day later the crowds forced officials at the stockyards and gasworks to sign promises to raise wages to $2 a day, while more dock and lumberyard workers struck. In the midst of this burgeoning activity, the Workingmen's Party proclaimed: "Fellow Workers . . . Under any circumstances keep quiet until we have given the present crisis a due consideration." . . .

. . . "This insurrection," said General Winfield Hancock, the commander in charge of all federal troops used in the strike, must be stifled "by all possible means." Not that the federal troops were strong and reliable. The Army was largely tied down by the rebellion of Nez Perce Indians, led by Chief Joseph. In the words of Lieutenant Philip Sheridan, "The troubles on the Rio Grande border, the Indian outbreak on the western frontier of New Mexico, and the Indian war in the Departments of the Platte and Dakota, have kept the small and inadequate forces in this division in a constant state of activity, almost without rest, night and day." Most of the enlisted men had not been paid for months, because Congress had refused to pass the Army Appropriations Bill to force the withdrawal of Reconstruction troops from the South. Finally, the Army included many workers driven into military service by unemployment. As one union iron molder in the Army wrote, "It does not follow that a change of dress involves a change of principle." No mutinies occurred, however, as the 3,000 available federal troops were rushed under direction of the War Department from city to city, wherever the movement seemed to grow out of control. "The strikers," President Hayes noted emphatically in his diary, "have been put down by *force*." More than 100 of them were killed in the process.

The Great Upheaval was an expression of the new economic and social system in America, just as surely as the cities, railroads, and factories from which it had sprung. The enormous expansion of industry after the Civil War had transformed millions of people who had grown up as farmers, self-employed artisans, and entrepreneurs into employees, growing thousands of whom were concentrated within each of the new corporate empires. Their work was no longer individual, but collective; they no longer directed their own work, but worked under control of a boss; they no longer controlled the property on which they worked or its fruits, and therefore could not find gainful employment unless someone with property agreed to hire them. The Great Upheaval grew out of workers' intuitive sense that they needed each other, had each other's support, and together were powerful.

This sense of unity was not embodied in any centralized plan or leadership, but in the feelings and action of each participant. "There was no concert of action at the start," the editor of *The Labor Standard* pointed out. "It spread because the workmen of Pittsburgh felt the same oppression that was felt by the workmen of West Virginia and so with the workmen of Chicago and St. Louis." In Pittsburgh, concludes historian Robert Bruce, "Men like Andrew Hice or Gus Harris or David Davis assumed the lead briefly at one point or another, but only because they happened to be foremost in nerve or vehemence." In Newark, Ohio, "no single individual seemed to command the . . . strikers. They followed the sense of the meeting, as Quakers might say, on such proposals as one or another of them . . . put forward. Yet they proceeded with notable coherence, as though fused by their common adversity."

The Great Upheaval was in the end thoroughly defeated, but the struggle was by no means a total loss. Insofar as it aimed at preventing the continued decline of workers' living standards, it won wage concessions in a number of cases and undoubtedly gave pause to would-be wage-cutters to come. Insofar as it aimed at a workers' seizure of power, its goal was illusory, for workers as yet formed only a minority in a predominantly agrarian and middle-class society. But the power of workers to virtually stop society, to counter the forces of repression, and to organize cooperative action on a vast scale was revealed in the most dramatic form.

It was not only workers who drew lessons from the Great Upheaval. Their opponents began building up their power as well, symbolized by the National Guard armories whose construction began the following year, to contain upheavals yet to come.

Certain periods, wrote historian Irving Bernstein, bear a special quality in American labor history. "There occurred at these times strikes and social upheavals of extraordinary importance, drama, and violence which ripped the cloak of civilized decorum from society, leaving exposed naked class conflict." Such periods were analyzed before World War I by Rosa Luxemburg and others under the concept of mass strikes. The mass strike, Luxemburg wrote, signifies not just a single act but a whole period of class struggle:

> Its use, its effects, its reasons for coming about are in a constant state of flux. . . .
> [P]olitical and economic strikes, united and partial strikes, defensive strikes and combat strikes, general strikes of individual sections of industry and general strikes of entire cities, peaceful wages strikes and street battles, uprisings with barricades—all run together and run alongside each other, get in each other's way, overlap each other; a perpetually moving and changing sea of phenomena.

The Great Upheaval was the first—but by no means the last—mass strike in American history.

# Remembering Haymarket: Chicago's Labor Martyrs and Their Legacy

### JAMES GREEN

On a rainy day in May 1886, as a squad of police marched to disperse a protest rally in Chicago's Haymarket Square, a ferocious explosion cut through the uniformed ranks. The bomb blast of May 4 that killed several policemen, the wild gun fire from police revolvers that took the lives of fifty or more workers, the sensational trial of the anarchists accused of the bombing, the public hanging of the four anarchist martyrs on Black Friday 11 November 1887, and the controversial pardon of the remaining defendants—all these dramatic events were remembered by workers engaged in the labor and radical movements for the next fifty years. During that time movement people were deeply divided about how to remember the Haymarket martyrs: as innocent victims of the grand struggle for the eight-hour day or as irresponsible anarchists who provoked a "red scare" that crippled the whole labor movement. . . .

## The City

The "milieu de mémoire" in this story is the booming city of Chicago in the 1870s and 1880s, "hog butcher, steel maker to the world," a city segmented along class lines after the Civil War as militant immigrant workers confronted aggressive entrepreneurs; it was the site of the first May Day general strike in 1867 when ten thousand workingmen, led by the molders at the McCormick Reaper works, took direct action for the eight-hour day. Social revolutionaries like Albert Parsons, a Confederate soldier later radicalized by Reconstruction politics in Texas, gained a following among Chicago workers in the years after the brutal repression of the 1877 railroad strike by the police, state militia, and federal troops. One historian even describes a "socialist hegemony over the local labor movement" in these years. Immigrant socialists were far more visible in public than the secretive Knights of Labor and their largely English-speaking leaders. Chicago's vast immigrant working class (76 percent foreign born in 1884) included many newcomers who responded to socialist ideas, especially when articulated by trade union organizers.

After joining the Marxist International Working People's Association (IWPA), Albert Parsons and other social revolutionaries affiliated with Michael Bakunin's breakaway Black International in 1883. While remaining loyal to the teachings of Karl Marx and the principles of communism, they broke with the Second Socialist International because of its emphasis on electoral politics. The Chicago revolutionaries agreed with Johann Most, the bombastic German anarchist, on the need for armed insurrection to overthrow the capitalist state. They also shared his enthusiasm for dynamite as the great equalizer, but unlike Most they believed in the revolutionary potential of the labor movement. The "Chicago idea" placed "the union at the

From James Green, "Remembering Haymarket: Chicago's Labor Martyrs and Their Legacy," in *Taking History to Heart: The Power of the Past in Building Social Movements* (Amherst: University of Massachusetts Press, 2000), pp. 121–144. Reprinted by permission.

center of revolutionary strategy and the nucleus of the future society," writes Paul Avrich, the historian of anarchism.

Socialists and communists of the IWPA influenced Chicago's German and Bohemian immigrants, who constituted many of the forty thousand members of the Central Labor Union (CLU), a dual union formed in 1884 by revolutionaries disaffected with the moderate leadership of the Knights of Labor and the craft unionism of the new Federation of organized Trades and Labor Unions led by pragmatic men. These social revolutionaries, who would later be called anarchists, looked back for inspiration to the Paris Commune, the anniversary of which they celebrated each year in March with remarkably popular ceremonies. In 1879 a "monster" rally attracted 100,000 people to the lake front where a surviving Communard spoke. Nourished by a rich social and cultural life, which included armed self-defense groups (the workers militias), countless picnics and dances, and a vibrant proletarian theater, these ceremonies took place annually for thirty-seven years and "became more elaborate every year," an example of how radical workers created an enduring memorial tradition.

The groundswell of enthusiasm for the eight-hour day among Chicago's unskilled and unorganized surprised even the revolutionaries. Though the shorter workday seemed like a mild reform to them, the radicals in the Central Labor Union took leadership of the new movement. In 1884 the Federation of Organized Trades made 1 May 1886 the date for a nationwide general strike, but its leaders acted reluctantly, as did the Knights of Labor. The social revolutionaries filled the void. IWPA women such as Lucy Parsons and Lizzie Swank-Holmes organized in the needle trades, while Albert Parsons, Michael Schwab, and other socialists spread the eight-hour fever to other trades. Skilled organizers and passionate orators, they injected drama into movement culture with daring actions that showed "a flair for the theatrical."

The socialist Central Labor Union caught the rising wave of eight-hour militancy and organized a demonstration on Easter Sunday 1886 in defiance of Christian values. A few days later on that first May Day, eighty thousand striking workers marched down Michigan Avenue demanding "eight hours for work, eight hours for rest and eight hours for play." On May 3 Chicago police shot and killed three pickets at the McCormick works, and that night Albert Parsons and his anarchist comrades met to plan a protest rally in Haymarket Square. That meeting, on the evening of May 4, attracted a smaller crowd than expected—perhaps three thousand—to hear Parsons and other radicals. The city's mayor, concerned about the violence that erupted at McCormick's, had ordered a large squad of police to preserve order. He attended the rally and left, believing the crowd to be calm and orderly. After Parsons spoke and departed, rain threatened to fall and the crowd began to disperse. Only three hundred people remained in the large square as the anarchist Samuel Fielden finished his remarks denouncing the law as being "framed for your enslavers." Suddenly, alarmed at Fielden's inflammatory language, two detectives hurried to the local police station where 176 police had been ordered to stand ready.

**The Event**

Soon a squad of 130 police marched out on the square in a military formation. The police captain asked Fielden to disperse the crowd and he agreed. Just as he stepped down from the hay wagon he used as a speakers' platform, someone (a perpetrator was never identified) threw an explosive device into the police ranks. The officers drew their pistols and began firing wildly, shooting blindly for five minutes. Seven police and an unknown number of rally participants and bystanders fell dead or wounded. One reporter estimated fifty civilian deaths. Sixty law officers were wounded and one of them died later. One policemen was killed by the bomb—six others died in the frenzied gunfire from their fellows' revolvers.

The Haymarket police riot lasted only a few minutes, but the explosion and what followed created the most powerful memory in U.S. labor history. And, unlike any other incident in nineteenth-century working-class history, except the Paris Commune, the Haymarket tragedy made an enduring international impact and became part of an oppositional memory constructed by workers outside of the United States where the official memory sought to criminalize the martyrs.

The chaos in the square provoked the first serious "red scare" in America. The *New York Times* editorial was typical: it called for a Gatling gun solution to the outbreak of anarchy and for the use of "hemp" in "judicious doses." In Chicago, where a state of martial law existed for two months, hundreds of men and women, mostly immigrants, were rounded up and interrogated. Employers and their allies seized on the bombing to discredit the eight-hour movement and the Knights of Labor, whose leaders failed to escape blame by denouncing the anarchists. Chicago's law officers and its press constructed a narration of what happened in the square to absolve the police of responsibility. They manufactured evidence of a horrible dynamite plot aimed at the complete destruction of Chicago.

The official interpretation of the Haymarket "riot" justified a massive assault on labor and radical movements in Chicago and elsewhere. As John Higham wrote in *Strangers in the Land:* "For years, the memory of Haymarket and the dread of imported anarchy haunted the American consciousness. No image prevailed more widely than that of the immigrant as a lawless creature, given over to violence and disorder." The bombing provoked a wave of anti-immigrant and anti-radical repression, including an Illinois "criminal syndicalism law" denying free speech to anarchists.

The memory of Haymarket caused awful problems for mainstream labor and socialist party leaders. The conservative Knights of Labor head Terence Powderly refused to plead clemency for the anarchists—a plea made from many foreign quarters, including a group from the French Chamber of Deputies. The German American leaders of the Socialist Labor Party denounced the Chicago anarchists and drew a lesson: given the "overwhelming superior strength" of the employers and their allies, any appeal "to physical force could only incur blood defeats" and retard the growth of socialism. American Socialists, even those like Joseph Buchanan who ardently defended the Haymarket "boys," reached similar conclusions. "The Chicago bomb" convinced Buchanan that until a working-class majority voted and was cheated out of the results, revolutionary action could not be justified. "Men who will not vote right," he used to say, "will not shoot right."

Samuel Gompers, president of the new American Federation of Labor, also condemned the anarchists' methods and blamed them for killing the eight-hour movement and for causing all unions to suffer. But Gompers also appealed for the convicts' lives on the grounds, he later wrote, that "labor must do its best to maintain justice for radicals or find itself denied the rights of freemen." In his clemency plea, Gompers warned the governor of Illinois not to create a memory that would be of use to the "revolutionary movement." Executing the Chicago anarchists would cause "thousands and thousands of labor men all over the world" to look upon the radicals "as martyrs," "executed because they were standing up for free speech and free press." This is exactly what happened as "labor men" invented a memorial tradition out of Haymarket, against the wishes of official leaders who wanted to forget the "catastrophe."

### The Hangings

However, trade union and socialist party leaders who disassociated themselves from the Haymarket martyrs discovered that memories of the Chicago anarchists and their travails were widely shared and deeply held among workers in many nations. Protests "swept the European continent" on 11 November 1887, the date when Albert Parsons and three anarchist comrades went to the gallows. Peter Kropotkin, the well-known Russian anarchist, reported no city in Spain and Italy worth naming "where the bloody anniversary was not commemorated by enthusiastic crowds of workers." In these places, he said, "The commemoration of the Chicago martyrs has almost acquired the same importance as the commemoration of the Paris Commune." When Gompers visited European cities in 1895 he noticed "in nearly every labor hall there were pictures of Parsons, Spies, Lingg, etc., and with an inscription: 'Labor's Martyrs to American Capitalism.'" On later visits, he saw "the same pictures still there."

Why did the memory of the Haymarket martyrs endure? The events themselves provide a starting point. The bombing was the most sensational news story of the era: The hunt for suspects also attracted intense press coverage. The spectacularly publicized trial of the eight anarchists accused of the "bombing" created a remarkable drama of its own, including a jailhouse romance between defendant August Spies and the daughter of a prominent Chicago businessman. Faced with the overwhelming power of the state in determining their fate and their memory, the defendants and their supporters plotted a narrative of their own, reversing everything the prosecution charged. "In their narrative interpretation [which became central to the working-class memory of Haymarket] . . . their persecution and even their execution were paradoxically empowering acts . . . that proved all their ideas to be true," Carl Smith writes. In the oppositional memory of Haymarket, the condemned men were recalled as martyrs who died for democracy and freedom while the state relied upon "lies, force and violence to hold it together."

The trial and the hangings of Albert Parsons, August Spies, George Engel, and Adolph Fischer, along with the suicide of Louis Lingg (who killed himself by exploding a dynamite cap in his mouth), produced a "drama without end," because, Smith explains, even those who condemned the anarchists had adopted their view that "urban industrial society [w]as a ticking bomb." After the hangings a prominent Chicago minister said no event since the Civil War had produced "such profound and long continued interest and excitement." These events attracted attention because they occurred in a "free America and [in] a time of peace" and because they evoked "an apprehensive concern"—a fear that they were but a first phase "of a widespread discontent upon the part of millions of poor people of this and other countries."

The press was obsessed with the anarchists, and some journalists, like the cartoonist Thomas Nast, portrayed them sensationally as demonic bomb throwers. But at the same time, the publicity generated curiosity about the anarchists and what they looked like. Some of the many drawings in the newspapers depicted them as normal human beings. In this melodrama the anarchists themselves played compelling theatrical roles, particularly Albert Parsons, who acted with power and passion in ways that many found unforgettable. Joseph Buchanan, whose rich life as a labor agitator involved many important events, vividly remembered Parsons's boldness many years after his execution. "Every man who has passed the half century mile post has stored away in his memory cabinets pictures which illustrate important events—mayhap crises—in his past life," he observed. "Sometimes they steal out from their hiding-places unbidden, and they lead the thought procession back to other days." In that "small cabinet" where Buchanan "stored the few pictures" he called "my tragedies," one often stole out: the scene recreated his audience with the governor of Illinois when Buchanan made one of the last clemency please for "the Haymarket boys." First, he read a letter from Spies, who offered to die in place of the others and appealed only to "the judgement of history." Buchanan then turned to a short note from Parsons that he had not yet seen in which the condemned man asked that if he was to die, he be granted a reprieve only so that his wife and two children could die with him. Everyone in the room gasped and Buchanan nearly broke down. Partly through such dramatic gestures, Parsons and his comrades found their way into "the memory cabinets" of many labor activists.

The Haymarket story reached a sensational climax on 11 November 1887 with the hanging of the four anarchists—the "Black Friday" long remembered in labor and radical movements. Perhaps the intensive media coverage of the executions (especially the graphic on the cover of *Leslie's Weekly*) perpetuated the event's memory. Public hangings were intended to dramatize punishment and memorialize pain. . . . [But in the] Haymarket case the defendants were presumed innocent even after "proven guilty"—an innocence proclaimed by important public figures like Congressman Robert Ingersoll, Senator Lyman Trumbull, William Dean Howells, Henry Demarest Lloyd, and Illinois governor John Peter Altgeld.

## The Martyrs

The innocence of the Haymarket martyrs seemed to make them especially tragic victims. Their heroism and stoicism added to their allure. Seeking to explain why the Haymarket episode "made such a powerful and lasting impression," one historian turned to Peter Kropotkin's observation that while others had died for labor's cause, none had been "so enthusiastically adopted by the workers as their martyrs." The moral qualities of the defendants appealed to workmen who believed the victims to be "thoroughly honest" as well as innocent. They "had no ambition," said Kropotkin, and "sought no power over others." Dedicated to their fellow workers and to their principles, they refused to plead for clemency on their own behalf during the entire year they awaited death. Even on the scaffold, "they hailed the day on which they died for those principles." As Kropotkin wrote one year after their execution: "Such men can inspire the generations to come with the noblest feelings."

But the anarchist movement did not depend solely upon inspiration to keep memories of Haymarket alive. The martyrs' families and supporters ritualized the act of remembering and began to do so immediately with a funeral many witnesses would never forget. After struggling with city officials who prohibited red flags and banned revolutionary songs, the anarchists led a large parade silently through Chicago's working-class neighborhoods on the long walk to Chicago's Waldheim Cemetery, a burial place for many of the city's German Jews. On Sunday 13 November 1887 thousands of workers marched in a funeral procession behind the bodies of the anarchists, past a half-million people who lined the streets to watch. Only when they reached the cemetery outside the city limits did they begin to sing "the Marseillaise"—the tune Parsons sang before his execution.

The mourners made Waldheim a "monumental memory site" partly because they were barred from access to the real "milieu de mémoire"—Haymarket Square. In his guide to the area for the Illinois Labor History Society, William Adelman describes the tempestuous history of this Square—a quintessential urban public space that like most markets, was a common gathering place for farmers, small traders, and plebeians of all sorts. It was so large that the Chicago anarchists chose it for the May 4 protest because they actually believed twenty thousand people would attend their rally. Nearby stood union halls so filled with eight-hour strike meetings the evening of May 3 that the anarchists planning the protest rally had to gather in the basement.

Soon after the Haymarket riot, the conservative *Chicago Tribune* started a fund drive to erect a statue in the square to memorialize the fallen police officers. The paper was owned by Cyrus McCormick, whose militant workers spearheaded the eight-hour movement. Many industrialists contributed and a statue of a policeman with an upraised arm was dedicated on Memorial Day 1889. The statue, which symbolized the authoritative memory of the bombing would experience a troubled history. In 1903 part of the inscription was stolen and later a streetcar operator ran his train off the track and knocked the statuary policeman off its base. The driver said he was tired of seeing that policeman with his arm raised in the air.

The police status symbolized an important activity for the forces of law and order: restricting urban public spaces from use by an insurgent working class. The labor movement could not reclaim the square itself for a memorial to mourn the workers who died there. But those who sought to preserve the memory of the martyrs could challenge official apportionments of "ceremonial space and time" by commemorating the anarchists' death every November 11 at Waldheim Cemetery.

## The Monument

In the years that followed the executions, the official story of the riot was tarnished when the very same Chicago police who led the charge on the square were discredited by charges of corruption. In 1893 the AFL's Chicago Trades and Labor Assembly joined radicals and progressives, including the famous defense attorney Clarence Darrow, in asserting that the defendants had been denied a fair trail and in demanding a pardon for the three anarchists who remained in prison. On 25 June 1893 thousands of unionists again converged on Waldheim to dedicate a statue at the gravesite. Many foreign visitors from the Columbian Exposition boarded special trains to attend the ceremony nine miles from Haymarket. The statue, inspired by a lyric in the "Marseillaise," was forged in bronze in the form of a hooded woman laying a laurel wreath on the brow of a dying worker. It resembled earlier art in the French republican tradition in which strong female figures symbolized liberty and justice. The martyrs' followers created a place of memory with a monument at Waldheim in order to advance the work of remembering.

The day after the dedication, the new populist governor of Illinois, John Peter Altgeld—himself a German immigrant—pardoned the three other Haymarket defendants and ensured his own political demise. The governor's statement—a remarkably radical one for a public official—blamed repressive police action for the bombing tragedy, claimed evidence had been fabricated, and accused the trial judge of "malicious ferocity." This courageous statement added enormous power to the memory of the Haymarket defendants as innocent victims of a "judicial hanging." Altgeld himself, "the forgotten eagle" in Vachel Lindsay's poem, was in fact remembered, perhaps longer than any other governor, as a politician who put truth and honesty above ambition.

These events heightened the significance of the Haymarket martyrs' grave as a site of memory. "Waldheim, with its hauntingly beautiful monument, became a revolutionary shrine, a place of pilgrimage for anarchists and socialists from all over the world," writes historian Paul Avrich. For decades, it drew more visitors than the statue of Illinois's favorite son, the martyred President Lincoln. Always ready to repress radicalism, the Chicago police drew more attention to the site by placing "restrictions on the annual memorial ceremonies" and threatening to ban them entirely—a sign of things to come. . . .

The martyrs' lives and deaths provided a redemptive narrative for a whole generation of radicals who told the anarchists' story repeatedly in speeches and writings that appeared in many languages. After the Chicago trial Emma Goldman "devoured every line on anarchism I could get, every word I could get about the men, their lives their work." Their execution "crushed her spirits" at first but then caused her "spiritual rebirth," giving her a "burning faith, a determination to dedicate myself to the memory of my martyred comrades, to make their cause my own." . . . Eugene V. Debs, who became a socialist after being imprisoned for leading the great Pullman rail strike of 1894, prayed at the martyrs' graves after his release from jail, just before he went to downtown Chicago to be greeted by a quarter-of-a-million workers. . . .

No one in that remarkable "traveling community of radicals" worked harder to keep the dead alive in memory than Albert Parsons's widow. Lucy Parsons dedicated her life to preserving the legacy of her martyred husband and his comrades. She became a cause célèbre in Chicago when the police chief vowed to prevent her from speaking in public. Her fame grew outside of Chicago when in 1889 she published *The Life of Albert Parsons,* a remarkable book that held a "weird fascination" for one reviewer who wrote that "few stories in our literature hold such dramatic power as this . . . a tale of chivalry so exalted, with an ending so tragic and pathetic," that it seemed like a classic romance. Throughout the grim nineties Lucy Parsons continued memorializing the martyrs during her speaking tours, especially on November 11 when the hanging was remembered in many cities. . . .

## The First Day of May

The memory of the martyrs also endured because many workers associated their deaths with the celebration of May Day and with the struggle for the eight-hour day—the issue that led to the choice of May 1 as a workers holiday by the 1889 International Socialist Congress in Paris. The Marxist champions of May Day had been active in the protests against the Haymarket executions and were well aware that the martyrs' memory was linked to the May 1 general strike of 1886. Many Italian immigrants in the United States observed May Day as "la pasgua dei lavora-tori" (The Easter of the workers). Some of them learned of the Chicago martyrs for the first time in picnic songs and in speeches by charismatic anarchists like Luigi Galleani who often referred to the incident as an example of how American democracy could be as oppressive as European tyranny. Radicals recalled that all the Haymarket defendants were immigrants, except Parsons, and predicted that their fate awaited others in this so-called land of liberty.

*[handwritten margin note: not quite, but more hypocritical]*

The remembrance of the Haymarket martyrs on May 1 was more than cere-monial. Their martyrdom became a keystone in constructing a homily of supreme sacrifice for workers' movements on the ascendancy in many capitalists nations dur-ing the 1880s. Confronting aggressive employers, hostile churches and newspapers, and militarized police forces, these movements needed issues like the eight-hour day, tactics like the mass strike, and heroes like the Haymarket martyrs. Movement builders found all these things in the tragic Chicago story.

More than at any time in the subsequent century, radical movements identified across national boundaries—sharing common issues like the eight-hour day, fight-ing common struggles for trade union legality, and using similar tactics like the militant strike. The Chicago martyrs became their common heroes. Revolutionaries excited by the worker insurgencies of the 1870s and 1880s exerted a remarkable influence on labor movements around the world; and among them, the anarchists of the Black International exercised an outsized influence. . . .

In the United States labor radicals found it more difficult to perpetuate Hay-market rituals. During the early 1900s anarchists maintained November 11 as a memorial day, but the occasion lost its power to attract pilgrims even before World War I. After 1890 anarchists and socialists failed to revive May Day as an occasion for remembering the martyrs—that is, until another sensational murder trial in 1906 promised to send three more labor radicals to the gallows. Pinkertons and law officers kidnapped [the prominent radical] Bill Haywood and took him with two other union militants to stand trial in Idaho for the dynamite murder of that state's former governor. The labor and socialist movements roused themselves in furious protest. They revived May Day in 1907 as an occasion of mammoth demonstrations, especially in New York where over 100,000 immigrants marched all day, and even in Boston, hardly a radical labor town, where nearly as many rallied on the common.

The "spectacular show trial" in Idaho not only allowed the socialist movement to resurrect May Day, it provided a powerful occasion for remembering Haymarket. The events of 1886 and 1887 were invoked in the Haywood trial by Clarence Darrow, the defense attorney who had helped win a pardon for the surviving "Haymarket boys," and by Eugene Debs, author of the inflammatory tract "Arouse Ye Slaves," who recalled Haymarket in a threat that infuriated President Theodore Roosevelt. "Nearly twenty years ago," Debs wrote in the *Appeal to Reason,* "the capitalist tyrants put some innocent men to death for standing up for labor. They are now going to try to do it again. Let them dare! There have been twenty years of revolutionary education, agitation, and organization since the Haymarket tragedy, and if an attempt is made to repeat it, there will be a revolution and I will do all in my power to precipitate it."

Haywood and his comrades were acquitted, May Day was recreated as a memory day, and in 1908 Lucy Parsons, carrying copies of the martyrs' *Famous Speeches,* made such a successful tour of eleven western cities that she decided to reprint the collection. Her tours became even more popular as the IWW preached the Chicago idea of direct-action unionism and reclaimed through dramatic free speech fights the public space closed down to radical labor after Haymarket. But Lucy Parsons also spoke to mainstream union members—for example in New York City where early in 1911 the Central Federated Union endorsed her talks before AFL locals. Then in two cross-country tours she sold ten thousand copies of the new edition of the Haymarket anarchists' *Famous Speeches.* In November, after her return to New York, she and Bill Haywood "spoke to packed November 11th meetings." At a time when many unions fought desperate struggles with the courts and the police and when the AFL adopted a "strong anti-statist outlook" and a posture of "semi-outlawry," trade unionists remembered the Haymarket tragedy as part of a state assault on the labor and eight-hour movements. . . .

A few years later, when anarchists, socialists, and Wobblies faced extinction amid the furies of war, there were other trials to remember—the McNamaras, Mooney and Billings, Carlo Tresca—and other victims to mourn, the women and children murdered at Ludlow, along with the Wobbly martyrs Joe Hill and Frank Little and their comrades massacred in Everett, Washington. The IWW began a new campaign to "remember" these victims in "Black November," but in the next decade, after the destruction of the labor left, few occasions survived in which movement heroes and heroines could be honored.

May Day celebrations were targets of state repression during World War I. Some laws actually banned the flying of the red flag that used to appear at the head of May 1 parades. During the red scare just after the war, May Day marches were violently attacked in several cities. In any case, this holiday had little hope for a revival in the patriotic fervor of the time, a time when the official culture created a very different holiday in May. Memorial Day, at the end of the month, created for the Civil War dead, now became an occasion for honoring soldiers killed in France and for recalling memories of World War I. May Day, as a time of remembering the Haymarket affair, suffered from outright suppression, while November 11, the memorial day of the hangings, faced a different fate in the court of official remembrance. After 1918 this day in November would be celebrated as Armistice Day, a major creation of "patriotic culture"—a veneration of the very state the martyrs had violently opposed and of the soldiers who had died for that nation-state.

## The History

Haymarket faded from working-class memory in the deeply repressive era of 1920s. Only private memories of Haymarket survived in individual "memory cabinets." "The act of remembering" Haymarket became an individual one, as is all the real work of remembrance. The memory of 1886–87 events now passed into recorded history. The Haymarket affair became a parable for the conservative interpretation of American history. In his influential six-volume history James Ford Rhodes concluded "that the punishment meted out to the anarchists was legally just." Another prominent historian concurred and added that the "wretches" who assumed "an impudent front" during the trial were found guilty and "merited" their "punishment." Thus did authoritative, academic history seek to negate the radical, proletarian memory of Haymarket.

But one historian unlocked the cabinets of private memory and made old movement recollections of Haymarket part of recorded history. In 1936, during a revival of progressive U.S. historiography, a young historian named Henry David published the first scholarly work on Haymarket that dismissed previous historians' judgments as "historically false." He demonstrated that the seven defendants could not have been guilty of murder given the evidence offered. He even questioned the possibility that the bomb could have been thrown by some other anarchist. The historian went on to challenge the interpretation of labor officials who blamed the anarchists for the failure of the Knights and the eight-hour movement. A scholar who studied at Columbia University, David absorbed the popular memory of Haymarket from Lucy Parsons; from George Schilling, the brilliant Chicago labor leader; and from his own immigrant father, who had an extensive personal knowledge of the American and European revolutionary movement; they passed their memory of the Haymarket directly to the historian. . . .

In 1937, a year after David's book appeared, a revived labor movement, with a historically conscious left wing, recalled the memory of 1887. In November union activists and leftists celebrated the fiftieth anniversary of the Haymarket executions in the Amalgamated Hall in Chicago. It was a year during which the cycle of conflict in the city turned again to anti-union violence. History seemed to be repeating itself. Lucy Parsons and others related to the martyrs spoke at the anniversary and at Waldheim. . . . Parsons referred to the newest tragedy in Chicago labor history. Just a few months before, the same city police who killed three strikers at the McCormick Works on 1 May 1886 shot down ten pickets at the Republic Steel Works on 31 May 1937—Memorial Day. For a short time, the memory of Haymarket became useful to the new industrial unions of the Committee of Industrial Organizations and to the Communists who led some of them.

The press and the authorities blamed the blood shed on Memorial Day 1937 on a "Communist riot," just as they had done after the Haymarket riot. But after a congressional committee viewed a suppressed newsreel of the shooting, the police were accused of killing peaceful strikers. Once again, a battle ensured over the memory of working-class martyrs in Chicago, and once again, influential voices sought absolution for innocent workers accused of being red rioters by the shapers of public opinion. Unexpectedly, the public response to the Memorial Day massacre helped create more protection for workers' rights and civil liberties. As a result, the memory of working-class martyrdom took on a different, less potent meaning. Cognizant of labor's violent past, and the effect of police actions at Haymarket and after, Chicago union leaders came to believe that workers' interests could only be protected by controlling or influencing the government. The Democratic mayor of Chicago repented for his decision to send police to guard Republic Steel's South

Chicago mill on Memorial Day and offered labor so much support that one of the strikers wounded by the police supported the Mayor's reelection campaign in 1939. As Democrats and as citizens, workers began to invest in "the state" because the government seemed to be standing by them in industry and in society as a whole.

## The Cemetery

When Lucy Parsons was buried with her husband, her son, and her beloved comrades at Waldheim in 1942, so was one of the last carriers of the "Chicago idea" of revolutionary unionism—an idea based on anarchist and syndicalist hostility to the capitalist state. A few years before her death, Lucy had joined the Communist Party, which now became the principal interpreter of Haymarket and its place of memory, Waldheim Cemetery—this despite the party's hostility to anarchism. During the popular front, Albert Parsons and the "anarchosyndicalists" of 1886 fit into the pantheon of Communist Party heroes as "martyrs of class struggle who gave their all for the emancipation of the working class"—heroes that included some who traced their political lives to Haymarket, notably "Big Bill" Haywood, who before he died in Moscow, asked that half of his ashes be buried in the Kremlin Wall and the other half "scattered at the site of the Martyrs Monument." In 1942 Jack Johnstone, a prominent Chicago Communist and respected labor organizer, asked to be buried with the Haymarket anarchists; so would other party leaders in later years, including William Z. Foster and Elizabeth Gurley Flynn, who as a teenager had been inspired by Lucy Parsons at the IWW founding convention. By sharing sacred ground and by writing labor history that linked anarchists, Wobblies and Communists in a kind of popular front, party intellectuals attempted to absorb the memory of Haymarket within their own tradition.

But during World War II, when the Communist Party disbanded, Waldheim faded as a site memory. It now embodied a "memorial consciousness" that barely survived because "the intimate fund of memory" had disappeared. . . . The Haymarket anarchists no longer served as heroes for a labor movement whose leaders had abandoned old anti-statist traditions. Many union officials, especially the immigrants who rose to power in the new unions, had decided to forget the bloody past of police and military repression, to regret their ancestors' militant radicalism, to block out memories of their rejection as immigrants—all in order to embrace a new version *compromise!* of "working-class Americanism" in which unions (with their ethnic membership) would take their place as a legitimate interest group in a pluralistic society.

By this time those who had experienced Haymarket had died. The oral tradition through which stories of Haymarket had been transmitted barely survived in Cold War America. It was a time when, Marianne Debouzy says, memories of working-class radicalism sank into oblivion as individuals were silenced and as left organizations were dismantled or outlawed, making it difficult for people to share oppositional memories. During the 1950s the grandson of Oscar Neebe, one of the Haymarket defendants pardoned in 1893, traveled to Mexico where he was shocked to learn that his grandfather was a revered proletarian hero. The memory of Oscar Neebe had been suppressed within his own family, which had suffered "many persecutions for Haymarket." Neebe's grandson inherited only his grandfather's name with no knowledge of his famous role in labor history. . . .

## The Reclamation

The memory of Haymarket was reclaimed in the 1960s by a new movement whose antiauthoritarian ideas were quite compatible with the beliefs of the Chicago martyrs. Like the anarchists of 1886, some antiwar radicals of the late 1960s believed in the propaganda of the deed; they declared war on a state that made war on Vietnamese insurgents and their supporters. On 4 May 1968, as antiwar demonstrators prepared for militant protests at the Democratic convention in Chicago, someone defaced the police monument in Haymarket Square. On 6 October 1969 the statue was blown up. The Weatherman faction of the Students for a Democratic Society took credit. An enraged Mayor Richard J. Daley promised to replace the edifice. On 4 May 1970—the anniversary of the 1886 bombing—a new statue was dedicated to the police.

While this violent struggle to memorialize the Haymarket victims pitted 1960s anarchists and the forces of law and order, the old voice of the labor movement arose taking its own stand on this site of conflict. The Illinois Labor History Society was formed in 1968 by union progressives like Les Orear, who worked for the Packinghouse Workers, and by labor historians like Bill Adelman, a labor educator. When the Teamsters and a few other unions contributed funds to rebuild the police statue blown up during the 1968 "days of rage," the Society was contacted by Bill Garvey, who edited the Steel Workers' union newspaper. He was dismayed that the scores of workers killed by the police in the 1886 riot had been totally forgotten in the controversy about the memory of the lawmen who died there. In 1969 he joined Labor History Society members in forming a Haymarket Workers' Committee to plan a memorial event in the Square to the innocent union members who lost their lives there simply by coming out to protest the shooting of fellow workers striking for the eight hour day. Garvey rented a hay wagon as a speakers' stand and asked radio personality Studs Terkel to keynote the memorial. The Labor History Society did not oppose the reconstruction of the police statue, but it demanded a compensatory place in Haymarket Square to mark the death of the workers who had gathered there for a peaceful protest in 1886. In 1970 Les Orear joined the Illinois State Historical Commission and persuaded its members to erect a memorial plaque in the square to honor the union dead. It was dedicated on May 4 of that year, but it was soon ripped down by vandals and never restored.

The struggle over Haymarket's divided memory escalated even further. On 6 October [1970] the newly dedicated police statue was bombed again.

Mayor Daley ordered round-the-clock security at the cost of $67,000 a year. Such protection became too costly, so city officials moved the official Haymarket icon indoors to police headquarters. On 4 May 1972 local anarchists and members of the IWW demonstrated at the site and attempted to erect on the empty pedestal of the police statue a paier-mâché bust of Louis Lingg, the anarchist who had cheated the hangman in 1887 by committing suicide in his jail cell. Once again, the Chicago police appeared to clear the square. . . .

Unable to mark the actual place where the workers died in the square, the Labor History Society acquired the deed to the Waldheim monument from the Pioneer Aid and Support Association of friends and family, which had had it constructed in 1893. It then maintained the site, which still attracted visitors from around the world. When the History Society organized a centennial event at the Cemetery in 1986, it even persuaded the Chicago Federation of Labor to endorse the commemoration. As Les Orear recalled, a younger generation now led the labor movement. These union officials were more open to the idea of honoring anarchists as innocent victims and less worried about identifying themselves with the memory of radical martyrs. But this was much too tame for a small band of anarchists who remained active in Chicago; they picketed the event because it was not organized to honor the martyrs as anarchists. Instead, it recalled the sacrifice of worker activists in the popular struggle for the eight-hour-day. Indeed, Chicago Mayor Harold Washington used the occasion to proclaim May Labor History Month, following the precedent of Black History Month in February. Rather than referring to the anarchists as men who died for their beliefs, he spoke to commemorate "the movement towards the eight-hour day, union rights, civil rights, human rights" and to the remembrance of the "tragic miscarriage of justice which claimed the lives of four labor activists."

Finally, . . . the monument at Waldheim gained official memorial status as a national landmark, but only after the directors of the labor-history theme study persuaded the park service to lift its ban on marking cemeteries and graves. . . . The long, patient work of the Illinois Labor History Society reached a successful climax as more than a thousand people came to Waldheim on 4 May 1998 for the official ceremony. The AFL-CIO presence was noticeable. Eight trade union leaders spoke—representative of a younger generation that had not inherited the criminalized memory of Haymarket.

However, unlike Waldheim Cemetery, Haymarket Square itself would remain unmarked, like many other sites of violence in American history. After the explosive events of the 1960s the site was neglected and forgotten, except by the Illinois Labor History Society. In 1982 Harold Washington became the first black mayor of Chicago after running against the old patronage system and its abuses, including police brutality. As part of the centennial anniversary in 1986, the Labor History Society proposed to Mayor Washington that the city recognize the martyrs of 1887 with a memorial park in the square. When Mayor Washington died in office, hopes for a Haymarket Square memorial faded, but not for Mollie West, a Chicago radical and survivor of the 1937 Memorial Day massacre, who clung to her belief that labor history sites, like Haymarket, can provide meaning for working people with no memory of struggles for social justice. She continued to advocate for a Haymarket Square memorial, but she could only imagine its construction through an act of resurrection: "We're waiting for Mayor Washington to come back," she said in 1993. "If he was here, this would've been done by now."

"Memory implies a certain act of redemption," writes John Berger. "What is forgotten has been abandoned . . . [and] with the loss of memory the continuities of meaning and judgment are also lost." More than any story told in American labor history, the Haymarket story preserved a memory of workers innocently victimized, of martyrs whose death gave meaning to the sacrifices made for labor rights and working-class empowerment, and of visionaries who created a labor movement to radically change capitalist society. Those who retold the story in this way rendered a harsh judgment on a city ruled by fear, a judiciary controlled by tyrants, a democracy defined by property.

# ⚘ F U R T H E R    R E A D I N G

Brecher, Jeremy. *Strike!* (1997).

Bruce, Robert V. *1877: Year of Violence* (1959).

Christie, Robert. *Empire in Wood* (1965).

Cooper, Jerry. *The Army and Civil Disorder* (1980).

Demarest, David, and Fannia Weingartner. *The "River Ran Red": Homestead 1892* (1992).

Dubofsky, Melvyn. *We Shall Be All: A History of the Industrial Workers of the World* (1969).

Dubofsky, Melvyn, and Warren Van Tine, eds. *Labor Leaders in America* (1987).

Fink, Leon. *Workingmen's Democracy: The Knights of Labor and American Politics* (1982).

Katzman, David M. *Seven Days a Week: Women and Domestic Service in Industrializing America* (1978).

Kaufman, Stuart. *Samuel Gompers and the Origins of the American Federation of Labor, 1848–1896* (1973).

Kazin, Michael. *The Barons of Labor: The San Francisco Building Trades and Union Power in the Progressive Era* (1987).

Krause, Paul. *The Battle for Homestead 1880–1950: Politics, Culture, and Steel* (1992).

Laslett, John. *Labor and the Left: A Study of Socialist and Radical Influences in the American Labor Movement, 1881–1924* (1970).

Licht, Walter. *Getting Work: Philadelphia, 1840–1950* (1996).

Mandel, Bernard. *Samuel Gompers: A Biography* (1963).

Messer-Kruse, Timothy. *The Yankee International: Marxism and the American Reform Tradition, 1848–1876* (1998).

Nelson, Bruce C. *Beyond the Martyrs: A Social History of Chicago's Anarchists, 1870–1900* (1988).

Oestreicher, Richard. *Solidarity and Fragmentation: Working People and Class Consciousness in Detroit, 1875–1900* (1986).

Salvatore, Nick. *Eugene V. Debs, Citizen and Socialist* (1982).

Saxton, Alexander. *Indispensable Enemy: Labor and the Anti-Chinese Movement in California* (1971).

Schneirov, Richard, ed. *The Pullman Strike and the Crisis of the 1890s: Essays on Labor and Politics* (1999).

Schwantes, Carlos. *Coxey's Army: An American Odyssey* (1997).

Shapiro, Karen. *A New South Rebellion: The Battle Against Convict Labor in the Tennessee Coalfields, 1871–1896* (1998).

Stowell, David. *Streets, Railroads, and the Great Strike of 1877* (1999).

Stromquist, Shelton. *A Generation of Boomers: The Pattern of Railroad Labor Conflict in Nineteenth-Century America* (1987).

Voss, Kim. *The Making of American Exceptionalism: The Knights of Labor and Class Formation in the Nineteenth Century* (1994).

# CHAPTER
## 6

# From Peasant to Proletarian

*During the forty years before the end of World War I, millions of peasants, rural laborers, and village tradesmen emigrated from Europe, the Mexican borderlands, French Canada, and the southern states. Most settled in the centers of industry and commercial agriculture that spread in a giant arc from New England through the Midwest and on to the great farms and mines of California. The transformation of rural people into a wage-earning proletariat was a worldwide phenomenon that swelled the populations of Shanghai, Buenos Aires, and Berlin as well as those of Chicago, Detroit, and Buffalo. By 1920 one out of eight U.S. residents had been born abroad; in many cities and regions, a large majority of the working class were either immigrants or the sons and daughters of immigrants.*

*Historians once conceived of America as a "melting pot" in which a process of cultural assimilation and upward mobility rapidly homogenized these newcomers. But today, scholars are more impressed with the vitality and integrity of these rural cultures, and with the remarkable struggle immigrant communities waged to nurture traditional values of work and family even in the midst of an urban, industrial environment over which they seemed to have so little control. A process of "chain migration" ensured that individual neighborhoods would long retain a particular ethnic flavor; in some instances, an entire block might be populated by the former residents of a single Sicilian village or North Carolina county. Likewise, choice and circumstance often linked particular immigrant groups to the job opportunities that opened up in specific regional industries: for example, French-Canadians in the textile mills of Woonsocket, Rhode Island; Finns along the Seattle waterfront; and Lithuanian Jews in the clothing factories of Baltimore. Black migrants from the U.S. South could find little work other than employment in personal service, although the labor shortages of World War I opened up thousands of jobs in meatpacking, steel, and other heavy industries to African American males.*

*What impact did these ethnic, racial, and gender divisions have on working-class America? Certainly some employers took advantage of this heterogeneity to structure their work forces along ethnically hierarchical lines that would enable them to suppress unions and more easily control those who toiled in their factories and mills. Protestant males of northern European extraction usually held the supervisory positions; unemployed blacks were sometimes recruited as strikebreakers. Racial prejudice, gender discrimination, and ethnic rivalry within the working*

*class also made organization and resistance difficult. But could the ethnic solidarity
of these same workers enhance their capacity for militancy and self-organization?
Did they find in their peasant heritage social values that they could use to question
the legitimacy of industrial capitalism itself?*

## ⚓ D O C U M E N T S

Much of what we know about the work life of immigrant labor was first recorded by
Progressive Era reformers eager to ameliorate deplorable workplace conditions. In
Document 1, Wisconsin labor economist John R. Commons, a pioneering historian
of American labor, offers a 1901 congressional investigating committee a structural
analysis of the sweatshop system in the Jewish garment trades. In Document 2,
industrial-relations investigator John Fitch describes the eighteen- to twenty-four-hour
"long turn" worked by pre–World War I immigrant steelworkers and notes its devastating impact on their family and community life. Lewis Hine's famous photographs
captured the evils of child labor and of unsanitary sweatshops for the National Child
Labor Committee. Document 3 presents two of Hine's tenement-life scenes.

Documents 4 and 5 provide an insight into the African-American migration
experience. In Document 4, we get a sense of why blacks moved north from letters
published in 1917 in the *Chicago Defender,* a major black newspaper. Document 5
records the argument made by some black leaders for opening up factory jobs to black
women, who were thought to adjust well to the pace of machine-driven work.

Documents 6 and 7 offer starkly contrasting views of the Asian workers who
came to the United States. In Document 6, California beet growers evaluate Chinese,
Japanese, and Mexican workers according to a demeaning set of racial stereotypes
in their report to a 1911 congressional commission. In Document 7, proletarian poet
H. T. Tsiang makes clear a few years later that Chinese immigrants clearly understood
the nature of their exploitation. Inspired by the Chinese revolution, Tsiang envisioned
an international working-class response to such racism and oppression.

## 1. Economist John R. Commons Denounces the "Sweating System," 1901

The term "sweating," or "sweating system," originally denoted a system of subcon-
tract, wherein the work is let out to contractors to be done in small shops or homes.
"In practice," says the report of the Illinois Bureau of Labor Statistics, "sweating
consists of the farming out by competing manufacturers to competing contractors
of the material for garments, which in turn is distributed among competing men
and women to be made up." . . . In the sweating system the foreman becomes a
contractor, with his own small shop and foot-power machine. In the factory system
the workmen are congregated where they can be seen by the factory inspectors and
where they can organize or develop a common understanding. In the sweating system they are isolated and unknown.

---

From John R. Commons, "Immigration and Its Economic Effects," Part III, *Reports of the Industrial
Commission on Immigration,* vol. 15 (Washington, D.C.: U.S. Government Printing Office, 1901).

The position of the contractor or sweater now in the business in American cities is peculiarly that of an organizer and employer of immigrants. The man best fitted to be a contractor is the man who is well-acquainted with his neighbors, who is able to speak the languages of several classes of immigrants, who can easily persuade his neighbors or their wives and children to work for him, and who in this way can obtain the cheapest help. During the busy season, when the work doubles, the number of people employed increases in the same proportion. All the contractors are agents and go around among the people. Housewives, who formerly worked at the trade and abandoned it after marriage, are called into service for an increased price of a dollar or two a week. Men who have engaged in other occupations, such as small business and peddling, but who are out of business most of the year, are marshaled into service by the contractor, who knows all of them and can easily look them up and put them in as competitors by offering them a dollar or two a week more than they are getting elsewhere. Usually when work comes to the contractor from the manufacturer and is offered to his employees for a smaller price than has previously been paid, the help will remonstrate and ask to be paid the full price. Then the contractor tells them, "I have nothing to do with the price. The price is made for me by the manufacturer, I have very little to say about the price." That is, he cuts himself completely loose from any responsibility to his employees as to how much they are to get for their labor. The help do not know the manufacturer. They cannot register their complaint with the man who made the price for their labor. The contractor, who did not make the price for their labor, claims that it is of no use to complain to him. So that however much the price for labor goes down, there is no one responsible for it.

There is always cutthroat competition among contractors. A contractor feels more dependent than any of his employees. He is always speculating on the idea of making a fortune by getting more work from the manufacturer than his neighbor and by having it made cheaper. Usually when he applies for work in the inside shop he comes in, hat in hand, very much like a beggar. He seems to feel the utter uselessness of his calling. Oftentimes the contractor is forced to send work back because he cannot make it under the conditions on which he took it; yet he does not dare to refuse an offer for fear the manufacturer will not give him more of his work. So he tries to figure it down by every device, and yet, perhaps, in the end is forced to send it back.

## 2. Investigator John Fitch Describes Steel's Long Shift, 1912

There is a very large class of workmen in the steel industry, many thousands of them throughout the country, who work consecutively either eighteen hours or twenty-four hours regularly every two weeks. This is so because the two shifts alternate working nights, the day shift of one week becoming the night shift of

From *Hours of Labor in the Steel Industry: A Communication to 15,000 Stockholders of the United States Steel Corporation* (Boston: privately printed, 1912), 6–8, 11–14.

the next and so on. When the plant works only six days, this can be accomplished without difficulty, but in a seven-day plant it is made possible only through the institution known as the "long turn." The night crew can change to the day shift by working through Saturday night until Sunday noon, an eighteen-hour period. The former day crew then relieves them and works until Monday morning, thus putting in another eighteen-hour period and getting itself on to the night shift for the week. The more general custom, however, is for the day shift to get in line for night work by working a full twenty-four-hour period, Sunday and Sunday night, finishing Monday morning. That puts the night crew on to Monday's day shift and allows them twenty-four hours off duty. Where the change is made every week, each crew works six days in one week and eight in the next.* In some plants the change is made only each two weeks. In that case, each man works the long turn once a month.

It is in the blast furnaces that the long turn comes with regularity. Federal census figures in 1910 show that there were 28,429 wage-earners employed in blast furnaces in the United States in 1909. The Federal Bureau of Labor investigators found that in a blast furnace plant nine-tenths of the employes [sic] work seven days a week. Nine-tenths of 38,429 is 34,586, which is the number of men in the blast furnaces who work either eighteen or twenty-four hours once or twice each month in 1909. But that isn't all. There were 647 open-hearth furnaces in 1909 with over 15,000 men tending them. Many of them work a part of every Sunday, and a considerable proportion are regular twelve-hour, seven-day workmen. And that isn't all. The number of mill wrights, engineers, yard laborers, furnace tenders, and guards in steel mills throughout the United States who have been regularly working twelve hours a day and seven days a week cannot be conjectured from data in my possession. It is a positive fact, however, that there is an enormous number of them. If we could ascertain the total number of seven-day workmen in 1910, we should find it to have been, I think, well over 50,000. A great majority of these worked twenty-four twice each month. . . .

## Social Effects of a 12-Hour Day

But all these things are more or less beside the point. Supposing it were true that the twelve-hour work is easy and that there were no physical indications of over-strain. The big fact, the only really vital and significant fact, remains that a twelve-hour schedule denies a man all true leisure. It isn't leisure for a man to sit on a bench in a steel mill waiting for his turn any more than it is for [a] motorman at a street crossing, waiting for the signal to proceed, or a machinist at his lathe, between times of increasing the tension. I have yet to hear of a steel company official choosing to spend his rest periods sitting on a bench beside a blooming mill, or picking out a blast furnace yard as a place to sleep. On the other hand, I am not recommending automobiles or golf as the necessary forms of recreation for the

---

*There are fourteen working days in one week—unless you think that a man who works twelve hours each twenty-four is doing only a half day's work at a time.

steel workers, but I do insist that it is the workman's right to spend his leisure hours outside the mill yard, and that is something that the twelve-hour day denies him.

In October, 1910, I talked with an employe of the Cambria Steel Company, an independent concern, who had one week a ten-hour day and next week a fourteen-hour night, and who every other Saturday night went out and worked through until Sunday night, a twenty-four-hour shift. It took him an hour to get from his home to the mill and another hour to go back. So his actual time away from home was twelve hours on day shift and sixteen hours at night.

"It's pretty hard to get rested in summer when you're on the night turn," he told me, "It's too hot to sleep well daytimes. But in the winter you can drop down and go to sleep anywheres, you're so tired. The day shift isn't so bad—ten hours long—but after you've worked the Sunday long turn, you're used up pretty bad. It takes several days to get over it." . . .

In November, 1910, I was in Lackawanna, NY., the home of the Lackawanna Steel Company, which is also an independent concern. It was there that I met the man . . . who worked fifty-six hours out of a possible seventy-two, at one time last fall. I called upon him in his home.

"Of course," he told me, "such a schedule is pretty hard on a man; I'm dead for a week after working the long shift. And then, you know, if you're a church man, it makes it pretty hard to attend services; I can't ever go Sunday morning. And Sunday night it's hard to go because I go to work extra early Monday morning. I get out to prayer-meeting only every other week, when I am on the day shift, and it's absolutely impossible to have a full meeting of the church at any time because the men work on different shifts." . . .

It was this man's wife who gave me a little insight into the burden of the long shift upon the housekeeper. "It's just about as hard for me as it is for him," she said. "He has to be at work at seven o'clock in the morning, so I have to get up at half past five to get his breakfast; and then he doesn't get home until after six and so it's pretty late before I get the work done. And on Monday mornings, when he goes to work earlier, I get up at half past four. But the worst thing about it all is that it's terribly uncertain. Sometimes he works a long turn when I don't expect it and sometimes he doesn't when I thought he was going to. If we plan for an evening out together, like as not he will come home early for supper and tell me that he has got to go back to the mill and work all night. We don't ever plan things any more; we just take an evening's pleasure together whenever we happen to have it."

"It's a great strain on a man," another at Lackawanna told me. "I could stand eight hours all right, but the twelve-hour schedule is a terribly nerve racking thing. I am only twenty-seven years old and my nerves are getting pretty bad. It's simply a killing pace in the steel works, and no pleasure in it. Most of the skilled men that I know are just trying to save their money until they get a stake and go out into something else before the industry kills them."

### 3.  Photographer Lewis Hine Depicts Child Laborers in the New York City Tenements, 1911

Children carried garments from the factory to be sewn at home. In fieldnotes accompanying this photograph, Lewis Hine wrote, "A load of kimonos just finished. Girl very reticent. Thompson St., N.Y." (National Archives)

From the Prints and Photographs Division, Library of Congress, Tenement House Scrapbook of Lewis Hine.

Reflecting on this New York City scene, Hine noted, "Mrs. Lucy Libertine and family: Johnnie, 4 years old, Mary 6 years, Millie 9 years, picking nuts in their basement tenement, 143 Hudson St. Mary was standing on the open mouth of the bag holding the cracked nuts [to be picked], with her dirty shoes on, and using a huge, dirty jacknife." (National Archives)

## 4. African Americans Seek Work in the North, 1917

Memphis, Tenn., May 5, 1917.

Dear Sir: I saw your add in the Chicago Defender papa and me being a firman and a all around man I thought I would write you. perhaps You might could do me lots of good. and if you can use me any way write me and let me No. in my trade or in foundry work. all so I got a boy 19 years old he is pretty apt in Learning I would Like to get him up there and Learn him a trade and I have several others would come previding if there be an opening for them. So this is all ans. soon

Algiers, La., May 16–17.

Sir: I saw sometime ago in the Chicago Defender, that you needed me for different work, would like to state that I can bring you all the men that you need, to do anything of work, or send them, would like to Come my self Con recomend all

From "Letters Home from Black Migrants to the North, 1916–1918," Emit Scott, ed., in *Journal of Negro History* 4 (July 1919), pp. 305–306. Reprinted by permission of the Association for Study of Afro-American Life and History, Inc.

the men I bring to do any kind of work, and will give satisfaction; I have bin fore-man for 20 yrs over some of these men in different work from R. R. work to Boiler Shop machine shop Blacksmith shop Concreet finishing or putting down pipe or any work to be did. they are all hard working men and will work at any kind of work also plastering anything in the labor line, from Clerical work down, I will not bring a man that is looking for a easy time only hard working men, that want good wages for there work, let me here from you at once.

Ellisville, Miss., 5/1/17.

Kind Sir: I have been takeing the Defender 4 months I injoy reading it very much I dont think that there could be a grander paper printed for the race, then the defender. Dear Editor I am thinking of leaving for Some good place in the North or West one I dont Know just which I learn that Nebraska was a very good climate for the people of the South. I wont you to give me some ideas on it, Or Some good farming country. I have been public working for 10 year. I am tired of that, And want to get out on a good farm. I have a wife and 5 children and we all wont to get our from town a place an try to buy a good home near good Schools good Churchs. I am going to leave here as soon as I get able to work. Some are talking of a free train May 15 But I dont no anything of that. So I will go to work an then I will be sure, of my leaving Of course if it run I will go but I am not depending on it Wages here are so low can scarcely live We can buy enough to eat we only buy enough to Keep up alive I mean the greater part of the Race. Women wages are from $1.25 Some time as high as $2.50. just some time for a whole week.

Hoping Dear Editor that I will get a hearing from you through return mail, giving me Some ideas and Some Sketches on the different Climate suitable for our health.

P.S. You can place my letter in Some of the Defender Columns but done use my name in print, for it might get back down here.

## 5. Helen B. Sayre Praises the Progress of Negro Women in Industry, 1924

The Negro woman's sudden entrance into industry is a new adventure and a dra-matic innovation. In the urgent quest for workers to "carry on" during the World War, she saw her longed-for opportunity, saw—as she visioned it—the end of the rainbow, and she came seeking it by thousands from her sunny, quiet southern home and plantation and placid housework and was at once swallowed up in the industrial centers in northern cities. Plucked so abruptly from the narrow spheres of such service as field hands, domestics and children's nurses, it is amazing to observe the transition and transformation of this same gentle, leisurely southern woman into the high-tension industrial worker in a large factory. Labor turnover, time clocks, piece work, output, maximum and minimum production, these words were unknown in her vocabulary a few years back. But today there are thousands

From Helen B. Sayre, "Negro Women in Industry," *Opportunity* 2 (August 1924): 242–244.

of these girls and women, working tirelessly and patiently and steadily in our large industrial plants,—and *making good.*

At the close of the War and during the general depression in business which followed, many Negro girls were released and replaced with white help. It was a tragedy to the Negro girl, as she had not had time to lay aside anything for the rainy day, to gain needed experience and skill, and to overcome the impatience of the average employer and an antagonistic foreman. She was hired in a period of crisis, to fill the gap at the bottom of the scale,—the most undesirable and unskilled jobs in the factory were assigned to her. The idea seemed very general that she could not be trusted to do the skilled work in any event—usually she was not given an opportunity if white help could be secured. Wet and sloppy work, heavy and tedious, with little chance for advancement, and if she did succeed, it was by sheer grit and determination, as many have told me. She had to be able to outdo her white competitor; sometimes she failed through lack of experience, and this would cause employers to say she was not capable, when in most cases it was simply due to poor selective instinct on his part or lack of intelligence or adaptability in her particular case.

Left to the mercy of ignorant, prejudiced, intolerant foremen, what could be expected? However, the whole story is not so dark. Though her progress was retarded by the turn in events, still we know that she did retain some very worthwhile places and she has progressed in them wherever possible to semi-skilled and skilled jobs. It is worthy of note, that wherever an employer was humane and appreciative and gave his Negro help a chance to advance and a square deal in wages and working conditions, he had steady, cheerful workers—which refutes a charge so prone to be made about their being undependable. Employers have found her amiable in disposition, intelligent and more adaptable than the unskilled foreign worker for whom white social agencies are engaged in season and out to aid them to adjust themselves, develop technique and become capable, highly skilled workers. For the Negro girl there are no such agencies outside of a small work being done by the Y.W.C.A. in the City of Chicago. In my experience with both white and Negro girls, I have found no difference between them in capacity for work. . . .

The story of the Negro women employed at the Nachman Springfilled Cushion Company of Chicago, Illinois, may be of some value in understanding the whole situation. It will also show the splendid growth of a business whose enviable record for superior quality and excellence in manufactured products is the output of these same women power machine operators, who make the durable covers for the softly resilient springs.

In the beginning this company employed less than fifty persons. It was a simple matter for the heads of the firm to know each individual worker. Today there are between six and seven hundred on the pay-roll. The employment of such large numbers has tended to destroy any personal relation between employer and employees, and there is practically no contact with the workers. The making of these cushion covers was also a simple process in the beginning; they were used mostly for chair seats and a perfectly "green" girl who had never seen a power machine before could learn in a very few days to sew them. Today this firm manufactures cushions for all kinds of upholstered furniture, day-beds, mattresses, and automobile seats. Each unit-spring is enclosed in a separate pocket and these covers are made in two operations.

When I tell you we have girls who can sew from five to seven thousand pockets in a day, you will realize that they have become "peppy" and mastered the speeding-up in industry. They are put on piece work in about three weeks and we have many girls making from twenty to thirty dollars per week. An average girl can make eighteen dollars per week. This is good pay for a year round job.

There came a time when this large group of girls, with no previous factory experience and no one to encourage and reprove them or give them any personal attention whatever, were doing about as they pleased. They were very irregular in attendance,—a very serious matter to the firm, in trying to give prompt service and keep up production.

The cushion is an unfinished product and is delivered in large quantities to factories to be upholstered. The girls would say, "If we stay out we are the only losers, being on piece work." So the week would go something like this: Monday—bad; Tuesday—a little better; Wednesday—very good, being pay day; Thursday—very poor; Friday—somewhat better; Saturday—a half-day and the worst day of the week. The company was about three months behind in delivery of orders due to the fact that girls were given a chance to learn to operate the machines with pay, and many stayed just long enough to learn. Continually employing new help, of course, was responsible for poor quality of work as well as large labor turnover and financial loss. The girls were disposed to be late for work and quit anywhere from a half-hour to fifteen minutes before closing time. There was considerable lack of respect for authority when it came to the forelady and inspector, as there was more or less a division of authority; so the firm had almost decided to release all the colored help, which meant a terrible blow to future opportunities. It was at this juncture that the Chicago Urban League was appealed to and they advised putting a Negro woman as Personnel Director in charge to save the situation if possible for these hundreds of girls. The work of this Director has been very interesting and to some considerable degree satisfactory to the firm. It must be acknowledged to the credit of the firm that they have done everything possible for the Director to carry out her plans.

Her first task was to establish confidence and good-will in the hearts of the workers for herself. This was done by bringing about some very needed improvements for the physical welfare of the workers, such as individual towels, rest-room, installing a wholesome lunch service, ice-water coolers on each floor during the summer months, having the space between the rows of machines widened seventeen inches so that the girls could swing the large work more easily in sewing, installation of ventilators. There was a need to develop a spirit of respect for those in authority and this has been brought about gradually by the careful handling of individual cases needing adjustment. It was necessary to educate those in authority as to their duty and responsibility as well as to require respect from the girls toward them.

The girls soon realized that if they had just cause for complaint, they were upheld; if they were in the wrong, their Director gave them a warning the first time that a second offense would mean dismissal, and it did mean just that. Misfits were gradually released; careless and poor operators were discharged; certain factory rules were established, such as for punctuality, attendance, general conduct. This was done after heart to heart talks with the girls and they were made to realize the necessity for these adjustments.

We have without doubt today, we believe, the best disciplined group of factory employees to be found. We have an average of 97% on time; 95%–98% on the job! Our production has increased steadily from about 250,000 pockets to an average of 400,000 per day and on special occasions when we have needed an increased production they have easily speeded up to 500,000. This is the output of about 170 operators. . . . Eighteen months ago we were three months behind in filling orders; today we guarantee a twenty-four hour delivery. Posting an hourly production scale on the bulletin board stimulates interest and it is great sport to watch the figures mount. We issue from time to time a printed bulletin or news sheet containing instructions and matters of general interest and information for the workers. We encourage the girls to larger earning effort by giving each girl a new dollar bill for every five dollars increase in her pay check; we also issue stars to the girls to wear on their caps, showing their rating,—one star for fifteen dollars; two stars for twenty dollars. . . .

Until the Negro woman in industry has had a longer factory experience, until she has acquired the modern industry complex, where they are employed in large numbers, they must be guided. In a few years they will have established themselves without question as to their ability and capacity for routine factory work. Then they may be counted upon to make their contribution and become an integral part of the great industrial systems of America. Give her time, give her guidance—most of all, give her opportunity.

## 6. California Employers Evaluate Foreign Beet Workers, 1911

The opinions of growers as to the general desirability as laborers of the different races employed vary, of course, according to individual prejudices and local race feeling, but they have certain striking features in common.

The consensus of opinion as to the Chinese is decidedly favorable, particularly when they are contrasted in certain respects with other races at present employed. The Chinese are regarded as thoroughly honest, faithful, conscientious, and efficient, though slow workers. They require no watching, and are said always to keep their contracts, regardless of losses to themselves. Furthermore, they take an interest in the outcome of the crop that often approaches servility toward their employers. For instance, it is said in one district that after they had finished the thinning they would often leave several of the old men at the camp to cut out weeds as fast as they grew. In this case the contract for each operation—thinning, hoeing, or harvesting—was apparently a separate one.

The chief criticism of the Chinese is based on their slowness and their reluctance to adopt new methods. In one district where they were employed for ten years they are said to have worked without tools for several seasons. They did

From Reports on the Immigration Commission, 61st Congress, 2nd Session, Senate Document 633, *Immigrants in Industries,* Part 25: Japanese and Other Immigrant Races in the Pacific Coast and Rocky Mountain States, vol. II: Agriculture (Washington, D.C.: U.S. Government Printing Office, 1911), 108–110.

not understand the kind of work desired, and consequently did all the thinning with their fingers. Later they consented to use hoes, and gradually became proficient workmen.

In weighing growers' opinions of the Chinese it must be remembered, however, that these opinions are expressed nearly a decade after the race had largely disappeared from the industry, and furthermore, that they refer to selected members of the race with years of experience in American methods of work and contractual relations. There is at least a question whether the Chinese have not risen in the appreciation of growers with their scarcity and at the expense of the reputations of the races at present employed.

The Japanese are commonly praised for their industry, quickness, steadiness, sobriety, cleanliness, adaptability, and eagerness to learn American ways and customs. They are condemned for lack of commercial honesty and for the pursuit of their own interests regardless of the cost to their employers. Many instances are reported of their disregard of contract obligations. The question as to whether a contract shall be kept or broken is apparently, in these cases, a commercial one, the answer depending upon the amount of money involved. If the contract price, less advances already made by the grower, is greater than the expense of completing the work the contract will be fulfilled; if it is less, the contract will be broken. One instance is reported where a bond was required from the contractor for the faithful performance of his agreement. This was in the case of a sugar company which employs nearly 300 Japanese for the hand work of its own fields. These men are all hired through a single contractor, a Japanese, who has been employed by the company for several years.

The company in its contract with this man requires from him a bond, to cover penalties provided for in the agreement in the following cases: (1) If at any time both the contractor and his foreman should be found absent from the fields by officials of the company during working hours; (2) if at any time the work should be stopped by disagreements between the contractor and his men. In the latter case the penalty is $100 for each day work is so interrupted. The company regards this contractor as a very reliable man and worthy of their entire confidence.

The average Japanese contractor is said to be very shrewd in choosing opportune moments for increasing his demands. It is said that one device used in the harvesting season is to postpone the work as long as possible on the pretext of a scarcity of laborers and then to demand increased prices because the beets have increased in size during the delay. The grower in such cases must usually acceded to the demands made or see his beets suffer from neglect in the fields. The bond in his contract (if the contract is so guaranteed) with the Japanese is rarely sufficient to recover the loss of his crop.

Sometimes when the contractor, contrary to the usual custom, hires his men by the day he is forced to demand an increase in the contract price because of the demands of his men for higher wages. Sometimes the contract price in such cases is contingent upon his ability to secure men at a certain rate. If the men succeed in securing a raise in wages the additional amount in either case is an expense, not to the contractor, but to the grower. The latter must harvest his crop or bear the large losses risked in an intensive culture like that of the sugar beet.

The extent to which the Japanese have forced prices up in the past ten years is illustrated by the history of prices paid for thinning in a certain district. For this work the men are paid by the hour for an eleven-hour day. When the Japanese first entered the district in large numbers in 1899, they worked at thinning for about $1 per day. Shortly after that they demanded and obtained 10 cents more per day. Since then their wages have gradually risen until in 1908 they were $1.65. During the thinning season of 1909 the men demanded 17 cents an hour, or $1.87 [sic] per day, but the "bosses" met and formally agreed to pay no more than $1.75 for eleven hours' work. The purpose of this agreement was to prevent overbidding for field workers. The men were forced to accept this rate of pay, but soon renewed their demands for the greater increase. At the time the special agent of the Commission visited this locality, no agreement had been reached.

In short, the Japanese are accused of the tactics pursued by other monopolists; that is, of local price cutting to repress competition, and of exorbitant increases in prices when, for the time being, competition is impossible.

In addition to lack of respect for contract obligations the Japanese are further accused of doing dishonest work. Often, when a flat rate has been made to cover the hand work of the entire season, it has been found that the Japanese would hoe out as many beets as possible in the thinning in order to make easier work of that operation and leave less work for the harvesting season. Sometimes, it is said, they would simply chop off the part of the beet showing above ground. Partly to remedy this evil the sliding scale of prices for topping and loading has been generally introduced. In justice to the Japanese, it should be said that they are not the only race accused of overthinning. The sliding scale is used in contracts with Mexicans in districts where only Mexicans are employed; and at present an attempt is being made to introduce this method of payment among the German-Russians in northern Colorado, for the same reason that led to its adoption among the Japanese in California.

As to Mexicans, conflicting opinions are expressed. Some employers complain that they are "hard to handle"; others say that they are much more tractable than the Japanese, who, they assert, are inclined to become conceited. All employers agree that the Mexicans lack ambition, and that they are addicted to the vices of drunkenness and gambling to an unusual degree. Consequently there is much complaint of their irregularity at work. In the face of this fact, however, some employers insist that the Mexican always keeps his contract. The reference here is doubtless to a practice of refraining from attempts to alter the terms of contracts rather than to the regularity with which the work called for is done.

In the two southern California districts where the force of field workers is predominantly Mexican, the Mexican is preferred to the Japanese. He is alleged to be more tractable and to be a better workman in one case. In the other he is said to be a quicker and better workman than the Japanese, but complaint is made that he in unreasonable. This is perhaps occasioned by a strike among the Mexicans for higher wages in the year 1908. This strike was broken by the temporary employment of German-Russians.

As previously stated, the Mexicans have been employed in several northern districts to provide competition against the Japanese. In at least one instance, already reported, it is said the Mexicans were soon "spoiled" by the Japanese, who persuaded them to be less careful in their work in order not to discredit Japanese standards.

To sum up, the Mexican is a fairly honest, efficient worker, whose usefulness is, however, much impaired by his lack of ambition and his proneness to the constant use of intoxicating liquor.

The East Indian has not yet had a fair trial in the industry. He is, of course, generally complained of on account of his uncleanliness, but this complaint is irrelevant in a consideration of his efficiency as a beet worker. So far as present experience goes, the East Indian is a slow but honest steady, and exceedingly tractable workman. He is averse to entering into contracts, because he does not understand the contract system, but it is said that this aversion can be overcome after his confidence has been gained by his employers.

In the amount of work done in a day by individuals of different races the Japanese are far in the lead. The average Japanese can be counted upon to care for at least 12 acres during the season. The Mexicans and East Indians never average more than 7 or 8 acres. The explanation is that the Japanese not only works more rapidly—and less thoroughly—but that he also works longer hours.

## 7. "Chinaman, Laundryman" Poet H. T. Tsiang Defends Chinese Immigrants, 1929

"Chinaman"!
"Laundryman"!
Don't call me "man"!
I am worse than a slave

Wash! Wash!
Why can I wash away
The dirt of others' clothes
But not the hatred of my heart?
My skin is yellow,
Does my yellow skin color the clothes?
Why do you pay me less
For the same work?
Clever boss!
You know
How to scatter the seeds of hatred
Among your ignorant slaves

Iron! Iron!
Why can I smooth away
The wrinkles of others' dresses
But not the miseries of my heart?

---

From H. T. Tsiang, "Chinaman, Laundryman," in *Poems of the Chinese Revolution* (New York: Self-published, 1929), 7–8.

Why should I come to America
To wash clothes?
Do you think "Chinamen" in China
Wear no dresses?
I came to America
Three days after my marriage.
When can I see her again?
Only the almighty "Dollar" knows!

Dry! Dry!
Why do clothes dry
But not my tears?
I work
Twelve hours a day,
He pays
Fifteen dollars a week
My boss says,
"Chinaman,
Go back to China
If you don't feel satisfied!
There,
Unlimited hours of toil:
Two silver dollars a week,
If
You can find a job."
"Thank you, Boss!
For you remind me.
I know
Bosses are robbers
Everywhere!"

Chinese boss says:
"You Chinaman,
Me Chinaman
Come work for me—
Work for your fellow countryman!
By the way,
You 'Wong,' me 'Wong'—
Do we not belong to the same family?
Ha! ha!
We are cousins!
Oh yes!
You 'Hai Shan,' me 'Hai Shan,'
Do we not come from same district?
O, come work for me;
I will treat you better!"
"GET away from here,

What is the difference,
When you come to exploit me?"

"Chinaman!"
"Laundryman"!
Don't call me "Chinaman"!
Yes, I am a "Laundryman"!
The workingman!
Don't call me "Chinaman"!
I am the Worldman
"The International Soviet
Shall be his human race"!

"Chinaman"!
"Laundryman"!
All the workingmen!
Here is the brush
Made of Marxism
Here is the soap
made of Leninism
Let us all
Wash with the blood!
Let us all
Press with the iron!
Wash!
Brush!
Dry!
Iron!
Then we shall have
A clean world.

## ✢ E S S A Y S

The first essay is a path-breaking study by historian Herbert Gutman, who helped to greatly expand the scope of labor history before his death in 1985. Gutman argues that American working-class history has been characterized by a clash between generation after generation of rural immigrants, who imported their traditional "customs, rituals, and beliefs" into the United States, and an industrial system that emphasized the rigid time and work discipline believed to be essential to factory production. In the second essay, Ronald Takaki, who teaches ethnic studies at the University of California at Berkeley, explores the work lives of Hawaii's multicultural proletariat in that territory's sugar cane fields in the late nineteenth and early twenties centuries.

Compare the functioning of the contract system in large-scale agriculture with its deployment in the garment trades, as described in the documentary section of the chapter. To what extent was the experience of Hawaiian laborers similar to that of Eastern European immigrants in the East? To what extent does a continuity between agricultural and industrial work mark the "diaspora" experience of Asians, Europeans, and African American southerners?

# The Cultures of First-Generation
# Industrial Workers

### HERBERT GUTMAN

Common work habits rooted in diverse premodern cultures (different in many ways but nevertheless all ill fitted to the regular routines demanded by machine-centered factory processes) existed among distinctive first-generation factory workers all through American history. We focus on two quite different time periods: the years before 1843 when the factory and machine were still new to America and the years between 1893 and 1917 when the country had become the world's industrial colossus. In both periods workers new to factory production brought strange and seemingly useless work habits to the factory gate. The irregular and undisciplined work patterns of factory hands before 1843 frustrated cost-conscious manufacturers and caused frequent complaint among them. Textile factory work rules often were designed to tame such rude customs. A New Hampshire cotton factory that hired mostly women and children forbade "spiritous liquor, smoking, nor any kind of amusement . . . in the workshops, yards, or factories" and promised the "immediate and disgraceful dismissal" of employees found gambling, drinking, or committing "any other debaucheries." . . . Manufacturers elsewhere worried about the example "idle" men set for women and children. Massachusetts family heads who rented "a piece of land on shares" to grow corn and potatoes while their wives and children labored in factories worried one manufacturer. "I would prefer giving constant employment at some sacrifice," he said, "to having a man of the village seen in the streets on a rainy day at leisure." Men who worked in Massachusetts woolen mills upset expected work routines in other ways. "The wool business requires more man labour," said a manufacturer, "and this we study to avoid. Women are much more ready to follow good regulations, are not captious, and do not clan as the men do against the overseers." Male factory workers posed other difficulties, too. In 1817 a shipbuilder in Medford, Massachusetts, refused his men grog privileges. They quit work, but he managed to finish a ship without using further spirits, "a remarkable achievement." . . .

Employers responded differently to such behavior by first-generation factory hands. "Moral reform" as well as . . . carrot-and-stick policies meant to tame or to transform such work habits. Fining was common. . . . Special material rewards encouraged steady work. A Hopewell Village blacksmith contracted for nineteen dollars a month, and "if he does his work well we are to give him a pair of coarse boots." In these and later years manufacturers in Fall River and Paterson institutionalized traditional customs and arranged for festivals and parades to celebrate with their workers a new mill, a retiring superintendent, or a finished locomotive. . . . Where factory work could be learned easily, new hands replaced irregular ones. A factory worker in New England remembered that years before the Civil War her employer had hired "all American girls" but later shifted to immigrant laborers because "not coming from country homes, but living as the Irish do, in the town, they take no vacations, and can be relied on at the mill all year round." Not all such devices worked to the satisfaction of workers or their employers. Sometime in the late 1830s merchant capitalists sent a skilled British silk weaver to manage a new mill in Nantucket that would employ the wives and children of local whalers and fishermen. Machinery was installed, and in the first days women and children besieged the mill for work. After a month had passed, they started dropping off in small groups. Soon nearly all had returned "to their shore gazing and to their seats by the sea." The Nantucket mill shut down, its hollow frame an empty monument to the unwillingness of resident women and children to conform to the regularities demanded by rising manufacturers.

First-generation factory workers were not unique to premodern America. And the work habits common to such workers plagued American manufacturers in later generations when manufacturers and most native urban whites scarcely remembered that native Americans had once been hesitant first-generation factory workers. To shift forward in time to East and South European immigrants new to steam, machinery, and electricity and new to the United States itself is to find much that seems the same. American society, of course, had changed greatly, but in some ways it is as if a film—run at a much faster speed—is being viewed for the second time: primitive work rules for unskilled labor, fines, gang labor, and subcontracting were commonplace. In 1910 two-thirds of the workers in twenty-one major manufacturing and mining industries came from Eastern and Southern Europe or were native American blacks, and studies of these "new immigrants" record much evidence of preindustrial work habits among the men and women new to American industry. . . . [S]killed immigrant Jews carried to New York City town and village employment patterns, such as the *landsmannschaft* economy and a preference for small shops as opposed to larger factories, that sparked frequent disorders but hindered stable trade unions until 1910. Specialization spurred anxiety: in Chicago Jewish glovemakers resisted the subdivision of labor even though it promised better wages. . . . American work rules also conflicted with religious imperatives. On the eighth day after the birth of a son, Orthodox Jews in Eastern Europe held a festival, "an occasion of much rejoicing." But the American work week had a different logic, and if the day fell during the week the celebration occurred the following Sunday. "The host . . . and his guests," David Blaustein remarked, "know it is not the right day," and "they fall to mourning over the conditions that will not permit them to observe the old custom." The occasion became "one for secret sadness rather than rejoicing." Radical Yiddish poets, like Morris Rosenfeld, the presser of men's clothing, measured in verse the psychic and social costs exacted by American industrial work rules:

> The Clock in the workshop,—it rests not a moment;
> It points on, and ticks on: eternity—time;
> Once someone told me the clock had a meaning,—
> In pointing and ticking had reason and rhyme. . . .
> At times, when I listen, I hear the clock plainly;—
> The reason of old—the old meaning—is gone!
> The maddening pendulum urges me forward
> To labor and still labor on.
> The tick of the clock is the boss in his anger.
> The face of the clock has the eyes of the foe.

The clock—I shudder—Dost hear how it draws me?
It calls me "Machine"—and it cries [to] me "Sew"!

Slavic and Italian immigrants carried with them to industrial America subcultures quite different from that of village Jews, but their work habits were just as alien to the modern factory. Rudolph Vecoli has reconstructed Chicago's South Italian community to show that adult male seasonal construction gangs as contrasted to factory labor were one of many traditional customs adapted to the new environment, and in her study of South Italian peasant immigrants Phyllis H. Williams found among them men who never adjusted to factory labor. After "years" of "excellent" factory work, some "began . . . to have minor accidents" and others "suddenly give up and are found in their homes complaining of a vague indisposition with no apparent physical basis." Such labor worried early twentieth-century efficiency experts, and so did Slavic festivals, church holidays, and "prolonged merriment." "Man," Adam Smith wisely observed, "is, of all sorts of luggage, the most difficult to be transported." That was just as true for these Slavic immigrants as for the early nineteenth-century native American factory workers. A Polish wedding in a Pennsylvania mining or mill town lasted between three and five days. Greek and Roman Catholics shared the same jobs but had different holy days, "an annoyance to many employers." The Greek Church had "more than eighty festivals in the year," and "the Slav religiously observes the days on which the saints are commemorated and invariably takes a holiday." A celebration of the American Day of Independence in Mahanoy City, Pennsylvania, caught the eye of a hostile observer. Men parading the streets drew a handcart with a barrel of lager in it. Over the barrel "stood a comrade, goblet in hand and crowned with a garland of laurel, singing some jargon." Another sat and played an accordion. At intervals, the men stopped to "drink the good beverage they celebrated in song." The witness called the entertainment "an imitation of the honor paid Bacchus which was one of the most joyous festivals of ancient Rome" and felt it proof of "a lower type of civilization." Great Lakes dock workers "believed that a vessel could not be unloaded unless they had from four to five kegs of beer." (And in the early irregular strikes among male Jewish garment workers, employers negotiated with them out of doors and after each settlement "would roll out a keg of beer for their entertainment of the workers." Contemporary betters could not comprehend such behavior. . . .

More than irregular work habits bound together the behavior of first-generation factory workers separated from one another by time and by the larger structure of the society they first encountered. Few distinctive American working-class populations differed in so many essentials (their sex, their religion, their nativity, and their prior rural and village cultures) as the Lowell mill girls and women of the Era of Good Feelings and the South and East European steelworkers of the Progressive Era. To describe similarities in their expectations of factory labor is not to blur these important differences but to suggest that otherwise quite distinctive men and women interpreted such work in similar ways. . . .

Historians of the Lowell mill girls find little evidence before 1840 of organized protest among them and attribute their collective passivity to corporation policing policies, the frequent turnover in the labor force, the irregular pace of work (after it was rationalized in the 1840s, it provoked collective protest), the freedom the mill

girls enjoyed away from rural family dominance, and their relatively decent earnings. The women managed the transition to mill life because they did not expect to
remain factory workers too long. Nevertheless frequent inner tension revealed itself
among the mobile mill women. In an early year, a single mill discharged twenty-
eight women for such reasons as "misconduct," "captiousness," "disobedience,"
"impudence," "levity," and even "mutiny." . . .

Aspirations and expectations interpret experience and thereby help shape behavior. Some Lowell mill girls revealed dissatisfactions, and others made a difficult
transition from rural New England to that model factory town, but that so few
planned to remain mill workers eased that transition and hampered collective protest.
Men as well as women, who expect to spend only a few years as factory workers
have little incentive to join unions. That was just as true of the immigrant male common laborers in the steel mills of the late nineteenth and early twentieth centuries
(when multiplant oligopoly characterized the nation's most important manufacturing
industry) as in the Lowell cotton mills nearly a century earlier. . . . In those years, the
steel companies successfully divorced wages from productivity to allow the market
to shape them. Between 1890 and 1910, efficiencies in plant organization cut labor
costs by about a third. The great Carnegie Pittsburg plants employed 14,359 common
laborers, 11,694 of them South and East Europeans. Most, peasant in origin, earned
less than $12.50 a week (a family needed fifteen dollars for subsistence). A stagger-
ing accident rate damaged these and other men: nearly 25 percent of the recent immigrants employed at the Carnegie South Works were injured or killed each year
between 1907 and 1910, 3,723 in all. But like the Lowell mill women, these men
rarely protested in collective ways, and for good reason. They did not plan to stay in
the steel mills long. Most had come to the United States as single men (or married
men who had left their families behind) to work briefly in the mills, save some
money, return home, and purchase farmland. Their private letters to European relatives indicated a realistic awareness of their working life that paralleled some of the
Lowell fiction: "if I don't earn $1.50 a day, it would not be worth thinking about
America"; "a golden land so long as there is work"; "here in America one must work
for three horses"; "let him not risk coming, for he is too young"; "too weak for America." Men who wrote such letters and avoided injury often saved small amounts of
money, and a significant number fulfilled their expectations and quit the factory and
even the country. Forty-four South and East Europeans left the United States for
every one hundred that arrived between 1908 and 1910. . . . Immigrant expectations
coincided for a time with the fiscal needs of industrial manufacturers. The Pittsburgh
steel magnates had as much good fortune as the Boston Associates. But the stability
and passivity they counted on among their unskilled workers depended upon steady
work and the opportunity to escape the mills. When frequent recessions caused recurrent unemployment, immigrant expectations and behavior changed. . . .[P]easant
"group consciousness" and "communal loyalty" sustained bitter wildcat strikes after
employment picked up. The tenacity of these immigrant strikers for higher wages
amazed contemporaries, and brutal suppression often accompanied them (Cleveland,
1899; East Chicago, 1905; McKees Rock, 1909; Bethlehem, 1910; and Youngstown
in 1915 where, after a policeman shot into a peaceful parade, a riot caused an estimated one million dollars in damages). The First World War and its aftermath
blocked the traditional route of overseas outward mobility, and the consciousness of

immigrant steelworkers changed. They sparked the 1919 steel strike. The steel mill had become a way of life for them and was no longer the means by which to reaffirm and even strengthen older peasant and village life-styles. . . .

Even though American society itself underwent radical structural changes between 1815 and the First World War, the shifting composition of its wage-earning population meant that traditional customs, rituals, and beliefs repeatedly helped shape the behavior of its diverse working-class groups. The street battle in 1843 that followed Irish efforts to prevent New York City authorities from stopping pigs from running loose in the streets is but one example of the force of old styles of behavior. Both the form and the content of much expressive working-class behavior, including labor disputes, often revealed the powerful role of secular and religious rituals. In 1857 the New York City unemployed kidnapped a musical band to give legitimacy to its parade for public works. After the Civil War, a Fall River cotton manufacturer boasted that the arrival of fresh Lancashire operatives meant the coming of "a lot of greenhorns here," but an overseer advised him, "Yes, but you'll find they have brought their horns with them." A few years later, the Pittsburgh courts prevented three women married to coal miners from "tin-horning" nonstrikers. The women, however, purchased mouth organs. ("Tinhorning," of course, was not merely an imported institution. In Franklin, Virginia, in 1867, for example, a Northern white clergyman who started a school for former slave children had two nighttime "tin horn serenade[s]" from hostile whites.) Recurrent street demonstrations in Paterson accompanying frequent strikes and lockouts nearly always involved horns, whistles, and even Irish "banshee" calls. These had a deeply symbolic meaning, and, rooted in a shared culture, they sustained disputes. A Paterson manufacturer said of nonstrikers: "They cannot go anywhere without being molested or insulted, and no matter what they do they are met and blackguarded and taunted in a way that no one can stand . . . which is a great deal worse than actual assaults." . . .

But the manufacturers could not convince the town's mayor (himself a British immigrant and an artisan who had become a small manufacturer) to ban street demonstrations. The manufacturers even financed their own private militia to manage further disorders, but the street demonstrations continued with varying effectiveness until 1901 when a court injunction essentially defined the streets as private space by banning talking and singing banshee (or death) wails in them during industrial disputes. In part, the frequent recourse to the courts and to the state militia after the Civil War during industrial disputes was the consequence of working-class rituals that helped sustain long and protracted conflicts.

Symbolic secular and, especially, religious rituals and beliefs differed among Catholic and Jewish workers fresh to industrial America between 1894 and the First World War, but their function remained the same. Striking Jewish vestmakers finished a formal complaint by quoting the Law of Moses to prove that "our bosses who rob us and don't pay us regularly commit a sin and that the cause of our union is a just one." ("What do we come to America for?" these same men asked. "To bathe in tears and to see our wives and children rot in poverty?") An old Jewish ritual oath helped spark the shirtwaist strike of women workers in 1909 that laid the basis for the International Ladies Garment Workers Union. A strike vote resulted in the plea, "Do you mean faith? Will you take the old Jewish oath?" The audience responded in Yiddish: "If I turn traitor to the cause, I now pledge, may this hand wither and drop off at the wrist from the arm I now raise." . . . Immigrant Catholic workers shared similar experiences with these immigrant Jews. A reporter noticed in 1910 at a meeting of striking Slavic steelworkers in Hammond, Indiana: "The lights of the hall were extinguished. A candle stuck into a bottle was placed on a platform. One by one the men came and kissed the ivory image on the cross, kneeling before it. They swore not to scab." Not all rituals were that pacific. That same year, Slavic miners in Avelia, Pennsylvania, a tiny patch on the West Virginia border, crucified George Rabish, a mine boss and an alleged labor spy. . . . That event was certainly unusual, but it was commonplace for time-honored religious symbols as well as American flags to be carried in the frequent parades of American workers. Western Pennsylvania Slavic and Italian coal miners in a bitter strike just east of Pittsburg (eighteen of twenty thousand miners quit work for seventeen months when denied the right to join the United Mine Workers of America) in 1910 and 1911 carried such symbols. "These rural marches," said Paul Kellogg [*Survey* editor], "were in a way reminiscent of the old time agrarian uprisings which have marked English history." But theirs was the behavior of peasant and village Slavs and Italians fresh to modern industrial America, and it was just such tenacious peasant-worker protests that caused the head of the Pennsylvania State Police to say that he modeled his force on the Royal Irish Constabulary, not, he insisted, "as an anti-labor measure" but be- cause "conditions in Pennsylvania resembled those in strife-torn Ireland." Peasant parades and rituals, religious oaths and food riots, and much else in the culture and behavior of early twentieth-century immigrant American factory workers were cultural anachronisms to this man and to others, including Theodore Roosevelt, William Jennings Bryan, Elbert Gary, and even Samuel Gompers, but participants found them natural and effective forms of self-assertion and self-protection.

The perspective emphasized in these pages tells about more than the behavior of diverse groups of American working men and women. It also suggests how larger, well-studied aspects of American society have been affected by a historical process that has "industrialized" different peoples over protracted periods of time. . . . Con- tact and conflict between diverse preindustrial cultures and a changing and increas- ingly bureaucratized industrial society also affected the larger society in ways that await systematic examination. Contemporaries realized this fact. Concerned in 1886 about the South's "dead"—that is, unproductive—population, the Richmond *Whig* felt the "true remedy" to be "educating the industrial morale of the people." The *Whig* emphasized socializing institutions primarily outside of the working class itself. "In the work of inculcating industrial ideas and impulses," said the *Whig,* "all proper agencies should be enlisted—family discipline, public school education, pulpit instruction, business standards and requirements, and the power and influence of the workingmen's associations." What the *Whig* worried over in 1886 concerned other Americans before and after that time. And the resultant ten- sion shaped society in important ways. . . .

The same process also affected the shaping and reshaping of American police and domestic military institutions. We need only realize that the burning of a Boston convent in 1834 by a crowd of Charlestown truckmen and New Hampshire Scotch-Irish brickmakers caused the first revision of the Massachusetts Riot Act since Shays' Rebellion, and that three years later interference by native firemen in a Sunday Irish funeral procession led to a two-hour riot involving upward of fifteen thousand persons (more than a sixth of Boston's population), brought militia to that city for the first time, and caused the first of many reorganizations of the Boston police force. The regular contact between alien work cultures and a larger industrializing or industrial society had other consequences. It often worried industrialists, causing C. E. Perkins, the president of the Chicago, Burlington, and Quincy Railroad to confide in a friend in the late nineteenth century. "If I were able, I would found a school for the study of political economy in order to harden men's hearts." It affected the popular culture. A guidebook for immigrant Jews in the 1890s advised how to make it in the New World: "Hold fast, this is most necessary in America. Forget your past, your customs, and your ideals. . . . A bit of advice to you: do not take a moment's rest. Run, do, work, and keep your own good in mind." Cultures and customs, however, are not that easily discarded. So it may be that America's extraordinary technological supremacy—its talent before the Second World War for developing labor-saving machinery and simplifying complex mechanical processes—depended less on "Yankee know-how" than on the continued infusion of prefactory peoples into an increasingly industrialized society. The same process, moreover, may also explain why movements to legislate morality and to alter habits have lasted much longer in the United States than in most other industrial countries, extending from the temperance crusades of the 1820s and the 1830s to the violent opposition among Germans to such rules in the 1850s and the 1860s and finally to formal prohibition earlier in this century. Important relationships also exist between this process and the elite and popular nativist and racist social movements that have ebbed and flowed regularly from the 1840s until our own time, as well as between this process and elite political "reform" movements between 1850 and the First World War.

The sweeping social process had yet another important consequence: it reinforced the biases that otherwise distort the ways in which elite observers perceive the world below them. When in 1902 *The New York Times* cast scorn upon and urged that force be used against the Jewish women food rioters, it conformed to a fairly settled elite tradition. Immigrant groups and the working population had changed in composition over time, but the rhetoric of influential nineteenth- and early twentieth-century elite observers remained constant. Disorders among the Jersey City Irish seeking wages due them from the Erie Railroad in 1859 led the Jersey City *American Standard* to call them "imported *beggars*" and "*animals*," "a mongrel mass of ignorance and crime and superstition, as utterly unfit for its duties, as they are for the common courtesies and decencies of civilized life." . . .

Although the Civil War ended slavery, it did not abolish these distorted perceptions and fears of new American workers. In 1869 *Scientific American* welcomed the "ruder" laborers of Europe but urged them to "assimilate" quickly or face "a quiet but sure extermination." Those who retained their alien ways, it insisted, "will share the fate of the native Indian." Elite nativism neither died out during the Civil War nor awaited a rebirth under the auspices of the American Protective Association and the Immigration Restriction League. In the mid-1870s, for example, the Chicago *Tribune* called striking immigrant brickmakers men but "not reasoning creatures," and the Chicago *Post-Mail* described that city's Bohemian residents as "depraved beasts, harpies, decayed physically and spiritually, mentally and morally, thievish and licentious." The Democratic Chicago *Times* cast an even wider net in complaining that the country had become "the cess-pool of Europe under the pretense that it is the asylum of the poor." Most Chicago inhabitants in the Gilded Age were foreign-born or the children of the foreign-born, and most English-language Chicago news-papers scorned them. . . . Here, as in the Jersey City *American Standard* (1859) and *The New York Times* (1902), much more was involved than mere ethnic distaste or "nativism." In quite a different connection and in a relatively homogeneous country, the Italian Antonio Gramsci concluded of such evidence that "for a social elite the features of subordinate groups always display something barbaric and pathologi-cal." The changing composition of the American working class may make so severe a dictum more pertinent to the United States than to Italy. Class and ethnic fears and biases combined together to worry elite observers about the diverse worlds below them to distort gravely their perceptions of these worlds. . . .

These pages have fractured historical time, ranging forward and backward, to make comparisons for several reasons. One has been to suggest how much remains to be learned about the transition of native and foreign-born American men and women to industrial society, and how that transition affected such persons and the society into which they entered. "Much of what gets into American literature," Ralph Ellison has shrewdly observed "gets there because so much is left out." That has also been the case in the writing of American working-class history, and the framework and methods suggested here merely hint at what will be known about American workers and American society when the many transitions are studied in detail. Such studies, however, need to focus on the particularities of both the groups involved and the society into which they enter. Transitions differ and de-pend upon the interaction between the two at specific historical moments. But at all times there is a resultant tension. [E. P.] Thompson writes:

> There has never been any single type of "the transition." The stress of the transition falls upon the whole culture: resistance to change and assent to change arise from the whole culture. And this culture includes the systems of power, property-relations, religious in-stitutions, etc., inattention to which merely flattens phenomena and trivializes analysis.

Enough has been savored in these pages to suggest the particular importance of these transitions in American social history. And their recurrence in different pe-riods of time indicates why there has been so much discontinuity in American labor and social history. The changing composition of the working population, the continued entry into the United States of nonindustrial people with distinctive cul-tures, and the changing structure of American society have combined together to produce common modes of thought and patterns of behavior. But these have been experiences disconnected in time and shared by quite distinctive first-generation native and immigrant industrial Americans. It was not possible for the grand-children of the Lowell mill girls to understand that their Massachusetts literary ancestors shared a great deal with their contemporaries, the peasant Slavs in the Pennsylvania steel mills and coals fields. And the grandchildren of New York City Jewish garment workers see little connection between black ghetto unrest in the 1960s and the kosher meat riots seventy years ago. A half-century has passed since Robert Park and Herbert Miller published W. I. Thomas's *Old World Traits Transplanted,* a study which worried that the function of Americanization was the "destruction of memories."

# Asian Immigrants Raising Cane:
# The World of Plantation Hawaii

RONALD TAKAKI

Paralleling the migration of Chinese to California was the movement of Chinese, Japanese, Korean, and Filipino laborers to Hawaii, an American economic colony that became a territory of the United States in 1900. Over 300,000 Asians entered the islands between 1850 and 1920. Brought here as "cheap labor," they filled the requisitions itemizing the needs of the plantations. Their labor enabled the planters to transform sugar production into Hawaii's leading industry. "It is apparent," declared the *Hawaiian Gazette* excitedly in 1877, "that Sugar is destined most emphatically to be "King."" But to be "King" the sugar industry required the constant importation of workers whose increasing numbers led to the ethnic diversification of society in the islands. For example, in 1853, Hawaiians and part-Hawaiians represented 97 percent of the population of 73,137 inhabitants, while Caucasians constituted only 2 percent and Chinese only half a percent. Seventy years later, Hawaiians and part-Hawaiians made up only 16.3 percent of the population, while Caucasians represented 7.7 percent, Chinese 9.2 percent, Japanese 42.7 percent, Portuguese 10.6 percent, Puerto Ricans 2.2 percent, Koreans 1.9 percent, and Filipinos 8.2 percent.

Hawaii was ethnically very different from the mainland. In 1920, Asians totaled 62 percent of the island population, compared to only 3.5 percent of the California population and only 0.17 percent of the continental population. Constituting a majority of the population in Hawaii, Asians were able to choose a different course than their mainland brethren. Powered by "necessity" yet buoyed by "extravagance," they responded in their own unique ways to the world of plantation Hawaii. . . .

Asian immigrants were not prepared for their experiences as plantation workers in Hawaii. They had come from societies where they labored to provide for their families within a context of traditions and established rules and obligations. They had greater control over their time and activities, working with family members and people they knew. "In Japan," a plantation laborer said, "we could say, 'It's okay to take the day off today,' since it was our own work. We were free to do what we wanted. We didn't have that freedom on the plantation. We had to work ten hours every day." The Filipino *tao,* or peasant farmer, followed the rhythm of the day, the weather, and the seasons in the Philippines. He worked in the fields with his wife and children, driving the carabao before him and urging his family workers to keep pace with him. *Hana-hana*—working on the plantation in Hawaii—was profoundly different.

Though laborers still awoke early as they did in the old country, they were now aroused by the loud screams of a plantation siren at five in the morning. . . .

After the 5:00 A.M. plantation whistle had blown, the *lunas* (foremen) and company policemen strode through the camps. "Get up, get up," they shouted as they knocked on the doors of the cottages and the barracks. "Hana-hana, hana-hana, work, work." A Korean remembered the morning her mother failed to hear the work whistle and overslept: "We were all asleep—my brother and his wife, my older sister, and myself. Suddenly the door swung open, and a big burly luna burst in, screaming and cursing, "Get up, get to work." The luna ran around the room, ripping off the covers, not caring whether my family was dressed or not." . . .

"All the workers on a plantation in all their tongues and kindreds, 'rolled out' sometime in the early morn, before the break of day," reported a visitor. One by one and two by two, laborers appeared from "the shadows, like a brigade of ghosts." From an outlying camp, they came on a train, "car after car of silent figures," their cigarettes glowing in the darkness. In front of the mill they lined up, shouldering their hoes. As the sun rose, its rays striking the tall mill stack, "quietly the word was passed from somewhere in the dimness. Suddenly and silently the gang started for its work, dividing themselves with one accord to the four quarters of the compass, each heading toward his daily task." The workers were grouped by the foremen into gangs of twenty to thirty workers and were marched or transported by wagons and trains to the fields. Each gang was watched by a luna, who was "almost always a white man." The ethnicity of the gangs varied. Some of them were composed of one nationality, while others were mixed. One luna said he had workers of all races in his gang, including Hawaiians, Filipinos, Puerto Ricans, Chinese, Japanese, Portuguese, and Koreans.

There were gangs of women workers, too, for women were part of the plantation work force—about 7 percent of all workers in 1894 and 14 percent in 1920. Most of the women workers—over 80 percent of them—were Japanese. Women were concentrated in field operations, such as hoeing, stripping leaves, and harvesting. My grandmother Katsu Okawa was a cane cutter on the Hana Plantation, and my aunt Yukino Takaki was an *hapaiko* worker, or cane loader, on the Puunene Plantation. Though women were given many of the same work assignments as men, they were paid less than their male counterparts. Japanese-female fields hands, for example, received an average wage of only fifty-five cents per day in 1915, compared to the seventy-eight cents. Japanese-male field hands received.

Women also worked in the camps: they washed laundry, cooked, and sewed clothes. "I made custom shirts with hand-bound button holes for 25 cents," recalled a Korean woman. "My mother and sister-in-law took in laundry. They scrubbed, ironed and mended shirts for a nickel a piece. It was pitiful! Their knuckles became swollen and raw from using the harsh yellow soap." On the Hawi Plantation, my grandmother Katsu Okawa operated a boarding house where she fed her husband and eight children as well as fifteen men every day. . . .

The most regimented work was in the fields. "We worked like machines," a laborer complained. "For 200 of us workers, there were seven or eight lunas and above them was a field boss on a horse. We were watched constantly." A Japanese woman, interviewed years later at the age of ninety-one, said: "We had to work in the canefields, cutting cane, being afraid, not knowing the language. When any *haole* [white] or Portuguese luna came, we got frightened and thought we had to work harder or get fired." . . .

One of the most tedious and backbreaking tasks was hoeing weeds. Laborers had to "hoe hoe hoe . . . for four hours in a straight line and no talking," said a worker. "Hoe every weed along the way to your three rows. Hoe—chop chop chop, one chop for one small weed, two for all big ones." They had to keep their bodies bent over. They wanted to stand up and stretch, unknotting twisted bodies and feeling the freedom of arched backs. The laborers cursed the lunas, "talking stink" about the driving pace of the work: "It burns us up to have an ignorant *luna* stand around and holler and swear at us all the time for not working fast enough. Every so often, just to show how good he is, he'll come up and grab a hoe and work like hell for about two minutes and then say sarcastically, 'Why you no work like that?' He knows and we know he couldn't work for ten minutes at that pace." The lunas were just plain mean "buggas." Laborers also did "hole hole" work, the stripping of the dead leaves from the cane stalks. To protect themselves against the needles of the cane leaves, they wore heavy clothing. Still, as they left the fields each day, they found their hands badly cut by the cane leaves. . . .

As they worked, laborers wore *bangos* hanging on chains around their necks—small brass disks with their identification numbers stamped on them. In the old country, they had names, and their names told them who they were, connecting them to family and community; in Hawaii, they were given numbers. The workers resented this new impersonal identity. Laborers were "treated no better than cows or horses," one of them recalled. "Every worker was called by number, never by name." . . .

When the cane was ripe, lunas on horseback led the workers out into the fields to harvest the crop. . . .

Cutting the ripe cane was dirty and exhausting work. As the workers mechanically swung their machetes, they felt the pain of the blisters on their hands and the scratches on their arms. "When you cutting the cane and you pulling the cane back," a worker said, "sometimes you get scratched with the leaves from the cane because they have a little edge just like a saw blade." Their heavy arms, their bent backs begged for a break, a moment of rest. . . .

Twelve feet in height, the cane enclosed and dwarfed the Asian workers. As they cleared the cane "forests," cutting the stalks close to the ground, they felt the heat of the sun, the humidity of the air, and found themselves surrounded by iron red clouds of dust. They covered their faces with handkerchiefs; still they breathed the dust and the mucus they cleared from their noses appeared blood red. "The sugar cane fields were endless and the stalks were twice the height of myself," a Korean woman sighed. "Now that I look back, I thank goodness for the height, for if I had seen how far the fields stretched, I probably would have fainted from knowing how much work was ahead. My waistline got slimmer and my back ached from bending over all the time to cut the sugar cane." . . .

Collecting the cane stalks, the workers tied them into bundles and loaded them onto railway cars. A train then pulled the cane to the mill where engines, presses, furnaces, boilers, vacuum pans, centrifugal drums, and other machines crushed the cane and boiled its juices into molasses and sugar. Inside the mill, laborers like my uncle Nobuyoshi Takaki felt like they were in the "hold of a steamer." The constant loud clanking and whirring of the machinery were deafening. . . .

At four-thirty in the afternoon, the workers again heard the blast of the plantation whistle, the signal to stop working. "Pau hana," they sighed, "finished working." Though they were exhausted and though they thought they were too tired to hoe another row of cane or carry another bundle of stalks, they suddenly felt a final burst of energy and eagerly scrambled to the camps. . . .

Planters claimed they treated their workers with "consideration and humanity," seeking "in every possible way to advance their comfort and make them contented and happy." But their purpose was not entirely humanitarian. Planters understood clearly that it was "good business" to have their laborers "properly fed": it "paid" to have a "contented lot of laborers," for they would then be able to extract a "good day's work" from them.

The paternalism of the planters was also intended to defuse the organizing efforts of the workers. A plantation manager explained how laborers were "capable of comprehending the difference between kind words, kind acts, kind wages generally and ruffian roughness and abuse." Paternalism was designed to pacify labor unrest. "We should avail to get our house in order before a storm breaks," planters told themselves. "Once the great majority of the laboring classes are busy under conditions which breed contentment . . . we can expect a gradual and effectual diminution of the power of the agitating [labor] element." Planters agreed that "humanity in industry pays."

Plantation paternalism also served to maintain a racial and class hierarchy. White plantation managers and foremen supervised Asians, constituting 70 to 85 percent of the work force. They saw their role as "parental" and described Koreans as "childlike" and Filipinos as "more or less like children" "by nature." The vice president of H. Hackfield and Company sent managers a circular informing them that the Filipino was "very incapable of caring for himself." Left entirely to his own resources, the Filipino was likely to spend his money on "fancy groceries" and consequently to be insufficiently nourished. Managers should "look after" Filipino laborers. Planters explained their paternalism in terms of white racial superiority. They had spread "Caucasian civilization" to Hawaii, where they as members of "a stronger race" had to supervise and care for Asian and Hawaiian laborers. "Where there is a drop of the Anglo-Saxon blood, it is sure to rule."

Behind paternalism was the "necessity" of coercion. Planters believed that they should control their workers with "the strong hand." "There is one word which holds the lower classes . . . in check," they declared, "and that is Authority." The plantation organization resembled a system of military discipline. . . .

As "generals," plantation managers devised an intricate system of rules and regulations for their "troops." They required their workers to be "industrious and docile and obedient," "regular and cleanly in their personal habits," punctual for work and rest, and present on the plantation at all times. To punish workers for violating the rules, planters developed an elaborate system of fines, which specified a charge for virtually every kind of misconduct. . . .

Where fines did not work, harsher penalties were employed. Asked how he would punish a contract laborer for idleness, a planter replied: "We dock him; we give him one one-half or three-quarters of a day of wages; and if he keeps it up we resort to the law and have him arrested for refusing to work." Sometimes planters used physical punishment to intimidate the workers. Chinese workers on the Olawalu Plantation were allowed five to fifteen minutes for lunch and were "kicked" if they did not return promptly to work. . . . The Hawaiian government had outlawed whipping, but the law did not always reflect reality. . . . A worker graphically described the tiered structure of strict supervision: "Really, life on the plantation is one of restrictions, unwritten rules and regulations imposed upon the inhabitants by the manager who is assisted by his various ranks of overseers and lunas to see to it that the people obey these regulations and do the amount and nature of the work that is expected of them. . . . In conclusion I say that life on a plantation is much like life in a prison."

To strengthen their authority over their ethnically diverse work force, planters developed an occupational structure stratifying employment according to race. Skilled and supervisory positions were predominantly occupied by whites. In 1882, for example, 88 percent of all lunas and clerks were white, while 28.5 percent of the laborers were Hawaiian and 48.3 percent were Chinese. None of the lunas were Chinese. In 1904, the Hawaiian Sugar Planters' Association passed a resolution that restricted skilled positions to "American citizens, or those eligible for citizenship." This restriction had a racial function: it excluded Asians from skilled occupations. They were not "white" according to federal law and hence ineligible to become naturalized citizens. In 1915, Japanese laborers were mostly field hands and mill laborers. There were only one Japanese, one Hawaiian, and two part-Hawaiian mill engineers; the remaining forty-one mill engineers (89 percent) were of European ancestry. A racial division was particularly evident in supervisory positions: of the 377 overseers, only two were Chinese and seventeen Japanese; 313 of all overseers, (83 percent) were white. . . .

After federal law terminated the contract-labor system in 1900, planters used their centralized organization, the Hawaiian Sugar Planters' Association, to institute mechanisms to keep wages low. In a "Confidential Letter" to plantation managers on July 24, 1901, the association called for island conventions of managers to form wage-fixing agreements: "The deliberations of Island conventions at which managers would meet should be behind closed doors as it would be embarrassing to have such proceedings published." To carry out this plan, the association established a central labor bureau to coordinate all employment of Asian laborers and to set wage rates. Laborers were warned they should not try to leave their assigned plantations to bargain for higher wages, for they would not be hired by another plantation unless they could show a certificate of discharge. To provide incentives for their workers to increase their productivity, the association introduced a "bonus system" in 1910. . . . But the bonus also kept the workers from leaving the plantation. The bonus was paid only once a year, and workers forfeited it if they left the plantation before bonus time. . . .

To control their workers, planters tied other "strings." They utilized a multitiered wage system, paying different wage rates to different nationalities for the same work. Japanese cane cutters, for example, were paid ninety-nine cents a day, while Filipino cane cutters received only sixty-nine cents. Planters also cultivated nationalistic consciousness among the laborers in order to divide them. They appealed to the "race pride" of the Filipino laborers to urge them to work as hard as the Japanese laborers. One Filipino work-gang leader, giving instructions in Ilocano, declared to his men: "We are all Filipinos, brothers. We all know how to hoe. So, let's do a good job and show the people of other nations what we can do. Let us not shame our skin!" The planters' divide-and-control strategy promoted interethnic tensions that sometimes erupted into fistfights in the fields and riots in the camps. On the Spreckelsville Plantation on Maui in 1898, for example, three hundred Japanese, wielding sticks and clubs, drove a hundred Chinese laborers from the camps. A year later, during a riot involving Chinese and Japanese workers on the Kahuku Plantation on Oahu, sixty Chinese were wounded and four killed.

But the plantation workers did not concentrate their discontent against each other; rather, they usually directed their rage outward against their bosses and the system, seeking to gain greater control over the conditions of their labor and a greater share of the profits they had produced. Not passive and docile as the managers wanted them to be, they actively struggled to improve the quality of their lives on the plantation in many different ways.

Occasionally workers fought back violently. They retaliated against mean overseers for physical abuse and mistreatment. Numerous instances of workers assaulting and beating up cruel and unfair lunas can be found in the records. On a Maui plantation in 1903, for example, after an Irish luna had hit a laborer, he was attacked by a gang of Chinese workers and buried under a ten-foot pile of cane stalks. In 1904, on the Waipahu Plantation, two hundred Korean laborers mobbed the plantation physicians, claiming he had killed a Korean patient with a kick to the abdomen. Sometimes workers aimed their anger at property, especially the dry cane fields that were easy targets for arson. After the police had broken up a demonstration of protesting Chinese laborers on the Waianae Plantation in 1899, a fire swept through its cane fields.

But while planters worried about direct labor resistance, they also had to watch for subtle and ingenious actions. . . .

. . . Everywhere workers engaged in day-to-day resistance, trying to minimize the amount of labor their bosses extracted from them. Many workers feigned illness in order to be released from work. . . . Laborers became skilled practitioners in the art of pretending to be working. On the Kohala Plantation on the island of Hawaii, a luna discovered that supervising Japanese women in the fields could be frustrating. In his diary, supervisor Jack Hall complained: "It always seemed impossible to keep them together, especially if the fields were not level. The consequence was that these damsels were usually scattered all over the place and as many as possible were out of sight in the gulches or dips in the field where they could not be seen, where they would calmly sit and smoke their little metal pipes until the luna appeared on the skyline, when they would be busy as bees."

To escape from work and daily drudgery, sliding numbly into recalcitrance, many plantation laborers resorted to drugs—opium and alcohol. . . . A Filipino worker remembered how "drinks were readily available because just about everyone knew how to make 'swipe wine.' You just ferment molasses with water and yeast and in a week it's ready. And if you distilled that, you got clear liquor ten times stronger than any gin you could buy from the store."

Planters complained that the use of drugs made it "impossible" to get from their laborers "anything like a fair day's work." "No employees can drink booze and do six honest days' work in a week," managers grumbled. . . . After saturating themselves with opium or alcohol on the weekends, laborers were "unfit for work" on Monday. Inspecting the camps on Mondays, plantation managers sometimes found a third of their men "dead drunk."

Drugs eased, perhaps made more bearable, the emptiness plantation laborers felt on the weekends as well as the boredom of their meaningless and routine work during the week. "There was very little to do when work was over," recalled a

Chinese laborer, "and the other fellows who were having a good time smoking asked me to join them, so then in order to be a good sport I took up opium smoking, not realizing that I would probably have to die with it." "If we don't smoke," another Chinese worker said, "we feel as if something were gnawing at our insides. The opium fumes will drive away that feeling and lift us out of our misery into a heaven of blissful rest and peace." Momentarily at least, drugs enabled workers to escape the reality of the plantation and to enter a dream world where they could hear again the voices of fathers, mothers, and other loved ones. . . .

But drugs were self-destructive and offered only temporary euphoria, and plantation workers often sought a more permanent form of escape—*ha'alele hana,* desertion from service. Until Hawaii became a U.S. territory in 1900, the contract-labor system was legal in the islands and plantation laborers under contract were bound by law to serve three-to-five-year terms. . . . Thousands of contract laborers fled from their assigned plantations before the completion of their contracts. In 1892, Marshal Charles B. Wilsom calculated that 5,706 arrests, or one third of the total arrests made between 1890 and 1892, were for desertion.

Planters constantly worried about their contract laborers running away. "On the island of Maui," the *Pacific Commercial Advertiser* observed in 1880, "scarcely a day passes which does not bring along some member of the police force in search of absconding Chinese plantation laborers, who are making quite a business of shipping [signing a labor contract], drawing large advances, and then 'clearing out' causing their employers much inconvenience and expense." . . .

. . . Generally staying on the plantations only as long as they were required by their contracts, Chinese workers moved in search of better employment opportunities. Many became rice farmers, making the swamplands yield rich harvests, and others settled in nearby villages and opened small stores. "My grandfather Len Wai worked on a plantation and operated a store during after-work hours," stated Raymond Len. "The store did well and he went full time into it after his contract was up." Most Chinese ex-plantation laborers went to Honolulu, where they lived in a bustling Chinatown.

Thousands of Japanese workers also left the plantations after their contracts had been fulfilled. . . . After annexation and the prohibition of contract labor in the Territory of Hawaii, laborers were no longer bound to the plantations, and planters anxiously witnessed an exodus of Japanese laborers to the mainland. In their camps, Japanese workers read circulars and advertisements about higher wages in California. In 1906 the *Hawaiian Star* reported: "The 'American fever,' as it is called among the Japs, appears to be causing a lot of agitation among them. Local Japanese papers contain the advertisement of Hasagawa, who recently got a license to solicit laborers, calling for 2,000 Japanese to go to the coast at once. The advertisement offers wages of from $1.35 per day up, stating that men who are good can make from $2 to $4 per day." In their efforts to stem the Japanese movement to the mainland, planters asked the Japanese Consul in Hawaii to issue circulars in Japanese instructing Japanese laborers to remain on the plantation. In 1903 the consul urged his countrymen to "stay at work steadily on the plantations and not go to an uncertainty on the mainland." Ignoring the consul's advice, Japanese laborers continued to migrate to the mainland in search of the highest bidder for their labor. By early 1907, 40,000 Japanese had left Hawaii for the West Coast.

But in March President Theodore Roosevelt suddenly issued an executive order prohibiting the passage of Japanese from Hawaii to the mainland. . . . At a mass meeting in Honolulu, Japanese laborers angrily denounced Roosevelt's restriction: "It enslaves us permanently to Hawaii's capitalists!" Trapped by law in Hawaii, Japanese workers saw they had no choice but to struggle for a better life in the islands.

Most of them saw that the struggle would have to be a collective one, and that their most powerful weapon was the strike. But they also realized the planters had the power to retaliate brutally. Past experiences had taught them some harsh lessons. In 1891, for example, two hundred striking Chinese laborers had protested unfair deductions from their wages and marched to the courthouse in Kapaau on the island of Hawaii. The plantation managers ordered them to return to their camps; late in the afternoon, the strikers left the courthouse. But as they were walking back to the camps, they were confronted by policemen armed with bullock whips. In fear, one or two of the strikers stooped to pick up stones. Suddenly, according to a newspaper report, the Chinese strikers found themselves "in the midst of a general onslaught," and were, "ruthlessly overridden and welted with the bullock whips." Pursuing the fleeing Chinese strikers, the policemen attacked the Chinese camp. They "demolished every window, strewed the premises inside and out with stones, seized every Chinaman they came across, and yanked forty or more by their queues. . . . Chinamen were seen with their tails twisted about the pommel of a saddle, dragged at a gallop."

Planters believed their repression of strikes had been justifiable because contract laborers could not legally strike; they were bound by contract to work for a specified term of years and could be arrested and punished in the courts for violating the agreement. But the Organic Act of 1900, which established Hawaii as a territory of the United States on June 14, abolished the contract-labor system.

Months before the Organic Act took effect, plantation workers anticipated their freedom. On April 4, Japanese workers in Lahaina struck. Upset over the deaths of three mill hands who had been crushed under a collapsed sugar pan, the laborers blamed management carelessness for the accident and refused to work. The strikers seized the mill and the town. For ten days, they defiantly "continued to meet, to parade in the town under Japanese flags, to drill, and even, unhindered by anyone, demolished the house and property of a store clerk who would not give them credit." . . .

In 1900, over twenty strikes swept through the plantations as 8,000 workers withheld their labor from the bosses. While the strikes were led and supported mainly by Japanese workers, two of them involved inter-ethnic cooperation. On June 22, Chinese and Japanese laborers on the Puehuehu Plantation struck to protest the retention of part of their wages, a provision contained in their original labor contracts. Five months later, forty-three Japanese and Portuguese women field hands on the Kilauea Plantation demanded that wages be raised from eight dollars to ten dollars a month. Though the striking women were locked out by the management, they stood together and won their wage increases.

After 1900, management-labor conflict became even more intense. As they organized themselves and initiated strike actions, workers found themselves facing the power of the state. This occurred during the 1906 Waipahu Plantation strike. Demanding higher wages, Japanese laborers struck, and plantation manager E. K. Bull immediately requested police assistance. Forty-seven policemen armed with rifles were assigned to the plantation. They functioned as Bull's private army. The policemen marched in review on the plantation grounds to intimidate the strikers with a show of force; patrolling the camps, they stopped and questioned all stragglers. During a tense moment of the negotiations, Bull threatened to use the police to evict the strikers from their homes in the camps. Unintimidated, the seventeen hundred Japanese strikers forced Bull to grant concessions in order to end the strike.

The Waipahu Plantation strike of 1906 underscored the importance of collective labor action. Labor violence and arson were individualistic as well as sporadic actions; they did not seriously undermine planter control. Recalcitrance and drunkenness represented resistance but did not change conditions in the workplace. Desertion enabled dissatisfied workers to escape, leaving intact the mechanisms of planter discipline and regimentation. But striking constituted a particularly effective expression of labor resistance, for it could lead to a positive transformation of the plantation structure. Moreover, striking could enable men and women of various nationalities to gain a deeper understanding of themselves as laborers, to develop a working-class identity and consciousness.

Divided by the political strategy of the planters and by their diverse national identities, workers initially tended to define their class interests in terms of their ethnicity. Thus, at first they organized themselves into "blood unions"—labor organizations based on ethnic membership: the Japanese belonged to the Japanese union and the Filipinos to the Filipino union.

The most important manifestation of "blood unionism" was the Japanese strike of 1909. Protesting against the differential-wage system based on ethnicity, the strikers demanded higher wages and equal pay for equal work. They noted angrily how Portuguese laborers were paid $22.50 per month while Japanese laborers earned only eighteen dollars a month for the same kind of work. "The wage is a reward for services done," they argued, "and a just wage is that which compensates the laborer to the full value of the service rendered by him. . . . If a laborer comes from Japan and he performs the same quantity of work of the same quality within the same period of time as those who hail from the opposite side of the world, what good reason is there to discriminate one as against the other? It is not the color of the skin that grows cane in the field. It is labor that grows cane." The Japanese strikers struggled for four long months. The strike involved 7,000 Japanese plantation laborers on Oahu, and thousands of Japanese workers on the other islands supported their striking compatriots, sending them money and food. Japanese business organizations such as the Honolulu Retail Merchants' Association contributed financially to the strike fund, and the Japanese Physicians' Association gave free medical service to the strikers and their families. A strong sense of Japanese ethnic solidarity inspired the strikers. Stridently shouting banzai at rallies, they affirmed their commitment to the spirit of Japan—*yamato damashii*. They told themselves they must "stick together" as Japanese to win the strike.

The strike reflected a new consciousness among Japanese workers, a transformation from sojourners to settlers, from Japanese to Japanese Americans. In their demand for a higher wage, the strikers explained: "We have decided to permanently settle here, to incorporate ourselves with the body politique [sic] of Hawaii—to unite our destiny with that of Hawaii, sharing the prosperity and adversity of

Hawaii with other citizens of Hawaii." Gradually becoming settled laborers, they now had families to support, children to educate, and religious institutions to maintain. Hawaii was becoming home for the Japanese laborers, and they asked what kind of home Hawaii would be for them. The strikers argued that the unsatisfactory and deplorable conditions on the plantations perpetuated an "undemocratic and un-American," class-divided society of "plutocrats and coolies." Such a pattern of social inequality was injurious to Hawaii in general. Fair wages would encourage laborers to work more industriously and productively, and Hawaii would enjoy "perpetual peace and prosperity." The goal of the strike was to make possible the formation of "a thriving and contented middle class—the realization of the high ideal of Americanism."

But the planters pressured the government to arrest the Japanese strike leaders for "conspiracy." Then they broke the strike by hiring Koreans, Hawaiians, Chinese, and Portuguese as scabs and began importing massive numbers of Filipinos to counterbalance the Japanese laborers. Three months after the strike, however, the planters eliminated the differential-wage system and raised the wages of the Japanese workers.

An ethnically based strike seemed to make good political sense to Japanese plantation laborers in 1909, for they constituted about 70 percent of the entire work force. Filipinos represented less than one percent. But the very ethnic solidarity of the Japanese made it possible for planters to use laborers of other nationalities to break the "Japanese" strike. Eleven years later, Japanese workers found that they had been reduced proportionately to only 44 percent of the labor force, while Filipino workers had been increased to 30 percent. Organized into separate unions, workers of both nationalities came to realize that the labor movement in Hawaii and their strike actions would have to be based on interethnic working-class unity.

In December of 1919, the Japanese Federation of Labor and the Filipino Federation of Labor submitted separate demands to the Hawaiian Sugar Planters' Association. The workers wanted higher wages, an eight-hour-day, an insurance fund for old retired employees, and paid maternity leaves. Their demands were promptly rejected by the planters. The Japanese Federation of Labor immediately asked the managers to reconsider their decision and agreed to declare a strike after all peaceful methods had been tried. The Japanese leaders knew there was "no other way but to strike." "Let's rise and open the eyes of the capitalists," they declared. "Let's cooperate with the Filipinos"—"back them up with our fund" and "our whole force." The Japanese leaders thought both labor federations should not act precipitously, however. Rather, both unions should prepare for a long strike and plan a successful strategy.

But the Filipino Federation of Labor felt the time for action had arrived. Consequently, on January 19, 1920, Pablo Manlapit, head of the Filipino union, unilaterally issued an order for the Filipinos to strike and urged the Japanese to join them. In his appeal to the Japanese Federation of Labor, Manlapit eloquently called for inter-ethnic working-class solidarity: "This is the opportunity that the Japanese should grasp, to show that they are in harmony with and willing to cooperate with other nationalities in this territory, concerning the principles of organized labor. . . . We should work on this strike shoulder to shoulder."

Meanwhile, 3,000 Filipino workers on the plantations of Oahu went out on strike. They set up picket lines and urged Japanese laborers to join them. "What's the matter? Why you hanahana [work]?" the Filipino strikers asked their Japanese co-workers. Several Japanese newspapers issued clarion calls for Japanese cooperation with the striking Filipinos. The *Hawaii Shimpo* scolded Japanese workers for their hesitation: "Our sincere and desperate voices are also their voices. Their righteous indignation is our righteous indignation. . . . Fellow Japanese laborers! Don't be a race of unreliable dishonest people! Their problem is your problem!" . . . On January 26, the Japanese Federation of Labor ordered the strike to begin on February 1. United in struggle, 8,300 Filipino and Japanese strikers—77 percent of the entire plantation work force on Oahu—brought plantation operations to a sudden stop. . . .

Aware of the seriousness of the challenge they faced and determined to break the strike, planters quickly turned to their time-tested strategy of divide and control. The president of C. Brewer and Company, one of the corporate owners of the sugar plantations, informed a plantation manager: "We are inclined to think that the best prospect, in connection with this strike, is the fact that two organizations, not entirely in harmony with each other, are connected with it, and if either of them falls out of line, the end will be in sight." The planters isolated the Filipino leadership from the Japanese Federation of Labor and created distrust between the two unions. They offered Manlapit a bribe, and suddenly, to the surprise of both the Filipino and Japanese strikers. Manlapit called off the strike, condemning it as a Japanese action to cripple the industries of Hawaii. But, on the rank-and-file level, many Filipinos continued to remain on strike with the Japanese. Escalating their attack on the Japanese, the planters slandered the Japanese strikers as puppets of Japan and claimed they were seeking to "Japanise" the islands. . . .

To break the strike directly, planters enlisted Hawaiians, Portuguese, and Koreans as strikebreakers. They knew that Koreans had a particular enmity for the Japanese, and the planters had consistently used Koreans to help break Japanese strikes. During the 1920 strike, Korean laborers under the leadership of the Korean National Association announced: "We place ourselves irrevocably against the Japanese and the present strike. We don't wish to be looked upon as strikebreakers, but we shall continue to work . . . and we are opposed to the Japanese in everything." More than one hundred Korean men and women organized themselves into a Strikebreakers' Association and offered their services to the Hawaiian Sugar Planters' Association.

Planters served forty-eight-hour eviction notices to the strikers forcing them to leave their homes and find shelters in empty lots in Honolulu. Crowded into encampments during the height of the influenza epidemic, thousands of workers and their family members fell ill and 150 died. . . . Under such punishing and chaotic conditions, the strikers could not hold out indefinitely and were compelled to call off the strike in July.

Though they had been soundly beaten, the workers had learned a valuable lesson from the 1920 strike. Filipinos and Japanese, joined by Spanish, Portuguese, and Chinese laborers, had participated in the first major interethnic working-class struggle in Hawaii. Men and women of different ethnicities, realizing how the 5:00 A.M. whistle had awakened all of them and how they had labored together in the fields and mills, had fought together for a common goal. And as they walked the picket lines and protested at mass rallies together, they understood more deeply the contribution they had made as workers to the transformation of Hawaii into a wealthy and profitable place.

During the strike, as the workers reached for a new unity transcending ethnic boundaries, leaders of the Japanese Federation of Labor questioned the existence of two separate unions—one for the Japanese and one for the Filipinos—and suggested the consolidation of the two federations into one union. They insisted that Japanese workers must affiliate with Filipino, "American," and Hawaiian workers, for as long as all of them were laborers they should mutually cooperate in safeguarding their standard of living. On April 23, the Japanese Federation of Labor decided to become an interracial union and to call the organization the Hawaii Laborers' Association— a new name trumpeting a feeling of multiethnic class camaraderie.

One of the leaders of the Hawaii Laborers' Association articulated this new and developing class perspective. The fact that the "capitalists" were "haoles" and the laborers Japanese and Filipinos was a "mere coincidence," explained Takashi Tsutsumi. Japanese and Filipinos had acted as "laborers" in "a solid body" during the 1920 strike. What the workers had learned from their struggle, Tsutsumi continued, was the need to build "a big, powerful and non-racial labor organization" that could "effectively cope with the capitalists." Such a union would bring together "laborers of all nationalities." The 1920 strike had provided the vision—the basis for a new union: in this struggle, Japanese and Filipino workers had cooperated against the planter class. "This is the feature that distinguishes the recent movement from all others." Tsutsumi observed. "There is no labor movement that surpasses the recent movement of Japanese and Filipinos." Tsutsumi predicted that a "big" interracial union would emerge within ten years springing from a "Hawaiian-born" leadership. "When that day comes," he concluded, "the strike of 1920 would surely by looked upon as most significant."

# ❖ *F U R T H E R    R E A D I N G*

Bao, Xiaolan. *Holding Up More Than Half the Sky: Chinese Women Garment Workers in New York City, 1948–92* (2001).

Barnett, James. *Work and Community in the Jungle: Chicago's Packinghouse Workers, 1894–1922* (1987).

Bodnar, John. *Workers' World: Kinship, Community and Protest in an Industrial Society* (1982).

Bodnar, John, Roger Simon, and Michael P. Weber. *Lives of Their Own: Black, Italians, and Poles in Pittsburgh, 1900–1960* (1982).

Camarillo, Albert. *Chicanos in a Changing Society: From Mexican Pueblos to Americans Barrios in Santa Barbara and Southern California, 1848–1930* (1979).

Cardosa, Lawrence. *Mexican Emigration to the United States, 1897–1931* (1980).

Cumbler, John. *Working-Class Community in Industrial America: Work, Leisure and Struggle in Two Industrial Cities (1979).*

Curtin, Mary Ellen. *Black Prisoners and Their World: Alabama, 1865–1900* (2000).

Deutsch, Sarah. *No Separate Refuge: Culture, Class, and Gender on an Anglo-Hispanic Frontier in the American Southwest, 1880–1940* (1987).

Diner, Hasia. *Erin's Daughters in America* (1983).

Foley, Neil. *The White Scourge: Mexicans, Blacks, and Poor Whites in Texas Cotton Culture* (1997).

Gabaccia, Donna R. *From Italy to Elizabeth Street* (1983).

Garcia, Mario. *Desert Immigrants: The Mexicans of El Paso, 1880–1920* (1981).

Glenn, Evelyn Nakano. *Issei, Nisei, War Bride: Three Generations of Japanese American Women in Domestic Service* (1986).

Gordon, Linda. *The Great Arizona Orphan Abduction* (1999).

Grossman, James. *Land of Hope: Chicago, Black Southerners, and the Great Migration* (1989).

Guerin-Gonzales, Camille. *Mexican Workers and American Dreams: Immigration, Repatriation, and California Farm Labor, 1900–1939* (1996).

Gutman, Herbert. *Power and Culture: Essays on the American Working Class* (1987).

———. *Work, Culture, and Society in Industrializing America* (1976).

Hahamovitch, Cindy. *The Fruits of Their Labor: Atlantic Coast Farmworkers and the Making of Migrant Poverty, 1870–1945* (1997).

Hareven, Tamara K. *Family Time and Industrial Time: The Relationship Between Family and Work in a New England Industrial Community* (1982).

Holt, Sharon Ann. *Making Freedom Pay: North Carolina Freedpeople Working for Themselves, 1865–1900* (2000).

Jones, Jacqueline. *The Dispossessed: American's Underclass from the Civil War to the Present* (1992).

———. *Labor of Love, Labor of Sorrow: Black Women, Work, and the Family from Slavery to the Present* (1985).

Katzman, David M. *Seven Days a Week: Women and Domestic Service in Industrializing America* (1978).

Korman, Gerd. *Industrialization, Immigrants, and Americanizers: The View from Milwaukee* (1967).

Letwin, Daniel. *The Challenge of Interracial Unionism: Alabama Coal Miners, 1878–1921* (1998).

Lewis, Earl. *In Their Own Interests: Race, Class, and Power in Twentieth-Century Norfolk, Virginia* (1991).

Moore, Barrington. *Social Origins of Dictatorship and Democracy: Lord and Peasant in the Making of the Modern World* (1966).

Ortiz, Altagracia, ed. *Puerto Rican Women and Work: Bridges in Transnational Labor* (1996).

Peck, Gunter. *Reinventing Free Labor: Padrone and Immigrant Workers in the North American West, 1880–1930* (2000).

Phillips, Kimberley. *Alabama North: African-American Migrants, Community, and Working-Class Activism in Cleveland, 1915–1945* (2000).

Piore, Michael J. *Birds of Passage: Migrant Labor and Industrial Societies* (1979).

Smith, Judith K. *Family Connections: A History of Italian and Jewish Immigrant Lives in Providence, Rhode Island* (1985).

Trotter, Joe W., Jr. *Black Milwaukee: The Making of an Industrial Proletariat, 1915–45* (1985).

Trotter, Joe W., Jr., and Earl Lewis, eds. *African Americans in the Industrial Age: A Documentary History, 1915–1945* (1996).

Vargas, Zaragosa. *Proletarians of the North: A History of Mexican Industrial Workers in Detroit and the Midwest, 1917–1933* (1993).

Walker, Melissa. *All We Knew Was to Farm: Rural Women in the Upcountry South, 1919–1941* (2000).

Yans-McLaughlin, Virginia. *Family and Community: Italian Immigrants in Buffalo, 1880–1930* (1977).

Zamora, Emilio. *The World of the Mexican Worker in Texas* (1995).

Zunz, Olivier. *The Changing Face of Inequality: Urbanization, Industrial Development, and Immigrants in Detroit* (1982).

# CHAPTER
## 7

# Cultures of the Workplace

✣

*Men and women bring to the workplace a set of deeply ingrained ideas and prac-
tices that shape their expectations and values when they get there. In recent years,
historians have become much more attuned to such cultural norms and constructed
identities, both inside their place of work and without. Influenced by cultural studies
and new scholarship on gender and race, labor historians pay almost as much attention to the dress, language, and leisure-time activities of workers as they do to their
pay, unions, strikes, and political activities. The workplace hierarchy established by
management has structured much of daily routine, but so too has the particular
work cultures of those employed, who carve out a relatively autonomous sphere of
action on the job, a realm of informal, customary values and rules that are changed
only slowly as one generation of workers merges into the next.*

*Of course, the range of such work cultures is enormously varied, and some are
far more pleasant and communal than others. The single greatest factor determining
the character of a work culture may well be the predominant gender in the work
force. Men and women often bring their own culture-bound expectations to the job
and socialize in different ways. Meanwhile, the organization of the work and the
technology of production structure the kinds of informal associations that one
worker can make with another. Thus the friendship pattern of a department-store
clerk might be quite different from that of a garment worker, not to mention a coal
miner. The vital cooperation of a longshore gang might evoke a sense of solidarity
far greater than the more individualized work practices of a long-haul truck driver
or computer programmer.*

*A focus on work culture and worker cultures prompts us to ask several questions.
What kinds of informal rules and behavioral norms guide the interaction among
workers and between employees and their supervisors, customers, and the general
public? Under what circumstances have informal mechanisms restricted the pace
and output of labor and socialized newcomers to the job? How have worker efforts to
resist or accommodate managerial demands become institutionalized through trade
unions, company employment policies, and off-the-job voluntary associations? How
do conceptions of manhood and womanhood define worker consciousness, political
activism, and the overall world of work? Why are most occupations sex segmented?
And to what extent have work cultures based on skill and a common working
environment, or on a shared popular culture, transcended the antagonisms of
gender, race, and ethnicity?*

In Document 1, United Mine Workers of America leader John Brophy recalls the work tradition and code of ethics that enabled him and his workmates to face the dangers inherent in early-twentieth-century coal mining. Unionized coal miners were proud of their autonomy and power at the point of production itself. But resistance to managerial authority was not limited to unionized workers. In Document 2, Antioch student Stanley Mathewson, describes how machinists, errand boys, and department-store clerks were among the wide range of employees who successfully deflected the supervisor's effort to increase the pace of production, thereby establishing an easier work routine and higher rate of pay. In response, many managers turned to the ideas of Frederick Taylor, often called the father of "scientific management," who distilled some of his most important ideas in a 1915 speech, reprinted here as Document 3. By then Taylor had become something of a cult figure among both industrial managers and certain Progressives, who believed that a socially informed, scientifically managed workplace might well transform working-class aspirations and thus ameliorate class antagonism.

Documents 4–6 reflect the tensions that arose out of the presence of women in a largely male work force and labor movement. In Document 4, published in 1897, prominent Boston craft unionist Edward O'Donnell argues for the exclusion of women workers from the industrial employment that he believes "must gradually unsex them." Document 5, Miriam Finn Scott's account of the triumphant conclusion of the 1909 garment workers' strike, demonstrates that women have a capacity for struggle and organization denied by O'Donnell. Finally, in Document 6, Alice Henry of the Women's Trade Union League argues that because of male sexism, and because of their own particular needs and aspirations, women workers need their own trade union locals.

## 1. Miner John Brophy Learns His Trade, 1907

I got a thrill at the thought of having an opportunity to go and work in the mine, to go and work alongside of my father. After . . . I got experience and some strength, and the ability to work with a little skill, I was conscious of the fact that my father was a good workman; that he had a pride in his calling. At that time all pit mining was hand work, as it were. But he not only was concerned with seeing that his rib—the left side of his workplace, which was known as the rib—was trimmed clean and clear so that he kept a straight line, as it were, cut just like a brick wall. Alongside the rib, paralleling it, would be the roadway on which the cars came to be loaded.

It was a great satisfaction to me that my father was a skilled, clean workman with everything kept in shape, and the timbering done well—all of these things: the rib side, the roadway, the timbering, the fact that you kept the loose coal clean rather than cluttered all over the workplace, the skill with which you undercut the vein, the judgment in drilling the coal after it had been undercut and placing the exact amount of explosive so that it would do an effective job of breaking the coal from the solid—indicated the quality of his work—it was all these things. . . .

From John Brophy, *Memoir,* Columbia Oral History Collection (1955), 95–104.

[I]t was skill in handling the pick and the shovel, the placing of timbers, and understanding the vagaries of the workplace—which is subject to certain pressures from the overhanging strata as you advance into the seam. It's an awareness of roof conditions. And it's something else too. Under the older conditions of mining under which I went to work with my father, the miner exercised considerable freedom in his working place in determining his work pace and the selection of the order of time in the different work operations. Judgment was everywhere along the line, and there was also necessary skill. It was the feel of all this. You know that another workman in another place was a good miner, a passable miner, or an indifferent one. . . .

While he had all that independence and exercise of individual judgment in his work, it's not to say that that was the total situation for the miner, because there are over-all control situations in the total mine system. There was the flow and distribution of mine cars, which constitute a turn of cars—that is, a share of work opportunity by which the miner earns his day's wages, because he was paid by the ton. That has an over-all controlling influence on him. He must meet this turn of the cars or his earnings declined. Also, unless there are very good reasons, such as adverse conditions developing in the workplace, he is inclined to lose face with his fellow workers if he misses his turn because of poor workmanship.

It's true too that many of the dangers in the mine are local and individual to the miner. That is, they occur in his working place. No one can safeguard him but himself using his own judgment in securing proper safeguards.

There are other conditions, like the matter of ventilation. If ventilation is poor, then all the miners are affected. If ventilation is bad, then of course, the distress becomes evident and there is considerable disturbance among the men and an attempt to do something about it. In the case of gas explosions, in mines where there are explosive gases, a small pocket of gas is ignited by a naked light or by the black powder explosive used to shatter the coal. It may be that they light just a small pocket of gas and create no danger, so that it just burns out the gas. But quite often the area of gas is so extensive that when ignited it has a widespread effect—that is, the violence of the explosion may kill not only the people in the workplace but others in the entire mine area. Such an explosion, if extensive, shatters the ventilating system, then after-damp follows, the poisonous residue left from the igniting of the gas, with all the oxygen burned out—suffocates the people that are left alive. . . .

The miner is always aware of danger, that he lives under dangerous conditions in the workplace, because he's constantly uncovering new conditions as he advances in the workingplace, exposing new areas of roof; discovering some weakened condition or break which may bring some special danger. There is also the danger that comes from a piece of coal slipping off the fast and falling on the worker as he lays prone on the bottom doing his cutting. The worker has got to be aware of all these conditions that may be in coal, that may be in the roof.

Then there is this over-all condition which controls his life. . . . It's an awareness of danger in all its various aspects and the recognition that in some of the larger areas of operation in the mine proper he must cooperate with his fellows at the price of life or to ward off or guard against danger. These are the peculiar complexes of the miner: he's a highly individualized worker—I'm speaking of the miner of my day and previous generations—who exercises a great deal of individual initiative in doing his work, in safeguarding himself in his individual workplace. He also must be concerned with his fellows in the larger aspects—the total mine—and he must be prepared to aid his fellows in time of danger. Everything else stops where there's danger. You react to the call for assistance at the moment when assistance may be required because while it may be somebody else today, it may be you tomorrow.

Then there is the further fact that the miner by and large lived in purely mining communities which were often isolated. They developed a group loyalty under all these circumstances. They were both individualists and they were group conscious. They had individual concerns and loyalties but they also had group concerns and group loyalties. It made them an extraordinary body of workers, these miners, because of these very special conditions, because involved in it was not only earning a livelihood, but a matter of health and safety, life and death were involved in every way. You find time and again miners, in an effort to rescue their fellow workers, taking chances which quite often meant death for themselves in an effort to rescue somebody else. . . .

Along with that is a sense of justice. There was the very fact that the miner was a tonnage worker and that he could be short weighed and cheated in various ways, and the only safeguard against it was organization. In that case it was important to have a representative of the miners to see that the weight was properly done and properly credited to the individual miner. There was the whole complex of circumstances that had been in the mining industry for generations which had been their experience. The miner in my day in the United States was aware that all knowledge didn't start with his generation, and that back of it were generations of other miners in other parts of the world, who had similar experiences, who had had their struggles, who had met situations in various ways and who had passed their knowledge on to their children and their children had passed it on.

Take my case. I think I have mentioned before that at least on one side of my family there are at least four generations of miners, and I say this with a sense of pride; very much so. I'm very proud of the fact that there is this long tradition of miners who have struggled with the elements. The nearest thing that I can compare it to—this miner's pride that grows out of his individual skill and his individual need and his cooperative relations with his fellows and his dependency upon the total operation to aid him in his daily output for his earnings—is the sailor. After all, the total operation for the seaman is the ship. He must maintain a certain standard, he must safeguard the ship because that's the element in which he operates, a changeable one. He has individual duties and he achieves individual skill as a sailor. But he must cooperate. There is a difference between a miner and a sailor. One is out on the surface; the other is underneath. The other thing is this, too. The difference is that every day a part of the miner's day is spent in his own small community with his family. It has certain elements of comparison, but there is that fundamental difference—that the miners live on the land in fixed communities and are there every day of the year, whereas the sailor does not. But both are equally dependent upon the good conduct on the operation, on the ship, in the mine. The miner depends upon good mine operation not only for a living but for life itself.

## 2. A Student's View of "Soldiering," 1931

The worker upon entering industry is, of course, first aware of the direct pressure exerted by his fellow-workmen. In fact, a new worker will often practice restriction for a long time for no other reason than that the working group insists upon it. Later, he usually becomes familiar with the underlying causes, the indirect factors which make "regulation," in the eyes of his fellows, necessary.

The cases which follow indicate how potent a factor for restriction the pressure of the group may be. . . .

"Red," a beginner in industry, was working on an assembly line in a phonograph factory, producing small motors, on hourly rate. The line was turning out an average of only 30 motors a day. "Red" found it so easy to keep up his part of the work that he would pile up parts ahead of the next worker in the line. He would then move over and help perform the next operation until the other worker caught up. This went on until "Red" was shifted by the foreman to the final operation in the assembly line. Here he was in a position to work as fast as he liked so far as passing on his completed work was concerned, but he was constantly waiting for the man behind. In order not to appear slow this man had to put through a few more parts, which had its effect all along the assembly line. The process of speeding up developed slowly until the gang, which formerly put through about 30 motors a day, was turning out an average of 120 a day. To "Red's" surprise, the men objected strenuously to this increase, argued with him and even threatened to "meet him in the alley" unless he slowed down his production. "Red" said that when production got up above 100 motors a day the threats became so insistent he began to fear "they might really mean something." However, "Red's" problem was "solved" by his transfer to another department. . . .

Tex, a southern boy, started to work for a mining company. He wanted to go into the mines, but he was too young to be put underground; so he was given a job in the electrical department running a coil-winding machine. He had never run such a machine, but found it quite easy to operate after he had been "shown how." The average output of the coils he was running had been 72 a day. When he began working, Tex knew no better than to make all the coils he could. The first day everything was new, but at the end of the second day he found that he had turned out 90 coils, 18 over the previous average output. If a new boy could produce as many as that on his second day, a much larger number might have been possible as he became better acquainted with his machine. Tex never found out what he might have done, however. He was frightened out of such an effort by two of the older workmen who approached him at the end of that second day and demanded, in a threatening manner, that he cut down his production.

On other jobs with this company, where Tex worked for several years, he encountered similar pressure. When he was given employment underground he was put to work with Tom, an experienced mine-electrician. One of their tasks was to get the material ready, haul it into the mine and put up about 600 feet of mine

Stanley Mathewson, *Restriction of Output Among Unorganized Workers* (New York: Viking, 1931), pp. 15–20.

trolley-wire. The preparations for such a job usually took about a half day. Tex suggested a way in which this time could be cut in half. He was delighted when Tom fell in readily with his suggestion. The material was prepared, hauled into the mine and under the new plan they were ready to put it in place before the morning was half gone. Then Tex got a shock! Tom, instead of going right ahead and putting up the wire, quit work and ordered Tex to do the same. They spent the time "just fooling around" until the hours which had been saved were used up unproductively. . . .

A messenger boy received a lesson in the principle of "cooperation" on his first job. The duties of the messengers took them to offices and shops where interesting people were at work and where interesting things went on. When he joined the group, the other messengers had a habit of stopping here and there on their rounds. This custom had established a sort of standard time for each round. The new boy found that he could make his rounds a lot faster than was usual if he did not stop to chat with the stenographers and watch the mechanics. The other boys soon explained to him that if he hurried from place to place they would have to do the same. This would necessitate giving up the interesting visits to which they were accustomed.

During the first six weeks of Ellen's employment in a large department store, she was at the bargain tables. Sometimes the merchandise sold itself so fast she could hardly handle the customers; at other times, her table would contain such unattractive goods that, try as she would, she could not interest any one. To keep either the extremely slow or the extremely fast pace was very hard for Ellen, and at times her tallies showed alarmingly small totals. She would probably have been dropped if her fellow-workers had not helped her out by sharing their sales with her.

Some time later Ellen was transferred to another department. Here, freed from the excessive peaks and lags, she made a sales record for the department. As a result, the other girls were censured by the buyer for not being able to keep up with her. She was later put at the head of a section and needed the coöperation of the girls. Accordingly, she split her sales with them so that they would not be criticized when their tallies were compared with hers. This plan worked all right until Ellen decided that she was foolish to work on that basis. She began to restrict her efforts, rather than give away the result of her extra work.

## 3. Frederick Winslow Taylor Explains the Principles of Scientific Management, 1916

By far the most important fact which faces the industries of our country, the industries, in fact, of the civilized world, is that not only the average worker, but nineteen out of twenty workmen throughout the civilized world firmly believe that it is for their best interests to go slow instead of to go fast. They firmly believe that it is for their interest to give as little work in return for the money that they get as is practical. The reasons for this belief are two-fold, and I do not believe that the workingmen are to blame for holding these fallacious views.

From *Bulletin of the Taylor Society,* reproduced in *Advanced Management Journal,* September 1963, 30–39.

If you will take any set of workmen in your own town and suggest to those men that it would be a good thing for them in their trade if they were to double their output in the coming year, each man turn out twice as much work and become twice as efficient, they would say, "I do not know anything about other people's trades; what you are saying about increasing efficiency being a good thing may be good for other trades, but I know that the only result if you come to our trade would be that half of us would be out of a job before the year was out." That to the average workingman is an axiom; it is not a matter subject to debate at all. And even among the average business men of this country that opinion is almost universal. They firmly believe that that would be the result of a great increase in efficiency, and yet directly the opposite is true. . . .

The . . . reason why the workmen of this country and of Europe deliberately restrict output is a very simple one. . . . If, for example, you are manufacturing a pen, let us assume for simplicity that a pen can be made by a single man. Let us say that the workman is turning out ten pens per day, and that he is receiving $2.50 a day for his wages. He has a progressive foreman who is up to date, and that foreman goes to the workman and suggests, "Here, John, you are getting $2.50 a day, and you are turning out ten pens. I would suggest that I pay you 25 cents for making that pen." The man takes the job, and through the help of his foreman, through his own ingenuity, through his increased work, through his interest in his business, through the help of his friends, at the end of the year he finds himself turning out twenty pens instead of ten. He is happy, he is making $5, instead of $2.50 a day. His foreman is happy because, with the same room, with the same men he had before, he has doubled the output of his department, and the manufacturer himself is sometimes happy, but not often. Then someone on the board of directors asks to see the payroll, and he finds that we are paying $5 a day where other similar mechanics are only getting $2.50, and in no uncertain terms he announces that we must stop ruining the labor market. We cannot pay $5 a day when the standard rate of wages is $2.50; how can we hope to compete with surrounding towns? What is the result? Mr. Foreman is sent for, and he is told that he has got to stop ruining the labor market of Cleveland. And the foreman goes back to his workman in sadness, in depression, and tells his workman, "I am sorry, John, but I have got to cut the price down for that pen; I cannot let you earn $5 a day; the board of directors has got on to it, and it is ruining the labor market; you ought to be willing to have the price reduced. You cannot earn more than $3 or $2.75 a day, and I will have to cut your wages so that you will only get $3 a day." John, of necessity accepts the cut, but he sees to it that he never makes enough pens to get another cut. . . .

## The Development of Scientific Management

There has been, until comparatively recently, no scheme promulgated by which the evils of rate cutting could be properly avoided, so soldiering has been the rule.

Now the first step that was taken toward the development of those methods, of those principles, which rightly or wrongly have come to be known under the name of scientific management—the first step that was taken in an earnest endeavor to remedy the evils of soldiering; an earnest endeavor to make it unnecessary for workmen to be hypocritical in this way, to deceive themselves, to deceive their employers, to live day in and day out a life of deceit, forced upon them by conditions—the very first step that was taken toward the development was to overcome that evil. . . .

What is scientific management? It is no efficiency device, nor is it any group or collection of efficiency devices. Scientific management is no new scheme for paying men, it is no bonus system, no piece-work system, no premium system of payment; it is no new method of figuring costs. It is no one of the various elements by which it is commonly known, by which people refer to it. It is not time study nor man study. It is not the printing of a ton or two of blanks and unloading them on a company and saying, "There is your system, go ahead and use it." Scientific management does not exist and cannot exist until there has been a complete mental revolution on the part of the workmen working under it, as to their duties toward themselves and toward their employers, and a complete mental revolution in the outlook of the employers, toward their duties, toward themselves, and toward their workmen. And until this great mental change takes place, scientific management does not exist. Do you think you can make a great mental revolution in a large group of workmen in a year, or do you think you can make it in a large group of foreman and superintendents in a year? If you do, you are very much mistaken. All of us hold mighty close to our ideas and principles in life, and we change very slowly toward the new, and very properly too.

Let me give you an idea of what I mean by this change in mental outlook. If you are manufacturing a hammer or a mallet, into the cost of that mallet goes a certain amount of raw materials, a certain amount of wood and metal. If you will take the cost of the raw materials and then add to it that cost which is frequently called by various names—overhead expenses, general expense, indirect expense; that is, the proper share of taxes, insurance, light, heat, salaries of officers and advertising—and you have a sum of money. Subtract that sum from the selling price, and what is left over is called the surplus. It is over this surplus that all of the labor disputes in the past have occurred. The workman naturally wants all he can get. His wages come out of that surplus. The manufacturer wants all he can get in the shape of profits, and it is from the division of this surplus that all the labor disputes have come in the past—the equitable division.

The new outlook that comes under scientific management is this: The workmen, after many object lessons, come to see and the management comes to see that this surplus can be made so great, providing both sides will stop their pulling apart, will stop their fighting and will push as hard as they can to get as cheap an output as possible, that there is no occasion to quarrel. Each side can get more than ever before. The acknowledgement of this fact represents a complete mental revolution.

## What Scientific Management Will Do

I am going to try to prove to you that the old style of management has not a ghost of a chance in competition with the principles of scientific management. Why? In the first place, under scientific management, the initiative of the workmen, their hard work, their good-will, their best endeavors are obtained with absolute regularity. . . . That is the least of the two sources of gain. The greatest source of gain under scientific management comes from the new and almost unheard-of duties and burdens which are voluntarily assumed, not by the workmen, but by the men on the management side. . . . These new duties, these new burdens undertaken by the management have rightly or wrongly been divided into four groups, and have been called the principles of scientific management.

The . . . first of the new burdens which are voluntarily undertaken by those on the management side is the deliberate gathering together of the great mass of traditional knowledge which, in the past, has been in the heads of the workmen, recording it, tabulating it, reducing it in most cases to rules, laws, and in many cases to mathematical formulae, which, with these new laws, are applied to the co-operation of the management to the work of the workmen. This results in an immense increase in the output, we may say, of the two. The gathering in of this great mass of traditional knowledge, which is done by the means of motion study, time study, can be truly called the science. . . .

The next of the four principles of scientific management is the scientific selection of the workman, and then his progressive development. It becomes the duty under scientific management of not one, but of a group of men on the management side, to deliberately study the workmen who are under them; study them in the most careful, thorough and painstaking way; and not just leave it to the poor, overworked foreman to go out and say, "Come on, what do you want? If you are cheap enough I will give you a trial."

That is the old way. The new way is to take a great deal of trouble in selecting the workmen. The selection proceeds year after year. And it becomes the duty of those engaged in scientific management to know something about the workmen under them. It becomes their duty to set out deliberately to train the workmen in their employ to be able to do a better and still better class of work than ever before, and to then pay them higher wages than ever before. This deliberate selection of the workmen is the second of the great duties that devolve on the management under scientific management.

The third principle is the bringing together of this science of which I have spoken and the trained workmen. I say bringing because they don't come together unless some one brings them. Select and train your workmen all you may, but unless there is some one who will make the men and the science come together, they will stay apart. The "make" involves a great many elements. They are not all disagreeable elements. The most important and largest way of "making" is to do something nice for the man whom you wish to make come together with the science. Offer him a plum, something that is worthwhile. There are many plums offered to those who come under scientific management—better treatment, more kindly treatment, more consideration for their wishes, and an opportunity for them to express their wants freely. That is one side of the "make." An equally important side is, whenever a man will not do what he ought, to either make him do it or stop it. If he will not do it, let him get out. I am not talking of any mollycoddle. Let me disabuse your minds of any opinion that scientific management is a mollycoddle scheme.

I have a great many union friends. I find they look with especial bitterness on this word "make." They have been used to doing the "making" in the past. That is the attitude of the trade unions, and it softens matters greatly when you can tell them the facts, namely, that in our making the science and the men come together, nine-tenths of our trouble comes with the men on the management side in making them do their new duties. I am speaking of those who have been trying to change from the old system to the new. . . .

The fourth principle is the plainest of all. It involves a complete redivision of the work of the establishment. Under the old scheme of management, almost all of the work was done by the workmen. Under the new, the work of the establishment is divided into two large parts. All of that work which formerly was done by the workmen alone is divided into two large sections, and one of those sections is handed over to the management. They do a whole division of the work formerly done by the workmen. It is this real cooperation, this genuine division of the work between the two sides, more than any other element which accounts for the fact that there never will be strikes under scientific management. When the workman realizes that there is hardly a thing he does that does not have to be preceded by some act of preparation on the part of management, and when that workman real-izes when the management falls down and does not do its part, that he is not only entitled to a kick, but that he can register that kick in the most forcible possible way, he cannot quarrel with the men over him. It is team work. There are more complaints made every day on the part of the workmen that the men on the man-agement side fail to do their duties than are made by the management that the men fail. Every one of the complaints of the men have to be heeded, just as much as the complaints from the management that the workmen do not do their share. That is characteristic of scientific management. It represents a democracy, co-operation, a genuine division of work which never existed before in this world.

## 4.  An A.F.L. View of Women Workers in Industry, 1897

The invasion of the crafts by women has been developing for years amid irritation and injury to the workman. The right of the woman to win honest bread is accorded on all sides, but with craftsmen it is an open question whether this manifestation is of a healthy social growth or not.

The rapid displacement of men by women in the factory and workshop has to be met sooner or later, and the question is forcing itself upon the leaders and thinkers among the labor organizations of the land.

Is it a pleasing indication of progress to see the father, the brother and the son displaced as the bread winner by the mother, sister and daughter?

Is not this evolutionary backslide, which certainly modernizes the present wage system in vogue, a menace to prosperity—a foe to our civilized pretensions? . . .

The growing demand for female labor is not founded upon philanthropy, as those who encourage it would have sentimentalists believe; it does not spring from the milk of human kindness. It is an insidious assault upon the home; it is the knife of the assassin, aimed at the family circle—the divine injunction. It debars the man through financial embarrassment from family responsibility, and physically, men-tally and socially excludes the woman equally from nature's dearest impulse. Is this the demand of civilized progress; is it the desire of Christian dogma? . . .

Capital thrives not upon the peaceful, united, contented family circle; rather are its palaces, pleasures and vices fostered and increased upon the disruption, ruin

From Edward O'Donnell, "Women as Bread Winners—the Error of the Age," *American Federationist* 4, no. 8 (October 1897): 186–187.

or abolition of the home, because with its decay and ever glaring privation, manhood loses its dignity, its backbone, its aspirations. . . .

To combat these impertinent inclinations, dangerous to the few, the old and well-tried policy of divide and conquer is invoked, and to our own shame, it must be said, one too often renders blind aid to capital in its warfare upon us. The employer in the magnanimity of his generosity will give employment to the daughter, while her brothers are weary because of their daily tramp in quest of work. The father, who has a fair, steady job, sees not the infamous policy back of the flattering propositions. Somebody else's daughter is called in in the same manner, by and by, and very soon the shop or factory are full of women, while their fathers have the option of working for the same wages or a few cents more, or take their places in the large army of unemployed. . . .

College professors and graduates tell us that this is the natural sequence of industrial development, an integral part of economic claim.

Never was a greater fallacy uttered of more poisonous import. It is false and wholly illogical. The great demand for women and their preference over men does not spring from a desire to elevate humanity; at any rate that is not its trend.

The wholesale employment of women in the various handicrafts must gradually unsex them, as it most assuredly is demoralizing them, or stripping them of that modest demeanor that lends a charm to their kind, while it numerically strengthens the multitudinous army of loafers, paupers, tramps and policemen, for no man who desires honest employment, and can secure it, cares to throw his life away upon such a wretched occupation as the latter.

The employment of women in the mechanical departments is encouraged because of its cheapness and easy manipulation, regardless of the consequent perils; and for no other reason. The generous sentiment enveloping this inducement is of criminal design, since it comes from a thirst to build riches upon the dismemberment of the family or the hearthstone cruelly dishonored. . . .

But somebody will say, would you have women pursue lives of shame rather than work? Certainly not; it is to the alarming introduction of women into the mechanical industries, hitherto enjoyed by the sterner sex, at a wage uncommandable by them, that leads so many into that deplorable pursuit.

## 5. The Shirtwaist Strikers Win, 1910

Any day last winter, from early morning till late at night, in rain or snow or sleet, in the district west of Fifth Avenue and south of Twenty-third Street, in New York, you could have seen hundreds of thin, pale-faced, ill-clad girls marching like sentinels up and down the sidewalk in front of certain doorways. And every day, had you watched, you could have seen scores of these half-starved girls beaten up by thugs and policemen, arrested, fined by magistrates, and even sent to the workhouse. These young girls, ever marching to and fro—if they stopped they were liable to arrest— were the pickets of the Ladies' Waist-Makers Union, which was a strike forty thousand strong—the biggest strike of women this country has known. The contest was

From Miriam Finn Scott, "What the Women Strikers Won," *Outlook* 95 (July 2, 1910): 480–481.

a bitter one; the odds seemed all against the girls. But, despite the menace and brutality of the police, despite cold and hunger, you would not have seen the number
of these young sentinels decrease. Some fell out, but there were volunteers in
plenty to take their places; and for a hundred days this desperate marching to and
fro went on unbroken.

Had you stood on Fifty Avenue in this same region on May Day, the international holiday of workers, you would have seen a strangely different procession.
Past you there would have tramped, as part of the May Day Parade, an army of
girls uniformed in white shirt-waists and red neckties—an army that was a full
hour in passing—an army three miles long. These were the girls who had desperately paced this same neighborhood half starved only a few months before; but
now, as they marched, they sang the workers' "Marseillaise," and on thousands of
faces was the look of victory, for they had won their strike.

This contrast is an epitome of what these girl strikers have achieved. To show
more definitely the extent and full significance of their victory it will be necessary
to recall briefly the working conditions that existed prior to the strike, and also to
recall the girls' equipment for a struggle. While in many shops the conditions were
good, in the majority the girls worked amid most pernicious sanitary surroundings,
they were the victims of a system of fines (for being late or damaging goods) that
were vastly disproportionate to any loss suffered by the employer; there was in
existence a subcontracting system which enabled the employer to pay as low as
two dollars a week of sixty hours; they worked ten, twelve, and even more hours a
day; in the busy season they did not get even one day's rest a week, and at the best
the majority of these girls could count on nothing better than a four months' season
of tense overwork, and eight months in which they would be more or less idle. As
to the preparedness of these girls for a great strike, perhaps I can suggest that by
saying that when I went to the office of the union a few days before the strike was
called, I found that the headquarters of the Ladies' Waist-Makers Union of New
York was a corner, mere "desk-room," in one very small office, and that the general
organizer, secretary, treasurer, and walking delegate were all combined in one not
very large man. This hard-working Pooh-Bah informed me that his union had an
irregular, unenthusiastic membership of about eight hundred, scattered throughout
Greater New York; that ninety per cent were of foreign birth, more than half did not
speak English, and that practically none of them had any knowledge or experience
in union organization. Such was the fighting condition of the union when the long
struggle with the four hundred manufacturers began.

. . . Though the union was so weak, the girls were ripe for revolt—and unyield-
ing revolt—and for fourteen weeks, amid the greatest hardships, they carried on
the fight, and at length carried it on to complete victory. At the time the strike was
declared off, 354 employers had signed the union's contract, and with a very few
exceptions all had agreed to a closed shop, to a fifty-two-hour week, to a raise of
wages from twelve to fifteen per cent, to do away with the sub-contracting system
and many other abuses, to limit night-work to two hours per day and not more than
twice a week, to pay week-workers for legal holidays, and in the slack season to
divide the work among all workers, instead of giving it to a favored few.

Important as are the direct economic results of the victory, there is another
result of even greater significance, and that is the existence of a real union where

before there had been but the shadow of one. Very recently I had occasion to visit the new headquarters of the union, and the contrast with the headquarters before the fight began was enough in itself to tell what a different thing the Ladies' Waist-Makers Union now is from the union of six months ago. Instead of a corner in one room, the union has a suite of two rooms, which it already finds too small for its purpose; instead of a few hundred scattered members, there are now twenty thousand girls in good standing, with new ones coming in daily; instead of the entire staff of officers being incorporated in one man, the union now has two organizers, two recording secretaries, two financial secretaries, nine walking delegates, one bookkeeper, and three stenographers. Besides, each organized shop has a voluntary chairman, and once a week all the chairmen meet with the walking delegates to report the conditions of the shops. In this way the union is kept in constant touch with each individual shop. Instead of an income of but little better than nothing a week, the average weekly income from dues and initiation fees is $2,400. The union has also established an employment bureau in its offices. When any girl is out of work, instead of tramping from shop to shop, she need only come to the bureau at the union's offices.

And, besides, the strike has had another result. There has been a tradition that women cannot strike. These young, inexperienced girls have proved that women can strike, and strike successfully.

## 6. Unionist Alice Henry Outlines Why Women Need Their Own Local Unions, 1915

The commonest complaint of all is that women members of a trade union do not attend their meetings. It is indeed a very serious difficulty to cope with, and the reasons for this poor attendance and want of interest in union affairs have to be fairly faced.

At first glance it seems curious that the meetings of a mixed local composed of both men and girls, should have for the girls even less attraction than meetings of their own sex only. But so it is. A business meeting of a local affords none of the lively social intercourse of a gathering for pleasure or even of a class for instruction. The men, mostly the older men, run the meeting and often are the meeting. Their influence may be out of all proportion to their numbers. It is they who decide the place where the local shall meet and the hour at which members shall assemble. The place is therefore often over a saloon, to which many girls naturally and rightly object. Sometimes it is even in a disreputable district. The girls may prefer that the meeting should begin shortly after closing time so that they do not need to go home and return, or have to loiter about for two or three hours. They like meetings to be over early. The men mostly name eight o'clock as the time of beginning, but business very often will not start much before nine. . . .

Where the conditions of the trade permit it by far the best plan is to have the women organized in separate locals. The meetings of women and girls only draw better attendances, give far more opportunity for all the members to take part in the

Alice Henry, "The Woman Organizer," *The Trade Union Woman* (New York: D. Appleton, 1915), 152–155.

business, and beyond all question form the finest training ground for the women leaders who in considerable numbers are needed so badly in the woman's side of the trade-union movement today.

Those trade-union women who advocate mixed locals for every trade which embraces both men and women are of two types. Some are mature, perhaps elderly women, who have been trade unionists all their lives, who have grown up in the same locals with men, who have in the long years passed through and left behind their period of probation and training, and to whose presence and active coöperation the men have become accustomed. These women are able to express their views in public, can put or discuss a motion or take the chair as readily as their brothers. The other type is represented by those individual women or girls in whom exceptional ability takes the place of experience, and who appreciate the educational advantages of working along with experienced trade-union leaders. I have in my mind at this moment one girl over whose face comes all the rapture of the keen student as she explains how much she has learnt from working with men in their meetings. . . . Always she is quick enough to profit by the men's experience, by their ways of managing conferences and balancing advantages and losses. . . .

But with the average girl today the plan does not work. The mixed local does not, as a general rule, offer the best training-class for new girl recruits, in which they may obtain their training in collective bargaining or cooperative effort. . . . Many of the discussions that go on are quite above the girls' heads. And even when a young girl has something to say and wishes to say it, want of practice and timidity often keep her silent. . . .

The girls, as a rule, are not only happier in their own women's local, but they have the interest of running the meetings themselves. They choose their own hall and fix their own time of meeting. Their officers are of their own selecting and taken from among themselves. The rank and file, too, get the splendid training that is conferred when persons actually and not merely nominally work together for a common end. Their introduction to the great problems of labor is through their practical understanding and handling of those problems as they encounter them in the everyday difficulties of the shop and the factory and as dealt with when they come up before the union meeting or have to be settled in bargaining with an employer.

## ✿ E S S A Y S

In the first essay, Yale University historian David Montgomery describes the rich, potent work culture of skilled, male industrial workers. He unveils a late-nineteenth-century world in which their unique knowledge of the labor process and their proud, "manly" values gave these autonomous craftsman substantial control of their workplace. Setting work rules, first informally and then through their unions, these machinists, iron molders, coal miners, and other skilled and semiskilled men developed an ethos of mutuality grounded in a self-confident masculine identity. Strikes, especially those undertaken to support other crafts, testified to their willingness to defend working-class institutions and values against employer encroachment.

The second essay, by historian Nan Enstad of the University of Wisconsin, Madison, deploys insights from cultural studies to reinterpret the 1909 shirtwaist strike of women garment makers. To understand the interplay between culture, politics, and working-class activism, she shifts the focus of her investigation to the patterns of consumption and public representation generated by this largely youthful, immigrant work group. Enstad uncovers a set of divergent social and political meanings that attach themselves to dress and fashion—to what these workers themselves sometimes called "ladyhood"—even as she interrogates the rebellious image these women strikers offered their supporters, no less than their opponents and the general public.

Are all work cultures as oppositional as those of the nineteenth-century crafts-man? To what extent did the work culture of the garment shops foster women's cultural practices? How did gendered assumptions influence the mentality of both mental craftsmen and shirtwaist workers?

# Work Rules and Manliness in the World of the Nineteenth-Century Craftsman

### DAVID MONTGOMERY

"In an industrial establishment which employs say from 500 to 1000 workmen, there will be found in many cases at least twenty to thirty different trades," wrote Frederick Winslow Taylor in his famous critique of the practices of industrial management which were then in vogue.

> The workmen in each of these trades have had their knowledge handed down to them by word of mouth. . . . This mass of rule-of-thumb or traditional knowledge may be said to be the principle asset or possession of every tradesman. . . . [The] foremen and superin-tendents . . . recognize the task before them as that of inducing each workman to use his best endeavors, his hardest work, all his traditional knowledge, his skill, his ingenuity, and his good-will—in a word, his "initiative," so as to yield the largest possible return to his employer."

Big Bill Haywood put the same point somewhat more pungently, when he declared: "The manager's brains are under the workman's cap."

Both Taylor and Haywood were describing the power which certain groups of workers exercised over the direction of production processes at the end of the nine-teenth century, a power which the scientific management movement strove to abol-ish, and which the Industrial Workers of the World wished to enlarge and extend to all workers. It is important to note that both men found the basis of workers' power in the superiority of their knowledge over that of the factory owners. It is even more important to note that they were referring not to "pre-industrial" work practices, but to the factory itself. . . .

My concern here [is] with the patterns of behavior which took shape in the sec-ond and third generations of industrial experience, largely among workers whose world had been fashioned from their youngest days by smoky mills, congested streets, recreation as a week-end affair and toil at the times and the pace dictated by the clock (except when a more or less lengthy layoff meant no work at all). It as such workers, the veterans, if you will, of industrial life, with whom Taylor was

David Montgomery, "Workers' Control of Machine Production in the Nineteenth Century," *Labor History,* 17 (Fall 1976): pp. 485–509. Reprinted by permission of Taylor & Francis, Ltd., http://www.tandf.co.uk/journals.

preoccupied. They had internalized the industrial sense of time, they were highly disciplined in both individual and collective behavior, and they regarded both an extensive division of labor and machine production as their natural environments. But they had often fashioned from these attributes neither the docile obedience of automatons, nor the individualism of the "upwardly mobile," but a form of control of productive processes which became increasingly collective, deliberate and aggressive, until American employers launched a partially successful counterattack under the banners of scientific management and the open shop drive.

Workers' control of production, however, was not a condition or state of affairs which existed at any point in time, but a struggle, a chronic battle in industrial life which assumed a variety of forms. Those forms may be treated as successive stages in a pattern of historical evolution, though one must always remember that the stages overlapped each other chronologically in different industries, or even at different localities within the same industry, and that each successive stage incorporated the previous one, rather than replacing it. The three levels of development which appeared in the second half of the nineteenth century were those characterized by (1) the functional autonomy of the craftsman, (2) the union work rule, and (3) mutual support of diverse trades in rule enforcement and sympathetic strikes. Each of these levels will be examined here in turn, then in conclusion some observations will be made on the impact of scientific management and the open shop drive on the patterns of behavior which they represented.

The functional autonomy of craftsmen rested on both their superior knowledge, which made them self-directing at their tasks, and the supervision which they gave to one or more helpers. Iron molders, glass blowers, coopers, paper machine tenders, locomotive engineers, mule spinners, boiler makers, pipe fitters, typographers, jiggermen in potteries, coal miners, iron rollers, puddlers and heaters, the operators of McKay or Goodyear stitching machines in shoe factories, and, in many instances, journeymen machinists and fitters in metal works exercised broad discretion in the direction of their own work and that of their helpers. They often hired and fired their own helpers and paid the latter some fixed portion of their own earnings.

James J. Davis, who was to end up as Warren Harding's Secretary of Labor, learned the trade of puddling iron by working as his father's helper in Sharon, Pennsylvania. "None of us ever went to school and learned the chemistry of it from books," he recalled. "We learned the trick by doing it, standing with our faces in the scorching heat while our hands puddled the metal in its glaring bath." His first job, in fact, had come at the age of twelve, when an aged puddler devised a scheme to enable him to continue the physically arduous exertion of the trade by taking on a boy (twelve-year old Davis) to relieve the helper of mundane tasks like stoking the furnace, so that the helper in turn could assume a larger share of the taxing work of stirring the iron as it "came to nature." By the time Davis felt he had learned enough to master his own furnace, he had to leave Sharon, because furnaces passed from father to son, and Davis' father was not yet ready to step down. As late as 1900, when Davis was living at home while attending business college after having been elected to public office, he took over his father's furnace every afternoon, through an arrangement the two had worked out between themselves.

The iron rollers of the Columbus Iron Works, in Ohio, have left us a clear record of how they managed their trade in the minute books of their local union from 1873 to 1876. The three twelve-man rolling teams, which constituted the union, negotiated a single tonnage rate with the company for each specific rolling job the company undertook. The workers then decided collectively, among themselves, what portion of that rate should go to each of them (and the shares were far from equal, ranging from 19¼ cents, out of the negotiated $1.13 a ton, for the roller, to 5 cents for the runout hooker), how work should be allocated among them, how many rounds on the rolls should be undertaken per day, what special arrangements should be made for the fiercely hot labors of the hookers during the summer, and how members should be hired and progress through the various ranks of the gang. To put it another way, all the boss did was to buy the equipment and raw materials and sell the finished product. . . .

Three aspects of the moral code, in which the craftsmen's autonomy was protectively enmeshed, deserve close attention. First, on most jobs there was a stint, an output quota fixed by the workers themselves. As the laments of scientific management's apostles about workers "soldiering" and the remarkable 1904 survey by the Commissioner of Labor, *Regulation and Restriction of Output,* made clear, stints flourished as widely without unions as with them. Abram Hewitt testified in 1867 that his puddlers in New Jersey, who were not unionized, worked 11 turns per week (5½ days), made three heats per turn, and put 450 pounds of iron in each charge, all by arrangement among themselves. Thirty-five years later a stint still governed the trade, though a dramatic improvement in puddling furnaces was reflected in union rules which specified 11 turns with five heats per turn and 550 pounds per charge (a 104% improvement in productivity), while some nonunion mill workers followed the same routine but boiled bigger charges.

Stints were always under pressure from the employers, and were often stretched over the course of time by the combined force of competition among employers and improving technology. In this instance, productivity under union rules expanded more than three per cent annually over three and half decades. But workers clung doggedly to the practice, and used their superior knowledge both to determine how much they should do and to outwit employers' efforts to wring more production out of them. In a farm equipment factory studied in 1902, for example, the machine shop, polishing department, fitting department and blacksmith shop all had fixed stints, which made each group of workers average very similar earnings despite the fact that all departments were on piecework. . . . Similarly, Taylor's colleague Carl Barth discovered a planer operator who avoided exceeding the stint while always looking busy, by simply removing the cutting tool from his machine from time to time, while letting it run merrily on.

"There is in every workroom a fashion, a habit of work," wrote efficiency consultant Henry Gantt, "and the new workers follows that fashion, for it isn't respectable not to." A quiver full of epithets awaited the deviant: 'hog,' 'hogger-in,' 'leader,' 'rooter,' 'chaser,' 'rusher,' 'runner,' 'swift,' 'boss's pet,' to mention some politer versions. And when a whole factory gained a reputation for feverish work, disdainful craftsmen would describe its occupants, as one did of the Gisholt turret lathe works, as comprised half "of farmers, and the other half, with few exceptions, of horse thieves." On the other hand, those who held fast to the carefully measured stint, despite the curses of their employers and the lure of higher earnings, depicted themselves as sober and trustworthy masters of their trades. Unlimited output led to slashed piece rates, irregular employment, drink and debaucher, they argued. Rationally restricted output, however, reflected "unselfish brotherhood," personal dignity, and "cultivation of the mind."

Second, as this language vividly suggests, the craftsmen's ethical code demanded a "manly" bearing toward the boss. Few words enjoyed more popularity in the nineteenth century than this honorific, with all its connotations of dignity, respectability, defiant egalitarianism, and patriarchal male supremacy. The worker who merited it refused to cower before the foreman's glares—in fact, often would not work at all when a boss was watching. . . .

Finally, "manliness" toward one's fellow workers was an important as it was toward the owners. "Undermining or conniving" at a brother's job was a form of hoggish behavior as objectional as running more than one machine, or otherwise doing the work that belonged to two men. Union rules commanded the expulsion of members who performed such "dirty work," in order to secure employment or advancement for themselves. When the members of the Iron Heaters and Rollers Union at a Philadelphia mill learned in 1875 that one of their brothers had been fired "for dissatisfaction in regard to his management of the mill," and that another member had "undermined" the first with the superintendent and been promised his rolls, the delinquent was expelled from the lodge, along with a lodge member who defended him, and everyone went on strike to demand the immediate discharge of both excommunicates by the firm.

In short, a simple technological explanation for the control exercised by nineteenth-century craftsmen will not suffice. Technical knowledge acquired on the job was embedded in a mutualistic ethical code, also acquired on the job, and together these attributes provided skilled workers with considerable autonomy at their work and powers of resistance to the wishes of their employers. On the other hand, it was technologically possible for the worker's autonomy to be used in individualistic ways, which might promote his own mobility and identify his interests with those of the owner. The ubiquitous practice of subcontracting encouraged this tendency. In the needle trades, the long established custom of a tailor's taking work home to his family was transformed by his employment of other piece workers into the iniquitous "sweat shop" system. Among iron molders, the "berkshire" system expanded rapidly after 1850, as individual molders hired whole teams of helpers to assist them in producing a multitude of castings. Carpenters and bricklayers were lured into piece work systems of petty exploitations, and other forms of subcontracting flourished in stone quarrying, iron mining, anthracite mining, and even in railroad locomotive works, where entire units of an engine's construction were let out to the machinist who filed the lowest bid, and who then hired a crew to assist him in making and fitting the parts.

Subcontracting practices readily undermined both stints and the mutualistic ethic (though contractors were known to fix stints for their own protection in both garment and locomotive works), and they tended to flood many trades with trained, or semi-trained, workers who undercut wages and work standards. Their spread encouraged many craftsmen to move beyond reliance on their functional autonomy to the next higher level of craft control, the enactment and enforcement of union work rules. In one respect, union rules simply codified the autonomy I have already described. In fact, because they were often written down and enforced by joint action, union rules have a visibility to historians, which has made me resort to them already for evidence in the discussion of autonomy per se. But this intimate historical relationship between customary workers' autonomy and the union rule should not blind us to the fact that the latter represents a significant new stage of development.

The work rules of unions were referred to by their members as "legislation." The phrase denotes a shift from spontaneous to deliberate collective action, from a group ethical code to formal rules and sanctions, and from resistance to employers' pretentions to control over them. In some unions the rules were rather simple. The International Association of Machinists, for example, like its predecessors the Machinists and Blacksmiths' International Union and the many machinists' local assemblies of the Knights of Labor, simply specified a fixed term of apprenticeship for any prospective journeyman, established a standard wage for the trade, prohibited helpers of handymen from performing journeymen's work, and forbade any member from running more than one machine at a time or accepting any form of piece work payment.

Other unions had much detailed and complex rules. There were, for example, sixty-six "Rules for Working" in the by-laws of the window-glass workers' Local Assembly 300 of the Knights of Labor. They specified that full crews had to be present "at each pot setting," that skimming could be done only at the beginning of blowing and at meal time, that blowers and gatherers should not "work faster than at the rate of nine rollers per hour," and that the "standard size of single strength rollers" should "be 40 × 58 to cut 38 × 56." No work was to be performed on Thanksgiving Day, Christmas, Decoration Day or Washington's Birthday, and no blower, gatherer or cutter could work between June 15 and September 15. In other words, during the summer months the union ruled that the fires were to be out. In 1884 the local assembly waged a long and successful strike to preserve its limit of 48 boxes of glass a week, a rule which its members considered the key to the dignity and welfare of the trade.

Nineteenth-century work rules were not ordinarily negotiated with employers or embodied in a contract. From the 1860s onward it became increasingly common for standard *wages* to be negotiated with employers or their associations, rather than fixed unilaterally as unions had tried earlier, but working rules changed more slowly. They were usually adopted unilaterally by local unions, or by the delegates to a national convention, and enforced by the refusal of the individual member to obey any command from an employer which violated them. Hopefully, the worker's refusal would be supported by the joint action of his shop mates, but if it was not, he was honor bound to pack his tool box and walk out alone, rather than break the union's laws. . . .

On the other hand, the autonomy of craftsmen which was codified in union rules was clearly not individualistic. Craftsmen were unmistakably and consciously group-made men, who sought to pull themselves upward by their collective boot straps. As unions waxed stronger after 1886, the number of strikes to enforce union rules grew steadily. It was, however, in union legislation against subcontracting that both the practical and ideological aspects of the conflict between group solidarity and upwardly mobile individualism became most evident, for these rules sought to regulate in the first instance not the employers' behavior, but that of the workers themselves. Thus the Iron Molders Union attacked the "berkshire" system by rules forbidding any of its members to employ a helper for any other purpose than "to skim, shake out and to cut sand," or to pay a helper out of his own earnings. In 1867, when 8,615 out of some 10,400 known molders in the country were union members, the national union legislated further that no member was allowed to go to work earlier than seven o'clock in the morning. During the 1880s the Brick Layers' Union checked subcontracting by banning its members from working for any contractor who could not raise enough capital to buy his own bricks. All building trades' unions instructed their members not to permit contractors to work with tools along side with them. . . . All such regulations secured the group welfare of the workers involved by sharply rejecting society's enticements to become petty entrepreneurs, clarifying and intensifying the division of labor at the work place, and sharpening the line between employer and employee.

Where a trade was well unionized, a committee in each shop supervised the enforcement in that plant of the rules and standard wage which the union had adopted for the trade as a whole. The craft union and the craft local assembly of the Knights of Labor were forms of organization well adapted to such regulatory activities. The members were legislating, on matters on which they were unchallenged experts, rules which only their courage and solidarity could enforce. On one hand, the craft form of organization linked their personal interests to those of the trade, rather than those of the company in which they worked, while, on the other hand, their efforts to enforce the same rules on all of their employers, where they were successful, created at least a few islands of order in the nineteenth-century's economic ocean of anarchic competition.

Labor organizations of the late nineteenth century struggled persistently to transform worker's struggles to manage their own work from spontaneous to deliberate actions, just as they tried to subject wage strikes and efforts to shorten the working day to their conscious regulation. "The trade union movement is one of reason, one of deliberation, depending entirely upon the voluntary and sovereign actions of its members," declared the executive Council of the AFL. Only through "thorough organization," to use a favorite phrase of the day, was it possible to enforce a trade's work rules throughout a factory, mine, or construction site. Despite the growing number of strikes over union rules and union recognition in the late 1880s, the enforcement of workers' standards of control spread more often through the daily self-assertion of craftsmen on the job than through large and dramatic strikes.

Conversely, strikes over wage reductions at times involved thinly disguised attacks by employers on craftsmen's job controls. Fall River's textile manufacturers in 1870 and the Hocking Valley coal operators in 1884, to cite only two examples, deliberately foisted severe wage reductions on their highly unionized workers in order to provoke strikes. The owners' hope was that in time hunger would force their employees to abandon union membership, and thus free the companies' hands to change production methods. As the treasurer of one Fall River mill testified in 1870: "I think the question with the spinners was not wages, but whether they or the manufacturers should rule. For the last six or eight years they have ruled Fall River." Defeat in a strike temporarily broke the union's control, which had grown through steady recruiting and rule enforcement during years which were largely free of work stoppages.

The third level of control struggles emerged when different trades lent each other support in their battles to enforce union rules and recognition. An examination of the strike statistics gathered by the U.S. Commissioner of Labor for the period 1881–1905 reveals the basis patterns of this development. Although there had been a steady increase in both the number and size of strikes between 1881 and 1886, the following 12 years saw a reversal of that growth, as stoppages became both smaller and increasingly confined to skilled crafts (except in 1894). With that change came three important and interrelated trends. First, the proportion of strikes called by unions rose sharply in comparison to spontaneous strikes. Nearly half of all strikes between 1881 and 1886 had occurred without union sanction or aid. In the seven years beginning with 1887 more than two-thirds of each year's strikes were deliberately called by a union, and in 1891 almost 75 per cent of the strikes were official.

Secondly, as strikes became more deliberate and unionized, the proportion of strikes which dealt mainly with wages fell abruptly. Strikes to enforce union rules, enforce recognition of the union, and protect its members grew from 10 per cent of the total or less before 1885 to the level of 19–20 per cent between 1891 and 1893. Spontaneous strikes and strikes of laborers and factory operatives had almost invariably been aimed at increasing wages or preventing wage reductions, with the partial exception of 1886 when 20 per cent of all strikes had been over hours. The more highly craftsmen became organized, however, the more often they struck and were locked out over work rules.

Third, unionization of workers grew on the whole faster than strike participation. The ratio of strike participants to membership in labor organizations fell almost smoothly from 109 in 1881 to 24 in 1888, rose abruptly in 1890 and 1891 (to 71 and 86, respectively), then resumed its downward trend to 36 in 1898, interrupted, or course, by a leap to 182 in 1894. In a word, calculation and organization were the dominant tendencies in strike activity, just as they were in the evolution of work rules during the nineteenth century. But the assertion of deliberate control through formal organization was sustained not only by high levels of militancy (a persistently high propensity to strike), but also by remarkably aggressive mutual support, which sometimes took the form of the unionization of all grades of workers within a single industry, but more often appeared in the form of sympathetic strikes involving members of different trade unions.

Joint organization of all grades of workers seemed most likely to flourish where no single craft clearly dominated the life of the workplace, in the way iron molders, brick layers, or iron puddlers did where they worked. It was also most likely to appear at the crest of the waves of strike activity among unskilled workers and operatives, as is hardly surprising, and to offer evidence of the organizational impulse in their ranks. In Philadelphia's shoe industry between 1884 and 1887, for example, the Knights of Labor successfully organized eleven local assemblies, ranging in size from 55 to 1000 members, each of which represented a different craft or cluster of related occupations, and formulated wage demands and work rules for its own members. Each assembly sent three delegates to District Assembly 70, the highest governing body of the Knights for the industry, which in turn selected seven representatives to meet in a city-wide arbitration committee with an equal number of employers' representatives. Within each factory a "shop union" elected by the workers in that plant handled grievances and enforced the rules of the local assemblies, aided by one male and one female "statistician," who kept track of the complex piece rates.

There is no evidence that local assemblies of unskilled workers or of semi-skilled operatives ever attempted to regulate production processes themselves in the way assemblies of glass blowers and other craftsmen did. They did try to restrict hiring to members of the Knights and sometimes regulated layoffs by seniority clauses. For the most part, however, assemblies of operatives and laborers confined their attention to wages and to protection of their members against arbitrary treatment by supervisors. On the other hand, the mere fact that such workers had been organized made it difficult for employees to grant concessions to their craftsmen at the expense of helpers and laborers. Consequently, the owners were faced simultaneously with higher wage bills and a reduction of their control in a domain where they had been accustomed to exercise unlimited authority.

Moreover, workers who directed important production processes were themselves at times reluctant to see their own underlings organized, and frequently sought to dominate the larger organization to which their helpers belonged. A case in point was offered by the experience of the Knights of Labor in the garment industry, where contractors were organized into local assemblies of their own, supposedly to cooperate with those of cutters, pressers, tailors, and sewing machine operators. Contractors were often charged with disrupting the unionization of their own employees, in order to promote their personal competitive advantages. Above all, they tried to discourage women from joining the operators' assemblies. As the secretary of a St. Louis tailors' local assembly revealed, contractors who were his fellow Knights were telling the parents of operators that "no dissent [sic] girl belong to an assembly."

On the other hand, the experience of the Knights in both the shoe and garment industries suggests that effective unionization of women operatives was likely to have a remarkably radicalizing impact on the organization. It closed the door decisively both on employers who wished to compensate for higher wages paid to craftsmen by exacting more from the unskilled, and on craftsmen who were tempted to advance themselves by sweating others. In Philadelphia, Toronto, Cincinnati, Beverly, and Lynn both the resistance of the manufacturers to unionism and the level of mutuality exhibited by the workers leapt upward noticeably when the women shoe workers organized along with the men. Furthermore, the sense of total organization made all shoe workers more exacting in their demands and less patient with the protracted arbitration procedures employed by the Knights. Quickie strikes became increasingly frequent as more and more shoe workers enrolled in the Order. Conversely, the shoe manufacturers banded tightly together to destroy the Knights of Labor.

In short, the organization of all grades of workers in any industry propelled craftsmen's collective rule making into a more aggressive relationship with the employers, even where it left existing styles of work substantially unchanged. The other form of joint action, sympathetic strikes, most often involved the unionized skilled crafts themselves, and consequently was more directly related to questions of control of production processes. When Fred S. Hall wrote in 1898 that sympathetic strikes had "come so much in vogue during the last few years," he was looking back on a period during which organized workers had shown a greater tendency to walk out in support of the struggles of other groups of workers than was the case in any other period in the history of recorded strike data. Only the years between 1901 and 1904 and those between 1917 and 1921 were to see the absolute number of sympathetic strikes approach even *one-half* the levels of 1890 and 1891. . . .

Eugene V. Debs was to extoll this extreme manifestation of mutuality as the "Christ-like virtue of sympathy," and to depict his own Pullman boycott, the epoch's most massive sympathetic action, as an open confrontation between that working-class virtue and a social order which sanctified selfishness. It is true that the mutualistic ethic which supported craftsmen's control was displayed in its highest form by sympathetic strikes. It is equally true, however, that the element of calculation, which was increasingly dominating all strike activity, was particularly evident here. As Fred S. Hall pointed out, sympathetic strikes of this epoch differed sharply from "contagious" strikes, which spread spontaneously like those of 1877, in two respects. First, the sympathetic strikes were called by the workers involved, through formal union procedures. Although figures comparing officials with unofficial strikes are not available, two contrasting statistics illustrate Hall's point. The construction industry was always the leading center of sympathetic strikes. In New York more than 70 per cent of the establishments shut by sympathetic action between 1890 and 1892 were involved in building construction. On the other hand, over the entire period of federal data (1881–1905) no less than 98.03 per cent of the strikes in that industry were called by unions.

Second, as Hall observed, the tendency toward sympathetic strikes was "least in those cases where the dispute concerns conditions of employment such as wages and hours, and [was] greatest in regard to disputes which involve questions of unionism—the employment of only union men, the recognition of the union, etc." The rise of sympathetic strikes, like the rise of strikes over rules and recognition, was part of the struggle for craftsmen's control—its most aggressive and far-reaching manifestation. . . .

. . . As craftsmen unionized, they not only made their struggles for control increasingly collective and deliberate, but also manifested a *growing* consciousness of the dependence of their efforts on those of workers in other crafts. They drew strength in this struggle from their functional autonomy, which was derived from their superior knowledge, exercised through self-direction and their direction of others at work, and both nurtured and in turn was nurtured by a mutualistic ethic, which repudiated important elements of acquisitive individualism. As time passed this autonomy was increasingly often codified in union rules, which were collectively "legislated" and upheld through the commitment of the individual craftsmen and through a swelling number of strikes to enforce them. Organized efforts reached the most aggressive and inclusive level of all in joint action among the various crafts for mutual support. When such actions enlisted all workers in an industry (as happened when women unionized in shoe manufacturing), and when they produced a strong propensity of unionized craftsmen to strike in support of each other's claims, they sharply separated the aggressive from the conservative consequences of craftsmen's autonomy and simultaneously provoked an intense, concerted response from the business community.

In an important sense, the last years of the depression represented only a lull in the battle. With the return of prosperity in 1898, both strikes and union organizing quickly resumed their upward spiral, work rules again seized the center of the stage, and sympathetic strikes became increasingly numerous and bitterly fought. Manufacturers' organizations leapt into the fray with the open shop drive, while their spokesmen cited new government surveys to support their denunciations of workers "restriction of output."

On the other hand, important new developments distinguished the first decade of the twentieth century from what had gone before. Trade union officials, who increasingly served long terms in full-time salaried positions, sought to negotiate the terms of work with employers, rather than letting their members "legislate" them. The anxiety of AFL leaders to secure trade agreements and to ally with "friendly employers," like those affiliated with the National Civic Federation, against the open shop drive, prompted them to repudiate the use of sympathetic strikes. The many such strikes which took place were increasingly lacking in union sanction and in any event never reached the level of the early 1890s.

Most important of all, new methods of industrial management undermined the very foundation of craftsmen's functional autonomy. Job analysis through time and motion study allowed management to learn, then to systematize the way the work itself was done. Coupled with systematic supervision and new forms of incentive payment it permitted what Frederick Winslow Taylor called "*enforced* standardization of methods, *enforced* adoption of the best implements and working conditions, and *enforced* cooperation of all the employees under management's detailed direction." Scientific management, in fact, fundamentally disrupted the craftsmen's styles of work, their union rules and standards rates, and their mutualistic ethic, as it transformed American industrial practice between 1900 and 1930. Its basic effect, as Roethlisberger and Dickson discovered in their experiments at Western Electric's Hawthorne Works, was to place the worker "at the bottom level of a highly stratified organization," leaving his "established routines of work, his cultural traditions of craftsmanship, [and] his personal interrelations" all "at the mercy of technical specialists."

Two important attributes of the scientific management movement become evident only against the background of the struggles of nineteenth-century craftsmen to direct their own work in their own collective way. First, the appeal of the new managerial techniques to manufacturers involved more than simply a response to new technology and a new scale of business organization. It also implied a conscious endeavor to uproot those work practices which had been the taproot of whatever strength organized labor enjoyed in the late nineteenth century. A purely technological explanation of the spread of Taylorism is every bit as inadequate as a purely technological explanation of craftsmen's autonomy.

Second, the apostles of scientific management needed not only to abolish older industrial work practices, but also to discredit them in the public eye. Thus Taylor roundly denied that even "the high class mechanic" could "ever thoroughly understand the science of doing his work," and pasted the contemptuous label of "soldiering" over all craft rules, formal and informal alike. Progressive intellectuals seconded his arguments. Louis Brandeis hailed scientific management for "reliev[ing] labor of responsibilities not its own." And John R. Commons considered it "immoral to hold up to this miscellaneous labor, as a class, the hope that it can ever manage industry." If some workers do "shoulder responsibility," he explained, "it is because certain *individuals* succeed, and then those individuals immediately close the doors, and labor, as a class, remains where it was."

It was in this setting that the phrase "workers' control" first entered the vocabulary of the American labor movement. It appeared to express a radical, if often amorphous, set of demands which welled up around the end of World War I among workers in the metal trades, railroading, coal mining, and garment industries. Although those demands represented very new styles of struggle in a unique industrial and political environment, many of the workers who expressed them could remember the recent day when in fact, the manager's brains had been under the workman's cap.

## French Heels and Ladyhood in the World of Early-Twentieth-Century Garment Strikers

### NAN ENSTAD

When more than 20,000 shirtwaist workers walked off their jobs in New York City in November 1909, the public debate immediately focused on the flamboyant fashion of the female strikers. "I had come to observe the Crisis of a Social Condition;" wrote one commentator for *Collier's* magazine, "but apparently this was a Festive Occasion. Lingerie waists were elaborate, [hair] puffs towered; there were picture turbans and di'mont pendants." Working women were well known for their exuberant embrace of consumer culture products, particularly fashion, but elaborately-dressed female strikers did not meet middle-class expectations for the proper demeanor of political participants, and the reporter for *Collier's* magazine did not immediately recognize them as political subjects. The shirtwaist strike is famous in labor history and women's history both because it was the largest female-dominated strike to that date and because it inaugurated a string of large, "women's strikes" in the 1910s that dramatically asserted working women's political participation and firmly established women's unionism. While women's fashion does not play a large role in the established histories of the strike, it did play a part in the unfolding events of the public strike debate. This article explores women's fashion in relation to the 1909 shirtwaist strike. . . .

Many working women by the turn of the century dressed in flamboyant styles that far exceeded middle-class standards of "taste." They would fashion commodities into a complex signifying practice of creating themselves as "ladies." In the early 1900s, they were well known for their large hats with a profusion of feathers, their "excessive" use of color, and their delicate and impractical french heels. Working women proudly declared themselves "ladies" when they dressed "high."

"Fashioning Political Identities: Cultural Studies and the Historical Construction of Political Subjects," *American Quarterly,* Vol. 50, No. 4 (December 1998), pp. 745–782. © 1998 American Studies. Reprinted by permission of The Johns Hopkins University Press.

Ladyhood was extremely widespread. While some working women, particularly those who joined middle-class sponsored clubs, eschewed the elaborate fashions of ladies, most of the largely Jewish and Italian immigrant shirtwaist workers successively participated in the consumer practices of ladyhood. The cultural experiences of Jewish and Italian women were not identical: young Jewish women enjoyed relative freedom of mobility compared to Italian women, tended to have more control over their paychecks, and more often attended dance halls and amusement parks. These public amusements served, as [Kathy] Peiss noted, as sites for the development of new styles and sexual mores. Italian parents expected daughters' leisure to be closely supervised, and young Italian women more rarely participated in the public amusements that Peiss studied. However, Italian women did dress in "style," a consumer practice which relied less upon autonomous mobility in the city than did dancing or amusement park attendance. Thus, the cultural experiences of Jewish and Italian women intersected in the purchase of fashion. Working women enacted ladyhood when they donned their dress and adopted mannerisms and a distinctive walk, and sometimes "high"-sounding names—all of which signaled that they were ladies.

When working women thus created themselves as ladies, they appropriated the status due to middle- and upper-class "ladies." Fashion served as a display of class distinction and taste, a cultural marker of privilege and difference. This marker served to express class hierarchies and differentiate middle-class women from working-class women and women of color, excluding the latter from the category of "lady." Working women did not simply dress for respectability; indeed their flamboyant styles regularly offended the middle class. Rather, they staged a daily carnivalesque class inversion by appropriating a key expression of class privilege for women: fashion and adornment. Ladyhood was a signifying practice, rooted in commodities, which allowed working women to occupy a creative space of cultural contradiction with a broad resulting range of meanings and implications. The practice of working ladyhood engaged gender, class, and ethnic exclusions that working women experienced daily, in a society which saw the heroic worker as male, the heroic women as middle-class, and the heroic American as a native-born Anglo-Saxon. Thus, the practice of working ladyhood created a site of multiplicity, a shifting identity that played off a range of cultural contradictions and instabilities in turn-of-the-century society.

Middle-class contemporaries of working ladies usually assumed that these practices simply revealed a lack of seriousness, a trivial concern with individual appearance or a reverence for the upper class. However, closer cultural study of these practices uncover fashion's place in a more complex set of social relations. . . .

When working women created the particular signifying practice of ladyhood, they necessarily built upon and modified already-established meanings associated with clothing in U.S. society. Fashion was a powerful meaning system to which working women had access, albeit limited, in a context in which their long hours of poorly paid labor quite dramatically circumscribed their world. Indeed, working women might feel a privileged access to fashion. They were, in their eyes, experts because so many of them produced, washed, or sold clothing. Through fashion, women borrowed from the cultural values placed on objects they produced to dignify their own de-valued labor. Working women knew from daily experience that owners subjugated workers' heath and welfare to the needs of industry in exchange for a wage which was usually inadequate. Working-class immigrant women learned daily what United States society had to teach them: the clothes they made, laundered, or sewed were more important than they themselves were. When they borrowed from the signifying logic of the display window to increase their own worth, they claimed a cultural franchise that they would otherwise lack.

Just as work experiences taught women that they held less value than the products they made, their social interactions taught them that, in the United States, appearance mattered more than character. Working women's encounters with bosses, wealthier Americans and men in general shaped their understanding of the ethnic, class, and sexual economies in which they had to find a place, all of which involved clothing. Many historical accounts have recounted this generation of urban immigrants' embrace of American fashion as a sign of "Americanization." These historians have focused primarily on the differences between customs in the United States, where ready-made clothing made it possible for most to dress with style, and the "old country," where fine dress often still signaled mobility. Indeed, in parts of Eastern Europe only women of the upper class could wear hats, coding a rigid caste system. When immigrants embraced "American" fashions, they imbued them with meanings rooted in a historical memory of oppression. But the social meanings of clothing were also embedded in day-to-day practices and hierarchies in the United States.

Immigrants soon learned of these hierarchies. One candy manufacturer, who primarily employed Italian women, admitted that he would not hire a woman who did not wear a hat when she applied for a job, but arrived bare-headed or wearing a shawl in the tradition of Italy. He claimed "Americanized" women were easier to work with. Lillian Wald similarly reported that many Lower East Side working women wore "paint" on their faces, not first out of a love for make-up, but because "employers did not like to have jaded-looking girls working for them." Perhaps employers did not like to see the daily effects of labor on their young, female employers. Whatever the logic of individual employers, however, they sent a consistent message that appearance, rather than experience, skill, aptitude, or attitude, was what mattered when applying for a job. In addition, they made it clear that appearance, rather than contribution to the nation's wealth as a worker, or participation in U.S. culture, was at the heart of Americanization.

Working women also regularly encountered members of the middle- and upper-classes who drew stark class distinctions on the basis of dress. Working women widely understood and resented that many people saw them as "unrefined," therefore less feminine and/or womanly, because of their labor and their income. . . .

Finally, women quickly learned that clothes played an economic role in romantic encounters with men as well. As one garment worker, who spent 25 percent of her wage of four dollars a week on clothing, said, "A girl who does not dress well is stuck in a corner, even if she is pretty." . . . Women knew the cultural value of clothing in a setting in which the labor market kept women's wages systematically lower than men's.

Given the value of commodities in U.S. culture, particularly in comparison to the value of working-class women's labor, and the currency of clothing in the face of nativism, classism and sexism, it is not surprising that fashion became important to working-class women. Indeed, dressing with style was a working-class tradition for white working-class women before and after the time period and context studied here, and it has been key to African Americans as well, for similar reasons. Nevertheless, the specific meanings that clothing held for working-class women took root in their particular circumstances. Clothing took on collective meaning in the practices of acquiring it, discussing and wearing it at work, as well as in the specific ways working women altered established styles, or the "content" of their fashion. . . .

Working women's ability to acquire ready-made clothes in the latest styles should not be heralded as the "democratization" of fashion due to industrialization. This oft-repeated thesis neglects the fact that the clothing available to working women, while stylish, was of decidedly inferior quality. Working women complained of cheap shirtwaists, suits, and shoes that came apart almost immediately. The possibilities offered to working women by consumer capitalism were matched by painful limitations. Furthermore, the availability of fashionable styles did not obliterate, but merely shifted, the role of clothing in class distinction.

When working women purchased clothing, they exercised their new entitlement as workers. As females, women traditionally worked to maintain the household; when they worked for pay, they owed the whole of their wages to the family economy. Parents expected daughters to hand over pay envelopes to the household financial manager, which in Italian and Jewish households was usually the mother. In return, most received a small allowance. Fathers and sons, however, could justly open their own envelopes before returning home and extract a sum for their own leisure. While most fathers also gave their pay envelopes to the household manager, they could remove a sum for their own portion. Many sons simply paid "board" to their mothers and kept the remaining money for themselves. Breadwinning still carried an association with a male role, and male breadwinning earned this right. . . . When women claimed their pay envelopes to purchase clothing, they laid claim to the status of "worker," enjoyed by their brothers but often denied to them, and made clothing a badge of their own labor.

While purchasing clothing could serve as an enactment of one's identity as "worker," women also drew upon their work skills and the knowledge of styles they gained at work to make and alter clothing. As stated earlier, working women could rarely do *all* of their own sewing: a tailored suit, jacket, or dress was a complicated and laborious process that demanded more time, and often more skill, than working women possessed. Nevertheless, working women often made shirtwaists and underwear and applied trimmings, lace, feathers, and other decorations to dresses and hats. Thus, they rescued from their labor additional personal value, and inflected their consumer practices with an element of their own creative production. . . .

. . . Department store workers were infamous for learning the styles from the clothing that they sold, and laundry workers saw a continual stream of fashionable clothing go through their machines. While some saw working women's knowledge of styles as morally threatening, giving women a taste for what they could not afford and potentially leading to prostitution, others saw a version of populism in the practice of wearing the styles one worked on during the day. . . . While paid little for their labor, working women elevated their own cultural value by wearing the clothing they produced.

Women not only used their knowledge of styles gained from their labor, they sometimes acquired materials, and actually made the clothing, while at work. The *New York Tribune* reported that one garment worker made her shirtwaist from fine, thin material bought from a Hester Street pushcart for twenty cents. But she used her skills as a neckwear worker, and materials from the ship, to give her shirtwaist distinction. . . . While this worker was reportedly "allowed" to take remnants from the shop, bosses regularly accused garment workers of stealing and some searched workers at the door for pilfered piece work materials. Besides the obvious opportunity to liberate some materials while at the shop, garment workers often took piece work home with them at night to complete before the next morning, in a frantic attempt to raise their wages, offering an additional opportunity to keep some materials for themselves. The written record registers women's outrage at searches and accusations of theft, and it is undeniable that many were falsely accused. However, women's sense of their right to the styles which they made can be seen as part of a "moral economy"—a way to recover unpaid wages or long hours lost to labor—and might have included directly absconding with workplace materials, whether remnants or whole pieces of fabric.

Some workers also used the workplace itself to make their own clothing. One worker reported that when the dull season hit their shop in May, workers would sit and wait for work that might come in, an experience that was typical in the small garment shops. They used this time to make their own clothes on the shop's machines. . . . Garment workers were paid by the piece in the vast majority of garment shops. This practice meant that bosses paid workers less when there was less work, transferring much of the risk and cost ensuing from a seasonal industry to the workers. In order to work at all, these women needed to sit and wait for the small amount of work they would get to perform. Their wages typically dropped by half during such periods. When workers made their own clothes, they were not literally taking time back from the owner, since they were not being paid at that moment. However, they did turn the oppressive piece work system to some value to themselves, and used machines otherwise not available to them. . . . These workers were not overtly challenging the labor system, but they were recapturing some of the value of their labor from its appropriation by capital.

When women bought or made clothing, then, their consumption was already infused with work-related meanings. The second aspect of consumption—the act of wearing the clothes—was also related to their workplace experiences. To be sure, women wore their fine clothes to dances, amusements parks, weddings, the movies, or to walk about in the evenings, activities that could build upon and augment the workplace culture. But women also wore their fine clothes to work.

Sometimes, women wore their fine clothes to work because they planned to go directly to dancehalls or other amusements after work. . . . Some women wore their stylish clothes to work because they had no other clothes to wear, having invested the whole of their budget into one outfit. Other women wore fine clothes to work because they wanted to look well when travelling to and from work. When [Dorothy] Richardson's "learner" at a box factory found she did not have an apron, she instructed her to turn her skirt inside out to protect it from the glue. When Richardson hesitated, her learner said, "The *ladies* I'm used to working with likes to walk home looking decent and respectable no difference what they're like other times." . . . When working women shed aprons and donned fine clothes for the trip home, they asserted that their labor did not lower their dignity or worth.

Whatever the reason women wore their fine clothes to work, one result was that they shared, and showed off, their clothes to each other, making clothing a central part of workplace culture. Additionally, the importance of "fashion" was larger than the products themselves, because women dreamed about and discussed them, imagining future purchases and styles seen in shop windows. When women discussed "swell evening pumps and lace petticoats," they shared information about styles, developed common "tastes" in clothing, and created a collective dream world centered in commodities.

The consumption of fashion, then, consisted of a number of related social practices which shaped the place of the particular clothing items in women's lives. These social acts of purchasing and making the products, of wearing clothing at the workplace, and of discussing fashion while working all had imaginative elements in themselves. To purchase a fashionable dress from a brightly lit pushcart or to dream together of a coveted outfit served to create a collective dream world of commodity consumption, one rooted in the painful limitations of daily life and labor. . . .

Working women dressed in fashion, but they exaggerated elements of style that specifically coded femininity: high-heeled shoes, large or highly decorated hats, exceedingly long trains (if trains were in style), and fine petticoats and shirtwaists. In addition, they used more color than was considered tasteful by the middle class to dress up their garments and heighten the element of display in their clothing. As one headline read: "East Side Fashions. They Keep Pace With Those of Fifth Avenue, and Perhaps Outrun Them a Little." . . . By appropriating and exaggerating the accoutrements of "ladyhood," they invested the category of "lady" with great imaginative value, implicity challenging dominant notions of ladyhood and filling the category with their own flamboyant practices. Working women created a cultural style similar in ways to gay camp or drag, in that they appropriated an overdetermined style of femininity that they were excluded from by the dominant culture. Like gay men in drag, working ladies seemed more absorbed in the element of display than in verisimilitude. Working ladies created their own distinctive style which implicitly denied that labor made them masculine, degraded, or alien. . . .

French heels also became popular with working women. These high heels received a mixed reception in the United States and never gained wide acceptance among the middle class. Rose Pastor rhetorically queried working women:

> If common sense bids one wear a low-heeled shoe and, fashion, a shoe with French heels that come about three inches high and makes one look like a trained dog walking on its hind legs—the body aslant forward and very expressive of a longing to drop on all fours and make walking easier, which ought one to choose?

French heels were often among the first purchases newly arrived immigrants made in America. . . .

Ladyhood was not something working women could shed at will like a suit of clothes. Rather, ladyhood, once enacted, was who they were. It was not an entirely "assigned" identity; nor was it a free choice. Many scholars accept the idea that identity is historically constructed rather than innate or natural. However, the ways in which this construction occurs and its implications for human agency are still very much under debate. In some scholars' works, this construction occurs simply through the assignment of identities of race, gender or class by a larger society. Agency in many of these works nevertheless is inherent in the individual, who manages to maximize his or her interests despite such assignments. Seeing ladyhood as an enacted cultural practice suggests a more complex view. . . .

. . . Once working women became ladies, ladyhood was part of their subjectivities, part of who they were, engaging their histories and their present placement in the web of power relations. When these women went out on strike, they inevitably did so, at least initially, *as ladies.* That is, working women carried the subjectivities formed through consumer practices into the context of the strike—they could not do otherwise.

The remainder of this article explores the relationship of ladyhood to strike public relations and an emerging image of the "girl striker." The sight of fashionably-dressed "ladies" out on strike surprised onlookers who did not understand their cultural practices and who expected honorable strikers to appear "rational," bringing serious complaints to the public attention. To many, fashionably-dressed working women could not be political subjects. The loose alliance of leaders in the International Ladies' Garment Union (ILGWU), the Women's Trade Union League (WTUL), and the Socialist Party (SP) responded by representing—and hailing—working women as strikers in terms that defended them as political actors but denied and conflicted with their established identities as ladies. Many striking women continued to identify as ladies and wound their subcultural practices into their overtly political identities as strikers. However, their identities as ladies conflicted with labor leaders' address and would not be represented in leaders' accounts.

When the strike began on 23 November 1909, working women were not automatically seen and accepted as political actors by the general public. While this strike would later become known as one of the many "women's strikes" of the 1910s, in November of 1909 a walkout of this magnitude had never before occurred in women-dominated industries and the sight of thousands of women striking on the streets of New York surprised labor leaders, employers and the general public alike. As the reporter for *Collier's* wrote:

> My preconceived idea of a strike was a somber meeting where somber resolutions were made, and there was always a background of mothers wiping their eyes with their aprons vowing that they would still endure for the Great Cause, and of babes who wept bitterly for a soup bone to suck. . . . "But they don't look as if they had any grievance," I objected. It is always painful to renounce a preconceived picture.

It was up to labor leaders to legitimate working women's positions as political actors to a middle-class public which, like the *Collier's* reporter, judged the seriousness and worth of the strikers' cause in part by their appearance. The *Collier's* reporter had a "preconceived picture" of strikers as "somber," and judged the validity of their claim by the presence or absence of her notion of rationality, a preconception of political subjectivity rooted in Enlightenment ideals. . . .

. . . [T]he elaborate fashion of shirtwaist strikers signaled femininity and irrationality: two qualities which disqualified one from being a political subject. In addition, many saw elaborate fashion on working-class women as evidence of wealth and desires "beyond the station" of the strikers, invalidating their claims that wages were too low. Women's flamboyant fashion thus would become a lightening rod for political debate about the central contests of the strike: women's right to act politically and the validity of their claims. . . .

The most visible aspect of women's political participation in the strike was picketing. While women certainly had picketed in the past, their visible and prolonged occupation of street corners was still seen by some as improper behavior for women. Indeed, early in the conflict the Triangle shop hired prostitutes to mock and harass picketers, knowing that this would intensify the association between female picketing and disreputable behavior. In addition, accounts of picketing in the press used portrayals of fashion on the picket line to represent a distinctively feminine, irrational disorder. On 26 November, only three days into the strike, the *New York World* reported a "riot" between strikers and strikebreakers in front of a large shop on Greene street in the Lower East Side. The *New York World* described picketing women as an "army of Amazons" who tore at the scabs with a fierceness and "steady grinding and ripping sounds produced by tearing clothing and scratching faces." The next day, the *New York Tribune* claimed that women used "the most approved feminine tactics" in the fight between picketers and scabs: "Hair was pulled out of heads by the handful, hats and coiffures were torn, cresses were disarranged, and many received marks of the fight from the nails of their antagonists." A later newspaper article described a "riot" in which "The girls kicked, scratched and pummelled [*sic*] each other until the street was littered with torn and tattered millinery." Labor leaders greatly protested articles which painted strikers as mobs of wild girls, rather than as workers with a right to picket, and denied charges of working women's violence. According to the union, employers hired thugs who attacked the picketers, giving the police excuse to harass and arrest them. Nevertheless, torn and dishevelled clothing in these descriptions probably signified irrationality and gender deviance for middle-class readers. In addition, articles about torn clothing and physically impassioned battles could carry a titillating element for an audience that was primed to see working women in public—that is, "streetwalkers"—in sexual terms.

Several female columnists in the popular press defended the striking women, countered the charge that they were interested only in fashion and fun, and provided a counterpoint to the predominant image of the strikers. However, their defense of the strikers did not represent them as political actors but as impoverished women in need of uplift. They accepted the formulation that fashionable dress signaled frivolousness and lack of need, and therefore directly contradicted charges that working women dressed fashionably. Beatrice Fairfax, reporting on one parade, insisted that the strikers "were all quietly and suitably dressed, there was no attempt at finery. Some of them were hatless." . . . An image of young women who had "no pleasure" and who made "no attempt at finery" fit nicely the preconception of the "deserving poor," consistent with an image of a strike in which, in the *Collier's* reporter's words, "babes . . . wept bitterly for a soup bone to suck." Such images of the strikers assured middle-class readers that striking women challenged poor working conditions but not the class structure itself. Middle-class journalists who supported the strikers thus represented them less as political actors and more as the needy poor.

Strike leaders responded to popular press representations of the strikers, and had little choice but to deal with the issue of clothing. Their strategy was to combine enlightenment ideals about rational political participation with quite different, charity-based notions of "needs." Leaders represented striking women as bringing rational claims to unionization, but bolstered their worthiness by emphasizing their abject poverty and exceptional physical need. Unlike middle-class journalists, they did not claim that strikers had never had a "pretty dress," for such a statement would ring false for any who had seen the strikers. Rather, leaders emphasized the poor *quality* of the clothing and avoided the issue of fashionable styles. . . . While the writers did not exaggerate the poverty of these underpaid workers, their accounts erased the participation of working ladies and their indigenous language of entitlement related to dress from much of the strike record. One article on the strike proved the need for higher wages through a meticulous discussion of working women's budgets, demonstrating that working women dressed "in scanty clothes" on very little money. . . .

. . . Theresa Malkiel . . . reassured readers that "It is not for riches or luxuries" that women struck, but simply for "a living wage, a little more freedom, the right to co-operate with each other for their common defense." Strike leaders' attempts to construct the strikers as rational political subjects affected the publicity they produced about the strikers' demeanor, particularly surrounding the "fun" of the strike and picketing. The popular press tended to represent the strikers as having fun on strike, dancing in holiday clothes. In direct contrast, Malkiel showed the strikers as rationally taking personal risks, not partying, when they walked off their jobs: "Of the 47,000 workers employed in the industry 35,000 laid down their scissors, shook the threads off their clothes and calmly left the place that stood between them and starvation." . . .

The strategic response of pro-union publications to the popular press representations of working women is understandable. The visible culture of working ladies could be used by the press to attack women's already shaky claims to a political voice. Middle-class columnists' defense created additional challenges for leaders, because they positioned strikers simply as charity cases in need of philanthropy and pity rather than as political actors. By representing strikers both as rational political actors and as charitable subjects, leaders softened the challenge that thousands of working-class immigrant women who demanded a political voice posed to gender, class and ethnic hierarchies. Striking women *as clients* made political claims that directly threatened shop owners' interests but that did not appear to threaten the class position of those that pitied them or took up their cause. As leaders cast striking women as supplicants, they tacitly placed middle-class observers in the powerful position of judge and, potentially, benefactor. Thus working women gained "a voice," that is, a recognized identity in relation to public and state power, partly via claims of defenselessness. However, by erasing women's subcultural practices, rather than building upon their meanings, they represented women in terms that striking ladies would find conflicted at best, insulting at worst. . . .

A number of articles and stories directed toward working women promoted the ideal of the rational girl striker in the years after the strike not only by erasing women's popular culture practices, but also by attacking them. . . . [R]egular articles by key organizers Gertrude Barnum and Pauline Newman (who had been a shirtwaist striker) urged women to give up their popular culture practices, which they saw as irrational, and to be more serious-minded. The attempts of some WTUL,

ILGWU and SP leaders to dissuade working women from consuming elaborated fashions reveal that their aim to construct working women as rational, enlightenment subjects was not entirely strategic. Rather, they believed that such a subjectivity was indeed necessary for political action, and that working women had to *reform* their cultural practices rather than build upon them. . . . Such representations did not simply describe actual women strikers, rather they called the rational girl striker into being. . . .

. . . [T]here are traces of evidence that for some working women, the cultural practices of ladyhood proved to be resources as they enacted formally-recognized political positions as strikers. Clara Lemlich, seasoned radical and striking shirtwaist worker, wrote the only article by a striking worker that appeared in the popular press, in order to convey the grievances of the working women. Lemlich's rhetoric in that article diverged markedly from the other leaders' rhetoric. Interestingly, approximately 40 percent of Lemlich's remarks conveyed these grievances through discussions of clothing, and reveal an emerging language of political entitlement that leaders in the ILGWU and the WTUL did not build upon. Lemlich first complained that there were no dressing rooms in the shops, forcing women to hang their coats and hats on hooks along the walls. "Sometimes a girl has a new hat," said Lemlich. "It never is much to look at because it never costs more than fifty cents, but it's pretty sure to be spoiled after it's been at the shop" Lemlich then used the issue of clothing rhetorically to counter the fact that, to the bosses, the women "are part of the machines they are running." . . . Lemlich was not simply arguing that women deserved to dress in a utilitarian way, but that they took pleasure and pride in the way that they dressed. They should be treated in accordance with the respect they showed themselves, that is, as "humans," not as machines.

Some might think that a demand for dressing rooms in the face of such oppressive and dangerous conditions was a trivial or even narcissistic concern. However, Lemlich's remarks would resonate with the concerns of working women who dressed as "ladies." She drew on the language and ideology common to working women and used it to articulate her grievance within a strike context. The "wish-image" embedded in the working ladies' fashion, that is, the utopian desire to be valued, was already tied to workplace practices and workplace culture, as women displayed, discussed and even made their clothing at work. Lemlich linked this working-class utopian imagination to the collective action of the strike. Her demand for dressing rooms was thus both literal and symbolic. Lemlich knew that for working women, such a demand would challenge the very ways that industrial labor devalued their lives. Thus, her grievance that shops should contain dressing rooms contained a complex defense of working women's humanity in opposition to workplace oppression. That even Lemlich, who had the discursive resources of socialism at her disposal, drew on the language of ladyhood to articulate grievances indicates the importance of working ladyhood to the strike culture as well as to workplace culture.

Labor leaders understood the threat of women's fashion to the public image of the strikers, and responded by strategically shaping a view of the strikers to match public expectations. They painted strikers as poor and needy, wearing thin and tattered clothing, and bringing rational grievances to public attention in a serious and calm way. They then worked to get striking women to match this image. Leaders thus obscured ladyhood and the fashion of the strikers, with three ramifications. First, they failed to build upon the indigenous practices and resistance of working women and urged women to adopt an image and subjectivity based in some tropes that they had already rejected. Most notably, they asked women who based their sense of self in the bright and proud clothing of ladyhood to embrace an image of poverty and tatters. In other words, union leaders hailed women in terms that would likely be highly conflicted, rather than simply emancipatory, for many. In doing so, leaders asked some strikers to fundamentally change who they were. Second, leaders thus narrowed the public image of labor union resistance and types of political identities. . . .

Finally, because the self-representation of working ladies did not become incorporated into union demands or rhetoric, it is largely hidden in the historical record of the strike. . . .

A rigid distinction between "politics" and "culture" would not benefit our analysis of these events. We need to understand the ways in which "ladyhood" already functioned at specific times as a political identity: it engaged central gender, class, and ethnic power dynamics, created solidarity, and provided a language that could be used to counter oppression. Ladyhood was certainly not entirely emancipatory: it could foster individualism as well as collectivity, and it reinforced women's loyalty to consumer industries which did not make working women's best interests their priority. However, if we refuse to acknowledge the political import of any identity that is contradictory or includes oppressive elements then we have few models in history for what we are looking for. We need to understand more about the relationships between identities formed within consumer culture and emerging subjectivities in arenas of formal political exchange. Working women's cultural practices of ladyhood defended their dignity in the face of oppression, and could thus become cultural resources as women created themselves as strikers. But this is not the only important question. Equally significant is how ladyhood interacted with the way strike leaders addressed . . . working women. Clearly, the ability of the union to effectively engage working women's identities and concerns could affect their ability to organize them for long-term union participation.

## ✣ F U R T H E R   R E A D I N G

Appier, Janis. *Policing Women: The Sexual Politics of Law Enforcement and the LAPD* (1998).

Aron, Cynthia Sondik. *Ladies and Gentlemen of the Civil Service: Middle-Class Workers in Victorian America* (1987).

Benson, Susan Porter. *Counter Cultures: Saleswomen, Managers, and Customers in American Department Stores, 1890–1940* (1986).

Cameron, Ardis. *Radicals of the Worst Sort: Laboring Women in Lawrence, Massachusetts, 1860–1912* (1993).

Cooper, Patricia Ann. *Once a Cigarmaker: Men, Women, and Work Culture in American Cigar Factories, 1900–1919* (1987).

Davies, Margery. *Woman's Place Is at the Typewriter: 1870–1930* (1982).

Dye, Nancy Schrom. *As Equals and as Sisters: Feminism, Unionism, and the Women's Trade Union League* (1980).

Eisenstein, Sarah. *Give Us Bread but Give Us Roses* (1983).

Enstad, Nan. *Ladies of Labor, Girls of Adventure: Working Women, Popular Culture, and Labor Politics at the Turn of the Twentieth Century* (1999).

Ewen, Elizabeth. *Immigrant Women and the Land of Dollars: Life and Culture on the Lower East Side, 1890–1925* (1985).

Fantasia, Rick. *Cultures of Solidarity: Consciousness, Action, and Contemporary American Workers* (1988).

Frank, Dana. *Purchasing Power: Consumer Organizing, Gender, and the Seattle Labor Movement, 1919–1929* (1994).

Gamber, Wendy. *The Female Economy: The Millinery and Dressmaking Trades, 1860–1930* (1997).

Garceau, Dee. *The Important Things of Life: Women, Work, and Family in Sweetwater County, Wyoming, 1880–1929* (1997).

Garrison, Dee. *Apostles of Culture: The Public Librarian and American Society, 1876–1920* (1979).

Glenn, Susan A. *Daughters of the Shtetl: Life and Labor in the Immigrant Generation* (1990).

Glickman, Lawrence B. *A Living Wage: American Workers and the Making of Consumer Society* (1997).

Green, Venus. *Race on the Line: Gender, Labor and Technology in the Bell System, 1880–1980* (2001).

Hall, Jacqueline Dowd, et al. *Like a Family: The Making of a Southern Cotton Mill World* (1987).

Halle, David. *America's Working Man: Work, Home, and Politics Among Blue-Collar Property Owners* (1984).

Halpern, Rick. *Down on the Killing Floor: Black and White Workers in Chicago's Packinghouses, 1904–54* (1997).

Hine, Darlene Clark. *Black Women in White: Racial Conflict and Cooperation in the Nursing Profession, 1890–1950* (1989).

Jensen, Joan, and Sue Davidson, eds. *A Needle, a Bobbin, a Strike* (1984).

Kuster, Ken. *Know-How on the Job: The Important Working Knowledge of "Unskilled" Workers* (1978).

Laslett, John H. M. *Colliers Across the Sea: A Comparative Study of Class Formation in Scotland and the American Midwest, 1830–1924* (2000).

Licht, Walter. *Working for the Railroad: The Organization of Work in the Nineteenth Century* (1983).

Melosh, Barbara. *"The Physician's Hand": Work Culture and Conflict in American Nursing* (1982).

Meyer, Stephen, III. *The Five Dollar Day: Labor Management and Social Control in the Ford Motor Company, 1908–1921* (1981).

Meyerowitz, Joanne. *Women Adrift: Independent Wage Earners in Chicago, 1880–1930* (1988).

Montgomery, David. *The Fall of the House of Labor: The Workplace, the State, and American Labor Activism, 1865–1925* (1987).

———. *Workers' Control in America* (1979).

Norwood, Stephen H. *Labor's Flaming Youth: Telephone Operators and Workers Militancy, 1878–1923* (1990).

———. *Strikebreaking and Intimidation: Mercenaries and Masculinity in Twentieth Century America* (2002).

Orleck, Annelise. *Common Sense and a Little Fire: Women and Working-Class Politics in the United States, 1900–1965* (1995).

Palmer, Phyllis. *Domesticity and Dirt: Housewives and Domestic Servants in the United States, 1920–1945* (1989).

Peiss, Kathy. *Cheap Amusements: Working Women and Leisure in Turn-of-the Century New York* (1986).

Reverby, Susan. *Ordered to Care: The Dilemma of American Nursing, 1850–1945* (1987).

Rosenzweig, Roy. *Eight Hours for What We Will: Workers and Leisure in an Industrial City, 1870–1920* (1983).

Ross, Steven. *Working-Class Hollywood: Silent Films and the Shaping of Class in America* (1998).

Ruiz, Vicki L. *Cannery Women, Cannery Lives: Mexican Women, Unionization, and the California Food Processing Industry, 1930–1950* (1987).

Sacks, Karen Brodkin. *Caring by the Hour: Women, Work and Organizing at Duke Medical Center* (1988).

Sharpless, Rebecca. *Fearless Ground, Narrow Choices: Women on Texas Cotton Farms, 1900–1940* (1999).

Strom, Sharon Hartman. *Beyond the Typewriter: Gender, Class, and the Origins of Modern American Office Work, 1900–1930* (1992).

Tax, Meredith. *The Rising of the Women: Feminist Solidarity and Class Conflict, 1880–1917* (1980).

Waldrep, G. C. *Southern Workers and the Search for Community: Spartanburg County, South Carolina* (2000).

Willett, Julie A. *Permanent Waves: The Making of the American Beauty Shop* (2000).

Zavella, Patricia. *Women's Work and Chicano Families: Cannery Workers of the Santa Clara Valley* (1988).

# Americans at Work in the Industrial Era

In this antebellum painting by Stanhope A. Forbes, *Forging the Anchor,* nineteenth-century work values and techniques are positively depicted. The work is cooperative and intrinsically important and engages both muscle and mind. On the right an apprentice stokes the fire while the tools of the blacksmith trade rest nearby. (Hagley Museum and Library)

In 1868 artist Stanley Fox offered *Harper's Bazaar* readers a sketch entitled *Women and Their Work in the Metropolis.* Note the homeworking mother who occupies the enlarged central panel. (Museum of American History)

In 1903 skilled workers in this Lynn, Massachusetts, shoe factory still cut and sorted leather with few tools and little direct supervision. (Hagley Museum and Library)

In a cotton field near Memphis, an early-twentieth-century plantation owner weighs the cotton picked by his hired hands after they have filled their hampers. (National Archives)

Black workers gather crude turpentine in a North Carolina pine forest in 1903. (Hagley Museum and Library)

During most of the twentieth century, office work has been organized according to Taylorite principles and segregated by gender, as in this office scene from the 1920s. (Culver Pictures)

Machinist Herman Backhoffer stands proudly beside his giant lathe at the Westinghouse turbine shop in Liston, Pennsylvania, just outside Philadelphia, in 1919. Such skilled northern European workers were among the most militant trade unionists in the World War I era and were often exceedingly hostile to the unskilled immigrants recently arrived from eastern and southern Europe. (Hagley Museum and Library)

By the early twentieth century, bread baking had moved from home to factory and had shifted from women's work to men's work, as this 1930 photograph of a commercial bakery near Philadelphia shows. (Hagley Museum and Library)

Anthracite miners in eastern Pennsylvania still used the pick, shovel, and hammer when this photograph was taken in 1930. Although the United Mine Workers of America would soon reorganize these coal fields and challenge the power of the Philadelphia-based railroads that owned these mines, the union could not forestall the postwar decline of anthracite as a heating fuel and the subsequent impoverishment of the region. (Hagley Museum and Library)

Wilmington, Delaware, leaders of the International Union of Marine and Shipbuilding Workers of America, CIO, sign their first contract with the Pusey and Jones Company in March 1941. Midcentury labor leaders often dressed as middle-class professionals, but in this bargaining ceremony the class divide is obvious. (Hagley Museum and Library)

Women steadily increased their proportion of the paid-labor force during the twentieth century, but light assembly and inspection remained a job "ghetto" where women factory workers were usually concentrated, as in this auto-parts assembly line of the late 1940s. (The Archives of Labor and Urban Affairs, Wayne State University)

Led by local president Paul Silver, center, these postwar shop stewards at Detroit Steel Products (UAW Local 351) made the union's democratic influence felt at the point of production. Silver is wearing a UAW bowling sweater, indicating his support of the union campaign to build an integrated bowling league at a time when the sport was otherwise racially segregated. (AFL-CIO Metro Detroit)

Although the Taft-Hartley Act was not the "slave labor" law denounced by most contemporary trade-union leaders, its passage in 1947 did help bring the growth of the labor movement to a halt. Here a Detroit Labor Day float dramatizes union opposition to the new law. (Archives of Labor and Urban Affairs, Wayne State University)

The time clock, here being punched by employees of the Lukens Steel Company about 1950, was one of the most common technical innovations devised by the scientific-management movement. In the years before the First World War, the time clock had replaced the factory whistle as a device for regulating the blue-collar workday. (Hagley Museum and Library)

In 1989 thousands of union miners and their supporters were arrested by Virginia state police during the Pittston strike in the southwest corner of the state. The United Mine Workers union struck to defend the health and pension benefits of its members, but the conflict proved most notable for the strikers' mass civil disobedience and their spirited solidarity, here signified by the fatigue-style hunting clothes that many strikers adopted as a uniform. (William E. Lester, United Mine Workers of America)

More than 70 percent of all American jobs are now categorized as service work, although wages, work responsibilities, and education levels can vary greatly within that employment sector. Wal-Mart and the Post Office are the largest employers in the United States. (Jim West)

At the end of the 20th century living wage campaigns blossomed on many university campuses. They were a response to the declining value of the minimum wage (one-third less than its real value in the 1960s) and difficulties faced by low-wage workers who sought to join trade unions. These students are sitting-in at the University of Virginia (Jim West)

The labor-intensive health-care industry was a frontier for union growth in the early 21st century. White women and people of color have therefore become a majority of all new union recruits. Here the Service Employees International Union demands a pay raise for Detroit nursing home workers. (Jim West)

# CHAPTER
## 8

# *Labor and the State During the Progressive Era*

The first two decades of the twentieth century are often called the Progressive Era. This era of social reform and economic regulation saw a broad coalition of reformers, including most of the labor movement, attempting to make the operation of American capitalism accord more closely with those democratic, republican virtues that many believed responsible for national well-being, even as that was defined according to principles privileging white, male, small-producer citizens. Given the strikes, the violence, the poverty, and the inequality associated with America's industrial regime, reformers often labeled the bundle of issues that confronted them "the labor question."

The Progressive Era labor question had two parts. First, unionists and their allies wanted a "living wage" sufficient to sustain a working-class family in dignity and comfort. The living wage idea was often shot through with patriarchal and racist assumptions, but it nevertheless generated a radical critique of the existing labor market. Reformers thought the price employers paid for their labor must be infused with a political and moral value that stood counterpoised to that of either the free market in labor or the presumptive right of the employer to contract with their employees for any wage or working condition independent of state regulation. Because women and children were not considered full citizens during the early years of the twentieth century, protective laws governing the wages and hours for these dependent groups were a favorite reform in the Progressive Era.

The second part of the Progressive Era labor question involved the very nature of American democracy. With the rise of big business late in the nineteenth century, the dichotomy between the rights and privileges of republican citizenship and the enormous power of concentrated capital became a question no Progressive could ignore. During the crisis-plagued second industrial revolution—the epoch of economic instability, corporate mergers, and mass strikes—working-class radicals won a wide audience when they called for an extension into the realm of production and the sphere of the market the basic civil and political rights embedded in the Constitution and its post–Civil War amendments. Unions and Progressives often called this extension "industrial democracy."

*Industrial democracy was not the same thing as socialism, which was predi-
cated on the collective ownership of the means of production, nor was it simply an
updated version of the nineteenth-century republican tradition, which celebrated
the artisan craftsman of manly bearing and looked with some suspicion on those
with lesser skill and independence. Rather, the advocates of industrial democracy
in the early twentieth century saw the new system as the next stage in the evolution
of American freedom. This Progressive Era impulse took the large industrial enterprise for granted as the basic building block of the new commonwealth and looked
for a solution to problems of authority, equality, motivation, and efficiency through
its reorganization and democratization.*

*The idea of industrial democracy flourished during World War I when the
administration of Woodrow Wilson demanded willing consent and workplace loyalty
from a working class whose members were more than half immigrant. The experience
of the Great War produced a generation of unionists, reformers, and governmental
experts who, fifteen years later, would play decisive roles in pushing forward New
Deal efforts to build a labor movement that could inject democratic norms and procedures into the offices, factories, and mines of Depression Era America.*

*Were Progressive Era reformers anticapitalist? Were they antiracist? Feminist?
Why might leaders of the American Federation of Labor (AFL) be hostile to their
reforms? And why might socialists scoff as well?*

## ✦ D O C U M E N T S

Documents 1–3 illustrate some of the ways in which the Supreme Court set national
labor policy before the New Deal of the 1930s. In 1894, the U.S. Army smashed a
nationwide railroad strike led by socialist Eugene V. Debs. In Document 1, lawyers
for Debs's American Railway Union argue for the lawfulness of the strike, whereas
the conservatives who dominated the high court insist that an injunction against the
strike, which halted mail delivery nationwide, is entirely necessary and constitutional.
Little more than a decade later, however, the Supreme Court sustained positive state
action on behalf of women workers, arguing in Document 2, from *Muller* v. *Oregon*
(1908), that Oregon's maximum-hour law was necessary to protect the health and
physical well-being of women workers. When it came to regulating wages, however,
the Court refused to embrace an expansive use of the state regulatory power, finding
in Document 3, from *Adkins* v. *Children's Hospital* (1923), that once women had won
the vote, they were no longer dependents who needed state protection. Individual
women were therefore "free" to make the same kind of employment contract with
an employer as were men.

The Great War that the United States entered in 1917 generated a surge of
patriotic activism. The government smashed radical, antiwar organizations like the
Industrial Workers of the World, but the labor shortage and the political requirements
of the production effort made it possible for women to enter many new occupations
and for unions affiliated with the AFL to double their membership. In Document 4, the
AFL calls for "equal pay for equal work" for women workers, not because of union
feminism, but because male labor leaders feared that employers would use the wartime
demand for workers to put low-wage women on heretofore higher-paying male jobs.

Documents 5 and 6 explore the wartime rhetoric of "industrial democracy," a concept embraced by many Progressive Era reformers. In Document 5, railway union lawyer
Donald R. Richberg, indicting industrial autocrats in 1917, proposes that wage earners

have the same kind of influence in their industries as do those who own the stock and bonds. Contrast his vision with President Woodrow Wilson's call for a "democratization of industry" in Document 6, from a May 1919 speech to Congress. Wilson's plea represented one of the last instances of Progressive Era idealism, which sought some way to raise living standards and give workers a state-sponsored mechanism to make their voice heard in a collective, democratic fashion. The postwar swing against the unions and the left forced the nation to wait almost a generation until such Wilsonian language again resonated among unionists, politicians, and business executives.

## 1. *In Re Debs,* 1895

### *Mr. Lyman Trumbull, for Petitioners.*

The bill states that the prisoners are officers and members of an organization known as the American Railway Union; that in May, 1894, a dispute arose between the Pullman Palace Car Company and its employés which resulted in the employés leaving the service of the company; that the prisoners, officers of the American Railway Union combining together, and with others unknown, with the purpose to compel an adjustment of the said difference and dispute between said Pullman Co. and its employés, caused it to be given out through the newspapers of Chicago, generally, that the American Railway Union would at once create a boycott against the cars manufactured by said Pullman Palace Co., and that in order to make said boycott effective, the members of the American Railway Union who were some of them employed as trainmen or switchmen, or otherwise, in the service of the railroads mentioned, which railroads or some of them are accustomed to haul the sleeping cars manufactured by the Pullman Palace Car Co., would be directed to refuse to perform their usual duties for said railroad companies and receivers in case said railroad companies thereafter attempted to haul Pullman sleeping cars.

Such is the gist of the bill. All that is subsequently alleged as to what was done by the prisoners, was for the purpose of compelling an adjustment of the difference between the Pullman Company and its employés. To accomplish this, the American Railway Union called upon its members to quit work for the companies which had persisted in hauling the Pullman cars. Was there anything unlawful in this? If not, then the prisoners and the members of the American Railway Union were engaged in no unlawful combination or conspiracy. The allegation that the prisoners, officers and directors of the American Railway Union did issue and promulgate certain orders and requests to the members of the unions in the service of certain railway companies in pursuance of said unlawful purpose or conspiracy did not make the purpose unlawful, when the facts stated in the bill show that the purpose was not unlawful. All that the prisoners are charged with threatening to do, or having done, was for the purpose, primarily, of bringing about an adjustment of the differences between the Pullman Company and its employés. It is only incidentally in pursuit of this lawful purpose that prisoners are charged with obstructing commerce.

The boycott of the Pullman sleepers was, as the bill shows, not to obstruct commerce, but for an entirely different purpose.

---

From *In Re Debs,* 158 US 564 (1895).

It was not unlawful for the American Railway Union to call off the members of the organization, although it might incidentally affect the operation of the railroads. Refusing to work for a railroad company is no crime, and though such action may incidentally delay the mails or interfere with interstate commerce, it being a lawful act, and not done for that purpose, is no offence. . . .

### *Mr. Justice Brewer, After Stating the Case, Delivered the Opinion of the Court.*

The case presented by the bill is this: The United States, finding that the interstate transportation of persons and property, as well as the carriage of the mails, is forcibly obstructed, and that a combination and conspiracy exists to subject the control of such transportation to the will of the conspirators, applied to one of their courts, sitting as a court of equity, for an injunction to restrain such obstruction and prevent carrying into effect such conspiracy. Two questions of importance are presented: First. Are the relations of the general government to interstate commerce and the transportation of the mails such as authorize a direct interference to prevent a forcible obstruction thereof? Second. If authority exists, as authority in governmental affairs implies both power and duty, has a court of equity jurisdiction to issue an injunction in aid of the performance of such duty. . . .

It must be borne in mind that this bill was not simply to enjoin a mob and mob violence. It was not a bill to command a keeping of the peace; much less was its purport to restrain the defendants from abandoning whatever employment they were engaged in. The right of any laborer, or any number of laborers, to quit work was not challenged. The scope and purpose of the bill was only to restrain forcible obstructions of the highways along which interstate commerce travels and the mails are carried. And the facts set forth at length are only those facts which tended to show that the defendants were engaged in such obstructions.

A most earnest and eloquent appeal was made to us in eulogy of the heroic spirit of those who threw up their employment, and gave up their means of earning a livelihood, not in defence of their own rights, but in sympathy for and to assist others whom they believed to be wronged. We yield to none in our admiration of any act of heroism or self-sacrifice, but we may be permitted to add that it is a lesson which cannot be learned too soon or too thoroughly that under this government of and by the people the means of redress of all wrongs are through the courts and at the ballot-box, and that no wrong, real or fancied, carries with it legal warrant to invite as a means of redress the coöperation of a mob, with its accompanying acts of violence.

We have given to this case the most careful and anxious attention, for we realize that it touches closely questions of supreme importance to the people of this country. Summing up our conclusions, we hold that the government of the United States is one having jurisdiction over every foot of soil within its territory, and acting directly upon each citizen; that while it is a government of enumerated powers, it has within the limits of those powers all the attributes of sovereignty; that to it is committed power over interstate commerce and the transmission of the mail; that the powers thus conferred upon the national government are not dormant, but have been assumed and put into practical exercise by the legislation of Congress; that in the exercise of those powers it is competent for the nation to remove all obstructions upon highways, natural or artificial, to the passage of interstate commerce or the carrying of the mail; that while it may be competent for the government (through the executive branch and in the use of the entire executive power of the nation) to forcibly remove all such obstructions, it is equally within its competency to appeal to the civil courts for an inquiry and determination as to the existence and character of any alleged obstructions, and if such are found to exist, or threaten to occur, to invoke the powers of those courts to remove or restrain such obstructions; that the jurisdiction of courts to interfere in such matters by injunction is one recognized from ancient times and by indubitable authority; that such jurisdiction is not ousted by the fact that the obstructions are accompanied by or consist of acts in themselves violations of the criminal law; that the proceeding by injunction is of a civil character, and may be enforced by proceedings in contempt; that such proceedings are not in execution of the criminal laws of the land; that the penalty for a violation of injunction is no substitute for and no defence to a prosecution for any criminal offences committed in the course of such violation; that the complaint filed in this case clearly showed an existing obstruction of artificial highways for the passage of interstate commerce and the transmission of the mail—an obstruction not only temporarily existing, but threatening to continue; that under such complaint the Circuit Court had power to issue its process of injunction; that it having been issued and served on these defendants, the Circuit Court had authority to inquire whether its orders had been disobeyed, and when it found that they had been, then to proceed under section 725, Revised Statutes, which grants power "to punish, by fine or imprisonment, . . . disobedience, . . . by any party . . . or other person, to any lawful writ, process, order, rule, decree or command," and enter the order of punishment complained of; and, finally, that, the Circuit Court, having full jurisdiction in the premises, its finding of the fact of disobedience is not open to review on *habeas corpus* in this or any other court. . . .

The petition for a writ of *habeas corpus* is

*Denied.*

## 2. *Muller* v. *Oregon,* 1908

### *Mr. Justice Brewer Delivered the Opinion of the Court.*

It is undoubtedly true, as more than once declared by this court, that the general right to contract in relation to one's business is part of the liberty of the individual, protected by the Fourteenth Amendment to the Federal Constitution; yet it equally well settled that this liberty is not absolute and extending to all contracts, and that a State may, without conflicting with the provisions of the Fourteenth Amendment, restrict in many respects the individual's power of contract. . . .

That woman's physical structure and the performance of maternal functions place her at a disadvantage in the struggle for subsistence is obvious. This is especially true when the burdens of motherhood are upon her. Even when they are not,

From *Muller* v. *Oregon,* 208 US 412 (1908).

by abundant testimony of the medical fraternity continuance for a long time on her feet at work, repeating this from day to day, tends to injurious effects upon the body, and as healthy mothers are essential to vigorous offspring, the physical well-being of woman becomes an object of public interest and care in order to preserve the strength and vigor of the race.

Still again, history discloses the fact that woman has always been dependent upon man. He established his control at the outset by superior physical strength, and this control in various forms, with diminishing intensity, has continued to the present. As minors, though not to the same extent, she has been looked upon in the courts as needing especial care that her rights may be preserved. Education was long denied her, and while now the doors of the school room are opened and her opportunities for acquiring knowledge are great, yet even with that and the consequent increase of capacity for business affairs it is still true that in the struggle for subsistence she is not an equal competitor with her brother. Though limitations upon personal and contractual rights may be removed by legislation, there is that in her disposition and habits of life which will operate against a full assertion of those rights. She will still be where some legislation to protect her seems necessary to secure a real equality of right. Doubtless there are individual exceptions, and there are many respects in which she has an advantage over him; but looking at it from the viewpoint of the effort to maintain an independent position in life, she is not upon an equality. Differentiated by these matters from the other sex, she is properly placed in a class by herself, and legislation designed for her protection may be sustained, even when like legislation is not necessary for men and could not be sustained. It is impossible to close one's eyes to the fact that she still looks to her brother and depends upon him. Even though all restrictions on political, personal and contractual rights were taken away, and she stood, so far as statutes are concerned, upon an absolutely equal plane with him, it would still be true that she is so constituted that she will rest upon and look to him for protection; that her physical structure and a proper discharge of her maternal functions—having in view not merely her own health, but the well-being of the race—justify legislation to protect her from the greed as well as the passion of man. The limitations which this statute places upon her contractual powers, upon her right to agree with her employer as to the time she shall labor, are not imposed solely for her benefit, but also largely for the benefit of all. Many words cannot make this plainer. The two sexes differ in structure of body, in the functions to be performed by each, in the amount of physical strength, in the capacity for long-continued labor, particularly when done standing, the influence of vigorous health upon the future well-being of the race, the self-reliance which enables one to assert full rights, and in the capacity to maintain the struggle for subsistence. This difference justifies a difference in legislation and upholds that which is designed to compensate for some of the burdens which rest upon her.

We have not referred in this discussion to the denial of the elective franchise in the State of Oregon, for while it may disclose a lack of political equality in all things with her brother, that is not itself decisive. The reason runs deeper, and rests in the inherent difference between the two sexes, and in the different functions in life which they perform. . . .

*Affirmed.*

## 3. *Adkins* v. *Children's Hospital*, 1923

### *Mr. Justice Sutherland Delivered the Opinion of the Court.*

In the *Muller Case* the validity of an Oregon statute, forbidding the employment of any female in certain industries more than ten hours during any one day was upheld. The decision proceeded upon the theory that the difference between the sexes may justify a different rule respecting hours of labor in the case of women than in the case of men. It is pointed out that these consist in differences of physical structure, especially in respect of the maternal functions, and also in the fact that historically woman has always been dependent upon man, who has established his control by superior physical strength. . . . But the ancient inequality of the sexes, otherwise than physical, as suggested in the *Muller Case* . . . has continued "with diminishing intensity." In view of the great—not to say revolutionary—changes which have taken place since that utterance, in the contractual, political and civil status of women, culminating in the Nineteenth Amendment, it is not unreasonable to say that these differences have now come almost, if not quite, to the vanishing point. In this aspect of the matter, while the physical differences must be recognized in appropriate cases, and legislation fixing hours or conditions of work may properly take them into account, we cannot accept the doctrine that women of mature age, *sui juris,* require or may be subjected to restrictions upon their liberty of contract which could not lawfully be imposed in the case of men under similar circumstances. To do so would be to ignore all the implications to be drawn from the present day trend of legislation, as well as that of common thought and usage, by which woman is accorded emancipation from the old doctrine that she must be given special protection or be subjected to special restrain in her contractual and civil relationships. In passing, it may be noted that the instant statute applies in the case of a woman employer contracting with a woman employee as it does when the former is a man. . . .

If now, in the light furnished by the foregoing exceptions to the general rule forbidding legislative interference with freedom of contract, we examine and analyze the statute in question, we shall see that it differs from them in every material respect. It is not a law dealing with any business charged with a public interest or with public work, or to meet and tide over a temporary emergency. It has nothing to do with the character, methods or periods of wage payments. It does not prescribe hours of labor or conditions under which labor is to be done. It is not for the protection of persons under legal disability or for the prevention of fraud. It is simply and exclusively a price-fixing law, confined to adult women (for we are not now considering the provisions relating to minors), who are legally as capable of contracting for themselves as men. It forbids two parties having lawful capacity—under penalties as to the employer—to freely contract with one another in respect of the price for which one shall render service to the other in a purely private employment where both are willing, perhaps anxious, to agree, even though the consequence may be to oblige one to surrender a desirable engagement and the other to dispense with the services of a desirable employee. The price fixed by the board need have no relation to the capacity

From *Adkins* v. *Children's Hospital,* 261 US 525 (1923).

or earning power of the employee, the number of hours which may happen to constitute the day's work, the character of the place where the work is to be done, or the circumstances or surroundings of the employment; and, while it has no other basis to support its validity than the assumed necessities of the employee, it takes no account of any independent resources she may have. It is based wholly on the opinions of the members of the board and their advisers—perhaps an average of their opinions, if they do not precisely agree—as to what will be necessary to provide a living for a woman, keep her in health and preserve her morals. It applies to any and every occupation in the District, without regard to its nature or the character of the work.

## 4. The American Federation of Labor Embraces Equal Pay for Equal Work, 1917

"Every labor organization in the country should be keenly interested in the welfare of women in industry," remarked a labor man in this city. "In all adaptable employments women have an equal right to positions. They should be encouraged rather than discouraged. With the transition of industry during the war period the employers, true to their well known concepts, will endeavor to substitute women at a lower wage scale than they are now paying their male employes. It is already being done. Patriotism is the cloak with which they are endeavoring to hide their financial gains by a lower labor cost. Women are being employed in railroad shops and other forms of employment entirely unsuited to them while thousands of men are available for these positions. The opportunity which the war affords unfair and unscrupulous employers to secure cheaper labor by the employment of women should be met by vigorous action by the unions of labor in the localities where this practice is being inaugurated. Equal pay for equal work should be the slogan. Every central body in the country should provide for a standing committee to collect data in its locality relative to the employment of women. If those who are substituting women for men are not paying wages formerly paid to men a local campaign should be inaugurated against the practice and the facts given the widest possible publicity and the officers of the American Federation of Labor informed. When a nation-wide campaign for equal pay is instituted by the labor unions the results will not only be beneficial to women who will enter industry, but the standards established by the unions will largely be maintained. We should not delay our efforts. It will be infinitely easier to check a tendency than correct an abuse."

## 5. Industrial Democracy Needed for the War Effort, 1917

There are in America, as there have been everywhere since governments began, two opposing faiths, one openly admitted—belief in the mass wisdom of democracy; the other openly denied, but the basis of our invisible government—belief in the class wisdom of oligarchy. The well advertised "efficiency" of Germany was the triumph

---

From "Slogan of Equal Pay for Women," *Jewelry Workers' Monthly Bulletin,* I (July 1917), p. 10.

From Donald R. Richberg, "Democratization of Industry," *New Republic,* Vol. II (May 12, 1917), pp. 49–51.

of benevolent autocracy. It was not an hereditary ruler but the united oligarchy of Germany's commercial and political rulers who developed that marvelous coöperative machinery of government and industry. In the forced competition of war the Allied nations have developed like oligarchies and it is hardly conceivable that the end of war will change the character of the governments so reorganized. We have a government in democratic form, and back of that government, and inevitably superior to that government, we have an industrial organization almost as oligarchic as the feudalism of the middle ages. Yet it is a truism that to obtain true democracy in government there must be true democracy in the economic life of the people. All Americans profess to desire the supremacy of democratic institutions. But to contend in the competitions of peace with nations now reorganized by war the industrial rulers of America will inevitably (and partly unconsciously) demand oligarchic expansion of the powers of our government to work in harmony with our oligarchically governed industries. In fact, demands for such extension of powers are already being pressed in order that we may play our part efficiently in the great war.

If those who are of democratic faith meet this drive against democracy only with defense of our political institutions, then, as our governmental power weakens with the incessant struggle for control, our industrial organizations which dominate our government will increase their anti-democratic power. To defend and perpetuate our political democracy we must submit our political faith to the final test, and establish democracy in the commercial government which is the real government of the nation.

Before considering the line of advance toward industrial democracy it may be desirable to demonstrate briefly the character of our present industrial control. Many independent workers may not realize how undemocratic industrial enterprises of large size are, and how completely an oligarchy of interwoven financial, manufacturing, distributing and selling interests dominates our commerce.

The modern corporation provides a means whereby a large amount of capital can be obtained from many investors and used for common profit by a directorate chosen by the stockholders and representing them. To this point a corporate business appears to be a democratic institution. This concentration of capital, however, permits the employment of a great amount of labor; and in the entire lack of any labor representation in the corporate control, the institution becomes wholly undemocratic. For example, $10,000,000 in capital may be invested in an enterprise which employs 5,000 men with a total payroll of $5,000,000 per year. If this $5,000,000 be regarded as a labor dividend at 5 per cent we find in the organization of this business a labor investment of $100,000,000 in contrast to a capital investment of $10,000,000. Yet that enormous labor investment has no representation in the control of the business. On the basis here outlined the Board of Directors represents, and governs the business primarily for the benefit of, 1/11 of the investment, and the other 10/11 is without representation in its government.

As the wage earners have come to realize their impotence under such management, naturally they have organized into unions in order that since their interests are not represented in business control they may at least be represented in effective opposition to such control. Here we find the sound and enduring basis of the warfare between capital and labor, a warfare which must persist until both parties are democratically represented in the control of their joint enterprise. The extreme partisans of each side embitter the struggle with their efforts at a partisan mastery which can only continue the destructive warfare. Those industrial rulers who oppose collective action by the workers and wage a ceaseless war on unionism are as hostile to democratic government as though they sought to reëstablish a feudal kingdom. The weapons of the middle ages have been discarded, but the methods of modern industrial feudalism are as tyrannical as those of the olden times. Economic violence has succeeded physical attack as a means of enforcing the autocratic will, but it is equally indefensible. In depressed times when dividends upon capital investment are likely to be impaired it is a common incident of big business to discharge large groups of workers, thereby depriving their families of any dividends on their labor investment. Yet upon what democratic theory can this preference of capital interest to labor interest be justified? A democratic industry would share the burdens of hard times as well as the benefits of prosperity with all its investors in proportion to their contributions, whether of labor or capital.

A long list of abuses of governmental aid could be presented to show the extension of this feudalistic control of industry over government. The misuse of official power by the courts and by the police and military authorities to support the abuse of private economic power are typical counts of the indictment that might be drawn. But it is unnecessary to multiply examples to prove the undeniable fact of the undemocratic organization of our industries. It is not only manufacturing laborers, but clerks, salesmen, agricultural employees, all those who might be broadly grouped in the salaried and wage-earning classes, who know from quick analysis of their unrepresented labor that we have industrial feudalism persisting in and dominating political democracy.

Where lie the roads to democratization of industry? Let it be repeated that legislation alone will not make the new highways. But tendencies in legislation show us in which direction popular understanding is moving. Social insurance limits the amount of economic violence which industrial rulers can visit upon employees. It also means that the labor interest in industry, backed by a democratic government, is demanding and receiving some recognition of its right to a voice in industrial control. Likewise the encouragement of collective action by the workers, support of the collective demands of the labor investors, is a proper function of democratic government. At present capital investors clamor against unionism because it means strikes. The strike is a powerful weapon of economic violence, crude and cruel but nevertheless a fit weapon in warfare where the employer still uses the battle-ax of wholesale and irresponsible discharge. The strike will remain a necessary weapon of economic violence for labor investors so long as economic violence is employed by capital investors. Not until both labor and capital have their representatives around the directors' table may we expect to see the end of economic violence on either side.

There is a negative part which a democratic government can play in this reorganization of industry which is perhaps more important than positive action.

There has been a widespread and just demand among business men that the government shall coöperate in their efforts to capture foreign trade. In tariff schedules, in ship-building, in diplomatic agreements, are some of the means whereby the government may assist effectively our commercial interests. It is a platitude of politics to assert that the wage-earners will share the benefits of such national aid. But why should not the government make this profit sharing reasonably certain? Why should not the government say to representatives of capital: You come to us representing an autocratic minority interest in your business, and this is a government by democratic majority. You wish government aid, and in due time after we have aided you we, the representatives of the people, must have our action approved by a democratic majority, convinced that we have acted for their benefit. Is it not therefore more fitting that the demand for aid should come from this majority? Are the labor investors, the democratic majority, represented in the control of this business which you ask the political representatives of that majority to aid? You say you speak for the wage-earners of your industry. Did they authorize you to speak for them or have you merely assumed that right? Is it not time for the political representatives of democracy to establish the principle that the directors of industry who represent an undemocratic control have only a limited right to ask the coöperation of a government whose principle of existence they oppose?

What is here suggested is no sudden revolution in government or industry but only certain principles of action by which we may hope in the coming years to work out the great problem of the rehabilitation of democracy. Political freedom has been achieved upon this continent through two great wars wherein our people staked their lives and fortunes upon that issue. Industrial freedom we possessed in the early days of an undeveloped country sparsely populated. But the day of the self-sufficient individualist is gone. The industrial organization of great masses of men and capital has been accomplished, as the great political organizations of the world were created, by the autocratic assumption of vast power by bold far-sighted men. Thus upon the very ruins of political oligarchies industrial oligarchies have been builded until they dominate by indirect means the governments which they should serve.

America has the established institutions of democracy through which her people can reorganize their industries into harmony with their government. Accompanying this advance the government can be mutualized to aid the general welfare. But to mutualize our government without at the same time democratizing our industries will be but sham statesmanship. To interweave our present industrial and governmental fabric will only weaken both. An industrial oligarchy and a political democracy will not work well together. Inevitably they will work largely in opposition until one or the other shall prevail. If we attempt to carry on this struggle while competing with the reorganized industrial oligarchies of Europe we shall surely degrade our national strength. We shall engage in world competitions enervated by internal disorders. Now is the time to strengthen our fibre while our future commercial rivals are wasting their material and human resources in the battle trenches. Our temporary profits in blood money mean spiritual loss. We may not decently rejoice in their accumulation. But, out of dreadful carnage, spiritual strength is being bred in Europe by the inspiration of which we may well and honestly profit.

This is our day of grace and if we fail now to prepare to meet our obligation we shall find out soon that our day is done. Billions of treasure and millions of lives we are ready to sacrifice to defend our country. Can we not have the vision to spend a fraction of that sacrifice to reorganize our industries and our government into an industrial democracy wherein all the interests of our people may be represented in the control of our political and economic government, and wherein our democratic directors may operate public and private business in the common interest of all the people?

DONALD R. RICHBERG.

## 6. President Woodrow Wilson on the Labor Question, 1919

The question which stands at the front of all others in every country amidst the present great awakening is the question of labour; and perhaps I can speak of it with as great advantage while engrossed in the consideration of interests which affect all countries alike as I could at home and amidst the interests which naturally most affect my thought, because they are the interests of our own people.

By the question of labour I do not mean the question of efficient industrial production, the question of how labour is to be obtained and made effective in the great process of sustaining populations and winning success amidst commercial and industrial rivalries. I mean that much greater and more vital question, how are the men and women who do the daily labour of the world to obtain progressive improvement in the conditions of their labour, to be made happier, and to be served better by the communities and the industries which their labour sustains and advances? How are they to be given their right advantage as citizens and human beings?

We cannot go any further in our present direction. We have already gone too far. We cannot live our right life as a nation or achieve our proper success as an industrial community if capital and labour are to continue to be antagonistic instead of being partners. If they are to continue to distrust one another and contrive how they can get the better of one another. Or, what perhaps amounts to the same thing, calculate by what form and degree of coercion they can manage to extort on the one hand work enough to make enterprise profitable, on the other justice and fair treatment enough to make life tolerable. That bad road has turned out a blind alley. It is no thoroughfare to real prosperity. We must find another, leading in another direction and to a very different destination. It must lead not merely to accommodation but also to a genuine cooperation and partnership based upon a real community of interest and participation in control.

There is now in fact a real community of interest between capital and labour, but it has never been made evident in action. It can be made operative and manifest only in a new organization of industry. The genius of our businessmen and the sound practical sense of our workers can certainly work such a partnership out when once they realize exactly what it is that they seek and sincerely adopt a common purpose with regard to it.

Labour legislation lies, of course, chiefly with the states; but the new spirit and method of organization which must be effected are not to be brought about by legislation so much as by the common counsel and voluntary cooperation of capitalist, manager, and workman. Legislation can go only a very little way in commanding what shall be done. The organization of industry is a matter of corporate and individual initiative and of practical business arrangement. Those who really desire a new relationship between capital and labour can readily find a way to bring it about; and perhaps Federal legislation can help more than state legislation could.

The object of all reform in this essential matter must be the genuine democratization of industry, based upon a full recognition of the right of those who work, in

From Woodrow Wilson, "A Special Message to Congress," in Arthur S. Link, ed., *The Papers of Woodrow Wilson* (Princeton: Princeton University Press, 1988), pp. 290–292. Reprinted by permission of Princeton University Press.

whatever rank, to participate in some organic way in every decision which directly affects their welfare or the part they are to play in industry. Some positive legislation is practicable. The Congress has already shown the way to one reform which should be worldwide, by establishing the eight hour day as the standard day in every field of labour over which it can exercise control. It has sought to find the way to prevent child labour, and will, I hope and believe, presently find it. It has served the whole country by leading the way in developing the means of preserving and safeguarding life and health in dangerous industries. It can now help in the difficult task of giving a new form and spirit to industrial organization by coordinating the several agencies of conciliation and adjustment which have been brought into existence by the difficulties and mistaken policies of the present management of industry, and by setting up and developing new Federal agencies of advice and information which may serve as a clearing house for the best experiments and the best thought on this great matter, upon which every thinking man must be aware that the future development of society directly depends. Agencies of international counsel and suggestion are presently to be created in connection with the League of Nations in this very field; but it is national action and the enlightened policy of individuals, corporations, and societies within each nation that must bring about the actual reforms. The members of the committees on labour in the two houses will hardly need suggestions from me as to what means they shall seek to make the Federal Government the agent of the whole nation in pointing out and, if need be, guiding the process of reorganization and reform.

# ✤ E S S A Y S

In the first essay, Columbia University historian Alice Kessler-Harris explores the gendered meanings of "free labor" as the concept was interpreted by male union leaders, conservative jurists, and feminist spokeswomen. Throughout much of the Progressive Era, women workers were thought to be fundamentally weaker and less resourceful than men. This belief opened the door to a set of "protective" labor laws that set minimum wages and maximum hours in many states. Laissez-faire ideology remained powerful, however, and when women got the vote, and hence a formal equality of citizenship, conservatives moved quickly to jettison the "separate sphere" ideology that had sustained even a minimal sort of social legislation.

In the second essay, historian Joseph McCartin of Georgetown University considers the origins and meaning of "industrial democracy" during the era of World War I. Worker militancy grew rapidly during the war, spawned in part by the officially sponsored patriotism that encouraged so many immigrant workers to think of themselves as rights-conscious citizens of state and industry. The rhetoric of war-era industrial democracy proved so powerful that it led to the nation's largest strike wave, as well as to a union-breaking employer counteroffensive that nevertheless incorporated many trappings of workplace participation and representation.

To what extent have labor laws, courts, or government agencies—that is, the state—liberated American workers? To what extent have they constricted worker activities? Were women workers excluded from laborite notions of "free labor" included in the quest for "industrial democracy," or do you think additional cultural constructions of gender came into play?

# Law and Free Labor

### ALICE KESSLER-HARRIS

Supreme Court decisions are frequently unpopular. Yet few have faced the storm of national derision that confronted the April 1923 opinion handed down in *Adkins* v. *Children's Hospital.* By a vote of 5 to 3 (Brandeis abstaining), the Court negated the constitutionality of a Washington, D.C., law that provided minimum wages for women and minors. With its act the Court also placed in jeopardy the minimum wage legislation of thirteen other states.

Newspaper editorials, public meetings, and placards denounced the decision. Mary Anderson, head of the Women's Bureau, called it "nothing short of a calamity." Samuel Gompers declared it to be a "logical next step in perfecting the doctrine that those who cannot help themselves shall not be helped." The *New York World* ran a cartoon that depicted Justice Sutherland handing the document to a woman wage earner, with the caption, "This decision, madam, affirms your constitutional right to starve." In the immediate aftermath of the decision, the National Women's Trade Union League called a conference to stave off what it feared would be "a wholesale reduction of wages for more than 1,500,000 women and girls." The "greatest wrong" in the decision, as Gompers and others pointed out, was that in describing labor as a commodity to be bought and sold Justice Sutherland had likened "the labor of a woman to the purchase of a shinbone over the counter to make soup." . . .

The response might have been louder because the decision was apparently so unexpected. Fifteen years earlier, in *Muller* v. *Oregon,* the Court had accepted the principle that women's health was a proper subject of state concern and therefore of state regulation. In the wake of that decision, most industrial states had taken it upon themselves to regulate the hours and working conditions of women and minors. These laws, quintessentially progressive in that they attempted to redress the imbalances of rapid industrial growth, had withstood many legal challenges and, just a year after Adkins, were to survive another. Though states were more cautious when it came to regulating wages, thirteen states and the District of Columbia had enacted minimum wage laws before 1923. Each was grounded in the assumption that the needs of working women for food, clothing, and shelter could be accurately determined and in the desire to maintain women's health and protect their morals by establishing wages at a level "adequate to supply the necessary cost of living."

. . . Why then had the Court so unexpectedly countered what seemed like a well-established trend?

The answer may lie in the competing paradigms embedded in the issue of minimum wages for women. Decisions about minimum wages were grounded both in legal precedents around labor and in those around women. Watching the judiciary confront these issues tells us something about the vital importance of the idea of gender differences in the progressive era. And looking at the evolution of the relationship between a doctrine grounded in changing theories of labor and one that

From Alice Kessler-Harris, *A Woman's Wage: Historical Meanings and Social Consequences* (Lexington: University of Kentucky Press, 1990), pp. 33–56. Reprinted by permission of the University of Kentucky Press.

rested on separate spheres may tell us something about the relationship of gender differences to other influential ideas in the construction of law and social policy. As we examine the roots of Adkins, we begin to understand something of how the gendered content of ideas governed an important set of political and judicial decisions and, not inadvertently, laid the groundwork for incorporating nineteenth century notions of workers' dignity and independence into the judicial system.

Minimum wage legislation derived its rationale from the gendered arguments used to gain passage of other regulatory legislation. Its purpose, as the title of the Oregon Act makes clear, was "to protect the lives and health and morals of women and minor workers . . . ," or, as the District of Columbia Act put it, "to protect women and minors from conditions detrimental to their health and morals, resulting from wages which are inadequate to maintain decent standards of living." As such, it was firmly rooted in progressive notions of women's separate sphere. . . . The widely accepted notion that women were mothers of the race provided more than adequate justification for the courts to regulate women's working lives. But although the courts in earlier decisions had accepted sex difference as a reasonable basis for restraining the freedom of women and employers to contract, and would subsequently continue to rely on sex difference, the Supreme Court rejected the idea in Adkins.

In so doing, the Court simply affirmed what had been well established by 1923, namely that an individual's freedom to contract was not subject to restraint by the state, unless the public welfare was affected. The decision was rooted in nineteenth century arguments over free labor. As Justice Sutherland noted, freedom of contract while not absolute was "the general rule, and restraint the exception." But the idea of free labor was not gender neutral. And therein lay the difficulty. For the Court, in this decision, insisted that women were individuals within the meaning of the law and thus overturned two decades of precedent that held that the requirements of gender difference superseded the right to freely contract their services. How had the two, so carefully reconciled for a generation, come into conflict?

We need to step back for a moment. Two alternative conceptions of "free labor" contested in the 1870s. The first, deriving from the early republic, had taken root in the period before the Civil War and, by the postwar period, was championed by such working class advocates as the Knights of Labor. In this view, labor was free when it had the capacity to participate independently in civic life. But that capacity inhered in the dignity and independence of the working person and therefore assumed that each person had equal rights or access to economic self-sufficiency. This doctrine of equal rights embodied at least a theoretical social equality that, workers and their representatives held, could not be sustained if workers were reduced to permanent wage-earning status. Implicit in this view was the notion that only economic independence could guarantee effective self-representation and the perpetuation of a democratic republic. The idea of free labor as it evolved in the nineteenth century thus assumed that, in order to participate effectively in the polity, workers required at least the possibility of escape from wage labor into self-directed employment.

From this conception of free labor, women as individuals were virtually excluded. They were not expected to be members of the polity in the same sense as men, nor was their wage work expected to offer access to independent judgment. In the eyes of male workers women's wage labor, while dignified and offering access to self-support, ought not to lead either to independence or to self-sufficiency. Rather, just as men's free labor was predicted on their capacity to support a family, so women's was assumed to sustain the family labor of men. As family members, women participated in the polity through their menfolk. Their wage work was encouraged only in occupational fields and at moments in the life cycle that did not violate customary conceptions of free labor. For women's wage work to threaten the male's capacity to be free was a problem just as it was a problem if women's wage work undermined the capacity of either men or women to be effective family members. . . .

But labor had rules that did not necessarily derive from families. In the late nineteenth century, a dramatic acceleration in the process of industrialization threatened possibilities for self-directed employment for men as well as for women. While the defenders of free labor confronted the challenges of a debilitating and all-encompassing wage system with such innovations as cooperative producer associations and political action, a new generation of industrialists and entrepreneurs battled them at every turn. Eager for a rapid transformation of control into their own hands and anxious to maximize the possibilities of cheap labor, entrepreneurs treated workers as individuals, each capable of negotiating and each protected by the Fourteenth Amendment's prohibitions on deprivation of property. Labor's freedom, they suggested, with the concurrence of the courts, inhered only in its right to freely contract to sell itself.

This view, commonly known as freedom of contract, challenged labor's notions of putative social equality and threatened the economic independence from which it derived. Within its perspective, equal rights were embedded in the capacity of each individual to compete freely. Workers (male and female) were free only to enter into contracts to sell their labor without restraint. In this position entrepreneurs were joined by the courts. As a matter of formal and legal principle, the courts, beginning in the 1880s, ignored the vulnerable position of workers and turned the Fourteenth Amendment's prohibition on depriving citizens of life, liberty, and property on its head. Consistently, they interpreted freedom of contract as a ban on state efforts to restrict the rights of employers to offer even the most debilitating working conditions. The courts thus effectively snuffed the political vision of free labor. . . .

The effort to limit labors' expectations by means of freedom of contract expressed the stake of a rapidly industrializing society in cheap and available labor. While theoretically, the tendency of such a system was to pull women into the labor force as individuals, there remained some questions as to whether they were "protected" by the Fourteenth Amendment as men were. For the same assault on free labor that had undermined notions of work as the locus of dignity relied upon, and perpetuated, the idea of the family as an economic unit and as the source of values by which a new generation of laborers would be raised. If, on the one hand, this provided a large pool of "cheap labor," on the other, even the most hardboiled advocates of freedom of contract could not be insensitive to the problem that women who were treated as individuals for the purpose of the workplace still needed to fulfill demanding roles as family members. Jobs that undermined the working class family by destroying women's health or fertility, or by encouraging women to compete for male jobs, could easily destroy the golden egg that produced cheap labor.

Advocates of freedom of contract differed from the champions of free labor on virtually every score. Yet both agreed to some sense of separate spheres. The content of women's roles differed for each. Labor's conception was rooted in the belief that effective civic participation demanded workplace dignity that in turn rested on an ordered and comfortable family life. Business's conception derived from the desire to preserve the family as an economic unit that could provide incentives to stable and loyal work force participation. Either way, ideas of gender difference defined women as family members whose work roles were secondary. Ideally, at least, this led to no contradiction for male workers: women, seen either as individuals who competed with them for jobs or as family members on whose household labor they relied, belonged at home. But for employers, placing women in separate spheres meant that they needed to treat women simultaneously as individuals with a sacrosanct freedom of contract and as family members in whom they and the state had a special interest. It was this contradiction that the courts were called upon to resolve in the minimum wage cases.

By 1908 they had successfully done so with regard to hours. Under pressure from coalitions of women workers, reformers, and trade unions, legislatures and courts had legitimized the now familiar device of making women "wards of the state." But what worked for hours had special consequences when applied to wages. Regulating hours, as the Court noted in Adkins, had "no necessary effect on the heart of the contract, that is, the amount of wages to be paid and received." The minimum wage, in contrast, touched its core. It was designed to defend freedom of contract by ensuring that women who could not otherwise survive did not undermine an ideology that relied on the fiction of a worker's liberty to negotiate fair terms for labor. At the same time the minimum wage threatened the idea of freedom of contract by clearly identifying some workers as lacking the appropriate liberty. Tracing the resolution of this dilemma will tell us something of how ideas of gender difference help to construct social reality. For in one of the wonderful ironies of history, judicial decisions and the legal system contributed to definitions of female difference that in the end threatened the idea of the free labor market they were meant to protect.

The progressive attempt to accommodate gender invigorated a free labor debate that had been all but lost. Arguably, it helped to alter the terms of the debate. In creating sex as a category outside the common expectation of labor and law, the courts opened the door to an evaluation of the proper relation of the state to labor as a whole. The language with which this struggle was enacted tells us something about the centrality of separate spheres in the lives of men and women and also about its competing functions. It enables us to watch how the notion of separate spheres first confronted and eventually helped to break down the pernicious idea of freedom of contract.

Let us begin with the case of Quong Wing, the Chinese laundry man who, in the winter of 1911–12, petitioned the United States Supreme Court for relief. Quong Wing, a male, had sued the treasurer of Lewis and Clark County, Montana, to return the $10 he had paid for a license to take in hand laundry. The Montana law, as cited by Justice Oliver Wendell Holmes in the Supreme Court decision, "imposed the payment upon all persons engaged in the laundry business, other than the steam laundry business, with a proviso that it should not apply to women so employed where not more than two women were employed." Because the law applied to all laundries except steam laundries, it taxed small enterprises while exempting large ones, and because it applied to all persons who worked in hand laundries except women who worked alone or in pairs, it in effect, taxed men who did what was considered women's work. There can be little doubt that the state meant to tax Chinese men, while exempting women and large operators; for, as Justice Holmes observed in his opinion for the Court, "hand laundry work is a widespread occupation of Chinamen in this country while on the other hand it is so rare to see men of our race engaged in it that many of us would be unable to say that they had ever observed a case." Yet Quong Wing did not charge racial discrimination—an issue on which Holmes thought he might well have won. Instead, he charged sexual discrimination—and lost. The Supreme Court upheld the Montana statute because, as Holmes put it,

> If the state sees fit to encourage steam laundries and discourage hand laundries that is its own affair. And if again it finds a ground of distinction in sex, that is not without precedent. . . . If Montana deems it advisable to put a lighter burden upon women than upon men with regard to an employment that our people commonly regard as more appropriate for the former, the Fourteenth Amendment does not interfere by creating a fictitious equality where there is a real difference. The particular points at which that difference shall be emphasized by legislation are largely in the power of the state.

This case is not the first to identify gender differences as a legal category. But, unlike the rationales for restricting women's working hours, on which the Court drew and which were rooted in the presumed physical disadvantages of women and the social benefits of legislation, the Court here asserted an arbitrary power to discriminate between men and women—not a new phenomenon but one that it did not even seek to justify except as a matter of legislative choice. Quong Wing thus extended Muller's standard of sex as an appropriate classification to assert a state's right to define which sex differences could be taken into account. In imposing a new standard for legislative review, the case raises many issues, among them how readily gender "difference" is deployed under circumstances that would have explicitly precluded ethnic "difference," and the content of the "distinction" or "difference" to which the Court so blithely refers and that it makes no attempt to define. But for our purposes the most interesting question is the way in which the decision illuminates the social meaning of men's and women's wages.

The decision in Quong Wing suggests that the "common regard" (or popular perceptions of women's roles) is determinative in legislative choice as to which differences shall be emphasized. But surely that is a problem. If we take seriously Justice Holmes's comment that "the particular points at which that difference shall be emphasized by legislation are largely in the power of the state," then we have little choice but to view gender difference as an idea with a political content that moves people to behave in certain kinds of ways—in short, as an ideological construct. The decision tells us quite clearly that male and female job choices, and the earnings that result, are subject to regulation to bring them into line with the "common regard." A look at the evidence suggests the ideological level at which gender entered the debate.

In 1912 the common regard held that women belonged in families. Employers freely (and largely falsely) expressed the belief that women did not need the incomes of males because they could rely on families to support them. More subtly, in the common regard, questions of masculinity entered into every decision on wages. For men the wage encompassed family support; for women it tended to incorporate only the self-support of a single person. . . . [I]t was appropriate for women to derive part of their support from families. This assumption found its way into *Adkins* where Justice Sutherland objected to the District of Columbia law because it failed to take account of "the cooperative economies of the family group, though they constitute an important consideration in estimating the cost of living, for it is obvious that the individual expense will be less in the case of a member of a family than in the case of one living alone." . . .

Because the battle was hard fought, the price of maintaining separate spheres was high. It took the form of a vicious and clearly ideological attack on women as workers that exaggerated their "natural" attachment to the home and belittled their ability to earn wages. The popular imagination conjured up pictures of wage-earning women who were helpless, dependent, weak, handicapped, ignorant, delicate, and exploitable. Portraits of wage-earning women depicted them as greedy and lazy as well. They had, it was said, a "natural longing for recreation . . . adornment" and luxury. At the same time, women lived in a world where unscrupulous employers did not hesitate to subject them to conditions "akin to slavery" and thus leave them vulnerable to peculiar dangers that threatened to lure them into vice and immorality. These conditions prevented women from living in "decency" or from enjoying "healthy and normal lives," and they inhibited the peace of a "satisfied mind" and a "wholesome existence." Worse, they threatened the "health and well-being" of future mothers and therefore held "the strength of the nation hostage." While these images expand upon those evoked to justify shorter hours for women but not for men, their consequences were not at all alike.

In the debate over the minimum wage, both sides had a stake in maintaining wage differentials, and so both resorted to this imagery. The terms of the debate thus contributed to depicting women in the extreme language of childhood and vulnerability. For example, both sides saw women as inefficient workers who lacked training. Proponents of the minimum wage argued that wage earners could be divided between those who "are earning what they receive or more" and those "whose services are worth little or nothing." Even sympathetic reformers like Florence Kelley held that too many untrained and unskilled women flooding the job market depressed women's wages. To raise wages required educating and training women to be more efficient and effective workers. That this had not happened as a natural result of the market was due to defects in women's character.

Women competed with each other. Like the notion that women workers were inefficient, the idea that female competition reduced wages pervaded the imagery. One side depicted women as "undutiful daughters" who, tempted by luxurious living, allowed their mothers to overwork themselves while they sought riches in the factory or department store. Or it imagined dissatisfied wives not content to live on their husbands' earnings. Though sympathetic to the minimum wage, the other constructed a picture of "women whose earnings are supplemented from other sources" and who are therefore a "constant drag on the wage level and offer formidable competition to the growing thousands of women dependent on their own labor for support. . . . " The circular logic of this argument appears when we place it in the form of a syllogism: Women do not earn enough, therefore they live with others, therefore they reduce the level of wages for all women, therefore women do not earn enough.

Another explanation was that women chose the wrong jobs. For example, opponents of the minimum wage suggested that women could easily save money and achieve mobility if they were willing to become domestic servants. Such jobs were widely available. But women, objecting to their endless hours, close supervision, and live-in conditions, frequently refused them. In view of their willingness to turn down these jobs, a minimum wage would only reinforce women's worst qualities, rewarding the inefficient without benefiting those who were oriented towards hard work and mobility. On the other side of this coin, a picture of women's inability to advance themselves could yield an argument for state aid as illustrated by the belief that they were in occupations not reachable in the normal course of trade union organization. "A great deal can be said for minimum wage laws and laws limiting the hours of labor for women," asserted feminist Crystal Eastman, who normally opposed special laws for women only, "on the ground that women's labor is the least adapted to organization and therefore the most easily exploited and most in need of legislative protection." Women who selected jobs that restricted their ability to bargain collectively and were, therefore, incapable of securing a fair return on their wages constituted, according to some labor leaders, "a helpless class of labor, broken in spirit." "Practically impossible to organize under existing conditions," they might be more readily organized once their "broken spirit had been reinforced by a minimum wage."

Women had weak characters. Opponents of a minimum wage suggested that legislation would increase immortality because it would give extra money to frivolous, unworthy people. Those who favored the minimum argued that weak women would succumb to vice and prostitution at the least temptation and needed higher wages to enable them to resist. Neither argument seemed to have much to do with reality. . . .

Arguments against the minimum wage were predicated heavily on the assumption that employers paid a natural wage that was the equivalent of the service rendered—that women were worth no more than what they earned. The neoclassical economic theory on which such arguments rested held the worker responsible for his or her place in the job market. In a free market, workers who could freely sell their labor earned the economic value of what they produced. Employers hired workers at different levels of wages calculated to reflect the value of the product created as well as the supply of workers willing to accept the wages offered. If women tended to work on low-value products (garments, paper flowers, boxes, textiles, shoes, for example), that was not the employer's fault but a result of women's choices. Business could not pay more than a "natural" wage without threatening the profits that enabled it to survive. If women's wages tended to be low, the logical explanation lay in a persistent assertion of a woman's "difference." A regulated minimum that forced employers to "supply individual needs . . . in excess of what the employee earns or is worth" would be disastrous. From this flowed a series of questions: Should the wage be determined not by the value of the

services rendered but by the cost of supporting women? Should industry be required to cover the deficit on women's wages? Was there a constitutional question
implicit in the issue of "whether an employer may be compelled to pay the cost of
maintaining the employer whose full services he voluntarily uses in the conduct
of an enterprise?" Since no employer would stay in business without profits, would
attempts to regulate wages (as a function of the cost of supporting women as
opposed to the value of the services they rendered) not drive employers out?

Circumventing the idea of freedom of contract by exacerbating women's
weakness and helplessness transformed the debate. Freedom of contract rested on
the notion that the wage was an abstraction—the product of agreement between
employer and employee. The argument over the minimum wage, because it was
gendered, exposed the social issue embodied in the wage and thus kept alive a
social meaning on which defenders of free labor had insisted. The Progressives
connected the wage argument to hours by suggesting that if women's wages were so
low as to undermine their childbearing and rearing capacities then the state as a
whole would suffer because its future citizens would be weak and without good discipline and values. Under those circumstances freedom of contract would threaten
the "future of the race." For the courts to accept this argument required suspending
wage theory and arguing for redistribution of income according to norms of social
justice that recalled the ideals of advocates of free labor.

In focusing so heavily on separate spheres, protagonists and antagonists alike
begged the question of social justice in the industrial sector, evoking fears that the
extreme solutions required to compensate for women's weakness might threaten
the free market. Thus, the argument over wages placed the judiciary squarely in the
position of deciding whether to concede separate spheres to women in order to
redistribute income sufficiently for women to maintain families (granting some
credence to the older free labor ideology and enabling women to keep open possibilities for gendered action) or whether to sustain freedom of contract in the face of
the apparent threat to families. The conundrum that this posed is revealed in the
language and arguments used during the course of the debate.

First, it raised the issue of the appropriate relationship between male and
female wages. If the natural wage was a male wage and women's wages were low
because they "could not earn a wage." then attempts to create an arbitrary minimum for women and not for men would threaten the balance between male and
female spheres. The alternative would be to raise male wages. But his begged the
issue of whether a state that could impose a minimum wage could not also impose
a maximum. Some who agreed that the public welfare was menaced by low wages
for women had to agree that it was equally vulnerable to low male wages. For if
higher wages were necessary to health and morality—if a law fixing wages was a
health law—surely then it was desirable for both men and women. If benefits
claimed for women were given to men after all, then whole families would benefit.
As one commentator put it, "If . . . a minimum wage law for women is constitutional because it tends to provide the race with healthy moral mothers, so would
a minimum wage law for men, because it would tend to provide the race with
strong honest fathers." Once opened, that Pandora's box could only produce a case
for a higher wage for all.

Closely related to the issue of health was that of morality. One of the basic arguments for minimum wages was that women with insufficient incomes were regularly tempted into amorous relationships or even into prostitution in order to make ends meet. Raising this issue involved not only questions of male morality but those of women's character as well. As Justice Sutherland put it, "It cannot be shown that well paid women safeguard their morals more carefully than those who are poorly paid." Then he added, "If women require a minimum wage to preserve their morals, men require it to preserve their honesty." . . .

If women could not earn their keep, then society, not women, would pay the cost of women's low wages. Again, women who worked were depicted as mere parasites who imposed a financial burden on the state and on other industries. Women's low wages, in this view, were nothing less than a "menace to public welfare." As Felix Frankfurter put it in the famous case of *Stettler* v. *O'Hara,* "Industries supporting male workers were being drawn upon to assist in supporting women workers engaged in other industries, which were refusing to carry their cost." Frankfurter, defending Oregon's minimum wage law, argued that the immediate effects of women's low wages were to impose financial burdens on the state, "which threatened excessive and unremunerative taxation." Women's wages, he argued, were a "community problem—a problem affecting the state in its pervasive entirety."

The degree to which arguments over women's wages threatened freedom of contract emerges most forcefully in the suggestion that depictions of women's difference that fueled a demand for the minimum wage would in the end raise false expectations as to the distribution of income and property. These expectations could not, according to some, be met under the limits of the constitution, for they required "A to give part of his property to B." Such an action would deny individual rights, destroy natural competition, and evoke the specter of social revolution. Minimum wage legislation, in the words of a June 1917 commentator, was "a new expression of the paternalistic and socialistic tendencies of the day. It savors of the division of property between those who have and those who have not, and the leveling of fortunes by division under governmental supervision. It is consistent with the orthodox socialist creed, but it is not consistent with the principles of our government which are based upon the protection of individual rights."

Champions of the minimum wage did not deny that individual rights were endangered by regulation. Rather, they argued that individual rights could not be allowed to supersede the rights of "women who must labor in order to live. It would seem," noted Justice Wendell Stafford, who had been part of the majority in the original D.C. Supreme Court decision that upheld the constitutionality of minimum wages, "that the right of this class to live on a barely decent level, and the right of the public to have them so live, should outweigh the right of those who do not need to work in order to live, and who therefore are merely asserting a right to earn money and thereby accumulate property."

The idea that weak women were at some level responsible for undermining a cherished principle of government was echoed and expanded by court decisions at all levels beginning in 1917. It finally became a key argument for invalidating the minimum wage. From 1912 to 1923, the minimum wage was more or less sustained. But by 1917 tensions provoked by the emphasis on gender difference became apparent. Writing for the District of Columbia Supreme Court in the penultimate round of *Children's Hospital* v. *Adkins,* Justice Van Orsdel declared that "legislation tending to fix the prices at which private property shall be sold, . . . places a limitation upon the distribution of wealth, and is aimed at the correction of the inequalities of fortune which are inevitable under our form of government, due to personal liberty and the private ownership of property. These principles are embodied in the Constitution itself."

Imposing a minimum wage was thus the equivalent of using the police power to "level inequalities of fortune." Van Orsdel made his own economic bias clear: "A wage based upon competitive ability is just, and leads to frugality and honest industry, and inspires an ambition to attain the highest possible efficiency, while the equal wage paralyzes ambition and promotes prodigality and indolence. It takes away the strongest incentive to human labor, thrift, and efficiency, and works injustice to employee and employer alike, thus affecting injuriously the whole social and industrial fabric." . . .

. . . Advocates of the minimum wage had couched their arguments in exaggerated assertions about the traditional roles of women. But to maintain those roles at the expense of freedom of contract would, in the view of a conservative judiciary, undermine the principle of individual rights and the economic system itself. To accommodate to the pressure would jeopardize the wages of men and of other women, the profits of industry, and the free enterprise system. Minimum wages, in short, would so alter the role of the state as to produce nothing less than the dreaded disease of sovietism.

Faced with a sharp conflict between two ideological systems, one had to give way. If women were to continue as paid workers, the courts could either deny the importance of gender difference or negate freedom of contract. In the event, the Supreme Court chose to sustain freedom of contract by declaring the minimum wage "to be wholly beyond legislative discretion." Divided 5 to 3 (with Brandeis abstaining because his daughter had been involved in preparing the brief), the Court declared that gender differences had come to the vanishing point, that there was no reason therefore to abrogate freedom of contract, and that the minimum wage was unconstitutional.

To some observers it appeared that the Court had done an "anomalous somersault." But in fact, a closer view reveals the decision to have been a logical consequence of the contradictions produced by the way in which women's differences had been incorporated into the social meaning of the wage. Speaking for the majority, Justice Sutherland evoked the underlying issues as he saw them: free enterprise was arrayed against motherhood. He concluded that free enterprise had to be preserved, even at the cost of wiping out the separate spheres. The wage, he asserted, was based on a "just equivalence of the service rendered," not on the need of the worker. No matter how pressing, the need of the worker could not avail. . . . Castigating those who did not pay attention to employers' needs and acknowledging that a women was worth little in the free labor market, he attacked the statute for failing to "require that the wage have any relation to the reasonable value of the workers' services."

Bold as the decision was, it might have been expected. It built upon what was implicit in Holmes's opinion in Quong Wing. Holmes had there asserted that the existence of sexual difference (or separate spheres) was the legitimate province of the state to define. In his view sexual difference was a legitimate classification for legislators. By 1923, in a new political environment, the Supreme Court, stymied by the tension between attributions of gender difference and an economic system that assumed freedom of contract, chose to take the opposite position. It simply defined sexual difference out of existence.

But the issue was not so simply put to rest. The rhetoric of the debate and the reality of women's lives conspired to keep it alive. In the dissents to Adkins and in the protest that ensued, a strong appeal to social justice, rooted in family and domestic life, persisted. Dissenting Chief Justice Taft, for example, thought the majority decision unwise because "it is not the function of this court to hold Congressional acts invalid simply because they are passed to carry out economic views which the Court believes to be unwise or unsound." To others it violated simple principles of social justice. "It demeans humanity," said Samuel Gompers, that "women and girl wage earners are to be bought over the counter." Confusion reigned over the Court's consistent affirmation of gender difference when it came to hours and working conditions and its equally consistent opposition to sex-based classifications when wages were at stake. Case after case came to the Supreme Court, only to be turned back. But by 1937 the Court once again reestablished an interest in women's difference as the opening wedge of a fight for social justice.

In *West Coast Hotel Co.* v. *Parrish,* the Court reversed itself. Chief Justice Hughes, speaking for the Court, rejected a freedom of contract defense against minimum wage legislation because, he said, "the Constitution does not speak of freedom of contract. It speaks of liberty. . . . But the liberty safeguarded is liberty in a social organization which requires the protection of law against the evils which menace the health, safety, morals and welfare of the people." Speaking in the language of nineteenth century advocates of free labor, he denied any "absolute" freedom of contract and argued that liberty did not imply "immunity from reasonable regulations and prohibitions imposed in the interest of the community." What were the interests of the community? They resided in protecting those parties that did not stand upon an equality and therefore in the state's interest in women.

Calling upon *Muller* v. *Oregon* and repeating the words of Quong Wing, that only a "fictitious equality" existed between men and women, the Court argued, in overturning Adkins, that women "are relatively defenseless against the denial of a living wage." Low wages were "detrimental to their health and well-being" and "cast a direct burden for their support upon the community." Echoing Holmes's insistence on the state's right to determine where difference shall be emphasized, the Court castigated selfish employers for disregarding the public interest, noted the anguish of the economic depression, and asserted that the "relative need" of women "in the presence of the evil, no less than the evil itself, is a matter for legislative judgment."

But the premonitions of Van Orsdel, Sutherland, and others had not been misplaced. For though Chief Justice Hughes used gender difference to highlight the state's interest in "the exploitation of a class of workers who are in an unequal position with respect to bargaining power and are thus relatively defenseless against the denial of a living wage," he explicitly utilized female difference as the entering wedge for judicial decisions about others in need. In so doing, he ensured that a new definition of liberty would prevail. Less than three years later, the Court relied on its decision in *West Coast Hotel* to sustain the constitutionality of the Fair Labor Standards Act which legislated minimum wages for men and women. But it abandoned sex difference as the crucial criterion for undermining freedom of contract. In *United States* v. *Darby,* the case that affirmed the FLSA and cleared the path for the social legislation of the modern period, the Court transcended gender and argued that "it is no longer open to question that the fixing of a minimum wage is within the legislative power."

How do we explain the shift? Part of the answer lies in the change in social conditions in the fourteen years between the two decisions. Sutherland, in dissent from the majority in *West Coast Hotel,* tried once again to make the case that there was no longer any reason why women "should be put in different classes in respect of their legal right to make contracts. Nor should they be denied, in effect, the right to compete with men for work paying lower wages which men may be willing to accept." This argument carried little weight in the depression climate. But much of the shift in Court opinion lies in the way that language about women and agitation around them had demonstrated the evident social purposes of such legislation. By the 1930s, when public opinion was once again ready to consider the search for social justice as part of the legitimate end of government, the idea that women constituted a separate and deserving class could and did serve to illustrate the rigidity of old doctrines of freedom of contract. Attention to gender differences had kept alive the possibility that all workers deserved state protection. As Justice Stone put it in his dissent from the Court's final attempt to preserve the sanctity of freedom of contract in *Morehead* v. *New York,* "In the years which have intervened since the Adkins case . . . we have had opportunity to perceive more clearly that a wage insufficient to support the worker does not visit its consequences upon him alone; that it may affect profoundly the entire economic structure of society and, in any case, that it casts on every taxpayer, and on government itself, the burden of solving the problems of poverty, subsistence, health and morals of large numbers in the community."

# Fighting for Industrial Democracy in World War I

### JOSEPH A. MCCARTIN

When a General Electric worker who helped organize a union in his plant in 1918 was asked by friendly government officials whether he had to hide his union sympathies on the job, his answers surprised them. "In a way, I didn't have any [union sympathies]," he replied, "only—I might say I had an American feeling, that is all. . . . I didn't have much thought in the matter . . . of union stuff." Upon further questioning, the examiners found that indeed this employee saw his union work as but an extension of the war effort that he loyally supported. That response signified something important about the industrial battle that rocked the United States in 1919, just months after this interview. . . .

From Joseph A. McCartin, " 'An American Feeling': Workers, Managers, and the Struggle over Industrial Democracy in the World War I Era," in Nelson Lichtenstein and Howell John Harris, eds., *Industrial Democracy in America: The Ambiguous Promise* (New York: Cambridge University Press, 1996), pp. 67–86. Reprinted by permission of Cambridge University Press.

This chapter argues that labor conflict of 1919 in the United States was in part a battle for legitimacy that was waged over language as well as over union organization. There is perhaps no clearer evidence that managers and workers battled over language in 1919 than the controversy that raged over *industrial democracy,* a term that, as historian David Brody points out, had become a "national byword" by the end of World War I. In developing their postwar American Plan attack, and in making their own version of industrial democracy an important feature of that plan, employers were not only trying to roll back trade unionism; they were attempting to reconstruct their legitimacy by incorporating the rallying cry of the wartime union upsurge into their managerial lexicon. For during the war, American labor militants had rallied behind industrial democracy—previously popularized by wartime government reformers—and successfully roused their followers with patriotic language. In doing so, militants cloaked labor protest—even demands that deeply challenged managerial authority—in a protective "American feeling." In 1919, the tasks of neutralizing that troublesome phrase, industrial democracy, and taking back the mantle of Americanism to which labor militants had laid claim, were integral to U.S. employers' counteroffensive against trade unionism. . . .

Paraphrasing E. P. Thompson, historian David Alan Corbin has observed that the "ideological impact of war propaganda on American workers may have been 'one of those facts so big,' . . . that it is easily overlooked, . . . and yet it indicates a major shift in the . . . 'subpolitical' attitudes of the masses." If the language of the wartime union movement is any indication, such a shift in attitudes indeed occurred in the United States during the era of the Great War. An important measure of that shift was the popularity of the slogan "industrial democracy," which, by the end of the war, was on the tongues of millions of American workers. While industrial democracy was not a new phrase—it had been used in the United States as early as the 1880s—wartime government labor reforms had given the term a new legitimacy, incorporated it into wartime propaganda, and spread it to virtually every corner of industry.

The federal government's role in spreading the industrial democracy slogan during the war derived from the Wilson administration's efforts to foster labor peace. Most historians agree that World War I constituted an important turning point in the relationship between American trade unionism and the state. Prior to the war, a hostile judiciary armed with the power of injunction offered American workers only what Christopher Tomlins in another context called a "counterfeit liberty." The massive strike wave of 1917 and the "inadequacy of the existent agencies for dealing with the industrial strife," however, pushed the Wilson administration toward important breakthroughs in the protection of trade union rights. These culminated with the creation by presidential authority of a powerful new agency, the National War Labor Board, in April 1918.

Set up as a kind of industrial court, the NWLB was chaired by William Howard Taft and labor attorney Frank P. Walsh and composed of an equal number of employers and AFL unionists. It adopted a set of progressive principles to serve as a bench mark in settling wartime labor disputes. These principles acknowledged the right to join a union, the duty to bargain collectively, and the impropriety of anti-union tactics. As a concession to open shop industry, the NWLB did not require employers to recognize unions if they had not done so prior to the war. In such cases, collective bargaining was to be accomplished through worker-elected shop committees. The installation of these shop committees may have been the most important policy the NWLB pursued.

Altogether the NWLB program represented a great leap forward for U.S. trade unionism. Intervening in over one thousand strikes before the war ended and applying its principles on a broad basis, the NWLB sharply limited the arbitrary power of employers. In his typically enthusiastic language, the NWLB's cochair, Frank P. Walsh, announced that the board was creating "a new deal for American labor." Trade-union membership figures support Walsh's assessment. Under the board's protection, union membership grew by nearly one million by the war's end. As one autoworker put it, "For once every citizen, no matter how humble, was made to realize that the government was a real thing and that it wielded power, enormous power."

Some scholars argue that the AFL's cooperation with the war effort and its submission of the NWLB's mediation undermined the AFL's militancy and independence. To be sure, the AFL's participation in the government's program helped legitimize the brutal suppression of the "disloyal" Industrial Workers of the World and Socialist party. However, to argue, as one scholar has done, that working with the NWLB "practically meant the transformation of the AFL from an independent trade union center to a government department which assumed the duty of preventing strikes and if necessary breaking them," is to overlook a central reality of the war for labor: the importance of language, symbolism, and ideology. When one examines the influence of the NWLB on the language of working-class militancy during the war, it becomes clear that the war had far more complex implications for labor than these critics have understood.

In promoting its program, the NWLB helped to popularize the slogan industrial democracy. That phrase fit the board's purposes well. Its mission was, as the president defined it, to end undemocratic management practices at home while troops ended autocracy overseas. No one did more to link the board's mission to the establishment of industrial democracy at home than its cochair Frank Walsh. "Political Democracy is an illusion," Walsh was fond of saying in his numerous speeches on behalf of the NWLB, "unless builded upon and guaranteed by a free and virile Industrial Democracy." He aimed to use the board to achieve such a vision, and Walsh firmly believed "the process of democratization [initiated by the NWLB] will continue until there remains not one single wage-earner in the country deprived of his voice in determining the conditions of his job and consequently his life."

Undoubtedly, official speeches about industrial democracy were often motivated by utilitarian concerns. The slogan was used along with a remarkable cult of the flag—including daily flag ceremonies at factories and workshops draped with hundreds of flags—to arouse maximum output. The word in many shops was: "Not Just Hats Off to the Flag, But Sleeves up for It." War production was the key. But by so closely linking work to patriotism, the government endowed labor with a new prestige, as when one official speaker told a group of Cleveland steelworkers: "Your greasy overalls . . . are as much a badge of service and honor in . . . the eyes of your country today as the uniform of the army or navy."

Such powerful rhetoric—which became increasingly common throughout 1918—had manifold implications. On the one hand, it served to chasten employers who were determined to persist in antiunion practices. On the other it reassured the AFL leaders who cooperated with the government that their loyalty was well placed. But at the same time, it evoked in millions of workers skyrocketing hopes for substantial change in their lives. Many came to believe that " 'Making the world safe for democracy' [would] go a long way toward lifting the burden of social and economic oppression" from their shoulders. The AFL's Matthew Woll later declared that as a result of the government's labor policy, "Men and Women came to think of democracy as they had never thought of it before. Democracy became the great, flaming religion of mankind." It was in this hopeful context that workers embraced the government's promised industrial democracy. . . .

By allowing workers to connect democracy in industry to democracy in Europe, the federal program had the effect of offering a potent vocabulary to the labor militants who had little trouble in seizing it to attack the authority of employers. If the NWLB implied that employers who opposed collective bargaining were subverting the war effort, on the shop floor union militants made the implication explicit, equating obstinate managers with the autocratic enemy. In the era when sauerkraut became "liberty cabbage," Bridgeport, Connecticut, machinists began referring to Remington Arms as "The American Junkers." The steelworkers of Birmingham, Alabama, called the Tennessee Coal and Iron Company the "Kaiser of Industrial America." "The American Hohenzollerns" was another favorite appellation. Most common of all, however, were the terms "prussian" and "autocratic." Indeed, the German "kultur," excoriated by George Creel's Committee on Public Information, seemed to offer a perfect analogy to industrial management and so bossism became "Kaiserism" in the language of union activists. By using this kind of language, the labor movement portrayed itself as demanding the "de-kaisering of industry," rather than merely seeking higher wages and shorter hours. Indeed, such language cast the labor movement as the agent of industrial democracy, making unionizing a patriotic act. . . .

Portrayed in this way, union organizing was as much an act of good citizenship as an act of self- or class-interest and workers could defend it as such. This gave activists a valuable ideological shield. When her foreman demanded to know whether Mrs. C. W. Brooks, an operative in the magazine department of a Colt firearms factory, had been attending union meetings, Mrs. Brooks could simply reply: "Yes, and as a free American citizen I have a right to go if I want to." For many labor militants it was a short step from identifying union organization as a citizen's right to defining it as a citizen's responsibility. The Machinists' organizing cry in Bridgeport was "Wake Up! Be Real Citizens!" With admonitions such as these sprinkling wartime union drives, it is little wonder that the GE activist mentioned above could claim that his union sympathies were really "an American feeling."

This "feeling," as the Wilson administration (and the AFL leadership for that matter) found, had many implications. It could be used by the union movement to ward off slanderous accusations that legitimate strikes were financed by the Kaiser's gold. Indeed, unions began to defend strikes as actions taken in defense of democracy at home and hence as *supportive* of the war effort. Thus, strikers at one electrical plant informed President Wilson that their walkout was "the only course of action that true Americans [could] pursue." But this same reasoning enabled militants to clothe in patriotic garments demands that challenged managerial authority; industrial democracy, militants proved, could serve subversive ends. Perhaps nothing illustrated this truth more clearly than the response of workers to the NWLB's shop committees.

While some government officials initially felt that shop committee representation "might help in getting hold of some [workers]," such was rarely the case. In practice, the shop committees came to represent a new covenant, the inauguration of "democracy in the shop." Thus, evidence indicates that shop committees encouraged rising expectations among the workers in the more than 125 factories where the NWLB installed them. Most workers apparently agreed that, as one put it, the creation of shop committees was "the most important thing the Board did." Government investigators confirmed this sense. "The interest of the employees [in the shop committee] was so great as to strike me as almost pathetic," reported one federal investigator about shop committee elections in munitions plants. . . . His counterpart at Bethlehem Steel agreed that shop committee elections put workers "in a mood of great hope."

In many shops, militants found it easy to translate these hopes into aggressive shop-floor organizations that sought to erode managerial prerogatives under the banner of industrial democracy. Union delegates swept the slates in almost all shop-committee elections held by the NWLB. And in many—particularly in the metal trades—radicals dominated the committees. In such cases, NWLB-created shop committees became major headaches to employers. Committee delegates "spent most of their time going from department to department and keeping things generally upset," groused one manager. His complaint found many echoes. In some shops—such as the GE plant in Lynn, Massachusetts—workers embraced the committee system as a mechanism to roll back the authority of the foreman and achieve greater autonomy in the workplace. The chief vehicles of the NWLB's promised industrial democracy, then, sometimes became the staging grounds for militant shop-floor organizations that did indeed demand something like [historian David] Montgomery's "workers' control." But, it is important to remember, even when this occurred, workers tended to call it not "workers' control" but "self-government in the workshop . . . part of the democracy for which our armies are fighting in France."

Nor should this surprise us. For the industrial democracy slogan and the rhetoric attacking "prussian" management provided a language both sweeping and flexible enough to accommodate the interests of semiskilled operatives as well as artisan radicals. Workers whose shop-floor experience and worldviews were not conducive to the development of a "workers' control" consciousness—women who worked as semiskilled operatives for example—could still find in the vague term industrial democracy legitimation for their desires for dignity on the job. Thus federal investigators found that women who were "afraid of the term unionism" were still "anxious to take advantage of committee representation" promised by the industrial democracy crusade.

Far from suppressing labor unrest, then, the rhetoric of the government's program empowered the workers' movement in ways no one could have foreseen. The spread of aggressive shop committees, the talk of industrial democracy, the hard-hitting attacks on "prussian management," it can be argued, helped shift the "sub-political" attitudes of American workers, igniting Woll's "flaming religion." By the end of the war, more workers were flooding into union ranks than served in the American Expeditionary Force in Europe. Many were simply swept up in the "pentecostal" mood that saw the lines between trade unionism and "American citizenship" blurred. . . .

By the time the Armistice was signed, not only were an increasing number of U.S. workers joining unions, they were doing so believing, as a Minneapolis trade-union paper put it, that "the dream of industrial democracy [was] coming true." Moreover, they looked to the postwar Reconstruction era, as most people termed it, for the fulfillment of that dream. As one steelworker told a Reading, Pennsylvania, throng during a celebration of the peace treaty, "You have been fighting for democracy, [but] there can be no peace until you have obtained . . . industrial democracy." Those kinds of statements led a contemporary observer, John Graham Brooks, to conclude that workers had "learned the troublesome liturgy about 'self-determination' " and were determined to have "something of it for themselves."

It was this "troublesome liturgy" as much as the growth of union organization that employers sought to reverse following the war. The task must have initially seemed awesome to them. So widespread had become the wartime demands for industrial democracy that reformers of many stripes, church groups, and trade-union leaders alike had adopted the term in their calls for "social Reconstruction" after the war. By 1919, industrial democracy had become, as one journalist at the time observed, a national "fetish," "the most ecumenically satisfying phrase now at large." Employers ignored the demand at their own peril.

But what had been labor's strength during the war turned out to be its weakness in peacetime. Industrial democracy provided an attractive organizing principle as long as the federal government—and specifically the NWLB—continued to play an active mediating role in labor conflict. While the government played that role, militants could even exploit its stance to advance a brand of radical workplace politics under the banner of industrial democracy. In effect, militants had labored in the ideological free space inadvertently created by Wilsonian labor reform. Following the war, however, the government's stance dramatically shifted toward demobilization, powerful labor allies—including Frank Walsh and Felix Frankfurter who headed the War Labor Policies Board—left government service, and as a result the free space within which workers had begun to organize was radically constricted.

Several factors account for this shift. First, the entire war labor administration had been created by emergency presidential initiative and lacked a solid legislative basis. Any hopes that the NWLB would be put upon sturdy legal footing after the war were quickly dispelled by the 1918 congressional elections that swept into office conservative legislators bent on hastily dismantling the war labor administration. At the same time, employers' hostility to wartime interference in their affairs by "petty government officials and shop committees" had coalesced into a powerful lobby for labor deregulation. But perhaps most importantly, President Wilson and his advisors concluded that postwar union demands would fuel spiraling inflation. Consequently, the administration set itself against postwar wage demands, using the remaining federal labor boards to block the unions (particularly in the railroad and mining industries) rather than defend them as they had done during the war crisis. Wilson thus threw the moral authority of the government against not "autocratic" employers but "unreasonable" unions.

That the shifting stance of the state was the crucial factor in American labor's defeat in 1919 is widely recognized. The impact of this shift on the language that workers had used during the wartime upheaval, however, has not been fully explored and is thus deserving of attention.

Labor's call for industrial democracy in 1918 was indeed a powerful rallying cry. But it was powerful partly because it was such an amorphous concept: to government administrators it promised greater war production; to AFL leaders it meant the acceptance of trade unionism; to rank-and-file militants it often symbolized "self-government in the shop." . . . In the absence of state support, labor found it impossible to prevent employers from applying a denuded definition of democracy to industrial democracy and then using that very phrase to battle trade unionism.

One employer put the postwar objectives of his class this way: "With labor crying for democracy," he wrote, "capital must go part way, or face revolution." Many employers had grasped this inevitability even before the war ended. As early as the ninth Yama conference of the National Industrial Conference Board, held in October 1918, there was evidence that an increasing number of employers were willing to go "part way." At that meeting, employers discussed demands for industrial democracy and debated possible counter strategies. Although conferees arrived at no consensus, many delegates returned to their respective companies to begin implementing representation plans or company unions like those pioneered by Midvale Steel and the Colorado Fuel and Iron Company in order to head off the demand for democracy in their shops. Soon the famous Special Conference Committee that included the executives of America's largest corporations was busily coordinating the spread of Employee Representation Plans (ERPs), the employers' alternative to shop committees and "self-government in the shop."

With the role of the state in guaranteeing workplace representation receding quickly, employers moved to implement ERPs "with a maximum of publicity and a minimum of interference." In doing so, employers played an important part in shaping what historian William Graebner has aptly characterized as a "new and profound appreciation for democratic modes of social control" in postwar America. Before 1919 was six months old, William Leiserson of the Labor Department reported that "a deluge of shop committees and employee representation plans [was] flooding the country." While such schemes bowed in the direction of democracy, they did so, as one of their proponents put it, "without surrendering any final authority" to the workers represented. Their purpose, the manager of a GE factory frankly acknowledged, was to "transmit the personality and character of the management to the men most effectively." Unions resisted the introduction of employee representation schemes, the hated "Rockefeller unions" that intended to "bunco . . . employees into thinking that they are getting a real taste of industrial democracy." When they were skillfully introduced, however, as at the Lynn plant of GE where nonradical AFL unionists were even encouraged to serve as delegates, the ERPs did gain approval from workers. In all, workers were in a poor position to resist the spread of ERPs in the industries where unions had secured only a tentative foothold before the war ended. By 1921, over seven hundred thousand workers labored in plants with this truncated version of shop committee representation.

The story of management's postwar representation movement has been well documented. Less thoroughly understood is the attempt by employers to capture the patriotic terminology that labor insurgents had used during the war. Yet this too was an important thrust of the postwar managerial counteroffensive; indeed, it was one of the factors that underlay the success of the employers' strategy. Following the war, employers proved that the patriotic language around which workers had built their movement could indeed be Janus-faced. If workers had begun to equate unionism with "an American feeling" during the war, employers made it their task to Americanize their version of employee representation. Thus their open shop movement became the American Plan. According to the propaganda of the open shop associations, their plan embodied "the spirit of the Declaration of Independence"; it constituted "a perfect manifestation of the American spirit."

Perhaps the most striking evidence of employers' attempts to capture the language of the wartime mobilization concerns their conscious use of the industrial democracy rhetoric that workers had used against them only months before. The employers' success in neutralizing or co-opting that rhetoric following the war revealed the fundamental ambiguity inherent in the language labor had used to articulate its wartime demands. During the war, the notion of industrial democracy had served as an instrument for both unions and employers. On the one hand, by linking war production and democracy it served as a tool for getting more work and greater loyalty out of workers. On the other hand, workers and unions used it to their own purposes. In this trade-off, employers had gotten more work at the cost of investing workers with new conceptions of citizenship; unions recruited more members at the cost of phrasing their demands in a language less working-class than American. During the war, labor had gained more than it lost in embracing industrial democracy; following the war, the tables were turned. In the language of industrial democracy, patriotism, citizenship, and Americanism were more at issue than class solidarity. Thus the phrase could be used with as much facility by employers following the war as it had been by labor militants during the war—a factor that helped to undermine labor's defense against the postwar open shop drive.

To be sure, this is not to suggest that the success of the employers' American Plan turned solely—or even largely—around the question of language. . . . But to ignore the importance of the postwar struggle over language—and employers' efforts to capture the industrial democracy slogan thus denying workers an effective language with which to both conceptualize and rally their movement—is to miss a central theme in the story of the employers' counteroffensive.

Employers themselves were surprisingly frank in their efforts to make the language of industrial democracy their own following the war. John Leitch, a theorist of the ERP movement, argued before the 1919 convention of the National Association of Manufacturers that employers could not afford to "let labor think that industrial democracy means anything like Bolshevism as it is run in Russia." Management's task, as Leitch understood it, was to make sure that the definition of democracy, implied by the term industrial democracy, did not challenge managerial prerogatives. . . .

Whether called an Industrial Democracy or an Industrial Assembly or simply a conference committee or employee representation committee, postwar ERPs all attempted to redefine the notion of industrial citizenship that union militants had attempted to construct during the war. While union organizers had rallied their followers with the cry "Wake Up! Be Real Citizens!" in 1919, employers introduced a new "citizenship theory of labor relations," as GE's Gerard Swope described it. If Americanism could serve as a language with which to unite workers during the war, it could also be wielded by employers seeking to foster division among workers after the Armistice. In 1919, steel mill owners circulated handbills that read: "WAKE UP AMERICANS!! ITALIAN LABORERS . . . have been told by labor agitators that if they would join the union they would get American jobs." If during the war workers challenged managerial authority by appealing to a higher loyalty—the nation's war effort—in peacetime, the government's antistrike stand allowed employers to claim that the country demanded loyalty to the company. Goodyear's Industrial Assembly drove home this point. "I want you to consider this company," Goodyear vice-president Paul Litchfield told his workers, "the same way as you would consider the United States." Litchfield aimed, he said, to create "a citizenship of the right type."

The Goodyear program, in fact, represented perhaps the most fully articulated effort by a corporation to clothe itself in the rhetoric and symbolism popularized by the war. Those who served as representatives in the Industrial Assembly took an oath of office that reinforced the dual loyalty to company and country Goodyear hoped to foster: they pledged to defend "the Constitution and laws of the United States and . . . the Industrial Representation Plan of the Goodyear Factory." "Loyal" employees earned the right to vote in Industrial Assembly elections. Significantly, however, while the NWLB allowed all workers to participate in shop committee elections, companies like Goodyear sharply restricted the franchise. Goodyear required voters to have been employed by the company for six months, to have obtained U.S. citizenship, and to have a command of the English language. In order to serve as Industrial Assembly delegates, longer tenure with the company was required. Those who could meet the requirements of Goodyear "citizenship" earned a new sobriquet designed by the company to describe its loyal employees: Goodyear called them "industrians." Goodyear "industrians," of course, enjoyed only a pale imitation of the "self-government in the shops" that the militant wartime industrial democracy movement had advocated.

The efforts of Goodyear and publicists like John Leitch to redefine industrial citizenship after the war direct our attention toward the importance employers placed on neutralizing the language and symbolism that served the wartime union upheaval. These efforts also indicate that U.S. labor's reversal between 1919 and 1922 was a more complex defeat than historians may have heretofore understood. For in that defeat, workers saw employers attack not only their organizations but the words and concepts upon which they had built them. The importance of this dimension of the conflict was not lost on the labor militants of that era. As employers laid their own claims to the language of the wartime upheaval, words such as industrial democracy and reconstruction that had fortified the wartime workers' movement left a bitter taste in the mouths of those who had once used them. Thus a textile union leader railed against the "57 varieties . . . of definitions of industrial democracy" that undermined labor's message. . . .

Labor militants did not abandon their claims to industrial democracy or their dreams of reconstruction after the war. Indeed, the wartime upheaval had in some ways permanently altered the language with which labor militants articulated their vision. Erstwhile labor radical turned scholar Frank Tannenbaum, for example, still hoped in 1921 for "the displacement of the capitalist system by industrial democracy." Railroad unions advocated the Plumb Plan under the banner of industrial democracy and the influential Intercollegiate Socialist Society rechristened itself the League for Industrial Democracy after the war. Industrial democracy thus remained a contested term even in the midst of postwar managerial ascendancy. The labor movement, however, would not soon be able to challenge successfully the definition of the phrase that American employers deployed in 1919. In the final analysis, that fact, as much as the trade-union defeats of that eventful year, defined the bitter legacy of the "Great War" for American workers.

# ⚓ *F U R T H E R    R E A D I N G*

Arnesen, Eric. *Brotherhoods of Color: Black Railroad Workers and the Struggle for Equality* (2001).

Boris, Eileen. *Home to Work: Motherhood and the Politics of Industrial Homework in the United States* (1994).

Brody, David. *Labor in Crisis: The Steel Strike of 1919* (1965).

Clark, Claudia. *Radium Girls: Women and Industrial Health Reform, 1910–1935* (1997).

Dawley, Alan. *Struggles for Justice: Social Responsibility and the Liberal State* (1991).

Dubofsky, Melvyn. *The State and Labor in Modern America* (1994).

———. *When Workers Organize: New York in the Progressive Era* (1968).

Ernst, Daniel. *Lawyers Against Labor: From Individual Rights to Corporate Liberalism* (1996).

Forbath, William. *Law and the Shaping of the American Labor Movement* (1991).

Gerstle, Gary. *American Crucible: Race and Nation in the Twentieth Century* (2001).

Hart, Vivian. *Bound by Our Constitution: Women, Workers, and the Minimum Wage* (1994).

Hoffman, Beatrix. *The Wages of Sickness: The Politics of Health Insurance in Progressive America* (2001).

Kessler-Harris, Alice. *In Pursuit of Equity: Women, Men and the Quest for Economic Citizenship in 20th Century America* (2001).

Lichtenstein, Nelson, and Howell John Harris, eds. *Industrial Democracy in America: The Ambiguous Promise* (1993).

McCartin, Joseph. *Labor's Great War: The Struggle for Industrial Democracy and the Origins of Modern American Labor Relations, 1912–1921* (1997).

McCormick, Charles. *Seeing Reds: Federal Surveillance of Radicals in the Pittsburgh Mill District, 1917–1921* (1998).

Milkman, Ruth, ed. *Women, Work, and Protest: A Century of U.S. Women's Labor History* (1985).

Mink, Gwendolyn. *Old Labor and New Immigrants in American Political Development: Union, Party, and State, 1875–1920* (1986).

———. *The Wages of Motherhood: Inequality in the Welfare State, 1917–1942* (1995).

Novkov, Julie. *Constituting Workers, Protecting Women: Gender, Law, and Labor in the Progressive Era and New Deal Years* (2001).

Orren, Karen. *Belated Feudalism: Labor, the Law, and Liberal Development in the United States* (1991).

Rodgers, Daniel. *Atlantic Crossings: Social Politics in a Progressive Age* (1998)

Skocpol, Theda. *Protecting Mothers and Soldiers: Materialist Origins of the American Welfare State* (1993).

Walkowitz, Daniel. *Working with Class: Social Workers and the Politics of Middle-Class Identity* (1999).

Wunderlin, Clarence, Jr. *Visions of a New Industrial Order: Social Science and Labor Theory in America's Progressive Era* (1992).

# Industrial Unionism
# During the Great Depression

*The 1930s are the pivot on which twentieth-century labor history turns. Millions of workers joined a newly energized trade union movement in these years, many of them under the banner of the Congress of Industrial Organizations (CIO), the breakaway union federation that burst on the national scene in 1936 and 1937.*

*The new unionism had three notable features. First, it organized mass-production industries like auto, steel, and electrical products and vital services like intercity truck transport, longshore freight handling, and municipal buses and subways, all of which stood at the core of the U.S. economy in the first half of the twentieth century. By 1945 the unions enrolled almost 15 million workers, five times the number at the depth of the Great Depression. About a third of all non-agricultural workers were now trade union members, a proportion far above that of any previous era in U.S. history.*

*Second, many of these unions were organized on an industrial basis. Therefore they enrolled all workers in a given plant or mill, regardless of their job title, skill level, or American Federation of Labor (AFL) claims that they belonged in one of its craft unions. Because of their inclusiveness, the new industrial unions enrolled many workers whom the AFL had spurned: Eastern European immigrants, African Americans, Mexican Americans, and white women in unskilled occupations.*

*Finally, the unionism of the 1930s had a radical flavor unseen since the era of Eugene V. Debs. Communists and socialists had played key roles in organizing workers in the maritime industries, in auto manufacturing, and in steel and electrical products. Once organized, these new unions often fought with foremen and managers to slow the pace of production, limit management prerogatives, and win a whole series of new rights, among them seniority, which had rarely before been codified in a binding collective-bargaining contract.*

*Of course, historians do not agree about the full meaning of this experience. How was it that these unions proved so successful at a time when unemployment rates stood at such high levels? Were the unions as radical as many of their contemporary opponents claimed? Were they an effective counterweight to managerial Taylorism? Did ordinary workers see the new unions as merely an instrument to increase their*

*pay and ameliorate the conditions under which they labored, or did they invest their
larger aspirations in this new social movement, finding in its struggles some of that
transcendant meaning hailed by anticapitalist radicals of old?*

## ⚓ D O C U M E N T S

Document 1 is the preamble to the National Labor Relations Act of 1935, more commonly known as the Wagner Act, named for its chief sponsor, New York senator Robert
Wagner. It justifies the rights of workers to choose their representatives democratically
and bargain collectively with employers. In Document 2, John Steuben, a Communist
organizer in Youngstown, Ohio, describes the Communist Party's large role in the
CIO's Steel Workers Organizing Committee (SWOC). Out of two hundred SWOC
organizers, about sixty were Communists. But many workers were hardly radicals. In
Document 3, the wife of a sit-down striker recalls her initial hostility to the union. In
Document 4, journalist Mary Heaton Vorse discusses why many white-collar workers
were indifferent to the new unionism, even at the depth of the Great Depression, but
why many might well join the Congress of Industrial Organizations.

Company recognition of the new unions hardly resolved conflict, either between
workers and managers or between workers themselves. In Document 5, the National
Labor Relations Board investigates the case of a textile-mill worker fired for his pro-
union views, and orders his reinstatement with back pay. In Document 6, Margaret
Nowak describes her husband's resourceful leadership in a 1937 slowdown strike in
Detroit. Disputes over pay, job content, transfers, and promotions remained endemic
in all workplaces, so most union contracts contained an elaborate grievance procedure
to resolve them. Union leaders often saw their shop-floor role in quite different ways,
as Documents 7 and 8 illustrate. Document 7 offers advice to United Automobile
Workers (UAW) shop stewards on how to win grievances, fight factory supervisors,
and strengthen the union. Document 8 reveals the far more conservative approach of
two high officials of the United Steelworkers, who successfully worked to transform
their union into one that cooperated with the corporation and tempered the militancy
of the rank and file.

# 1. Preamble of the National Labor
# Relations Act, 1935

The denial by employers of the right of employees to organize and the refusal by
employers to accept the procedure of collective bargaining lead to strikes and other
forms of industrial strife or unrest, which have the intent or the necessary effect of
burdening or obstructing commerce by (a) impairing the efficiency, safety, or operation of the instrumentalities of commerce; (b) occurring in the current of commerce;
(c) materially affecting, restraining, or controlling the flow of raw materials or manufactured or processed goods from or into the channels of commerce, or the prices
of such material or goods in commerce; or (d) causing diminution of employment
and wages in such volume as substantially to impair or disrupt the market for goods
flowing from or into the channels of commerce.

---

From *Public Laws of the United States,* 74th Congress, Session 1, 1935–1936, 449–450.

The inequality of bargaining power between employees who do not possess full freedom of association or actual liberty of contract, and employers who are organized in the corporate or other forms of ownership association substantially burdens and affects the flow of commerce, and tends to aggravate recurrent business depressions, by depressing wage rates and the purchasing power of wage earners in industry and by preventing the stabilization of competitive wage rates and working conditions within and between industries.

Experience has proved that protection by law of the right of employees to organize and bargain collectively safeguards commerce from injury, impairment, or interruption, and promotes the flow of commerce by removing certain recognized sources of industrial strife and unrest, by encouraging practices fundamental to the friendly adjustment of industrial disputes arising out of differences as to wages, hours, or other working conditions, and by restoring equality of bargaining power between employers and employees.

It is hereby declared to be the policy of the United States to eliminate the causes of certain substantial obstructions to the free flow of commerce and to mitigate and eliminate these obstructions when they have occurred by encouraging the practice and procedure of collective bargaining and by protecting the exercise by workers of full freedom of association, self-organization, and designation of representatives of their own choosing, for the purpose of negotiating the terms and conditions of their employment or other mutual aid or protection.

## 2. Communist John Steuben Organizes Steel, 1936

Youngstown, Ohio
August 31, 1936

Dear Comrade Stachel:

. . . The drive in the Youngstown steel district like throughout the country has not yet assumed a mass character. However, this does not express the real sentiment of the steel workers, meeting hundreds of them every week, both American and foreign-born, I have yet to find one case of real hostility towards the union. On the contrary, I am met with open arms and the steel workers are keenly interested in the drive and are anxiously hoping to see the drive go over big. I am absolutely convinced that the greatest majority of the steel workers will join the union in the next few months to come.

Why then is there their great discrepancy between the favorable sentiment and the actual growth of the union? The way I see it, these are some of the reasons:

1. The open warning of the companies to fire the men who join the union, still constitute the greatest obstacle. Although we can already observe a definite break down of this fear.

2. Many old foreign-born workers are still bitter against the American steel workers who didn't back them in the 1919 strike and want to see the Americans come in first.

From Max Gordan, "The Communists and the Drive to Organize Steel, 1936" in *Labor History* 23 (Spring 1982), pp. 260–265. Reprinted with permission of Taylor & Francis, Ltd., http://www.tandf.co.uk/journals.

3. The self-satisfaction of the SWOC [Steel Workers Organizing Committee] on the top with the progress of the drive. This results in a failure to press the field organizers to produce better results. . . . These people on the top (SWOC) also picture the steel drive as a mere series of mass meetings and a mechanical signing up of members without developing any partial struggles and obtain certain initial victories for the workers, without necessarily calling local strikes. . . .

4. The work of the organizers, especially the UMWA [United Mine Workers of America] organizers, is perhaps one of the weakest links in the whole drive. . . .

This is so important a question that I therefore must deal with it in detail. The organizers' staff in Youngstown can be divided into two categories: The UMWA organizers and the Party forces. There is a vast difference between the two. It is amazing how people can be so long in the labor movement and know so little! Not only are they political babies, they are not even good union organizers. To give you an example, a UMWA official from the anthracite (Gwyn) was in Youngstown five weeks and recruited three men. Another from the soft coal (Buhaley) was here six weeks and recruited five men and these were supposed to be well trained organizers. Then take the man who is in charge here (Frank Shiffka) completely incompetent and if not for our forces he would have left the field long ago. . . . On the other hand our forces that are on the staff are the best organizers and produce more results than any of them. I, personally, have established myself as the best recruiter and on the average I recruit close to fifty percent of the total recruits. Our youth organizer and the other comrades are also doing fine.

In face of such a vast difference between our and the UMWA forces, it was necessary to establish a proper relationship. Having in mind that these people don't know what criticism and self-criticism means, we have to avoid any head-on-collision with them. Instead we pursued a policy of winning their confidence. This was fully accomplished with the result that our suggestions and our policies are unquestionably accepted. We have also from the very start, decided that the Party comrades must be the best organizers and by our example bring up the rest of the crew. This is just what is happening now.

A few remarks about the methods of organization. . . . If you receive accurate reports from the field you then know that as yet in no place are the mass meetings a real success and in many places these "mass" meetings only expose the weaknesses of the union and sometimes make it look even worse than it really is. For example, I think it is crazy to now call mass meetings in towns like Alliquippa. On the basis of the experiences in other places and on the basis of Foster's lessons in Youngstown (1919), we have decided not to call any mass meeting until we have at least two thousand men signed up. Then when we have such a number of workers signed up and these are involved in preparation for a mass meeting, we are sure that at least five thousand steel workers will attend the meetings. The workers like this policy very much, as they would be afraid (and with full justification) to attend open meetings. However, we have engaged a radio station in Akron and we broadcast from there twice a week, this will go on till after Labor Day and then we will fight for a further allowance for the radio. The radio and STEEL LABOR are the medium through which we are reaching thousands of workers with the voice of the union. . . .

A few words on the method of recruiting. Of course we are using Comrade Foster's three point theory of organization as our starting point. On the basis of this theory, I have developed a method which has been proven and tested to be the best and the whole crew in Youngstown is now practicing it. I call it the "chain form of recruiting." In brief, it works like this—when I sign up a worker, I ask him to recommend three or five other men from his department. Then I ask him to talk to these workers in the mill and prepare the ground for me. Then two days later I visit these workers, most of them already expect me and when I come to their house and present my credential, they already know who I am and I find no difficulty in signing them up. These men in turn recommend others and the chain is endless. Right now, for example, over a hundred workers are expecting me at their homes. This week, every house that I went to, as soon as I present my credential, the reply was, "Come in, I have been waiting for you." My list is already so big that another organizer will be attached to me so that the workers will not be kept waiting too long. Those organizers that begun to practice this chain form of organizing are also meeting with similar success.

Another method that I am using is not to spread out too much. Instead, I am concentrating on certain departments. For example, I have already signed up the majority of the men in the Condroit Department of the Ygstn Sheet and Tube (over 40 men). From there I began to move into the 40 inch mill. The experience is that once you establish a base in one department it is much easier to spread out into the other departments.

To summarize this point: the tempo in recruiting depends entirely on the organizers, the methods they use, the hours they put in, the ability to convince the worker not to fear signing up and even enthusing them for active participation in the drive. . . .

While it is absolutely correct to discourage local strikes at this stage of the game and even be on guard against any strikes that may be contemplated by the steel companies, yet, the union must already begin to develop certain partial struggles that will result in some immediate victories for the workers. These can be developed through progressive company union representatives, through committees and petitions. The companies are terribly nervous and it is possible to obtain all kinds of concessions that in turn will help to build the union. It is unfortunate that the SWOC don't realize the importance of such actions. Then, there is another aspect to the same problem: when a worker joins the union he expects some kind of help and if this is not forthcoming he will fall for the company propaganda of "Why pay dues?" I think that our forces on the staff should raise this question everywhere and bring it to the attention of the CIO. . . .

## Press Policies of Steel Corporations

Our secret method of recruiting and organization created a very difficult situation for the companies. They are really not aware of the degree of progress we have made so far. The decentralized form of organization is an additional obstacle to them. However, we know that they are careful in firing union men. Sixteen of our people were uncovered . . . including many of our comrades. But so far only the YCL [Young Communist League] organizer was fired out of the Sheet & Tube. All the others were called in, warned but not yet fired.

Through a friendly federal man we have also learned that the companies have brought in a lot of ammunition inside the mills. Sheet & Tube has deputized 151 men, Republic 50 men. We have also learned that when the first public meeting is held, they will provoke a fight and open a barrage of tear gas.

Meanwhile, they are publishing every Sunday a full page ad. I will send you a sample of this Sunday ad. They are also circulating a petition among wives of steel workers against the CIO. The spies continue to shadow the organizers and all our wires are tapped. Recently I moved to a new house hoping to keep it secret, several days later two cars with the stool pigeons were in front early in the morning. I figure it is no use to move again, I have arranged for another sleeping place in case of emergencies. I have also learned from the same source that they are especially out to get us and to link us up with the CIO and then make a big splash in the papers. We are now expecting it to break soon and we are prepared for it. . . .

**On the Party**

. . . The functioning of the Party is very unsatisfactory. . . . At present I devote all my time to the drive. However, as soon as I personally recruit 500 into the union (I have already reached the 200 mark) and the other comrades recruit another 500 steel workers, it will no longer be necessary for me to devote my time on individual recruiting and I will have more time for direct Party work. However, I have already established dozens of splendid contacts for the Party. I look forward that within six months from now the bulk of the Party will be composed of powerful nuclei inside the mills. We have already made a start by recruiting one of the organizers into the Party. . . . I am now working on several other leading people in the drive and I am sure we will soon have them in the Party.

The Party comrades inside the mills are doing splendid work and they are coming forward very nicely. Up to now the active comrades were busy with putting the Party on the ballot, now we're through with this work, we will get busy on stabilizing the units and involve our Party forces in the steel drive. . . .

Comradely yours,

Steuben

# 3. Mrs. Violet Baggett Joins the Union, 1937

A month ago today I knew nothing and cared less about the Automobile Union. My husband being a member of the United Auto Workers, attended meetings, but just before this sit-down strike at Cadillac it seemed to me that about all he thought about was going to union meetings. I'd heard about the Reds and had been told that this gang were Reds with leaders in Russia. I'd also been informed they met in beer gardens with plenty of short-haired girls to entertain them.

So when the strike was called and my husband stayed in all day and then came home, only to start out next morning for the picket line, I decided it was time I stopped this union business for good, in our home anyway. So I started out as soon as I knew he was well on his way. It didn't take long to find the place but on the

From *The United Auto Worker,* 1937. Reprinted by permission of *The United Auto Worker* (official publication of the International Union, UAW).

door was a card saying Use Side Door Please. Sure enough the side door opened into a beer garden. By that time I was mad all over.

The man in charge seemed surprised when I demanded the Cadillac strikers and told me they were upstairs. By then I wasn't only mad but tired as well, and climbing those stairs didn't improve my disposition—not much. I met a lady coming down from the kitchen and before I could make up my mind just what to say first she smiled and asked me if I'd come to help. Instead of flappers and empty beer bottles I saw half a dozen women peeling vegetables, others washing dishes.

I thought I'd stick around a little before starting my little riot. I peeled onions while my eyes wept tears of agony, then potatoes, then we cut bread till my hands blistered, sorted and cut and packed pies, hundreds of them. By night I was almost too tired to go home and I'd completely forgotten to speak my piece. The other women didn't seem to mind the long hours. I kept this up for seven whole days, sometimes from seven to seven. I soon learned everyone was too busy to bother about how I felt, so I got busy, too.

I found a common understanding and unselfishness I'd never known. These people are real people and I'm glad I'm one of them. I only wish I'd got mad long ago and investigated, but I didn't have time for anything outside of my own small circle. I'm living for the first time with a definite goal. I want a decent living for not only my family but for everyone. Just being a woman isn't enough any more. I want to be a human being. I'm ready and glad to wear my green beret and Women's Emergency Brigade armband anytime, anywhere I'm needed. I hope if anyone chances to read this they'll take the time to find out as I did what women can and are doing to help men in their fight for decent wages and working conditions.

Mrs. Violet Baggett, President
West Side Local Women's Auxiliary, Detroit

## 4. White-Collar Workers Organize, 1938

The First National Conference of the Insurance Agents Union was held in New York, December, 1937. This meeting was in a sense a more revolutionary development than the organization of steel and auto workers. That insurance agents from all over the country, from New England to California, should have begun a militant organization showed that a profound change in thinking was going on among the middle-class workers.

The very calling of such a conference has historic significance. Here, for the first time, was provided a parallel for the practical organization of the giant insurance companies. Through their investment of policyholders' funds these huge companies constitute a vast reservoir of financial capital. Though there are 382 insurance companies in America, ten major concerns hold over 70 per cent of all insurance assets. And nine of these giant firms are directly influenced by the house of Morgan, which shares control in some instances with the Rockefeller interests.

This meeting was an illustration of the fact that the white collar and professional people are joining the onward march of labor. While the number of factory

From Mary Heaton Vorse, *Labor's New Millions* (New York: Modern Age Books, 1938), 182–189.

workers reached its peak in 1919, the employment peak for white collar workers was not reached until ten years later. Now both groups are equally subject to lay-offs and wage cuts and they are at last recognizing this crucial fact. Politically, and from the standpoint of a sound labor movement, this is nearly the most important development that the labor renaissance of the last years has produced. For it is through the unions' penetration of the white collar and professional workers that the middle class will at last awaken to its place in history.

One of the most discouraging things about the labor movement in the past has been that this enormous group, composed of nearly a sixth of the workers of this country, looked at labor's efforts to organize with the same indifference with which the white Capetown dwellers regard the muffled drumming of the African in the bush.

The small-town dweller, the people engaged in small businesses, that army of people who are employed one year and who are in business for themselves the next, and all those who are steadily leaving the ranks of the employers to become them-selves employed, have been in ignorance, not only of the labor movement, but of their own relation to the world in which they live. There are literally thousands of towns in the United States composed almost exclusively of working people of one kind or another; towns where scarcely a score of people make or spend over $2,000 a year, who, fed as they are on information furnished by the manufacturers' associations, regard labor as something remote from them, an unruly group composed of people who make strikes, engage in riots, and whose leaders are mostly racketeers.

The ignorance of the middle class and the white collar worker is as dense in industrial towns. In Anderson, Indiana, during the General Motors strike, office girls by the score, firmly believing that the unionization of the auto workers would destroy business in Anderson, signed the cards furnished them by the [antiunion] Citizens Committee.

One of the most potent ways of dispelling this ignorance is through the or-ganization of the white collar and professional people. But this organization to be successful must carry with it a large measure of education designed to show this class its true relation to the modern business and industrial scene. Through the C. I. O.'s progressive approach, the impetus given to it by militant young leaders, and guided by the judgment of mature minds long in the labor movement, educa-tion and organization are being carried on together.

The technician, the draftsman, the great army of workers in the financial dis-tricts, the great army of employed girls starting out to the office every morning, the teachers, the musicians, and all those engaged in the amusement trades have in the past considered themselves as belonging to the propertied class instead of regarding themselves as workers. The lag of thought behind reality is nowhere more clearly seen than among white collar workers who still act as though they were living in the days when in office or workshops the young clerk or apprentice was presently taken into the firm and had the opportunity of marrying the employer's daughter.

The largest white collar union, the Brotherhood of Railway and Steamship Clerks, Freight Handlers, Station and Express Employees, though having a member-ship at its best of 135,000 workers, refused to have Negro members in its ranks. The same was true of government employee unions under the A. F. of L. They remained stagnant and inactive and in no wise saw their struggle as labor's struggle.

The failure of the amusement groups and the government employees to relate themselves to the struggle of labor was largely the fault of the A. F. of L. Its conception of labor was as narrow as that of the salaried worker. A distrust of "intellectuals" has always been characteristic of it. Since the earliest days of Gompers' rule the A. F. of L. never made any effort to penetrate the hostility or ignorance of the middle class.

Among the white collar people, organization even for the most exploited office help was feeble and ineffectual. In industrial disputes no attempt was made by the workers to organize the office staff who almost invariably sided with the management; and when the hotel workers formed unions, it was the women in the hotels' employ who could often be counted on to scab, and take the places of the waiters on strike.

Until the depression, the white collar workers sailed along unconscious of their place in the world; their clean hands and clean collars gave them the illusion of superiority. Actually the changing economic scene with its closed frontier, huge aggregations of capital and steadily shrinking opportunities for small ownership, had completely altered the status of these workers. Unwittingly they became "salary slaves." The depression shattered the world in which they lived and revealed to them that they were as insecure as any man who has nothing to sell but the work of his two hands.

There is no record of all the thousands of middle-class young people who lost their houses, their furniture, their cars, and who subsisted on the charity of their families or public relief during the depression. In New York City alone it was estimated that 40 per cent of the women on relief had formerly held clerical jobs. In 1932 it was estimated that nearly 20 per cent of the nation's four million clerical workers were unemployed. Salaries fell. The average $20 and $22-a-week job now netted only $15. Qualified chemists could be had for only $14 a week. Four-fifths of the three million and a half professionals and technicians are salaried people. The toll that the depression took on their jobs was tremendous. Statistics for 1933 show 98 per cent of the architects unemployed, 85 per cent of the engineers and 65 per cent of the chemists. Many of these, finding employment only under the W. P. A., learned that their lot was even more precarious than that of the industrial workers. . . .

During the depression they swelled the relief rolls as surely as did the industrial workers or the small-pay stenographers. The depression was writing a lesson on the walls of history: that all workers are subject to the same economic laws; that the brain worker who has invested a small fortune in his training is no more insured against destitution than is the lowest paid typist or laborer.

Some of the professional and white collar people read the lesson and began forming unions after 1931, but it is necessary to remember that a vast number sought relief for their economic ills in crackpot panaceas. There is only a beginning, so far, in the organization of this important group of people who are the logical ones to interpret labor's new identity and purpose to the middle class.

For the moment professional people organize, their identification with all of labor becomes apparent to them. What has happened to the Newspaper Guild is one of the most important developments that has occurred in recent years.

Under the fierce attack of the American Newspaper Publishers Association, after some hard-fought strikes, and after it had seen its members fired for union activity, the Guild membership learned rapidly.

The Guild's swift gain in numbers is remarkable, but not so remarkable as the span it has covered in its thinking. When it first started, the news writers didn't think of themselves as workers. They considered the organization as a sort of club. They had not analyzed their position. They did not realize that the average newspaperman throughout the country was receiving a smaller salary than the government-paid garbage man.

At their last convention . . . they voted to join the C. I. O. and to include as eligible to the Guild all workers from circulation men to copy boys. Their stand was questioned by the opposition and a referendum was taken which overwhelmingly confirmed this action of the convention. . . .

Another union which has come along rapidly is the Federation of Architects, Engineers, Chemists, and Technicians. The first professional union to affiliate with the C. I. O., it grew rapidly. It included in its ranks unemployed members and workers employed on the professional projects of the W. P. A. and has been in the forefront of the line by which the old antipathy and ignorance of the middle class can at last be expelled. . . .

In the W.P.A. and outside it many small professional unions have been formed. They have been about equally divided between the A. F. of L. and the C. I. O. They include social workers, dental laboratory technicians, nurses, librarians, research workers, pharmacists, etc. . . . [T]he C. I. O. hopes ultimately to form strong industrial unions of government employees. Such injustices as occurred in 1932—when through economy measures men in the prime of life, in customs or immigration, coast guard, etc., were put on the retired list with small pensions—would never have occurred had there been a union to speak for them.

Both the A. F. of L.'s narrow, "vested interest" outlook and those earlier opportunities for advancement into ownership from white collar work are responsible for the present serious lag in thinking that stops a swifter organization in this field. Salaried workers are still reluctant to acknowledge their common interest with industrial workers and learn from organized labor new lessons in economic history. Nevertheless, the pressure of reality is steadily bringing these facts home to white collar employees.

The rapid progress of the white collar unions and their education of the middle-class people from whom they spring will be one of the greatest insurances that this country can have against fascist movements.

In estimating the importance of this movement we must remember that the middle class has been the recruiting ground of the fascist movement.

When the bottom dropped out of the economy of the middle class in Germany, its members did not join the ranks of the workers. Not understanding what had happened to them, they maintained the illusion of their superiority to the manual workers and became easy dupes of Hitler's propaganda. He was financed by the employers, just as we have seen elsewhere in this book that the little Fuehrers in America are financed by the Weirs and the Graces. Hitler derived his rank and file support from the economically ignorant middle class. How true it is that the middle class when in distress inclines toward adventurers can be seen by the fact that such adventurers as Huey Long, Gerald K. Smith, and Father Coughlin got their support from just such distressed people as those who supported Hitler in Germany.

Hunting a solution to their economic disarray, these groups readily swallowed the various eccentric schemes and plans offered to a gullible public. Our bewildered middle class has supported the Townsend Plan, share-the-wealth moves, social credit plans and the like, just as the frightened salaried classes in Germany turned to Hitler for relief from their economic misery. The pattern repeats itself.

Only by labor's telling its story plainly, by pointing out the democratic and practical aspects of its program, will these middle-class workers be brought to see where they belong in the economic picture, and transfer the weight of their influence from the side of the employer who has so assiduously courted them to the side of the worker with whom their interests dovetail.

And only when they do transfer their interests, only when they have ceased to be on the side of the management and the bosses, will they cease to be food for such fascist ventures as the Citizens Committees. Only when they realize that their economic salvation lies in organization, together with all salaried and industrial workers, will the importance of the labor movement be understood throughout the country and a true unity of all workers be achieved. Without the support of the middle class, the farmers, and white collar groups, the organized industrial worker cannot lead all labor finally to economic and political maturity.

## 5. A Union Man Gets His Job Back, 1938

Pursuant to notice, a hearing was held in Greenville, South Carolina, on October 4 and 5, 1937, before D. Lacy McBryde, the Trial Examiner duly designated by the Board. The Board and the respondent were represented by counsel and participated in the hearing. Full opportunity to be heard, to examine and cross-examine witnesses, and to produce evidence bearing upon the issues was afforded all parties. . . .

The respondent, a South Carolina corporation, is engaged in the manufacture of cotton cloth. It operates three plants, all in Greenville County, South Carolina. The main plant, known as the Woodside plant, with which this case is concerned, is located at Greenville while the other two are located at Simpsonville and Fountain Inn. . . .

Textile Workers Organizing Committee is a labor organization affiliated with the Committee for Industrial Organization and admits to membership employees of the respondent at its Woodside plant. The predecessor of the unit of the Textile Workers Organizing Committee here involved was known as United Textile Workers of America, Local 1684, and was affiliated with the American Federation of Labor. In 1936 the local was absorbed by the Textile Workers Organizing Committee. . . .

On October 10, 1935, John R. Kirby, an employee of the respondent at the Woodside plant, was discharged. Kirby had been a member of the Union since 1934, then holding the office of warden. During September of that year there was a general strike in the cotton textile industry, affecting also the Woodside plant. At that time Kirby acted as captain of the pickets around the Woodside plant. In November 1934, following the strike, Kirby was elected president of the Union for 1 year, an office he held at the time of his discharge. Avery Hall, an employee at the Woodside plant, in response to the question whether he knew Kirby to be an active Union man replied, "I sure did." And when asked whether this fact was generally known in the plant Hall testified, "Most all the hands knowed it." Another witness,

From *National Labor Relations Board Report*, vol. 5, 1938.

Roy Dryman, an employee at the Woodside plant, when asked whether and how he knew Kirby was a Union man testified, "Because he told me he was and he asked me I guess fifty times to join." Dryman further testified, "I don't guess there was a half dozen people in the mill who didn't know he was an active Union man." From the record it is clear that Kirby was an active Union member and that this fact was generally known throughout the plant.

The Woodside plant was divided into two sections, known as Mill No. 1 and Mill No. 2, though both were in the same building. Prior to Kirby's discharge each section had worked on a day and night shift. In February 1935, pursuant to a pre-determined plan, the respondent commenced to make alterations in the plant by which the production would be so changed that the night shift in Mill No. 2, as well as 22 jobs, including those of 15 frame hands, would be eliminated. . . .

On Monday, September 23, 1935, which was the next working day, Kirby started at his regular job when S. N. McConnell, at that time the second hand in Mill No. 1, told Kirby he was wanted by Bray. Grover Hardin, until then employed on the night shift in Mill No. 2, was placed in Kirby's position. Kirby reported to Bray and was told that he was to be transferred to the night shift in Mill No. 2, that being the shift which was to be eliminated as soon as the improvements had been completed. Kirby asked Bray why this was being done, and when no reason was given said, "Mr. Bray, I know why you are transferring me out there. It is because I belong to the Union." From the inception of the improvements in the plant the night shift in Mill No. 2 had been continually reduced until at the time of the transfer only three employees were working there. Kirby was the only man to be transferred from the carding room in Mill No. 1 to the carding room in Mill No. 2, where he took Hardin's place. The Monday following his transfer Kirby was notified by the respondent that his services would be terminated at the end of that week, as the particular set of frames on which he was working were not to be used longer. Accordingly, about 2 weeks after his transfer Kirby was discharged. Shortly thereafter the night shift in Mill No. 2 ceased operating.

Bray testified that in eliminating the night shift in Mill No. 2 he tried to retain the best men. He testified he tried "to pick out the people [he] thought would fit better . . . from an efficiency standpoint, and the people that could get along with people, and cause no confusion in the mill . . . regardless of the time they have been there." Bray testified that neither the pay nor the employment was regulated by seniority, but "everything being equal we try to take care of the people that has been there."

We shall endeavor to apply this test of the respondent to Kirby, on the basis of the evidence presented in the record. Kirby started to work for the respondent during the latter part of April 1933, having had previous experience elsewhere. Though it was up to Bray to make the selection of the men to be kept, the second hand was the employee most familiar with the relative efficiency of the various frame hands in the carding department as he was their immediate superior, worked with them continuously, and kept a written record of their mistakes. From the time of the strike in 1934 to the time Kirby was transferred to Mill No. 2, McConnell was the second hand in charge of the night shift in Mill No. 1. Prior to McConnell's arrival as second hand, the evidence adduced at the hearing was to the effect that Kirby's work was always satisfactory. McConnell testified that Kirby was an average hand, that of the group of approximately 16 frame hands on the night shift in Mill No. 1 there were "two or three that would get better production," but there were "Some didn't get the production he got, couldn't get about as well." Bray admitted he did not seek McConnell's advice before deciding to remove Kirby from the night shift in Mill No. 1 and discharging him shortly thereafter. Bray testified he did not want McConnell's advice because McConnell was Kirby's uncle. . . .

The respondent tried to imply that Kirby did not work regularly by endeavoring to show in his cross-examination that he was not regular in his attendance at the plants at which he had worked since his discharge by the respondent. But if any conclusion is to be drawn from the only record available, the pay-roll record . . . , it would seem that Kirby was rarely absent. For the period of 16 weeks noted in the record he was absent but 2 days. . . .

On the basis of his efficiency, his ability to "get along with people," and his attendance at the plant, it appears that Kirby was one of the better frame hands of the 16 on the night shift in Mill No. 1. This being so, and "everything" not "being equal" as to this group of 16, the question of seniority need not be considered. It must be noted that Kirby was the only man to be transferred from the carding room in Mill No. 1 to the carding room in Mill No. 2. On the basis of the respondent's own test it is clear that if anyone were to be transferred Kirby should not have been that one. . . .

The Union, besides admitting employees of the Woodside plant, also admitted employees from other cotton mills in Greenville. However, there were more members from the Woodside plant than from the others. Though at the time of the strike the membership was quite large, after the strike it had become fairly small. Nevertheless the Union under Kirby held regular meetings and continued active. Following his discharge and departure from Greenville to find other work, however, it became inactive. A few weeks after his departure the Union did not hold further meetings.

The respondent contended that it never knew Kirby was president of the Union and did not even know he belonged to it until his comment to Bray at the time of the transfer. We find, however, in view of the clear testimony that Kirby took an active part in the 1934 strike, and that almost everyone about the plant knew Kirby was active in Union affairs, that the respondent must have been aware of his Union activities. From the record it is clear that Kirby was discharged for his activities in behalf of the Union and the employees of the respondent at the Woodside plant.

We find that by the above acts the respondent has discriminated in regard to the hire and tenure of employment of Kirby, and that it has thereby discouraged membership in the Union. We also find that by the above acts the respondent has interfered with, restrained, and coerced its employees at the Woodside plant in the exercise of the rights guaranteed in Section 7 of the Act. . . .

Upon the basis of the findings of fact and conclusions of law and pursuant to Section 10(c) of the National Labor Relations Act, the National Labor Relations Board hereby orders that the respondent, Woodside Cotton Mills Co., Greenville, South Carolina, and its officers, agents, successors, and assigns shall:

1. Cease and desist from:

(a) Discouraging membership in Textile Workers Organizing Committee or any other labor organization of its employees at its plant in Greenville, South Carolina, by discrimination in regard to hire or tenure of employment or any terms or conditions of employment;

(b)  In any other manner interfering with, restraining, or coercing its employees at its plant in Greenville, South Carolina, in the exercise of their right to self-organization, to form, join or assist labor organizations, to bargain collectively through representatives of their own choosing, and to engage in concerted activities for the purpose of collective bargaining or other mutual aid or protection, as guaranteed in Section 7 of the Act.

2. Take the following affirmative action which the Board finds will effectuate the policies of the Act:

(a)  Offer to John R. Kirby immediate and full reinstatement to his former position or to a position corresponding to that formerly held by him at the plant in Greenville, South Carolina, with all rights and privileges previously enjoyed;
(b)  Make whole said John R. Kirby for any loss of pay he has suffered by reason of his discharge by repayment to him of a sum of money equal to that which he would have earned as wages during the period from the date of his discharge to the date of such offer of reinstatement, less the amount he has earned during such period;
(c)  Post notices in conspicuous places throughout its plant at Greenville, South Carolina, and maintain such notices for a period of at least thirty (30) consecutive days from the date of posting, stating that the respondent will cease and desist as aforesaid;
(d)  Notify the Regional Director for the Tenth Region in writing within ten (10) days from the date of this order what steps the respondent has taken to comply therewith.

## 6. Stanley Nowak Organizes a Slowdown Strike, 1937

Ternstedt's was one of the greatest aggregations of women workers in the automotive industry. The vast majority of the twelve thousand employees were women, and all previous organizing attempts had netted only about a dozen members. On some floors of Main Plant No. 18 hardly a man was to be seen, as men worked mainly in the tool and die section.

At the organizational meeting, considerable doubt was expressed as to whether women could be organized, especially since previous attempts had accomplished so little. Finally Stanley spoke up. "I disagree," he said, "that women are difficult to organize. In every shop I have organized, and in every activity in which women have participated with me, I have found them very dependable, vocal, and militant, often more so than men."

"Well, you can have it, Stanley," said the others, who willingly turned over to him the Ternstedt assignment. . . .

Stanley began stopping in at a neighborhood bar, where he learned of grievances in Ternstedt's different departments and featured them in the next day's leaflet. This caught the attention of the workers, and some of them began to stop for a word or two.

From Margaret Collingwood Nowak, *Two Who Were There: A Biography of Stanley Nowak* (Detroit: Wayne State University Press, 1989), pp. 103–104, 109–114. Reprinted with permission of Wayne State University Press.

The tool and die men and some of the machine repair men began to stop at the sound truck to ask questions. Because of their skills they were less vulnerable than other workers, and soon they began to sign applications and hand out leaflets to fellow employees.

Stanley felt it was time to call meetings. The Slovenian Benefit Society owned the Slovene Hall on Livernois and South streets, about a block away. The sympathetic and cooperative manager permitted the hall's use as a temporary union headquarters and meeting place. Membership meetings grew until forty or fifty people were attending after each shift. . . .

One reason for so many women employees was that the company manufactured small parts easily manipulated by women—door handles, chromium trim, and so on. Many women hired during World War I had been allowed to remain because they would work for less than men. Ternstedt's reputation for low wages was widely known. The bonus system was juggled so that it was almost impossible to earn more than the hourly rate, no matter how much production was turned in. . . .

Another unfair practice was the "shape-up." Employees coming to work gathered around in a semicircle while the foremen selected workers for certain machines or tasks. After all the jobs for that shift were assigned, the remaining workers went home without pay, not even for carfare, since they were paid only for actual working time no matter how many hours they had waited for assignment. . . .

Since Ternstedt was a division of GM [General Motors], the successful ending of the Flint sit-down on 11 February gave a tremendous boost to the Ternstedt organizing drive. The master contract between GM and the UAW [United Auto Workers] covered all GM plants, thus entitling Ternstedt workers to union recognition. . . .

The workers had begun to publish a paper, the *Ternstedt Flash*. When it announced the coming meeting between [plant manager S. E.] Skinner and the Bargaining committee, a wave of enthusiasm swept the plants, resulting in hundreds of new members. This meeting was regarded as the first step toward victory. However, the workers soon discovered the truth of the old adage, "You can lead a horse to water, but you can't make him drink." Skinner complied with that part of the agreement calling for meeting with the bargaining committee, but granted no concessions. This went on for weeks, creating a serious crisis.

Workers had joined the union for its benefits, yet Skinner refused to agree to any of the demands presented. The new GM contract specifically ruled out strikes. Moreover, there was tremendous antistrike agitation in the press. What could be done to compel Skinner to bargain, short of a strike? . . .

Shop stewards were now functioning in every department at Ternstedt's, numbering almost two hundred, all impatiently demanding action. Unless something was done quickly, further organizing would be stymied, and membership would drop. Stanley anxiously turned the matter over in his mind. Then he recalled reading about a strike in Vienna before World War I, where workers stood at their machines and went through the motions of working, yet produced very little. An old Polish worker in Chicago, who had participated in that strike, had told him about it years before and had given him a book in Polish describing it. He located the book in our library and spent most of the night reading it long after I was asleep. The next morning he seemed relieved.

Smiling, he said over breakfast, "Since the union contract cannot compel Skinner to grant concessions at the bargaining table, neither can it compel workers to produce while at their machines. If Skinner can make a farce of bargaining, I don't see why we can't use this tactic in return." . . .

And so was born the first slowdown in UAW history. The problem now was to organize the new tactic. Of the twelve thousand Ternstedt workers, only a handful had any union experience. They had never heard of a slowdown but were ready for any kind of action.

The new technique was first carefully explained to the bargaining committee, then to the two hundred or more stewards, who then had to explain and demonstrate the idea to trusted workers in each department—all this while maintaining absolute secrecy. Fortunately, there were no company agents in the union leadership in the plants. Finally, the plan was ready to be put into operation. Production was not to be cut all at once in all plants but rather in each department at a different time. On the appointed day and hour, the cue was to be given successively in each department. A meeting of the bargaining committee with Mr. Skinner had been scheduled for the very morning when all this was to take place, and there was some apprehension among the group as they headed for Mr. Skinner's office.

"Good morning, Stanley," greeted Skinner as Stanley came in with his committee that morning in early April 1937.

"Good morning to you, Mr. Skinner," returned Stanley.

The committee members filed into the office and took their places around the big table in the center. Mr. Skinner looked every inch the business executive in his smart suit with his sleek, graying hair and trim build. He sat at his desk a few feet away, greeting each one with a great display of amiability, waving his long cigarette holder and moving papers around as he made conversation. At the bargaining table, small talk and laughter masked an undertone of uneasiness and tension. Skinner's unusual affability and exaggerated courtesy made the committee members wonder, "Does he know?" A surreptitious wink or shrug in reply to questioning glances expressed their hopes and uncertainty. . . .

As each demand was presented, Skinner appeared to weigh it carefully, discussed it with the group, then turned it down for one reason or another. This had been the pattern of the meetings for weeks.

As the farce proceeded, a telephone call interrupted Mr. Skinner. The committee members looked at each other hopefully, and listened eagerly. Skinner was somewhat less genial when he returned to the table, but he continued with negotiations. In a few moments another call came. Skinner looked searchingly around the table as he resumed his seat. His good humor had vanished. Two more calls came. With each one he grew more disturbed. As he hung up the receiver from the last one, his face contorted with anger and he pointed an accusing finger at Stanley.

"You son of a bitch, *you* did this to me!"

"I did what?" Stanley asked innocently.

"*You* know what I'm talking about. How dare you have the gall to come here and go through the motions of bargaining when there's a strike in the plant?"

"A strike?" Nowak repeated. "Aren't the workers on the job? We don't know of any strike."

"Oh yes you do!" insisted Skinner.

"I don't believe it, Mr. Skinner. Take me through the shop and show me where there is a strike."

"Like hell, I will! Get out of here! All of you! You have a hell of a nerve to negotiate with a strike going on." . . .

That night, the day-shift workers joyfully reported what had taken place in their departments. It hadn't taken long for department heads to notice the lag in production and reprimand the workers.

"I'm doing the best I can," workers maintained. "Maybe it's the machine."

Machines checked out okay, but production was still slow. At first, workers were somewhat clumsy at appearing to work while producing little; however, they soon caught on, and then it became a wonderful game, each worker trying to outdo the others in making as many motions as possible and doing the least work. Production slowly dropped. Management had been taken completely by surprise. A new wave of enthusiasm brought hundreds of new union applications, until more than 80 percent of the work force had joined. . . .

The slowdown continued. Production dipped to about 40 percent or 50 percent of the norm. In some departments it dropped to as low as 5 percent or 10 percent on some days. Skinner still refused to budge.

UAW vice president Wyndham Mortimer later told Stanley that William F. Knudsen, GM's president, had approached him and asked if he couldn't pressure Ternstedt workers to end their slowdown.

"They wouldn't even listen to such an idea," Mortimer declared, "unless Skinner begins to bargain in good faith."

Skinner must have been advised to abandon his hard-nosed attitude, for when Stanley phoned him soon after, he said, "Well, Stanley, I guess it's about time we got together again. Bring your bargaining committee and we'll get down to business."

In one three-hour session more was accomplished than in all previous meetings combined. Apparently Skinner realized that he was the one "over the barrel" this time. Union recognition was granted at once, and piecework was abolished, with hourly rates to be negotiated in place of piecework. . . .

## 7. For UAW Shop Stewards: "How to Win for the Union," 1941

[The] power of organized labor is brought to bear against management through the shop stewards and plant committeemen, who are the elected representatives of the organized workers. *On these committeemen or stewards depends the success or failure of labor in the automobile industry.*

But the conduct of negotiations with management is only half the job of these committeemen and stewards. Not only must they carry the union's grievances to management: they must insure the continued organization of the men whom they represent.

---

From *How to Win for the Union: A Discussion for UAW Stewards and Committeemen,* 1941. Reprinted by permission of UAW Education Department.

The best negotiator in the world will not get to first base if he allows the men he represented to fall away from the union. Without organization behind him and working with him, no steward, no committeeman, no officer can win victories from management. Unless he speaks for solidly organized workers, he is as futile and helpless as the individual auto worker back in the days of the open shop.

In other words, the committeemen and stewards have a double responsibility: responsibility for conduct of negotiations and for the men whom he represents united behind the policy of organized labor. He is at once a diplomat negotiating with a foreign power and a general preparing his troops for possible conflict. . . .

In plants where contracts have been signed between the UAW and management a procedure for handling grievances is usually written into the contract itself. In all plants where collective bargaining is carried on, a good steward knows the contract practically by heart.

The contract is a constitution governing union-management relationships. No one can hope to handle grievances successfully without a full knowledge of its provisions. A lawyer must know something of the law before he is allowed to plead cases in court. You must know your plant law before you handle grievances. . . .

The contract is your constitution, and the settlement of grievances under it are the decisions of an industrial supreme court. *A complete record of such decisions is sometimes more important than the contract itself.* . . .

The best contract in the world may be signed between union officers and corporation executives; but, unless that contract is enforced and put into life throughout the shop it is worth a little bit less than the paper it's written on. This is the job of the steward in his dealing with company foremen.

Where union organization is new, the problem of educating foremen to collective bargaining may be one of the toughest jobs the union has to face. Before organization came into the plant, foremen were little tin gods in their own departments. They were accustomed to having orders accepted with no questions asked. They expected workers to enter into servile competition for their favors.

With the coming of the union, the foreman finds the whole world turned upside down. His small-time dictatorship has been overthrown, and he must be adjusted to a democratic system of shop government. Naturally many foremen resent this change and continue a hostile attitude toward the union even after higher company officials may have decided to "work along with the union."

This makes the steward's problem difficult. He must convert the foreman to the democratic processes of collective bargaining and establish a sound working relationship with him as an individual.

Many inexperienced committeemen and stewards feel that the way to do this is to get tough with their foremen. They feel that threats and fistbanging will do the job for them. In 1937 some UAW committeemen used these methods.

Experience has shown that this approach does not work forever. . . .

Although the foreman represents the interests of the company as opposed to the workers, he is also a human being. Approach him like one. Find out what he is interested in. If he is a baseball fan, a little talk about batting averages won't hurt anything. Or if he likes fishing, you can discuss that. Occasional talk of this kind will not make it any harder to get down to business on grievances.

Don't give your foreman reason to believe that you are trying to bluff him. A reputation for honesty and good judgment is essential to your success in collective bargaining.

Hold down on personalities and name-calling. It won't help to settle grievances. And you can be even more forceful, when the occasion demands, if you have something in reserve. Try to avoid personal spite against a foreman because of unfair policies he is ordered to carry out by top management.

If a foreman tries to bully you or talk you down, talk back quick and hard, but keep your temper. A lost temper usually means a lost argument.

Various forms of pressure will bring results from foremen who are trying to be hard. With some men publicity in local union papers or bulletins brings results. With others, reports to top management on trouble-making foremen are the best medicine.

In plants where top management is sincerely anxious to work along with the union, a chronically disruptive foreman will be disciplined by his superiors.

Your relationship with the foreman should be that of equals seeking a solution to a common problem. But don't forget: the stronger the organization behind you, the more powerful your arguments will be. . . .

The steward's greatest difficulty will come on grievances which do not appear to be covered by the terms of the contract. On a demand for action from a worker which is directly contrary to the written contract, the steward has no choice but to say no. But many cases will arise in which justifiable complaints do not seem to be covered one way or another by provisions of the contract.

In such a situation the steward or plant committeeman goes through his contract with a fine-tooth comb to find some provision which will cover this particular situation. If the issue is one of any importance he will get the help of his local union officers in this.

In practically all cases where a worker has a legitimate complaint it will be possible to find some clause of the contract which, with a little pulling and hauling, can be made to cover the situation. Lawyers have been able to use a Constitution written over 150 years ago to cover the complex issues of modern life. A bright steward should be able to do just about as well with his contract. . . .

The union's system of shop stewards and committeemen is a weapon of democracy. That is its fundamental meaning. Where the foreman's power is handed down to him from the corporation owner on top, the steward's power comes from the workers below. The foreman, in the last analysis, is responsible to the directors of the corporation. His job is done successfully when their interests are served. In the same way the steward is responsible to the majority—to the workers; and his job, likewise, is well done when their interests are well served. . . .

A steward or committeeman cannot take action without the backing of the men in his department. This is a truth which cannot be repeated too often.

But this fact is no excuse for inaction. No steward can sit on his hands and allow the company to break down union conditions, simply because the men in his department have not taken the bit in their teeth to demand action of him.

*It is the steward's job to go out and win democratic support for the union policies which his experience and knowledge of the labor movement prove to be right.*

The steward should remember that forces hostile to labor inside and outside the plant are at all time seeking to win influence over his men. Unless the steward gives positive leadership in behalf of CIO principles, he will find his men pulled away from him.

To make democracy work, therefore, the steward or committeeman must be prepared to put a solid program before his men and, if need be, fight for its support. He must awaken and encourage his men to take part themselves in working out union policy. He should fight at all times against the "card carrier" spirit. He should know, and teach others, that the union is no slot machine into which men drop a dollar a month and receive automatic returns in the form of better wages, hours, and conditions. . . .

The union is opposed to unauthorized strikes. This is not because a milk and water policy has been adopted. It is primarily because the unauthorized strike or stoppage is undemocratic.

Were the unauthorized strikes to be tolerated it would mean simply that any small group within the union would have the power to dictate to the union as a whole. A handful of men in a single plant cannot be given the right of involving tens of thousands of workers, without their consent, in a costly and dangerous struggle. That would mean that a contract covering thousands of workers could be broken down at the whim of a few individuals. To give a minority such power is the very opposite of democracy. It would mean that the UAW-CIO could not exist as a stable organization—could not prepare itself for meeting the tremendous problems that loom in the future of the industry.

That is why every steward, committeeman and officer is duty-bound to fight for the observance of the Constitution and rulings of the International Executive Board for the elimination of all unauthorized stoppages and strikes.

## 8. Union Leaders Oppose Shop-Floor Agitators, 1941

On Sunday, March 2, 1941, Stanley Orlosky, lifelong union worker, a pipe fitter in a steel mill, was expelled from his union after a trial on charges of "violation of obligation to the Steel Workers Organizing Committee." To add to his disgrace, Stanley was tried by union officers whom he had solicited to join the union a few years earlier. He came to our office to appeal the decision of the trial board of his local union. Stanley was powerfully built, stood six feet tall, and the few strands of gray in his black hair belied his forty-five years. He exhibited a soiled membership card in the United Mine Workers of America, Local 405, Loyalhanna, Pennsylvania, dated March 17, 1911. This was secured in his first strike. He lost out in it. Stanley worked the coal fields until 1928, when he was blacklisted and forced to go into the steel mills. The ABC Steel Company fired him in 1933 for being president of the NRA local union, but hired him back in 1934 when the union died. In 1936 he became vice-president of the SWOC [Steel Workers Organizing Committee] local union in his section of the mill and was chairman of the grievance committee until 1940, when the SWOC director removed him from office for violating the contract.

Excerpt from *The Dynamics of Industrial Democracy,* by Clinton Golden and Harold Ruttenberg. Copyright 1942 by Clinton Golden and Harold Ruttenberg. Reprinted by permission of HarperCollins Publishers, Inc.

"Being a good union man is agitating—that's what I always knew as a union man—and I got fired for agitating," Stanley complained to us. "The union was organized to have freedom, and not to be fired for talking. The men that tried me in the local, I had a hard time getting to join the union a few years ago. Now they're big union shots. The company has had it in for me since 1933. I'm a thorn in the flesh to it. Now the union sides with the company, and I'm out. That ain't justice. The national office should give me another hearing, and give me back my membership card," he pleaded.

We investigated his case. The talking for which Stanley was fired consisted of charging the incumbent union officers with "selling the men down the river," since they settled grievances on their merits. His idea of a grievance settlement was to get everything or strike. Stanley's leadership was essential to the establishment of the union against bitter resistance, but after it had been fully accepted by management such leadership was a handicap to the development of co-operative union-management relations. His expulsion was sustained by the SWOC national officers.

In this huge mill of more than ten thousand workers, SWOC has five local unions, instead of one, to facilitate the administration of union affairs. Two of the locals are still led by leaders of Stanley's type. Carl Rossi, young high-school graduate, is president of one of the remaining belligerently led locals. He boasts, "I've never lost a grievance case." At joint meetings of the officers from the five locals Carl charges the co-operative ones with "running company unions." He disposes of arguments that costs do not permit granting a particular request with "They're always crying poor mouth." When told his unrelenting pressure for wage adjustments might cut employment, might even put the company out of business, Carl smiles. "Them birds are always crying wolf, and you guys [SWOC district director and co-operative leaders] fall for that scarefish stuff. Not me—that mill will be there when I got whiskers a mile long." Carl and the countless other local union leaders he typifies view the union's relations with management as being predicated upon a continual fight. In those cases, unfortunately still a majority, where management keeps the union at a respectful distance, such a union approach is unavoidable; but where the union has been taken into management's confidence, greater responsibilities face the union and its leaders.

Carl has only one concern in pressing a case of a union member: get for the member what he wants or as close to it as possible. The problem of finding the means to meet the demand is exclusively management's. In winning a case Carl takes all the glory; in losing one Carl gives management all the blame. But Carl never loses a case. A negative reply merely puts the case on the unfinished-business agenda; Carl keeps pressing it until management yields or the member dies. Management . . . encourages this kind of approach by insisting that union membership be voluntary, despite the union's majority enrollment. Repeatedly we have been told by management, "It is your job to sell the union to the employees." Local union leaders know no better way to do this than to "get things" for their followers, and let management worry about how to pay for them.

Eventually this honeymoon comes to an end. Carl's company has taken SWOC into its inner councils, abandoned its policy of keeping the union at a distance, and says to SWOC's top leaders, "We are co-operating fully with SWOC, have granted the union shop as evidence of our sincerity; but some of your local union leaders still serve us with ultimatums to grant demands by a certain time or they will strike. What are you doing to have them approach these problems in a co-operative spirit, as matters for which they must assume joint responsibility?"

At this point union members, their national officers, intermediary field staffs, and local union leaders face the acid test. They have to demonstrate that under a union shop unions can assume and discharge their responsibilities to the best interests of both their members and the business enterprises upon which they depend for a livelihood. This is primarily the job of top union leaders, since they must show to their followers, on the union staff and in the mines, mills, and factories, the way toward industrial peace and fruitful union-management relations. Before this, however, they must show newly recognized unions how to make collective bargaining work under the difficult conditions of partial union membership.

There are two stages in the development of labor leadership: one is the contract stage; the other is the union-shop stage. In signing the initial contract with a firm, top union leaders automatically assume the task of showing the local union involved, and the union field staff directing its affairs, how to bargain contractually. Likewise in signing a union-shop contract, the national union leadership automatically assumes the responsibility for directing the union involved toward co-operative relations with management. We find ourselves in the peculiar position of having to do both jobs simultaneously with different groups of workers, because SWOC's relations with the eight hundred and twenty-six firms under contract are in varying stages of maturity.

## ✢ E S S A Y S

The following two essays offer sharp contrasts as to what the union movement meant in the 1930s. In the first essay, historian Melvyn Dubofsky of the State University of New York at Binghamton offers a provocative interpretation emphasizing the failures and limits of the new unionism, both as a political institution and as a vehicle for transforming popular consciousness. He points out that most workers did not take part in militant strike actions, that the Congress of Industrial Organizations' (CIO) union leadership was often quite conservative, and that the decade ended with the social and political structures of American life fundamentally unchanged. Most important, Dubofsky asserts a social inertia at the heart of working-class consciousness that failed to engender a cultural or ideological value system capable of standing apart from that of marketplace capitalism.

In contrast, in the second essay, historian Bruce Nelson of Dartmouth College celebrates what he calls the Pentecostal era of worker militancy and class consciousness that transformed the social and economic world of West Coast longshoremen after the Big Strike of 1934. Nelson finds that many workers willingly followed the leadership of political radicals, that oppositional values did emerge, and that working conditions were so changed that some longshoremen now referred to themselves as the "Lord of the Docks."

Did the meaning of working-class Americanism change during the 1930s? Do these two historians define worker militancy and political radicalism in the same fashion? To what extent is the CIO an heir to the tradition of the Knights of Labor, the Industrial Workers of the World, or the American Federation of Labor in the Gompers era?

# Not So Radical Years:
# Another Look at the 1930s

## MELVYN DUBOFSKY

Our conventional view of the 1930s was aptly caught in the title of Irving Bernstein's history of American labor during that decade, *Turbulent Years,* a title that the author borrowed from Myron Taylor's annual report to the Board of Directors of the United States Steel Corporation in 1938. That liberal historians and corporate executives perceive the 1930s as a "turbulent" decade should today occasion no surprise. For the American business elite especially, their social, economic, and political world had turned upside down during the Great Depression and New Deal. After nearly a full decade of corporate hegemony, class collaboration, and trade union retreat, the United States during the 1930s seemed chronically beset with class conflict, violence, and ubiquitous labor radicalism. In the words of one of the decade's radicals, Len DeCaux, a "new consciousness" awakened workers from lethargy. . . .

The picture one has of the 1930s, then, whether painted by a liberal scholar such as Bernstein, an activist like DeCaux, or a tycoon like Taylor, is of conflict and struggle. The foreground is filled with militant and radical workers, the masses in motion, a rank and file vigorously, sometimes violently, reaching out to grasp control over its own labor and existence.

Given the conventional portrait of the American 1930s, conventional questions arise, the most obvious of which are the following: (1) Why did labor militancy decline? (2) Why did militant, radical rank-and-file struggles produce old-fashioned, autocratically controlled trade unions in many cases? (3) Why did the turbulence create no lasting, mass radical political movement? . . .

In examining the 1930s, how should we go about creating the history of that era? Two convenient models are at hand. In one we can seek lessons for the present in an instrumental view of the past. That approach suggests the might-have-beens of history. If only Communists had behaved differently; if nonsectarian radicals had pursued the proper policies; if the militant rank and file had been aware of its true interests (as distinguished from the false consciousness inculcated by trade-union bureaucrats and New Deal Democrats); then the history of the 1930s would have been different and *better.* The second approach to our turbulent decade has been suggested by David Brody. "The interesting questions," writes Brody, "are not in the realm of what might have been, but in a closer examination of what did happen." Brody's approach, I believe, promises greater rewards for scholars and may even be more useful for those who desire to use the past to improve the present and shape the future. As Karl Marx noted in *The Eighteenth Brumaire,* man indeed makes his own history, but only "under circumstances directly encountered, given and transmitted from the past. The tradition of all the dead generations weighs like a nightmare on the brain of the living." . . .

---

From Melvyn Dubofsky, "Not So 'Turbulent Years' A New Look at the 1930s," in Charles Stephenson and Robert Asher, *Life and Labor: Dimensions of American Working Class History,* 1986, pp. 205–223. Reprinted by permission of State University of New York Press.

Let us now see if we can uncover or glimpse the reality of the American 1930s. Certainly, the turbulence, militancy, and radicalism of the decade existed. From 1920 through 1939, the American economic and social system remained in crisis. Despite two substantial recoveries from the depths of depression, unemployment during the decade never fell below 14 percent of the civilian labor force or 21 percent of the nonagricultural work force. Those workers who once believed in the American myth of success, who dreamed of inching up the occupational ladder, acquiring property of their own, and watching their children do even better occupationally and materially, had their hopes blasted by the Great Depression. . . .

The thwarted aspirations of millions of workers combined with persistent mass unemployment produced a decade of social unrest that encompassed every form of collective and individual action from mass marches to food looting. One historian has pointed out that between February 1930 and July 1932, at least seventeen separate incidents of violent protests occurred. In Chicago in 1931, after three persons were killed during an anti-eviction struggle, sixty thousand citizens marched on City Hall to protest police brutality. Indeed in nearly every city in which the unemployed organized and protested, violent confrontations with the police erupted.

More important and more threatening to the established order than protests by the unemployed and hungry, which punctuated the early depression years, were the more conventional forms of class struggle which erupted with greater incidence after the election of Franklin Roosevelt and the coming of the New Deal. In 1934, after twelve years of relative quiet on the labor front, industrial conflict broke out with a militancy and violence not seen since 1919. In Toledo, Ohio, National Guardsmen tear-gassed and drove from the city's streets Auto-Lite Company strikers who had the support not only of the radical A. J. Muste's American Workers party and Unemployed League, but also of the citywide central labor council, an AFL affiliate. And the following month, July 1934, witnessed still more violent struggles. A strike by maritime workers in the San Francisco Bay area brought battles between police and longshoremen, several dead strikers, and the dispatch of state troops. In protest, the San Francisco central labor council declared a citywide general strike for July 16. Here, too, a labor radical, Harry Bridges, an Australian immigrant and a Marxist, led a strike unsanctioned by the AFL. Only a day after the San Francisco general strike ended, Americans read in their newspapers of July 21 that on the previous day in Minneapolis, Minnesota, fifty men had been shot in the back as police fired on strikers. Within a week of the bloody July 20 battle between police and teamsters in the city's main square, Minnesota Governor Floyd Olson placed the Twin Cities under martial law. Once again, in Minneapolis, as earlier in Toledo and San Francisco, left-wing radicals led the strike, in this instance the Trotskyists, Farrell Dobbs and the brothers Vincent, Miles, Grant, and Ray Dunne. And only a week after the shootings in Minneapolis, on July 28, 1934, deputy sheriffs in the company town of Kohler, Wisconsin, killed one person and injured twenty in what the New York *Times* characterized as a "strike riot."

Few areas of the nation seemed untouched by labor militancy in 1934. In the spring a national textile strike called by the United Textile Workers of America brought out 350,000 workers from Maine to Alabama, and violent repression of the strikers proved the rule in the South's Piedmont mill towns. Throughout the spring auto and steel workers flocked into trade unions, like coal miners the previous year, seeming almost to organize themselves. And when auto manufacturers and steel barons refused to bargain with labor, national strikes threatened both industries. Only direct presidential intervention and the equivocal actions of AFL leaders averted walkouts in autos and steel.

If 1934, in Irving Bernstein's chapter title, amounted to a "Eruption," 1937 experienced an epidemic of strikes. The year began with the famous Flint sit-down strike in which the United Auto Workers conquered General Motors; saw United States Steel surrender to the Steel Workers Organizing Committee (SWOC)-CIO without a struggle less than three weeks after the General Motors strike ended; and culminated in the late spring with perhaps the most violent and bloodiest national strike of the decade: the Little Steel conflict that led to the Memorial Day "massacre" outside Republic Steel's South Chicago plant. In between Flint and Little Steel, more than four hundred thousand workers participated in 477 sit-down strikes. Twenty-five sit-downs erupted in January 1937, forty-seven in February, and 170 in March. "Sitting down has replaced baseball as a national pastime," quipped *Time* magazine.

The labor militancy and strikes of 1934 and 1937 created a solidarity that hitherto eluded American workers. During the 1930s, it seemed, the United States had developed a true proletariat, more united by its similarities than divided by its differences. Mass immigration had ended in 1921, and hence the last immigrant generation had had more than a decade to integrate itself into the social system and for its children to have been "Americanized" by the public schools and other intermediate social agencies. Male-female role conflicts appeared notable by their absence, and strikers' wives provided their husbands with substantial assistance as members of women's auxiliaries. "I found a common understanding and unselfishness I'd never known in my life," wrote the wife of one Flint sitdowner. "I'm living for the first time with a definite goal. . . . Just being a woman isn't enough any more. I want to be a human being with the right to think for myself." "A new type of woman was born in the strike," noted an observer of the struggle in Flint. "Women who only yesterday were horrified at unionism, who felt inferior to the task of speaking, leading, have, as if overnight, become the spearhead in the battle for unionism."

Even racial tensions among workers seemed to diminish during the 1930s, especially after the emergence of the CIO whose "new unionists" often crusaded for civil rights as vigorously as for trade unionism. The changes wrought by CIO led two students of black labor to conclude in 1939 "that it is easier to incorporate Negroes into a new movement . . . than to find a secure place in an older one." . . .

One must not, however, romanticize working-class solidarity and thus lose sight of the tensions that continued to pit American workers during the 1930s against each other rather than a common enemy. In New Haven, Connecticut, American-born workers still denigrated Italians as "wops," and "it's dog eat dog all right," retorted an Italian-American machinist "but it's also Mick feeds Mick!" A Hollywood film of the late 1930s, *Black Legion,* starring Humphrey Bogart as a frustrated white American-born Protestant machinist, captured the still lingering resentment harbored by the American-born against the foreign-born (and even their children), and depicted the sort of worker more likely to listen to Father Coughlin [conservative radio priest] than to John L. Lewis [United Mine Workers president], Franklin D. Roosevelt, or perhaps [the Communist party's] William Z. Foster. Or, listen to an official of an AFL union with jurisdiction in an industry that employed many Afro-Americans. "I consider the Negroes poor union men. You know as well as I do that they are shift-less, easily intimidated and generally of poor caliber. . . . What should have happened is what is being done in Calhoun County, Illinois, where Negroes are not allowed to stay overnight. As a result there are no Negroes there and no Negro problem."

But it was the CIO, not the AFL, that symbolized the labor upheaval of the 1930s. And in 1937 when CIO-organized autos, steel, rubber, and other former bas-tions of the open shop, between three and a half and four million workers joined the labor movement, a larger number than the entire AFL claimed as of January 1, 1937. Now, for the first time in its history, organized labor in America wielded power in the strategic core of mass-production industry, and it did so under the aegis of a labor federation (CIO) whose leaders consciously repudiated the AFL tradition of class accommodation and collaboration. The CIO during the late 1930s exemplified solidarity rather than exclusiveness, political action in place of nonpartisanship, biracialism and bisexualism instead of racial and sexual chauvinism, and militancy rather than opportunism. "CIO started as a new kind of labor movement," recalled Len DeCaux in his autobiography. "A challenge to the old AFL and the status quo it complacently guarded. It was new in its youth and fervor, new in the broad sector of the working class it brought into action, new in the way it accepted and integrated its radicals, new in its relative independence of corporate and government control, new in its many social and political attitudes." . . .

Had Lewis decided to lead . . . an independent political movement, the time never seemed riper. The Great Depression and the New Deal had wrought a veri-table political revolution among American workers. Masses of hitherto politically apathetic workers, especially among first-generation immigrants and their spouses, went to the polls in greater numbers. And Roosevelt broke the last links that bound millions of workers across the industrial heartland from Pittsburgh to Chicago to the Republican party. Lewis exulted at the results of the 1936 election in which for the first time since the depression of the 1890s, Democrats swept into power in the steel and coal towns of Pennsylvania and Ohio, winning office on tickets financed by CIO money and headed by CIO members. . . .

All this ferment, militancy, radicalism, violence, and perhaps even an altered working-class consciousness were part of American reality during the 1930s. Yet, as we know, American socialism expired during the depression decade, communism advanced only marginally, Roosevelt seduced the farmer-laborites and populists, the CIO came to resemble the AFL, and John L. Lewis once again reverted to be-having like a "labor boss of the most conventional kind." Why? To answer that ques-tion we have to examine other aspects of social, economic, and political reality during the 1930s. . . .

Just as one can claim that the 1930s represented a crisis for American capitalism that expressed itself most overtly in the eagerness and militancy with which workers challenged their corporate masters, one might just as easily assert that for most Americans, workers included, events during the decade reinforced their faith in the "justness" of the American system and the prospects for improvement without fun-damental restructuring. For many workers capitalism never collapsed; indeed, for those employed steadily, always a substantial proportion of the work force, real wages actually rose as prices fell. For other workers, the tentative economic recovery of 1933–34 and the more substantial growth of 1937 rekindled faith in the Ameri-can system. The two great strike waves of the decade, 1934 and 1937, erupted not in moments of crisis, but when hope, profits, employment, and wages all revived. Crisis, in other words, induced apathy or lethargy; economic recovery, a sign that the system worked, stimulated action. And when the recovery of 1936–37 was followed by the "Roosevelt depression," a more rapid and deeper decline than the Great Crash of 1929–33, the number of strikes diminished markedly and the more militant CIO affiliates concentrated in the mass-production industries suffered severe membership and financial losses. Perhaps this final crisis of the depression decade left unresolved might have snapped whatever bonds still tied workers to the American system. That, however, remains a problematic historical might-have-been, as the coming of World War II resolved the contradictions in American capitalism and substituted patriotic unity for class conflict.

An analysis of the statistics of working-class militancy during the 1930s—the incidence of strikes, the number of workers affected, the man-days lost—also leads to divergent interpretations. One can stress the high level of strike activity, the fact that only 840 strikes were recorded in 1932 but 1,700 erupted in 1933, 1,856 in 1934, 2,200 in 1936, and in the peak strike year, 1937, 4,740. One can argue that no area of the nation and, more importantly, no major industry escaped industrial conflict. For the first time in United States history, strikes affected every major mass-production industry and paralyzed the towering heights of the economy: steel, auto, rubber, coal, electrical goods; the list goes on and on. For the nation and its workers, the 1930s were indeed "turbulent years."

But the statistics of industrial conflict reveal another story, an equally interesting one. When the 1934 strike wave erupted, President Roosevelt sought to understand its origins and implications. He asked the Commissioner of Labor Statistics, Isidore Lubin, to analyze and interpret the 1934 outbreak. Lubin prepared a report that he transmitted to the President in late August 1934. Seeking to place the 1934 strikes in historical perspective, Lubin acted logically. He compared what had happened in the first half of 1934 to the last previous year in which the United States had experienced such massive labor militancy, 1919. And he concluded that the 1934 strike wave could not match 1919 in intensity, duration, or number of workers involved. More than twice as many strikes began each month in the first half of 1919, reported Lubin, than in the same period in 1934; moreover, more than two and a half times as many workers were involved in the 1919 strikes. He then proceeded to assure the President that July 1934; the month of the San Francisco and Minneapolis general strikes, witnessed no mass working-class upheaval. Only seven-tenths of one percent, or seven out of every thousand wage earners, participated in strikes. Only four-tenths of one percent of man-days of employment were lost as a result of strikes. "In other words," Lubin reassured the President, "for every thousand man-days worked four were lost because of strikes." . . .

But what of 1937, the decade's premier strike year, when more than twice as many workers struck as in 1934? Well, according to official statistics, only 7.2 percent of employed workers were involved in walkouts (practically the same percentage as in 1934) and their absence from work represented only 0.043 percent of all time worked.

Questions immediately arise from a reading of such strike statistics. What was the other 93 percent of the labor force doing during the great strike waves of 1934 and 1937? More important, how were they affected by the upsurge of industrial conflicts which did not involve or affect them directly?

Such questions are especially important when one bears in mind the continental size of the United States. Geography could, and did, easily dilute the impact of industrial conflict nationally. The United States lacked a London, Paris, Berlin, or Rome, where massive, militant strikes affected the national state directly as well as private employers. Few of the major strikes of the 1930s occurred even in state capitals, most of which were isolated from industrial strife. When teamsters tied up Minneapolis and longshoremen closed down San Francisco in July 1934, truckers continued to deliver goods in Chicago and Los Angeles, and waterfront workers remained on the job in New York, Baltimore, and San Pedro. For trade unionists and radicals it was exceedingly difficult . . . to transform well-structured local and regional organizations into equally effective national bodies. Just as the millions of unemployed during the 1930s did not experience the shock of joblessness simultaneously, so, too, different workers experienced industrial conflict at different times and in different places. As we will see below, what workers most often experienced in common—participation in the American political system—was precisely what most effectively diluted militancy and radicalism.

Despite the continental size and diversity of the American nation, it is possible to glimpse aspects of working-class reality in local settings that disclose uniformities in belief and behavior which do much to explain the dearth of durable radicalism in the United States. We are fortunate that two truly excellent, perceptive sociological field studies were completed during the 1930s that dissect the social structure and culture of two characteristic smaller American industrial cities. We are even more fortunate that the two cities investigated—Muncie, Indiana, and New Haven, Connecticut—proved so unlike in their economic structures, population mixes, and regional and cultural milieus. Muncie was dominated by two industries—Ball Glass and General Motors—characterized by an almost totally Americanborn, white Protestant population, and situated in the heartland of American agriculture, individualism, and evangelical Protestantism. New Haven, by contrast, claimed no dominant employers, encompassed a population differentiated by nationality, race, and religion as well as class, and was set in a region traditionally urban (also urbane) and non-evangelical in culture. Yet after one finishes reading Robert and Helen Lynd on Muncie and E. Wight Bakke on New Haven, one is more impressed by the similarities rather than the differences in working-class attitudes and behavior.

Let us examine Muncie first. The Lynds had initially gone to Muncie in the mid-1920s in order to discover how urbanization and industrialization had affected American culture, how the city and the factory had altered beliefs and behavioral patterns developed in the country and on the farm. They returned a decade later in order to see what impact, if any, the "Great Depression" had had on local culture and behavior. Surprisingly, for them, at least, they found labor organization weaker in 1935 than it had been in 1925, yet the Muncie business class seemed more united and more determined than ever to keep its city open shop (nonunion). The Lynds discovered objectively greater class stratification in 1935 than in 1925 and even less prospect for the individual worker to climb up the ladder of success. . . , yet they characterized Muncie's workers as being influenced by "drives . . . largely those of the business class: both are caught up in the tradition of a rising standard of living and lured by the enticements of salesmanship." As one Middletown woman informed the sociologists: "Most of the families that I know are after the same things today that they were after before the depression, and they'll get them the same way—on credit."

Union officials told the Lynds a similar tale of woe. Union members preferred buying gas for their cars to paying dues, and going for a drive to attending a union meeting. Local workers were willing to beg, borrow, or steal to maintain possession of their cars and keep them running. Despite seven years of depression, Muncie's workers, according to the Lynds, still worshipped the automobile as the symbol of the American dream, and, as long as they owned one, considered themselves content.

"Fear, resentment, insecurity and disillusionment has been to Middletown's workers largely an *individual* experience for each worker," concluded the Lynds,

> and not a thing generalized by him into a "class" experience. . . . Such militancy as it generates tends to be sporadic, personal, and flaccid; an expression primarily of personal resentment rather than an act of self-identification with the continuities of a movement or of a rebellion against an economic status regarded as permanently fixed. The militancy of Middletown labor tends, therefore, to be easily manipulated, and to be diverted into all manner of incidental issues.

So much for Muncie—what of New Haven with its more heterogeneous and less culturally individualistic working class that, in some cases, the investigator could interview and probe after the CIO upheaval of 1936–37? Again we see in Bakke's two published examinations of the unemployed worker in New Haven an absence of mass organization, collective militancy, or radicalism, despite an apparent hardening of class lines. New Haven's workers, unlike Muncie's, apparently did not share the drives of the business class and they did in fact develop a collective sense of class. "Hell, brother," a machinist told Bakke, "you don't have to look to know there's a workin' class. We may not say so—But look at what we do. Work. Look at where we live. Nothing there but workers. Look at how we get along. Just like every other damned worker. Hell's bells, of course, there's a workin' class, and it's gettin' more so every day." Yet New Haven, like Muncie, lacked a militant and radical working class. Why?

Bakke tried to provide answers. He cited the usual barriers to collective action and working-class radicalism: ethnic heterogeneity; fear of the alien; fear of repression; and capitalist hegemony that was cultural as well as economic and political. Yet he also discovered that answers to the absence of militancy and radicalism lay embedded deep within the culture of New Haven's workers. In most cases, their lives had disproved the American dream; rather than experiencing steady upward mobility and constantly rising material standards of living, Bakke's interviewees had lived lives of insecurity and poverty. They regularly had had to adjust their goals to actual possibilities, which almost always fell far below their aspirations. As one worker after another informed Bakke, life involved putting up with it, grinning and bearing it, and using common sense to survive. Explaining how the unemployed managed in a period of general economic crisis, a brass worker noted in a matter of fact fashion, "The poor are used to being poor." . . .

Just so with New Haven's workers. For the majority of them, alternatives to the existing system seemed most notable for their absence. The only alternatives the city's workers cited, German Nazism, Italian Fascism, and Soviet Communism, none of which to be sure they had experienced, held no allurement, promised them "no better, more just social order." Workers repeatedly referred to Soviet Russia to explain both Socialism's and Communism's lack of appeal. . . .

Ah, one might say, Muncie and New Haven were atypical and their working class more so.

Look at Flint and Youngstown, Akron and Gary, Minneapolis and San Francisco. In those cities workers acted collectively and militantly. But a closer look at even such *foci* of labor struggle reveals a much more complex reality than suggested by conventional romanticizations of working-class solidarity and rank-and-file militancy.

Without militants, to be sure, there would have been no Flint sit-down strike, no San Francisco general strike, no walkout by Akron's rubber workers. Without rank-and-file participation, that is, collective struggle, there would have been no union victories. Yet, in reality, solidarity rarely produced collective action; rather, more often than not, action by militant minorities (what some scholars have characterized as "sparkplug Unionism") precipitated a subsequent collective response. And rank and filers frequently resisted the radicalism of the militant cadres who sparked industrial confrontations. In Flint . . . only a small minority of the local workers belonged to the UAW and paid dues on the eve of the strike, and the sit-down technique was chosen consciously to compensate for the union's lack of a mass membership base. . . . Lee Pressman, general counsel to the Steel Workers Organizing Committee, recalls that as late as the spring of 1937, after the UAW's success at Flint and United States Steel's surrender to SWOC, labor organizers had still failed to enroll in SWOC more than a substantial minority of the steelworkers employed by firms other than United States Steel. For most rank and filers, then, militancy consisted of refusing to cross a picket line, no more. As one observer noted of the Flint sit-downers, a group more militant than the majority of auto workers, "Those strikers have no more idea of 'revolution' than pussy cats."

Even the most strike-torn cities and regions had a significantly internally differentiated working class. At the top were the local cadres, the sparkplug unionists, the men and women fully conscious of their roles in a marketplace society that extolled individualism and rewarded collective strength. These individuals, ranging the political spectrum from Social Democrats to Communists, provided the leadership, militancy, and ideology that fostered industrial conflict and the emergence of mass-production unionism. Beneath them lay a substantial proportion of workers who could be transformed, by example, into militant strikers and unionists, and, in turn, themselves act as militant minorities. Below them were many first- and second-generation immigrant workers, as well as recent migrants from the American countryside, who remained embedded in a culture defined by traditional ties to family, kinship, church, and neighborhood club or tavern. Accustomed to following the rituals of the past, heeding the advice of community leaders, and slow to act, such men and women rarely joined unions prior to a successful strike, once moved to act behaved with singular solidarity, yet rarely served as union or political activists and radicals. And below this mass were the teenage workers caught halfway between liberation from their parental families and formation of their own new households, more attracted to the life and rituals of street gangs and candy-store cronies than to the customs and culture of persistent trade unionists and political activists.

A word must now be added concerning those scholars who have argued that during the 1930s a spontaneously militant and increasingly radical rank and file was either handcuffed or betrayed by bureaucratic and autocratic labor leaders. For those who accept the Leninist thesis that trade unions are, by definition, economist and hence nonrevolutionary, there is no problem in comprehending the behavior of American trade unions and their members during the 1930s. But for those who seek to understand why the militant beginnings of the CIO terminated in an ideological and institutional deadend, why, in Brody's words, "the character of American trade unionism . . . made it an exploiter of radicalism rather than vice versa"—questions remain. And it may seem easiest to answer . . . that the blame for the failure of radicalism rests with such labor leaders as John L. Lewis and Sidney Hillman who sold out to the New Deal, collaborated with employers, and restrained rank-and-file militancy through the instrument of the nonstrike union contract. That hypothesis, commonly subsumed under the rubric "corporate liberalism," contains a grain of truth. But the small truth tends to obscure a greater reality. As J. B. S. Hardman [labor intellectual] observed a half century ago, labor leaders are primarily accumulators of power; and, need it be said, no man was more eager to accumulate power than John L. Lewis. A businessman's power flowed from his control of capital; a politician's from influence over voters and possession of the instruments of government; and a labor leader's power derived from his union membership, the more massive and militant the rank and file, the more influential the labor leader. Bereft of a mass membership or saddled with a lethargic rank and file, the labor leader lost influence, and power. All labor leaders, then, necessarily played a devious and sometimes duplicitous game. Sometimes they rushed in to lead a rebellious rank and file; other times, they agitated the rank and file into action; whether they seized leadership of a movement already in motion or themselves breathed life into the rank and file, labor leaders obtained whatever power they exercised with employers and public officials as a consequence of their followers' behavior. Yet, while they encouraged militancy, labor leaders also retrained their troops, in John L. Lewis's phrase, "put a lid on the strikers." They did so for several reasons. First, not all rank-and-file upheavals promised success; and nothing destroyed a trade union as quickly or diluted a labor leader's power as thoroughly as a lost strike. Second, leaders had to judge at what point rank-and-file militancy would produce government repression, an ever-present reality even in Franklin D. Roosevelt's America. Third, and more selfishly, rank-and-file upheavals could careen out of control and threaten a labor leader's tenure in office as well as strengthen his external power. Throughout the 1930s such labor leaders as John L. Lewis alternatively encouraged the release of working-class rebelliousness and "put the lid back on." The labor leader was truly the man in the middle, his influence rendered simultaneously greater and also more perilous as a result of working-class militancy.

A final word must also be said about the union contract, the instrument that allegedly bound workers to their employers by denying them the right to strike. With historical hindsight, such seems to be the end result of the union-management contract under which the union promises to discipline its members on behalf of management. But one must remember that during the 1930s ordinary workers, the romanticized rank and file, risked their jobs, their bodies, and their lives to win the contract. And when they won it, as in Flint in February, 1937, a sit-down striker rejoiced that it "was the most wonderful thing that we could think that could possibly happen to people." . . .

Paradoxically, the one experience during the 1930s that united workers across ethnic, racial, and organization lines—New Deal politics—served to vitiate radicalism. By the end of the 1930s, Roosevelt's Democratic party had become, in effect, the political expression of America's working class. Old-line Socialists, farmer-labor party types, and even Communists enlisted in a Roosevelt-led "Popular Front." Blacks and whites, Irish and Italian Catholics, Slavic- and Jewish-Americans, uprooted rural Protestants and stable skilled workers joined the Democratic coalition, solidifying the working-class vote as never before in American history. Roosevelt encouraged workers to identify themselves as a common class politically as well as economically. As with David Lloyd George in Britain's pre–World War I Edwardian crisis, Franklin D. Roosevelt in the American crisis of the 1930s found revolutionary class rhetoric indispensable. It panicked the powerful into concessions and attracted working-class voters to the Democratic party. Just as Lloyd George intensified the earlier British crisis in order to ease its solution, Roosevelt acted similarly in New Deal America. By frightening the ruling class into conceding reforms and appealing to workers to vote as a solid block, Roosevelt simultaneously intensified class consciousness and stripped it of its radical potential.

The dilemma of John L. Lewis showed just how well Roosevelt succeeded in his strategy. During the 1930s, no matter how much Lewis preferred to think of himself as an executive rather than a labor leader, however little he associated personally with the working class, he functioned as the leader of a militant working-class movement. Whereas Roosevelt sought to contain working-class militancy through reforms, militant workers pressured Lewis to demand more than the President would or could deliver. The more evident became the New Deal's economic failures, the more heavily labor militants demands a fundamental reordering of the economy and society, demands that Lewis, as leader of CIO, came to express more forcefully than any other trade unionist. "No matter how much Roosevelt did for the workers," recalls DeCaux, "Lewis demanded more. He showed no gratitude, nor did he bid his followers be grateful—just put the squeeze on all the harder." But Lewis, unlike the British labor leaders of Lloyd George's generation who found in the Labour Party an alternative to the Prime Minister's "New Liberalism," had no substitute for Roosevelt's New Deal. In the United States, the President easily mastered the labor leader.

Lewis's lack of a political alternative to the New Deal flowed from two sources. First was the refusal of most American leftists to countenance a third-party challenge to the Democrats and the intense loyalty most workers felt to Roosevelt. Between the winter of 1937–38 and the summer of 1940, however much Lewis threatened to lead a new third party, his public speeches and private maneuvers failed to create among workers a third-party constituency. It was Lewis's radical speeches that made his eventual endorsement in 1940 of Wendell Wilkie so shocking to many of the labor leader's admirers. Had those Lewis sycophants known that in June 1940, the CIO president plotted to win the Republican nomination for Herbert Hoover, they might have been even more startled. And it was his support first of Hoover and then of Wilkie that exposed the second source for Lewis's lack of a radical alternative to the New Deal. That was the extent to which Lewis, other labor leaders, and perhaps most workers had assimilated the values of a business civilization. This union, Lewis told members of the United Mine Workers at their 1938 convention, "stands for the proposition that the heads of families shall have a sufficient income to educate . . . thee sons and daughters of our people, and they go forth when given that opportunity. . . . They become scientists, great clergymen . . . great lawyers, great statesmen. . . . Many of our former members are successful in great business enterprises." And two years later in 1940, he told the same audience: "You know, after all there are two great material tasks in life that affect the individual and affect great bodies of men. The first is to achieve or acquire something of value or something that is desirable, and then the second is to prevent some scoundrel from taking it away from you." Notice the substance of Lewis's remarks to a trade-union crowd, the combination of urging the children of the working class to rise above it, not with it, and the materialistic stress on possessive individualism. Lewis, the most militant and prominent of the depression decade's labor leaders, remained too much the opportunist, too much the personification of vulgar pragmatism and business values to lead a third-party political crusade.

What, then, follows logically from the above description of the 1930s and the implied line of analysis? First, and perhaps obviously, however turbulent were the American 1930s, the depression decade never produced a revolutionary situation. Second, one observes the essential inertia of the working-class masses. Once in motion, the mass of workers can move with great acceleration and enormous militancy—but such movement remains hard to get started. Such social inertia combined with the inability of most workers and their leaders to conceive of an alternative to the values of marketplace capitalism, that is, to create a working-class culture autonomous from that of the ruling class, was more important than trade-union opportunism, corporate cooptation, or New Deal liberalism (though the last factor was clearly the most potent) in thwarting the emergence of durable working-class radicalism. Third, and finally, it suggests that a distinction must be drawn between class struggle as a historical reality and workers as a class fully aware of their role, power, and ability to replace the existing system with "a better, firmer, more just social order [than] the one to be torn down."

## Radical Years: Working-Class Consciousness on the Waterfront in the 1930s

### BRUCE NELSON

This essay will examine the activity and consciousness of maritime workers—longshoremen and seamen—on the Pacific Coast of the United States during the 1930s. In many ways, the thirties were decisive years in the history of the American working class. Perhaps nowhere else was the turbulence, or the distance travelled, greater than in the maritime industry, where workers who had long been regarded as social

From "Radical Years: Working-Class Consciousness in the 1930s," by Bruce Nelson from Maurice Zeitlin, ed., *Political Power and Social Theory* (Los Angeles: JAI Press, 1984), pp. 141–152, 154–162, 165–170, 174. Reprinted by permission of the author.

scum suddenly developed an exhilarating sense of power and self-respect; unions that had been moribund for many years were infused with new energy or, in some cases, pushed aside in favor of more dynamic labor organizations; and a working-class subculture that had often displayed evidence of militancy and rebellion provided the foundation of a renaissance of consciousness that affected many workers beyond the confines of the waterfront. In particular, the experience of the maritime workers on the West Coast provides a portrait that contrasts sharply with the recent historiographical emphasis on the narrow, episodic character of worker militancy and the allegedly deep "social inertia" beneath the turbulent surface of events in the 1930s. . . .

Because Communists played an important role in the maritime industry throughout the 1930s, it has been common to attribute the upheaval on the waterfront to their influence and to discuss the development of maritime unionism from the standpoint of the sharp changes in Communist line and program which occurred from 1929 to 1941. . . . [H]owever, my focus will be quite different. This essay will concentrate mainly on the middle years of the 1930s, when the maritime union movement displayed an independent dynamic which, to some degree, eludes the usual periodization of "Third Period," "Popular Front," etc. The key to this independent dynamic is the coming together of a way of life and work with a set of distinct historical factors that included the desperate conditions brought on by the Great Depression, the sense of opportunity and hope generated by New Deal labor legislation, and the worldwide rise of fascism and its apparent manifestations in the United States. The coalescence of these sparks with an already volatile subculture was more important than the influence of a particular left-wing party or trade union leader in shaping this era of insurgency.

In the early 1930s conditions on the West Coast waterfront were barbaric, even by the standards of the Great Depression. Among the longshoremen, the defeat of a number of local strikes in 1919 and 1920 had destroyed the International Longshoremen's Association (ILA) in almost every port and left the men at the mercy of the employers. In San Francisco, the stevedores were forced to endure a despised company union, a notorious speed-up, and the degrading "shape-up," where a few men were "hired off the streets like a bunch of sheep," as longshore leader Harry Bridges put it, while hundreds of others were turned away without work. Depression conditions aggravated the problem of an already swollen work force, and the ILA later recalled that many experienced longshoremen were forced to seek government relief while others "worked like slaves in shifts from 24 to 36 hours without sleep." As the "favored" few worked themselves into a state of exhaustion, crowds of hungry men would hover by the pierheads, on the chance that someone would get hurt on the job or fail to keep pace with the speed-up.

The seamen fared no better than the dockworkers. The humiliating loss of a nationwide strike in 1921 had reduced the venerable International Seamen's Union (ISU) to an empty shell. Wages were slashed and many of the favorable working and living conditions which had been won during an earlier period of insurgency were eliminated. In most ports, seamen were forced to hire through employer-controlled "Fink Halls," where a union partisan, or anyone else who "kicked," was systematically blackballed. When the Great Depression hit the shipping industry, many veteran seamen found themselves in the ranks of the unemployed, while inexperienced "workaways"—who agreed to ship out in exchange for a bunk, sub-standard food, and a wage payment of one dollar a month—received an alarming proportion of the available jobs. . . .

But, more importantly, the men themselves were not mere flotsam who lacked the capacity to resist the shipowners' ruthless hegemony. The twenties were lean years to be sure, and conditions in the early 1930s were leaner still. But there was among the longshoremen and a seamen a tradition of militancy and spontaneous radicalism that was bound to surface again when the historical conditions were ripe. This tradition had its roots in the structure of life and work among the maritime workers and the seamen in particular. Seafaring men had long been victimized by low wages and abysmal conditions of life and work. They knew well the meaning of deprivation and were keenly aware of the enormous distance between the lifestyles of rich and poor. Moreover, they lived on the fringes of society and had little or no recourse to family, religious, ethnic, and other institutions which served the purpose of reconciling working people to the hegemony of the employing class or of creating a stable subculture which reinforced an alternative value system. Although many seamen were literate and well-read, few had had much formal education. Likewise, the transiency inherent in their calling meant that few seamen voted or showed much interest in the activity of the major political parties. The very nature of their trade made it difficult to lead a normal family life, and their low wages made it nearly impossible to support themselves, not to mention wives and children. They were, in the words of *Fortune,* "homeless, rootless, and eternally unmoneyed"—free of the responsibilities of home and family and yet, in many cases, wistful for the comfort and security of a more normal life.

While the seaman lived on the fringes of American society, he routinely saw a good deal more of the rest of the world than his shoreside counterpart. Oftentimes this experience opened his eyes to the breadth of injustice and suffering and rendered him somewhat cynical about conventional representations of reality. Harry Bridges, who came from a comfortable British middle-class family which had emigrated to Australia, grew restless with a clerk's life and went to sea at the age of fifteen. Long after he had settled down on the San Francisco waterfront and become the principal leader of the West Coast longshoremen, Bridges vividly recalled the profound effect that his stint as a seaman had had upon his outlook:

> I took a trip that gave me a look at India and another at Suez, and what I saw there didn't seem to line up with what my father had told me about the dear old British. Then I got "home" and saw London. It was the filthiest, most unhealthy place I had ever seen. . . . I kept traveling around, and the more I saw the more I knew that there was something wrong with the system.

. . . Of course, not every seaman was radicalized by such encounters. Some shipped mainly in the coastwise trade, along the shores of North America, and many in the foreign trade confined themselves to the "gin mills" and whorehouse that were meant to ensnare the sailor in every port. But a breadth of experience, a worldliness, existed among seafaring men, and it undoubtedly contributed to their relative openness to radical and revolutionary ideas. . . .

The structure of life and work among longshoremen and seamen naturally gave rise to a syndicalist orientation. The close affinity between working and living conditions, the rootlessness and isolation from mainstream American institutions, and the cosmopolitanism of the waterfront created the elements of a mood that, in its most dynamic form, sought to transform the world by fundamentally reshaping the patterns of authority and organization in the realm of work. However, this impulse was at once broader and more elusive than the program of American syndicalism as represented by the Industrial Workers of the World (IWW). The Wobblies focused a lot of energy on the waterfront, and they were able to maintain a foothold among marine workers long after they had become little more than a fading memory in most other industries. The "mood of syndicalism" had at least four readily identifiable dimensions: first, the impulse toward workers' control of production; second, the belief that "direct action" at the point of production was the most effective means for the achievement of working-class objectives; third, the determination to cross traditional craft union barriers in order to build solidarity with other workers; and, finally, a striving for fundamental social transformation embodied in the Wobblies' exhortation to "bring to birth a new world from the ashes of the old." But this "mood of syndicalism" in maritime went far beyond the Wobblies' limited appeal, and survived their eventual demise, because it was rooted not in the doctrine of a particular Left organization but in the subculture of life and work on the waterfront. In the thirties, as in earlier periods of syndicalist upsurge, the world of work became the principle focus and arena of struggle and transformation. As we shall see, it was mainly from this base that the marine workers sought not only to transform conditions on the job, but also to affect the outcome of more overtly political struggles. . . .

Every year, in early March, International Seamen's Union President Andrew Furuseth sent an anniversary message to the ISU's pioneer affiliate, the Sailors' Union of the Pacific [SUP], to commemorate its founding in 1885. In 1929, when the union's fortunes were at an all-time low, Furuseth's letter to the few diehard members and their guests burned with a zeal that was peculiarly out of character with the times. "*I wish we could all of us be saturated with the spirit of the crusader,*" he said. "Let us make this meeting a Pentecostal one, and go away from it with the determination to achieve, to live up to the highest and best that is in us."

Five years and two months later, maritime workers erupted with the "spirit of the crusader," and for 83 days they waged one of the great battles in the history of the American working class. Even by the standards of 1934, one of the most extraordinary years in the annals of labor, the "Big Strike" fully merited the superlatives which its partisans assigned it. For this drama transformed labor relations in the Pacific Coast maritime industry, ushered in a "Pentecostal" era of unionism and workers' self-activity that confounded and alarmed the AFL old guard as much as it did the employers, and triggered the formation of the Maritime Federation of the Pacific, an organization that many hoped would be a stepping stone toward "One Big Union" of all the marine crafts.

The upheaval began on May 9 as a coastwide longshore strike, but almost immediately seamen began walking off the ships and joining the ILA picket lines. Within ten days virtually all of the maritime unions were on strike, and rank and file Teamsters, in defiance of their officials, were refusing to haul cargo to or from the docks. This remarkable solidarity continued to grow and reached its high point in the San Francisco General Strike in mid-July.

On July 3 the employers declared the port open and the waterfront became "a vast tangle of fighting men" as 700 police tried to move scab cargo through massive picket lines. After regrouping on the July 4th holiday, both sides resumed the battle on July 5, or "Bloody Thursday," as it was soon to become known. The strikers defended themselves and their cause with magnificent courage and discipline. As one observer put it, "In the face of bullets, gas, clubs, horses' hoofs, [and] death . . . [t]hey were fighting desperately for something that seemed to be life for them." But in a physical confrontation of this magnitude, the workers were no match for the superior firepower at the employers' disposal. By the end of the day, two pickets were dead, shot in the back by police; hundreds more were injured, and National Guard troops patrolled the waterfront. It appeared that the strikers had been defeated.

However, "Bloody Thursday" was about to take on a new symbolic meaning. In the funeral procession for the strike's martyrs, tens of thousands of people took to the streets in a silent tribute that must surely rank as one of the most dramatic moments in the history of the American working class. Eyewitness spoke of "a river of men flowing up Market Street like cooling lava" and of "a stupendous and reverent procession that astounded the city." One employer spokesman acknowledged this event as "the high tide of . . . united labor action in San Francisco." It was, indeed, the general strike in embryo.

A week later more than 100,000 workers "hit the bricks" in solidarity with the maritime unionists. . . .

The general strike ended inconclusively after four days, with both sides claiming victory. By the end of July, an arbitration procedure had been established, and the maritime workers returned to the job, with none of their demands resolved. To many, it appeared that the strikers were exhausted, and that the inconclusive termination of the general strike had been a setback to the cause of unionism. The *New Republic* complained that "fighting spirit and funds have been used up" and "public opinion has been alienated." The *Nation* expressed the fear that "the maritime unions have now been abandoned to their fate." San Francisco banker William H. Crocker exulted that "Labor is licked." But appearance and reality were sharply at variance. The 83-day maritime and general strike had been but a prelude. The "Pentecostal" era was about to begin. . . .

The Big Strike had involved particular demands that now faced the prospect of arbitration. The National Longshoremen's Board appointed by President Roosevelt would soon make important concessions to the stevedores on the questions of wages, hours, overtime, and control of hiring. But, meanwhile, longshoremen and seamen demonstrated that they had an additional agenda requiring immediate attention. This agenda included the determination to rid the docks and ships of men who had scabbed during the strike, a campaign to make every work unit 100 percent union and to extend unionism into the ranks of unorganized waterfront workers, and the determination to tame the gang bosses and ships' officers who had driven the marine workers with relative impunity during the long non-union era.

Any confusion, fear, and tendencies toward recrimination generated in the aftermath of the general strike seem to have been swept aside as soon as the men returned to work. Longshoreman Henry Schmidt recalled that "somehow or another the men discovered . . . when they went back to work that morning that they had terrific power; they also had some courage, and they changed the working conditions immediately." Bill Rutter, another longshoreman, remembered that "some very good [working] rules . . . were made up, on the pierhead before we went into work that morning." Rutter was a member of a gang scheduled to load sacks of barley, and the men informed their bosses that they would work only fifteen sacks, rather than the customary twenty, per load. After about an hour, a load with twenty sacks came down, and then another. "The guys all went and got their coats and were standing there waiting to pull out," when the bosses relented and agreed to the gang's demand.

Moreover, there was widespread agreement with the opinion of a rank and file stevedore that "we must have a good housecleaning on the waterfront" because "it is filthy with rats, finks, [and] scabs." The "housecleaning" also began immediately. On the American-Hawaiian docks in San Francisco, for example, more than a dozen longshore gangs shut the piers down for a few days until the company agreed to fire several notorious scabs. Employer spokesman Gregory Harrison stated that from July 31, the day the men returned to work, until the day the presidential mediation board rendered its decision on the longshore dispute, "there were repeated strikes and stoppages of work along all of the waterfronts of the Pacific Coast." According to Harrison, "Twenty-nine such strikes and stoppages were actually recorded" during this 74-day period. . . .

The first major confrontation came on September 20, when 600 longshoremen and seamen struck in support of the latter's demand that the Dollar Line fire seventeen non-union workers who had sailed on the *President Taft* during the maritime strike. When the company balked at this demand, 200 seamen walked off the ship, and 400 longshoremen working the Dollar Line docks immediately joined them. Ship scalers and teamsters soon rallied to the walkout, and union taxi drivers refused to bring passengers to the pier. According to one report, "a crowd of over a thousand men" picketed the docks. After several hours of stalemate, the Dollar Line capitulated and provided the non-union men with a police escort from the ship. The *President Taft* then sailed with a crew that was 100 percent union. . . .

One of the major focal points of rank and file combativeness concerned the pace of work, the weight of sling loads, and relations between gang bosses and men on the docks. In the aftermath of the Big Strike, many of the gang bosses assumed that conditions on the docks would quickly return to "normal" and that they would be free once again to drive the men at the old relentless pace. But the longshoremen quickly introduced them to a new reality. In one instance, a boss demanded that his gang increase the weight of their sling loads, or "you can go home." No longer intimidated by such threats, the gang started to walk off the job; and when the outraged boss took a swing at the gang steward, the union representative "grabbed the big fink around the neck and put him to the floor."

This confrontation and its outcome provide an apt symbol of the enormous change taking place on the West Coast waterfront. The results can be measured in many ways, including statistics on productivity. Spokesmen for the shipowners were soon complaining that the cost of handling cargo in San Francisco had become "probably the highest in the world." Almon Roth, the president of two major waterfront employers' associations, claimed that "a gang of longshoremen used to handle as high as 3,000 sacks of sugar per hour in the unloading operations at Crockett," but that a recent check-up showed "we were getting only 950 sacks her hour per gang. . . . Observation of this operation proved that the men in the hold were resting 60 percent of their time." Roth acknowledged that "there was a day when employees complained of speed-ups." Now, however, "the pendulum has swung the other way. Today employers suffer from deliberate slow-downs."

The transformation lamented by Roth was not the result of spontaneous up-surge alone. The unions established rules designed to spread the work evenly and to prevent "chiselers" from spearheading a return to the old order. Among the long-shoremen, there were numerous examples of entire gangs walking off the job early in order to abide by the regulation limiting hours of work to 120 per month. The membership of the ILA voted a $25 fine for anyone who worked more than the 120-hour limit without the union's permission, and there were also penalties for other infractions. While most of these rules were job-related, some were consider-ably broader in focus. The San Francisco ILA local placed a gang boss on trial for "slandering colored brothers." Among the sailors, there was a regulation firing any union member who set foot in the Seamen's Church Institute, which symbolized shipowner paternalism and a "pie in the sky" attitude toward the seamen's condi-tions of life and work. The Marine Firemen's Union placed a severe penalty on any of its members caught buying a Hearst newspaper.

Soon after the conclusion of the Big Strike the ILA organized a system of dock and gang stewards to coordinate the activity of the men on the front. According to the employers, this brought about a virtual revolution in the locus of effective power on the docks. Gregory Harrison complained that, because of the steward system,

> authority to direct work upon the docks passed from the hands of the foremen into the hands of dock and gang stewards. The dock and gang stewards are appointed by the Union. They have an organization of their own. They meet regularly; they adopt rules; they establish the manner in which, and the speed at which, work is to be performed on the waterfronts of the Pacific Coast.

Although Harrison may have exaggerated the extent of the longshoremen's control of the work process, he was certainly correct in indicating that a dramatic transformation had taken place. . . . The most eloquent testimony about the depth of this change came from the workers themselves. A longshoreman's wife stated that:

> Before the strike my husband was always complaining about conditions on the water-front, how hard he was working and how much the bosses were hollering and so forth.
> Since returning to work after the strike he is a changed man entirely. He seems different and happier, and even finds time to pay a little attention to his wife. . . .
> Thanks to the strike, a change for the better has come for the men on the front and a change has taken place in our home life.

. . . A rank and file longshoreman recalled that "not so very long ago, when we first organized, I was fired and discriminated [against] for being a union man and wearing an I.L.A. button. I have seen my wife and two daughters go hungry." But, he proclaimed, "the old order of things shall never come back to us. . . . We are all brothers now—one for all, and all for one. The spirit of comradeship and Unionism prevails amongst us and we have learned a bitter lesson."

An "Admiral Line Stevie" [a worker on the Admiral Line docks] declared that "We must all fight to the last man to see to it that the old conditions shall never come back to the waterfront again." This determination to put the misery of the past behind them forever was strengthened in the longshoremen and their families by an almost lyrical sense of the glories of the emerging new era. The "Admiral Line Stevie" was convinced that "at this time on the waterfront we have the finest conditions in the world." An "Oldtimer" who had first joined the ILA in 1915 declared that "we are the most militant and organized body of men the world has ever seen." In a letter to the *Waterfront Worker,* a group of "stevies" proclaimed that the longshoremen had truly become the "Lords of the Docks." . . .

For longshoremen and seamen alike, the foundation of the new order was control of hiring. The dock workers had established the union hiring hall as their number one demand during the strike. Although the arbitration award of October 1934 provided for the establishment of hiring halls operated in each port by labor relations committees of employer and union representatives, the ILA won the sole right to select the job dispatchers. With the union in charge of dispatching, and the men on the docks ready to "hang the hook" on any employer who refused to accept candidates sent from the hall, full control of hiring quickly passed into the hands of the ILA. The shipowners were soon complaining that "the award provisions for [joint] operation of the longshore hiring halls, and the rights of employers thereunder, have been entirely defeated . . . , although the employers have always contributed one-half of the expense of their maintenance." . . .

. . . [I]f this example and many others have demonstrated a significant transformation of work relations and practices, what of the realm of consciousness? Did the maritime workers of the 1930s fit the allegedly normative American mold of "job consciousness" and "militant pragmatism," or were they moving in the direction of a more thoroughly radicalized consciousness? . . .

In a study of workers in a specific industry and geographic location at a particular historical moment, it is perhaps all the more important to acknowledge that their ideology does not possess normative dimensions that can and should be measured against an enclosed ideal category called "working-class consciousness." On the other hand, it would be equally wrong to take refuge in pure empiricism. For, as English historian E. P. Thompson has reminded us, there is a *logic* if not a *law* in "the responses of similar occupational groups undergoing similar experiences." Without falling prey to notions of historical inevitability, it is possible to affirm that history has demonstrated a persistent if uneven tendency on the part of working people toward the formation of ideas, institutions, and values that have transcended time periods and national boundaries and have reflected a striving toward a collective affirmation of self. At some moments, this tendency has resulted in an inwardly-focused, politically passive subculture. In other circumstances, it has led to an expansive consciousness, based on a lively sense of class relations and class struggle, and seeking to create a more just social order.

For many years our understanding of working-class consciousness was circumscribed by rigid and essentially static models. The two most prominent examples, the Leninist model and that of the Commons/Perlman school of labor economists in the United States, have much in common in spite of their ideological antagonism. Both view the normal focus of working-class activity as essentially narrow and pragmatic, and both regard the intellectual as playing a crucial role in changing the workers' consciousness. Lenin declared that "the history of all countries shows that

Lenin
→

the working class, exclusively by its own efforts, is able to develop only trade union consciousness." In the Leninist idiom, the Marxist section of the intelligentsia rescues the workers from the narrow economism and parochial immediacy of the factory world by bringing them the "scientific" truths of socialism. The Commons/Perlman school would agree with Lenin's declaration, but far from denigrating the spontaneous perceptions of the workers, sees their alleged pragmatism as appropriate and beneficial. For Commons and his disciples, the normal outlook of the worker is "job consciousness," seeking only "an enlarged opportunity measured in income, security, and liberty in the shop and industry." When the worker deviates from this normative path, it is because of the intrusion of intellectuals and their abstract, essentially alien formulas. While Lenin characterized the true working-class spokesman as a revolutionary "tribune of the people," Commons and Perlman exalted the "philosophy of organic labor" which had its roots in the craft guilds of the Middle Ages and was developed to its highest level by Samuel Gompers and the American Federation of Labor in the United States.

The last two decades have witnessed a powerful challenge to these static conceptions of working-class consciousness. The most formidable assault has come from Thompson, whose studies of the "making" of the English working class have demonstrated the existence of humane traditions, deeply-held values and powerful currents of thought which shaped the response of working people to changing forms of exploitation. Although intellectuals sometimes played an important role in articulating the ideas and aspirations of the common people, they were not the motive force in the development of working-class consciousness. Rather, Thompson has stressed the richly-textured traditions and the often disciplined and creative self-activity of millions of ordinary folk who too often have been regarded as inert and inarticulate.

The worldwide popular insurgency of the 1960s provided further impetus for a major assault on the reigning orthodoxies. With millions of people taking to the streets on behalf of civil rights and in opposition to U.S. intervention in Vietnam, many young historians in the United States developed a new appreciation for the dynamic role of class struggle and other forms of conflict in American history. The widespread labor militancy of the 1930s once again became a focal point of admiration and study, although there was much speculation and controversy about why the upsurge did not result in a more thoroughgoing social transformation and a more enduring Left movement. In some quarters, the Communist Party and the leadership of the CIO unions came in for a good deal of criticism for allegedly blunting and undermining the spontaneous radicalism of millions of industrial workers. . . .

In a provocative essay . . . Melvyn Dubofsky offers "another look" at what he calls the "Not So 'Turbulent Years'" of the 1930s. Dubofsky explores the widespread "passivity beneath the turbulent surface of violent events as well as the persistence of many pre-depression era beliefs and behavioral patterns of American workers." For him it is not the Communists and the CIO leaders who are responsible for the circumscribed outcome of the 1930s upsurge, but rather the workers themselves, or "the essential inertia of the working-class masses." . . .

The experience of the maritime workers challenges several major themes of the new labor history, including its emphasis on the distance between the aspirations of workers and the goals of trade unions and union leaders. In the case of the hidebound International Seamen's Union, there certainly was such a distance even when the

.tiative of rank and file seafarers and joined them on the picket
strike. But to suggest a similar pattern in the case of militants
maritime workers from whose ranks they emerged would be
ıing, "Unionism" became almost a sacred cause on the West
ιe great majority of longshoremen and seamen flocked into the
ι the period surrounding the Big Strike. For another, the resurgent
ιcame vivid examples of rank and file democracy in action. Their
ιneetings were well attended—often to the point of overflowing—and
were generally characterized by vigorous debate, with broad participation from the
ranks. Moreover, the unions submitted most major policy questions to coastwide
membership referendums. In this setting, it was precisely the militant activists who
emerged as elected officials and whose leadership was endorsed by the rank and file
over and over again, in the face of frequent attempts by the employers and the media
to discredit these "radicals" and replace them with more amenable representatives.
In a typical broadside, the San Francisco *Examiner* characterized "the line-up in the
waterfront labor situation" as

Harry Bridges vs. responsible union labor

Harry Bridges vs. the shipping industry

Harry Bridges vs. San Francisco, the Pacific Coast, the entire American
seaboard.

Put in one phrase—the issue is:

COMMUNISM VS. AMERICAN LABOR.

Bridges denied being a Communist Party member, but he solicited advice and
assistance from Communists and openly endorsed much of the Party's program.
Some of the insurgent maritime unionists *were* Communists. Others moved in the
direction of self-conscious syndicalism and claimed to be more consistently radical
than the Communists. While there remained an inevitable distance between the militant strains in the maritime subculture and the commitment to a specific left-wing
program, it is clear that the radical affiliations of Communists and syndicalists did
not isolate these activists from their fellow workers in the marine industry. To some
degree, the radicalism of the leadership was a reflection of the insurgent spirit and
ideological ferment in the ranks. . . .

The record of the West Coast maritime workers indicates a pattern that differs
markedly from the portrait which emerges from Dubofsky's essay and the recent
studies of the auto workers. In the Big Strike and the "Pentecostal" era that followed
on the Pacific Coast, we see not only militant pragmatism but the flowering of radical
class consciousness among significant numbers of workers in the marine industry.
There were indeed strong syndicalist overtones to their movement, but the character
of their activity was often dramatically different from the shop-floor syndicalism
. . . among auto workers during the CIO upsurge. The longshoremen and seamen
did not limit their sights to the maritime equivalent of a single plant or department.
Increasingly, they believed that their struggle rightly included not only walkouts
and job actions to transform the world of work, but strikes to defend workers faced
with stiff legal penalties, the refusal to load cargo designed to aid Mussolini's war
effort in Ethiopia, and opposition to German ships bearing the hated swastika.
Moreover, to the growing dismay of the employers, the government, and the press,

they insisted on engaging in much of this political activity right at the "point of production." . . .

The shipowners were quick to blame this ideological ferment on the Communist Party and its representatives within the maritime unions. To the employers, the ideas and activity of the marine workers represented a deviation from the "safe, sound Americanism" which allegedly had prevailed on the waterfront before the 1934 strike. They longed for the more congenial unionism of the AFL's old guard, even though for more than a decade they had refused to recognize the unions headed by these men. What the shipowners conveniently overlooked, however, was the fact that the consciousness and activity of the longshoremen and seamen in the new era had long been an inherent part of the subculture of the marine industry and had been expressed by the workers, episodically if not consistently, during the 50 years that maritime unionism had had a foothold on the Pacific Coast. The tendency to override craft separation and form cooperating federations—at its highest level, the demand for "One Big Union" in the industry—had existed side by side with craft divisions and jealousies and had often swept aside the latter during periods of upsurge. Moreover, the marine workers' internationalism was as much a product of their subculture as it was a reflection of "derived" ideas brought to the men from without. And, given the long history of harsh exploitation, and the fact that there were few institutions that served to mitigate their suffering and draw them closer to the American mainstream, longshoremen and seamen did not need Communists to tell them about the reality of the "class struggle.". . .

Although the maritime workers demonstrated a strong sense of internationalism, they often justified their activity in terms of "Americanism." On the surface, this may seem paradoxical, and it certainly does not conform to the dogma which places working-class consciousness in opposition to any form of nationalism or patriotism. But, in fact, the maritime workers were expressing a very different form of Americanism from their employers, who often wrapped themselves in the flag while they endeavored to thwart the most elementary demands of labor. Early in the maritime strike, a major spokesman for capital had defined the conflict as one between "American principles and un-American radicalism." This kind of invective continued to characterize the shipowners' and the news media's descriptions of the marine unions and their leadership for several years. Every insurgent act on the part of the longshoremen and seamen was presented as evidence of the "alien" and subversive" character of their movement.

The maritime workers were only too well aware that their bitterest enemies voiced their opposition to the new unionism in the language of "Americanism." Even acts of criminal violence and the denial of basic human rights were justified in terms of the defense of "American principles." But in spite of the way their opponents degraded the term, the maritime workers were by no means ready to concede the mantle of Americanism to the shipowners. On the contrary, the workers saw themselves as true patriots, defenders of democracy, and inheritors of the progressive and revolutionary dimensions of America's historical experience. In the eyes of the marine workers, it was the capitalists and their allies who were "unAmerican," because they were trying to deny broad sections of the people their fundamental democratic rights and to rob the workers of an "American standard of living." A resolution passed unanimously by the San Francisco Bay Area District Council of the Maritime Federation stated: ". . . the growth of fascist tendencies and organizations in the State of California . . . [is] in direct opposition to the Democratic principles upon which our government was formed, which guarantee the right of free speech, assembly, the right to organize and fight for better conditions." The *Voice of the Federation* declared that "American citizens are now faced with the choice of fighting for their Liberties or being crushed under the iron heel of a ruthless mob despotism, organized and led by 'unAmerican' employers." . . .

. . . In concluding, it is necessary to acknowledge that the "Pentecostal" era was relatively short-lived. It foundered on the rocks of resurgent craft antagonism, clashing personalities, and divergent strategic orientations within the Maritime Federation. As the alliance between the San Francisco longshoremen and the Sailors' Union of the Pacific gradually came apart, so did the threads which had given the Federation its distinctive radical hue. What we are left with, then, is a brief renaissance of consciousness that burned brilliantly for an historical moment. From the standpoint of the conventional wisdom in labor relations, it has been judged as an era of massive "irresponsibility" which gradually gave way to a more "reasonable" pattern of behavior. But, viewed from the standpoint of the workers themselves, this renaissance represents a long overdue festive upheaval, a search for more humane and just patterns of work relations, a struggle between labor and capital that invaded the realms of culture and politics and provoked a vigorous and healthy debate on the meaning of Americanism and the place of workers in the social hierarchy.

Moreover, in important and enduring ways, the victories of the 1930s transformed the lives of the maritime workers. Conditions on the waterfront changed to the point where, in Henry Schmidt's words, "the supervisorial personnel had practically nothing to say." The longshoremen were no longer merely "laborers." Now they proclaimed themselves "Lords of the Docks." The seamen were no longer transients and pariahs. They struggled for years to create the conditions which made it possible for them to have homes and families. The material gains and their new sense of pride turned these workers into widely respected members of the larger community. In fact, among many of their fellow workers, the longshoremen and seamen took on the stature of heroic proletarian rebels. "The Staccato Beat of Marching Feet" became a vivid symbol of their historic advance. The acknowledgement that this forward march was to some degree disrupted and diverted should not detract from our appreciation of the power of the "Pentecostal" era and the indigenous foundation upon which this historical moment was constructed.

# ✣ *F U R T H E R   R E A D I N G*

Babson, Steve. *Building the Union: Skilled Workers and Anglo-Gaelic Immigrants in the Rise of the UAW* (1991).
Bernstein, Irving. *A Caring Society: The New Deal, the Worker, and the Great Depression* (1985).
———. *Turbulent Years: A History of the American Worker, 1933–1941* (1970).
Bodnar, John. *Workers' World: Kinship, Community, and Protest in an Industrial Society, 1900–1940* (1982).
Brattain, Michelle. *The Politics of Whiteness: Race, Workers, and Culture in the Modern South* (2001).

Brody, David. *Workers in Industrial America: Essays on the Twentieth Century Struggle* (1981).

Bucki, Cecelia. *Bridgeport's Socialist New Deal, 1915–36* (2001).

Chateauvert, Melinda. *Marching Together: Women of the Brotherhood of Sleeping Car Porters* (1997).

Cochran, Bert. *Labor and Communism: The Conflict That Shaped American Unions* (1977).

Cohen, Lizabeth. *Making a New Deal: Industrial Workers in Chicago, 1919–1939* (1990).

Denning, Michael. *Cultural Front: The Laboring of American Culture in the Twentieth Century* (1998).

Dubofsky, Melvyn, and Warren Van Tine. *John L. Lewis: A Biography* (1977, 1987).

Faue, Elizabeth. *Community of Suffering & Struggle: Women, Men and the Labor Movement in Minneapolis, 1915–1945* (1991).

Fine, Sidney. *Sitdown: The General Motors Strike of 1936–1937* (1969).

Fraser, Steven. *Labor Will Rule: Sidney Hillman and the Rise of American Labor* (1994).

Freeman, Joshua. *In Transit: The Transport Workers Union in New York, 1933–1966* (1989).

Friedlander, Peter. *The Emergence of a UAW Local, 1936–1939: A Study in Class and Culture* (1975).

Gall, Gilbert. *Pursuing Justice: Lee Pressman, the New Deal, and the CIO* (1999).

Gerstle, Gary. *Working-Class Americanism: The Politics of Labor in a Textile City, 1914–1960* (1989).

Gordon, Colin. *New Deals: Business, Labor and Politics in America, 1920–1935* (1994).

Hunnicutt, Benjamin. *Work Without End: Abandoning Shorter Hours for the Right to Work* (1988).

Irons, Janet. *Testing the New Deal: The General Textile Strike of 1934 in the American South* (2000).

Kazin, Michael. *The Populist Persuasion: An American History* ((1995).

Kelley, Robin. *Hammer and Hoe: Alabama Communists During the Great Depression* (1990).

Kessler-Harris, Alice. *In Pursuit of Equity: Women, Men, and the Quest for Economic Citizenship in 20th Century America* (2001).

Lichtenstein, Nelson. *Walter Reuther: The Most Dangerous Man in Detroit* (1996).

Lynd, Alice, and Staughton Lynd, eds. *Rank and File: Personal Histories by Working-Class Organizers* (1973).

Lynd, Staughton. *"We are All Leaders:" The Alternative Unionism of the Early 1930s* (1996).

Markowitz, Gerold, and David Rosner. *"Slaves of the Depression": Workers' Letters About Life on the Job* (1987).

Nelson, Bruce. *Workers on the Waterfront: Seamen, Longshoremen, and Unionism in the 1930s* (1988).

Preis, Art. *Labor's Giant Step: Twenty Years of the CIO* (1964).

Ruiz, Vicki. *Cannery Women, Cannery Lives: Mexican Women, Unionization, and the California Food Processing Industry, 1930–1940* (1987).

Scharf, Lois. *To Work and to Wed: Female Employment, Feminism, and the Great Depression* (1980).

Schatz, Ronald. *The Electrical Workers: A History of Labor at General Electric and Westinghouse, 1923–1960* (1983).

Simon, Bryant. *A Fabric of Defeat: The Politics of South Carolina Millhands, 1910–1948* (1998).

Storrs, Landon R. Y. *Civilizing Capitalism: The National Consumers' League, Women's Activism, and Labor Standards in the New Deal Era* (2000).

Tomlins, Christopher. *The State and the Unions: Labor Relations, Law, and the Organized Labor Movement in America, 1880–1960* (1985).

Weber, Devra. *Dark Sweat, While Gold: California Farm Workers, Cotton, and the New Deal* (1994).

Zieger, Robert. *The CIO, 1935–1955* (1955).

# CHAPTER 10

# Race, Gender, and
# Industrial Unionism:
# World War II
# and Its Aftermath

World War II lasted only half a decade, and most of the killing and destruction took place far away from the United States, yet this most massive of all twentieth-century military conflicts had an enormous impact on American society. Above all, the war ended the Great Depression. With the military accounting for about 47 percent of all production and services at the peak of the fighting, the gross national product doubled in the wartime years. And unlike so much contemporary military spending, this war was a metal-bending, engine-building, gasoline-powered con-flict that required an enormous amount of relatively unskilled labor. Unemployment, still 14 percent in 1940, vanished in just a couple of years. Wages went up, infant mortality declined, and life expectancy increased. Indeed, jobs were created for 17 million new entrants into the work force, enabling millions of people once consigned to the bottom of the labor market—white women, black laborers, teenagers, and older workers—to take high-paying defense-related jobs for the first time; or if they were already employed in industry, to improve their positions and their pay.

But how much of a social revolution did this full-employment economy generate? The war clearly had a huge impact on the status of black workers. _The unprecedented demand for new sources of industrial labor, combined with Allied denunciations of Nazi racism, weakened longstanding racist structures within the workplace._ Three million blacks surged out of the rural South and into factories, shipyards, steel mills, and military training camps where union contracts and government policy gave them a measure of industrial citizenship. Blacks were increasingly well organized and self-confident, and their advances generated enormous tensions. By the summer of 1943, race riots and "hate strikes" convulsed many war industry centers. But the modern civil rights era clearly had dawned.

*Historians of American women have been fascinated as well by the new demographic patterns generated by the war. The imagery of Rosie the Riveter has been a compelling one, but just what were the thoughts and opinions of the millions of housewives, sales clerks, and female farm laborers who took over traditionally male jobs? Were they motivated by wartime propaganda or by a proto-feminist consciousness? Or did they merely respond to the lure of higher pay and new jobs? And scholars are puzzled because this great migration of female labor seems unaccompanied by the kind of change in social consciousness that made the movement of black workers into industry so politically and socially explosive. After the war many women simply left, or were forced out of, high-profile, heavy-industry jobs. Despite popular myths about the 1950s, there was no wholesale return to the kitchen: within less than a decade, a higher proportion of women were at work—about 35 percent—than at the height of World War II.*

*And while the trade union movement itself boomed during the war, it found itself ambiguously transformed. The powerful War Labor Board (WLB) guaranteed unions protection against hostile managers, raised the wages of many lower-paid workers, and called on employers to offer equal pay for equal work. But the government also put a ceiling on wages and demanded a no-strike pledge from union leaders. This difficult arrangement tended to transform union officials into mere contract administrators who enforced the will of the bureaucrats in Washington. As might be expected, many workers objected to the wage limits, long WLB delays in resolving their disputes, and the effort wartime managers now made to restore discipline in their shops and mills. By 1944 a wildcat-strike movement had emerged, largely centered in cities such as Detroit, Akron, and Chicago, where unionists sought to defend the power of the shop-floor organizations they had built in the 1930s.*

*Is war always good for jobs and unions? Should strikes during wartime be banned as "unpatriotic"? To what extent was World War II a "watershed" in industrial relations, economic restructuring, and working class advancement?*

## ✣ D O C U M E N T S

When A. Philip Randolph, an African American trade unionist, threatened to organize a 1941 "March on Washington" demanding that defense jobs be open to blacks, President Franklin D. Roosevelt responded with a historic executive order, reprinted here as Document 1. In Document 2, Mildred Keith, an African American typist, complains to her local Fair Employment Practice Commission office. In Documents 3 and 4, the War Labor Board (WLB) mandates equal pay for equal work, regardless of an employee's race or gender. But compare the WLB's use of a sweeping ideological argument to attack the idea of racial discrimination in Document 3 with the far narrower grounds on which the WLB endorses women's rights at work in Document 4.

World War II–era civil rights activism is apparent in Document 5, an excerpt from an article in the NAACP's (National Association for the Advancement of Colored People) *The Crisis,* which confidentially, and correctly, predicted that the Detroit branch of this organization would soon enroll twenty thousand members. The interplay of ideology and organization was crucial to the rise of a civil rights consciousness among black workers, but the entrance of white women into the work force generated no mass women's movement. In Document 6, Marie Baker, the recently divorced mother of a small child, describes her successful work life in a southern California aircraft factory, which ended abruptly and with little protest on Baker's part at the war's end.

# 1. President Franklin D. Roosevelt Establishes a Committee on Fair Employment Practice, 1941

WHEREAS it is the policy of the United States to encourage full participation in the national defense program by all citizens of the United States, regardless of race, creed, color, or national origin, in the firm belief that the democratic way of life within the Nation can be defended successfully only with the help and support of all groups within its borders; and

WHEREAS there is evidence that available and needed workers have been barred from employment in industries engaged in defense production solely because of considerations of race, creed, color, or national origin, to the detriment of workers' moral and of national unity.

1. All departments and agencies of the Government of the United States concerned with vocational and training programs for defense production shall take special measures appropriate to assure that such programs are administered without discrimination because of race, creed, color, or national origin;

2. All contracting agencies of the Government of the United States shall include in all defense contracts hereafter negotiated by them a provision obligating the contractor not to discriminate against any worker because of race, creed, color, or national origin;

3. There is established in the Office of Production Management a Committee of Fair Employment Practice, which shall consist of a chairman and four other members to be appointed by the President. The chairman and members of the Committee shall serve as such without compensation but shall be entitled to actual and necessary transportation, subsistence and other expenses incidental to performance of their duties. The Committee shall receive and investigate complaints of discrimination in violation of the provisions of this order and shall take appropriate steps to redress grievances which it finds to be valid. The Committee shall also recommend to the several departments and agencies of the Government of the United States and to the President all measures which may be deemed by it necessary or proper to effectuate the provisions of this order.

> FRANKLIN D. ROOSEVELT
> THE WHITE HOUSE
> June 25, 1941

---

From "Executive Order 8802," in Samuel Rosenman, ed., *The Public Papers and Addresses of Franklin D. Roosevelt,* vol. 10 (New York: Harper & Brothers, 1950), 233–235.

## 2. Mildred Keith Protests Discrimination, 1942

Mr. Thomas M. Jackson
1219 8th Street
Oakland, California

Dear Sir:

. . . Here is the statement of my trying to obtain employment as typist.

At present I am on W.P.A. as senior typist and have had the rating of senior typist for the past three years. I have been threatened to be taken off W.P.A. by a Miss Gale and placed in domestics as she stated I am young and able to do domestics. (She has a statement from my family physician contradicting this statement.) She further stated my classification was domestic. I showed Miss Gale my I.D. card from the employment office and my classification read typist. I was asked by her just where do I think a colored person could get a job as typist. I told her any place as we are all American citizens, and as long as the employer wasn't prejudiced like she. I was told I should try some of the colored business men in this area, surely there must be some who would need a typist. I explained to Miss Gale I didn't need a high school education and a year in college to do domestics, and as she was so interested in finding employment for me, please get me something in my classification.

On February 10, 1942, I took a civil service examination for junior typist, I passed with a rating of 85.91. After receiving my rating, I was called two places for personal interviews. One at the Naval Supply Depot in Oakland and one at the Naval Material Inspector's office in San Francisco. Both without results. I have also received two letters from the Civil Service asking if I would accept a position in Washington, D.C. I answered stating that obligations prevented me from accepting the position from home. Since then I have received nothing else from Civil Service. On May 22, 1942, I wrote the manager of the civil service asking if there was a possibility of my being placed. To date I have received no reply. I have filed applications at Fort Mason in Oakland and also at the Quartermaster's Headquarters in Oakland. Only to be told all positions were filled and I would have to be referred to them by Civil Service. I was asked if I had taken any examinations and when I showed them my rating I was told I would be placed on file.

I know for a fact girls have been placed that received a lower rating than I and some that haven't taken an examination.

I would appreciate greatly anything that can be done in aiding me to obtain employment in this status.

Respectfully yours

Mildred Keith (Mrs.)

---

From Mildred Keith to Thomas M. Jackson, July 23, 1942, Papers of C. R. Dellums, 72/132, Carton 25, Folder "Bay Area Committee Against Discrimination," University of California, Berkeley, Bancroft Library. Courtesy of the Bancroft Library, University of California, Berkeley.

## 3. The War Labor Board Assails Workplace Racism, 1943

In this small but significant case the National War Labor Board abolishes the classifications "colored laborer" and "white laborer" and reclassifies both simply as "laborers" with the same rates of pay for all in that classification without discrimination on account of color. The Negro workers in this classification are hereby granted wage increases which place them on a basis of economic parity with the white workers in the same classification. This wage increase is made without regard to the "Little Steel" formula, but with regard simply for the democratic formula of equal pay for work equal in quantity and quality in the same classification. This equalization of economic opportunity is not a violation of the sound American provision of differentials in pay for differences in skills. It is rather a bit of realization of the no less sound American principle of equal pay for equal work as one of those equal rights in the promise of American democracy regardless of color, race, sex, religion, or national origin.

The unanimous decision is in line with the President's Executive Order 8802; with the general policy of the Board; with the union's request; . . . with the unanimous recommendation of the review committee composed of representatives of labor, industry, and the public; with prophetic Americanism; and with the cause of the United Nations. To the credit of the Company this decision, along with other decisions in the case, is accepted by management in good faith and spirit.

Economic and political discrimination on account of race or creed is in line with the Nazi program. America, in the days of its infant weakness, the haven of heretics and the oppressed of all races, must not in the days of its power become the stronghold of bigots. The world has given America the vigor and variety of its differences. America should protect and enrich its differences for the sake of America and the world. Understanding religious and racial differences make[s] for a better understanding of other differences and for an appreciation of the sacredness of human personality, as a basic to human freedom. The American answer to differences in color and creed is not a concentration camp but cooperation. The answer to human error is not terror but light and liberty under the moral law. By this light and liberty, the Negro has made a contribution in work and faith, song and story, laughter and struggle which are an enduring part of the spiritual heritage of America.

There is no more loyal group of our fellow citizens than the American Negroes, north and south. In defense of America from attack from without, they spring to arms in the spirit of Dorie Miller of Texas, the Negro mess boy, who, when the machine gunner on the Arizona was killed, jumped to his unappointed place and fired the last rounds as the ship was sinking in Pearl Harbor.

It is the acknowledged fact that in spite of all the handicaps of slavery and discrimination, the Negro in America has compressed more progress in the shortest time than any race in human history. Slavery gave the Negro his Christianity. Christianity gave the Negro his freedom. This freedom must give the Negro equal

From U.S. Department of Labor, *The Termination Report of the National War Labor Board,* vol. 1 (Washington, D.C.: U.S. Government Printing Office, 1947), 152.

rights to home and health, education and citizenship, and an equal opportunity to work and fight for our common country.

Whether as vigorous fighting men or for production of food and munitions, America needs the Negro; the Negro needs the equal opportunity to work and fight. The Negro is necessary for winning the war, and, at the same time, is a test of our sincerity in the cause for which we are fighting. More hundreds of millions of colored people are involved in the outcome of this war than the combined populations of the Axis Powers. Under Hitler and his Master Race, their movement is backward to slavery and despair. In America, the colored people have the freedom to struggle for freedom. With the victory of the democracies, the human destiny is toward freedom, hope, equality of opportunity and the gradual fulfillment for all peoples of the noblest aspirations of the brothers of men and the sons of God, without regard to color or creed, region or race, in the world neighborhood of human brotherhood.

## 4. The War Labor Board Orders Equal Pay for Equal Work, 1944

Adjustments which equalize the wage or salary rates paid to females with the rates paid to males for comparable quality and quantity of work on the same or similar operations . . . may be made without the approval of the National War Labor Board. . . .

The application of the Order is quite plain and simple in cases where women are employed to replace men on jobs which are not changed.

Where the plant management, in order to meet the necessity of replacing men by women, has rearranged or lightened the job, perhaps with the employment of helpers to do heavy lifting or the like, a study of job content and job evaluation should afford the basis for setting "proportionate rates for proportionate work." Such questions require a reasonable determination, by collective bargaining or arbitration, of the question whether, or how far, the newly arranged job is of equal quantity and quality with the old job. The new wage set on such a basis does not require the approval of the National War Labor Board. . . .

We have found from experience that there has been some tendency to abuse this rule of equal pay for equal work.

This refers particularly to job classifications to which only women have been assigned in the past. The rates for such jobs, especially when developed by collective bargaining, are presumed to be correct in relation to other jobs in the plant.

Whether a job is performed by men or women, there may be a dispute over correctness of its wage rate in relation to rates for other jobs in the same plant. These are the so-called intra-plant inequality cases. Their discrimination should not be related to the "equal pay for equal work" question; they should be determined on the basis of maintaining or developing a proper balance of wage rates for various jobs based upon job evaluation.

We have even seen instances in which the workers have demanded, or the employers have proposed, that the wages being paid to women in one plant should be increased on the ground that in some other plant similar work is being done by men

---

From U.S. Department of Labor, *The Termination Report of the National War Labor Board,* vol. 1 (Washington, D.C.: U.S. Government Printing Office, 1947), 291.

at a higher wage. Such proposals tend to overlook the fact that wages paid to men in the same occupation generally vary from plant to plant. In such cases, the question whether the work is done by men or women is irrelevant. The claim for increased wages immediately reduces itself to a single question of different wage rates for the same work in different plants. Interplant inequalities in wage rates are quite common in American industry, and often well established. They afford a basis for a wage increase only in very exceptional cases. If the interplant inequality is in fact one that should be corrected at all, its correction is independent of any question of men and women workers.

## 5. *The Crisis* Predicts a Surge in NAACP Membership, 1943

The question has been raised, "Can Detroit get 20,000 NAACP members in 1943?"

Yes—is the answer echoed by the president of the branch, Dr. James J. McClendon, the executive board, the membership committee, the labor committee and interested citizens of Detroit. . . .

Detroit takes pride in building powerful organizations. The largest industrial union in the world—Ford Local 600, UAW-CIO, of which a Negro, Shelton Tappes, is recording secretary—is located in the "motor city." The United Automobile, Aircraft and Agricultural Implement Workers of America, CIO, one of the largest international unions in the world, got its start in Detroit, once an open shop town.

Today, Detroit is a worker's town—dynamic in every respect. The CIO and the AFL embrace a majority of the Negro workers and these organizations are reflected in the NAACP membership. AFL teachers, sanitary workers, street car and bus motormen, conductors and conductorettes, laborers, carpenters, postal employees; CIO rubber workers, retail and restaurant employees, maintenance workers, autoworkers, state, county and municipal workers, make up a major portion of the present membership of more than twelve thousand NAACP members. . . .

The labor committee is the largest and most active committee of the branch. Meeting regularly each Sunday afternoon, it hears grievances of workers from plants and industries throughout the city, takes them up through regular union channels, always reserving the NAACP as the court of last appeal. It was the labor committee which saw the need for a demonstration against mounting discrimination, and, together with the Inter-Racial Committee of the UAW-CIO, sponsored the largest gathering held recently on the question of employing more Negro women in Detroit's war industries.

### War Brings Problems

Since 1941, more than 300,000 workers have come into the metropolitan area to man the industries, some of them newly created, which are producing the materiel

From "20,000 Members in 1943," *The Crisis,* Vol. 50 (May 1943), pp. 140–141. The publisher wishes to thank The Crisis Publishing Co., Inc., the publisher of the magazine of the National Association for the Advancement of Colored People, for use of this work that was first published in the May 1943 issue of *The Crisis.*

for victory. More than 50,000 Negro workers are a part of this new group. Bursting at its seams, the city's problems of housing, recreation, delinquency and employment have risen in alarming proportions. Perhaps this accounts for the willingness of Detroit citizens to tackle *any* problem of discrimination with a vitality that amazes the nation—especially Washington!

Aroused by the slow upgrading of trained Negro men, the reluctance of war industries to utilize available Negro woman power, the NAACP labor committee and the Inter-Racial Committee of the UAW-CIO co-sponsored a demonstration in Cadillac Square, Sunday, April 11. More than 10,000 people paraded from the Detroit Institute of Arts to the Square where stands the monument of Sojourner Truth.

The parade was colorful. Huge banners cried: "Down with discrimination," "Jim-Crow must go!" "Bullets and Bombs are Colorblind." Air raid wardens, Women's Volunteer Corps, OCD people, marched in uniform to show that the Negro is taking part in civilian defense activities. The Boy Scouts and the "Majorettes," a group of young girls twirling batons behind the American Legion Drum and Bugle Corps, added youthful color to the parade.

5,000 people marched for more than five miles on a warm Sunday afternoon to give vent to their feelings against jim-crow practices in Detroit. As the procession passed the USO, 24 Negro soldiers on weekend leave from a nearby airfield proudly walked from the building and calmly fell into the line of march. Their action clearly showed that they felt: "This is our fight too!" . . .

Embodying the desire to have democracy practiced at home as well as abroad, the huge assembly ratified the *Cadillac Charter,* which called for: abolition of discrimination in government, housing, the armed forces; abolition of the poll tax; security from mob violence, lynching, police brutality and physical violence; equal treatment in hiring, upgrading and training. The preamble stated that "as people of all races" we "declare ourselves wholeheartedly behind the effort of the government to prosecute the war to an ultimate victory." The charter further pointed out that "full and equal participation of all citizens is fair, just and necessary for victory and an enduring peace. . . . [D]iscriminatory practices cannot be maintained if America is to hold out to the world hope of freedom."

## 6. Women's Work in a California Warplane Factory, 1941–1945

I needed a job because I was going to be very independent. I wasn't going to ask for any alimony or anything. I was just going to take care of myself. There was no jobs in Mojave in the desert; you had to come down here.

Women, everyone, was going to work at that time. We were really patriotic in those days. 'Course, we were in a real war. We were being attacked; you know, Pearl Harbor and all. I think the people came together better than they did during Vietnam. 'Course, Vietnam was such a mess; I mean, it was a real tragedy. But during World

---

From "Interview with Marie Baker," in Sherna Berger Gluck, *Rosie the Riveter Revisited: Women, the War, and Social Change* (Boston: Twayne Publishers, 1987).

War II, everybody got real patriotic and got in there and worked. Grandmothers, mothers, daughters, everybody. I was real patriotic and I wanted to help. I was going to work right out in the factory. I wasn't going in for an office job. No, no, I didn't want that.

So I came down and had an interview and went to work at North American. I had a friend and I had a room at her house in L.A. My daughter stayed in Mojave with my sister until I could have her down here.

I started after just a day or two. I was very nervous. I had the impression that women were tough that worked in factories, and I was scared to death, hoping nobody would hit me. That was silly. But it didn't seem like nice people worked in factories. I don't know where I got that idea. So I was nervous about going. Because I had been so sheltered. I was a Caspar Milquetoast, I really was.

Anyway, I just went straight into the plant. You get your badge and someone takes you up to your department, introduces you to the supervision, sets you down to this little table where you're going to sit for all these hours. It was such a huge place and we were upstairs, not near any planes, of course, because it was just this little section where you did all the buffing of the tubes. But it was exciting. In spite of being nervous, it was exciting. Here I was, being a war worker.

The first day I worked at a machine that had like sandpaper on it. When the tubes are cut, they're rough and not smoothed off at the ends. So this is a wheel that goes around and you'd hold the tube up to it to try to smoothe it off. Morons could have done it, sitting there just buffing the tubing.

I was so excited about a job that I didn't really care. But when I got a chance to go into another department, I was delighted. I was hoping that I would be transferred because it was boring, but you didn't think much about that because you were so busy being so patriotic and doing something for your country.

They put me in the empennage department, which is the tail section of the plane, the B-25 bomber. We put the de-icer boot on the vertical and the horizontal stabilizers of the bomber. The men had been doing that and they weren't quite as neat as the women. So we were doing a better job. They just showed us what to do and we did it; it was quite a few little operations. They'd bring in the stabilizers, the horizontal ones, and we had to get a template to put on there—that was like a pattern—and fasten it on. Then we took a drill and drilled holes. When that was taken off, we got a notcher and we'd notch the holes. And then we'd get the boot—made of rubber—and we'd powder it, and then we'd place it on this horizontal stabilizer and use pins to hold it in. Then we'd take out each pin and put a screw in to hold it. Then we'd turn it over and do the other side. And it had to be real smooth. The purpose of the de-icer boot, the planes were going to the countries where ice would form, and from the cockpit they could press a button or something and it would make it expand and the ice would break and fall off because it was rubber.

This girl that came with me from the tube-bending department, she and I got real good at it. Seems like we had it mastered real fast. I think we were the first two in there, and then they kept bringing more girls in and we showed them. The men were thrilled to pieces to get away from that job because they didn't like it. They'd rather be putting the plane together than just standing there putting the boots on.

They were bringing in more girls to do this—because the bombers were really going out fast—and they needed a leadgirl. So they made me a leadgirl. I did have

some special training because I had some paperwork to do. At that time Mr. Kindel-
berger was the president of North American, and his secretary, Bobby Waddell, gave
a class on office procedures. It was given through the University of Southern California, and we went right on company time during the day into one of the offices. I
think it was once a week for six weeks.

I went in April and this was about August. By that time, there was eighteen girls
working in there and eight of them were Negro girls. There were men, too, because
the rudders and all that went on right there in the department. After we finished the
boots on the stabilizers, then the men put them on the tail sections of the plane. But
I just supervised the women.

There was a leadman, a foreman, and an assistant foreman over me, but I had
to see if the girls were working and get supplies to do the work and see if they got
along. There was a girl from the South. I guess she had never been around Negroes
and she didn't want to work near them. I told her I had four brothers out in the
Pacific and they were all fighting at the same time, and why couldn't she stand in
there and work next to someone no matter who they were? Kind of made me a little
angry. Then another girl, she didn't like the perfume one of the girls was wearing.
She'd put up a big fuss about that! So minor! But otherwise, they got along pretty
good. They finally got over their little funny ways.

I had no problems with the black women. I got along fine with them. The only
problem was when two of them got into a fight. The men in the department, the
supervision, they're the ones that broke it up. It was a silly fight to begin with. I was
terribly upset when I had to go in and be a witness. The union lawyer started throwing questions at me. I was so nervous! They put words in your mouth. By the time I
got out of there, I went straight to the little girls' room and had a good cry. It just
really shook me up, terribly. But because I was the leadgirl, I had to tell. I didn't like
that part at all! . . .

Well, North American had to find me a house because I was a war worker—
which they did. A brand new two-bedroom apartment here in Rodondo Beach for
$46.50 a month. And my girlfriend, Gwen Thomas, lived in the single apartment
downstairs, and we lived in the big one upstairs. She had two children and her husband was in the navy and, of course, gone all the time. My mother was to take care
of the two children. . . .

My mother did the cooking and the housekeeping and looked after Barbara. So
it was wonderful having her with me. She stayed with me until after I got married
the second time. Coming home, mother always had dinner ready for us, and we'd
just sit around and listen—we didn't have television, just radio. Sometimes we'd
go to the show, or on Saturdays, we'd go into L.A. once in a while, look around.
That's about it. And then we had company a lot because my brothers would sometimes come. And there was other friends who were in the service and would drop in
once in a while unexpectedly. . . .

Later on, when they quit putting the de-icer boot on the bomber because it was
going to a hot country and they didn't need it, then they gave me a choice. I could
work on the line, which was putting things together, or I could be the general foreman's clerk. Naturally, I took that. I could stay clean, I could stay dressed. I could
do the paperwork which I had been doing anyway, keeping track of each worker. I
was right there in the same area. It was just elevated two steps, to like a little box

thing. The general foreman sat up there and the foreman, and I had a little desk there looking down into the department.

When a new-start came in, I'd go to the front office and pick them up and bring them back and introduce them to the supervision and show them where to get the tools. And when someone terminated, I'd take them out. And then I got supplies for the department, even for the men. I'd keep a record on each employee and when they were entitled to a raise, I'd type it up for the general foreman. Things like that. I liked it. And I had a shop pass. I could roam around a little if I didn't have anything to do. By that time, I had a sister, two brothers, and a sister-in-law working in the plant.

I thought I would continue as long as I could. I hoped that I would. We didn't think they'd be making that many planes after the war and wouldn't need that many workers, but I'd been there so long and I was pretty sure that they still needed a clerk out in the plant. So I figured that I'd probably still have a job. If I hadn't married, I think I'd still be there. In fact, I did stay for a while until my husband came back. He was an officer in the Merchant Marine. We were married [in] April '45, and he left and he was gone until August. . . .

He was all ready to teach when the war started, but didn't have a chance to. When he came back, he applied at different schools and he was accepted at San Bernardino. I had to terminate—I hated to do it, but I had to. So we left my mother and my daughter in my house here and we went to San Bernardino and he worked there for a semester.

So at the end of the war, I wasn't thinking about working again. I was just thinking of being a wife and maybe a mother, future mother. I wanted another child, but I was happy to be a housewife.

## ✦ E S S A Y S

In the first essay, historians Robert Korstad of Duke University and Nelson Lichtenstein of the University of California, Santa Barbara argue that in the 1940s, the organization of thousands of black workers laid the basis for a union-led civil rights movement whose dimensions approached that of the better-known insurgency that so transformed race relations in the 1960s. Korstad and Lichtenstein show how the formation of a black-led union at the Reynolds Tobacco Company in Winston-Salem, North Carolina, empowered the black community and transformed the politics of that southern city. Such victories proved difficult. Anticommunism and antiradicalism were obstacles, but as historian Eileen Boris of the University of California, Santa Barbara demonstrates in the second essay, the opponents of racial equality during the 1940s deployed a powerful set of sexually charged prejudices and stereotypes that stood athwart the antidiscriminatory work of union liberals, the Fair Employment Practice Commission, and the War Labor Board. Racial discrimination was a profoundly gendered phenomenon during the midcentury decades.

Did the war advance the struggle for civil rights and in what ways? How did wartime migrations from the South into cities such as Detroit and Los Angeles influence race and gender relations in the workplace as well as outside of it? Did the war change women's place in society? Why might white women have benefited more than other women?

# How Organized Black Workers Brought Civil Rights to the South

### ROBERT KORSTAD AND NELSON LICHTENSTEIN

Most historians would agree that the modern civil rights movement did not begin with the Supreme Court's decision in *Brown* v. *Board of Education.* Yet all too often the movement's history has been written as if events before the mid-1950s constituted a kind of prehistory, important only insofar as they laid the legal and political foundation for the spectacular advances that came later. Those were the "forgotten years of the Negro Revolution," wrote one historian; they were the "seed time of racial and legal metamorphosis," according to another. But such a periodization profoundly underestimates the tempo and misjudges the social dynamic of the freedom struggle.

The civil rights era began, dramatically and decisively, in the early 1940s when the social structure of black America took on an increasingly urban, proletarian character. A predominantly southern rural and small town population was soon transformed into one of the most urban of all major ethnic groups. More than two million blacks migrated to northern and western industrial areas during the 1940s, while another million moved from farm to city within the South. Northern black voters doubled their numbers between 1940 and 1948, and in the eleven states of the Old South black registration more than quadrupled, reaching over one million by 1952. Likewise, membership in the National Association for the Advancement of Colored People (NAACP) soared, growing from 50,000 in 355 branches in 1940 to almost 450,000 in 1,073 branches six years later.

The half million black workers who joined unions affiliated with the Congress of Industrial Organizations (CIO) were in the vanguard of efforts to transform race relations. The NAACP and the Urban League had become more friendly toward labor in the depression era, but their legal and social work orientation had not prepared them to act effectively in the workplaces and working-class neighborhoods where black Americans fought their most decisive struggles of the late 1930s and 1940s. By the early forties it was commonplace for sympathetic observers to assert the centrality of mass unionization in the civil rights struggle. A Rosenwald Fund study concluded, not without misgivings, that "the characteristic movements among Negroes are now for the first time becoming proletarian"; while a *Crisis* reporter found the CIO a "lamp of democracy" throughout the old Confederate states. "The South has not known such a force since the historic Union Leagues in the great days of the Reconstruction era."

This movement gained much of its dynamic character from the relationship that arose between unionized blacks and the federal government and proved somewhat similar to the creative tension that linked the church-based civil rights movement and the state almost two decades later. In the 1950s the *Brown* decision legitimated much of the subsequent social struggle, but it remained essentially a

From Robert Korstad and Nelson Lichtenstein, "Opportunities Found and Lost: Labor, Radicals, and the Early Civil Rights Movement," *Journal of American History,* 75 (December 1988): 786–793, 799–806, 811.

dead letter until given political force by a growing protest movement. In like manner, the rise of industrial unions and the evolution of late New Deal labor legislation offered working-class blacks an economic and political standard by which
they could legitimate their demands and stimulate a popular struggle. The "one
man, one vote" policy implemented in thousands of National Labor Relations
Board (NLRB) elections, the industrial "citizenship" that union contracts offered
once-marginal elements of the working class, and the patriotic egalitarianism of
the government's wartime propaganda—all generated a rights consciousness that
gave working-class black militancy a moral justification in some ways as powerful
as that evoked by the Baptist spirituality of Martin Luther King, Jr., a generation
later. During the war the Fair Employment Practice Committee (FEPC) held little
direct authority, but like the Civil Rights Commission of the late 1950s, it served to
expose racist conditions and spur on black activism wherever it undertook its well-
publicized investigations. And just as a disruptive and independent civil rights
movement in the 1960s could pressure the federal government to enforce its own
laws and move against local elites, so too did the mobilization of the black working
class in the 1940s make civil rights an issue that could not be ignored by union
officers, white executives, or government officials.

This essay explores . . . the workplace-oriented civil rights militancy that arose
in the 1940s, in particular the unionization of predominantly black tobacco workers
in Winston-Salem, North Carolina. The remarkable collective activism of these
workers made Winston-Salem a center of black working-class activism in the upper
South, but similar movements took root among newly organized workers in the cotton compress mills of Memphis, the tobacco factories of Richmond and Charleston,
the auto plants of Detroit, the steel mills of Pittsburgh and Birmingham, the stockyards and farm equipment factories of Chicago and Louisville, and the shipyards of
Baltimore and Oakland. . . .

Winston-Salem had been a center of tobacco processing since the 1880s, and
the R. J. Reynolds Tobacco Company dominated the life of the city's eighty thousand citizens. By the 1940s whites held most of the higher paying machine-tending
jobs, but blacks formed the majority of the work force, concentrated in the preparation departments where they cleaned, stemmed, and conditioned the tobacco.
The jobs were physically demanding, the air was hot and dusty, and in departments
with machinery, the noise was deafening. Most black workers made only a few
cents above minimum wage, and benefits were few. Black women workers experienced frequent verbal and occasional sexual abuse. Reynolds maintained a determined opposition to trade unionism, and two unsuccessful American Federation of
Labor (AFL) efforts to organize segregated locals had soured most black workers
on trade unionism.

But in 1943 a CIO organizing effort succeeded. Led by the United Cannery,
Agricultural, Packing and Allied Workers of America (UCA-PAWA), a new union
drive championed black dignity and self-organization, employing several young
black organizers who had gotten their start in the interracial Southern Tenant Farmers
Union. Their discreet two-year organizing campaign made a dramatic breakthrough
when black women in one of the stemmeries stopped work on June 17. A severe
labor shortage, chronic wage grievances, and a recent speedup gave the women both
the resources and the incentive to transform a departmental sit-down into a festive,

plant-wide strike. The UCAPAWA quickly signed up about eight thousand black workers, organized a committee to negotiate with the company, and asked the NLRB to hold an election.

The effort to win union recognition at Reynolds sparked a spirited debate about who constituted the legitimate leadership of the black community in Winston-Salem. Midway through the campaign, six local black business and professional men—a college professor, an undertaker, a dentist, a store owner, and two ministers—dubbed "colored leaders" by the *Winston-Salem Journal,* wrote a long letter to the editor urging workers to reject the "followers of John L. Lewis and William Green" and to remain loyal to Reynolds. In the absence of any formal leadership, elected or otherwise, representatives of Winston-Salem's small black middle class had served as spokesmen, brokering with the white elite for small concessions in a tightly segregated society. The fight for collective bargaining, they argued, had to remain secondary to the more important goal of racial betterment, which could only be achieved by "good will, friendly understanding, and mutual respect and co-operation between the races." Partly because of their own vulnerability to economic pressure, such traditional black leaders judged unions, like other institutions, by their ability to deliver jobs and maintain a precarious racial equilibrium.

The union campaign at Reynolds transformed the expectations tobacco workers held of the old community leadership. Reynolds workers responded to calls for moderation from "college-trained people" with indignation. "Our leaders," complained Mabel Jessup, "always look clean and refreshed at the end of the hottest day, because they work in very pleasant environments. . . . All I ask of our leaders is that they obtain a job in one of the factories as a laborer and work two weeks. Then write what they think." W. L. Griffin felt betrayed. "I have attended church regularly for the past thirty years," he wrote, "and unity and co-operation have been taught and preached from the pulpits of the various Negro churches. Now that the laboring class of people are about to unite and co-operate on a wholesale scale for the purpose of collective bargaining, these same leaders seem to disagree with that which they have taught their people." Others rejected the influence of people who "have always told us what the white people want, but somehow or other are particularly silent on what we want." "We feel we are the leaders instead of you," asserted a group of union members.

Reynolds, the only major tobacco manufacturer in the country not under a union contract, followed tried and true methods to break the union. Management used lower-level supervisors to intimidate unionists and support a "no union" movement among white workers, whose organizers were given freedom to roam the company's workshops and warehouses. That group, the R. J. Reynolds Employees Association, sought a place on the NLRB ballot in order to delay the increasingly certain CIO victory. Meanwhile, the white business community organized an Emergency Citizens Committee to help defeat the CIO. In a well-publicized resolution, the committee blamed the recent strikes on "self-seeking representatives of the CIO" and warned that continued subversion of existing race relations would "likely lead to riots and bloodshed."

In earlier times, this combination of anti-union forces would probably have derailed the organizing effort. But during World War II, black workers had allies who helped shift the balance of power. The NLRB closely supervised each stage of the election process and denied the company's request to divide the work force into two bargaining units, which would have weakened the position of black workers. When local judges sought to delay the election, government attorneys removed the case to federal court. In December 1943 an NLRB election gave the CIO a resounding victory. But continued federal assistance, from the United States Conciliation Service and the National War Labor Board, was still needed to secure Reynolds workers a union contract in 1944.

That first agreement resembled hundreds of other wartime labor-management contracts, but in the context of Winston-Salem's traditional system of race relations it had radical implications, because it generated a new set of shop floor rights embodied in the seniority, grievance, and wage adjustment procedures. The contract did not attack factory segregation—for the most part white workers continued to control the better-paying jobs—but it did call forth a new corps of black leaders to defend the rights Reynolds workers had recently won. The one hundred or so elected shop stewards were the "most important people in the plant," remembered union activist Velma Hopkins. They were the "natural leaders," people who had "taken up money for flowers if someone died or would talk to the foreman [even] before the union." Now the union structure reinforced the capabilities of such workers: "We had training classes for the shop stewards: What to do, how to do it. We went over the contract thoroughly." The shop stewards transformed the traditional paternalism of Reynolds management into an explicit system of benefits and responsibilities. They made the collective bargaining agreement a bill of rights.

The growing self-confidence of black women, who constituted roughly half of the total work force, proved particularly subversive of existing social relations. To the white men who ran the Reynolds plants, nothing could have been more disturbing than the demand that they negotiate on a basis of equality with people whom they regarded as deeply inferior—by virtue of their sex a well as their class and race. When union leaders like Theodosia Simpson, Velma Hopkins, and Moranda Smith sat down at the bargaining table with company executives, social stereotypes naturally came under assault, but the challenge proved equally dramatic on the shop floor. For example, Ruby Jones, the daughter of a railway fireman, become one of the most outspoken shop stewards. Perplexed by her newfound aggressiveness, a foreman demanded, "Ruby, what do you want?" "I want your respect," she replied, "that's all I ask."

By the summer of 1944, Local 22 of the reorganized and renamed Food, Tobacco, Agricultural and Allied Workers (FTA) had become the center of an alternative social world that linked black workers together regardless of job, neighborhood, or church affiliation. The union hall, only a few blocks from the Reynolds Building, housed a constant round of meetings, plays, and musical entertainments, as well as classes in labor history, black history, and current events. Local 22 sponsored softball teams, checker tournaments, sewing circles, and swimming clubs. Its vigorous educational program and well-stocked library introduced many black workers (and a few whites) to a larger radical culture few had glimpsed before. "You know, at that little library they [the city of Winston-Salem] had for us, you couldn't find any books on Negro history," remembered Viola Brown. "They didn't have books by Aptheker, Dubois, or Frederick Douglass. But we had them at *our* library."

The Communist party was the key political grouping in FTA and in Local 22. FTA president Donald Henderson had long been associated with the party, and many organizers who passed through Winston-Salem shared his political sympathies. By

1947 party organizers had recruited about 150 Winston-Salem blacks, almost all tobacco workers. Most of these workers saw the party as both a militant civil rights organization, which in the 1930s had defended such black victims of white southern racism as the Scottsboro boys and Angelo Hearndon, and as a cosmopolitan group, introducing members to the larger world of politics and ideas. The white North Carolina Communist leader Junius Scales recalled that the "top leaders [of Local 22] . . . just soaked up all the educational efforts that were directed at them. The Party's program had an explanation of events locally, nationally, and worldwide which substantiated everything they had felt instinctively. . . . It really meant business on racism." The party was an integrated institution in which the social conventions of the segregated South were self-consciously violated, but it also accommodated itself to the culture of the black community. In Winston-Salem, therefore, the party met regularly in a black church and started the meetings with a hymn and a prayer.

The Communist party's relative success in Winston-Salem was replicated in other black industrial districts. In the South a clear majority of the party's new recruits were black, and in northern states like Illinois and Michigan the proportion ranged from 25 to 40 percent. The party's relative success among American blacks were not based on its programmatic consistency: during the late 1940s the NAACP and other critics pointed out that the wartime party had denounced civil rights struggles when they challenged the Roosevelt administration or its conduct of the war effort, but that the party grew more militant once Soviet-American relations cooled. However, the party never abandoned its assault on Jim Crow and unlike the NAACP, which directed much of its energy toward the courts and Congress, the Communists or their front groups more often organized around social or political issues subject to locally initiated protests, petitions, and pickets. Moreover, the party adopted what today would be called an affirmative action policy that recognized the special disabilities under which black workers functioned, in the party as well as in the larger community. Although there were elements of tokenism and manipulation in the implementation of that policy, the party's unique effort to develop black leaders gave the Communists a special standing among politically active blacks.

Tobacco industry trade unionism revitalized black political activism in Winston-Salem. Until the coming of the CIO, NAACP attacks on racial discrimination seemed radical, and few blacks risked associating with the organization. A 1942 membership drive did increase branch size from 11 to 100, but most new members came from the traditional black middle class: mainly teachers and municipal bus drivers. The Winston-Salem NAACP became a mass organization only after Local 22 conducted its own campaign for the city branch. As tobacco workers poured in, the local NAACP reached a membership of 1,991 by 1946, making it the largest unit in North Carolina.

Unionists also attacked the policies that had disenfranchised Winston-Salem blacks for more than two generations. As part of the CIO Political Action Committee's voter registration and mobilization drive, Local 22 inaugurated citizenship classes, political rallies, and citywide mass meetings. Union activists challenged the power of registrars to judge the qualifications of black applicants and insisted that black veterans vote without further tests. The activists encouraged the city's blacks to participate in electoral politics. "Politics IS food, clothes, and housing," declared the committee that registered some seven hundred new black voters in the months before the 1944 elections. After a visit to Winston-Salem in 1944, a *Pittsburgh Courier* correspondent wrote, "I was aware of a growing solidarity and intelligent mass action that will mean the dawn of a New Day in the South. One cannot visit Winston-Salem and mingle with the thousands of workers without sensing a revolution in thought and action. If there is a 'New' Negro, he is to be found in the ranks of the labor movement."

Organization and political power gave the black community greater leverage at city hall and at the county courthouse. NAACP and union officials regularly took part in municipal government debate on social services for the black community, minority representation on the police and fire departments, and low-cost public housing. In 1944 and 1946 newly enfranchised blacks helped reelect Congressman John Folger, a New Deal supporter, against strong conservative opposition, In 1947, after black registration had increased some tenfold in the previous three years, a minister, Kenneth Williams, won a seat on the Board of Aldermen, becoming the first black city official in the twentieth-century South to be elected against a white opponent. . . .

By the mid-1940s, civil rights issues had reached a level of national political salience that they would not regain for another fifteen years. Once the domain of Afro-American protest groups, leftist clergymen, and Communist-led unions and front organizations, civil rights advocacy was becoming a defining characteristic of urban liberalism. Thus ten states established fair employment practice commissions between 1945 and 1950, and four major cities—Chicago, Milwaukee, Minneapolis, and Philadelphia—enacted tough laws against job bias. Backed by the CIO, the Americans for Democratic Action spearheaded a successful effort to strengthen the Democratic party's civil rights plank at the 1948 convention.

In the South the labor movement seemed on the verge of a major breakthrough. *Fortune* magazine predicted that the CIO's "Operation Dixie" would soon organize key southern industries like textiles. Black workers proved exceptionally responsive to such union campaigns, especially in industries like lumber, furniture, and tobacco, where they were sometimes a majority of the work force. Between 1944 and 1946 the CIO's political action apparatus helped elect liberal congressmen and senators in a few southern states, while organizations that promoted interracial cooperation, such as the Southern Conference for Human Welfare and Highlander Folk School, experienced their most rapid growth and greatest effectiveness in 1946 and 1947.

The opportune moment soon passed. Thereafter, a decade-long decline in working-class black activism destroyed the organizational coherence and ideological élan of the labor-based civil rights movement. That defeat has been largely obscured by the brilliant legal victories won by civil rights lawyers in the 1940s and 1950s, and by the reemergence of a new mass movement in the next decade. But in Winston-Salem, Detroit, and other industrial regions, the time had passed when unionized black labor was in the vanguard of the freedom struggle. Three elements contributed to the decline. First, the employer offensive of the late 1940s put all labor on the defensive. Conservatives used the Communist issue to attack New Deal and Fair Deal reforms, a strategy that isolated Communist-oriented black leaders and helped destroy what was left of the Popular Front. The employers' campaign proved particularly effective against many recently organized CIO locals with disproportionate numbers of black members. Meanwhile, mechanization and decentralization of the most labor intensive and heavily black production facilities sapped the self-confidence of the black working class and contributed to high rates of urban unemployment in the years after the Korean War.

Second, the most characteristic institutions of American liberalism, including the unions, race advancement organizations, and liberal advocacy organizations, adopted a legal-administrative, if not a bureaucratic, approach to winning citizenship rights for blacks. The major legislative goal of the union-backed Leadership Conference on Civil Rights in the 1950s was revision of Senate Rule 22, to limit the use of the filibuster that had long blocked passage of a national FEPC and other civil rights legislation. The UAW and other big unions cooperated with the NAACP in the effort, but the work was slow and frustrating and the struggle far removed from the shop floor or the drugstore lunch counter.

Finally, the routinization of the postwar industrial relations system precluded efforts by black workers to mobilize a constituency independent of the leadership. Focusing on incremental collective bargaining gains and committed to social change only if it was well controlled, the big unions became less responsive to the particular interests of their black members. By 1960 blacks had formed oppositional movements in several old CIO unions, but they now encountered resistance to their demands not only from much of the white rank and file but also from union leaders who presided over institutions that had accommodated themselves to much of the industrial status quo. . . .

Like most labor intensive southern employers, R. J. Reynolds never reached an accommodation with union labor, although it signed contracts with Local 22 in 1945 and 1946. Minimum wage laws and collective bargaining agreements had greatly increased costs of production, especially in the stemmeries, and the black women employed there were the heart and soul of the union. Soon after the war, the company began a mechanization campaign that eliminated several predominantly black departments. When the factories closed for Christmas in 1945 new stemming machines installed in one plant displaced over seven hundred black women. The union proposed a "share the work plan," but the company was determined to cut its work force and change its racial composition by recruiting white workers from surrounding counties. The black proportion of the manufacturing labor force in Winston-Salem dropped from 44 to 36 percent between 1940 and 1960.

The technological offensive undermined union strength, but by itself Reynolds could not destroy Local 22. When contract negotiations began in 1947, the company rejected union demands for a wage increase patterned after those won in steel, auto, and rubber earlier in the spring. Somewhat reluctantly, Local 22 called a strike on May 1. Black workers and virtually all of the Negro community solidly backed the union, which held out for thirty-eight days until a compromise settlement was reached. But, in a pattern replicated throughout industrial America in those years, Communist influence within the union became the key issue around which management and its allies mounted their attack. The *Winston-Salem Journal* soon denounced Local 22 as "captured . . . lock, stock and barrel" by the Communist party, warning readers that the strike would lead to "open rioting." This exposé brought Local 22 officers under the scrutiny of the House Committee on Un-American Activities (HUAC), which held a highly publicized hearing on the Winston-Salem situation in the summer of 1947.

Communist party members contributed to the volatility of the situation. In the late 1940s, Local 22 found itself politically vulnerable when foreign policy resolutions passed by the shop stewards' council followed Communist party pronouncements. The party's insistence on the promotion of blacks into public leadership positions sometimes put workers with little formal education into union leadership jobs they could not handle. Moreover, the party's obsession with "white chauvinism" backfired. After the 1947 strike, Local 22 made a concerted effort to recruit white workers. Some young veterans joined the local, although the union allowed most to pay their dues secretly. The party objected, remembered North Carolina leader Junius Scales, "'If they got any guts,' they would say, 'let them stand up and fight,' not realizing, as many black workers and union leaders realized, that for a white worker to just *belong* to a predominantly black union at that time was an act of great courage."

With its work force increasingly polarized along racial and political lines, Reynolds renewed its offensive in the spring of 1948. Black workers remained remarkably loyal to the union leadership, but the anticommunist campaign had turned most white employees against the union and erode support among blacks not directly involved in the conflict. The company refused to negotiate with Local 22 on the grounds that the union had not complied with the new Taft-Hartley Act. The law required union officers to sign an affidavit swearing they were not members of the Communist party before a union could be certified as a bargaining agent by the NLRB. Initially, all the CIO internationals had refused to sign the affidavits, but by 1948 only Communist-oriented unions such as FTA still held out. When Reynolds proved intransigent, there was little the union could do. FTA had no standing with the NLRB, and it was too weak to win another strike.

At the same time, Local 22 began to feel repercussions from the conflict within the CIO over the status of unions, like the FTA, that had rejected the Marshall Plan and endorsed Henry Wallace's Progressive party presidential campaign in 1948. A rival CIO union, the United Transport Service Employees (UTSE), sent organizers into Winston-Salem to persuade black workers to abandon Local 22. In a March 1950 NLRB election, which the FTA requested after complying with the Taft-Hartley Act, UTSE joined Local 22 on the ballot. The FTA local retained solid support among its black constituency, who faithfully paid dues to their stewards even after the contract had expired and in the face of condemnation of their union—from the company, the CIO, and HUAC. Even the black community leader Alderman Williams asked workers to vote against the union and "send the Communists away for good." Yet Local 22 captured a plurality of all the votes cast, and in a runoff two weeks later it won outright. But when the NLRB accepted the ballots of lower-level white supervisors, the scales again tipped against the local.

Local 22 disappeared from Winston-Salem's political and economic life, and a far more accommodative black community leadership filled the void left by the union's defeat. Beginning in the mid-1940s, a coalition of middle-class blacks and white business moderates had sought to counter the growing union influence within the black community. They requested a study of local race relations by the National Urban League's Community Relations Project (CRP). Largely financed by Hanes Hosiery president James G. Hanes, the CRP study appeared in late 1947 and called for improved health, education and recreational facilities, but it made no mention of workplace issues. The Urban League foresaw a cautious, "step by step approach" and proposed that an advisory committee drawn from the black middle class discuss community issues with their white counterparts and help city officials and white philanthropists channel welfare services to the black community. The *Winston-Salem Journal* called the CRP's recommendations a "blueprint for better community relations" but one that would not alter "the framework of race relations."

The Urban League's program helped make Winston-Salem a model of racial moderation. Blacks continued to register and vote in relatively high numbers and to elect a single black alderman. The city high school was integrated without incident in 1957, while Winston-Salem desegregated its libraries, golf course, coliseum, and the police and fire departments. But the dynamic and democratic quality of the black struggle in Winston-Salem would never be recaptured. NAACP membership declined to less than five hundred in the early 1950s, and decision making once again moved behind closed doors. When a grievance arose from the black community, group of ministers met quietly with Hanes; a few phone calls by the white industrialist led to desegregation of the privately owned bus company in 1958.

A similar story unfolded in the plants of the R. J. Reynolds Tobacco Company. After the destruction of Local 22, the company blacklisted several leading union activists, yet Reynolds continued to abide by many of the wage standards, benefit provisions, and seniority policies negotiated during the union era. The company reorganized its personnel department; rationalized procedures for hiring, firing, and evaluating employees; and upgraded it supervisory force by weeding out old-timers and replacing them with college-educated foremen. To forestall union activity, Reynolds kept its wages slightly ahead of the rates paid by its unionized competitors.

In February 1960, when sit-ins began at segregated Winston-Salem lunch counters, the voices of black protest were again heard in the city's streets. But the generation of blacks who had sustained Local 22 played little role in the new mobilization. College and high school students predominated on the picket lines and in the new protest organizations that confronted white paternalism and challenged the black community's ministerial leadership. NAACP membership rose once again; more radical blacks organized a chapter of the Congress of Racial Equality (CORE). Public segregation soon collapsed.

The subsequent trajectory of the freedom struggle in Winston-Salem was typical of that in many black communities. Heightened racial tensions set the stage for a 1967 riot and a burst of radicalism, followed by the demobilization of the protest movement and years of trench warfare in the city council. The political career of Larry Little, the son of Reynolds workers who had been members of Local 22, highlighted the contrasts between the two generations of black activists. Little moved from leadership of the North Carolina Black Panther party in 1969 to city alderman in 1977, but despite the radicalism of his rhetoric, crucial issues of economic security and workplace democracy were not restored to the political agenda in Winston-Salem. Because black activists of his generation confronted the city's white elite without the organized backing of a lively, mass institution like Local 22, their challenge proved more episodic and less effective than that of the previous generation. . . .

E. P. Thompson once asserted that most social movements have a life cycle of about six years. And unless they make a decisive political impact in that time, that "window of opportunity," they will have little effect on the larger political structures they hope to transform. For the black freedom struggle the mid-1940s offered such a

time of opportunity, when a high-wage, high-employment economy, rapid unionization, and a pervasive federal presence gave the black working class remarkable self-
confidence, which established the framework for the growth of an autonomous
labor-oriented civil rights movement. The narrowing of public discourse in the early
Cold War era contributed largely to the defeat and diffusion of that movement. The
rise of anticommunism shattered the Popular Front coalition on civil rights, while
the retreat and containment of the union movement deprived black activists of the
political and social space necessary to carry on an independent struggle.

The disintegration of the black movement in the late 1940s ensured that when
the civil rights struggle of the 1960s emerged it would have a different social character and an alternative political agenda, which eventually proved inadequate to
the immense social problems that lay before it. Like the movement of the 1940s,
the protests of the 1960s mobilized a black community that was overwhelmingly
working-class. However, the key institutions of the new movement were not the
trade unions, but the black church and independent protest organizations. Its community orientation and stirring championship of democratic values gave the modern
civil rights movement a transcendent moral power that enabled a handful of organizers from groups like the Student Nonviolent Coordinating Committee, SCLC, and
CORE to mobilize tens of thousands of Americans in a series of dramatic and crucial
struggles. Yet even as this Second Reconstruction abolished legal segregation and
discrimination, many movement activists including Martin Luther King, Jr., recognized the limits of their accomplishment. After 1965 they sought to raise issues of
economic equality and working-class empowerment to the moral high ground earlier
occupied by the assault against de jure segregation. In retrospect, we can see how
greatly they were handicapped by their inability to seize the opportunities a very
different sort of civil rights movement found and lost twenty years before.

## Racialized Bodies on the Homefront

### EILEEN BORIS

*There were a lot of women workers on board, mostly white. Whenever I passed the*
*white women looked at me, some curiously, some coyly, some with open hostility.*
*Some just stared with blank hard eyes. Few ever moved aside to let me pass. . . .*
*Now and then some of the young white women gave me an opening to make a pass,*
*but I'd never made one: at first because the coloured workers seemed as intent on*
*protecting the white women from the coloured men as the white men were, probably*
*because they wanted to prove to the white folks they could work with white women*
*without trying to make them.*

—BOB JONES IN CHESTER HIMES, *IF HE HOLLERS LET HIM GO,* 1945

Racialized bodies dominate Chester Himes' homefront novel of social rage just as
they provided a terrain of struggle in the wartime industry that forms its setting. Obsessed with manhood and color, protaganist Bob Jones chafes under cultural notions

"'You Wouldn't Want One of 'Em Dancing with Your Wife': Racialized Bodies on the Job in World
War II," by Eileen Boris, *American Quarterly,* Vol. 50, no. 1 (March 1998): 77–98. Copyright © 1998
American Studies Association.

of gender and race. This angry young African American migrant from Cleveland is a leaderman at a Los Angeles shipyard. Yet whites constantly undermine his authority as a supervisor. A white woman secretary keeps his blueprints locked away. A white Georgian foreman refuses to release a white woman tacker to Jones's all-black crew. Madge, "a peroxide blonde with a large-featured, overly made-up face" from Texas, taunts him through her whiteness, sure that white men "had to protect her from black rapists." Her insulting refusal to work for Jones (she calls him "nigger") provokes him to curse her ("screw you then, you cracker bitch!), leading to his demotion.

At the novel's climax, Madge locks Jones into a cabin berth, crying "rape" when inspectors discover them. Though rejecting the sexual overtures of this southern temptress, he becomes ensnarled anyway in the rape-lynching complex that has colonized his mind as well as the imagination of white co-workers. The novel ends when Madge withdraws her charge of rape—"a patriotic gesture comparable only to the heroism of men in battle," the shipyard President explains, that would avoid the racial conflict ever threatening to disrupt industrial output. Jones is forced to enter the army, a no-choice plea bargain for possessing a concealed gun.

Jones views himself trapped by forces of whiteness blocking his dream "to be accepted as a man—without ambition, without distinction, either of race, creed, or colour . . . without any other identifying characteristics but weight, height, and gender." This was the promise of federal employment policy during the war: an executive order against discrimination passionately embraced by African Americans. The President's Committee on Fair Employment Practice (FEPC) omitted sex as a covered category, sharing the mode of thought expressed by Jones whose listing of acceptable "identifying characteristics" naturalizes gender even as he questions the significance of racial difference. In keeping with the cultural pluralism of American social science, Jones holds contradictory positions. On the one hand, race is nothing but biology, so unimportant when it comes to the rights of citizenship. On the other hand, African Americans possess a culture and history that generates both racial pride and victimization. So race matters most of all.

Caught in fantasies of revenge, marking his manhood through violence, Jones vacillates over accepting the integrationist accommodation proposed by his light-skinned and "better class" social worker girlfriend. He feels betrayed by the American creed of "liberty and justice and equality," the set of national ideals upon which A. Philip Randolph based black demands for defense jobs and the end of the Jim Crow army. . . . Blackness negates Jones's masculinity, challenged on the highways and in the ship's hole, symbolized by the workman's overalls and hardhat that "made me feel rugged, bigger than the average citizen, stronger than a white-collar worker—stronger even than an executive." Difference mocks African American male claims to citizenship—claims that Himes associates with the masculine itself.

*If He Hollers Let Him Go* echoes the shopfloor and sidewalk conflict experienced by working people in the crowded production centers of the second World War. It dramatizes the psychological hurt among African American men that fatter wartime paychecks failed to [assuage]. "Fair" employment—that is, without discrimination—did not necessarily bring dignity. It was not the same as "equal" employment—similar job placements—in a society still burdened by legalized segregation and cultural constructions that differentiated people by their race *and* gender. Racialized understandings of manhood and womanhood—of the black male rapist, the pure white female, and the uncleanly black woman—provided an arena for the wartime debate over fair employment, one connected to larger structures of power and authority.

Central to this story are the ways that the specter of social equality haunted the federal government's wartime mobilization. With the end of reconstruction and the reimposition of white rule in the former Confederacy, sexualized language served as a powerful means to sustain white supremacy. Defenders of lynching deployed it, justifying mob violence in defense of white female purity. Southern historians have noted, as Nell Irvin Painter contends, that "sex was the whip that white supremacists used to reinforce white solidarity." This discourse relied upon fears of despoliation and tarnishment; its talk of miscegenation suggested that whites and blacks belonged to different species. Too often, white women themselves embraced their role as signifiers of purity, posing actual as well as symbolic obstacles to interracial action at the ballot box and on the job. Often presented through the question, "Would you want your daughter to marry a 'Negro?'" social equality for its distractors represented the pollution of white bodies. It meant a lessening of white male ability to control access to women, especially their own, a control that justified disenfranchisement and segregation.

With the migration of southerners of both races out of the region, this system of knowing reinforced racial hierarchies. . . . Wartime patriotism offered an avenue for eastern and southern European ethnics to become American; like the Irish before them, part of that process involved becoming white and differentiating themselves from African Americans. Moreover, the politics of total war in the 1940s, which gave untold powers to the federal government, threatened racial separation and states' rights, setting the stage for political assaults against fair employment in terms of the bodily intimacy dreaded by segments of white America. Rhetorical assaults became physical. Shipyard diarist Katherine Archibald described this attitude on the part of white workers: "[T]he ancient fear of despoliation of women of the privileged race by men of inferior blood, which has played so large a part in the establishment and elaboration of caste systems in all societies, prevailed."

The field investigations and complaints of discrimination to the FEPC during the war, like Archibald's participant enthology and Himes's imaginative novel, serve as lenses into the complex dynamics of race and gender within class society. . . . Those who defended segregation and dreaded social equality . . . associated sexuality, bodies, and race. Southern newspapers responded to FEPC hearings with charges that the goal was "to see that Negroes are put in all sorts of positions where they, as white-collar workers, may associate with white men and women who work in similar capacities, and thus to break down social barriers." Southern politicians, like Birmingham's Eugene "Bull" Connor, warned President Roosevelt that "any effort now by any person connected with the federal government officially, or socially to destroy segregation and bring about amalgamation of the races will hinder the Southland in its war efforts." . . .

During World War II, African Americans sought equality of treatment, the end of legal segregation and unequal facilities, an integrated army, and better paying defense jobs. But they struggled to be heard against a discourse that displaced demands for economic equity into openings for sexual intimacy. This article deviates from the dominant economistic reading of industrial conflict during the second

World War by focusing on what cultural theorist Robyn Wiegman has called "the transformation of the economic into the sexual" through analysis of confrontations sparked by bodily closeness on shopfloors, streetcars, and other public spaces. Some of these involved white women who refused to share toilet and dressing facilities with black ones; some were rank and file workers defying their unions; employer strategies to divide the laboring force encouraged others. In doing so, it begins to study white resistance to the African American quest for equality by moving from the workplace through the neighborhood to confront "fears of sexual mixing and its consequences."

Though bound by the rules of segregation, blacks and whites in the South had lived in closer proximity than elsewhere in the nation. Many white Northerners and Westerners had little contact with African Americans. Wartime population shifts and labor needs pierced such boundaries and generated interaction, especially in such expanded production centers as Los Angeles, California's East Bay, and Detroit, precisely at a time when accelerated entrance of white women into factories also challenged women's and men's proper places. Still, as subordinate workers, wives, canteen hostesses, and other objects of the male gaze, white and black women often stood as bodies through which black as well as white men constructed their own masculinity. . . .

## The President's Committee on Fair Employment Practice

Through Executive Order 8802, President Franklin D. Roosevelt created the FEPC in June 1941 to end discrimination in employment related to the war effort. FEPC targeted African Americans and other racial minorities, Jews and other religious minorities, and non-citizens or those not of United States nationality. However, African Americans filed more than 90 percent of the complaints. FEPC did not include women as a separate category, only as members of other, covered groups. . . .

FEPC was a weak agency; it worked by complaint only and could not impose sanctions or file its own court cases. It held public and private hearings, attempting to jawbone adherence to the Presidential order. It often failed to upgrade the jobs of black workers or even get them hired. But its dedicated biracial staff of administrators and field officers tirelessly investigated business, unions, the military, and government, including the Federal Employment Service, creatively bring recalcitrants to the attention of agencies that had enforcement teeth. Thus the Atlanta *Journal* complained in 1944, "So adroit are its maneuvers that it is usually out of the picture when any trouble it has started is full-blown. It calls on other governmental agencies to enforce its decrees and whip dissenters in line." In actuality, the WMC [War Manpower Commission] and other agencies usually placed a higher priority on wartime efficiency over nondiscrimination, fearing the conseqences of white walkouts in protest over black hires. Labor shortages, rather than the FEPC, probably accounted for the tripling of the number of African Americans in war work to 8 percent of the entire workforce. FEPC was less a powerful remedy than a symbolic threat to the racial structure of employment. For it legitimized black demands and emboldened protest.

Throughout its lifetime (1941–1946), the FEPC faced challenges from opponents. Southern Democrats filibustered its appropriations and blocked legislation to create a permanent agency; conservative northern Republicans agreed that it undermined "freedom of contract," linking government regulation of industry with government interference with personal association. A Mississippi congressman expressed this connection when he declared: "the relation between the employer and the employee is intimate"; one from Louisiana spoke of forcing "employers of the Nation, particularly in the South, to intermix the Negro along with his white employees."

These congressmen fought against the agency as an attempt to "saddle social equality upon Dixie," as the African American *Pittsburgh Courier* described Southern white opinion. Senator Richard Russell (D-Georgia) in 1946 attacked FEPC as a "measure . . . which would have a tendency to bring about social equality and intermingling and amalgamation of the races." A Texas Democratic candidate for Congress condemned the agency for having 60 percent of its personnel as "negroes. Some of the black executives have white women for secretaries," he charged. Others lambasted FEPC for making white and black women use the same bathrooms. Georgia Governor Eugene Talmadge charged "Negroes of the North, finding a lot of craven politicians amenable to their desires, have succeeded in creating a condition under which white and colored persons are mixed indiscriminately in various departments at Washington." FEPC was unsettling the natural order of things, further abetting a social liberalism symbolized by First Lady Eleanor Roosevelt's support for civil rights.

This defensiveness against "social equality" suggests how wartime conditions threatened the racialized gendered regime, in part by undermining the southern system of cheap labor. Black migration to war production centers cut the supply of field workers, but so too did money sent home from defense work and the military. Black women became less dependent on field work just as the greater options of black men led them to demand more control over tenancy. Labor shortages meant that white farm wives took to the fields during harvest time. Black women also left domestic service, which led to rumors of "Eleanor Clubs" or "Disappointment Clubs" with the "motto 'A white woman in every kitchen by Christmas.'" Such clubs would allow members to 'get even' with their former white employers for past grievances."

During a time when the behavior of African American soldiers—their courage in combat and their dating of British, Australian, and other "white" women—further upset inherited expectations, the homefront also offered possibilities for disruption and protest, spaces to contest sexualized representations of African Americans and challenge the use of social equality as a barrier to economic equality. The "Double Victory" campaign, after all, connected battlefront and homefront, defeat of the Nazis with victory against Jim Crow.

### The Homefront as a Site of Intimacy

Men as well as women had their bodies racialized in the contest over fair employment during World War II. Congressional investigation of the "checkerboarding" of the merchant marine, or sending to sea racially mixed crews, illuminates how the discourse of social equality justified job discrimination. In some workplaces, like mines, black and white men labored beside each other, but ships were particular places of intimacy, with homosocial—if not homoerotic—undertones. Secretary of the Navy Frank Knox, who refused to use black men for anything other than mess crews, rejected the idea that "Negro and white sailors should be compelled to live together." The Seafarers' International Union admitted black members, but complained to a special investigative committee under the conservative Virginia Democrat Howard W. Smith that the War Shipping Administration (WSA) deliberately sent out black and white men for the same ships. This bypassed the union's "rotary hiring hall system," which union spokesmen called, "fair and equitable in every way, which enables whites to share ships' quarters with whites and Negroes with Negroes." The union claimed equal wages, working conditions, and membership rights for African Americans, but black workers suffered from occupational segregation by race and held lesser paying jobs in the Steward's Department. Because their task was to cook and serve food, they did not eat with the rest of the crew.

Yet the union charged the WSA with

> misrepresenting or concealing the facts when it recruits boys from American homes and then tries to compel them to depart abruptly from old-time family traditions to share eating and sleeping quarters on American ships with members of another race, particularly when such a condition is not at all necessary and is disruptive of rather than helpful to the war effort.

Or as one congressional opponent of the FEPC put it, "human nature" meant that white men "have set ideas as to how they want to sleep or how they want to live. They haven't any prejudice against the colored men." In this tale, not only did racial separation (in the form of separate but equal) aid the war by maintaining full efficiency, but "family," "tradition," and "American" stood apart from men of African descent. Economic power, as well as social authority, was at stake.

All parties to the seafarers' dispute felt, as another congressman explained, "the colored men ought to have the right to work just like the white man." Defenders of the union claimed equality of opportunity, while asserting that the circumstances of shiplife determined which men went to which ship. Administration officials clashed with congressmen over this interpretation of "equality." One Assistant Deputy Administrator of the WSA dodged inquiries over whether the FEPC executive orders "require[d] in any way the social intermingling of different races" by arguing that FEPC sought "full manpower utilization," but felt unable to answer if there was "any emphasis at all . . . on social equality." However, the Atlantic Coast Regional Representative admitted that "the order does not require" social intermingling, though "full utilization of manpower" included "employment" which took place "aboard ship" as well as "ashore" and "in the Government." Men who work on ships lived on them at the same time. Congressional inquisitors pushed him to admit that such employment would lead to social equality. In this case, equal opportunity and "social intermingling" merged into each other. But Representative Claire Hoffman (R-Mich.) was unsatisfied that social equality was anything but another name for intermarriage. A hearing about men on ship degenerated into questions about whether men and women of different races could choose to marry each other. The (il)logic became: men on ships lead to miscegenation.

Rumors of social equality countered African American assertiveness. During the Spring of 1944 in Dallas, "a large group of Negroes," whose votes had ushered in the Congress of Industrial Organization (CIO) at their plant, became dissatisfied with both the union contract and the pace of War Labor Board (WLB) deliberations over an equal pay complaint. They went to the WLB offices, "acting in their own behalf"—"an extraordinary occurrence" in Texas, according to the FEPC regional director. They protested in a context in which "rumors, the dissemination of leaflets, news articles tending to rile up the people" poisoned relations between white and black workers. Employees heard "that a Negro worker passed a note to a white woman worker in which he asked her to meet him after work." White workers could read the leaflet, "Do You Want Your Daughter to Marry a Negro?" which had "been spot dropped all over Texas." The FEPC sought to defuse tensions prior to the July Democratic National Convention, but the presence of black men and white women at the same workplaces offered kindling to those who desired to enflame white racial interests in the face of black economic demands.

Senator Theodore Bilbo (D-Miss.) was such a flame thrower. A segregationist . . . , Bilbo fumed against blacks "force[ing] the white employees in the departments in Washington to eat with them and use the same toilet facilities." "The most disgusting thing in Washington life," he charged, "is to see nice sweet girls from North Dakota being forced to use the same stools and toilets used by the Negroes who come from the slums of Washington, a large percentage of them affected by Negro diseases." The FEPC, he argued,

> is not intended to do away with discrimination. It is a smooth, deliberate plan, and scheme to integrate the Negro race into the life of the American laboring world. It is one step in the great drive for social equality, social commingling, social intermingling, intermarriage—interbreeding, if you please!

. . . Fear of bodily closeness was real. . . . Rumors of black " 'bumpers' and 'pushers' clubs" circulated among whites in Detroit and other cities, some spread by "an upper-middle class white group." A Los Angeles shipfitter recorded a conversation with his AFL representative who justified a "Negro Auxiliary" by reminding him, "Our unions give social affairs. You wouldn't want one of 'em dancing with your wife, would you." . . .

From management's perspective, forced integration might disrupt shopfloor routines. From that of labor militants, lack of integration reinforced divisions within the union that would curtail a solidarity which might be needed against the company. By separating themselves socially, workers undermined the equality promised by the CIO and the quest for a more democratic America. Though the CIO tried to promote a "culture of unity" through dances and other social events, . . . rank and file unionists did not necessarily include African Americans in that culture. Black social scientists St. Clair Drake and Horace R. Cayton discovered resistance even in the late 1930s to "social extensions of economic contact." . . .

"Race mixing," when it involved black men and white women, could lead to violence. . . . Radio reports that "a Negro had attempted to rape a white girl on a bus, and had been caught and beaten up by some white men" fanned the Detroit race riot on 20 June 1943. . . . For their part, African Americans had heard "that some white man—a Southerner, of course—had thrown a negro woman and her baby off the Belle Isle bridge." . . . A fight started on a bus traveling from the Belle Island Park to Detroit that was crowded "with sailors, unescorted white girls (mostly factory workers on a holiday) and young negro men." According to a federal government report, racial overcrowding and female sexuality touched off the melee:

> One of the girls, the story goes, was a bit high; all were singing. Finally the tipsy girl jumped up and yelled, "I want to dance." A Negro boy sitting nearby jumped up, grabbed her, and started to dance with her, provoking no objection from the girl. This incensed the sailors. They made the driver stop the bus, and, according to the story, pulled the Negro out and heaved him over the bridge railing into the water, about one hundred feet below.

. . . [W]hite servicemen sought to defend their masculinity, challenged in their minds by black men's new public assertiveness. Whites complained about black servicemen "roaming Chicago streets every weekend with no place to go at night to sleep," hanging out in parks, on the streets, and in taverns. Such charges ignored discrimination access to off-base facilities and instead expressed the subtext of the menacing black man as a rationale for blaming such men for their temporary homelessness. Senator James Eastland (D-Miss.) drew such a picture during a 1945 filibuster against the FEPC when he charged [that] black soldiers . . . "disgrac[ed] the flag of their country" by raping French women.

Black men also sought to protect their women against abuse by white men. Military police had to join civil officers "to disperse a crowd . . . when city police-men tried to arrest a negro woman" in Savannah near the railroad station. Following a strike over the upgrading of black male workers at a General Motors engine plant outside of Indianapolis, "Zoot Suit" youth rescued a black woman from plain-clothes policemen who were trying to pick her up as a prostitute. This incident sparked an evening of street skirmishes between black men, white male bystanders, and white policemen. In other cities Zoot Suiters sought to shield their women against "predatory" white men. Their countercultural style defied the notion of wartime sacrifice for a white man's war—their clothes required more cloth than rationing allowed. They asserted an independent manhood.

Black men suffered from what historian George Lipsitz has called "the con-nections between masculine self-affirmation, racial identities, and control over women." Author Chester Himes had failed to find a good job, but his wife was codirector of USO activities. He remembered:

> It hurt me for my wife to have a better job than I did and be respected and included by her white co-workers, besides rubbing elbows with many well-to-do blacks of the Los Angeles middle class who wouldn't touch me with a ten-foot pole. That was the begin-ning of the dissolution of our marriage. I found that I was no longer a husband to my wife; I was her pimp. She didn't mind, and that hurt all the more.

Like his protagonist Bob Jones, Himes experienced "the fear of being unable to support and protect his wife in a world where white men could do both." Wanting "to be the 'man' in bed that he could not be in a war plant," he felt "castrated" by the pressure.

These fears and apprehensions occurred against a backdrop of sexual harrass-ment and brutality toward African American women that fully matched the vile rhetoric of Southern Democratic Congressmen. The *Pittsburgh Courier* noted the hypocrisy of Bilbo's call for racial purity when respectable black women in Wash-ington, D.C., "schoolteachers, professionals, war-widows, co-eds . . . are so molested by white men (to whom all colored women are simply objects of prey) that they cannot walk a single block . . . without being invited to 'come go for a nice ride.'" A serviceman's wife had to leave a better paying job at the Pennsylvania Railway after refusing the advances of the white foreman. White men raped black school-girls and soldiers' wives; they beat and sometimes killed black women. But they never received punishment equal to the long prison sentences and occasional lynching that black men still faced for even calling a white woman on a phone. These white assailants included policemen and landlords intent on enforcing southern racial and social hierarchies. A partial exception to the degrading treat-ment of black women came with the response to the Abbeville, Alabama kidnap and rape of Recy Taylor, "22-year-old mother and wife of a U.S. soldier." After northern radicals and southern liberals created a *cause celebre,* the governor promised "to press charges." The rhetorical protection of white women continued to mask attacks on black women into the 1940s. But such incidents also suggest that wartime rhetoric and economic change encouraged black women to challenge the place set aside for them in the white South.

## Shopfloor Confrontations

Southern white males certainly defined physical proximity between white women and black men as objectionable. At a Birmingham, Alabama sheet metal mill, white union members struck for a day because "the clocking lines for Negroes and whites had been placed too close together." As the committeeman for the steel-workers union noted, black men "had no business in the line with the white ladies and wished they would segregate them." Although black workers had other things on their minds—"to get out and take a bath and go home"—than sharing a line with "ladies" (the customary appellation for white women), "Negro Sam" report-edly told him, "if one stubbed his toe and happened to brush against a white woman they could not make her or any one believe it was not done on purpose." White men defended white womanhood, their control of the shopfloor, and their hold on skilled jobs. The company responded by segregating facilities.

White women themselves objected to working with both black men and women. According to the vice-president of the Mobile-based Alabama Dry Dock and Shipbuilding Company, white "young bucks and girls" attacked black men up-graded to welding jobs on 24 May 1943. The company had hired white women over black men and women after they had "scraped the bottom of the barrel as far as [white] men are concerned." Such women would come to constitute 11.6 percent of the workforce, numbering over 3,000. They became socialized into aspects of the work culture of the shipyards. So perhaps it was not surprising that "Women Joined Men in Clubbing and Stoning Negro Ship Workers," reported the liberal New York daily *PM.* They used "bricks and iron bars." "A white lady," one black man noted, "hit me over the head with a broom handle." In surveying the incident, a national official of the Marine and Shipbuilding Workers of America suggested that white women had started the violence by "belabor[ing] colored women with sticks and stones and *then* white men began to beat colored male workers." Among the precipitating rumors was one that "a Negro welder had killed a white woman the night before." The *Mobile Register* blamed "indiscreet mingling of white and negro workers." What appeared as economic conflict expressed fears of proximity and took violent physical form. . . .

The toilet and bathroom, places for the most private bodily functions, became sites of conflict; their integration starkly symbolized social equality. Atlanta segregationists attempted to block the opening of a regional office of the FEPC in November 1943 by refusing office space to the FEPC's biracial staff, who would not only interview black plaintiffs there but also share the building's toilets with other federal agencies. After pressure from regional congressmen failed and the office opened, newspaper and political harrassment persisted. Cries of " 'brazen negress' and 'carpetbaggers' " greeted the hiring of an African American woman secretary. Talmadge fanned white opinion when he spoke of the introduction of "a flat-nosed mulatto" and reported, "the white girls were stunned at first." After appealing to his successor, Governor Ellis Arnall, to stop a travesty, Talmadge claimed that "the white woman painted a large sign on the rest room door that said 'White Only,' but this 'BRAZEN LITTLE NEGRO' ignored it." A new toilet built for FEPC black employees ended the commotion. A former FEPC official told historian Merl Reed that the Regional Director "became so exasperated that he sent to Eleanor Roosevelt memoranda drafted on toilet paper."

Concepts of purity that distinguished white women from African Americans lay behind discriminatory acts. White workers based moral judgments on physical appearance; as one woman admitted, "I always thought colored people were not clean and smelled bad and weren't as good as white people." Manuals for managers attempted to counter notions fanned by racist southern politicians. . . . A New York State handbook reminded managers that "the possibility of acquiring a venereal disease by contact with a toilet is exceeding remote." Such manuals also pointed out that black women and men not only cleaned public and private toilets but care for children, prepare food, and "handle much of the linen and make up the beds of many white Americans." A domestic's touch could be ignored in ways that bodily closeness at the job apparently could not; private service work reinforced racialized gender hierarchies in ways that public intimacy undermined them.

Despite the attempt by some managers to alleviate fears, "the cleanliness taboo" generated resistance to using the same toilet, shower, and locker room facilities, especially on the part of white women. Sometimes these resisters merely threatened to leave work to see if they could push management to remove black women, but "had no intention of really going through with their threat because they knew it might jeopardize their own jobs," as happened at a Buffalo, New York aircraft factory. Other times they shut down production. Fifteen hundred United Automobile Union members walked out in the spring of 1944 when Chevrolet Motors refused "to rehire seven woman workers who had balked at working alongside four Negro women," who presumably would use the same toilets. When more than half the labor force of the U.S. Rubber Company in Detroit struck a few months before, they demanded that black women machinists "be transferred" or the company provide separate toilets for them. In contrast, lack of racial friction at Pullman's railroad operations may have derived from company adherence to segregated toilets and related facilities.

The hearing before the WLB over the December 1943 strike at the Baltimore Western Electric plant illuminates the racialized gendered subtext behind contests over employment discrimination. Toilet integration was central to this job action. Though only 200 out of 6,000 eligible employees participated in the strike vote, the presence of picket lines dropped attendance to about 30 percent of the workforce, with almost all black workers crossing the lines. The U.S. army took over this plant deemed vital to the war effort.

Western Electric's Superintendent of Industrial Relations emphasized economic reasons for integrated facilities—the need to maintain a flexible workforce that could be transferred between buildings. The lawyer for the Employees Association argued that shared toilets undermined production goals since white workers refused to accept them. He suggested that separate facilities "could be established without violating the Executive Order, and . . . the union would take action in behalf of Negroes if the company failed to set up facilities for them which would be equal to those established for whites." But later he justified the majority's "astounding" willingness to interrupt production with the stereotyped scare: "It goes without saying that among the colored race venereal disease is greater than among whites."

Eugene Barnes, an African American member of the Employees Association, placed the conflict in perspective when he argued that the union—run by officers who called only one meeting a year—merely existed to maintain the power of its leaders. The Association "had stimulated the petition among the workers and had told many persons that they were voting for separate facilities and not for a strike." The goal was "to keep the colored employee out of their department altogether." With vital war production undermined, the company built locker units with attached washrooms and toilets at opposite sides of the building, assigning blacks to one unit and whites to another even though no designating racial signs limited use of toilets. The company would give tests for venereal disease, but the cafeteria would remain integrated. An FEPC investigator concluded that black employees "felt rather bitter about the treatment which they received from the white employees." The FEPC argued, "such installing of segregated duplicate facilities *cannot* but lead to discriminatory employment practices and would be in violation of [the] Executive Order." Members of the African American Non-Partisan Committee at the plant "privately" opposed the establishment of the separate facilities in the spring of 1944. But faced with the prospect of a strike when the army left, the company succumbed to white community norms and ignored the FEPC finding that separate was discriminatory.

The experience of discrimination was gendered. Previously crowded into service and agricultural labor and thus thought of as a nonindustrial workforce, African American women labored against stereotypical images of their bodies, against representations as Mammy or Sapphire. Not only did they receive "the left-over and undesirable jobs in war industries," but they confronted barriers of "physical types . . . and intangibles not imposed on white female workers." Personnel managers drew upon the picture of the fat black woman to reject applicants. As one such woman recalled, "one time they say we was too old and the next time we were too fat. I only weight 165—5 feet 3 inch—46 years and still these [white] women weight 200 pound and some much older then 50 years." African American women had to engage in additional maintenance or survival labor, a form of self and community care work, to reproduce themselves as neater, pleasanter, more cooperative than their white counterparts, to make whites feel more comfortable around them.

They had to dress well and act respectable in public, whether engaging in the activities of everyday life or protesting discrimination.

Regarded as different, black and white women saw each other as racialized bodies, not merely gendered ones, and so would develop insults that impugned the womanhood of the other. One group of black women at General Electric refused to work after a white woman inspector allegedly "called a colored woman worker either 'Black Son of a Bitch' or 'Black Heifer.'" The army feared "possible violence." At the Fisk Tire and Rubber Company, Chicopee Falls, Massachusetts, a white woman "alleged that the colored girl was in a state of pregnancy. The girl happens to be unmarried," the FEPC regional director reported, "and the rumor spread like wildfire through the shop. It affected the girl so badly that she went to her doctor and procured a certificate stating that she was not in a state of pregnancy." Given feelings of racial superiority, that white women rejected black women having any authority over them hardly surprises. At a California draft board, a white man was promoted supervisor rather than a black woman because white women rejected the notion of "a Negro [telling] white people what to do." The belief that women could not get along with each other—that "we needed a man to keep peace and harmony between the girls"—reflected the reality of some workplaces and offered an excuse for discrimination in others. Men continued to predominate as supervisors, with gender-mixed black crews coming under male leadership.

### The Specter of Social Equality

Worker responses to wartime integration occured in a political context in which demagogic politicians vilified the FEPC. Working people worried about social equality. "As the friendships became more intimate the white employee speculated as to how friendly he might become with a Negro employee without admitting him to 'social equality,'" participant observer Bernice Reed noted of a West coast aircraft factory. "A white female employee" wondered, "'If I go to X's house to visit his wife and babies will that be socializing? I wouldn't call that socializing, would you, just to go by to see his babies?'" Most interracial friendships stopped at the plant gate, but Reed concluded that "management accommodated to integration of Negro employees less readily than non-supervisory employees."

The promise of social equality—confused by its opponents with nondiscrimination in the workplace—challenged the larger social and political hierarchies that gripped the nation. Shopfloor integration—where black and white, male and female bodies labored in close proximity—stood as the material and symbolic embodiment of social equality. In seeking to exclude African Americans from war jobs, white workers reacted to what they perceived to be more than an economic threat. Women as well as men recoiled from "black skin." Fear of the other, of different bodies, encapsulated wartime tensions, disruptions, and insecurities. This is not to argue that all or most white workers responded to racial pornography; racial demagogues had no monopoly on image painting. Alternative signifiers certainly existed and trade union leadership, from the CIO and especially from its left-led unions, at times provided a counterpoint to both local union racism and the fear of social equality.

Throughout the Jim Crow era, white supremacists had embodied opposition to social, political, and economic equality in the menacing figure of the black male rapist and the demeaning image of the uncleanly black woman. What was new during WWII was an official ideology of pluralist inclusion that facilitated the transformation of the foreign born into the American but also delegitimated racism in the face of Nazism. The federal government, however tentative, became involved in combating workplace discrimination among employers as well as unions. State action further encouraged the aspirations of African Americans who demanded fair treatment from a country for which their men were dying. Black workers claimed the rights of citizenship on the job as well as in the community. They believed in fairness, and asked to be "treated as an American and not as a Negro," to be just a man, as Bob Jones dreamed.

## ✤ F U R T H E R     R E A D I N G

Anderson, Karen. *Wartime Women: Sex Roles, Family Relations and the Status of Women in World War II* (1981).

Atleson, James. *Labor and the Wartime State: Labor Relations and the Law During World War II* (1998).

Bates, Beth Tompkins. *Pullman Porters and the Rise of Protest Politics in Black America, 1925–1945* (2001).

Bloom, Jack. *Class, Race and the Civil Rights Movement* (1987).

Daniel, Cletus. *Chicano Workers and the Politics of Fairness* (1991).

Gabin, Nancy. *Feminism in the Labor Movement: Women and the United Auto Workers, 1935–1975* (1990).

Gamboa, Erasmo. *Mexican Labor and World War II* (1990).

Garfinkel, Herbert. *When Negroes March: The March on Washington Movement in the Organizational Politics of FEPC* (1959).

Gould, William. *Black Workers in White Unions* (1977).

Griffith, Barbara. *The Crisis of American Labor: Operation Dixie and the Defeat of the CIO* (1988).

Gross, James A. *The Making of the NLRB: A Study in Economics, Politics, and Law* (1974).

———, *The Reshaping of the National Labor Relations Board: Nation Labor Policy in Transition, 1937–1947* (1981).

Harris, Howell. *The Right to Manage: Industrial Relations Policies of American Business in the 1940s* (1982).

Harris, William. *The Harder We Run: Black Workers Since the Civil War* (1982).

Helper, Allison L. *Women in Labor: Mothers, Medicine, and Occupational Health in the United States, 1890–1980* (2000).

Hill, Herbert. *Black Labor and the American Legal System: Race, Work and the Law* (1985).

Honey, Maureen. *Creating Rosie the Riveter: Class, Gender and Propaganda During World War II* (1984).

———, *Bitter Fruit: African American Women in World War II* (1999).

Honey, Michael. *Southern Labor and Black Civil Rights: Organizing Memphis Workers* (1993).

Jacobson, Julius, ed. *The Negro in the American Labor Movement* (1969).

Johnson, Marilyn S. *The Second Gold Rush: Oakland and the East Bay in World War II* (1993).

Kelley, Robin. *Race Rebels: Culture, Politics, and the Black Working Class* (1996).

Kersten, Andrew Edmund. *Race, Jobs, and the War: The FEPC in the Midwest, 1941–46* (2000).

Kesselman, Amy. *Fleeting Opportunities: Women Shipyard Workers in Portland and Vancouver During World War II and Reconversion* (1990).

Klare, Karl E. "Judicial Deradicalization of the Wagner Act and the Origins of Modern Legal Consciousness, 1937–1941," *Minnesota Law Review* 62 (1978), 265–339.

Kryder, Daniel. *Divided Arsenal: Race and the American State During World War II* (2000).

Lemke-Santangelo, Gretchen. *Abiding Courage: African American Migrant Women and the East Bay Community* (1996).

Lichtenstein, Nelson. *Labor's War at Home: The CIO in World War II* (1982).

Lipstz, George. *Rainbow at Midnight: Labor and Culture in the 1940s* (1994).

Meier, August, and Elliott Rudwick. *Black Detroit and the Rise of the UAW* (1979).

Milkman, Ruth. *Gender at Work: The Dynamics of Job Segregation by Sex During World War II* (1987).

Moore, Shirley Ann Wilson. *To Place Our Deeds: The African American Community in Richmond, California, 1910–1963* (2000).

Nelson, Bruce. *Divided We Stand: American Workers and the Struggle for Black Equality* (2000).

Reed, Merl. *Seedtime for the Civil Rights Movement: The President's Committee on Fair Employment Practice, 1941–1946* (1991).

Skocpol, Theda. "Political Response to Capitalist Crisis: Neo-Marxist Theories of the State and the Case of the New Deal," *Politics and Society* 10 (1980), 155–201.

Stone, Katherine Van Wezel. "The Post-War Paradigm in American Labor Law," *Yale Law Journal* 90 (1981), 1509–1580.

Tolliday, Steven, and Jonathan Zeitlin, eds. *Shop Floor Bargaining and the State: Historical and Comparative Perspectives* (1985).

Tomlins, Christopher. *The State and the Unions: Labor Relations, Law, and the Organized Labor Movement in America, 1880–1960* (1985).

# CHAPTER
## 11

# Trade Unions in
# the Postwar Years

Historians once wrote as if labor history ended in about the year 1950. The giant
strikes and factional struggles of the 1930s and 1940s were over, and many companies, once bitterly antilabor, bargained routinely with the big trade unions, whose
members enjoyed the highest standard of living in the world. At this point the social
scientists and economists took the lead. These scholars recognized that change could
still take place, but they nevertheless thought of the relationship among workers,
unions, employers, and the state as a relatively fixed and harmonious system. Indeed,
by the mid-1950s, most observers thought that the union movement had grown up,
almost as an adolescent moves inevitably into adulthood. Thus, Richard Lester, an
influential industrial-relations expert of the early postwar years, entitled one of his
books As Unions Mature.

But social systems do not simply evolve; they are the product of economic change
and political struggle. And in recent years this postwar "settlement," or "labor-
capital accord," has come under sharp attack. The end of liberal, political hegemony
and the decline in the fortunes of the union movement have prompted many historians to take a closer and more critical look at the peculiarly American interclass
accommodation that jelled in the late 1940s: a decentralized system characterized by
extremely detailed, firm-centered collective-bargaining contracts; management power
at the point of production; and a labor movement whose procapitalist, antiradical
politics placed it far to the right of any other in the industrial world. Compared with
other advanced industrial countries, the United States offers its workers a low "social
wage": that is, no system of national health insurance, relatively low public pensions
and unemployment payments, and few restraints on the mobility of capital.

How was this system created? First, the inauguration of the Cold War brought
enormous pressures to bear on the labor movement, especially on the Congress of
Industrial Organizations (CIO), whose leadership concluded that the very survival
of their organizations depended on the exclusion of those unions in which the Communists still played an influential role. This purge proved a disaster, not because
Communist-influenced unionists themselves represented a workable alternative leadership for the labor movement, but because the bureaucratic ejection of these radicals
so decisively narrowed the limits of internal political debate within the unions.

Second, the rightward shift in national politics after World War II blocked the labor-liberal effort to construct an American version of the European welfare state. Unions like the auto workers and the steelworkers had to turn to the bargaining table to secure those welfare benefits—health insurance, pensions, inflation protection, and so forth—that in other countries were the nearly exclusive responsibility of the government. The system worked well for a couple of decades, but it gradually became clear that the collective-bargaining relationship could not support this burden. Not all firms were equally profitable, and not all workers were enrolled in unions that could win such generous contracts. By the 1970s, the wage scales and benefit schedules of American workers were characterized by far greater inequality than a quarter-century before.

Finally, American managers successfully restored much of their ability to control production at the shop-floor and office level. It was here, far from the bargaining tables, that shop stewards and supervisors waged a bitter and protracted conflict. During World War II, the War Labor Board (WLB) had encouraged unions and managers to collaborate in a system of routine grievance-handling that proscribed the tradition of militant self-help often characteristic of shop bargaining in the 1930s. The postwar Taft-Hartley Act advanced this process, as did the system of centralized bargaining and grievance arbitration that evolved in these same years.

What were the key events that made this process irreversible? What impact did this postwar system have on the activity and consciousness of ordinary workers?

## ⚓ D O C U M E N T S

The Congress of Industrial Organizations' 1949 indictment of the United Electrical, Radio and Machine Workers of America (UERMWA, or often just UE) is reprinted as Document 1. This 600,000-member union, the third largest in the industrial union federation, was expelled on the grounds that its leadership followed the Communist line. The charge was rendered in brutal language, and in the 1950s and afterwards, such anticommunist sentiment worked its way deeply into the consciousness of American workers. The shop floor was also an arena of struggle. In Document 2, Betty Friedan, a radical UE staffer in 1952 and later one of the founders of the modern feminist movement, puts forth her union's case for gender equality in the factories.

But shop activism soon became more difficult. In Document 3, Harry Shulman, the influential arbitrator who adjudicated disputes between the United Auto Workers and Ford Motor Company, admonishes union militants for failing to respect the authority of the company's supervision. Although Chrysler had one of the best traditions of shop-floor activism in the auto industry, even here strict adherence to the contract could become a trap, as chief shop steward B. J. Widick indicates in Document 4. In Document 5, the conventional labor-relations wisdom of the era is summed up by a 1951 *Fortune* magazine essay applauding the conservatism of the union movement and asserting the embourgeoisement of American workers.

## 1. The CIO Attacks a Communist-Led Union, 1949

We can no longer tolerate within the family of CIO the Communist Party masquerading as a labor union. The time has come when the CIO must strip the mask from these false leaders whose only purpose is to deceive and betray the workers. So long

From CIO, *Proceedings of the 11th Constitutional Convention*, Cleveland, October 31–November 4, 1949, pp. 302–303.

as the agents of the Communist Party in the labor movement enjoy the benefits of affiliation with the CIO, they will continue to carry on this betrayal under the protection of the good name of the CIO.

The false cry of these mis-leaders of labor for unity and autonomy does not deceive us.

In the name of unity they seek domination.

In the name of autonomy they seek to justify their blind and slavish willingness to act as puppets for the Soviet dictatorship and its foreign policy with all its twists and turns from the Nazi-Soviet Pact to the abuse of the veto in the UN, the Cominform attack upon the Marshall Plan, . . . the Atlantic Treaty and arms aid to free nations.

Now that they are at the end of the trail, these Communist agents cry out against "raiding and secession." What they call raiding and secession is simply a movement of workers throwing off their yoke of domination. These workers seek refuge from a gang of men who are without principle other than a debased loyalty to a foreign power.

Their masters have long decreed the creation of a new labor federation into which they hope to ensnare the labor unions they think they control. This has already taken place in many countries of the world. It will not happen in America.

When they saw that their attempt to use UERMWA to subvert the CIO was failing, they resorted to the typical Communist tactic of systematic character assassination against the National CIO, our President, Philip Murray, and all affiliated unions and officers who opposed the Cominform policy.

Their program of vilification reveals the degradation of men who have surrendered the right and lost the ability to think for themselves. It brands them as unfit to associate with decent men and women in free democratic trade unions.

The CIO is a voluntary association of free trade unions dedicated by its constitution to the protection and extension of our democratic institutions, civil liberties, and human rights. Free unions are voluntary associations of free men, held together by common loyalties and the elements of decency and honesty. We will fight with conviction and vigor against all enemies within or without the CIO who would trample or seek to destroy these sacred principles.

The certificate of affiliation of the CIO is a symbol of trust, democracy, brotherhood and loyalty in the never-ending struggle of working men and women for a better life. There is no place in the CIO for any organization whose leaders pervert its certificate of affiliation into an instrument that would betray the American workers into totalitarian bondage.

By the actions of its leadership, by their disloyalty to the CIO, and their dedication to the purposes and program of the Communist Party, contrary to the overwhelming sentiment of the rank and file membership who are loyal Americans and loyal CIO members, the leadership of the United Electrical, Radio and Machine Workers of America have rendered their union unworthy of and unqualified for this certificate of affiliation.

The UERMWA has been selected by the Communist Party as its labor base from which it can operate to betray the economic, political, and social welfare of the CIO, its affiliates and the general membership. The program of the UERMWA leadership that has gradually unfolded is but an echo of the Cominform. At the signal of the Cominform, the Communist Party threw off its mask and assumed its true role as a fifth column. Its agents in the labor unions followed the Communist Party line. The UERMWA leadership abandoned any pretense of loyalty to the CIO and its program. The record is clear that wherever the needs of the Communist Party in the Soviet Union dictated, the leadership of the UERMWA was always willing to sacrifice the needs of the workers.

## 2. Betty Friedan Argues for Trade Union Feminism, 1952

In advertisements across the land, industry glorifies the American woman—in her gleaming GE kitchen, at her Westinghouse laundromat, before her Sylvania television set. Nothing is too good for her—unless she works for GE, or Westinghouse, or Sylvania or thousands of other corporations throughout the U.S.A.

As an employee, regardless of her skill she is rated lower than common labor (male). She is assigned to jobs which, according to government studies, involve greater physical strain and skill than many jobs done by men—*but she is paid less than the underpaid sweeper, the least skilled men in the plant.* She is speeded up until she may faint at her machine, to barely earn her daily bread.

Wage discrimination against women workers exists in every industry where women are employed. It exists because it pays off in billions of dollars in extra profits for the companies. According to the 1950 census, the average wage of women in factories was $1,285 a year less than men. Multiply this by the 4,171,000 women in factories and you get the staggering total of 5.4 billion dollars. In just one year, U.S. corporations made *five billion four hundred million dollars in extra profits* from their exploitation of women. . . .

From the very beginning, the UE has challenged industry's double wage standard. For 15 years this union has fought, more than any other union and against bitter company resistance, to eliminate lower rates for women. . . .

A historic precedent for all labor was set by the UE in a National War Labor Board case against GE and Westinghouse in 1945, advancing the principle of equal pay for equal work not only where women were doing the same jobs as men but on those jobs regarded by the company as exclusively "women's jobs."

The government at that time published an exhaustive document establishing the fact that "exploitation" of women workers was taking place in both companies and recommending that it "should be ended." But it took the UE strike of 1946 and constant national, local and shop battles to make the bosses even start to narrow the rate differentials.

As a result of union activity over the years, the discriminatory lower rates for women have been raised and on some jobs equal pay has been won. But the majority of women workers in lamp, radio and television production and in packing operations, so-called light assembly, so-called simple machine and finishing operations in all plants, are still being exploited at rates of pay below common labor. They are

From *UE Fights for Women Workers,* by Betty Friedan. (New York: United Electrical, Radio and Machine Workers of America, 1952). Reprinted by permission of United Electrical, Radio and Machine Workers of America (UE).

still segregated on jobs the companies set aside as exclusively "women's jobs" so that they may continue to under-rate them as compared to jobs held by men.

Today, the UE is engaged in an intensified campaign to end the rate discrimination against women. For these rates below common labor threaten every rate in the plant. The companies, as part of their general rate-cutting offensive, are putting in new machines and processes to be run by women at rates below common labor, replacing higher-paid men. And because the women's base rate is so low, they are at the mercy of the company's speed-up drive—the women are being used as a wedge to speed up and cut rates of all workers.

That's why in collective bargaining today, a major UE demand is to abolish all rates below common labor and end the rate discrimination against women. The full weight of the union is being thrown behind this battle. . . .

## The Companies Say:

"Women are young, temporary workers. They quit after a few years to get married." "The greater turnover of women, the special services they require, make it necessary to pay them lower rates."

## The Facts Are:

The U.S. Census Bureau reveals that one out of every two women workers in American industry is at least 35 years old, and most of these older workers have held onto their present jobs for at least five years.

The National War Labor Board rejected these company arguments in World War II, laying down the principle that "intangible alleged cost factors incident to the employment of women could not legitimately be used to reduce the rates to which the women would otherwise be entitled on the basis of job content." In the GE and Westinghouse cases, the Board said "no evidence of such costs was introduced."

## The Companies Say:

"Women don't have families to support. They work for pin money." "General sociological factors justify lower pay for women."

## The Facts Are:

According to government figures, one out of every four women workers have children under 18 whom they must support. One out of every five is either widowed, divorced or separated from her husband. Many have to work because they are war widows, wives of disabled veterans, or of men now in the army. But most women work because their husband's pay is inadequate to support the family needs. *93% of all women work because they have to support themselves or their families.* . . .

## The Companies Say:

"Women aren't as strong as men. They need extra help for heavy lifting etc."

**The Facts Are:**

The over-emphasis on physical effort is a trick often used by companies to justify sex differentials. Actually, physical effort alone has little to do with the value of a job on the company's own scales, which place common labor digging ditches at the lower end and tool and die makers at the top. . . .

It's true that women can't lift as heavy weight as men, even though the companies used to demand it of them before they had the protection of a UE contract.

But the ability to lift heavy weights is actually only a very small part of the valuation placed on a job by the companies themselves. Out of 33 sample jobs rated by the National Electrical Manufacturers Association, only two were given as many as 40 points for "physical effort" out of a total possible evaluation of 500 points. Physical effort at the most constitutes less than 10% of the evaluation the company places on the job. . . .

The situation of Negro women workers today is even more shocking.

Even more than white women, Negro women have to work to live. For the discrimination that keeps Negro men at the bottom of the pay scale forces their wives to work to supplement the pitifully inadequate income of the family.

But Negro women are barred from almost all jobs except low-paying domestic service in private homes, or menial outside jobs as janitresses and scrubwomen. In the basic sections of the electrical, radio and machine industry, as in industry generally, Negro women are not employed. In lamp plants and others where Negro women have been hired as a source of cheap labor, they suffer the exploitation of all women working under discriminatory rates of pay because of their sex. . . .

UE's fair practices committees in many local unions have been fighting the discrimination against hiring of Negro women in the electrical and machine industry, and the discriminatory practices that restrict Negro women to the most menial, lowest-paid jobs. But electrical apparatus plants and other basic sections of the industry still discriminate on a large scale against Negro women, and for the most part today Negro women are not employed in the industry. Negro women workers have a real stake in the UE's fight to end rate exploitation of women in the industry, but their problems also require a special fight to lift the double bars against hiring of Negro women.

Companies make so much extra profit out of their exploitation of women that they bitterly resist attempts to make them stop it. That's why over the years they've filled men workers and even the women workers themselves with propaganda that women aren't worth as much as men in a factory—and that if women got more they'd be taking money or jobs away from the men. The last thing the companies want is for the women and men to get together to fight this profitable double standard on wages, as they are doing today in UE.

That's why the UE can't fight this battle merely over the bargaining table with the company but must conduct an educational campaign in the shop and the community to expose the bosses' propaganda and show how the exploitation of women hurts all the workers in the plant.

*It's an actual fact that lower rates for women are being used by the companies today to cut rates for men.* In Westinghouse, East Pittsburgh, the company took jobs paying $1.45 to $1.48 an hour when done by men and put women on them for $1.30 to $1.38 an hour. . . .

It's obvious that as long as these discriminatory women's rates below common labor exist, all men's rates are endangered. It's an established principle that the lowest rates in a plant are the basis upon which all other rates are constructed. Thus low rates for women hold down the entire rate structure. . . .

It works the same way with speedup. *Because women's base rates are so low, they are forced to speedup to make a living wage. The company is then able to force the men in the plant to speedup accordingly.*

Along with the battle to end discrimination against women, UE is fighting to eliminate double seniority lists wherever they exist and to win for women equal opportunities for upgrading to jobs throughout the plant.

Double seniority lists are a part of the whole pattern of discrimination the companies use to keep women segregated as "inferior" workers and confined to certain under-rated jobs so that their low pay rates can be used to keep all wages down. They are a way of keeping the workers divided and weakening the strength of the union.

The companies don't want to put women on "men's jobs"—not because they don't have the skill, but because the *segregation* of women is the only way they can maintain the discriminatory rates of pay from which they reap those extra profits. They don't want to put men on "women's jobs" in time of layoff because they'd lose the sex excuse for lower rates and they know they'd have to raise the rates for the job.

UE men and women have fought together in a number of plants recently to end these discriminatory practices in seniority and job opportunities. At Westinghouse Airbrake in Pittsburgh, UE Local 610 eliminated the dual seniority list that had existed in the plant and established in their contract that layoffs be conducted strictly in accordance with length of service, guaranteeing to both men and women the right to bump into any job in any department for which they had seniority, regardless of sex.

Recently 1500 workers were laid off. The company wanted to transfer women only into jobs that they considered "women's jobs"—which would have meant that long-service women would have been laid off. The union told the company that the only principle operating was seniority, not sex—and that women, and men, must be laid off and transferred according to seniority throughout the plant.

As a result, 150 women were transferred into jobs and departments where no women had even worked before—into the machining department, assembling departments, into turret lathe, milling machine, drill press, and grinding jobs. In one department 29 long-service women went in as grinders where never before had there been women grinders. Women replaced sweepers—and men from the machine shop who might otherwise have been laid off replaced shorter service women in the rubber department on what had formerly been "women's jobs."

The women who transferred into these machine, drill press and grinding jobs, etc. were given a breaking in period, just as the men were. The fact that women are working alongside men on these skilled jobs in a heavy industry plant like Westinghouse Airbrake shows that it can be done in any plant in the industry. . . .

One third of the UE membership are women. If all the women who work in UE plants belonged to the union, the percentage would be even higher. This single fact shows how important for the strength of the union is the fight to end discrimination against women in our plants.

The companies want to keep the women segregated, on separate lower paying jobs with separate seniority, so that they may use them as part of their plan to drive down wages and destroy union gains under their war program. In the layoffs that are resulting from the war economy and the big business runaway shop drive, they want to pit women against men, married women against single workers, older women against younger, etc.

Segregation of women is the handle of a dangerous union-smashing weapon in the hands of the company. The only way to fight it is to end the segregation, integrate the women's jobs in their proper place in the rate structure, make it possible for women to be upgraded to any job in the plant, and establish identical seniority rights based on length of service without regard to age, sex, marital status, race or color.

*Women in UE are determined to win the rates and job rights to which they are entitled.* They have been meeting in conferences all over the country to discuss urgent problems of meeting the high cost of living on paychecks even lower than other workers . . . of physical suffering caused by growing speedup in the plant, coupled with care of home and children after the full workday. They resolved to fight to end the double wage standard that enables the companies to make an extra profit on their sex while they have such a hard time getting along. And these UE women have real fighting power, as they have demonstrated on many a picket-line across the country.

*But fighting the exploitation of women is men's business too, as more and more men workers faced with rate cuts and speedup in GE, Westinghouse and other plants now realize. In every local and shop, and in the national chains, the whole weight of the union is being thrown into the fight to end the double wage standard against women.*

UE is fighting and winning this battle in many plants today, despite all company argument and prejudice. It can be won in your plant, too. For the strength of the union, it must be won.

## 3. Arbitrator Harry Shulman Upholds the Authority of Ford Supervision, 1944

As a result of the blockade of Gates 9 and 10 of the Rouge Plant, incident to the memorable disturbance in the Aircraft Building on March 15, 1944, many employees in other buildings were unable to report to work. The Spring & Upset building was undermanned by some forty per cent that day. It was desirable to keep the Supercharger job going in that building, not only because of the great need for that product in the war effort, but also to avoid the shutting down of jobs involving numerous men in other buildings which were dependent on the Supercharger job. Accordingly, Spring & Upset Supervision sought to assign men temporarily to work out of their classifications on the Supercharger and other jobs. The Company

From Ford Motor Company–UAW Opinion A-2, June 17, 1943, as quoted in Neil Chamberlain, ed., *Sourcebook on Labor* (New York, 1958), 641.

found that X, a district committeeman in this unit, had instructed employees not to work out of their classifications and that, as a result of his instructions, certain employees, though otherwise willing to accept the assignments, refused to do so, with the consequence that the needed production was not maintained—at least not until top officers of Local 600 came into the building and straightened the matter out. X was thereupon suspended pending further investigation and on March 24th he was discharged. The grievance in this case protests his discharge.

Some men apparently think that when a violation of contract seems clear, the employee may refuse to obey and thus resort to self-help rather than the grievance procedure. That is an erroneous point of view. In the first place, what appears to one party to be a clear violation may not seem so at all to the other party. Neither party can be the final judge as to whether the Contract has been violated. The determination of that issue rests in collective negotiation through the grievance procedure. But in the second place, and more important, the grievance procedure is prescribed in the Contract precisely because the parties anticipated that there would be claims of violations which would require adjustment. That procedure is prescribed for all grievances, not merely for doubtful ones. Nothing in the Contract even suggests the idea that only doubtful violations need be processed through the grievance procedure and that clear violations can be resisted through individual self-help. The only difference between a "clear" violation and a "doubtful" one is that the former makes a clear grievance and the latter a doubtful one. But both must be handled in the regular prescribed manner.

Some men apparently think also that the problems here involved are evils incident to private profit enterprise. That, too, is a totally mistaken view, as a moment's reflection will show. The problems of adjustment with which we are concerned under the Contract are problems which arise and require adjustment in the management of an enterprise under any form of economic or social organization. Any enterprise—whether it be a privately owned plant, a governmentally operated unit, a consumer's cooperative, a social club, or a trade union—any enterprise in a capitalist or a socialist economy, requires persons with authority and responsibility to keep the enterprise running. In any such enterprise there is need for equality of treatment, regularity of procedure, and adjustment of conflicting claims of individuals. In any industrial plant, whatever may be the form of the political or economic organization in which it exists, problems are bound to arise as the method of making promotions, the assignment of tasks to individuals, the choice of shifts, the maintenance of discipline, the rates of production and remuneration, and the various other matters which are handled through the grievance procedure.

These are not incidents peculiar to private enterprise. They are incidents of human organization in any form of society. On a lesser scale, similar problems exist in every family: who shall do the dishes, who shall mow the lawn, where to go on a Sunday, what movie to see, what is a reasonable spending allowance for husband or daughter, how much to pay for a new hat, and so on. The operation of the Union itself presents problems requiring adjustment quite similar to those involved in the operation of the Company—problems not only in the relations of the Union to its own employees but also in the relations between the members of the Union. Anyone familiar with seniority problems knows that the conflict of desires within the Union are quite comparable to those between the Union and the Company. And any active member of Local 600 knows that the frictions and conflicts within a large Union may be as numerous and difficult as those between the Union and the Company. Such "disputes" are not necessarily evils. They are the normal characteristics of human society which both arise from, and create the occasion for, the exercise of human intelligence. And the grievance procedure is the orderly, effective and democratic way of adjusting such disputes within the framework of the collective labor agreement. It is the substitute of civilized collective bargaining for jungle warfare.

But an industrial plant is not a debating society. Its object is production. When a controversy arises, production cannot wait for exhaustion of the grievance procedure. While that procedure is being pursued, production must go on. And someone must have the authority to direct the manner in which it is to go on until the controversy is settled. That authority is vested in Supervision. It must be vested there because the responsibility for production is also vested there; and responsibility must be accompanied by authority. It is fairly vested there because the grievance procedure is capable of adequately recompensing employees for abuse of authority by Supervision.

It should be definitely understood, then, that a committeeman has no authority to direct or advise an employee to disobey Supervision's instructions; that his authority is expressed in the duty to take the matter up with Supervision and seek an adjustment through negotiations and the grievance procedure; that an employee must obey Supervision's instructions pending the negotiations or the processing of his grievance, except only in the rare case where obedience would involve an unusual health hazard or similar sacrifice; and that disobedience by the employee, or counsel of disobedience by a committeeman, is proper cause for disciplinary penalty.

## 4. Shop Steward B. J. Widick Outlines the Frustrations of the Contract System, 1954

I have been elected Chief Steward for six consecutive years. Being a Chief Steward has a lot of advantages. Some days you do not have any grievances. It's not too exhausting if you know your way around. Under the Chrysler Contract the stewards have more freedom than under the Ford or GM contracts because the form is vague. It says in effect: "A chief steward is to work when not engaged in grievance procedure." This is given a very elastic interpretation. In the 1948 negotiations, Chrysler tried to put in the GM system with specific time limits. They were not able to do that, mainly due to our local union, so that we still have this flexible, vague wording, which means in effect that a man takes the time for union business that he can get away with, and in practice it means that most of the stewards never work. . . .

We had a very famous case on trim work. Back in Dodge in 1946 they changed from tacking trim on with hammer and tacks to using an instrument like a putty knife and sticking the trim in, and they changed the rate since it was no longer a

From George Heliker interview of B. J. Widick, March 6, 1954, Frank Hill Papers, Ford Motor Company Historical Collections, Henry Ford Museum, Dearborn, Michigan.

"trim job," which is where a man uses a hammer and tacks. They cut the men's wages ten cents an hour. That went to Umpire, who ruled that the new operation was an assembly operation—just ordinary, unskilled labor. . . .

It is difficult to get at these issues via the "strikeable issues" (clause in the UAW-Chrysler contract) because the strike is a very, very limited weapon, too costly in most cases, and has in the past, in view of all the great strikes we have had since the war, exhausted the people in the shops. It's a bluff. You can't get the rank and file to strike on those kinds of issues for a very good reason: things are too tight. The Company knows that, they know the feeling of the people as well as we do. All of this changes depending on the economic situation, how steady the work is, etc. In the first postwar years, when the Company could sell anything it could build, they were too busy making money to bother with disputes on minor grievances, or trying to take things away from us, or anything like that—we had our own way. Now, the opposite is true, and the Company knows it. It will take something like the guaranteed annual wage issue to mobilize the workers for any kind of serious struggle.

Although it is a rule of the Contract, supported by the International Union, that grievances are to be written, we never write them. I have had only one written grievance in six years. I do not believe in them. If I can't win it on the floor—this is our way of looking at it—you can't win it. The Company seldom deliberately violates the Contract. Actually, our fights are almost always around this business of the "fat" we have built up. If you are going to keep that fat, you are going to keep it only by not going into the bargaining procedure, because you can't win there.

I do not have any objection to the Umpire system in principle. I think that the Umpire should have limited authority on certain limited issues. But I think our contracts are becoming such legalistic documents as to be unworkable in terms of real, genuine labor relations; and we are getting this whole new body of law, which is just fantastic. With that and the Taft-Hartley Law we are getting a complexity which is out of this world. The average Chief Steward is incapable of bargaining seriously under our Contract, on many issues. . . . In the old days, he was the Union, he was the Contract. Everything he did was decisive in the plant. Now he is a Philadelphia lawyer. It's embarrassing. Time and again Management does things that I know it has a right to do under the Umpire system, but the men don't know it. If I explain to them that the Company has that right under four or five rulings made previously, they get sore at me. They will say, "You don't represent us; you represent the Company."

As a result—in our setup, and I'm sure its true elsewhere—the Stewards tend to become demagogues. They tend to fake on all this stuff. They write grievances when they know they shouldn't. All he does by that technique is avoid his responsibility by passing it on to the Shop Committeeman. . . . Instead of an education in the actual meaning of the Contract and the establishing of a decent relationship in the shop, you get the art of buck-passing to the nth degree, and that's really why we have all this trouble in the plants. The Stewards, instead of being real leaders, tend to become more and more political fakers, and that's how they win elections.

[*Like so many other long-time union radicals, chief shop steward B. J. Widick eventually left the shops. After 1960 he taught, wrote, and lectured on union and industrial relations subjects.*]

## 5. *Fortune* Magazine Applauds the U.S.
## Labor Movement, 1951

The transformation of American capitalism has been due in large part . . . to the rising power of labor, which has forced a revision of capitalist thinking and capitalist practices. Yet the fact that this change has been no more than a *transformation,* the fact that capitalism in America has not been overthrown or seriously damaged by the power of the workers, is of equal importance to a real understanding of America. And this fact, which can scarcely be duplicated anywhere in the world, can be accounted for only by reference to the U.S. labor movement itself.

What utterly baffles the European intellectual concerning the American labor movement is its stubborn refusal to behave in accordance with the so-called "laws of history." American labor has exhibited none of the ideological uniformity that characterizes continental or British labor. A vast philosophical distance separates arch-Republican Bill Hutcheson of the carpenters from ex-Socialist Dave Dubinsky of the ladies' garment workers; yet they work together as vice presidents of the American Federation of Labor. And while the younger Congress of Industrial Organizations shows greater cohesion, the differences between Emil Rieve of the textile workers and Walter Reuther of the automobile workers might be enough to disrupt most European trade-union organizations. This diversity runs all the way to the individual local. Within the same union, within the same industry, within the same city, union practices, union policies, and even union oratory vary all over the lot.

American labor is not "working-class conscious"; it is not "proletarian" and does not believe in class war. Some parts of it are as uncompromisingly wedded to rugged individualism as the National Association of Manufacturers. Others want to "reform capitalism." If there were a standard or typical labor view on this subject, it would probably come close to that of George W. Brooks of the strong and tough pulp, sulfite, and paper-mill workers (A.F. of L.), who says "labor's objective of 'making today better than yesterday' is predicated on its acceptance of capitalism."

Yet the American union is a militant union—more militant, perhaps, than its European counterparts. Not only can the average union point to steadier gains for its members in the form of wages and benefits than any counterpart of it elsewhere; it has also been demanding for itself more and more managerial power within the business enterprise. And it is capable of fighting for both its economic and its power demands with a ferocity and bitterness (to say nothing of a vocabulary) that could hardly be matched by any class-war union.

For however much similarity there may be between the objective conditions that gave rise to unionism throughout the industrialized world, the American union is unique in the meaning it has for its member, in the purpose and function it serves for him: *it is his tool for gaining and keeping as an individual the status and security of a full citizen in capitalist society.* That the union has made the worker to an amazing degree a middle-class member of a middle-class society—in the plant, in the local community, in the economy—is the real measure of its success. . . . Never have left-wing ideologies had so little influence on the American labor movement

From Russell Davenport, *The Permanent Revolution* (New York: Time-Life Books, 1951), pp. 91–93. Reprinted by permission of *Fortune Magazine,* © 1951, Time, Inc.

as they have today. The Communists still control a small but strategic sector of American labor and have scattered but dangerous beachheads elsewhere, notably in the Ford local of the automobile workers. But in glaring contrast to twenty or even to ten years ago, the Communists stay in control only by claiming to be "bona fide unionists"; the mask is dropped only in the closed conventicles of the faithful. David Dubinsky pointed out in 1950 that the old radical, socialist, and idealist movements which formerly were the source of union leaders have been drying up. There are no Wobblies today, no Jewish Bund, no Italian anarchists, no Debs, no Mother Jones. If there is any ideological influence in American labor today it is Catholic union theory—spread by a growing number of labor priests and Catholic labor schools. It is of considerable importance in several C.I.O. unions as well as in the building trades of the A.F. of L.

In historical perspective it appears that the flare-up of left-wing ideologies in the middle thirties was a freak, no more typical of the basic trends of American unionism since the 1890s than the economic stagnation of the period was typical of the basic trends of the American economy. In origins (Knights of Labor, etc.) the American labor movement was more socialist than the British, and in 1902 the A.F. of L. convention barely defeated a resolution endorsing socialism (4,897 to 4,171). This date corresponds to the date when British labor took the opposite turning— 1899, when Keir Hardie committed the [Trade Union Congress] T.U.C. to the borning Labor party. Since then British labor has been increasingly dominated by the socialist intellectual. By contrast, the creed of the American labor movement, as summed up in that famous sentence of the Clayton Act of 1914, "The labor of a human being is not a commodity or article of commerce," traces back not to the *Communist Manifesto* but to that blackest of "black Republicans," Mark Hanna, whom Gompers joined in the leadership of the National Civic Federation. There is a price for these achievements of democratic unionism. The less class war, the more group greed: a quiet division of loot or assumption of privilege at the expense of less organized members of society. Here is the peculiar danger posed by American labor to a free and mobile society: the danger of social thrombosis, of union feudalism.

Last November, Pan American Airways pilots threatened to strike. Their objective was not higher wages, shorter hours, or different working conditions. It was to deny jobs and benefits to a group of fellow pilots. Pan American had just acquired American Overseas Airlines. But the Pan American pilots refused to let the American Overseas pilots come in except at the very bottom. Union leaders and government agencies both urged full acceptance of the seniority gained by the American Overseas men during their years of service—in vain. The demand of the Pan American pilots was not motivated so much by fear of damage as by desire to gain a better position for themselves—at the expense of fellow pilots who had been unlucky enough to work for the less successful company.

The pressure for *exclusive* kinds of job security usually comes from the men and is often resisted by union leaders. It is in part an instinctive assertion of the property right—a property right in a certain job. The blame, if blame there be, lies not at the door of unionism but in the technical conflict between machine modes of production and American democratic ideals. It seems harder nowadays (though it may not be) to reach the top through individual effort in an industrialized economy. The workers respond to this supposed sacrifice of vertical mobility by claiming more security—and when this claim is asserted in a particular job, the result may be a real loss of horizontal mobility.

Union policy is not responsible for this danger, but the structure of U.S. unionism has paralleled and sharpened it. The value of the union card is highest in a small unit: there is one local per company, if not per plant or even per department. Seniority rights tend to be bounded by the local's membership. So are the "fringe benefits"—pension rights, severance pay, vacations, sick pay, profit shares, life insurance, etc.—benefits worth as much as 30 cents in some companies for every dollar paid in straight wages. The growing demand for these benefits is in itself a sign of the middle-class character of the American worker and of his union. They are among our major tools of integrating the worker into industrial capitalism as a full and responsible citizen. And they are necessarily grounded in his membership in one particular enterprise or in one particular industry. But these privileges and benefits are usually not transferable. They thus create the danger of tying the worker to his job. After a few years of service a man has amassed too big a stake to be willing to leave, even for a better job. They may also tend to convert the job into a property and the work group into a closed guild. In the typographical union a "priority system" protects a preferred job for a linotype operator even if the worker is forced out for years by illness—or, as in the last war, even leaves the industry for a defense job. Companies with generous pension or profit-sharing plans are under increasing pressure to restrict the hiring of new workers to sons or relatives of their present employees. The fear of just such "un-American" developments was partly responsible for the no-closed shop provision of the Taft-Hartley Act.

But to halt or reverse this trend will require more than restrictive legislation. It will require considerable imagination in devising new techniques and procedures—above all, techniques to make job benefits transferable. It may also require enabling legislation, the kind that encourages and rewards voluntary action. In attempting to solve this problem we will have to be careful not to weaken the desire of the American worker and of his union for a stake in the enterprise.

# ✣ *E S S A Y S*

In the first essay, Yeshiva University's Ellen Schrecker, one of the foremost historians of American anticommunism, discusses the vital, if often exaggerated, role played by the Communists in the life of the industrial union movement. She then follows with a sweeping analysis of the ways in which McCarthyism, a term that has entered the vocabulary as a synonym for mean-spirited antiradicalism, crippled not only those unions that were led by Communists after World War II, but the entire progressive union movement.

In the second essay, historian Nelson Lichtenstein of the University of California, Santa Barbara outlines the expansive postwar vision of the industrial unions and the political developments that gradually forced the unions to abandon this vision. Taking the New Deal and the World War II experiences as a guide, unionists like the United Auto Workers' Walter Reuther had hoped to exert direct political influence on the government for favorable regulation of wages, prices, and the postwar deployment of capital. This gambit failed, and in its wake came a struggle with the big corporations in the field of collective bargaining alone, a terrain far narrower and less advantageous than that of the policymaking political arena.

What is the relationship between the fight against the Communists and the evolution of postwar collective bargaining? Why were business leaders so hostile to even noncommunist union leaders? Was the Taft-Hartley Act really a "slave labor law," as many unionists charged?

# Labor Encounters the Anticommunist Crusade

### ELLEN SCHRECKER

For . . . fifty years, McCarthyism has . . . haunt[ed] organized labor. Because it rarely got the attention that went to the rest of the flamboyant career of Joe McCarthy or the high-profile spy cases of Alger Hiss and the Rosenbergs, labor's encounter with the anticommunist crusade of the 1940s and 1950s has long been overlooked. Yet, as the labor movement struggles to reenergize itself and reconnect with a broader political agenda, it may have to exorcise the ghosts of the McCarthy era. Obviously, we cannot blame all of labor's current problems on the purges of the early Cold War. Still, many—from labor's declining percentage of the workforce to its poor public image—had their roots in that grim moment. Moreover, by preventing American unions from building a broad-based social movement that challenged corporate values and championed social justice, the anticommunist furor narrowed political options for all Americans.

Labor was involved from the start. Not only was it the most important institutional victim of the Cold War red scare, but many individual victims had union ties. Complicating the issue, however, was the fact that some labor leaders collaborated with the witchhunt. Driving Communists out of organized labor would, they believed, promote freedom and protect unions. They were wrong; in the long run, all sides suffered. McCarthyism weakened the entire labor movement, damaging Communists and anti-Communists alike.

There were many reasons labor was targeted during the Cold War. Anticommunism was, after all, a useful tactic for a business community seeking to roll back the gains unions had made since the 1930s. McCarthyism, however, which encompassed much more than the bizarre behavior of the junior senator from Wisconsin who gave it his name, was not just a union-busting device. It was above all an attempt to destroy the influence of every institution, idea, and individual connected to American communism—and it succeeded. For, despite the widely disseminated notion that the victims of the anticommunist crusade were "innocent liberals" or apolitical folks whose names had gotten on the wrong mailing lists, most of the men and women who were targeted during the McCarthy era were or had been in or near the Communist party, and many of them were union activists.

This should not surprise us. After all, whatever else it stood for, the Communist party claimed to speak for the working class and understandably sought a niche within those institutions that most directly represented the interests of American

From Ellen Schrecker, "McCarthyism's Ghosts: Anticommunism and American Labor," *New Labor Forum* (Spring/Summer 1999), pp. 7–17. Reprinted by permission of the author.

workers—their unions. At least for a few years in the 1930s and 1940s before McCarthyism drove them out, Communists did have some influence within American labor. That influence, though never as extensive as its supporters hoped or its enemies feared, was nonetheless significant; eliminating it affected the rest of the labor movement in ways that we are just coming to understand.

## Communism and the Labor Movement

American communism was such a demonized and contradictory movement that, despite the end of the Cold War, it still provokes impassioned debate. On the one hand, the party was an authoritarian political sect whose adherents tried to conform to an inappropriate Soviet model and closed their eyes to the horrors of Stalin's Russia. On the other hand, it was the most dynamic force on the American left during the 1930s and 1940s, attracting an entire generation of activists and idealists who believed that communism might help them bring about a better world. These people flung themselves into the main political struggles of the time. They organized labor unions, opposed racial inequality, and fought fascism, imperialism, and war. At the same time, they hid their party membership, repressed internal opposition, and, in a few cases, even spied for the Soviet Union. The record, in short, is mixed.

Within the labor movement, the party threw its most devoted cadres into the early organizing campaigns of the CIO. Communists were energetic, experienced organizers who helped build unions within the maritime, automobile, steel, and electrical industries, as well as among white-collar and professional workers. Though the party won over few ordinary workers, individual Communists often rose to leadership within the unions they had built. They were honest, hard-working union leaders and were recognized as such by the men and women they served. As a result, by the late 1940s Communists and their allies controlled about 20 percent of the unions within the CIO and had a sizable, though dwindling, pocket of influence within the UAW. The party dominated the largest electrical workers' union, the United Electrical, Radio, and Machine Workers (UE), as it did the International Longshoremen's and Warehousemen's Union (ILWU), the International Union of Mine, Mill, and Smelter Workers, and about a dozen smaller unions that represented workers everywhere, from ships and canneries to department stores and federal bureaucracies.

To what extent the party shaped the unions it controlled is hard to say. Many Communist labor leaders were clearly more committed to their unions than to the party. Some, in fact, were to quit the party when they felt that its demands would hurt their unions. Others, especially at the local level, though not explicitly defying party directives, worked around them. For many of these people, building a strong labor movement was the most effective way to achieve the goals they had joined the party to accomplish. They did not try to transform their unions into revolutionary organizations but often limited their support for the party's nonlabor policies to what one ex-Communist called "the resolution bit"—endorsing party causes at their annual conventions or inserting pro-Soviet editorials in union newspapers.

Still, the communist-led unions did differ from the non-communist ones. Their leaders were better educated, more militant, more class-conscious, and usually more democratic than most non-communist union leaders. In addition, they rejected the bread-and-butter unionism of mainstream labor, committing their unions to a broad range of social reforms.

Nowhere was that commitment as striking as in the area of race relations. For much of the 1930s and 1940s, the Communist party was one of the few political organizations not specifically dedicated to civil rights to call for racial equality. At a time when the American workplace was largely segregated, the party pressed its labor cadres to fight discrimination on the job. This was not a popular position. In some unions, like New York City's largely Irish Transport Workers Union, communist leaders initially hesitated to confront their members on the matter. The issue was too central to American communism to be avoided, however, and ultimately the TWU began to seek the hiring of black motormen and bus drivers. During World War II, when African-Americans broke the color line in previously closed industries, some left-wing unions pioneered an early form of affirmative action to help these newly hired workers keep their jobs after the war.

The Communists' support for racial equality did not endear them to white workers, but it did appeal to minority ones, enabling some left-led unions like the Longshoremen, the Food, Tobacco, and Agricultural Workers Union (FTA), and Mine-Mill to gain a foothold in the South and in such racially diverse areas as Hawaii and the Southwest. Not only did these unions promote minority group members to leadership positions, but in some areas they even functioned as civil rights organizations. The Communist-led FTA Local 22 in Winston-Salem, North Carolina, exemplified this type of rights-based unionism. In addition to making its economic demands, the local gave a new sense of self-worth to the thousands of African-American women who held menial jobs in the R. J. Reynolds company's huge tobacco plant, empowering them to challenge the demeaning way in which the company had traditionally treated them. The union also encouraged its members to vote and to join the NAACP—efforts that helped elect an African-American to Winston-Salem's Board of Aldermen and obtain better services for the city's black residents.

Local 22's concern for women was characteristic of the left-wing unions. From the tobacco factories of North Carolina to the welfare agencies of New York City, unions within the party's orbit sought out the subjugated, poorly paid, and often nonwhite female workers that the rest of the labor movement had largely overlooked. They also organized clerical workers and other denizens of the nation's "pink ghetto." The unions addressed women's issues and allowed strong female leaders to emerge. The UE was the pioneer in this era. During and immediately after World War II, the union, which had more female members than any other major industrial union, consciously fought for women's rights. Not only did it call for equal pay for equal work, but it also opposed the inequities involved in shunting women off into poorly paid "women's jobs." During the late 1940s and early 1950s, the UE continued to press gender issues in policy statements and in the articles that Betty Friedan, then a reporter for the union's newspaper, was writing.

## The Anticommunist Crusade

The Anticommunist crusade brought most of these efforts to a halt. Betty Friedan was an indirect victim; she lost her UE job when the beleaguered union downsized and dropped her from the paper. Though the UE was one of the few left-led unions to survive the anticommunist onslaught, it emerged seriously debilitated and no longer in a position to push for women's rights or any of the other social reforms it had once championed. Most of the other left-wing unions went under, unable to withstand the unrelenting assault against them. What made the anticommunist crusade against the labor left so effective was that it came from so many sources and employed so many different weapons. Employers, federal officials, rival union leaders, Catholic priests, ex-Communists, right-wing journalists, and politicians all sought to drive Communists out of organized labor. Many of these people had been fighting communism for years, often as part of an informal network of dedicated anti-Communists. The Cold War gave their efforts greater legitimacy and brought new forces into the field, including a wide array of federal agencies.

From the late 1940s on, the Communist-led unions were under constant attack. Few indeed were the left-wing unions whose leaders were not called before congressional investigators and grand juries, shadowed by the FBI, denied security clearances, subjected to criminal prosecution, audited by the IRS, or, if they were foreign born, threatened with deportation. Beset by internal schisms and external raids, stiff-armed by employers, denied legal protection by the National Labor Relations Board (NLRB), and finally expelled from the CIO, these unions were so beleaguered and preoccupied with self-defense that they could barely fulfill their basic economic functions, let alone devote any resources to ambitious programs for social reform.

The most serious damage was done by the 1947 Taft-Hartley Act. Anticommunism was only a subsidiary concern of the act's authors, who had long been trying to reverse the union gains of the late 1930s and early 1940s. Nonetheless, by the time the measure reached the floor of Congress, the consensus about the need to eliminate Communists from the labor movement was so overwhelming that the only issue discussed was how it could be done. The provisions that were finally enacted in Section 9(h) of the new legislation required all union officials to sign a non-Communist affidavit affirming that they did not belong to or sympathize with any communist or subversive organization. Unions whose officers did not sign the affidavit would be denied the protection of the NLRB.

In the beginning, it was unclear how damaging Section 9(h) would be. Many mainstream union leaders opposed the affidavit as both a violation of civil liberties and an unfair burden on labor. In addition, because of the law's vague and presumably unconstitutional language regarding belief in and support for communism, several unions including the Steelworkers challenged it in court as a violation of the First Amendment. Finally, in the aftermath of Harry Truman's upset victory in the 1948 presidential election, it was possible that Taft-Hartley might be repealed. The Truman administration and the mainstream unions soon learned to live with the measure, however, especially when they realized how much it hurt the left-wing unions.

The unions' refusals to let their officers sign the affidavits meant that they could not participate in NLRB elections or have the board process their unfair labor practices complaints. Antagonistic employers, recognizing that the NLRB would no longer intervene against them in such cases, simply refused to bargain, often forcing the unions into unpopular and debilitating strikes. At the same time, rival unions, which had been raiding the communist unions for years, stepped up their attacks. While the left-led unions had formerly been able to fend off most such raids, once they were barred from the NLRB's elections they became much more vulnerable. Internal battles also escalated, as the weakened left-wingers faced challenges from anticommunist factions which now got help from such allies as the House Un-American Activities Committee (HUAC) and the Catholic Church.

By the middle of 1949, the left-led unions capitulated and let their officers sign the affidavits. Their constitutional challenge was going badly, there was little chance that Taft-Hartley would be repealed, and their very survival required compliance. There was a problem, however. Some of the leaders of these unions were in fact Communists. Thus, in order to bring their unions into compliance, these leaders publicly resigned from the party, insisting, however, that their political beliefs remained unchanged. Naturally, their opponents questioned the authenticity of their resignations. Hostile employers refused to bargain with their unions, while NLRB officials prodded the Justice Department to indict them for perjury.

At the same time, the CIO was preparing to oust its left-wing members. Its president, Philip Murray, had resisted such a move for years, reluctantly endorsing it only after the Communists and their allies defied the CIO by backing the third-party candidacy of Henry Wallace in the 1948 presidential election. At its 1949 convention, the CIO expelled the UE and pressed charges against ten other unions, citing their failure to repudiate their Communist leaders and their refusal to back American foreign policy. Each union then received a hearing before a three-man tribunal. As in so many of the anticommunist investigations of the late 1940s and the 1950s, the evidence of these unions' transgressions consisted of the testimony of former Communists and literary texts, in this case convention resolutions and newspaper editorials that paralleled the party's line. No one questioned the unions' activities in the field of labor relations.

By the summer of 1950, when the Supreme Court finally ruled that Section 9(h) of the Taft-Hartley law was constitutional, the pathetic condition of the ostracized and marginalized unions was obvious. Nonetheless, in its decision, the Court's majority echoed the prevailing wisdom that restrictions on Communists and their unions were justified because of the threat they posed to the nation's security. If the United States went to war against the Soviet Union, the Communist-led unions might, so it was believed, encourage their members to sabotage vital installations or call political strikes to shut down defense plants. The outbreak of the Korean War intensified these fears.

Even before the Korean War, however, federal officials and private businessmen had invoked national security whenever they sought to crack down on the labor left. In 1948, for example, the Atomic Energy Commission refused to let the UE represent workers at a General Electric plant that made nuclear reactors. Even at those factories where the union remained in place, the denial of security clearances to its shop stewards and other activists was just as crippling.

The left-wing unions were also harassed by congressional investigators who subpoenaed their leaders and subjected them to hostile questioning about their communist ties. Unlike most of the committees' other unfriendly witnesses, these union officials usually kept their jobs, but the unfavorable publicity that accompanied the investigations often benefited the union's internal and external enemies, especially when the hearings coincided with a strike or union election.

When Local 22 of the Food, Tobacco, and Agricultural Workers Union went out on strike against the R. J. Reynolds company in 1947, HUAC intervened. By exposing the Communist connections of the local's leaders, these hearings weakened its support within the broader community. At the same time, rival unions took advantage of the FTA's failure to sign the Taft-Hartley affidavits to raid the local, while the company redesigned its manufacturing process to eliminate the jobs of the union's most loyal members. As a result, by the time the CIO expelled its parent union, Local 22 was no longer functioning.

A similar set of hearings by HUAC and the House Education and Labor Committee broke a 1947 strike against the Allis-Chalmers Company outside Milwaukee and destroyed the militant UAW local that conducted it. Years of bitterness had plagued the relationship between Allis Chalmers and its left-led union. Even if the leaders of Local 248 had not been close to the Communist Party, the company's hostility to organized labor would probably have turned them into militants. As it was, red-baiting and work stoppages were endemic. A seventy six-day strike in the spring of 1941 had precipitated widely circulated charges that the local was following party orders to sabotage the nation's defense effort. The company reiterated those charges when Local 248 walked out again in April 1946. It mounted a massive public relations drive, planting fifty-nine articles about the union's Communist connections in a local newspaper and feeding material to congressional investigators, journalists, and the FBI.

At its hearings in March 1947, the House Education and Labor Committee grilled the local's president and former president about their political affiliations. Both men denied that they were Communists; but the committee produced a leading ex-Communist witness to rebut their testimony and recycle the story that the former president, Harold Christoffel, had called the 1941 walk-out at the party's behest. HUAC then repeated the process, and a Labor Committee subcommittee showed up in Milwaukee to reinforce the message. A week later the strike was over. Within six months Local 248, the largest union in Wisconsin, had fallen from mor than 8,000 members to 184.

The hearings also landed Harold Christoffel in prison. Indicted for perjury after denying party membership, Christoffel was one of several left-wing labor leaders to face criminal prosecution during the 1950s. Perjury and contempt of Congress were the most common charges, as they were for most of the people prosecuted during the McCarthy period. Though Christoffel and a handful of other left-wing labor leaders went to prison, most of the other defendants won their cases on appeal. Even so, their struggles dragged on for years, draining their own resources and those of their unions.

Deportation proceedings were equally debilitating. The most notorious case was that of the Australian-born West Coast Longshoremen's leader Harry Bridges, who was the target of three separate deportation proceedings as well as a perjury indictment for denying that he was a Communist at the time he was naturalized. Although Bridges and most of the other foreign-born union leaders threatened with deportation ultimately escaped exile, especially if they kept their cases in the courts long enough for the Supreme Court to have second thoughts about political deportations, the defense effort was again costly.

The harassment continued. The IRS investigated some left-wing union leaders for tax evasion. The Justice Department brought charges before the Subversive Activities Control Board against UE and Mine-Mill. The federal government's loyalty-security program decimated the United Public Workers of America, while the port security program inaugurated during the Korean War did the same for the West Coast Marine Cooks and Steward's Union. Though the affected unions and their attorneys often fought back successfully, the struggles were draining. As one left-wing lawyer who argued many of these cases recalled, he was lucky if his labor clients could cover his train fare.

By the time McCarthyism finally wound down in the 1960s most of the Communist-led unions had disappeared. The smaller ones had either been absorbed by larger unions or else they had merged with a rival. Ultimately, only the ILWU survived more or less intact. The once-powerful UE remained independent, but it had lost the bulk of its members and most of its clout. Obviously, McCarthyism did not cause every setback the left-led unions encountered. Many of these unions were, after all, in declining industries such as shipping or the fur business. Still, it is clear that the hardships imposed by the anticommunist crusade increased the difficulties these unions faced and made it impossible for them to fulfill their normal trade union functions.

## The Impact of McCarthyism

Those most directly affected were the workers the unions had represented. The communist-led unions were on the whole well-run, honest, and effective organizations that won work rules and economic packages as good as, and often better than, those of other unions. The multi-pronged assault they faced, however, made it hard for them to serve their members as well as they once had. Weakened by schisms and raiding, they often accepted unfavorable contracts rather than mount strikes they knew would be lost. At the same time, the strain of defending themselves and their leaders had seriously drained the already diminished resources of the unions. Ultimately, as one ILWU leader explained, the fight against McCarthyism became "too damn expensive," because it began "to preempt the economic struggle where the guy's bread and butter and paycheck are on the line."

The rest of the labor movement suffered as well. Anticommunism proved to be a costly diversion from other union issues. Though its sponsors had used red-baiting to help get the 1947 Taft-Hartley Act through Congress, the measure attacked all of organized labor, not just its Communist elements. Many of the act's provisions such as the exclusion of supervisors from collective bargaining and the prohibition of secondary boycotts, were even more damaging than its non-Communist affidavit. They rolled back many of the gains that organized labor had made since the 1930s and made it harder for unions to recruit new members or take them out on strike. Nonetheless, instead of mobilizing a coalition to repeal Taft-Hartley, labor squabbled over Section 9(h).

This was a serious mistake. Taft-Hartley created an unfavorable legal environment that forced the entire labor movement onto the defensive. Unable to employ the aggressive organizing tactics that had been successful in the 1930s, unions found it difficult to expand. As a result, by the 1970s, when the postwar boom began to falter and the well-paid blue-collar jobs of its members began to disappear, labor was unable to mobilize either the political or the economic clout to protect its earlier gains. Its numbers dropped and its percentage of the overall workforce declined drastically. In 1945, 35 percent of the nation's nonagricultural workers were unionized. By the early 1990s that figure had fallen to below 16 percent (10 to 11 percent if government workers were excluded).

Debilitating as Taft-Hartley was, it was not solely responsible for labor's failure to replenish its ranks. Here again the anticommunist crusade bears much of the blame, for it diverted the mainstream unions from organizing the unorganized. Instead of reaching beyond its traditional white male constituency in the heavy industry and skilled trades of the Northeast, Midwest, and West, labor raided its own left wing. Not only did that raiding distract the mainstream unions from recruiting new members, but it also disrupted the often left-led organizing drives within those areas of the economy, like the service sector, where the labor movement most needed to grow. The Communist-influenced unions had, after all, been wooing white-collar workers and professionals for years. They had also appealed to groups, such as women and people of color, that the traditional unions largely ignored.

The attenuation of organized labor was not entirely the result of the anticommunist purges. Business was strong, well organized, and determined to reassert its dominance. The passage of the Taft-Hartley Act was only part of a larger corporate effort to destroy the legitimacy and power of American unions. Nonetheless, the ouster of its left-wingers weakened the labor movement by limiting its options and depriving it of just those activists who might have mounted a stronger defense of collective action against the corporate sector's promotion of privatization and individual gain.

The Communists and their allies were, after all, labor's most militant voices. Their ideology encouraged them to champion workers against bosses. They understood how capitalism operated and were often willing to challenge management at every level. They were, for example, among the first unionists to raise such crucial issues as deindustrialization and runaway plants. In addition, because they recognized the importance of retaining the loyalty of their rank-and-file members, they tried to create a broader union community to involve those members in union affairs. A typical left-wing local, like the one Harold Christoffel organized at Allis-Chalmers, ran dances, held classes, and also aggressively pursued grievances. Moreover, as long as the Communist Party retained a presence, its opponents also had to work the grassroots.

Once the left-wingers were gone, labor lost its spark. The radical organizers who had built and sustained the CIO were ousted, replaced by less imaginative individuals with neither their predecessors' vision nor drive. The labor movement became more centralized, corrupt, and distant from its members. Not surprisingly, the members reciprocated. They lost interest in their unions, stopped going to meetings, and no longer viewed belonging to a union as central to their own identity. That apathy forced the labor movement to rely increasingly on federal intervention instead of the support of its own members. When the government turned against organized labor, as it did during the Reagan administration, the AFL-CIO was blindsided.

The labor movement's retrenchment and its failure to expand in the 1940s and 1950s also had consequences that extended far beyond the ranks of organized labor. In particular, the absence of strong unions in the South made it all but impossible to challenge the power of the conservative Southern Democrats in Congress. The CIO's main attempt to organize the region, its ill-fated "Operation Dixie" organizing drive in 1946–47, foundered in part because it refused to challenge the region's power structure or dominant values. It focused mainly on white workers and distanced it-self from the Communist-led unions that had successfully recruited Southern blacks. Whether "Operation Dixie" would have succeeded had it been more militant and less skittish about engaging African-Americans and the left is unclear. There was so much opposition to unionization in the South that, moderate as the CIO's venture was, it did not escape either red- or race-baiting, and it folded within six months. Without a strong labor movement to anchor it, Southern liberalism withered, diminishing the range of political options in that part of the country and strengthening the forces that were (and still are) pushing national politics to the right.

The civil rights movement was also affected. Not only did the decline of Southern liberalism deprive it of its strongest allies within the white community, but the demise of the labor left destroyed the unions that were the movement's main institutional base within the black working class. Fearful of red-baiting, the largely middle-class civil rights leaders no longer sought economic change, concentrating instead on calling for legal and political rights. These were demands that the anticommunist liberals within the labor movement could readily endorse. Yet, despite their rhetorical support for desegregation in the South, few shared the Communists' genuine commitment to the cause. Accordingly, though labor leaders like Walter Reuther bankrolled much of the civil rights movement, they were rarely willing to put their mouths where their money was and confront the discrimination within their own organizations. It is hard to say whether left-led unions could have overcome the racism of white workers, but at the very least they would not have ignored the severing of race from class that has had such a disastrous effect on contemporary American politics.

McCarthyism cost labor its political independence. The purge of its left-wing dissidents deepened the labor movement's identification with the Democratic party. It also overcame the final obstacles to labor's enlistment in the Cold War. Abandoning all critical distance from the Truman administration's foreign policy, organized labor let itself become so thoroughly coopted that it even lent its support to the undemocratic machinations of the CIA. By the mid-1960s, the AFL-CIO was endorsing the Vietnam War.

On domestic issues as well, McCarthyism constricted labor's agenda and hastened its transformation from a social movement into a special interest group. Though labor often functioned as the left wing of the Democratic party, it was a very timid left that had long since abandoned its advocacy of major social and economic reforms. Such had not always been the case. During the 1940s, the CIO (and not only its left-led unions) had urged an expansion of the New Deal welfare state. While never questioning the legitimacy of the capitalist system, it demanded universal health insurance, public housing, and economic security for all Americans. The left-led unions actively supported this agenda, encouraging their more moderate labor allies to champion what was in effect a social democratic program of expanded welfare reforms.

Once the labor movement purged its left-wingers, however, its center of gravity shifted to the right. In addition, the fear of being politically tainted for backing the same measures as Communists made it retreat. Thus, instead of seeking legislation that would benefit the rest of society, labor turned inward, seeking higher wages and benefits for its members. Moreover, by developing its own essentially private welfare systems, the labor movement not only abandoned its role as the nation's main institutional proponent of social reform, but also contributed to the growing delegitimization of state action that is eroding so much of the public sector today.

While we cannot turn back the clock to the mid-1940s and recoup the opportunities for social change that disappeared during the anticommunist purges, today's labor movement may well have to reconnect with the legacy of its former radicals if it is to regain the relevance and vitality that it once enjoyed. Above all, if it is to become the basis for a broader revitalization of American society, it must shed the political constrictions that McCarthyism imposed and transform itself into the broad movement for social justice that its lost left wing once dreamed it could be.

## The Union's Retreat in the Postwar Era

### NELSON LICHTENSTEIN

The dramatic growth of the organized working class put the American system of industrial relations at a crossroads in 1945. In the years since 1933 the number of unionized workers had increased more than fivefold to over fourteen million. About 30 percent of all American workers were organized, a density greater than at any time before and a level that for the first time equaled that of northern Europe. Unions seemed on the verge of recruiting millions of new workers in the service trades, in white collar occupations, across great stretches of the South and Southwest, and even among the lower ranks of management. "Your success has been one of the most surprising products of American politics in several generations," Interior Secretary Harold Ickes told a cheering CIO convention just after Roosevelt's 1944 reelection. "You are on your way and you must let no one stop you or even slow up your march." Three years later, the sober-minded Harvard economist Sumner Slichter still counted U.S. trade unions "the most powerful economic organizations which the country has ever seen."

It was not size alone that contributed to this assessment. The élan so noticeable in many sections of the labor movement rested upon a degree of union consciousness, in some cases amounting to working-class loyalty, that would today seem quite extraordinary. The mid-1940s were no period of social quiescence, for the war itself had had a complex and dichotomous impact on working Americans. On the one hand it had provided them with a taste of postwar affluence and had attuned them to the daily influence of large, bureaucratic institutions like the military and the government mobilization agencies. But the labor shortages of that era and the social patriotic ideology advanced by government and union alike engendered a self-confident mood that quickly translated itself into a remarkable burst of rank-and-file activity. Led by shop stewards and local union officers, hundreds of thousands of workers had taken part in a wildcat strike movement that had focused on a militant defense of union power in the workplace itself. And the now forgotten series

From Steven Fraser and Gary Geistle, eds., *The Rise and Fall of the New Deal Order, 1930–1980.* Copyright © 1989 Princeton University Press. Excerpt pp. 123–124, 137–145 reprinted with permission of Princeton University Press.

of postwar general strikes called by central labor councils in Oakland, California; Lancaster, Pennsylvania; Stamford, Connecticut; and Akron, Ohio are indicative of the extent to which working-class activity still retained an occasionally explosive character even in the later half of the 1940s.

The economic power wielded by American trade unions was by its very nature political power, for the New Deal had thoroughly politicized all relations between the union movement, the business community, and the state. The New Deal differed from previous eras of state activism not only because of the relatively more favorable political and legislative environment it created for organized labor but, perhaps even more important, because the New Deal provided a set of semipermanent political structures in which key issues of vital concern to the trade union movement might be accommodated. Although the industry codes negotiated under the National Recovery Administration were declared unconstitutional in 1935, the Fair Labor Standards Act established new wage and hour standards three years later. The National Labor Relations Board established the legal basis of union power and provided the arena in which jurisdictional disputes between the unions might be resolved, while the National War Labor Board had provided a tripartite institution that both set national wage policy and contributed to the rapid wartime growth of the new trade unions. The successive appearances of these agencies seemed to signal the fact that in the future as in the past, the fortunes of organized labor would be determined as much by a process of politicized bargaining in Washington as by the give and take of contract collective bargaining.

As a result of the wartime mobilization the United States seemed to advance toward the kind of labor-backed corporatism that would later characterize social policy in northern Europe and Scandinavia. Corporatism of this sort called for government agencies, composed of capital, labor, and "public" representatives, to substitute rational, democratic planning for the chaos and inequities of the market. The premier examples of such corporatist institutions in 1940s America were the War Labor Board and its wartime companion, the Office of Price Administration—administrative regimes that began to reorder wage and price relations within and between industries. Although union officials often denounced both agencies for their accommodation of politically resourceful business and producer groups, the maintenance of institutions such as these were nevertheless seen by most liberal and labor spokesmen as the kernel of a postwar "incomes" policy. That policy would continue the rationalization of the labor market begun during the war, set profit and price guidelines, and redistribute income into worker and consumer hands. These agencies were usually staffed by individuals somewhat sympathetic to their consumer and trade union constituencies and headed by New Dealers like Chester Bowles and William H. Davis who recognized the legitimacy of labor's corporate interests. . . .

Since contemporary trade unions have often been equated with "special interest politics," it is important to recognize that the American trade union movement of the immediate postwar era, and especially its industrial union wing, adopted a social agenda that was broad, ambitious, and not without prospects for success. The unions thought the welfare of the working class would be advanced not only, or even primarily, by periodic wage bargaining but through a political realignment of the major parties that would give them a powerful voice in the management of industry, planning the overall political economy and expansion of the welfare state. The union agenda was never an entirely consistent one, but its thrust meshed well with the corporatist strain that characterized late New Deal social policy.

This perspective was most graphically manifest in the demand for tripartite industry governance, embodied in the Industry Council Plan put forward by CIO president Philip Murray early in the war. The industry council idea represented an admixture of Catholic social reformism and New Deal era faith in business-labor-government cooperation. Under the general guidance of a friendly government, the Industry Council Plan contemplated the fusion of economic and political bargaining at the very highest levels of industry governance. Here was the essence of the CIO's corporatist vision: organized labor would have a voice in the production goals, investment decisions, and employment patterns of the nation's core industries. "The Industry Council Plan," wrote Philip Murray, "is a program for democratic economic planning and for participation by the people in the key decisions of the big corporations." Such important elements of the union movement's wartime agenda as the Guaranteed Annual Wage, industry-wide bargaining, and rationalization of the wage structure could be won only through this initiative.

If the CIO plan had something of an abstract air about it, the proposals put forward by the young autoworker leader, Walter Reuther, had a good deal more political bite. Reuther rose to national prominence in 1940 and 1941 with a widely publicized "500 planes a day" plan to resolve the military aviation bottleneck through a state-sponsored rationalization of the entire auto/aircraft industry. Reuther proposed a tripartite Aircraft Production Board that would have the power to reorganize production facilities without regard for corporate boundaries, markets, or personnel. It would conscript labor and work space where and when needed and secure for the United Auto Workers (UAW) at least a veto over a wide range of managerial functions. Winning wide support among those New Dealers who still retained a commitment to social planning, the Reuther plan was ultimately delayed and then defeated by an automobile industry both hostile to social experimentation and increasingly well represented within the government's wartime production agencies.

The Reuther plan nevertheless cast a long shadow, for it contained hallmarks of the strategic approach so characteristic of labor-liberalism in the 1940s: an assault on management's traditional power made in the name of economic efficiency and the public interest, and an effort to shift power relations within the structure of industry and politics, usually by means of a tripartite governmental entity empowered to plan for whole sections of the economy. Thus did auto executive George Romney declare, "Walter Reuther is the most dangerous man in Detroit because no one is more skillful in bringing about the revolution without seeming to disturb the existing forms of society."

Indeed, the union movement defined the left wing of what was possible in the political affairs of the day. Its vision and its power attracted a species of political animal hardly existent today, the "labor-liberal" who saw organized labor as absolutely central to the successful pursuit of his political agenda. After 1943 the CIO's new Political Action Committee put organizational backbone into the northern Democratic party, and the next year its "People's Program for 1944" codified many of the central themes that would define liberalism in the immediate postwar years: big-power cooperation, full employment, cultural pluralism, and economic planning.

"Labor's role in our national progress is unique and paramount," affirmed Supreme Court justice William O. Douglas as late as 1948. "It is labor, organized and independent labor, that can supply much of the leadership, energy and motive power which we need today."

The CIO hoped to take the tripartite, corporatist model of wage-price bargaining that had emerged during the war and use it to bridge the uncertain political currents of the reconversion era. The industrial union federation wanted a National Production Board that would preside over the reconversion of defense plants to civilian production, maintain a semblance of price control, and establish a set of wage guidelines designed to defend working-class incomes. As CIO president Philip Murray told a 1944 labor meeting, "Only chaos and destruction of our industrial life will result if employers look to the war's end as an opportunity for a union-breaking, wage cutting, open-shop drive, and if labor unions have to resort to widespread strikes to defend their very existence and the living standards of their members." To forestall such a prospect, the CIO in March 1945 sponsored a "Labor-Management Charter" with William Green of the AFL and Eric Johnston, the corporate liberal president of the U.S. Chamber of Commerce. Consisting of a list of often irreconcilable platitudes hailing the virtues of unfettered free enterprise and the rights of labor, the charter nevertheless symbolized the CIO's hope for cooperation with the liberal wing of American capitalism in stabilizing postwar industrial relations along roughly the lines established during the war. "It's Industrial Peace for the Postwar Period," headlined the *CIO News*. In return for management support for the unamended Wagner Act and a high-wage, high-employment postwar strategy, the unions pledged to defend "a system of private competitive capitalism" including "the inherent right and responsibility of management to direct the operations of an enterprise."

The businessmen with whom the CIO hoped to work were collective bargaining progressives and moderate Keynesians who favored a counter-cyclic fiscal policy and a degree of structural reform as the minimum program necessary to stabilize postwar capitalism. Often influenced by the Committee for Economic Development and the Twentieth Century Fund, they also supported the 1946 Full Employment Act in something like its original, liberal form. Among these progressive industrialists with whom the CIO sought an alliance, in addition to the Chamber of Commerce's Eric Johnston, who called for a "people's capitalism" in the postwar era, was Paul Hoffman of the Studebaker Corporation, who took pride in his company's harmonious relationship with organized labor. But the most famous of these progressives was undoubtedly Henry J. Kaiser, the maverick West Coast industrialist who had built his empire on New Deal construction projects and wartime contracts. Hardly an opponent of government planning or public works spending, Kaiser's good relations with the unions and the pioneering health-care facilities at his shipyards and mills added to his reputation as a social liberal. In 1945 he won strong UAW cooperation for a well-publicized effort to convert the gain Willow Run bomber plant to civilian car production.

Implementation of a new wage-price policy was one of the key elements in such an accord with the liberal wing of the business community, so state action was essential. The CIO wanted a 20- or 30-percent increase in real wages to make up for the elimination of overtime pay at the end of the war, and many New Dealers like

Commerce Secretary Henry Wallace and William Davis, now head of the Office of Economic Stabilization, considered such a wage boost essential to maintaining living standards and avoid the long-feared postwar downturn.

Such forecasts were music to CIO ears, but the political and social base for such a liberal postwar prospect had already been eroded. Since 1938 labor-liberalism had been on the defensive, stymied by the defection of Southern agriculture from the New Deal coalition, by the political rejuvenation of a conservative manufacturing interest during World War II, and by the reemergence of long-standing ethnic and social tensions within the urban Democratic party. Certainly emblematic of this stalemate was Harry Truman's selection as vice-president in 1944, replacing Henry Wallace, the labor-liberal favorite. FDR's successor was not a New Dealer, but a border-state Democrat, a party centrist whose political skill would lie in successfully presiding over an increasingly factionalized party coalition. . . .

The CIO had also profoundly misjudged the tenor of the postwar business community. The progressive industrialists with whom the industrial union federation hoped to achieve an accord were in fact a relatively uninfluential minority. Key business spokesmen were those practical conservatives who presided over the core manufacturing firms in the unionized steel, electrical, auto, rubber, and transport industries. Led by men such as John A. Stephens of U.S. Steel, Ira Mosher of the National Association of Manufacturers, and Charles E. Wilson of General Motors, these industrialists had emerged from the war with enormous sophistication and self-confidence. Unlike their counterparts in continental Europe, or even in the British Isles, who had been tarred with the brush of collaboration or appeasement, American business leaders found the wartime experience one of both commercial success and political advance. They felt in little need of the kind of state-sponsored labor-management collaboration that helped legitimize a mixed capitalist economy in Germany, France, and Italy in the immediate postwar era.

These industrialists recognized the potential usefulness of the new industrial unions as stabilizers of the labor force and moderators of industrial conflict, but they also sought the restoration of managerial prerogatives that wartime conditions had eroded in the areas of product pricing, market allocation, and shop-floor work environment. They were intensely suspicious of the kind of New Deal social engineering favored by labor, and only with some reluctance did they accommodate themselves to the modest degree of economic stimulation that would later go by the name "commercial Keynesianism." Looking forward to a postwar boom, they wanted to be free of government or union interference in determining the wage-price relationship in each industry. Thus the long-awaited Labor-Management conference that President Truman convened in November 1945 was doomed to failure. No accord proved possible on either the prerogatives of management or the scope of legitimate union demands, and on the critical issue of a general wage policy, the CIO got nowhere. Philip Murray offered industry a de facto policy of labor peace in return for a pattern wage increase, which Truman had endorsed in a speech of October 30, but the opposition was so great that the issue never secured a place on the formal conference agenda.

The CIO faced resistance not only from industry but from within the labor movement itself. The AFL unions had never been as committed as the CIO to the tripartite bargaining arrangements of the war era, and these unions demanded a return to free and unrestricted collective bargaining. In part this stemmed from the AFL's tradition of Gompersarian voluntarism, but it also reflected the contrasting organizational base of the two labor federations. The CIO industrial unions were overwhelmingly concentrated in the manufacturing sector of the economy where they faced oligopolistically organized employers who where themselves capable of imposing a new wage pattern. But only 35 percent of AFL membership lay in this heavy industrial sector, while construction, transportation, and service trades proved the federation's most important centers of strength. These decentralized, and now booming, sectors of the economy were less subject to the pattern-setting guidelines established by core firms like General Motors and U.S. Steel. With almost seven million members in 1945, the AFL was not only 30 percent larger than the CIO but actually growing more rapidly, in part because its flexible model of mixed craft and industrial unionism seemed to fit more closely the actual contours of the postwar economy than did the CIO brand of mass organizations. This meant that, although CIO unions like the Steelworkers and the UAW remained innovative and powerful institutions, their political and organizational weight was often less impressive than it seemed.

Although he was an industrial unionist, John L. Lewis spoke most forthrightly for the AFL viewpoint. Repeated clashes between the United Mine Workers (UMW) and the Roosevelt administration during the war had soured the mine leader on the kind of state-sponsored industrial planning arrangements he had once advocated as the CIO's first president. Lewis was now determined to exercise his union's power unfettered by a new set of federal regulations. "What Murray and the CIO are asking for," declared Lewis at the Labor-Management conference, "is a corporate state, wherein the activities of the people are regulated and constrained by a dictatorial government. We are opposed to the corporate state."

This stalemate led directly to the General Motors strike, actually begun while the conference remained in session, and then to the general strike wave that spread throughout basic industry in the winter of 1946. Like Walter Reuther's other wartime "plans," the GM strike program made a strong appeal to the "national" interest, this time not so much in terms of rationalized production and democratic control, but as part of the emerging Keynesian consensus that a substantial boost in mass purchasing power would be necessary to avoid a postwar depression. The UAW's demand that industry pacesetter GM raise wages by some 30 percent without increasing the price of its product seemed adventuresome in a collective bargaining negotiation; even more so was its demand that GM "open the books" to demonstrate its ability to pay. The company quickly denounced these UAW demands as European-style socialism, but they were in fact little more than standard OPA price-setting procedures now translated into the language of collective bargaining.

While this program was formally directed against the giant automaker, it was in practice a union demand against the state as well, for its ultimate success rested upon the ability of an increasingly embattled OPA to resist industry pressure and enforce price guidelines well into the postwar era. This program won Reuther a wave of support, both within the UAW, where it prepared the way for his election as union president, and among influential liberals who identified with the union effort. A union-sponsored "National Citizens Committee on the GM-UAW Dispute" lauded the UAW's determination to lift "collective bargaining to a new high level by insisting that the advancement of Labor's interest shall not be made at the expense of the public." And a strike support committee, headquartered at NAACP offices in New York, quickly enrolled such luminaries as Eleanor Roosevelt, Wayne Morse, Reinhold Niebuhr, Walter White, and Leon Henderson.

Reuther and the rest of the CIO won an 18.5-cent wage increase during the postwar round of strikes and negotiations that ended in the late winter of 1946. But the effort to turn this struggle into a downward redistribution of real income was decisively repulsed, first by the adamant opposition of industrial management, second by Truman administration vacillation, and finally by division and timidity within trade union ranks, especially after Philip Murray made it clear that the Steelworkers' union would not turn its mid-winter strike into a political conflict with the Truman administration over the maintenance of price controls.

The 1946 strike settlement ended left-liberal hopes that organized labor could play a direct role in reshaping class relations for the society as a whole. Thereafter Reutherite social unionism gradually tied its fate more closely to that of industry and moved away from a strategy that sought to use union power to demand structural changes in the political economy. Instead the UAW worked toward negotiation of an increasingly privatized welfare program that eventually succeeded in providing economic security for employed autoworkers. But just as postwar liberalism gradually reduced its commitment to national planning and eschewed issues of social and economic control, so too did the UAW abandon the quest for labor participation in running the automobile industry. And just as liberalism increasingly came to define itself as largely concerned with the maintenance of economic growth and an expansion of the welfare state, so too would the UAW and the rest of the labor movement define its mission in these terms.

Although the immediate postwar strike wave had proven the largest since 1919, the pattern wage increases won by the UAW and other major unions soon evaporated under the galloping inflation let loose when government price controls were cut back during the summer. In the fall, therefore, all the major unions had to return to the bargaining table to demand another round of wage increases. Unions that sought to improve on postwar wage patterns, such as the Railway Brotherhoods and the UMW, now found that "free" collective bargaining of the sort advocated by John L. Lewis brought them into bitter confrontations with the government. The frequent strikes and annual pay boosts of this era, which industry used to raise prices, were at least partially responsible for creating the conservative, antilabor political climate that gave Republicans their large victory in the 1946 elections and then culminated in the passage of the Taft-Hartley Act in 1947.

Passage of the Taft-Hartley Act over President Truman's veto proved a milestone, not only for the actual legal restrictions the new law imposed on the trade unions, but as a symbol of the shifting relationship between the unions and the state during the late 1940s. The law sought to curb the practice of interunion solidarity, eliminate the radical cadre who still held influence within trade union ranks, and contain the labor movement to roughly its existing geographic and demographic terrain. The anti-Communist affidavits, the prohibition against secondary boycotts, the enactment of section 14b allowing states to prohibit the union shop, the ban on foreman unionism—all these sections of the law had been on the agenda of the National Association of Manufacturers and other conservative groups since 1938.

Of course, Taft-Hartley was not the fascist-like "slave labor law" denounced by the AFL and CIO alike. In later years, unions like the Teamsters prospered even in right-to-work states, while the bargaining relationship between employers and most big industrial unions was relatively unaffected by the new law. But if Taft-Hartley did not destroy the union movement, it did impose upon it a legal/administrative straitjacket that encouraged contractual parochialism and penalized any serious attempt to project a classwide political-economic strategy.

This explains the union movement's enormous hostility to Taft-Hartley. As CIO counsel Lee Pressman put it in 1947, "When you think of it merely as a combination of individual provisions, you are losing entirely the full impact of the program, the sinister conspiracy that has been hatched." Union leaders correctly recognized that the act represented the definitive end of the brief era in which the state served as an arena in which the trade unions could bargain for the kind of tripartite accommodation with industry that had been so characteristic of the New Deal years. At the very highest levels a trust had been broken, which is why Philip Murray declared the law "conceived in sin." . . .

The cold war's chilling effect on domestic politics . . . sealed the fate of labor-liberal efforts to find an effective vehicle that could stem the rightward drift in national politics. Until the spring of 1948 labor-liberals almost uniformly repudiated Truman as their presidential candidate and proposed replacing him with men as different as Dwight D. Eisenhower and William O. Douglas. More significant, the structure of the Democratic party also came under scrutiny. The CIO, the new Americans for Democratic Action, and the AFL favored its "realignment," either by liberalization of the South or, if that failed, the expulsion of the Dixiecrats. Moreover, there was still enough interest in the formation of a third party to create at least a serious debate within some of the major unions—notably the UAW—and within sections of the liberal community.

Ironically, it was the actual formation of a third party—the Progressive party, which ran Henry Wallace for president—that put a decisive end to such political experimentation and brought the industrial union wing of the labor movement even closer to the Democratic party. . . . His candidacy brought into sharp relief two issues that would prove crucial to the political reformulation of postwar labor-liberalism. The first was the Marshall Plan, and more generally the effort to integrate into an American-dominated world order the shattered economies of the industrialized West and commodity-producing South. Although initially greeted with some skepticism even by anti-Communist union leaders like Walter Reuther, the Marshall Plan won strong endorsement from most liberals as their hopes for the construction of a purely domestic full-employment welfare state declined, and as the Truman administration advanced the European Recovery Program as a key to international trade and North Atlantic prosperity.

The second issue raised by the Wallace candidacy was the legitimacy of the Communists in American political life, and more broadly the possibility that Popular Front politics might have a continuing relevance in postwar America. Wallace refused to accept the postwar settlement that was emerging abroad and at home. He wanted détente with the Soviet Union (accepting its control of Eastern Europe) and saw the Marshall Plan as little more than an effort to drive Western Europe into the straitjacket constructed by a newly hegemonic American capitalism. At home he denounced Taft-Hartley, defended those unions that defied its sanctions, and tried to ally himself with the most advanced forms of civil rights militancy.

By 1948 the Wallace candidacy was therefore anathema, for it represented a break with what was becoming fundamental in postwar America: alignment with the government in the battalions of the new cold war and exclusion of the Communists from the political arena. This was made explicit in a January 1948 CIO executive council resolution rejecting the Progressive party and endorsing the Marshall Plan. A powerful Wallace movement threatened to taint the CIO with the badge of disloyalty. "The real issue," asserted the ever cautious Philip Murray, "is the jeopardy in which you place your Unions." Truman's well-crafted opening to the labor-liberals—his Taft-Hartley veto message in June 1947, his accommodation of the urban coalition's pressure for federal civil rights action in the summer of 1948, and his pseudopopulist "Give 'm Hell, Harry" presidential campaign in the fall—solidified labor-liberal ties with the Democratic party. Although the trade unions might still differ privately on bargaining goals or even their approach to Taft-Hartley, any divergence from the CIO election strategy was tantamount to organizational treason, which was in fact one of the charges leveled against several unions expelled from the CIO in 1949.

Organized labor's failure to build its own political party may well have been overdetermined, even in an era when its organizational strength reached a twentieth-century apogee. The peculiarities of the American electoral system, the concentration of union strength in a relative handful of states, the ideological pressures generated by the cold war, and the continuing ethnic and racial divisions within the working class are but the most obvious factors that sealed labor's alliance with the Democratic party. But the costs of this political marriage still require calculation. Even in the urban North the Democratic party rarely offered the representatives of organized labor more than a subordinate role in the development of its political program. The CIO bargained with the Democratic party "much as it would with an employer," admitted Political Action Committee (PAC) head Jack Kroll in the early 1950s.

Two important consequences flowed from this dilemma. At the level of national policy formation, organized labor had no effective vehicle through which it could exert systematic pressure upon either the Democratic party or the state apparatus. The trade unions maintained an extensive lobbying operation in Washington and in most state capitals, but on any given issue of interest to their membership, they were forced to rebuild the labor-liberal coalition all over again. Thus labor took justifiable credit for the reelection of Truman in 1948, but it proved incapable of translating this vote into a coherent congressional majority after Congress convened three months later. In turn, this radical disjunction between the relative solidity of the working-class vote and the weakness of its political representation contributed to the demobilization and depoliticization of a large part of the American working class in these years. Denied access to a political leadership that could articulate their specific class-oriented interests, workers found their consciousness shaped either by the parochial interests of their union, or, more likely, by the vaguely populist rhetoric of mainstream Democrats.

After 1947 the defensive political posture adopted by even the most liberal of the CIO unions enhanced the apparent appeal of a narrowly focused brand of private-sector collective bargaining. For example, the conservative victory in the 1946 congressional elections had a dramatic impact on Walter Reuther's own thinking. In a radio debate of May 1946, well before the elections, Reuther told his audience that rhetoric about a "government controlled economy" was a big-business scare tactic. The real question, he said, is "how much government control and for whose benefit." But in the wake of the massive Republican victory of November 1946 Reuther made a rhetorical about-face, now urging "free labor" and "free management" to join in solving their problems, or a "superstate will arise to do it for us." Or as Reuther put it in another context, "I'd rather bargain with General Motors than with the government. . . . General Motors has no army."

General Motors and other big companies also sought a long-range accommodation with their own unions. General Motors wanted to contain unionism within what it considered its "proper sphere"; otherwise, declared Charles Wilson, the "border area of collective bargaining will be a constant battleground between unions and management." To executives like Wilson this fear was exacerbated by the realization that inflationary pressures generated by cold war military spending would be a permanent feature of the postwar scene. The UAW effort to link company pricing policy to a negotiated wage package in 1946 had been staved off by GM, but the company realized that disruptive strikes and contentious annual wage negotiations, especially if couched as part of a broader offensive against corporate power, merely served to embitter shop-floor labor relations and hamper the company's long-range planning.

Therefore in the spring of 1948—just after the Czech coup and during the months when Congress debated an administration request for a $3.3 billion military procurement package—GM offered the UAW a contract that seemed to promise social peace even in an era of continuous inflation. Two features were central to the new social order: first, an automatic cost-of-living adjustment keyed to the general price index; second, a 2-percent "annual improvement factor" wage increase designed to reflect, if only partially, the still larger annual rise in GM productivity. To GM, such permanently escalating labor costs would prove tolerable because this industrial giant faced little effective competition, either foreign or domestic, so it could easily "administer" any price increases made necessary by the new labor contract.

The agreement was a dramatic, even a radical, departure from past union practice. Reuther himself had rejected wage escalation until early 1948, and a Twentieth Century Fund survey of union leaders taken later the same year revealed that more than 90 percent opposed COLA clauses in their contracts. With the general wage declines of 1921, 1930–32, and 1938 still a living memory, most union leaders instinctively rejected the premise upon which the GM-UAW contract was based: the emergence of a new era of inflationary prosperity and relative social peace. Labor leaders thought such schemes foreclosed the possibility of a large increase in the real standard of living, and they continued to fear that such a wage formula would become a downhill escalator when the inevitable postwar depression finally arrived. The UAW, for example, described the 1948 GM pact as only a "holding action" that protected GM workers until the labor-liberal coalition could replace it with more comprehensive sociopolitical guidelines.

But when the 1949 recession turned out to be less that the depression many had expected, the gateway was open to the further elaboration of such an accommodation between the big unions and the major corporations. Again, the UAW pioneered the way, with a new agreement, a five-year "Treaty of Detroit" that provided an improved COLA, a wage increase, and a $125-a-year pension. *Fortune* magazine hailed the 1950 UAW-GM contract as "the first that unmistakably accepts the existing distribution of income between wages and profits as 'normal' if not as 'fair.' . . . It is the first major union contract that explicitly accepts objective economic facts—cost of living and productivity—as determining wages, thus throwing overboard all theories of wages as determined by political power and of profits as 'surplus value.'" By the early 1960s the COLA principle had been incorporated in more than 50 percent of all major union contracts, and in the inflationary 1960s and 1970s it spread even wider: to Social Security, to some welfare programs, and to wage determination in some units of the government and nonunion sector.

Just as the negotiation of COLA agreements came in the wake of the union movement's forced retreat from the effort to reshape the Truman administration's early economic policy, so too did the new interest in pension and health and welfare plans represent a parallel privatization of the labor movement's commitment to an expanded welfare state. Initially, American trade unionists overwhelmingly favored a public, federal system for financing social benefits like pensions, health care, and unemployment insurance. Both the CIO and AFL worked for the passage of the Wagner-Murray-Dingell bill, a 1945 proposal that would have liberalized and federalized the American social welfare system in a fashion not dissimilar to that envisioned by the British government's pathbreaking Beveridge Report of 1942, which laid the basis for the welfare state constructed by the postwar Labour government.

But the same forces that gutted the Full Employment Act of 1946 also destroyed labor-backed efforts to raise the social wage in these same postwar years. "Nothing more clearly distinguishes the post-war political climate of the USA from that of Great Britain than the almost unqualified refusal of its legislature to respond to proposals for social reform," wrote the British political scientist Vivian Vale. The United States devoted about 4.4 percent of GNP to Social Security in 1949, a proportion less than half that of even the austere economies of war-torn Western Europe.

Organized labor still found company-funded pension and health schemes distasteful—their coverage was incomplete, their financing was mistrusted, and they smacked of old-fashioned paternalism—but the political impasse faced by postwar unionists seemed to offer no alternatives. . . .

Indeed, mainstream union leaders never abandoned their formal commitment to an expanded welfare state, but at the same time they retreated, if more subtly, to a more parochial outlook. Immediately after the disastrous midterm elections of 1946, CIO leaders announced that they were not going to wait "for perhaps another ten years until the Social Security laws are amended adequately." Instead they would press for pensions and health benefits in their next collective bargaining round. Some unionists of a more explicitly social democratic outlook, like Walter Reuther and William Pollock of the Textile Workers, theorized that if employers were saddled with large pension and health insurance costs, they would join "shoulder to shoulder" with labor-liberal forces to demand higher federal payments to relieve them of this burden. But such assumptions proved naive. The big unions themselves no longer saw an increase in federal welfare expenditures as an urgent task. And after the steel and auto unions established the heavy-industry pension and health benefit pattern in 1949, employers were more than ready to fold these additional costs into their product prices. Moreover, managers recognized that company-specific benefits built employee loyalty, and at some level they understood that a social wage of minimal proportions was advantageous to their class interest, even if their own firm had to bear additional costs as a consequence. . . .

The weakness of the postwar welfare state and the extreme fragmentation inherent in the American system of industrial relations did much to redivide the American working class into a unionized segment that until recently enjoyed an almost Western European level of social welfare protection, and a still larger stratum, predominantly young, minority, and female, that was left out in the cold. Because so much of the postwar social struggle has taken place at the level of the firm rather than within a broader political arena, this American system has reinforced the postwar economy's tendency to construct segmented and unequal labor markets. This multi-tiered system of industrial relations has served to erode solidarity within the working class and has made it difficult to counter claims that welfare spending and social equity are harmful to economic growth. The classic resentment felt by many blue-collar workers toward those on state-supported welfare has one of its roots in the system of double taxation the organized working class has borne in the postwar era. Union workers pay to support two welfare systems: their own, funded by a "tax" on their total pay periodically renegotiated in their contract, and that of the government, paid for by a tax system that grew increasingly regressive as the postwar years advanced. In turn, organized labor has come to be perceived (and all too often perceives itself) as a special-interest group, in which its advocacy of welfare state measures that would raise the social wage for all workers has taken on an increasingly mechanical quality.

Among other consequences, these divisions within working class and between labor and its erstwhile allies have progressively weakened political support for the structures of the welfare state erected in the New Deal era. American unions remain supporters of Social Security, national health insurance, and minority-targeted welfare programs, but their ability to mobilize either their own members or a broader constituency on these issues declined during most of the postwar era. A militant civil rights movement, not the unions, put these issues back on the national agenda for a time in the 1960s. Moreover, labor's postwar abdication from any sustained struggle over the structure of the political economy has had its own debilitating consequences. As older industries decline, it has both sapped the loyalty of the labor movement's original blue-collar constituency and at the same time deprived the unions of any effective voice in the contemporary debate over the reorganization of work technology or the reindustrialization of the economy.

## ✦ *F U R T H E R   R E A D I N G*

Amberg, Steven. *Labor and the Postwar Political Economy* (1992).
Bell, Daniel. *The End of Ideology: On the Exhaustion of Political Ideas in the West* (1960).
Boyle, Kevin. *The UAW and the Heyday of American Liberalism, 1945–1968* (1995).
———, ed. *Organized Labor and American Politics, 1894–1994* (1998).
Brody, David. *Workers in Industrial America: Essays on the Twentieth Century Struggle* (1980).

Buhle, Paul. *Taking Care of Business: Samuel Gompers, George Meany, Lane Kirkland, and the Tragedy of American Labor* (2000).

Caute, David. *The Great Fear: The Anti-Communist Purge Under Truman and Eisenhower* (1978).

Chinoy, Ely. *Automobile Workers and the American Dream* (1955, 1992).

Clark, Daniel. *Like Night and Day: Unionism in a Southern Mill Town* (1997).

Davis, Mike. *Prisoners of the American Dream* (1987).

Deslippe, Dennis. *"Rights, Not Roses": Unions and the Rise of Working-Class Feminism, 1945–1980* (2000).

Fones-Wolf, Elizabeth. *Selling Free Enterprise: The Business Assault on Labor and Liberalism, 1945–1960* (1994).

Foster, James. *The Union Politic: The CIO Political Action Committee* (1975).

Freeman, Joshua. *Working-Class New York: Life and Labor Since World War II* (2000).

Greenstone, J. David. *Labor in American Politics* (1969).

Halpern, Martin. *UAW Politics in the Cold War Era* (1988).

Horowitz, Daniel. *Betty Friedan and the Making of the Feminine Mystique: The American Left, the Cold War, and Modern Feminism* (1998).

Horowitz, Roger. *"Negro and White, Unite and Fight!": A Social History of Industrial Unionism in Meatpacking, 1930–1990* (1997).

Jacoby, Sanford. *Modern Manors: Welfare Capitalism Since the New Deal* (1997).

Levenstein, Harvey. *Communism, Anticommunism, and the CIO* (1981).

Lichtenstein, Nelson. *State of the Union: A Century of American Labor* (2002).

———. *Walter Reuther: The Most Dangerous Man in Detroit* (1995).

Lichtenstein, Nelson, and Stephen Meyer, eds. *On the Line: Essays in the History of Auto Work* (1989).

McAuliffe, Mary Sperling. *Crisis on the Left: Cold War Politics and American Liberals, 1947–1954* (1978).

Metzgar, Jack. *Striking Steel: Solidarity Remembered* (2000).

Meyer, Stephen. *"Stalin over Wisconsin": The Making and Unmaking of Militant Unionism, 1900–1950* (1992).

Mills, C. Wright. *The New Men of Power: America's Labor Leaders* (1948, 2001).

Minchin, Timothy. *What Do We Need a Union For? The TWUA in the South* (1997).

Radosh, Ronald. *American Labor and United States Foreign Policy* (1969).

Richards, Yevette. *Maida Springer: Pan-Africanist and International Labor Leader* (2000).

Rosswurm, Steve, ed. *The CIO's Left-Led Unions* (1992).

Schrecker, Ellen. *Many Are the Crimes: McCarthyism in America* (1998).

Stebenne, David. *Arthur J. Goldberg: New Deal Liberal* (1996).

Zieger, Robert. *American Workers, American Unions, 1920–1985* (1995).

CHAPTER
12

# *Rights-Conscious Unionism*
# *in the Public Sector*

Beginning in the late 1950s, public employees rode a wave of rights consciousness to
build collective organizations of considerable size and power. Teachers, hospital staff,
and workers in municipal and state government had been largely unorganized in
the years before 1960. Their employment security, white-collar status, and legal
standing outside the labor law seemed to make them immune to collective action.
Unlike the blue-collar working class, public employees often sat behind a desk, took
a regular paid vacation, and kept their fingernails clean.

But two things happened after World War II to transform the status and expectations of public employees. All of a sudden, many blue-collar workers received more
pay, equal job security, and some of the same perks as white-collar employees, such
as paid vacations. Most levels of government let wages and benefits lag. Thus by the
early 1960s, truck drivers earned more than schoolteachers and auto workers more
than post office clerks.

Second, the ranks of these workers exploded after World War II. The permanent
federal work force doubled in size, but among the eighty thousand units of state and
local government, payrolls tripled and quadrupled in the quarter-century after the
end of the war. Public employment became increasingly black and brown, not only
because administrators sought a low-wage work force, but because racial minorities,
still excluded from so many good private sector jobs, valued year-round government-
paid work.

The offices, classrooms, and hospital hallways of New York City proved the
birthplace of modern public employee unionism. Despite their exclusion from Wagner
Act protections, indeed despite state laws that severely penalized public employee
work stoppages, the teachers, social workers, and sanitation men of the city pushed
forward the frontiers of collective action all during the late 1950s and early 1960s.
City employees in heavily Jewish and Italian occupations were soon joined by the
increasingly large number of African Americans and Puerto Ricans who worked in
blue-collar city services and on hospital, food, and cleaning staffs. The most startling
expression of the new militancy erupted in the postal system in March 1970, when
200,000 workers struck urban post offices. Their strike amounted to a revolt—not

*only against their employer, the federal government, but also against their own union leaders, who had long functioned largely as Capitol Hill lobbyists.*

*Public sector unionism thereafter grew rapidly; soon many long-standing employee groups, including those that enrolled police, firefighters, teachers, and state civil servants, transformed themselves into de facto unions. This form of rights-conscious public employee unionism was aided by a new set of laws that legalized collective bargaining in many northern and western states, as well as in federal employment. By the 1980s, union density among schoolteachers reached an extraordinary 80 percent, which was greater than in coal mining and auto production. Indeed, by the end of the twentieth century, public sector unionism, over 4 million strong, represented about 40 percent of all organized workers.*

*How does work for the government differ from that in the private sector? Why have many racial and ethnic minorities, from nineteenth-century Irish to twentieth-century African Americans, gravitated to such work? What are the differences between unionism in government employment and the corporate economy?*

### ⚓ D O C U M E N T S

Public school teachers became increasingly frustrated in the immediate postwar years. In Document 1, teacher-unionist Selma Borchart demonstrates that by 1951, the paternalism of so many public school superintendents and principals undermined the dignity and professionalism classroom teachers sought to cultivate. Public employee unionism was greatly advanced by the rise of a powerful civil rights movement in the early 1960s. In Document 2, we reprint the original demands of the August 1963 March on Washington for Jobs and Freedom, venue for Martin Luther King Jr.'s famous "I Have a Dream" oration. Note the degree to which the demands of the march organizers weave together, civil, labor, and economic rights. This same imbrication is clear in Document 3, an account by union leader Taylor Rogers of the 1968 Memphis sanitation strike, where the slogan "I Am a Man" reflected the rights-conscious potency of the union struggle for an all-male group of some 1,300 African American strikers. In Document 4, Cesar Chavez, president of the United Farm Workers, deploys the rights language and ethos of King and the civil rights movement in defense of the effort by a largely Latino group of farm workers to organize a union in the California grape and lettuce fields.

## 1. The American Federation of Teachers on the Rights of Teachers, 1951

The American Teacher is not free today. [The] [t]eacher shortage is due not only to low salaries. It is due to the lack of freedom of the teacher; to the petty tyrannies to which teachers are subjected.

Teachers are told how to dress, how to play, what to eat, how to spend their leisure time. Teachers are told which organizations they must join, and which

From "The Teachers' Rights," in Selma Borchart Papers, Folder 113–17, "Teachers' Salary and Rights," AFT Papers, Walter Reuther Library, Wayne State University, Detroit. Reprinted by permission of Walter Reuther Library.

organizations they may not join. They are officially urged, in every state, to join the state education association, which actually is the Company Union, in education. In many states teachers are required, as a condition of employment, to join this Company Union at the national, state and local level. In many places, the check-off is used; dues for the administratively controlled teacher's association—The Company Union—are deducted from the teacher's salary before the teacher is paid. On the other hand teachers are dismissed, in many places, for forming or joining a union. Teachers are penalized in many ways. They may be assigned to badly located schools; they may be given an extra heavy teaching load; they may be denied promotions; they may be insulted in teachers' meetings by their superior officers, simply because they choose to join a union.

A significant case with far-reaching implications is the North Carolina case. Here, the teachers finding no possible chance to better their conditions of employment through the state educational association (the Company Union), formed a union, a local of the American Federation of Teachers. The Superintendent of Schools [then] called the teachers together and warned them of the dire consequences they would suffer, if they joined a union. Yet in spite of his threats, many teachers joined the new Union. Ironically, this Superintendent of Schools, who had threatened them, was then selected as a member of a delegation which was being sent to Japan, to "teach democracy," to the Japanese teachers. The strong protest of the American Federation of Labor kept this Superintendent from going to Japan to teach his brand of American democracy.

But the North Carolina case is but one of the many similar attacks on teachers. The state federations of labor in Virginia, Iowa, Florida, Idaho, California, as well as in North Carolina—just to mention a few—are, at this moment, actually engaged in a determined struggle to help make the teacher free to join any legal organization of his own choosing.

Teacher tenure laws are essential to protect the teacher on the job from political pressures. Yet, in many legislatures the fight for teacher tenure laws has been made more difficult by the opposition to such laws from the very organization the teachers are told to join.

The teacher, like every other worker, must be economically more free than he is today. Teachers' salaries are woefully small. No professionally trained worker should be asked to begin work at less than $3000 per year. The salary should be graduated by annual increments, until in about five or six years, he reaches a salary worthy of the services he renders.

The teacher must be relatively more free in his contemplation of his old age security than he is today. His small salary does not enable him to save much. Teachers' pensions in most cases are not adequate. . . .

The teacher must have enough free time—unassigned time, to enable him to work closely with the individual pupil, to give to his work that inspiration which must come from close personal work with the individual child and youth. The teacher must in addition have adequate leisure time, for his relaxation and to continue his personal professional growth.

The teacher must be free to use his professional training and experience in helping shape administrative school policy. The tragic waste inherent in a system which denies the teacher—the professional worker who is most closely identified with actual child training—a right to participate in planning the educational program for a school system, is certainly disturbing.

The teacher must be free from the all-too-prevalent petty tyrannies of school administrators. A person to whom parents entrust their children should certainly be regarded as capable of running his personal affairs without interference from school authorities. The petty, personal indignities to which teachers are often subjected would not be tolerated by any good trade unionist on his job. Teachers certainly are entitled to protection against such indignities.

A case in point, is the situation in Pawtucket, Rhode Island. The teachers there sought through their union to negotiate a very badly needed wage increase. They could not get even an adequate hearing to present their case. All efforts to attempt to negotiate their differences with their employers were for weeks met by evasion and rebuffs, and threats; threats of loss of job; threats of adverse legislative action.

This case shows the urgent need for the development of special machinery through which teachers and, incidentally other public employees, may seek to adjudicate their problems without threats or reprisals against them, for any protective action which they may take, in their own interests. Surely the teacher as a worker with heavy professional responsibilities should have representation of his own choosing in a machinery established to help settle administrative disputes in the community. But the teacher is not free.

It is only a free teacher who can help train free men and women.

## 2. The March on Washington Demands Jobs and Freedom, 1963

# MARCH ON WASHINGTON FOR JOBS AND FREEDOM
## AUGUST 28, 1963

## LINCOLN MEMORIAL PROGRAM

### WHAT WE DEMAND*

1. Comprehensive and effective *civil rights legislation* from the present Congress—without compromise or filibuster—to guarantee all Americans

> access to all public accommodations
> decent housing
> adequate and integrated education
> the right to vote

2. Withholding of Federal funds from all programs in which discrimination exists.

3. *Desegregation of all school districts in 1963.*

4. Enforcement of the *Fourteenth Amendment*—reducing Congressional representation of states where citizens are disfranchised.

5. A new *Executive Order* banning discrimination in all housing supported by federal funds.

6. Authority for the Attorney General to institute *injunctive* suits when any constitutional right is violated.

7. A massive federal program to train and place all unemployed workers—Negro and white—on meaningful and dignified jobs at decent wages.

8. A national *minimum wage* act that will give all Americans a decent standard of living. (Government surveys show that anything less than $2.00 an hour fails to do this.)

9. A broadened *Fair Labor Standards* Act to include all areas of employment which are presently excluded.

10. A federal *Fair Employment Practices Act* barring discrimination by federal, state, and municipal governments, and by employers, contractors, employment agencies, and trade unions.

---

*Support of the March does not necessarily indicate endorsement of every demand listed. Some organizations have not had an opportunity to take an official position on all of the demands advocated here.

---

Leaflet reprinted in National JOBS FOR ALL Coalition, "Jobs for All Season," 1998. Reprinted courtesy of the National JOBS FOR ALL Coalition, 475 Riverside Drive, Suite 832, New York, NY 10115-0050.

# 3. Union Leader Taylor Rogers Relives the Memphis Sanitation Strike (1968), 2000

*You keep your back bent over, somebody's gonna ride it.*

Twenty-seven years after Martin Luther King, Jr.'s death, I spoke with Taylor Rogers about the traumatic events of 1968. He and his wife lived in a pleasant home in a north Memphis neighborhood where the respectable working poor and the "underclass," without employment, skills, or prospects for change, lived almost side by side. Rogers had barely escaped that fate himself through unionization, which he felt gave dignity to a life of hard work and little pay.

. . . I finally got a job with the city in 1958, at the Sanitation Department. There wasn't too much opportunity for a black man at that time. Really wasn't no other jobs hardly to be found. I was at a point I had to take what I could get. That was the situation with most of the men.

At that time working conditions were terrible. We had all kinds of things to go through with the boss. Whatever the boss said was right. You didn't have no rights to speak up for nothin'. We'd go out in the morning, we'd stay out until they'd tell us we could come in. Had roll call in the morning. If the guy didn't like the way you answered your name, he'd send you home. . . .

I was workin' on the trucks. Now you see all these garbage cans on the street. Back then, everybody had a 50-gallon drum in the backyard. We had to go in those backyards with tubs. You carried those tubs on your head and shoulders. Most of those tubs were leakin' and that stuff was fallin' all over you. You got home you had to take your clothes off at the door 'cause you didn't want to bring all that filth in the house. We didn't have no decent place to eat your lunch. You didn't have no place to use the restroom. Conditions was just terrible. We didn't have no say about nothing. Whatever they said, that's what you had to do: right, wrong, indifferent. Anything that you did that the supervisor didn't like, he'd fire you, whatever. You didn't have no recourse, no way of gettin' back at him. We just got tired of all that.

Most of the supervisors was white people. All the better jobs the whites had, bulldozer drivers, heavy-equipment people, supervisors, and stuff like that. They didn't have to do too much of nothin'. They would send us home when it was rainin' and we didn't get no pay. But the white guys could sit around and they would get their full day. The men working was 99 percent black. About 1966, I believe it was, we pulled a work stoppage. But we was on the picket line for about an hour, and T. O. Jones [leader of the unrecognized union] came around and told us we had to go in because they put out an injunction on us. Once they found out that we was out there, that's when they got the injunction. So we all went back to work the next day. We kept on. We took things and took things. . . .

We finally got to a point where we had lots of followers. We had talked with the city, we had tried to get organized, get some recognition, get some things done that we needed done, and we always got turned down. We just finally got tired of it.

---

From Michael Honey, *Black Workers Remember: An Oral History of Segregation, Unionism, and the Freedom Struggle* (Berkeley: University of California Press, 2000), excerpts from pp. 293–296, 298–302. Reprinted by permission of the Regents of the University of California and the University of California Press.

We had some guys that worked over on a kind of a packer where you put your garbage. One rainy day they were up in there and something triggered that thing off, and it just crushed them. We just got tired. Thirteen hundred men decided they was tired and wasn't gonna take no more. . . .

[But before that] nobody really had paid no attention but the men. This was a strike that *we* called. Labor didn't call it, *we* called it. I don't think nobody knowed too much about our problems. They see us out there doing this dirty work, but I don't think they paid no attention. But we were the men who did it, we got together and decided it. But you keep your back bent over, somebody's gonna ride it. We decided we gotta do what we have to do and we withdrew our services from the city.

[Mayor] Loeb went all off the wall and everything. He did a lot of things. He had strikebreakers. They had police and fire trucks there every day. Some of the men was goin' back in [as strikebreakers] and we'd have a "prayer meetin' " with them, and they didn't go back no more. We'd talk to them and tell them, "It's our job y'all are trying to take out there." We'd talk to them wherever we'd meet them. Right on the spot we'd tell them so, trying to tell them not to go back. The ones that the city was hiring at the time, we didn't bother with them too much. Everywhere they'd go they had to have a police squad car escorting them. We wasn't trying to be violent or anything. We just wanted decent working conditions. But we had to do whatever we had to do to try to keep things goin'. Some of them wouldn't go back the next day. Some of them wouldn't go. We never resorted to violence, to do anything to nobody.

Every Sunday, churches was taking up money for the strikers. We'd go out to Firestone or International Harvester on Friday and stand outside the gate when the men were coming out, and they gave us a lot of money. We'd just stand there with a bucket and they'd come by and drop the money in. We'd have mass meetings out at Mason Temple and then we'd pass garbage cans around. Those garbage cans were just filled with money. It brought the black community together more so than anything I've seen. That's how we survived.

In the white neighborhoods they'd put the garbage out where people [strikebreakers] could get it. In the white community they would put it in the can and put it out on the street, and somebody could come along and pick it up. . . . All they had to do was drive by, dump it in the truck, and keep on going. But in the black neighborhoods, they'd dump it in the street. It would be such a mess they couldn't get to it, they couldn't pick it up. That would put pressure on the city, too, because then the health department started getting down because of the uncleanness. The streets were filled with garbage. People would just go out the door and dump their garbage in the street, pile it up on the curb. . . .

You were determined. But sometimes you got weary and things looked bad, it looked like we wasn't making no progress. It dragged out so long some of the men started going back. Some of them were losing spirit, losing confidence. It got a little rough. That's when Reverend Lawson got Dr. King involved. When Dr. King came in, he made some speeches and things, and that built the morale back up and men started comin' out again. . . .

When Dr. King came the first time and gave his speech, like he was saying, "Don't worry about what would happen to me but [worry] what would happen to the garbagemen if we didn't [win]." It made the community more up and ready and made the men more up and ready to keep on pushing to get something done. His speech brought people out, brought poor people together.

All those marches were kind of crucial. Right after the first march, we marched with the national guard with fixed bayonets and tanks, but we kept marchin'. . . . We marched every day from Clayborn Temple to the city hall and back. The black ministers were leading this.

After King was killed, all over the country everybody was puttin' pressure, the president, everybody else was puttin' pressure on Henry Loeb for lettin' this kind of thing happen. So he signed it. We finally got a contract, an agreement signed.

Loeb was such a hardnose, I don't know what would have happened if King hadn't got killed. I don't know whether he would have gave in or what. He had support from the white people here in Memphis. That's what kept him so strong. Everywhere he'd go the whites would tell him, "Hang on in there, Henry." It was bad for him. When you get that kind of support, it's hard for you to pull out. He had so much pressure on him then. If he didn't have that support he probably would have gave in. . . . The city council had three blacks, but they were always overruled.

. . . So when King got killed, I think that's when the pressure came down on Memphis, and Loeb had to move. Because people from all over the country started comin' in, and unions from all over the country. Walter Reuther brought fifty thousand dollars from the auto workers. So Loeb had to give in.

Even if it had been poor white workers, King would have done the same thing. That's just the kind of person he was. He stopped what he was doin.' He was plannin' this big march to Washington. All his staff thought it was outrageous of him to stop and come to Memphis. But he went where he was needed, where he could help poor people. . . .

And that's what he did, he dropped all that and come and dealt with it. That's when the first march was. Then he had to continue on. He had to let people know that he could come back to Memphis and have a nonviolent march. But before that nonviolent march, that's when they assassinated him, before that second march. After his death we did have that nonviolent march, we had a silent march, all you could hear was people's footsteps hittin' the pavement. It was a silent march.

He didn't get all accomplished he wanted accomplished, but I don't think he died in vain. Because what he came here to do, that was settled. There was a lot of other things he wanted done, things that needed to be done, and a lot of things have got done.

What a lot of people in Memphis don't realize, white folks and people with good jobs, is that black folks wouldn't be in the position they're in now if it had not been for King comin' here and dyin'. All the banks have got colored tellers, and school principals. Before that, we didn't have that. [Today] city hall is full of blacks, even to the mayor. From the top all the way through. So some of the things he was about happened. And things are still happening. But it's a slow process. I think there's been a big change in Memphis.

The Local AFSCME 1733 grew from 1,300 workers to about 7,000. We organized a number of others after we got that all settled. We got [workers at the] fire commission, city court clerks, auto inspection stations, both city and county school boards, Liberty Land [amusement park]. Sanitation had their chapter, park commissioner has their chapter. Each chapter had a chairperson, and those people made up the executive board of the whole Local 1733. All of them come under the umbrella of 1733. I started off as a steward, then I went to chief steward. From chief steward to chapter chairperson for sanitation, from that to president of the local in 1972. And I stayed there until 1992. . . .

Sanitation workers had strength because of their unity. We'd have lots of things going on in city hall, we'd ask all the other chapters to show up. Even if it was for their chapter, the sanitation workers would always be there. There would be more of the sanitation people there than [other] workers, because we was the backbone and we was the strength.

## 4.  Cesar E. Chavez, Good Friday Message, 1969

Good Friday 1969.

E. L. Barr, Jr., President
California Grape and Tree Fruit League
717 Market St.
San Francisco, California

Dear Mr. Barr:

I am sad to hear about your accusations in the press that our union movement and table grape boycott have been successful because we have used violence and terror tactics. If what you say is true, I have been a failure and should withdraw from the struggle; but you are left with the awesome moral responsibility, before God and man, to come forward with whatever information you have so that corrective action can begin at once. If for any reason you fail to come forth to substantiate your charges, then you must be held responsible for committing violence against us, albeit violence of the tongue. I am convinced that you as a human being did not mean what you said but rather acted hastily under pressure from the public relations firm that has been hired to try to counteract the tremendous moral force of our movement. How many times we ourselves have felt the need to lash out in anger and bitterness.

Today on Good Friday 1969 we remember the life and the sacrifice of Martin Luther King, Jr., who gave himself totally to the nonviolent struggle for peace and justice. In his "Letter from Birmingham Jail" Dr. King describes better than I could our hopes for the strike and boycott: "Injustice must be exposed, with all the tension its exposure creates, to the light of human conscience and the air of national opinion before it can be cured." For our part I admit that we have seized upon every tactic and strategy consistent with the morality of our cause to expose that injustice and thus to heighten the sensitivity of the American conscience so that farm workers will have without bloodshed their own union and the dignity of bargaining with their agribusiness employers. By lying about the nature of our movement, Mr. Barr, you are working against nonviolent social change. Unwittingly perhaps, you may unleash that other force which our union by discipline and deed, censure and

From *Christian Century,* Vol. 86 (April 23, 1969), p. 539. Copyright © 1969 Christian Century Foundation. Reprinted with permission the April 23, 1969 issue of the *Christian Century.*

education has sought to avoid, that panacean shortcut: that senseless violence which honors no color, class or neighborhood.

You must understand—I must make you understand—that our membership and hopes and aspirations of the hundreds of thousands of the poor and dispossessed that have been raised on our account are, above all, human beings, no better and no worse than any other cross-section of human society; we are not saints because we are poor, but by the same measure neither are we immoral. We are men and women who have suffered and endured much, and not only because of our abject poverty but because we have been kept poor. The colors of our skins, the languages of our cultural and native origins, the lack of formal education, the exclusion from the democratic process, the numbers of our slain in recent wars—all these burdens generations after generation have sought to demoralize us, to break our human spirit. But God knows that we are not beasts of burden, agricultural implements or rented slaves; we are men. And mark this well, Mr. Barr, we are men locked in a death struggle against man's inhumanity to man in the industry that you represent. And this struggle itself gives meaning to our life and ennobles our dying.

As your industry has experienced, our strikers here in Delano and those who represent us throughout the world are well trained for this struggle. They have been under the gun, they have been kicked and beaten and herded by dogs, they have been cursed and ridiculed, they have been stripped and chained and jailed, they have been sprayed with the poisons used in the vineyards; but they have been taught not to lie down and die nor to flee in shame, but to resist with every ounce of human endurance and spirit. To resist not with retaliation in kind but to overcome with love and compassion, with ingenuity and creativity, with hard work and longer hours, with stamina and patient tenacity, with truth and public appeal, with friends and allies, with mobility and discipline, with politics and law, and with prayer and fasting. They were not trained in a month or even a year; after all, this new harvest season will mark our fourth full year of strike and even now we continue to plan and prepare for the years to come. Time accomplishes for the poor what money does for the rich.

This is not to pretend that we have everywhere been successful enough or that we have not made mistakes. And while we do not belittle or underestimate our adversaries—for they are the rich and the powerful and they possess the land—we are not afraid nor do we cringe from the confrontation. We welcome it! We have planned for it. We know that our cause is just, that history is a story of social revolution, and that the poor shall inherit the land.

Once again, I appeal to you as the representative of your industry and as a man. I ask you to recognize and bargain with our union before the economic pressure of the boycott and strike takes an irrevocable toll; but if not, I ask you to at least sit down with us to discuss the safeguards necessary to keep our historical struggle free of violence. I make this appeal because as one of the leaders of our nonviolent movement, I know and accept my responsibility for preventing, if possible, the destruction of human life and property. For these reasons and knowing of Gandhi's admonition that fasting is the last resort in place of the sword, during a most critical time in our movement last February 1968 I undertook a 25-day fast. I repeat to you the principle enunciated to the membership at the start of the fast: if to build our union required the deliberate taking of life, either the life of a grower or his child, or the life of a farm worker or his child, then I choose not to see the union built.

Mr. Barr, let me be painfully honest with you. You must understand these things. We advocate militant nonviolence as our means for social revolution and to achieve justice for our people, but we are not blind or deaf to the desperate and moody winds of human frustration, impatience and rage that blow among us. Gandhi himself admitted that if his only choice were cowardice or violence, he would choose violence. Men are not angels, and time and tide wait for no man. Precisely because of these powerful human emotions, we have tried to involve masses of people in their own struggle. Participation and self-determination remain the best experience of freedom, and free men instinctively prefer democratic change and even protect the rights guaranteed to seek it. Only the enslaved in despair have need of violent overthrow.

This letter does not express all that is in my heart, Mr. Barr. But if it says nothing else it says that we do not hate you or rejoice to see your industry destroyed; we hate the agribusiness system that seeks to keep us enslaved, and we shall overcome and change it not by retaliation or bloodshed but by a determined nonviolent struggle carried on by those masses of farm workers who intend to be free and human.

Sincerely yours,
Cesar E. Chavez

## ✣ E S S A Y S

The upsurge of trade unionism in the 1930s and 1940s had taken place largely among private sector blue-collar workers. But such men and women hardly encompassed more than a third of the entire U.S. working class. In the first essay, historian Majorie Murphy of Swarthmore College describes how many schoolteachers, especially in big cities like New York, began to think of themselves as both workers and professionals in the years after World War II. Many were women, many were the sons and daughters of immigrants. They sought middle-class respect and income, but since almost all public workers were uncovered by any labor law, their early struggles were illegal and highly controversial.

In the second essay, historian Michael Honey of the University of Washington, Tacoma, traces the linkages between economic justice, trade unionism, and the civil rights movement in the life and thought of Martin Luther King Jr. Honey then describes the epic struggle of African American sanitation men to form a union and to win recognition, dignity, and a higher standard of living in Memphis. Their strike became world-famous after an assassin struck down King in that city when he traveled there to aid the union cause.

Was the conflict in Memphis about civil rights or unionism? Or can any such distinction be made? In the years after 1968, why did the American Federation of Teachers seem an opponent of some goals of the civil rights movement, while the American Federation of State, County, and Municipal Employees became closely identified with African American aspirations?

# Collective Bargaining: The Coming of Age
# of Teacher Unionism

### MARJORIE MURPHY

Collective bargaining changed the fundamental relationship between teachers and administrators. It promised teachers more say in the conduct of their work, more pay, and greater job security. It essentially refined and broadened the concept of professionalism for teachers by assuring them more autonomy and less supervisory control. Before 1961 unions in less than a dozen school districts . . . [bargained collectively]. By the late seventies, 72 percent of all public school teachers were members of some form of union that represented them at the bargaining table.

For elementary teachers, collective bargaining meant breaks from the constant pressure of being in front of the classroom for six hours; for high school teachers it meant time to prepare for classes; for junior high school teachers it meant relief from extra lunch guard duties. Teachers were no longer told arbitrarily when they had to appear at school and when they could leave; surprise faculty meetings after school disappeared; and administrators could no longer appear suddenly in a teacher's classroom. Teachers still had to report to school at a prescribed time, they still had to attend meetings, they still had to welcome in outsiders to their classes, but what changed was the arbitrariness, the complete absence of control on the job that teachers had incessantly complained of. If the fundamental object of unionism is to give workers dignity on the job, unionization achieved that much for teachers and more.

Of the two teachers' organizations, the AFT [American Federation of Teachers] was the first to embrace collective bargaining. The NEA [National Education Association] thought collective bargaining would destroy professionalism; leaders in the NEA warned that if teachers behaved like trade unionists they would lose all respect and status in the community. In contrast, the AFT pointed out that teachers would gain respect because at last their salaries would be commensurate with their preparation. As collective bargaining laws were introduced, the union and the association began a bitter contest for representation in hundreds of school districts throughout the country. To prove that one organization had more clout than the other, the two organizations became more and more militant, and the number of school strikes rose dramatically. This new teacher militancy often tested old anti-strike legislation for public employees, and as a result of the teachers' contest these laws were liberalized.

## Postwar Prospects for Collective Bargaining

Collective bargaining was an issue of discussion within the AFT after World War II, as teachers struck for higher wages. The national acceptance of unionization emboldened the teachers to expect similar acceptance of their desires to fully join

Reprinted from Marjorie Murphy, *Blackboard Unions: The AFT and the NEA, 1900–1980* (Ithaca, N.Y.: Cornell University Press, 1991), pp. 209–231. Copyright © 1991 by Cornell University. Used by permission of the publisher, Cornell University Press.

the labor movement. As teacher strikes increased, especially within the AFT, a long discussion over strikes ended with the union reaffirming its no-strike policy at the outset of the postwar red scare. Still, strong arguments were raised against the old policy: first, that teachers had a right to a decent standard of living and needed the means to get it; second, that teachers had an obligation to rescue children from intolerable conditions in the schools; and finally, that citizens were so apathetic about school problems that they needed drastic action before they would respond to the teachers' needs. By 1952, even though a divided AFT convention reaffirmed the policy in sweeping language, change was in the air. Carl Megel's election as AFT president that year was seen as a call for more aggressive leadership on economic issues. He began his term by pointing out that "the average salary for teachers in the United States during the past year was approximately $400 less than the income for the average factory worker." Megel did not attack the strike policy right away, but under his leadership a series of articles appeared in the *American Teacher,* between 1954 and 1958, devoted to explaining what collective bargaining was, how it worked in labor, and what teachers could expect.

The union wanted to make it clear that there was a big difference between the way that most locals were bargaining (by attending school-board meetings and making formal requests, which were often ignored) and the way most unions bargained, with formal negotiations within a limited time frame. As one Chicago teacher put it, "Collective bargaining is not waiting months for a reply."

In an editorial entitled "Collective Bargaining v. Collective Begging," Megel outlined the benefits that real collective bargaining could bring to teachers once boards of education had to recognize union representatives and bargain in good faith. This program of internal education introduced the prospect of changing the relationships between teachers and their employers. Teachers, often chastened under McCarthyism, cautiously pursued a change in the hierarchical and often destructive line-to-staff methods of supervision in the schools. They were also concerned about their low salaries and their poor working conditions—issues that, since the turn of the century, they had claimed a right to criticize.

In 1958 the AFT urged the repeal of no-strike legislation in various states and edged closer to sanctioning the idea of unlimited collective bargaining, though without mentioning strikes. In contrast, the NEA maintained its no-strike policy: "There is no question of the attitude of NEA members in the past: they have been and remain, preponderantly against the use of the strike by teachers."

The move toward collective bargaining, from roughly the end of postwar teacher militancy in 1952 to the New York City schoolteachers' strike in 1962, can be characterized as a slow, often discouraging, and sometimes extraordinarily frustrating battle of wits between young, dedicated, idealistic organizers and a stubbornly ensconced bureaucracy that was bent on ignoring them. In this important decade teachers were able to gain procedures for dismissal that guaranteed due process, procedures that would have saved the jobs of hundreds if teachers had had such rights before McCarthyism. Teachers were also able to get rid of the discriminatory laws regarding married women teachers while strengthening tenure and pension laws. On the local level, teachers confronted their stringent boards of education and, in an age of the greatest prosperity in the history of the nation, heard fantastic reasons why they could not share in this growth. Sometimes teachers had sufficient luck, organization, and determination to gain small wage increases. Teachers made gains before collective bargaining, but they did so under the slowest conditions imaginable. In this decade, the *American Teacher* faithfully recorded every tedious gain and every disappointing loss.

## The New York Teachers

David Selden was one of the young organizers working to turn the tide for collective bargaining. A schoolteacher in Dearborn, Michigan, Selden was impressed by the success of the United Auto Workers and its president, Walter Reuther. Selden began union organizing in the national AFT office before going to New York City to organize in 1953. At that time Charles Cogen, a scholarly man who had taught in private high schools after several years in the New York City public school system, served as president of Local 2. Selden worked well with Cogen, often pushing his boss to take bold stands for collective bargaining. As Selden describes it, the union was still functioning much as the Teachers' Guild had; that is, it was primarily interested in social issues (opposition to prayer in schools, for example) rather than in bread-and-butter questions of salaries and pensions. Selden argued and won a reorientation of union efforts in the direction of collective bargaining, and then began to press issues that could attract new members. The strength of the union was in the junior high schools, so Selden's goal was to organize elementary and high school teachers. For the elementary school teachers he discovered the issue of having a free lunch period. Elementary school teachers had no break from their early morning arrival until dismissal, often after long faculty meetings late in the afternoon. Selden was able to successfully press the board for free time, while maintaining the goal that teachers would eventually receive a full hour off in the middle of the day.

The high school teachers were a bit more difficult to organize. In New York they had long been organized by the unaffiliated High School Teachers' Association (HSTA). They resisted a move by the Board of Education to introduce a single salary schedule in the schools, a move that many boards of education made in the late forties to equalize teachers' salaries in elementary and high schools. High school teachers, many but not all of whom had more education than elementary school teachers, considered this a further erosion of their status and fiercely resisted it. . . . The change for New York came in 1948, but it was not a welcome one for the male high school teachers who led HSTA.

More men were entering high-school teaching after the war, thus equalizing the numbers of men and women in high school faculties. As the G.I. Bill brought more men onto college campuses they began to compete with women for teaching jobs at the highest pay levels. In the same period the ratio of men to women elementary school teachers remained fairly constant, as it did throughout the twentieth century. Nationally men earned more money than women in the schools, but because of the early equal pay suits brought by Grace Strachan in 1910, in most cases this disparity could be explained not by legal differences in allocations but by the different ratios of men in higher-paid high school teaching jobs. Although women teachers tended to be slightly older than men teachers, and to have more seniority, the median income levels were $3,456 a year for men and only $2,394 for women.

Inflation after the war tended to exaggerate effects of the transition from dual salary schedules to single salary schedules. High school teachers noted that elementary teachers had received an increase in income of 62 percent above 1939 pay levels, while high school teachers had received an increase of only 25.6 percent. . . . Teachers in both the union and the association raised the question whether they were being adequately compensated for the extracurricular and cocurricular activities they participated in, especially as the nation focused on problems of juvenile delinquency and the need for afternoon activities. The New York High School Teachers' Association boycotted extra duties in 1954, and in 1958 evening high school teachers struck for extra pay. Selden convinced Local 2 to support the strike, and early in 1959 merger talks began which were to culminate in the formation of the United Federation of Teachers (UFT). As part of the merger agreement, the UFT would support salary differentials based on "merit," that is, on level of education achieved.

With these organizing efforts bringing in new teachers and swelling the ranks of Local 2 to five thousand teachers, Selden began to plan a teachers' strike for collective bargaining, to take place on 16 May 1960. Before teachers walked out, the Board of Education agreed to make arrangements for collective bargaining. After a summer of waiting, however, the union leadership announced a strike for election day, 7 November 1960. The strike threat had the Democratic city leadership at the point of despair, but the Board of Education was adamant and the teachers walked out. To be sure, Selden's organizing drive had left many of the city's forty thousand teachers untouched, and many schools were unaffected by the teachers' walkout. But the publicity given the teachers' demands and the effective strikes in junior high schools and high schools forced the city to give in to the UFT. After one day out the teachers returned to work victoriously, knowing that in one year an election would be held and that a collective bargaining arrangement would follow. It was a stunning victory that raised teachers' hopes for change nationally.

The daring one-day strike of New York teachers forced a collective bargaining election on the Board of Education in a union town where the city administration under Mayor Robert Wagner was fairly sympathetic to public employee unions. But at roughly the same time other states had begun to recognize the need for collective bargaining for public workers. The first collective bargaining law for public employees had appeared in Wisconsin in 1959. Wisconsin was the state where the first American Federation of State, County, and Municipal Employees organized in 1934. With a long history of progressive public employee unions and a strong lobby in Madison, it was possible to pass a strong collective bargaining law, which was amended in 1961. The new statute gave public employees the right to form their own organizations, and it provided for a form of fact finding in the event of an impasse in negotiations. The law explicitly prohibited strikes.

President Kennedy issued Executive Order 10988, entitled "Employee-Management Co-operation in Federal Service," on 17 January 1962, giving federal employees the right to organize and bargain collectively. The presidential endorsement nudged along the cause of collective bargaining so that by 1966 seven states had collective bargaining statutes on the books. These laws were not uniformly promising for teacher organizations. In California, for example, the Winton Act provided for a council of representatives of all teacher organizations to meet with employers. Administrators were quick to exploit the rivalry between the association and the union and effectively paralyzed negotiations. Other states failed to provide for fact finding or other forms of mediation, thereby leaving the often prohibited strike as the only avenue of resolving disputes. Teachers without collective bargaining laws were able to negotiate grievances and begin informal negotiations, but without an enabling law there was little that teachers could do except force their districts, usually through a strike, to recognize their organizations and bargain with them. The rise in teacher militancy in the midsixties moved other states to revise their statutes and recognize public employee rights. The breakthrough in the sixties came only because of the success of the New York City local.

**The New York Strike**

In the spring of 1961, the New York City Board of Education authorized a collective bargaining election. Despite efforts on the part of the NEA, . . . and various other teachers factions in the city, the UFT won. . . . Negotiations for a contract began immediately, but the inexperience of both the board and the teachers conspired to slow things to a near halt. By the spring of 1962 it became apparent that New York teachers would go out on strike for their demands. Unlike the election-day strike of 1960 or the various threats of work stoppages in the fifties, this strike would not be symbolic in any way: teachers had to force the Board of Education to make concessions by every means at their disposal. The first contract would set the pattern, the scope, and the degree of latitude for the work force. Just as the auto workers had to illustrate their solidarity and determination in the great sit-down strikes of the thirties, public employees had to demonstrate their mettle to an equally determined Board of Education.

Unlike private sector workers, public school teachers operated under a variety of legal restraints. In New York the particular constraint was the Condon-Waldin law, which . . . set forth a variety of sanctions against public workers who took their grievances to the streets. Under its provisions, teachers could lose their jobs if they struck, and if the board rehired them they would lose all tenure rights for five years and not be able to get a pay raise for six. Condon-Waldin also struck out at union leaders, providing stiff jail terms and fines. Mike Quill of the New York City Transit Workers devoted his energy to narrowing the scope of this legislation. But teachers' strikes had been gestures of defiance of the law, not direct confrontations with it. Work stoppages, boycotts of extracurricular activities, and one-day, no-work demonstrations were means of getting around the law, weakening it to the point where few public officials felt comfortable in applying its stiff sanctions to any public employee group.

The organizational leaders of the union were Cogen, Selden, and Albert Shanker, who joined the staff in 1958. A former junior high school mathematics teacher, Shanker was influenced by Selden, and the two lived in the same apartment building for many years. Assured that they had the majority of teachers behind them, the two young organizers gambled that they could pull off a more serious strike in 1962. They had reasons to be optimistic in betting that the law would not constrain them. Paramount among these was President Kennedy's executive order in 1962, which broadly defined collective bargaining rights for public workers. Despite this assurance, Kennedy's secretary of labor, Arthur Goldberg, was adamantly opposed to public employee strikes and warned the teachers "to resolve your difference by means other than strikes." Union leaders responded militantly to these warnings. "At the present moment," Cogen said, "we are looking for a contract with the Board of Education, not a strike." And yet the UFT president, paraphrasing Kennedy's own language, repeated, "Government must act like government and unions must act like unions."

Twenty thousand teachers struck the New York City public school system on 12 April 1962. It was a surprising turnout of half the teaching force, many picketing the schools while five thousand others rallied at city hall. The issues were very clear: teachers wanted a substantial pay raise, free lunch periods, check-off union dues, and one hundred and forty-seven other items dealing with work-place conditions. The teachers argued that conditions in the schools had demoralized the staff. Non-teaching chores, inadequate textbook supplies, and detailed lesson plans prepared for visiting administrators were extra burdens that could easily be eliminated. Teachers also focused on supervision as a chief grievance: "Staff conferences often find principals lecturing to teachers dogmatically on organizational details rather than encouraging the kind of academic exchange of views that marks faculty meetings at colleges." With a long list of grievances and a recalcitrant Board of Education, the union decided to focus attention first on the salary issue.

The Board of Education was perfectly willing to settle an amount of money and then go together with teachers to local and state officials to lobby a new budget request. But the UFT pointed out that such an approach had been the practice in times past, when teachers won salary concessions from the local board of education only to find that the coffers were empty. . . . New York schoolteachers argued that with collective bargaining they wanted a contract, a written and legally binding agreement that said teachers would get the money regardless of the lobbying and taxing problems of the local government. Although the newspapers focused on the money issue, they missed this structural change. The change would give organized teachers some guarantees that their organizing efforts would not be wasted. It had been common . . . for school boards to agree to teachers' demands during election season only to renege on those agreements afterward, when the teachers could no longer mobilize political support for their salaries.

First the union leaders were served with injunctions. Board president Max Rubin announced that all twenty thousand teachers were fired under Condon-Waldin and that the New York State Commissioner of Education was looking into the possibility of lifting the striking teachers' licenses. Union leaders also anticipated jail terms. On the other side of the coin, the schools were in disarray. The teachers were again most effective in the junior high schools and high schools, where disciplinary problems were rampant and baby boomers were overcrowding the classes. Several fistfights and incidents of rambunctious behavior among the undersupervised students had parents worried for the safety of their children at school. Many kept their children at home, thereby strengthening the strike. No injunction was filed under New York's Condon-Waldin Act, thus making it easier for the board and the union to settle their first dispute without long legal battles.

In order to give the raises teachers demanded, the city needed $13 million, money that had been promised to Democratic mayor Robert Wagner for educational improvements but had been cut by the efforts of the Republican governor Nelson Rockefeller. It was rumored that the popular Wagner intended to challenge Rockefeller for the governor's seat. If Wagner could blame the strike on Rockefeller, as he was clearly doing, then Rockefeller's fiscal stringency could backfire at the polls. Rockefeller had begun to pay careful attention to New York City problems.

David Selden suggested that the governor could lend the city $13 million by using a precedent set in the depression when the state had forwarded money based on anticipated income in the following year. It was an emergency measure to be sure, but it put real money on the bargaining table. Mayor Wagner, Governor Rockefeller, and the UFT negotiating team met to make the deal only hours after Charles Cogen had urged the teachers to go back to work. The settlement was a major victory for the UFT. Teachers had won real money on the table, and they had successfully defied Condon-Waldin without tough reprisals. But there was more to this strike victory than appearances. The avoidance of reprisals under Condon-Waldin meant that a new labor law would have to be drawn up, and as it turned out this revision proved no more conducive to labor peace than had previous legislation.

In assessing the strike, it is important to keep in mind that it was not just a local affair. News of the strike "crippling" the schools was a banner headline in the *New York Times*. Hundreds of thousands of other teachers and public employees in other parts of the country looked to the New York strike as an important precedent. "This is the greatest day in the history of education in New York City," Charles Cogen told rallying teacher strikers. . . . New York teachers . . . spoke of the strike as something revolutionary: "Nothing like this had ever happened before," Simon Beagle recalled. . . .

In November 1960 when the first one-day walkout occurred in New York, there were three teacher work stoppages in the entire nation, and clearly the New York City teachers were the focus of teacher-strike activity. Between 1953 and 1956 there were only fourteen strikes, whereas in 1947, at the height of the postwar strike era, there were twenty strikes involving 4,720 teachers. The New York revolution in 1962 involved 20,000 and opened up a new era of strike activity. In 1964 there were nine teacher strikes involving 14,400 teachers, and in 1965 teachers walked out in nine school districts, including Newark, New Jersey, where union leaders faced stiff jail terms. The big jump came in 1966 when thirty strikes were recorded by the U.S. Department of Labor. "Strikes and threats of strikes by public employees, particularly schoolteachers, are proving a virulent fever," the *Detroit Free Press* observed, "and the fever spreads." In 1967 the number of strikes rose to 105 and the strikes were getting longer. Although there were slightly fewer strikes in 1968, the number of idle teaching days rose to an all-time high of 2,190,000.

### Gender and Explanations of Militancy

Although most explanations of teacher militancy were based on economic justice, analysts found that salary issues did not fully explain the rise in militancy, especially since salaries seemed to be on the rise before strike fever hit the schools. The most dramatic structural change in the teaching industry between 1954 and 1964 was the 94-percent growth of the number of male schoolteachers compared with the 38-percent growth of female teachers in the same period. In 1951 men were only 21.3 percent of classroom teachers, whereas in 1964 they were 31.4 percent. We have already seen that most of these new male recruits poured into the higher-paying high school positions, but researchers also found that these men were younger than women in teaching and that 36.2 percent of secondary teachers but only 25.5 percent of elementary school teachers were under thirty years of age. Young people, sociologists have argued, tend to be more militant and radical than older people. An NEA study in 1966 identified an angry young man who had joined a profession with steadily increasing salaries but no longer felt that teaching would provide sufficient financial rewards; since 80 percent were married and 66 percent had children to support, their disillusionment did not come quickly enough for them to switch careers. Finally, researchers found that men were more likely than women to join unions, often concluding that men had greater needs for benefits than female teachers, but also suggesting that until men became teachers in large numbers, unionization had been insignificant.

None of the researchers in these studies knew the history of Margaret Haley and the early years of the teachers' union; their oversight of the contribution of women to the revival of militancy in the union reinforced cultural stereotypes about women. Some attention was paid to the fact that women tended to teach in the elementary schools, but none of the investigators looked into the issue of union membership and the union's position on single salary issues. In Stephen Coles's study of New York militancy, no mention was made of the issue of single salary schedules, and yet the resentment of elementary teachers can be easily documented. What is surprising is that despite the agreement between the High School Teachers' Association and the Teachers' Guild on salary schedules in 1959, more than 50 percent of elementary school teachers supported the strike in 1962. Another explanation for the sociologists' contention that men had caused teacher militancy was that male teachers came from lower-class backgrounds, whereas women came from higher-class backgrounds. Because teachers who came from lower-class homes were more likely to have fathers who were Democrats and union members, they tended more toward union membership and militancy. But the gender differences in class origins were not as great as the investigators indicated. Coles found that 61 percent of men and 47 percent of women thought of themselves as working or lower-middle class, yet in a footnote he observed that there was only a small difference in actual social origins of men and women teachers: 31 percent of the women were from the working class and 39 percent of the men were from the working class. . . .

If one were to dismiss the gender argument as an explanation of militancy yet agree that economic factors alone did not explain the rising militancy of teachers, there was one other issue, explored in all the studies, that can serve as a less gender-biased explanation of what was happening in the schools. . . . [T]eachers were fed up with the centralized bureaucracy of the schools. Teachers complained about oversupervision, increasing bureaucratization, inappropriate assignments, and a lack of control over licensing, training, and assignments. These grievances go back to the beginnings of unionization; after tenure laws had been effectively introduced, teachers were willing to strike for those same demands (as well as higher pay) after World War II. Viewed from the historical perspective, teachers seemed to resume in the sixties the militancy of the late forties, which had been interrupted by the red scare.

## Organizational Warfare

The first response of the NEA to the 1962 strike was to denounce the tactics of the AFT as unprofessional. NEA executive secretary [William] Carr remarked that "industrial practices cannot be copied in a doctrinaire manner in public enterprises." He specifically directed his comments toward the New York City strike threat in 1962 by saying that such tactics "do not represent values that can be taught to American public school children."

The defeat of the NEA in the collective bargaining election of 1961 seemed especially humiliating to the NEA leadership. T. M. Stinnett, an NEA participant, described how inept the NEA was in the first confrontation with AFT organizers. An AFT plant supplied the union with information on every NEA move, while at national headquarters the ever cooperative Research Division was sending out salary information, which the clever AFT organizers were using in their union publications. Shaken by the experience and pressed from within his own organization for reform on desegregation, Carr delivered what he called his "turning point" speech to the 1962 NEA convention. He said that the NEA had been through three crises before, citing the reorganization after World War I, the depression, and World War II; but the fourth great crisis, he said, was before them. "Some labor leaders may plan to use their considerable economic and political power to affiliate all public school teachers in a white-collar union," Carr warned. The AFL-CIO, he said, had declared war on the teachers and apparently was prepared to attack the NEA at its weakest point: the cities.

In 1964 Carr characterized the union attempt as "an assault on professional independence." He continued, "The AFL-CIO program, as defined by its leadership, would, if successful, destroy the NEA and its state and local affiliates." He urged teachers to keep the educational profession an "independent one" and warned delegates to "know the difference between professional association and a teachers' union and how to tell why the former is better. You should know this as well as your own phone number." He further argued that AFL-CIO labor councils and affiliates had opposed taxes for schools and implied that teachers could expect that once the AFL-CIO had triumphed over the NEA, teachers could expect to live under an "Iron Curtain" of labor control. In keeping with NEA tradition, Carr never mentioned the AFT, which was, after all, the actual source of the challenge to the NEA. The NEA always treated the AFT as though it were a satellite, independent in name only.

The NEA did not stand idly by as the AFT proclaimed its victory in New York. Yet the teachers' strike fever spread so quickly in the cities that the association had difficulty in catching up to the union's impressive takeoff. William Carr was quick to notice that the gains were made in urban areas where the NEA had been weak because of its statewide structures. Most urban leaders considered state executive secretaries to be conservatives, interested only in legislation, and the executive secretaries in turn saw the urban leaders as troublemakers not truly interested in the association. The NEA's Urban Project aimed in part at solving this problem. By

1968 the Urban Project ran on a million-dollar budget explicitly to help organize local city chapters in competition with the AFT. . . .

Despite its weakness in the push for collective bargaining, the midsixties was hardly a time of gloom for the association. Its major advances came elsewhere, in Washington. Carr had invested heavily in the early sixties in federal legislation. This was his primary program, and indeed it had been the main focus of the organization since it located in Washington in the early twenties. The strength of the NEA was in its ability to lobby, and it had sought a federal education bill . . . [for many years].

The irony is that federal legislation had been stymied since the early fifties in the last collapse of the coalition of civil rights groups, labor, the NEA, and the AFT. *Sputnik* in 1957 reawakened interest in federal aid and produced the National Defense Education Act in 1958, but this bill fell far short of the goals and expectations of the NEA. Now, with the election of John F. Kennedy, things were looking up for educational funding. In 1962 the Manpower and Development Training Act promised $435 million in funds for vocational schools, a large sum but not what the NEA wanted. Carr and other educational reformers had their eyes on a general school-aid bill that would provide $2.5 billion in aid. Kennedy, who endorsed the bill, visited with NEA leaders shortly before his assassination to discuss lobbying efforts for the bill, but even his tragic death would not save the bill, which was defeated in December 1963.

After years of begging, teachers found a friend in Lyndon B. Johnson. A former schoolteacher himself, Johnson came into office with the promise that he could deliver what Kennedy had failed to accomplish: a federal aid bill for education. . . . At first Johnson's aid followed the pattern of the New Deal. Educational programs were attached to his multibillion-dollar war on poverty, especially the Economic Opportunity Act of 1964, which included job corps, work study, and aid to urban and rural community-action programs. Johnson was also able to expand the National Defense Education Act of 1958 to include history, English reading, and geography in addition to mathematics, science, and languages, which had been targeted in the original act. These programs were largely part of Kennedy's unfinished term of office; Johnson's own imprint was really felt only after his 1964 landslide electoral victory. The Elementary and Secondary Education Act of 1965 brought $1.3 billion in grants to schools for textbooks, community centers, and audiovisual materials. "No law I have signed, or ever will sign, means more to the future of America," the veteran congressional legislator, remarked. Annual appropriations of this bill from $5 billion to $7 billion gave education its first general federal subsidy.

Although the Johnson bill was not everything the NEA had hoped for, most educators agreed that it was a major commitment to federal aid to education, the long-sought goal of both the union and the association. In July 1965 Johnson was warmly received at the NEA convention to discuss the more than sixty pieces of federal legislation, from Head Start to graduate school programs, that his administration had supported. It would seem to Carr that his patience in lobbying efforts had paid off and all that the association had to do was to maintain its good reputation and the favor of Congress to promote the long-lost dream of the association—a department of education.

Victories in the early Johnson years seemed to reinforce Carr's conservatism. His fears were that the unbridled militancy of the teachers could lead to a cooling off on the part of Congress—and to some degree he was right—but Congress reneged on further educational funding not so much because of the teachers' actions but rather because in the late sixties the prohibitive costs of the Vietnam War had forced Johnson to do what he had been loathe to do: raise taxes to protect his domestic reforms and continue the war. Meanwhile, the NEA lobbyists seemed unresponsive to Johnson's political problem and continued with its general lobbying efforts. The commitment to these lobbying efforts had the effect of hampering the efforts of the teachers, who were counseled to look to legislative victories rather than collective bargaining to achieve their salary goals. Indeed, some of the NEA staff saw the rise in militancy and strikes as dangers jeopardizing years of efforts to gain goodwill. This orientation was not merely Carr's personal style; it was, and remains, one of the chief characteristics of the modern NEA. The whole point of locating in Washington in 1920 was to gain national recognition and federal legislation to improve the profession. The NEA could not shift its orientation from lobbying to collective bargaining without a major internal reorganization.

### Professionals into Unionists

The real obstacle for the NEA in its crisis of competition with the AFT was not the union, nor was it NEA weakness in urban centers, nor even the problem of membership. Collective bargaining itself presented the NEA with its deepest concern; it was an ideological construct that fundamentally challenged the association's long-cherished concepts of professionalism. Although the association had affiliates that struck in the late forties, and even though it had representative organizations that regularly petitioned boards of education to adjust salaries, protect teachers' academic rights, and apply grievance procedures, it was anathema to the association to engage in collective bargaining because the term itself was embedded in unionism. Instead it was more in the style of the NEA to declare "professional day" strikes, where teachers would call in sick for one day. Teachers in Kentucky stages a statewide "professional day" under the auspices of the state association.

Instead of striking, however, the NEA promoted the idea of sanctions, according to which if a state or a district refused to negotiate or respond to demands for higher pay, then the NEA would declare sanctions against that district or state, under which other teachers were urged not to take jobs in the state or district. To facilitate this, in 1967 the NEA set up a computer bank of jobs and teachers, a service that might have better served the growing number of unemployed teachers but was begun to bolster the sagging reputation of professional sanctions. Sanctions did not work because they were difficult to mobilize teachers behind, extremely difficult to maintain, and easily dismissed by cost-conscious districts and states. Sanctions declared against Utah in 1964 lasted for three hundred days when—after teachers helped elect a new governor, a new legislature came to power and after NEA organizers invested a great deal of expense and time—the NEA gained a modest salary increase. Finally, in 1967 the NEA passed a resolution stating that though strikes were to be avoided, the association recognized that under certain circumstances teachers were forced to strike, in which case the association would come to their aid. Even as the association came closer to union activity, the careful language obscured its change in direction. Euphemisms for bargaining activity like "co-operative determination," "collective determination," and "democratic persuasion" preceded the association's favorite euphemism for collective bargaining, "professional negotiations."

However comforting the adoption of indirect language may have been, it accomplished little in the way of confronting the problem that, willy-nilly, the association was being dragged into a process of unionization, and unless it adopted the weapons of labor, it faced oblivion. James Carey, secretary-treasurer of the Industrial Union Department of the AFL-CIO, the same organization that had helped fund the New York City drive, addressed the NEA convention in 1962 and explicitly spoke to this question. "One of the prime troubles—if not the chief curse of the teaching industry, is precisely the word 'profession.' That term, as it is used so frequently here, implies that your craft is somewhat above this world of ours; it implies a detachment, a remoteness from the daily battles of the streets, in the neighborhoods and cities."

Carey's remarks angered some of the association's members, but others were willing to listen and pushed for organizational changes. The biggest push of all came from the successes of the AFT. Between January 1961 and September 1965 the NEA and the AFT completed in forty different elections to determine who would represent teachers at the bargaining table. The NEA won twenty-six elections and the AFT won fourteen, but the AFT represented 74,000 teachers, whereas the NEA could bargain for only 21,000 teachers. In suburban and rural districts the association won, but the statistics failed to raise the spirits of association organizers. Association leaders knew that they had to face the AFT challenge more aggressively. Even though they still had a substantial membership lead, 943,000 to 110,000, they could see that the union would gain hegemony if it continued its successes.

In each collective bargaining campaign the AFT made two very effective charges against the NEA which made a substantial difference to urban public school teachers: administrative domination and foot-dragging on civil rights. Well over 85 percent of the NEA's members were classroom teachers, but school superintendents and district supervisors remained prominent in national meetings until the midsixties. Some state associations insisted that local chapters have administrators in their organizations, although some chapters were able to limit membership to classroom teachers only. As for the AFT, it allowed principals into separate locals, but the national constitution specifically forbade membership to supervisors. Teacher unionists were quick to argue that administrators represented management in negotiations and that it was an obvious conflict of interest to allow them into the deliberations of teachers.

The NEA hesitated to adopt such industrial language. Negotiations for teachers were simply discussions between professionals, NEA leaders reasoned, and therefore they could see no value in abandoning their administrators. Yet in 1967, when members of the Association of American School Administrators (AASA) on the NEA Board of Trustees moved to nominate a replacement for William Carr, the Representative Assembly prevented them from acting and thus opened the door for a shift in power within the organization. Internally there was no discussion of the "administrator-dominated organization" charge made by the AFT. The AASA continued to work with the NEA leadership to work out a compromise position and in 1969 went so far as to announce that it would stay in the association even though it deplored teachers' strikes. The drift away from the administrative orientation was just that: there was no final breach. Instead there was a slow shift in emphasis from the more hierarchical educational elite organization to a far more democratic structure that drew more teachers into organizational deliberations.

On the issue of civil rights, the NEA clearly accelerated its integration program in 1965. In the next few years the NEA underwent a complete transformation, a change in structure and outlook that was indeed profound. As time passed, the NEA's ideological barriers to collective bargaining became psychological barriers, which were more easily overcome. The organization became less reticent about union tactics, and even the term "union" was no longer anathema as it had once been. The last vestige of the old NEA philosophy, the "professional organization," changed in its meaning too, as the competition between organizations heated up in the late sixties.

# Martin Luther King Jr. and the Memphis Sanitation Strike

MICHAEL HONEY

On the twenty-fifth anniversary of the death of Martin Luther King, Jr., several hundred people from across the nation met at the National Civil Rights Museum in Memphis. Built on the site of the Lorraine Motel, where King was shot on April 4, 1968, in an impoverished district where he helped to lead a strike of black sanitation workers, the museum highlights King's deep commitment to movements of the poor. In this setting, participants at a three-day symposium on King criticized popular treatments of him, which typically focus on his role in the early desegregation struggles and victories from 1955 to 1965 and cite his "I Have a Dream" speech in 1963 as the high point of his career. While affirming the importance of King's early role, participants viewed King not as a dreamer but as a pragmatist and a movement strategist, one who had an economic analysis and who sought to mobilize movements from below. King's radicalism became especially apparent during his later career from 1965 to 1968 and particularly during the Poor People's Campaign and the Memphis sanitation workers' struggle in the last months of his life. Many symposium participants felt that King must be understood more fully, as a minister to the poor and the working class, as well as a civil rights leader, if his legacy is to be useful to new generations struggling with blatant disparities between rich and poor. This perspective suggests, among other things, the need for closer assessment of the significance of King's role in the events in Memphis and of the struggles of black workers in that city.

By the time of the sanitation strike in 1968, King believed that movements by those at the bottom, allied with unions and middle-class people of good will, could regenerate what seemed to be a flagging struggle for freedom and equality. Since the mid-1950s, he had put his life on the line repeatedly to end southern segregation, but increasingly he had come to believe that desegregation by itself could not

From "Martin Luther King, Jr., the Crisis of the Black Working Class, and the Memphis Sanitation Strike," in *Southern Labor in Transition, 1940–1995,* ed. Robert H. Zieger (Knoxville: University of Tennessee Press, 1997), pp. 205–223. Copyright © 1997 by the University of Tennessee Press.

end black oppression. The Watts rebellion and other uprisings of the urban black poor after 1965 forced King to focus on questions of economic justice. In numerous speeches and writings of this period, he repeatedly warned of economic trends throwing black workers into crisis, even as they strode toward legal and civic freedom. He spoke of the deep roots of black economic distress in slavery and segregation. He probed the effects of a global economy which increasingly mechanized and marginalized people of color, the uneducated, and the poor; and he criticized unions for failing to address the needs of African Americans. He saw trends creating a crisis of the poor and the black working class that neither civil rights organizations nor the established labor unions by themselves could address. King hoped that poor people's movements would focus renewed energy on reforming an oppressive racial and economic order that placed disproportionate numbers of African Americans on the bottom. He saw the Memphis sanitation strike as one such movement. . . .

Although King spent most of his time working in the top-down organizational style of the Baptist Church, via the Southern Christian Leadership Conference (SCLC), his Ghandian understanding of the role of masses in history caused him to view both labor and the civil rights movements, at their best, as grassroots rebellions evolving from the bottom up. Long before the 1968 sanitation strike, King had made speech after speech to unions, pointing to the common methods and goals of labor and civil rights movements, and calling for a grand alliance of the two. He presumed not only that civil rights and voter registration would break segregation, but also that black and white workers' votes would combine to end state restrictions on union organizing and replace reactionary southern legislators with liberals. The high point of his own alliances with unions came in June 1963, with a mass freedom march in Detroit, cosponsored with the UAW, with over 125,000 participants; and with the August 28 March on Washington, to which the UAW and many other unions (although not the AFL-CIO) gave crucial support. By 1965, King and SCLC even went so far as to propose to UAW President Walter Reuther that unionists collaborate with SCLC to train a new generation of southern organizers for placement in the field, to "bring Unions into every sphere of labor activity here in the South w[here] Unions do not now exist"

King relished the glowing promise of a civil rights-labor alliance, but he also expressed growing unease with its limitations, which became more apparent as the 1960s wore on. Unions and the civil rights movement needed each other but often had separate and competing concerns. Like other black leaders, King saw unions as fundamental allies in the freedom struggle, but he also recognized clearly the role white unionists frequently played in marginalizing blacks economically. . . . In speeches to union gatherings, he repeatedly described the cause of black economic crisis as rooted partly in automation, which in the 1950s and 1960s eliminated hundreds of thousands of unskilled jobs. After a long history of employer and union discrimination, these positions had only begun to provide accessible, high-wage, unionized employment for black workers; racism still blocked African-American advancement into more skilled production and craft jobs. In his speeches, King stressed the vulnerability of the black working class and called upon unions to do away with all vestiges of discrimination within their own organizations. If the unions did not find a way to raise the living standard of all workers, and not just those under union contract, the proportion of unionized workers would continue to shrink; black workers would continue to be impoverished; and the strength of both labor and civil-rights organizations would ebb. . . .

Memphis exhibited all the racial and economic problems which King had pointed to in his speeches before union audiences. It is not surprising, then, that in the winter and spring of 1968 the mounting socioeconomic grievances of African-American workers erupted into a dramatic and far-reaching confrontation. In February, more than thirteen hundred black sanitation men launched what became a sixty-four-day strike, seeking nothing more than what many other workers had gained long before: union recognition, decent conditions, improved wages and benefits. The uprising of such men shocked white Memphians, as even those older workers who presumably had resigned themselves to their condition rose *en masse* to support the strike. The strike quickly developed into a stark confrontation, pitting supporters of the old racial-economic order against practically the entire Memphis African-American community and major portions of the city's organized labor movement.

The condition of the thirteen hundred sanitation men who worked for the city epitomized the plight of the black urban poor. Many sanitation workers lived below the poverty level, even as they worked two or more jobs. A large portion of them came from rural Fayette County, Tennessee, where control of the cotton economy had shifted from planters using black unskilled labor to corporations using machines. There black unemployment reached nearly 70 percent, and 80 percent of the housing lacked plumbing. According to one of the men who moved from Fayette County to become a sanitation worker in Memphis, "There is no worst job. I would take anything." Such individuals usually obtained sanitation work through friends or family members already employed. At one time, rural blacks had used low-wage jobs in Memphis as stepping stones to jobs in Chicago or elsewhere in the North. But as employment opportunities in northern cities slackened, those who remained in Memphis were locked into dead-end jobs. They soon discovered that, no matter how long they might work as sanitation men, they remained classified as unskilled day laborers and could not become foremen or supervisors. Only whites held these positions, and most of them had little more than contempt for African Americans, who did backbreaking work compensated by low wages, few benefits, and no job security. Forty percent of sanitation workers were so poor that they qualified for welfare to supplement their salaries. In the 1960s, conditions worsened, as successive city governments economized by sending them home without pay on rainy days (it typically rained 60 inches a year in Memphis), refusing to replace obsolete and dangerous trucks and other equipment, and refusing to increase wages even to keep up with the cost of living.

Unionization for these men represented a break from their past of peonage and sharecropping in the countryside and urban poverty and caste-system status in the city. Their organizing efforts also directly conflicted with long-entrenched anti-union policies of the city government. True, the Crump machine always had used craft unions as a vehicle for patronage and as a political auxiliary, and the machine had allowed whites to organize in the building trades and other areas where the city let contracts. Even then, however, it had made its agreements with the white unionists orally. It had violently resisted industrial unions, encouraging and even organizing beatings and expulsion of organizers. It also . . . opposed public employee unions, and city officials repeatedly had vowed never to sign an agreement with a labor organization. In the 1930s and 1940s, when city employees, including teachers, firefighters, and police, tried to organize, the municipal authorities fired and black-listed them. From the 1930s into the 1960s, municipal judges issued injunctions freely, crippling organizing campaigns and disrupting even the most militant strikes of white workers. Given this history, the idea that poor black sanitation workers would breach the barriers to form a public employee union seemed unthinkable.

Union organizing among sanitation workers reflected the heroic and dogged efforts of a few individuals. In 1947 and again in 1960, outsiders had attempted to unionize sanitation workers, but both times city authorities had scared them off. However, with help from the Retail Clerks International Association, garbage worker T. O. Jones, a Memphis native who had returned to the city in 1958 when a recession in West Coast shipyards had eliminated his job, began another attempt to help the sanitation workers. In 1963, acting on the basis of tips from informants, the Public Works Department fired Jones and thirty-three other workers. Over the next several years, however, Jones continued to meet with workers in this homes and to collect union dues. By 1964, aided by ministers and a black businessman and civic leader, O. Z. Evers, Jones and a number of workers had formed an Independent Workers Association of Memphis. With help from Secretary-Treasurer Bill Ross of the Memphis Trades and Labor Council, Jones succeeded in getting several of the dismissed unionists rehired. The American Federation of State, County, and Municipal Employees (AFSCME) put him on its payroll as an organizer, and he soon succeeded in gaining a charter for Local 1733. The Trades and Labor Council supported this initiative and called on the city to grant a written contract and dues check-off. City Commissioners rejected the council's demand, claiming that the city charter forbade formal recognition of any union.

City politics also helped the sanitation workers to press their case. Unlike their counterparts in most of the South, Memphis's African-American citizens never had been disfranchised, although for decades the poll tax and the Crump machine had controlled their vote. Civil rights protesters had made modest gains in desegregating the downtown stores, and in 1964 black voters provided the winning margin in the election of racial moderate William Ingram as mayor, giving Jones encouragement to press on. Hoping for a reasonable response, in August 1966, the workers were on the verge of a strike. But even during Ingram's regime, the courts issued a severe injunction, and the Public Works Department threatened to replace the workers if they ignored it. At this point, black community leaders remained reluctant to endanger that progress toward desegregation that had been made during Ingram's regime and took little action to support the union.

By 1968, however, things had changed dramatically. . . . In the mid-sixties, racial progressives saw signs of real change under Mayor Ingram. The 1966 shift from a commission to a mayor-council form of municipal government would, they believed, facilitate Ingram's progressive reforms. And in 1967 three blacks gained seats on the new city council. At the same time, however, the 1967 mayoral election split black and working-class white voters. Previously they had joined to elect Ingram, but now the black vote divided between incumbent Ingram and black mayoral candidate A. W. Willis, while Henry Loeb won by campaigning openly as a white supremacist, gaining virtually no support from the eighty thousand African-American

voters. Loeb's election hardened white resistance to further black gains and especially frustrated and angered the city's historically moderate black middle class
and religious leaders. "After all these years of being cooperative citizens, there
were not enough white people to join with us to give us a decent mayor," recalled
Rev. Benjamin Hooks.

Under Loeb, a fiscal conservative who vowed to cut the city's costs, conditions
worsened considerably for both the sanitation workers and the African-American
community. The city's refusal to provide modern equipment meant that workers had
to carry leaking tubs of garbage on their heads. White residents considered these
workers "garbage men," not hard-working fellow citizens providing essential services. In the neighborhoods, they were treated as servants who should be grateful for
gifts of cast-off clothing as a "fringe benefit" of the job. City authorities refused to
entertain the idea that their work might be worth more than $1.60 an hour. To save
money, Loeb's administration reduced the workforce in the sanitation division of
the Public Works Department, an act that vastly increased the workloads of those
who remained and forced them to toil extra hours without compensation. . . . In one
episode at the end of January, the sanitation division sent black workers home without pay during a rainstorm, while allowing the few white supervisors and drivers
who worked for the division to remain on the job and collect wages. Such behavior
by white bosses was typical, as was their refusal to allow blacks to take shelter during storms. On February 1, this disdain for black workers' safety and comfort had
tragic consequences, when two African-American sanitation workers took refuge
from a storm in a truck's compactor, which malfunctioned and crushed them to
death. Having no insurance, the men's families were left destitute, while the city
took more than a week to pay for their burial expenses. Meanwhile, the deeply racist
Loeb regime continued to scorn—when it did not simply ignore—black sanitation
workers' efforts to organize and thus seek to ameliorate their condition.

Following a chain of accumulated grievances, the deaths of the two black
workers and the failure of the Public Works Department to pay wages to the men
sent home in January set off a spontaneous walkout by outraged workers on February 12. Almost immediately, the local chapter of the National Association for the
Advancement of Colored People (NAACP) and many black ministers voiced their
support for the job action. In response, for the next two months, Loeb's government
refused to bargain with the men as long as they were on strike and hauled out every
means at its disposal to break the union. Its methods included an injunction that
prohibited union leaders from almost all public activities, continual police intimidation of strikers and their supporters, permanent replacement of many strikers by
scabs of both races, and refusing to talk to union representatives or to recognize the
right of city workers to organize. The city's two daily newspapers supported these
policies and ignored the perspectives of the strikers and the black community. The
press failed to explain the underlying causes of the strike and ran racist cartoons
and headlines that further offended black sensibilities. Powerful city elites saw
the dispute as an opportunity to teach lower-class blacks that while their counterparts in other places, such as Detroit and New York, might demonstrate and strike,
this could not happen in Memphis. White citizens seemed to support Loeb's hard-
line stance, helping with garbage collection and applauding the city's intransigent
stance. The city government even gave the impression that those who interfered

with strike-breakers might be shot in the streets, as newspapers pictured white replacement workers carrying guns while they picked up garbage.

Confusion on the part of the city council heightened tensions. Its Committee on Public Works first told strike supporters that it would recommend a settlement to the council, but instead the council, on February 23, without permitting public comment, adopted a hostile substitute resolution. Finding the council meeting closed, strikers and their supporters flooded from the City Hall into the streets for a march, only to be attacked by truncheon-wielding, mace-spraying police. This incident, more than any other, demonstrated the limits of the black political empowerment and civil rights victories that had been achieved in Memphis. It demonstrated in a visceral way that black economic powerlessness remained the main fact of life, and it fused festering economic grievances with fundamental questions of civil and human rights.

The blatant racism of the city administration now galvanized black ministers, politicians, and civil rights leaders and energized a hitherto somnolent local labor movement. On the day after the police attacks, black community leaders and organizations, long at odds with each other, put aside their divisions and organized a group called Community on the Move for Equality (COME). Over the next six weeks, this organization proceeded to unite the African-American community behind the strikers with mass meetings, daily picketing, and a boycott of downtown businesses (particularly targeting the Loeb family's laundries), and the newspapers. Whites and blacks from the Memphis Trades and Labor Council and the United Rubber Workers and other industrial unions joined to support the strike.

All in all, the walkout triggered a degree of mobilization of both the African-American community and progressive whites rarely seen in Memphis or anywhere in the South. As the conflict in Memphis became both more dramatic and more desperate, the struggle drew in Roy Wilkins of the NAACP, Bayard Rustin of the AFL-CIO's A. Philip Randolph Institute, and AFSCME President Jerry Wurf, as tacticians and speakers at huge mass rallies. On March 14, a crowd variously estimated at between nine thousand and twenty-five thousand Memphians attended a rally featuring Wilkins and Rustin. Behind the scenes, debates whirled over whether to emphasize the strike as a workers' struggle, with hopes of drawing in more white unionists, or as a civil rights struggle, in order to solidify the black community behind it. For AFSCME, the outcome of the struggle represented the success or failure of its efforts to organize blue-collar public workers, especially in the South. For national civil rights leaders, the struggle in Memphis provided a crucial test of white America's willingness to come to grips with black economic demands or to recognize the dignity of African Americans in a more general sense. Many local people concluded that the strike was *both* a labor and a civil rights struggle and that the two could not be separated. With this perspective in mind, on March 17, Rev. James Lawson, a long-time Memphis religious and civil-rights leader, called his friend and colleague Martin Luther King, Jr., for the second time to ask him to come to the city and speak on behalf of the workers.

King's labor perspective led him naturally to support the Memphis union struggle. His staff at SCLC, in the midst of frenzied preparations for the Poor People's Campaign, opposed his involvement in Memphis, while King identified the situation as emblematic of the dilemmas facing poor people and especially poor blacks. As workers, the sanitation men fought for union recognition; for the right to vacations, decent wages and benefits, rest breaks, and health and safety precautions; and for recognition of their right to belong to a union. King commented that these men, like most of the working poor, had none of the benefits that made a job worthwhile. Yet, more than that, he realized, black sanitation workers fought for dignity and respect as human beings. King understood that the conditions of the Memphis strikers typified the harsh realities facing the black working poor and unemployed all over America. . . .

King used Memphis as an example of how the nation had devalued the labor of the working poor. "You are reminding the nation that it is a crime for people to live in this rich nation and receive starvation wages . . . this is our plight as a people all over America," King said. "We are living as a people in a literal depression," but one unrecognized by most whites or the government. "Do you know that most of the poor people in our country are working every day?" he asked the crowd. "And they are making wages so low that they cannot begin to function in the mainstream of the economic life of our nation. These are the facts which must be seen, and it is criminal to have people working on a full-time basis and [in] a full-time job, getting part-time income." It was the powerlessness of workers and the unemployed, especially people of color, said King, that accounted for the widespread poverty in America. "We are tired of being at the bottom," he said; we are tired of "wall-to-wall rats and roaches" instead of wall-to-wall carpeting; "we are tired of smothering in an airtight cage of poverty in the midst of an affluent society. We are tired of walking the streets in [a] search for jobs that do not exist."

King also explained the sanitation strike as emblematic of the freedom movement's evolution from civil-rights demands to more systemic demands. According to King, the struggle for black equality logically had brought the movement to Memphis. While the Selma march and the Voting Rights Act of 1965 had brought to an end one phase of the struggle, "now our struggle is for genuine equality, which means economic equality. For we know that it isn't enough to integrate lunch counters. What does it profit a man to be able to eat at an integrated lunch counter if he doesn't earn enough money to buy a hamburger and a cup of coffee?" Civil rights gains had been only a down payment on the fulfillment of the American Dream. Returning to a theme of his 1963 "I Have a Dream" speech, King demanded payment on the "promissory note" for life, liberty, and happiness that originated in the documents of the American Revolution. "We are saying now is the time," King told Memphians, "to make real the promises of democracy."

King's plea for African-American racial unity in support of working-class demands resonated deeply in Memphis; his call for the "haves" to join hands with the "have-nots" already had become a central theme of the strike. Even before his appearance, the confrontation between ill-treated workers and a racist city administration had lessened divisions based upon conflicting political loyalties and organizational turf battles among African-American leaders in Memphis, particularly among black ministers. As Rev. Ralph Jackson, a key leader and negotiator in the conflict, later told interviewers, he and other members of the black middle class had been distant from black workers and had not understood their plight at all. His eyes had been opened by thirteen hundred sanitation strikers carrying placards proclaiming "I Am a Man" and demanding to be treated not as "boys" or as servants but as citizens with rights equal to those of the wealthy and white. Moreover, the experience of being maced by the police had brought Jackson and other better-off blacks sharply up against the racial system and taught them how it felt to be both black and poor. The strike drew ministers and professionals away from a focus purely on civil-rights concerns and into the daily lives of poor people, where economic and racial injustice went hand in hand. Thus, a struggle that the poorest of the poor had initiated became central to the achievement of intraclass black unity in the Memphis of the late 1960s. . . .

King had placed the sanitation strike not only into the context of the movement for black unity, but into an almost classic labor context. King's presence in Memphis awoke the national media to the importance of the strike there and brought many international unions into the picture. More than any other group, AFSCME, whose future in the South, if not nationally, hung on the outcome of the strike, provided the core of support. In addition, however, once King and other civil-rights leaders had made the strike a national issue, the AFL-CIO and its members unions sent substantial financial support—well over one hundred thousand dollars by the end of the strike. Fifty union officials from ten southern states meeting in Memphis for an AFL-CIO Social Security conference backed the strike and called the conduct of the city government "a throw-back to the Dark Ages."

At the local level, attention from the national AFL-CIO galvanized many white union leaders to take a stronger position in support of the strike. The white-led Memphis Trades and Labor Council, the local AFL-CIO coordinating body, backed the strike with donations of funds and by mobilizing a March 4 march of some five hundred white unionists. The *Memphis Union News,* edited by Bill Ross, sharply and repeatedly denounced Mayor Loeb and "the ultra-conservative community leaders" he represented and supported the boycott of downtown stores and "the labor-hating press." The Labor Council and its Amalgamated Meat Cutters and Butcher Workman's Union President Tommy Powell called for a petition drive to recall Loeb. And some local white leaders challenged white workers' racism. George Clark, white president of United Rubber Workers of America Local 186, responded to criticism from white members of his union with a ringing denunciation of "the right-wing people in our plant, that are supposed to be union members," stating that they "will not prevent this union from supporting this, or any other group of workers, in their efforts to have a union."

Black unionists also were forthright in their support of the strike. Leroy Clark, president of Local 282 of the United Furniture Workers of America, and other African-American trade unionists encouraged community and union picketing and support, while black members of the rubber workers' local provided space for meetings and moral support to the sanitation workers from the beginning. William Lucy played a key role as an international AFSCME organizer. George Holloway and a few other black members of UAW Local 988 at the International Harvester plant supported the strike wholeheartedly, despite the disapproval of whites at the plant. One perspective, then, held that a labor-civil rights coalition had in fact been created in Memphis. Labor economist F. Ray Marshall, for example, concluded that the support of organized labor, black and white, combined with an aroused civil-rights community, provided "a significant element leading to the [eventual] settlement of the dispute."

However, at the same time that labor and civil rights solidarity seemed to be growing, white workers' responses were ambivalent, even contradictory. While some white unionists engaged in arms-length solidarity, others expressed outright hostility to the strike. The AFL-CIO's regional political organizer Dan Powell recalled that African-American workers could win only when their strike became a racial issue, making it possible to mobilize the African-American community behind them. Yet, as he and AFSCME leader Lucy noted, while white union leaders supported the strike as an economic issue, as soon as it became a racial struggle, many rank-and-file whites abandoned it. AFSCME organizer Jesse Epps and Rev. Lawson both observed that white workers generally stayed out of the struggle. On March 4, when they did march in support of the sanitation workers, white workers began their march separately from blacks, took a different route, and stayed to themselves when the groups came to a common destination. Worse, the building trades and many craft unions, always a conservative force in Memphis, took no official position on the sanitation strike but unofficially sided with Mayor Loeb. Many white workers did not want to pay the increased taxes that wage increases for sanitation workers would have necessitated. Nor did national union support necessarily translate into support at the local level. Although the national UAW had a strong record of support for Dr. King, . . . whites in UAW Local 988 had a long history of militant racism and largely opposed the sanitation workers' struggle. In short, the resistant racialized consciousness of the white working class surfaced clearly during the strike.

The schizophrenic character of organized labor in Memphis reflected a growing racialization of white worker consciousness in the late 1960s which had become apparent to King, who found himself increasingly at odds with many white union members and much of the established union leadership. The 1955 merger of the AFL craft unions and the CIO industrial unions may have strengthened organized labor; but, as Lucy later commented, its leadership, starting with AFL-CIO President George Meany, "was not vested in the more progressive side of labor." King wanted labor leaders to take up the challenge of poverty in America, but he felt that, for the most part, they had not done that. King's opposition to the Vietnam War and his unwillingness to condemn Black Power also distanced him, and many grassroots activists, from mainstream liberals, especially many top union leaders with institutional ties to the American foreign-policy establishment. . . .

Long before the Memphis strike, King had realized that the coalition he sought between the civil rights movement and the unions was problematic. At the same time, King lacked a real grounding in the labor movement, making it difficult to conceive or execute the Poor People's Campaign, which included few unions in the coalition of the poor. Neither King nor his lieutenants had built a strong working-class base for the campaign, nor did they seem to know how to do so. King's conception of the campaign rested on the idea of an alliance among poor whites and poor people from racially oppressed minorities, few of whom belonged to unions and many of whom were without jobs. Most unions in high-wage sectors of the economy, on the other hand, long since had opted out of poor people's politics.

Even more worrisome to King, the ability of such racial polarizers as George Wallace to stimulate "backlash" among white voters had increasingly come to define two-party politics. In a May 1967 speech titled "Civil Rights at the Crossroads," delivered to shop stewards of the Teamsters Union, which in the past had pledged funds to SCLC, King identified the racial undercurrents eroding potential coalitions. Few whites, unionized or not, said King, recognized or welcomed the new phase of the movement that . . . would cost billions of dollars in taxes, at a time when many in the white population, including many white workers, increasingly saw their interests as being in conflict with those of the poor and people of color. . . .

King's move into the second phase of the civil rights revolution had elicited hostility toward him from many quarters, particularly the media and the federal government. . . . On March 28, media hostility climaxed after black Memphis teenagers began breaking store windows on Beale Street during an attempted mass march led by King. Using this disorder as their excuse, Memphis police unleashed an indiscriminate and violent attack against all marchers and citizens in the area of the march. In their enthusiasm to repress the gathering, police killed black youth Larry Payne with a shotgun and beat scores of others. Following this incident, the mayor placed the African-American community under curfew, and the state brought in four thousand members of the National Guard, while the courts enjoined King from leading any more marches. With FBI encouragement, both federal officials and national news media barraged the public with unfavorable images of King's abilities and character. The events in Memphis now brought King's national leadership into question. This onslaught convinced King that he must defy the court order against him and return to Memphis to lead a massive and nonviolent public demonstration, even under the most unfavorable of circumstances. Failure to do so, he feared, would destroy the Poor People's Campaign and his own status as a national leader.

The Memphis strike thus brought King, and in many ways the movements of the 1960s, to a point of crisis that entailed both opportunity and danger. On the night of April 3 at Mason Temple in Memphis, . . . King issued his last testament before the black poor and dispossessed of Memphis, saying, "I may not get there with you, but I want you to know tonight that we as a people will get to the promised land." The next day he was dead, victim of an assassin's bullet.

King's death led to massive bad publicity for Memphis and to rapid defeat for Mayor Loeb, who had resisted or sabotaged every effort by the city council or citizens to resolve the sanitation strike. On April 2, white business leaders already had begun to pressure Loeb to soften his opposition to collective bargaining; after King's death, a delegation of them came to him and demanded that he settle the strike. Meanwhile, cities all over the U.S. went up in flames in response to King's death. In Memphis alone, nearly a million dollars in property damage (including 275 stores looted) and three deaths resulted from turmoil in the streets. On April 7, some eight thousand Memphians, most of them white, held a "Memphis Cares" memorial. Then, on April 8, thousands of labor, civil rights, and religious leaders converged on the city from around the country for a completely silent march by between twenty and forty thousand people. Some one hundred thousand people marched the next day at King's funeral procession in Atlanta. At the Memphis rally, the UAW's Walter Reuther pledged fifty thousand dollars to the sanitation workers, and the AFL-CIO's Meany set aside twenty thousand dollars as the first installment in a special fundraising drive among unions to support the sanitation strike. President Lyndon B. Johnson sent Undersecretary of Labor James Reynolds to impress upon local officials the urgency of the need for a strike settlement; Tennessee's Gov. Buford Ellington likewise pressed for resolution of the dispute. Although unrepentant to the end, Loeb finally removed himself as an obstacle to negotiations, and on April 16 union members ratified a proposed settlement in which the city capitulated to virtually all of the union's demands, including union recognition and dues check-off. The union had won. . . .

. . . In the aftermath of the strike victory, the black community and civil rights forces in Memphis surged forward. AFSCME 1733 became the largest single local in the city, consolidating nearly six thousand members, 90 percent of them black. In 1969, Local 1733, along with other Memphis unions, the NAACP, and the black community went on to instigate support of union organizing at Saint Joseph's Hospital. Although this drive failed, the city eased its opposition to collective bargaining; and in 1972 and 1973, white fire fighters and, ironically, the police (the vast majority of them white) created officially recognized unions. In 1978, both groups won strikes. In the early 1970s, an aroused African-American community elected blacks to the school board and elected the first black congressmen from the Mid-South since Reconstruction. By virtue of their prestige and the size of their union, the lowly sanitation workers became power brokers of a sort. In 1975, according to scholar Thomas Collins, "Local 1733 was the largest and by far the most powerful black political organization in town." . . . [A]lthough the union's political power weakened in subsequent years, . . . the strike victory and its aftermath brought a significant change in power relations in Memphis, leading in the 1990s to the election of an African American, Willie Herrenton, as mayor and also to a degree of black-white power sharing.

The 1968 strike victory had ramifications beyond Memphis as well. "A new kind of respect and a new kind of recognition" of the role of garbage workers in municipal economies emerged after the Memphis strike, according to William Lucy. An upsurge of sanitation-worker organizing in several southern cities followed the Memphis struggle, and public-employee unionism became the fastest-growing sector of the union movement in the 1970s. . . . The Memphis formula of maximum community involvement in union battles, the "Memphis spirit," as Lucy called it, also inspired other efforts to build labor-civil rights coalitions, most notably in the dramatic struggle between black hospital workers organized into Local 1199B Hospital Workers Union, joined by King's Southern Christian Leadership Conference, and white city leaders in Charleston, South Carolina, in 1969.

By the end of the 1970s, the upsurge in civil-rights unionism had receded, along with the SCLC itself. The Charleston strike, for example, led to no consolidation of union power. The model of a labor-civil rights coalition and a maximum community involvement in strikes remained, but their implementation seemed uncertain. Nonetheless, the death of King amid a labor struggle in Memphis left an ideological imprint on history which is an important legacy of the 1960s. Memphis and the Poor People's Campaign represent the culmination of King's search for a means to shake the foundations of American racism and economic injustice. . . . King sought to turn the civil rights movement toward an economic agenda that finally would address black economic demands that the United States had neglected ever since Reconstruction. At the same time, he tried to bring together the economic grievances of poor whites, blacks, and other people of color. The legacy of civil rights unionism remained uncertain in a subsequent era in which Republican and corporate strategies of divide-and-rule dominated the American landscape. Nonetheless, King's struggle . . . [for a] coalition politics aimed at uniting poor and working people with other potential allies continued to offer an alternative road map for labor, civil rights, and reform movements, one based on King's admonition to striking sanitation workers in Memphis: "We can all get more together than we can apart . . . and this is the way we gain power."

## ✢ *F U R T H E R    R E A D I N G*

Aaron, Benjamin, Joyce Najita, and James Stern, eds. *Public-Sector Bargaining* (1988).
Appy, Christian. *Working-Class War: American Combat Soldiers in Vietnam* (1993).
Aronowitz, Stanley. *From the Ashes of the Old: American Labor and America's Future* (1998).
Davidson, Chandler. *Race and Class in Texas Politics* (1990).
Ferriss, Susan, et al. *The Fight for the Fields: Cesar Chavez and the Farmworkers Movement* (1997).
Fink, Leon, and Brian Greenberg. *Upheaval in the Quiet Zone: A History of Hospital Workers Union, Local 1199* (1989).
Gould, William B. *Black Workers in White Unions: Job Discrimination in the United States* (1977).
Graham, Hugh Davis. *The Civil Rights Era: Origins and Development of National Policy, 1960–1972* (1990).
Honey, Michael. *Black Workers Remember: An Oral History of Segregation, Unionism and the Freedom Struggle* (1999).
Isserman, Maurice, and Michael Kazin. *America Divided: The Civil War of the 1960s* (1999).
Lemann, Nicholas. *The Promised Land: The Great Black Migration and How It Changed America* (1992).
Levy, Peter. *The New Left and Labor in the 1960s* (1994).
Murphy, Marjorie. *Blackboard Unions: The AFT and the NEA, 1900–1980* (1990).
Pfeffer, Paula. *A Philip Randolph, Pioneer of the Civil Rights Movement* (1990).
Thompson, Heather. *Whose Detroit? Politics, Labor, and Race in a Modern American City* (2001).
Weiner, Lois. *Preparing Teachers for Urban Schools* (1993).

C H A P T E R
13

# *White Collars, Pink Collars,*

# *and Hardhats*

*In the three decades following World War II, the American working class under-
went a profound transformation. The standard of living of the average family just
about doubled, high school graduation became the norm for most working-class
youth, and college enrollments tripled. Manufacturing employment rose gradually,
but employment in offices, retail trade, and services of all sorts increased far more
rapidly. By 1975 more than twice as many workers were categorized as service
workers than as factory operatives or foremen. Impressed with the success of
U.S. capitalism and the rise in education levels and white-collar jobs, some social
scientists and journalists argued that the demise of factory labor and the rise of
office work signaled the arrival of a middle-class majority in the United States.
This vast new army sat behind a desk or stood behind a counter, they wore
white or pink collars, they kept their hands clean, and they were paid by the
week, not the hour.*

*But such social prognostication was premature. After 1945 the American
class structure, as measured by relative income distribution, remained static.
And within the working class, the difference between a good job and a poor one
grew larger. Work at the core of the economy—in the big firms, the middle reaches
of the government bureaucracies, and the military—was relatively well paid lifetime employment. This sector expanded modestly in the quarter-century after the
war; the corporations were earning money, the government hired more teachers
and policemen, and the unions made many once transient and unstable job
situations more secure. But there were still millions of jobs—perhaps as many
as 40 percent of all positions—that shared none of these characteristics. Farm
laborers, insurance-company clericals, cab drivers, cannery workers, and dime
store clerks were poorly paid, held insecure jobs, and had few prospects for
promotion. Many economists have come to see these jobs as part of a distinct and
fast-growing "secondary" labor market, rigidly segregated from the more secure
work of the core economy yet essential to the functioning of the ever-changing
business system itself.*

*Of course, such casual and insecure employment has always been a part of
the American working-class experience. However, in the postwar era, the typical*

*worker in this sector was not the ditch digger or farm hand, but the female office or sales clerk. Despite the celebration of the male wage earner at the head of a nuclear family, as in early television shows like* Father Knows Best, *or the hardhat construction workers that came to symbolize working-class masculinity after 1970, the growth of women's employment was by far the most dramatic development in the world of work during the early postwar decades. By 1955 the proportion of women in the work force—33 percent—was greater than at the height of World War II, and by 1980 this proportion had more than doubled, even among women between the ages of twenty-five and thirty-four, the prime childrearing years.*

*Although the entrance of college-educated women into male-dominated professions like law, medicine, and academe had captured much attention, women's wages actually dropped relative to those of men in most occupations. And women continued to work in sex-segregated jobs. In fact, 95 percent were employed in just five traditional job categories: light manufacturing, retail trade, clerical, health, and education. Not unexpectedly, the high-status work within these sectors was usually male; low-status work, female. Thus the job of bank clerk, once an exclusively male preserve (when money handling carried high status) abruptly shifted to an almost exclusively female occupation in the mid-1950s, when bank managers routinized and downgraded the job.*

*What determines the class standing of a family: its total income, lifestyle, or occupation of the breadwinner(s)? Why are some jobs still considered "male" and some "female" despite the rise of feminism and the enactment of antidiscrimination laws? Is gender equality more likely at the bottom or at the top of the occupational hierarchy?*

## ⚘ D O C U M E N T S

Among the most influential students of the postwar working class was sociologist Daniel Bell. In Document 1, Bell argues that the long-term shift from agriculture to manufacturing to service- and information-based enterprises culminated in a "post-industrial society," whose class structure differed from that of the traditional occupational hierarchy. But a glimpse inside some service industry jobs reveals a more prosaic world of work. In Document 2, accountant Fred Roman describes the steep and treacherous career ladder at his large accounting firm. In Document 3, airline reservations agent Lee Radler Archacki, a married mother of two, explains why she chose nightshift work in an attempt to juggle jobs, childcare, and marriage. Her "choice" embodied the economic and professional costs faced by women and mothers in the work force. Document 4 offers a revealing look inside the world of a McDonald's restaurant, which employs more young people than any other institution in the United States.

Documents 5 and 6 demonstrate the way in which sex-typed occupations were being transformed during the 1960s and 1980s. In Document 5, at a 1967 hearing before the Equal Employment Opportunity Commission, the Transit Workers Union argues against the age and marriage criteria that airline carriers sought to sustain as "a bona fide occupational qualification" for the jobs filled by "young and pretty" flight attendants. And in Document 6, engineering managers open war on that citadel of blue-collar power, the construction unions, whose level of organization, job control, and high wages would be slashed during the 1970s and 1980s.

# 1. Sociologist Daniel Bell's
# "Post-Industrial" Vision, 1973

In *The Communist Manifesto,* which was completed in February 1848, Marx and Engels envisaged a society in which there would be only two classes, capitalist and worker—the few who owned the means of production and the many who lived by selling their labor power—as the last two great antagonistic classes of social history, locked in final conflict. In many ways this was a remarkable prediction, if only because at that time the vast majority of persons in Europe and the United States were neither capitalist nor worker but farmer and peasant, and the tenor of life in these countries was overwhelmingly agrarian and artisan. . . .

Marx's vision of the inexorable rise of industrial society was thus a bold one. But the most important social change in Western society of the last hundred years has been not simply the diffusion of industrial work but the concomitant disappearance of the farmer—and in a Ricardian world of diminishing returns in land, the idea that agricultural productivity would be two or three times that of industry (which it has been in the United States for the last thirty years) was completely undreamed of.

The transformation of agrarian life (whose habits had marked civilization for four thousand years) has been the signal fact of the time. In beholding the application of steam power to a textile mill, one could venture predictions about the spread of mechanization and the extension of factory work. But who would, with equal confidence, have made similar predictions following the invention by Cyrus McCormick of the reaper in 1832 and its exhibition at the Crystal Palace in London in 1851? Yet in the United States today, only 4 percent of the labor force is engaged in agriculture; the work of little more than three million persons (as against more than twice that number two decades ago) feeds 207 million persons, and if all crop restraints were released, they could probably feed fifty million more.

In place of the farmer came the industrial worker, and for the last hundred years or so the vicissitudes of the industrial worker—his claims to dignity and status, his demand for a rising share of industrial returns, his desire for a voice in the conditions which affected his work and conditions of employment—have marked the social struggles of the century. But beyond that, in the utopian visions of Marx and the socialist movement, the working class, made conscious of its fate by the conditions of struggle, was seen as the agency not only of industrial but of human emancipation; the last great brakes on production and abundance would be removed when the working class took over control of the means of production and ushered in the socialist millennium.

Yet if one takes the industrial worker as the instrument of the future, or, more specifically, the factory worker as the symbol of the proletariat, then this vision is warped. For the paradoxical fact is that as one goes along the trajectory of industrialization—the increasing replacement of men by machines—one come logically to the erosion of the industrial worker himself. In fact by the end of the century the proportion of factory workers in the labor force may be as small as the proportion of farmers today; indeed, the entire area of blue-collar work may have diminished so greatly that the term will lose its sociological meaning as new categories, more appropriate to the divisions of the new labor force, are established. Instead of the industrial worker, we see the dominance of the professional and technical class in the labor force—so much so that by 1980 it will be the second largest occupational group in the society, and by the end of the century the largest. This is the new dual revolution taking place in the structure of occupations and, to the extent that occupation determines other modes of behavior (but this, too, is diminishing), it is a revolution in the class structure of society as well. This change in the character of production and of occupations is one aspect of the emergence of the "post-industrial" society. . . .

A post-industrial society is based on services. Hence, it is a game between persons. What counts is not raw muscle power, or energy, but information. The central person is the professional, for he is equipped, by his education and training, to provide the kinds of skill which are increasingly demanded in the post-industrial society. If an industrial society is defined by the quantity of goods as marking a standard of living, the post-industrial society is defined by the quality of life as measured by the services and amenities—health, education, recreation, and the arts—which are now deemed desirable and possible for everyone.

The word "services" disguises different things, and in the transformation of industrial to post-industrial society there are several different stages. First, in the very development of industry there is a necessary expansion of transportation and of public utilities as auxiliary services in the movement of goods and the increasing use of energy, and an increase in the non-manufacturing but still blue-collar force. Second, in the mass consumption of goods and the growth of populations there is an increase in distribution (wholesale and retail) and finance, real estate, and insurance, the traditional centers of white-collar employment. Third, as national incomes rise, one finds . . . that the proportion of money devoted to food at home begins to drop, and the marginal increments are used first for durables (clothing, housing, automobiles) and then for luxury items, recreation, and the like. Thus, a third sector, that of personal services, begins to grow: restaurants, hotels, auto services, travel, entertainment, sports, as people's horizons expand and new wants and tastes develop. But here a new consciousness begins to intervene. The claims to the good life which the society has promised become centered on the two areas that are fundamental to that life—health and education. The elimination of disease and the increasing numbers of people who can live out a full life, plus the efforts to expand the span of life, make health services a crucial feature of modern society; and the growth of technical requirements and professional skills makes education, and access to higher education, the condition of entry into the post-industrial society itself. So we have the growth of a new intelligentsia, particularly of teachers. Finally, the claims for more services and the inadequacy of the market in meeting people's needs for a decent environment as well as better health and education lead to the growth of government, particularly at the state and local level, where such needs have to be met.

The post-industrial society, thus, is also a "communal" society in which the social unit is the community rather than the individual, and one has to achieve a "social decision" as against, simply, the sum total of individual decisions which, when aggregated, end up as nightmares, on the model of the individual automobile and collective traffic congestion. But cooperation between men is more difficult than the management of things. Participation becomes a condition of community, but when many different groups want too many different things and are not prepared for bargaining or trade-off, then increased conflict or deadlocks result. Either there is a politics of consensus or a politics of stymie.

As a game between persons, social life becomes more difficult because political claims and social rights multiply, the rapidity of social change and shifting cultural fashion bewilders the old, and the orientation to the future erodes the traditional guides and moralities of the past. Information becomes a central resource, and within organizations a source of power. Professionalism thus becomes a criterion of position, but it clashes, too, with the populism which is generated by the claims for more rights and greater participation in the society. If the struggle between capitalist and worker, in the locus of the factory, was the hallmark of industrial society, the clash between the professional and the populace, in the organization and in the community is the hallmark of conflict in the post-industrial society.

This, then, is the sociological canvas of the scheme of social development leading to the post-industrial society. . . .

## 2. Fred Roman on the Life of an Accountant, 1972

I usually say I'm an accountant. Most people think it's somebody who sits there with a green eyeshade and his sleeves rolled up with a garter, poring over books, adding things—with glasses. (Laughs.) I suppose a certified public accountant has status. It doesn't mean much to me. Do I like the job or don't I? That's important.

*He is twenty-five and works for one of the largest public accounting firms in the world. It employs twelve hundred people. He has been with the company three years. During his first year, after graduating from college; he worked for a food chain, doing inventory.*

The company I work for doesn't make a product. We provide a service. Our service is auditing. We are usually hired by stockholders or the board of directors. We will certify whether a company's financial statement is correct. They'll say, "This is what we did last year. We made X amount of dollars." We will come in to examine the books and say, "Yes, they did."

We're looking for things that didn't go out the door the wrong way. Our clients could say, "We have a million dollars in accounts receivable." We make sure that they do, in fact, have a million dollars and not a thousand. We ask the people who owe the money, "Do you, in fact, owe our client two thousand dollars as of this date?" We do it on a spot check basis. . . .

Reprinted from Studs Terkel, *Working: People Talk About What They Do All Day and How They Feel About What They Do,* Pantheon Books. Reprinted by permission of Donadio & Olson, Inc. Copyright © 1972 by Studs Terkel.

We work with figures, but we have to keep in mind what's behind those figures. What bugs me about people in my work is that they get too wrapped up in numbers. To them a financial statement is the end. To me, it's a tool used by management or stockholders.

We have a computer. We call it Audex. It has taken the detail drudgery out of accounting. I use things that come out of the computer in my everyday work. An accountant will prepare things for keypunching. A girl will keypunch and it will go into the monster. That's what we call it. (Laughs.) You still have to audit what comes out of the computer, I work with pencils. We all do. I think that's 'cause we make so many mistakes. (Laughs.) . . .

I'm not involved in keeping clients or getting them. That's the responsibility of the manager or the partner. I'm almost at the bottom of the heap. I'm the top class of assistant. There are five levels. I'm a staff assistant. Above me is senior. Senior's in charge of the job, out in the field with the client. The next level is manager. He has overall responsibility for the client. He's in charge of billing. The next step is partner. That's tops. He has an interest in the company. Our owners are called partners. They have final responsibility. The partner decides whether [a debt] is going to go or stay on the books.

There are gray areas. Say I saw . . . five hundred thousand dollars as a bad debt. The client may say, "Oh, the guy's good for it. He's going to pay." You say, "He hasn't paid you anything for the past six months. He declared bankruptcy yesterday. How can you say he's gonna pay?" Your client says, "He's reorganizing and he gonna get the money." You've got two ways of looking at this. The guy's able to pay or he's not. Somebody's gotta make a decision. Are we gonna allow you to show this receivable or are we gonna make you write it off? We usually compromise. We try to work out something in-between. The company knows more about it than we do, right? But we do have to issue an independent report. Anyway. I'm not a partner who makes those decisions. (Laughs.)

I think I'll leave before I get there. Many people in our firm don't plan on sticking around. The pressure. The constant rush to get things done. Since I've been here, two people have had nervous breakdowns. I have three bosses on any job, but I don't know who's my boss next week. I might be working for somebody else.

Our firm has a philosophy of progress, up or out. I started three years ago. If that second year I didn't move from SA–3, staff assistant, to SA–4, I'd be out. Last June I was SA–4. If I hadn't moved to SA–5, I'd be out. Next year if I don't move to senior, I'll be out. When I make senior I'll be Senior–1. The following year, Senior–2. Then Senior–3. Then manager—or out. By the time I'm thirty-four or so, I'm a partner or I'm out. . . .

It's a very young field. You have a lot of them at the bottom to do the footwork. Then it pyramids and you don't need so many up there. Most of the people they get are just out of college. I can't label them—the range is broad—but I'd guess most of them are conservative. Politics is hardly discussed.

Fifteen years ago, public accountants wore white shirts. You had to wear a hat, so you could convey a conservative image. When I was in college the big joke was: If you're going to work for a public accounting firm, make sure you buy a good supply of white shirts and a hat. They've gotten away from that since. We have guys with long hair. But they do catch more static than somebody in another business.

And now we have women. There are several female assistants and seniors. There's one woman manager. We have no female partners.

If you don't advance, they'll help you find another job. They're very nice about it. They'll fire you, but they just don't throw you out in the streets. (Laughs.) They'll try to find you a job with one of our clients. There's a theory behind it. Say I leave to go to XYZ Manufacturing Company. In fifteen years, I'm comptroller and I need an audit. Who am I gonna go to? Although their philosophy is up or out, they treat their employees very well. . . .

When people ask what I do, I tell them I'm an accountant. It sounds better than auditor, doesn't it? (Laughs.) But it's not a very exciting business. What can you say about figures? (Laughs.) You tell people you're an accountant—(his voice deliberately assumes a dull monotone) "Oh, that's nice." They don't know quite what to say. (Laughs.) What can you say? I could say, "Wow! I saw this company yesterday and their balance sheet, wow!" (Laughs.) Maybe I look at it wrong. (Slowly emphasizing each word) *There just isn't much to talk about.*

### 3. Lee Radler Archacki Explains Why She Chose the Night Shift, 1979

Watching Lee Radler Archacki zip through her 16-hour, double-duty schedule is like watching an Olympic gymnast perform, It looks effortless. It isn't.

From Monday through Friday, this lithe, exuberant, right-down-to-the-roots blonde fills two full-time jobs: a day shift as a stay-home mother at her six-room house in Colonia, New Jersey, and a night shift as a reservations agent at Eastern Airlines, two and a half miles away.

Obviously, this routine must be buttressed by a sturdy constitution and exceptional stamina. Lee, 31, has both. "I feel good," she says. "I very seldom feel really tired. And if I do, it's toward the end of the week."

That's a bit of an exaggeration. Lee prefers to forget the many occasions when she's been steeped in exhaustion. But once she checks in at Eastern at four in the afternoon, she gets her second wind and starts to perk up, her energy level steadily rising. When she returns home shortly after midnight to sleeping children and a husband who has usually zonked out on the sofa while waiting for her, Lee is riding high.

"It takes me a couple of hours to unwind," she says. "I wake Billy [her husband] and tell him to go to bed. I have a drink. Then I get out a book and read for at least an hour. I'm tired in the morning, but I'm not tired when I come home. That's the only time I really have for myself—and I need it."

Bill and Lee take turns parenting their children. By the time Lee leaves for work, Bill is back home, ready to take over. Their system works. The secret ingredients that overcome the inevitable stresses and strains are a marital partnership, a triumphant sense of organization and an invincible motivation. "We don't want our children brought up by strangers," Lee says decisively. . . .

From Fern Marja Eckman, "I Chose the Night Shift," *Working Mother,* September 1979, pp. 70, 89, 110.

Bill and Lee try to share their responsibilities. "We had guests over for dinner last Sunday night," Lee says. "After coffee, Billy helped me clean off the table. His friend said, 'What are you doing that for?' And Billy said, 'In this house there's no such thing as a man's work and a woman's work. The two of us do both.'"

But the Archackis realize that Lee carries the heavier load: From 7:30 A.M. to 2:30 P.M., after five and a half hours of sleep, Lee, who is not a lick-and-promiser, puts in a full round of household chores. She serves breakfast to the youngsters. (Bill usually leaves early.) Then she sends Steve off to school, a block away. She chauffeurs Susie to nursery school and shops. When she returns home, Lee makes the beds, does the laundry and cleans. She picks up Susie at 11:30, gives both kids lunch (two lunches, in fact, because they like different foods), shoos Steve back to school and prepares dinner for Bill to heat or cook in the evening.

At 3:30 in the afternoon, freshly showered and dressed, Lee kisses the children and Bill, who has returned from his fieldwork and is now digging into a mound of paperwork. Scooting out to the garage, Lee jumps into her cherished new, sky-blue Ford Granada. At 5 feet 8 inches and 130 pounds, she looks chic enough in her boutique clothes to be a model.

"Sometimes," Lee says, "if it's been a really hectic day, I just sit behind the wheel for a little while. I take a deep breath and say to myself, 'Okay, I'm going to work now and I can relax. For the next eight hours, I'll be away from everything that is hectic and humdrum. I'm going to a job I like, to work with people I like.'"

Soothed by her own minitherapy, she backs her car into the street. Stephen, who hates to see his mother leave, always waves to her from the porch or the living room window. Lee waves back. Then she drives off to Iselin, in Woodbridge Township, New Jersey, where she happily immerses herself in her duties on Eastern's 4 P.M.-to-midnight shift. But unfailingly, at 8:45 she takes time out to call home to say goodnight to Steve and Susie.

Lee loves her job, which earns her a little more than $15,000 a year. "Every passenger who calls in has a different question," she reports, laughing. "The classic one is, 'How much does it cost to go to Florida?' You say, 'Where in Florida?' And the voice at the other end says, 'Miami, of course,' as though Florida had no other cities."

Eight hours of similar questions could prove monotonous, even with two 15-minute breaks and a half hour for lunch. But Lee has been with Eastern 11 years, long enough to have gained experience and competence in other sections. More often than not, she is on loan to another department. She enjoys the variety.

"A lot of the people who started out with me are now making $18,000 a year as managers," Lee volunteers. "Managers change hours often. I can't be flexible that way because of the children. In two years, when Susie is in school full time, I'll be able to work days. It bothers me that I can't go anywhere on my job until then." Pause. "Two years isn't very long." Another pause. "Or I may go back to working part time." . . .

. . . To this day, Stephen gets up in the morning and says, 'Mommy, do you really have to work tonight?'"

But Lee considers herself a good wife and a good mother. "I feel I'm doing what's best for my family, but mainly what's best for me," she says. It's difficult to avoid the impression that she is giving herself a little pep talk. "If I'm happier, I'll make them happier. I just hope that I'm not trying to do it in the wrong way."

The Archackis combined income is comfortably over $30,000 a year. "There's no doubt about it," Lee says. "We could live on my husband's salary. But I'll be honest with you, I don't want to stop working.

As each of Lee's two maternity leaves expired, Bill made it clear he would prefer her to concentrate on the children and let him support the family. Lee, who has worked since she was 17, compromised by cutting back to working part time.

"I thought, 'Well, I'll give that a try for about a year until we get a little ahead financially,'" Lee says. "Then the cost of living rioted. We knew we wanted to buy a house. A new house needs more furniture, okay?" There is always the lure of a money-consuming project on the family's horizon. . . .

When Lee felt she was ready to resume her full-time schedule at Eastern in 1977, Bill promptly suggested they hire a housekeeper. Lee just as promptly vetoed his proposal, even though it would have allowed her more leisure time. "I can keep my house better than a stranger can," she says.

"The fact that Bill and I don't see much of each other during weekdays, that we're not together every night, makes us appreciate the time we are together. Just a couple of days ago he said, 'You know, you really look nice—but you always look nice.' I don't think I would take care of myself the same way if I weren't working. I never want to get into the rut where you're not going anywhere so you just let yourself go. If I have an evening off, I shower and dress and put on fresh makeup. Billy says, 'How come you're all dressed up?' I figure if I can do it for my job, I can do it for my husband." . . .

Infrequently, an unexpected and joyous event—unpaid undertime—drops into the family's collective lap like a wonderful gift. The opposite of overtime, undertime occurs when an employee has the option of leaving early on a slow day or evening.

"Last night, about 8:30," Bill says, "Lee called to tell me to keep the children up. 'I'm leaving right now—I have undertime,' she said. I didn't tell the kids, in order to surprise them. I had the garage door open for Lee. When she pulled in, I turned to Steve and said, 'Go see who that is outside.' He looked out and screamed, 'It's Mommy!'"

A media star couldn't have had a more rousing welcome or a more appreciative audience. "The kids made a big fuss over her," Bill says. His own pleasure can be gauged by the breadth of his grin. And for once, Lee didn't have to telephone Steve and Susie at 8:45 to say goodnight.

## 4. Computerized Order Taking at McDonald's, 1988

I waited on line at my neighborhood McDonald's. It was lunch hour and there were four or five customers at each of the five open cash registers. "May I take your order?" a very thin girl said in a flat tone to the man at the head of my line.

"McNuggets, large fries and a Coke," said the man. The cashier punched in the order. "That will be—."

"Big Mac, large fries and a shake," said the next woman on line. The cashier rang it up.

"Two cheeseburgers, large fries and a coffee," said the third customer. The cashier rang it up.

"How much is a large fries?" asked the woman directly in front of me.

The thin cashier twisted her neck around trying to look up at the menu board.

"Sorry," apologized the customer, "I don't have my glasses."

"Large fries is seventy-nine," a round-faced cashier with glasses interjected from the next register.

"Seventy-nine cents," the thin cashier repeated.

"Well how much is a *small* fries?" . . .

By then it was my turn.

"Just a large fries," I said.

The thin cashier pressed "lge fries." In place of numbers, the keys on a McDonald's cash register say "lge fries," "reg fries," "med coke," big mac," and so on. Some registers have pictures on the key caps. The next time the price of fries goes up (or down) the change will be entered in the store's central computer. But the thin cashier will continue to press the same button. I wondered how long she'd worked there and how many hundreds of "lge fries" she'd served without learning the price.

Damita, the cashier with the glasses, came up from the crew room (a room in the basement with lockers, a table and a video-player for studying the training disks) at 4:45. She looked older and more serious without her striped uniform.

"Sorry, but they got busy and, you know, here you get off when they let you."

The expandable schedule was her first complaint. "You give them your availability when you sign on. Mine I said 9 to 4. But they schedule me for 7 o'clock two or three days a week. And I needed the money. So I got to get up 5 in the morning to get here from Queens by 7. And I don't get off till whoever's supposed to get here gets here to take my place. . . . It's hard to study with all the pressures."

Damita had come to the city from a small town outside of Detroit. She lives with her sister in Queens and takes extension courses in psychology at New York University. Depending on the schedule posted each Friday her McDonald's paycheck for a five-day week has varied from $80 to $114. . . .

The flexible scheduling at McDonald's only seems to work one way. One day Damita had arrived a half hour late because the E train was running on the R track.

"The assistant manager told me not to clock in at all, just to go home. So I said O.K. and I left."

"What did you do the rest of the day?" I asked.

"I went home and studied, and I went to sleep."

"But how did it make you feel?"

"It's like a humiliating feeling 'cause I wasn't given any chance to justify myself. But when I spoke to the Puerto Rican manager he said it was nothing personal against me. Just it was raining that day, and they were really slow and someone who got here on time, it wouldn't be right to send them home."

"Weren't you annoyed to spend four hours travelling and then lose a day's pay?" I suggested.

"I was mad at first that they didn't let me explain. But afterwards I understood and I tried to explain to my sister: 'Time waits for no man.'"

"Since you signed on for 9 to 4," I asked Damita, "and you're going to school, why can't you say, 'Look, I have to study at night, I need regular hours'?"

"Don't work that way. They make up your schedule every week and if you can't work it, you're responsible to replace yourself. If you can't they can always get someone else."

"But Damita," I tried to argue with her low estimate of her own worth, "anyone can see right away that your line moves fast yet you're helpful to people. I mean, you're a valuable employee. And this manager seems to like you."

"Valuable! $3.35 an hour. And I can be replaced by any [pointing across the room] kid off the street." I hadn't noticed. At a small table under the staircase a manager in a light beige shirt was taking an application from a lanky black teenager.

"But you know the register. You know the routine."

"How long you think it takes to learn the six steps? Step 1. Greet the customer, 'Good morning, can I help you?' Step 2. Take his order. Step 3. Repeat the order. They can have someone off the street working my register in five minutes."

"By the way," I asked, "on those cash registers without numbers, how do you change something after you ring it up? I mean if somebody orders a cheeseburger and then they change it to a hamburger, how do you subtract the slice of cheese?"

"I guess that's why you have step 3, repeat the order. One cheeseburger, two Cokes, three. . . ."

"Yeah but if you punched a mistake or they don't want it after you get it together?"

"Like if I have a crazy customer,which I do be gettin' 'specially in this city, and they order hamburger, fries and shake, and it's $2.95 and then they just walk away?"

"I once did that here," I said. "About a week ago when I first started my research. All I ordered was some French fries. And I was so busy watching how the computer works that only after she rang it up I discovered that I'd walked out of my house without my wallet. I didn't have a penny. I was so embarrassed."

"Are you that one the other day? Arnetta, this girl next to me, she said, 'Look at that crazy lady going out. She's lookin' and lookin' at everything and then she didn't have no money for a bag of fries.' I saw you leaving, but I guess I didn't recognize you. [I agreed it was probably me.] O.K., so say this crazy lady comes in and orders French fries and leaves. In Michigan I could just zero it out. I'd wait till I start the next order and press zero and large fries. But here you're supposed to call out 'cancel sale' and the manager comes over and does it with his key.

"But I hate to call the manager every time, 'specially if I got a whole line waiting. So I still zero out myself. They can tell I do it by the computer tape, and they tell me not to. Some of them let me, though, because they know I came from another store. But they don't show the girls here how to zero out. Everybody thinks you need the manager's key to do it."

"Maybe they let you because they can tell you're honest," I said. She smiled, pleased, but let it pass. "That's what I mean that you're valuable to them. You know how to use the register. You're good with customers." . . .

McDonald's computerized cash registers allow managers to determine immediately not only the dollar volume for the store but the amount of each item that was sold at each register for any given period. Two experienced managers, interviewed separately, both insisted that the new electronic cash registers were in fact slower than the old mechanical registers. Clerks who knew the combinations—hamburger, fries, Coke: $2.45—could ring up the total immediately, take the cash and give change in one operation. On the new registers you have to enter each item and may be slowed down by computer response time. The value of the new registers, or at least their main selling point (McDonald's franchisers can choose from several approved registers), is the increasingly sophisticated tracking systems, which monitor all the activity and report with many different statistical breakdowns.

"Look, there," said Damita as the teenage job applicant left and the manager went behind the counter with the application, "If I was to say I can't come in at 7, they'd cut my hours down to one shift a week, and if I never came back they wouldn't call to find out where I was.

"I worked at a hospital once as an X-ray assistant. There if I didn't come in there were things that had to be done that wouldn't be done. I would call there and say, 'Remember to run the EKGs.' Here, if I called and said, 'I just can't come by 7 no more,' they'd have one of these high school kids off the street half an hour later. And they'd do my job just as good."

## 5. Sex Discrimination in the Skies, 1967

If the EEOC [Equal Employment Opportunity Commission] should declare sex to be a bona fide occupational qualification for the position of Flight Cabin Attendant, it would put TWU's [Transport Workers Union's] fight against discrimination on account of sex back to the frustrating days when the fight began and it would undo all the progress that has been made thus far in eliminating such discrimination. Industry representatives would be in a position to assert and would assert that the EEOC's determination is justification—governmental justification, no less—for continuing and even enlarging its discriminatory practices based on sex. We make no bones about it; our collective bargaining strength, which must also and primarily be asserted for obtaining improved working conditions and higher wages for all employees regardless of sex, would be hardput to . . . overcome effectively the savage blow which such a finding and decision would deliver to our struggle against discrimination at this critical-period in our bargaining history.

We therefore want no finding by the EEOC that sex is a bona fide occupational qualification.

We go further and emphasize that sex is not a valid basis for imposing discriminatory terms of employment and that any determination by this Commission which would support a contrary proposition is unsound, unreasonable, contrary to the evidence and contrary to the term and principles of the Equal Employment Opportunity Act and the Regulations adopted by this Commission in implementation of the Act.

From Asher W. Schwartz, "Statement at Hearing, September 12, 1967," Equal Employment Opportunity Commission, "Stewardess Employment by the United States Air Transport Industry. Robert F. Wagner Labor Archives, New York University. Records of the Transport Workers Union of America, Box 32, Local 550, 1987.

The men who run the airline industry like and admire young, pretty and single girls. We all do. But they can attract them to their industry successfully because they can provide them with stewardess jobs which are glamorous, well-paid and possessed of superior working conditions through Union contracts. They also like to keep them young, so in large part they have been discarding them at 32 or 35 years of age. I don't yet know what their objection to young and pretty married girls is, except perhaps that they have husbands. Whatever the reasons may be, they have nothing to do with the qualifications of a flight cabin attendant, except allegedly and theoretically in terms of employer and customer preferences, which the Commission has ruled will not warrant the application of a bona fide occupational qualification. . . .

The fact is that experience shows that the job of flight attendant is filled equally well by males and females. Most, if not all, foreign airlines as well as many American airlines employ both males and females with equal effectiveness and efficiency. Even the concept that pretty and gracious hostesses are preferred by passengers is under serious question. In May 1966, the Wall Street Journal inquired into the matter and found that some stewardesses complain that "faster trips and bigger planes have changed gracious hostesses into harried waitresses."

However, our area of concern here is not whether the flight attendant is a male or female, or whether she is gracious or harried, but whether the female flight attendant is being illegally discriminated against because of her sex. The airlines have admitted discrimination. That is why they have applied to this Commission for a bona fide occupational qualification. If there were no discrimination a bona fide occupational qualification would be irrelevant and unnecessary.

Whatever the reasons the carriers may have for establishing sex as a bona fide occupational qualification, valid or otherwise, they have nothing to do with the discriminations which the carriers are seeking to justify; namely, age and marriage limitations. An age limit of 32 and a hard and fast rule against marriage are not conditions of employment which necessarily or even reasonably follow from sex being declared a bona fide occupational qualification, if it is. . . .

For the moment, I will assume that the airlines are justified in selecting only females for the position of flight attendant. The graciousness, strength, vitality and beauty of a woman is not any less after 32 than before 32. . . .

Most jobs require physical exertions and mental alertness and the capacity to meet these requirements is reduced with increasing age in varying degrees with different persons, male and female. Yet in the absence of specific proof of incapacity, an age disqualification—not a retirement age—is almost unheard of in American industry and there is certainly none at the age of 32. None of our Union contracts in the airline industry or elsewhere recognize any such limitation.

The carriers press their case further for fixing "the young and pretty girl" test as a bona fide occupational classification by asserting a competitive basis. It may be realistic to accept the proposition that an airline with unattractive flight attendants could not enjoy a competitive advantage over another airline and that an airline employing young and pretty girls would have a competitive advantage over an airline employing unbecoming flight attendants. But this would be due solely to customers' preferences rather than because of any quality of the job. This would be true of any business in which employees have contact with customers. If, however, all the airlines are uniformly restricted in their use of sex as a device, this competitive factor would not be affected. The carriers may still choose their own employees, male and female. . . .

Marriage is no greater employment handicap to the female than it is to the male employee, except upon the conception and arrival of children. This exception can be and is met by appropriate terms affecting employment of females after marriage which are easily established and agreed to. Husbands may be a problem of course, but wives can be too. Sex is no ground for making marriage a disqualification of employment. . . .

We can understand that certain jobs can be or should be performed only by members of one sex or the other. There is no question but that sex would be a bona fide occupational qualification for the appointment of a Sales Clerk of a Girdle or Brassiere Department in a Department Store. There is no logic, however, to the contention that therefore the female employee in that department may be subjected to more disadvantageous terms of employment than the Saleswomen in the Handbag Department, the Salesmen in the Men's Clothing Department or an employee in a department in which employees are both male and female. . . .

We do not believe that the choice of young girls as flight attendants is a necessary one. The airline carriers are operating on outdated concepts. Passengers no longer need the presence of a young and pretty girl, if they ever did, to reassure them that flying is safe. Travel by air is no longer really an alternative method of transportation. Passengers no longer fly airplanes for status, pleasure or thrill, if they ever did, but rather to get from one place to another.

But whether the airlines employ men or women, TWU is emphatically opposed to any measures which will validate discriminatory practices in terms of employment which are not necessary to the performance of the work of a flight attendant. We think it clear that age and marriage limitations are of that character and since these are the limitations which the airlines are asking to support by their application to this Commission, we urge the Commission to deny that application.

## 6. The Scandal Behind Soaring Construction Costs, 1972

On a construction project in the East last year, Joe W., a union-selected master mechanic who never uses a tool of any sort, had earnings above $94,000—about $18,000 in base salary, plus $76,000 in overtime. What does he do to earn this much? For part of his working time he directs a staff of largely nonworking assistants whose pay rate is almost as big as his own. The rest of his time he spends on the telephone, arranging for outside service men to repair machines on his job.

The total amount of his pay stems from a union requirement that he be paid for every hour that any man—either one of his mechanics or an outside service

From Edward M. Young, "Low Productivity: The Real Sin of High Wages," *The Engineering News-Record,* February 24, 1972. Copyright. © 1972 by McGraw-Hill, Inc. Reprinted in condensed form from *The Engineering Record,* copyright The McGraw-Hill Companies, Inc. February 24, 1972. All rights reserved.

man—is working on the job. And when the total time spent in maintenance exceeds the basic 35 hours in any week, he receives double-time, even though he may be home sleeping.

An extreme case, to be sure. But it serves to illustrate a major complaint of many building contractors today: that the high salaries required by union contracts frequently bear no reasonable relation to value received or to time and energy expended.

Records of many construction companies verify that as wages have risen, productivity in the nation's largest industry has fallen, often greatly. An excessive—but certainly common—example is found in a study of pay and production records of a Chicago-based general contractor. In 1926, when masons were getting $1.50 an hour (with no fringe benefits), one mason could lay 600 blocks a day. Today, with masons getting about $9 an hour—and two masons required to handle the block—the contractor says he is lucky to get 100 blocks a day from the pair. In 1926, when concrete was finished by hand, the contractor figured on getting 2000 square feet of finished concrete per man per day. Today, with the help of labor-saving vibrators, mechanical screeds and power trowels, he gets 600 square feet.

According to a survey by *Engineering News-Record,* low productivity wastes from 15 to 40 percent of every construction payroll dollar. Since construction now has an annual volume of about $115 billion, and since the labor factor is about 40 percent of the total in-place cost, Americans this year are spending from $7 billion to $18 billion for something they aren't getting.

**Fair Day's Work?**

Contractors blame low productivity in construction mainly on restrictive labor-union practices. (Low productivity is not restricted to union labor, but it is considerably greater on jobs where men have the protection of unions.) In extent, these practices range from overly long coffee breaks to outright falsification of payroll records. In their lesser ranges, they are accepted by contractors as a way of life. In their extremes, they are foisted on employers by strikes, slow-downs, threats of violence and outright sabotage. The result is that labor does not give a fair day's work for a fair day's pay.

Contractors defend their acceptance of featherbedding union work rules by citing their high overhead, expensive equipment rentals, contract completion deadlines and often costly penalty clauses. They are in no position to withstand a prolonged strike. Labor thus has the upper hand in imposing such restrictive practices as:

• *Prohibiting labor-saving devices and requiring unnecessary manpower.* Bans on the use of speedily assembled plastic pipe and of powder-activated tools for installing pipe anchors are but two of the countless legalities seized on by unions to delay construction. . . .

The most common example of requiring unneeded manpower involves the operation of welding machines and compressors. Although these machines are started and turned off by the push of a button and run unattended all day, unionized contractors in every part of the country report that for each such machine on a job they must have an operating engineer on hand at all times at $7.50 to $10 an hour. . . .

In some sections of California and in several Eastern states, unions require that large cranes be attended by two operators and an oiler, or by an operator and two oilers. In either case, three men are being paid while only one works.

Electricians have their own version of this arrangement. They require that a union electrician be on hand during any hours in which temporary lights are used. On many jobs the lights are never turned off, and attending electricians are paid $7 to $10 an hour around the clock week in, week out, to watch them burn. . . .

• *Excessive non-productive time.* Almost every union contract provides for coffee breaks, morning and afternoon, and most contractors approve, because they say the breaks decrease fatigue and increase efficiency. But where a union contract provides for a 10- or 15-minute break, on many jobs the men take 20 minutes to a half-hour. This means that a man working a seven-hour day can spend almost 15 percent of his time taking breaks.

Travel and show-up time are two other big cost raisers. The actual distance traveled rarely has anything to do with the size of the travel payment. That is based on the distance of the job from the contractor's office the union hall or, in some cases, from the center of a city. . . .

Show-up time in money paid to men who come to a site but, because of bad weather or other circumstances, do not work or work for only a short time. Minimum pay for show-up is generally two hours, but some job classifications receive a day's pay just for appearing on the job. One contractor says, "I've had men show up without tools or work clothes when they knew the weather was so bad they couldn't possibly work. Their families wait for them in the car." . . .

## Headaches for Contractors

While many labor abuses are thus agreed to by contractors through acceptance in labor agreements, some others are nothing short of extortion. A frequent abuse involves the rental, at unconscionable prices, of employe[e]-owned equipment, usually trucks.

One New England contractor reports that at the start of a job several of his operating engineers (including the master mechanic) suggested that, since the men already owned pickup trucks needed to service equipment, it would be cheaper for the contractor to rent these than to buy new ones. Because the rentals demanded were excessive, the contractor refused; instead, he provided the men with new, company-owned trucks. Within a few months, these pickups were in such bad condition that they were virtually useless.

Aware now of the situation, the contractor scrapped his own trucks and rented those of mechanics. However, the price set was now considerably higher than in the beginning—on the premise that at the start the mechanics had "no idea the job would be so hard on trucks."

Another industry headache is the jurisdictional dispute that puts the contractor helplessly in the middle. A common dispute of this type is between operating engineers and elevator installers as to who shall run elevators in buildings under construction. Usually, operating engineers run the elevators carrying tools and equipment, and elevator installers run those carrying men. Often there is a demand from both unions to have a man on any elevator carrying men with tool boxes. The problem is generally resolved by keeping two elevators manned at all times, so that each union can be represented on the project, even though there is never more than one elevator in operation at any given time. . . .

## Help Wanted

In the face of such union practices, the country has seen a rise in open-shop operations unprecedented since the Depression of the '30s. The Associated General Contractors of America reports that today 35 percent of its members do more than half their work under open shops. Even on jobs that remain in the domain of construction unions (representing three million members), labor is losing ground as architects and engineers, contractors and owners, fed up with labor excesses, seek and find better, faster and cheaper ways to build. Dry-wall construction has completely replaced lath and plaster in many places. Pre-cast concrete structures have so greatly reduced the need for bricklayers and cement finishers that in many parts of the country there is a surplus of these tradesmen. Pre-fabricated steel buildings are increasingly gaining favor because of their economy and speed of erection.

Responsible labor leaders, faced with public outcry against them and the tremendous increase in open-shop operations, have begun to accept the need for internal controls—if only to prevent new labor laws. And contractors are beginning to stand up to unreasonable demands if for no other reason than that they are being hurt financially.

The picture must change before high wages and low productivity price construction—and badly needed homes, schools and hospitals—right out of the market.

## ✤ E S S A Y S

The first essay, by historian Joshua B. Freeman of Queen's College, City University of New York, situates the 1970 attack of "hardhats" on antiwar protestors in the context of a declining construction industry. Though popular stereotypes often miss the complexity of worker subjectivity, the hardhat did not merely symbolize a certain rough-hewn masculinity but actually stood for a workplace culture that excluded men of color and white women. Freeman imaginatively unpacks the social construction of white manhood in the post-war years.

Historian Dorothy Sue Cobble of Rutgers University turns to female-dominated service industries in the second essay, gauging the impact of the new feminism on the women who challenged managerial paternalism in airlines, offices, and private households. Flight attendants left the male-dominated transportation unions to forge their own organizations to fight more effectively against corporate efforts to promote them as mere sex objects in the sky. Inspired by second-wave feminism, office workers also demanded "raises, not roses," while household workers, who drew much of their energy from the African American freedom struggle, sought to dismantle the historic "mammy" stereotypes that structured so much domestic service.

To what extent was the hard-hat a typical "blue-collar" worker? How would you characterize the politics of the building trades in the early 1970s? Why have construction workers come to seem so conservative and so typical of the American working class? Why is so much service work "sexualized" at the point of personal contact? How do such gender criteria, for both men and women, shape the employer-employee relationship?

# Construction Workers Defend Their Manhood

JOSHUA FREEDMAN

When in the spring of 1970 construction workers in New York and St. Louis violently attacked anti-war demonstrators, an image of the "hardhat" was fixed in popular consciousness: journalists, politicians, social scientists, novelists, and moviemakers portrayed building tradesmen as the rudest, crudest, and most sexist of all workers. The stereotyped brawny, flagwaving construction worker became a pivot of national cultural and political debate. For some, hardhats were "real men," more willing than other Americans to defend their country and its values from enemies abroad and political dissidents, racial minorities, and counterculturalists at home. For others, hardhats were ominous figures: politically reactionary, pathologically violent, and deeply misogynist. The general public was ambivalent: by a 40% to 24% plurality those polled indicated more sympathy for the hardhats than for the students they attacked, but 53% disapproved of their use of violence.

The hardhat image was of considerable importance because the construction worker was commonly presented in the mass media, public discourse, and commercial iconography as the archetypical proletarian. Although building tradesmen occasionally had filled that role before, from the 1920s through the 1950s it was the auto worker, associated with the ethos of mass production and modernity, and belonging to a key, pattern-setting union, whom academics, artists, and businessmen generally studied, celebrated, and negotiated with as the leading blue-collar worker. However, as the composition of the work force shifted away from manufacturing, the assembly line lost its glamour, and the influence of the United Automobile Workers diminished, construction workers eclipsed auto workers in emblematic importance. By the 1970s, the hardhat itself became—and still is—the central symbol of American labor, a role earlier filled by the leather apron, the lunch pail, and the worker's cap. Furthermore, construction workers were widely held forth as prime examples of "Middle Americans" (or alternatively, "The Silent Majority"), a vast, vague group that was key to conservative designs for political realignment during the Nixon and post-Nixon eras.

The multiple symbolic meanings of the hardhat—both the piece of apparel and the person wearing it—were intensely gendered. The manliness of construction workers was so taken for granted by imagemakers and their audiences that the hardhat was treated as a magical object, conferring masculinity on its wearer. Beer companies, trying to convince men that drinking a particular brand of beer would confirm their manhood, began featuring hardhat-wearing actors in their advertisements, while political candidates, worried that they were perceived as "wimps," donned hardhats and posed near industrial equipment.

While the hardhat identity is universally recognized, it has yet to be seriously investigated. When, why, and how did construction workers come to be associated with aggressive, crude masculinity? Were they significantly different from other workers in this regard, and if so why? And what does the case of construction

---

From Joshua B. Freeman, "Hardhats: Construction Workers, Manliness, and the 1970 Pro-War Demonstrations," *Journal of Social History,* Vol. 26 (Summer 1993), pp. 725–737.

workers tell us about the changing place and meaning of manliness in the image, self-understanding, and culture of American workers? . . .

Even a cautious assessment of the available evidence . . . reveals the world of post–World War II construction workers, especially on large urban projects, as not only remarkably male in composition—even today women make up under 2% of the workforce—but also remarkably male in culture and remarkably sexualized. Take its very language. In building trades argot, circa 1970, easy work was "tit work," heavy labor "bull work." Loafing was "fucking the dog," while a very small measurement was a "cunt hair." A tool used to reshape wire was known as the "bull's dick," while calls for diagonal cutters—"dia x" for short—were the occasion for endless jokes about "dykes." Even routine griping came out in sexual terms. One ironworker complained that: "You freeze your balls right up into your belly in the winter and seat 'em down to your knees in the summer."

Of course, earthy, profane language was heard at non-construction worksites as well. Testicles were as central—if in a somewhat different way—to the speech and worldview of left-wing painter and former United Electrical Workers organizer Ralph Fasanella as to Tommy and Chubby De Coco, the conservative construction electricians and "fifty-year-old pussy chasers" in Richard Price's 1976 novel *Bloodbrothers* (made into a movie three years later). But if far from unique, the profanity and sexualization of language among post–World War II construction workers seem extreme. Furthermore, because the public was more likely to see building tradesmen at work than most other blue-collar groups, profanity was more widely associated with hardhats than with workers in more isolated occupations who might curse mightily among themselves.

Proximity to the public made possible another type of sexually-related construction workers behavior, "watching the windows." This consisted of peering from structures being built into adjacent apartments or hotel rooms to spy on naked women or couples engaged in sex. Often elaborate preparations—bringing binoculars to work, building hiding places or even bleachers—were made to facilitate such voyeurism, which was widespread and almost always a group activity. When live women were unavailable for viewing, pornographic magazines, books, or even movies shown in on-site trailers might substitute. Pasted-up pictures of nude women—"paper pussy"—were virtually a norm in American industry, but peeping as a regular part of work culture was highly unusual.

Still more evidence of the gendered sexualized nature of construction work comes from the women who entered it after 1978, when the federal government began requiring construction companies and apprenticeship programs to develop affirmative action programs for recruiting female workers. Pioneer building tradeswomen reported over and over again being harassed on the job both sexually and in non-sexual ways meant to drive them away, up to and including serious physical assaults.

The hardhat image, then, perhaps exaggerated the extent to which construction workers were "macho" and different from other workers, but clearly there was something intensely male about the culture of post–World War II construction work. In and of itself this was not new; it was also the case for late nineteenth-century and New Deal–era construction work. What was different was the changing meaning of manliness, to both construction workers and those who observed them.

For the turn-of-the-century skilled construction worker, manliness meant independent, mutuality, and pride in craft. Worksite photographs of early twentieth-century carpenters, for example, show nearly dressed men, wearing derby hats and sometimes white shirts and ties, carefully maintaining an erect dignified bearing. This self-presentation (even in apparently unposed photographs workers usually were aware of the camera) corresponded to a political construct in which building tradesmen, like other craftsmen, closely linked self-respect, manhood, and citizenship. Reinforcing one another, all three ultimately rested on economic independence, which was seen as the fruit of skill, hard work, sobriety, and organization.

Within this craft tradition, manhood apparently did not have an explicitly sexual meaning. . . . These notions of manliness grew out of a gender system and an industrial system in flux. Long-term developments away from the workplace, such as the female suffrage and temperance movements, had profound implications for thinking in all classes about what it meant to be a man. Working-class ideas of manhood and manliness also were affected by changes at work, especially the introduction of new technologies that made venerated skills outmoded, the greater use of female or child labor, and the rise or fall of union power. While the pattern varied from industry to industry, generally it seems that as the nineteenth century drew to a close, physical strength and specific craft skills became less important in working-class male identity, while the ability of a worker to provide for his family became more so. This might explain why photographic portraits of workers posed with symbols of their trade declined in popularity, while those of workers and their families dressed in their finest clothes became favored.

Literary as well as visual evidence suggests that for the late-nineteenth-century craft worker, the concept of manliness was firmly attached and even subsumed to ideas of respectability and domesticity. Skilled workers—including building tradesmen—were not immune from the temptations of drink, gambling, and extra-marital sex. But apparently most sought to temper themselves, to control such impulses, and thereby disassociate themselves from the "rough working-class culture" dominated by less-skilled, more poorly-paid workers. Many found an alternative to plebeian rowdiness in the huge fraternal orders that sprang up all over postbellum America. Typically these joined together skilled artisans and small proprietors around ritualized expressions of male solidarity, promoting a link between manliness, respectability, and economy standing. These groups were racially exclusionary and often nativist. For many native-born white workers, manhood was as much a racial and ethnic category as one of gender: African-Americans and immigrants from many regions were considered incapable of behaving in manly ways.

Construction unions built on, embodied, and promoted the idea of respectable manliness. Many building trades unions called themselves brotherhoods, and like other craft unions borrowed extensively from the fraternal movement. The oath of the Bricklayers was typical in calling on its members to "solemnly and sincerely pledge by my honor as a man that I will not reveal any private business . . . of this union." The International Association of Bridge and Structural Iron Workers, while not hesitant to use explosives against open-shop employers, took it upon itself to promote bourgeois respectability among its members in other regards. One business agent claimed: "The organization has made men [out] of a lot of irresponsible bums. . . . I remember when a bridgeman wearing a white collar couldn't get a job. The foreman would say that he was a dude, who didn't know his trade. It's different now. If a man is well dressed . . . the foreman will size him up and conclude that he is a decent fellow."

This quest for respectability, to dress well, was both an expression of workers' sense of their dignity and an effort to meet middle-class norms, part and parcel of the struggle by workers and unions, as Sidney Hillman once put it to "establish themselves as a full-fledged part of organized society." It was evident at the top of the labor movement in the pleasure leaders like Samuel Gompers, John Mitchell, and John L. Lewis took in rubbing elbows with the rich while decked out in their finery. At the bottom it could be seen in the jackets and ties unionists so often wore to demonstrations.

The ironworkers in the most famous photographs of construction workers ever taken—those by Lewis W. Hine of the raising of the Empire State Building—did not wear white shirts and ties, but like the turn-of-the-century carpenters they projected a strong sense of dignity and self-possession. While the photographs they appear in are more candid than earlier ones—Hine more deeply penetrated the worksite than previous photographers—their image nonetheless was carefully crafted; Hine frankly wrote that his purpose in making these and the other photographs in his 1932 collection, *Men at Work,* was to win respect for the "men of courage, skill, daring and imagination" who "make. . . . and manipulate" the machinery of modern life.

"Constructive heroism"—to use Alan Trachtenberg's characterization of the Empire State Building photographs—was typical of artistic representations of labor during the 1930s, both in North America and Europe. Caught up in a cult of productivity, liberals and leftists worshipped giant industrial enterprises and the men who built and operated them, regardless of their social or economic context. The Soviet White Sea Canal and the American Grand Coulee Dam, the auto plants at River Rouge and Gorky, were all seen as part of the great Faustian drama of man conquering nature.

And man it was. It can hardly be a coincidence that in Hine's pre–World War I photographs, documenting the exploitation of labor, women and children figured prominently, but in his later celebration of work only adult men appear, beautiful men, strong and vigorous, hanging high in the air like Icarus, challenging the gods themselves. Hine's pictures of bare-chested ironworkers, with their hint of eroticism, are informed by "the fetish of masculinity." . . .

The increased use of a male worker's body to symbolize the working class—and masculinity—may have been a reaction, at least in part, to continuing changes in industrial life and gender relations, including increased mechanization, a further decline of craft labor, the ever-greater dominance of the corporation over the individual, rising female labor force participation, and increased social and political freedom for women. . . . It was as if artists and other imagemakers were trying to bolster a male role in deep peril. Significantly, the workers portrayed by New Deal–sponsored sculptors and muralists tended to be in precisely those occupations hardest hit by unemployment and automation: the building trades, mining, and factory work.

How much the labor imagery of the 1930s corresponded to working-class reality is unclear. The workers in Hine's photographs and in New Deal public art seemed poised between the turn-of-the-century republican craftsman and the socialist-realist worker-hero. The detached, formal bearing and sexual coolness of both archetypes is far removed from the earthiness of the immigrant bricklayers in the best-selling 1939 novel, *Christ in Concrete,* written by Pietro Di Donato, a bricklayer and son of a bricklayer who presumably had a better sense of life at construction sites than most artists.

On and off the job Di Donato's workers were fountains of ribaldry and sexual reference. But this in itself was not a mark of their manhood, for the women in the book were almost as open in their joyful, rustic sexuality. To be a man was to be sexual, but sexuality was seen as an attribute of all healthy, natural beings in the profoundly familial—but not puritanical—outlook of these workers. More than sexuality, craft, strength, and the ability to endure made a man a man. . . .

The construction workers Di Donato describes are in many ways different from modern ones, but one incident in his novel previews a scene strongly associated with the hardhat image. When a "tall slim girl with dancing ripe breasts" walked past a construction site, one bricklayer "stood up, rolled his sleepy eyes and drawled from loose lips in American, 'Ahhhhbye-bee, you make-a-me seeck . . . uhmnnnnnn bye-bee you make-a me die-a . . . .'" Another "bared his horse teeth and stuttered ecstatically, 'Ma-Ma-Madonna mine, what grapes she has!'" Two other workers admonished them for being disrespectful, but they too joined in the watching.

This scene has a number of elements that figure in explanations of post–World War II hardhat behavior. Most obvious is ethnicity. Di Donato's workers are almost all Italian, and some commentators—from sociologists to filmmakers—have strongly associated postwar plebeian vulgarity with Italian-American culture. . . . Without ruling out the possible relevance of ethnicity—it is notable that *Blood-brothers* also was set in an Italian-American milieu—in the absence of systematic, comparative studies it seems dangerous, and pat, to place too much weight on ethnicity as an explanation for the sexual stance of construction workers, especially given anecdotal evidence that participants in the demonstrations that helped establish the hardhat image came from varied backgrounds.

In explaining construction worker behavior, others have pointed to the peculiar social geography of urban building sites—another element in Di Donato's "girl" watching scene. Such sites are self-enclosed spaces, off-limits to passersby, yet surrounded by, and literally looking out on, well-used public areas. This creates the possibility for spying on, ogling, or verbally harassing nearby women (and men) from within a zone of psychological and physical safety. . . . Protected from outsiders by fence, hardhats, and each other, construction workers have a sense of invulnerability unlike, say, bus drivers or waiters. Sociologists and journeymen electrician Jeffrey W. Riemer further argues that the primitive conditions on construction sites contribute to crude behavior of all kinds, including "urinating in public, farting, wearing dirty clothes daily, excessive profanity, spitting, [and] throwing one's lunch garbage to the wind."

Riemer contends that construction worker job behavior dubbed deviant—including sexually-related behavior—is actually quite normal and largely benign. Other workers, he argues, would act similarly if they had the chance. To some extent he undoubtedly is right; physical setting and work organization play a role in what might be called "hardhatism." Other groups of male workers who operate with only loose supervision on the borders between protected private space and busy public space—for example truck drivers—also have been notorious for sexist behavior. But Riemer's tendency to treat the crude behavior he observed as being the result of natural male impulses freed from normal inhibitory structures is naive at best and ahistoric. Unless we believe in a genetic masculinity programmed for such behavioral detail as shouting "Ahhhh bye-bee," we need to look further.

One place to look is at the danger of construction work, a central theme of *Christ in Concrete* and almost all other writing about the building trades. For workers in occupations like mining, police work, and construction, which combine high risk with small team organization, safety and survival depend on the establishment of mutual trust. When the work force in such situations was all male, or virtually so, trust often was built through a decidedly male idiom of physical jousting, sexual boasting, sports talk, and shared sexual activities. This had a particularly strong impact in construction for two reasons. First, in contrast to mining, where work and residential communities heavily overlapped and women played a prominent role in supporting worker struggles, in construction, work and home life were usually quite separate. In fact, many construction workers were semi-itinerant, living long stretches away from their families. Second, because construction jobs were of limited duration, informal work groups had to be continually recreated; workers often found themselves working alongside people they never had met, yet on whom their lives and safety depended. Shared masculine activities—from peeping to whoring to whistling at women—were a way to glue together a work force in an endless process of recombination. In an era when no outward signs generally distinguished gay men from straights, aggressive heterosexual behavior also was a way of ensuring that close male bonding was not seen as evidence of homosexuality. Solidarity, safety, and sexism thus reinforced one another.

In the post–World War II era, as in the more distant past, construction unions actively encouraged a shared sense of manhood—often specifically white manhood—as a mode of worker bonding and solidarity. Apprenticeship programs, through hazing, surveillance, common experience, and the exclusion of women and non-whites, were used to build this collective identity; as much as a process of skills acquisition, apprenticeship was an "initiation into the fraternity of tradesmen." . . . On the job, apprentices—often called "punks"—faced numerous rites of passage to full occupational manhood, in the process reinforcing the maleness of the trade. Not surprisingly, it was young workers—full of anxieties about their own status—who were the most hostile to women when they began entering the construction trades. . . .

Employers encouraged an intensely male work culture as well, for example by tolerating sexual shenanigans on the job and distributing nude calendars at Christmas. Many believed that male bonding increased the motivation, productivity, and stability of their work force. For this reason, contractors long resisted hiring women; one told an interviewer that "a lot of these guys [construction workers] are ex-service guys. They don't want a woman around—they'll just distract them . . . the guys start competing for their attention or whistling or fighting over them." Also, some employers believed a shared sense of maleness eased antagonisms between workers and themselves (much in the way that the fraternal movement helped bridge the gap between skilled workers and higher social orders).

Ethnicity, worksite ecology, occupational structure, and union tradition, then, all to one degree or another contributed to the hardhat phenomenon. However, they do not explain why it emerged when it did nor the intensity of the hostility some construction workers displayed toward women, homosexuals, and anti-war demonstrators in the late 1960s and early 1970s. What makes that rage particularly puzzling is that it came at the end of a long period when construction workers, by objective measures and their own assessments, had done exceedingly well.

The years between the end of World War II and the early 1970s constituted a golden age for American workers, when earnings, benefits, and living standards rose to unprecedented heights. Construction workers especially prospered; a long build-ing boom, a labor shortage, an astounding unionization rate of over 80 percent, and a sympathetic legal and political environment (including the Davis-Bacon Act and similar state laws), enabled skilled tradesmen to push their hourly wages to the point that the over-paid construction worker became a stock figure in postwar culture.

In an era when studies of workers' attitudes towards their jobs stressed their alienation (in spite of their growing affluence)—the much discussed "blue collar blues"—construction workers were notable for their high level of job satisfaction. Unlike almost everyone else, building tradesmen apparently liked their jobs. In addition to high pay and good benefits, they repeatedly cited the challenge of their work, its variety, and their independence. Equally important was the pride they had in their crafts and in the products of their labor. Often workers would visit build-ings they had worked on, sometimes bringing along their families, to admire the tangible product of what they considered their "honest work." . . .

Not especially interested in upward mobility, postwar construction workers had no particular admiration for those above them in the social hierarchy. Unlike their predecessors, they did not feel the need to create a respectable self-presentation when in the presence of middle-class observers. Rather, they often did the oppo-site, deliberately flouting middle-class notions of decorum by wearing rough work clothes as a badge of honor, riddling their speech with curses, and harassing women who passed by construction sites. Ironworker Mike Cherry recalled his pleasure at the "weekly dumb show" when his coworkers building a midtown New York skyscraper went to cash their checks, evoking "the uncomprehending, often half-frightened stares of Chase Manhattan's more typical customers as the . . . hoards of construction workers—various oily, muddy, or dusty and all irrepressibly and vulgarly gregarious—poured in."

While this desire to shock reflected craft pride, fraternity, and a healthy con-tempt for elites, it also was rooted in the resentment many construction workers felt about their social invisibility. After World War II construction workers no longer needed to seek economic and political power; collectively they already had won it. Yet during these same years construction workers—like other manual workers—virtually disappeared from popular culture, political discourse, even advertising. This was understandably galling to building tradesmen, with their acute sense of their social contributions and accomplishments. Public rowdiness was one way for them to make themselves socially visible. As a strategy, it worked brilliantly with the pro-war hardhat demonstrations.

Social status, however, was not the only cause of construction worker con-cern. Even during good times, workers in construction never felt completely secure because of the limited duration of their jobs. In the late 1960s, although the economy and construction continued to boom, there were particular reasons for anxiety. Profit rates for American businesses had begun to fall, leading to a drive for higher productivity. In some building trades this meant efforts to standardize tasks and force greater specialization, diminishing needed skill. At the same time, accelerating inflation—a by-product of the Vietnam War—impacted construction in a number of ways. First, it threatened to wipe out wage gains. Second, it led the largest purchasers of new buildings, the major national corporations, to form the Constitution Users Anti-Inflation Roundtable (which later became the Business Roundtable) to press for lower construction labor costs. And third, it exposed the industry to unaccustomed political pressure as President Nixon, in September 1969, suspended most federal construction spending as an anti-inflationary measure, insisting that labor and management find a way to control costs before money would be released.

Falling profits, a productivity drive, and inflation on the one hand, and workers made confident by low unemployment, years of prosperity, and powerful unions on the other, led to an increase of strikes of all kinds in the late 1960s, including in the construction industry. In New York, for example, in 1969 there were strikes by steamfitters, sheet metal workers, hoisting engineers, rigging and machinery movers, and construction teamsters. The combination of confidence and anxiety that fed the late 1960s strike wave contributed to the aggressive masculinity associated with the hardhat image. In fact, one of the key groups initiating the New York hardhat demonstrations were elevator constructors, who the previous year had struck for three-and-a-half months, tying up work at dozens of high-rise worksites.

Both anxiety and confidence also could be seen in the sharp, occasionally violent response to efforts to desegregate the construction industry. As a result of sustained pressure by civil rights activists, by 1969 various public agencies were pressing contractors and construction unions—many of which were all white or virtually so—to open their ranks to African-Americans. In September of that year the Nixon Administration announced the Philadelphia Plan, a model program requiring contractors to set specific goals for minority hiring. Many white construction workers opposed such efforts. In some cases immediate self-interest was involved. Suburban and out-of-town workers on big city projects feared losing their jobs to inner-city residents. Also, many building tradesmen wanted to reserve training and job slots for their kin. Other objections were ideological and psychological, ranging from pure and simple racism to workers' belief that their own early struggles—real or imagined—would be rendered meaningless if black workers were given new, supposedly easier ways to enter the industry.

In 1969, in at least two cities, white construction workers held raucous anti-desegregation demonstrations that had many similarities with the better-known pro-war demonstrations the following year. In Pittsburgh some 4,000 white workers rallied against a decision by the mayor to shut down local construction while negotiations were held with black protestors. In Chicago over 2,000 building tradesmen gathered outside a building where a federal hearing was being held on alleged union discrimination, jeering at witnesses, scuffling with police, and rushing Jesse Jackson and his wife as they entered the building. Later part of the crowd invaded the Chicago *Sun-Times-Daily News* building chanting "we want the truth," while others taunted a group of demonstrators supporting the Chicago 8 anti-war activist, then on trial.

The impressive 1970 mobilization of construction workers in support of U.S. foreign policy thus built on earlier struggles against employers and integration. Some observers believed that the pro-war demonstrations themselves were linked to the issue of racial discrimination. Almost immediately after the New York demonstrations Assistant Secretary of Labor Arthur A. Fletcher suggested that there was "an ulterior motive" for the pro-war marches. "I believe they feel if they can support the President on this one issue," he said, "they can get inside the White House and be a formidable opponent of the Philadelphia Plan."

Part of the power of the race issue lay in its relationship to workers' sense of self-worth. Craft identity, union membership, and earning power—all established partly by exclusion—were linked in workers' minds to their social position and patriarchal authority. Efforts by non-whites to enter the building trades thus threatened white workers' sense of status as producers, citizens, and men. So did the growing drive by women for legal and social equality. In the late 1960s this threat was not job-related; until the end of the following decade there was no significant push to allow women into the building trades. But it was everywhere else: in the streets, in the media, and, most important, in the home. In 1968, for example, radical feminists received extensive publicity in connection with their protest against the Miss America contest, women were allowed for the first time to serve on juries in Mississippi, and Princeton University tenured its first female professor. . . . And only days before the 1970 hardhat demonstration, the Senate, under pressure from women's groups, held the first hearings on the Equal Rights Amendment in twelve years, the prelude to its passage two years later.

Many construction workers saw themselves as surrounded by overly-assertive women and uppity blacks. One plumber commented to sociologist E. E. Le Masters: "I don't mind [women] being equal, but some of them want to run the whole damn show. They're just like niggers—give them an inch and they'll take a mile." Le Masters reported that the construction workers he studied in the early 1970s were deeply frightened by women's liberation. While these workers did not object to their wives working for wages, which about half did, or having separate social lives, which the men actually preferred, they had not interest in egalitarian marriages. Non-white men imperilled the patriarchal notions of white workers who equated manliness and whiteness, but feminists presented a more direct and serious challenge. When modest desegregation finally did come to the construction industry, white male workers generally accepted non-white male colleagues more easily than female ones. . . .

If new notions of womanhood were seen as threatening by many construction workers, new notions of manhood were likewise unsettling. On popular music stages, at "be-ins," and on college campuses a new figure appeared in the 1960s, the long-haired young man who explicitly rejected the idea that manhood meant physical strength and aggressiveness. Instead these counter-culturalists linked manhood to such traditionally female notions as sensuality and sensitivity. Even more startling were the growing number of men, particularly after the June 1969 Stonewall Inn riot, who proudly announced their homosexuality. To love other men, they proclaimed, was not to be a sissy—a feminized male—but to be male in the purest form.

Initially these new images of manhood had a particular class content; they were associated with privilege, with those who did not have to labor all day in the heat and cold like hardhats did, with those who were using their class position to dodge the draft and the war in Vietnam (a particularly touchy issue for construction workers, since many were World War II or Korean War veterans and some had sons in the armed forces). It was the combination of class resentment and perceived threat to patriarchal notions of manliness that gave the hardhat demonstrations that: "Here were these kids, rich kids, who could go to college, who didn't have to fight, they are telling you your son died in vain. It makes you feel your whole life is shit, just nothing." Tellingly, pro-war construction workers singled out male and anti-war protestors with the longest hair for assault and shouted at New York's patrician mayor, John Lindsay—a special target of their wrath—that he was a "faggot."

In the Spring of 1970 a variety of factors—from long-standing characteristics of construction work to recently developed racial, class, cultural, political, and sexual tensions—combined to shape construction worker behavior and spark the hardhat demonstrations. The mass media—newspapers, magazines, television, and movies—then fixed the hardhat image in the public eye. The widespread publicity they gave the hardhats reflected the dramatic nature of the New York and St. Louis events, which were the first substantial physical clashes between groups of civilians over the Vietnam War. But the media also found in the hardhat image a powerful metaphor for the deepening conflicts that had developed during the 1960s over politics, gender roles, and cultural values.

The hardhat image endured in part because it resonated with a crisis of *middle-class* masculinity. . . . Anxiety over this dilemma made it safer for middle-class artists and imagemakers to explore the meaning of manhood metaphorically rather than though self-examination. Thus moviemakers, writers, and advertisers became fascinated by the white, ethnic working-class, which was portrayed, for better or for worse, as the last enclave of traditional manliness. . . . [E]ven as the specific political events surrounding the initial prominence of the hardhat receded into the past, the hardhat continued to serve as a symbol of masculinity. At least in this respect the 1970s replicated the 1930s, when the muscular, sensuous, blue-collar male was used to represent the strength, self-confident, defiance, and virility that many artists and intellectuals yearned for.

The particular historical moment that created the hardhat in all his splendor was a short one. Within a few years the construction boom, along with the rest of the economy, collapsed. Taking advantage of changed economic and political circumstances, a fierce anti-union drive succeeded by the late 1980s in reducing the unionization rate for construction workers to 22 percent, one of the most remarkable reversals of class power in American history. The sense of confidence and well-being that allowed construction workers to snub their noses at what the middle class considered acceptable behavior turned out to rest on shaky economic foundations.

The cultural foundations of the hardhat phenomenon also proved shaky. By the mid-1970s a long-haired young man was more likely to be a construction worker than a college student. Though neither side realized it at first, there was common ground between hardhats and long-haired, middle-class protestors: both rejected bourgeois respectability. But when the American Century came to an end . . . the middle-class longhairs could and did run for the shelter of conventional careers and social acceptability. It was not so easy for the young workers who by then had adopted some of their style. So the counterculture made its last stand not among the children of privilege but in the working class. In the process of class migration it lost its expansive, optimistic character—no long-haired construction worker ever thought that the age of Aquarius was dawning—and took on a sullen aspect, a statement of difference and diffidence. Ironically, the longhair became the heir of the hardhat.

## Feminism Transforms Women Service Workers

### DOROTHY SUE COBBLE

In 1972, a group of tired stewardesses tried to explain their concerns to the incredulous male transit union officials who led their union. No, the primary issues were not wages and benefits, they insisted, but the particular cut of their uniforms and the sexual insinuations made about their occupation in the new airline advertisements. Their words fell on deaf ears. Despite their commonalities as transportation workers, the gender gap separating the two groups was simply too wide to cross. Indeed, male subway drivers could not understand why the stewardesses would object to their glamorous sex-object image. Deeply held gendered notions of unionism and politics also stood in the way of communication. For even if the complaints of stewardesses were accepted as "real," to many male union leaders they seemed petty: matters not deserving of serious attention, let alone concerted activity. . . .

I focus here on the organizing efforts among three groups of female service workers—flight attendants, clericals, and household workers (or according to 1970s terminology: stewardesses, secretaries, and maids)—groups which experienced significant collective organization on a national basis for the first time in this period. These groups provide a rich evidentiary base for an exploration of the content and form of activism among female service workers. In the 1970s, women composed ninety-five percent of flight attendants, ninety-seven percent of secretaries (the largest group of office workers), and ninety-seven percent of domestic workers. Not surprisingly, the organizations they created were almost exclusively female. . . .

Moreover, these three occupations allow for speculation about the differences among women by race, class, age, and family status. Women from many different ethnic and economic backgrounds entered clerical work in the twentieth-century as it replaced domestic service as the largest single occupation among women. Over a third of all working women held clerical positions in the 1970s. African-American women did not enter clerical work in any appreciable numbers before World War Two, but by the 1970s almost as large a percent of African-American women were

From Dorothy Sue Cobble, " 'A Spontaneous Loss of Enthusiasm': Workplace Feminism and the Transformation of Women's Service Jobs in the 1970s," © 1999, *International Labor and Working-Class History,* No. 56 (Fall 1999), pp. 23–29. Reprinted by permission of Cambridge University Press.

in clerical jobs as held jobs in the overall labor market. In contrast to the hetero-geneity of clerical workers, only certain categories of women were hired as flight attendants or domestic workers. Although age and marriage bars fell in the 1960s, the airlines continued to prefer young, single, white women for their flight atten-dant positions. Conversely, domestic work was an occupation composed dispro-portionately of women of color and older women heads of households. In 1968, of the million and a half women working as private household employees, some sixty-four percent were African American. By the mid-1970s, the percentage of African Americans had dropped to fifty-three percent but the numbers of Hispanic and other ethnic minority women had increased. The median age of household workers was forty-six, some six years older than the typical woman worker, and over one-third were either divorced or separated or widowed. . . .

## The Reform Decades

. . . The 1960s witnessed the passage of federal legislation which prohibited em-ployment discrimination on the basis of race and sex and promoted the unioniza-tion of public-sector workers, the majority of whom were minority and/or female. By the late 1960s, however, the civil rights movement was ebbing and the wave of public-sector unionization had subsided.

The women's movement, however, was just taking off. It too drew on prior efforts of gender reformers, although these efforts were not as widespread nor as visible as those on behalf of racial justice. Female reformers had called for an eco-nomic and political agenda that was partially realized in the establishment of the Presidential Commission on the Status of Women and the Equal Pay Act of 1963, but this network of social and labor feminists was in disarray by the late 1960s. The passage of the 1964 Civil Rights Act brought long-simmering disagreements over the support of sex-based state protective laws into the open. In 1969, the Equal Employment Opportunities Commission ruled that most sex-based state protective legislation conflicted with Title VII and hence was illegal. Virtually overnight, the principal basis for a half century of opposition to the Equal Rights Amendment (ERA)—defense of protective laws—disappeared. The collapse of this cornerstone of the older labor feminism made possible the emergence of a new, transformed workplace-based feminism.

Like their middle-class counterparts, working-class and union women engaged in widespread gender activism in the 1960s and 1970s. . . . [B]lue-collar factory women in the late 1960s . . . embraced a new vision of gender equality and for the first time en masse rejected the sex-typing of jobs as discriminatory. Rank-and-file union women flooded the Equal Employment Opportunity Commission (EEOC) offices with sex discrimination claims in the 1960s and forced the agency to take the issue seriously. Once stirred into action, the EEOC sought and won majority court decisions designed to end sex segregation and discriminatory practices by such prominent employers as AT&T and US Steel.

Working women relied on workplace-based organizing as well as the courts to advance gender equality. Nonprofessional as well as professional women organized workplace caucuses that took up issues of affirmative action and employment dis-crimination. They also sought to transform the bargaining and legislative agenda of the labor movement. By 1974, union women had established the Coalition of Labor Union Women (CLUW). A self-consciously feminist organization, CLUW supported the Equal Rights Amendment as well as women's reproduction rights, and the founders' goals included moving women into union leadership, increased attention to organizing women workers, and an end to sex segregation and other discriminatory workplace practices based on sex.

What is less known, however, is the activism among women in female-dominated jobs during this period and the ways in which their reform movements changed the longstanding familial and paternalistic norms governing female-dominated service jobs. These women took older reform traditions and reworked them to suit their own realities as women service workers. They built upon the past, but they broke with it as well. They expanded the vocabulary of workplace rights, made a public and political issue of the gendered construction of women's jobs, and invented new forms of workplace representation.

### "Sex Objects in the Sky Unite"

Unlike most women in the female service ghetto, the majority of flight attendants had joined unions in the 1940s and 1950s. The unions representing stewardesses included the Stewards and Stewardesses (S&S) Division of the Air Line Pilots Association (ALPA), the Teamsters, and the Transport Workers Union. These unions had secured moderate advances in wages, hours, and working conditions for flight attendants, and under growing pressure from the flight attendants themselves and the impetus of new antidiscriminatory legislation, they had helped undermine the airline policies restricting the occupation to white young single, and childless women. Airlines hired a small number of minority women as attendants in the late 1950s, and by the end of the 1960s, flight attendants could marry, have children, and work past age thirty-two.

But by the early 1970s, flight attendants wanted more: They wanted economic rights and opportunities equal to men as well as the right to control and define their own sexuality and "personhood." To secure these rights, flight attendants put increasing pressure on their male-dominated unions and formed the first all-female national organization of flight attendants, Stewardesses For Women's Rights (SFWR). As Sandra Jarrell, cofounder of SFWR, explained, "the most obvious tool available for remedying the injustices we are subject to are [*sic*] the unions. Unfortunately, unions do not have the reputation of representing the interests of women." The male leadership, she continued, blamed stewardesses, but they "will obtain rank and file support only if they stop limiting [themselves] . . . to economic issues."

The emergence of this new militancy among flight attendants in the 1970s was spurred in part by the new feminist sensitivity to employment discrimination and to male control over female sexuality. Flight attendants, however, were as much feminist leaders as followers. They helped invent the new feminism in the 1960s, and they were instrumental in the 1970s in demonstrating the power of these ideas when applied to women's jobs.

The rise of activism among flight attendants was also a product of the transformation of the occupation and the kind of women who entered it. By the early 1970s, for the first time, the majority of flight attendants were married and expected to stay in their job longer than the earlier average of eighteen months. Moreover, working conditions had deteriorated. Flight attendants' real wages fell as higher fuel costs and recession-related declines in business travel cut into airline profits.

But most galling, the occupation was sexualized as companies came to rely upon female sexuality to sell seats. The fantasy image of flight attendants in the 1950s had been the fresh-faced girl next door—the kind you wanted to marry. By the early 1970s, however, the image had shifted from the attractive young woman available for marriage to the attractive young woman available for sex. Airlines routinely required flight attendants to wear hot pants and other sexually alluring uniforms. National's rules called for all stewardesses to wear "Fly Me" buttons. The company maintained with a straight face that no sexual innuendo was intended, despite their ad campaign featuring stewardesses panting, "Hi, I'm Linda, and I'm gong to FLY you like you've never been flown before." . . .

Historically, attendants had taken pride in their appearance and the company's celebration of their attractiveness, but the more crass approach was objectionable to many. The new sexy image encouraged harassment by male passengers; it also meant that they had become less respectable. As one explained: "It represents a lack of respect for hostesses. We have always projected pride, a class kind of image and this slogan is barroom talk. We're professional career women and mothers . . . not fly girls."

Flight attendants initially took their concerns to the three chief unions that represented them, but they made little headway. In exasperation and somewhat reluctantly, stewardesses began organizing in opposition to their unions as well as their employers. Not only did they form their own national organization in 1972, SFWR, but by the end of the 1970s they had deserted the male-dominated transportation unions in droves, setting up a bewildering array of independent flight attendant unions.

The SFWR dedicated itself to "fighting the policies of the airlines which strip us of our individuality and dignity," chiefly the airlines' manipulation of the flight attendant's sexual image. The SFWR attacked the problem from a number of angles. They picketed films that depicted flight attendants as hypersexual women. They filed lawsuits against Continental and National alleging that their airline ads created a hostile work environment. They distributed buttons reading, "Go Fly Yourself" and "National, Your Fly is Open" bumper stickers.

And they initiated an elaborate media campaign to publicize their alternative image of the flight attendant as a career woman and professional. The campaign culminated in the release of a "countercommercial" aimed at ending what they called "sexploitation." In it, they defined themselves as professionals responsible for passenger safety, not passenger sexual titillation. "The sexpot image is unsafe at any altitude," the script proclaimed, because "people do not obey the safety orders of their sexual fantasies." Or, as one SFWR leader put it in a letter to *Time* magazine: "We're in the business of saving tails, not serving them. The airlines are ass-king for pecuniary returns with a part of my anatomy that is not for sale."

Although the SFWR took the lead in this campaign, they were joined by some union officials, particularly those leading the Association of Flight Attendants (AFA), the former S&S Division of ALPA which had decided to go independent. The SFWR also worked with flight attendant unions to change the rules governing appearance, demanding that airlines change stewardesses' uniforms and abolish their archaic grooming and weight requirements. The S&S Division of ALPA had led the battle in the 1960s with some success. Girdle checks disappeared as did most airline charm classes. In the 1970s, SFWR and union pressure helped convince airlines to let flight attendants choose their own make-up and hair style.

But the airlines drew the line at weight: Thinness was one nonnegotiable aspect of female attractiveness. Airlines weighed attendants weekly, held them to weight standards which were detrimental to their health, refused to adjust requirements as women aged, and fired more flight attendants for violations of weight regulations than for any other reason. The SFWR argued that such rules were discriminatory since only female attendants were required to be pencil thin, that the airline "appearance supervisors" used highly arbitrary standards, and that the only acceptable work rules an employer should impose were those related to a person's ability to perform his or her assigned job.

Other issues included demands for enforcement of affirmative action policies and the end of mandatory layoffs during pregnancy. Their health and safety task force objected to the airline's claim that stewardesses' health problems were "primarily self-inflicted and psychosomatic" and called for a serious research program "to find out just what is happening to our bodies." . . .

When the SFWR folded in 1976, many former SFWR activitsts turned fulltime attention to union work. A number ran for union office and won. In their new capacity as union officers and activists, they continued the flurry of lawsuits and press releases. They also threatened airlines with strikes, sick-ins, and the old International Workers of the World (IWW) tactic of slowdowns—what Kelly Rueck of the AFA described as "a spontaneous loss of enthusiasm" for the job. By the end of the 1980s much had changed. Weight restrictions were lifted; new, more dignified uniforms appeared; and flight attendants no longer looked like mass-produced lifesize Barbie dolls.

## Office Wives Organize

Like flight attendants, clericals' working conditions were declining as their needs and expectations rose, spurring protest. According to some chroniclers, clerical work had been in decline since the late nineteenth century as female workers replaced male, and wages, status, and promotional opportunities plummeted. But conditions deteriorated further in the post–World War Two decades. As larger, more bureaucratic organizations became the norm and the new office technologies spread, many secretaries found themselves reorganized into office clerical pools. Others saw their jobs downgraded to a monotonous routine of typing and filing.

Accompanying this decline was a shift in the needs and expectations of the women employed as clericals. The majority were married (as they had always been), but a growing proportion were single or heads of families without a partner. They spent more years at work and felt frustrated by their "secondary earner" wages and the lack of promotional opportunities.

In addition, the messages of the new feminism stirred discontent. If flight attendants did not take kindly to being seen as mistresses, many secretaries no longer found solace in their role as "office wives." Not only did they have to attend to the bosses' personal needs, but like housewives their labor was rarely acknowledged or respected. And since few job descriptions for secretarial positions existed, there were not protective boundaries, emotional or otherwise. Of course, secretaries did have their one day of token recognition, National Secretaries Day, begun in 1951. Being taken out to lunch and given roses by the boss once a year was supposed to compensate for poor working conditions the rest of the year.

Organized clericals set out to change this state of affairs. Public-sector clericals had organized along with teachers, maintenance workers, and others in the 1960s; now the focus shifted to the millions of unrepresented office workers in the private sector. Margie Albert, a twenty-five-year office veteran and a steward for the Distributive Workers of America spoke of a "new spirit" sweeping America's secretaries in a 1973 *New York Times* opinion editorial piece; New York Congresswoman Bella Abzug had it read into the *Congressional Record.*

Albert claimed the movement erupted in 1969 when employers imposed a "no pants, dresses only" rule on office staff. Women rebelled, she reported, signing petitions, organizing delegations to the boss, and threatening mass walkouts. Albert may have exaggerated the extent of the discontent, but certainly the acceptance of conventional office etiquette was eroding.

Within the next few years, over a dozen independent office-worker organizations sprang up, perhaps the most effective being 9to5. Launched in 1973, 9to5 grew quickly from its origins as a luncheon gripe session for Harvard secretaries (led by fellow University of Chicago refugees Karen Nussbaum and Ellen Cassedy) to a citywide organization with hundreds of members. Similar groups emerged in Chicago (Women Employed), New York (Women Office Workers), San Francisco (Women Office Employees), and elsewhere. By the end of the decade, twelve local groups (with a total membership of some ten thousand) had united under the umbrella of the National Association of Working Women. Like flight attendants, clerical wanted higher wages and promotions; they also wanted their occupation professionalized and upgraded. The objectionable quality of interpersonal relationships in the office or "insulting male behavior," however, angered women the most.

As Karen Nussbaum remembered it, the "most powerful motivator was the issue of respect. Women did not want to feel they were office wives. They were real workers with real jobs." They also wanted their personhood acknowledged. Nussbaum recalled with chargin her experience of being looked "dead in the eye" and asked, "Isn't anybody here?" Other clericals spoke bitterly of being "invisible," of having people not "really look at you as a person," and of the indignity of the "servant role." In short, clericals rejected being an "office maid" as well as an "office wife." . . .

. . . In many ways, the office-worker movement looked to modernize and depersonalize the boss-secretary relationship. They called for evaluations based on more objective criteria, such as skills in typing, office management, and budget administration, rather than on a pleasing personality or good looks. They wanted to be promoted on their own merits rather than rise as appendages to their boss. More "precise job descriptions," some thought, would limit the almost total discretion bosses had over them.

At the same time, the office-worker movement also believed that bureaucratization and depersonalization were not the ultimate solution. Rather than banish the personal, they sought to transform it. They hoped to rewrite the cultural scripts governing office relationships and change the larger cultural norms that underlay the "micro-inequities" of daily office encounters. In brief, they sought to change attitudes as well as practices.

To effect these ends, office-worker groups relied on a range of tactics: lawsuits, petitions, pickets, as well as more unorthodox tactics—described by one reporter as a combination of "street theatre and Madison Avenue hype." Their public relations skills served them particularly well in their attempt to "repossess" National Secretaries Day. Their demand for an office-worker "Bill of Rights" and their slogans "Respect, rights, and raises" and "Raises not roses" instigated a public debate over the working conditions of clericals and the cultural norms governing boss and secretary interaction. Their call for secretaries to refuse participation in such a longstanding and widespread public ritual as National Secretaries Day set off confusion in offices nationwide. Did secretaries really prefer raises to roses? As with the male union officers who had represented flight attendants, few male bosses could understand why their female support staff would want to reject what many saw as flattering forms of male attention. But for a significant segment of the clerical work force, National Secretaries Day represented an outmoded paternalism perfectly symbolized in the demeaning rituals of one-way gift-giving.

9to5 and other groups also devised innovative tactics to draw attention to the non-job-related duties often required of clericals—the duties, as one secretary explained, "that have no purpose but to make the boss seem, and feel, important." They held "worst boss contests" to publicize the most outrageous requests bosses made of secretaries and on occasion they picketed individual bosses. . . .

Office-worker groups like the SFWR had an impact way beyond their small numbers. By the end of the 1970s, the movement had helped win millions of dollars in back pay and equity raises, spurred the development of employer affirmative action plans, turned National Secretaries Day into a contested ritual, and inspired a hit "9 to 5" song, movie, and TV show.

Ultimately, the office-worker movement helped transform the daily office encounters that had done so much to humiliate and demean secretaries. As *Business Week* noted in 1980, 9to5 changed public "notions of fairness," of "what a boss may fairly ask a[n] office worker to do." Personal errands, coffee-making, and numerous other requests were no longer acceptable business practice in most offices. By the 1990s, even the time-honored tradition of "rug-ranking," or basing a secretary's pay on her boss's status rather than on the content of her job, was in retreat. Like their counterparts in the home, secretaries were no longer a perk of the powerful or a mere appendage; they were emerging as individuals.

These gains, as significant as they were, left many problems unresolved. Countless office workers got raises, promotions, and enhanced job control. . . . The women relegated to the more impersonal, assembly-like conditions stayed put; not surprisingly, women from the working-class and women of color held a disproportionate number of these jobs.

From the beginning, however, many office-worker activists had pushed for changes affecting "the entire class of women who are being discriminated against," not just the few. And, by the end of the 1970s, many office-worker groups turned to unionization as a way of broadening the movement and addressing the particular concerns of the lower echelons of the clerical sector.

9to5, through its new sister organization Local 925 (later Service Employees International Union [SEIU] District 925), decided to focus on organizing women in insurance and banking, because, as Nussbaum explained, it was "the heart of the clerical workforce—some 30 percent" and "the majority came from working-class neighborhoods." District 65 and other unions also targeted clericals in banking and insurance as well as publishing, legal offices, and universities. Their decision reflected in part the more union-minded orientation of clericals and their new willingness to self-organize.

Employers fought with every weapon available, particularly in the insurance and banking sector. "We never knew what hit us," Nussbaum remembered some fifteen years later. "We got smashed over and over. These businesses [insurance and banking] had not traditionally been unionized, and they were damned if they were going to be the first ones in the new wave." By the end of the 1980s, the banking industry had changed some of its most egregious discriminatory pay and promotion policies, but union density had actually fallen over the course of the decade. The insurance industry was equally invincible. After a hard-fought organizing and contract victory at the Syracuse offices of Equitable Life, the company closed its Syracuse branch and laid off all its unionized workers.

The major successes were among university clericals, especially at prestigious schools such as Harvard, Yale, Vassar, and Columbia. Even these privileged institutions, however, balked at the notion of sharing control and wealth with their largely female clerical staff. Harvard, for example, engaged its support staff in an exhausting twelve-year campaign before conceding defeat. Nevertheless some seventy percent of the campaigns among university clericals conducted in the 1970s and 1980s emerged with union contracts despite employer opposition.

By the end of the 1980s, office-worker unionization (sixteen percent) was comparable to the work force as a whole (seventeen percent). The 1980s did not witness the reversal of union decline—one that began for the private-sector work force in the 1950s—but the fault cannot be laid at the door of office workers.

### "Taking the 'Mammy' Out of Housework"

The household-worker movement also burst into public view in the early 1970s. In 1971, some six hundred mostly black and middle-aged women gathered for the first national conference of household employees. Under the banner, "pay, protection, and professionalism," they applauded enthusiastically as speaker after speaker spoke of a new day for domestics. The conference received extensive press coverage, encouraging hope that a fundamental shift in the employment relations governing domestic work was underway.

The events of the 1970s were the culmination of trends long in motion. Household employment had changed fundamentally over the course of the twentieth century. By World War Two, day work predominated over live-in arrangements, and outside the South, African-American and other women of color replaced Irish and Scandinavian immigrants as the typical domestic. In the decades following the war, wages and working conditions also improved slightly for household workers as demand exceeded supply and opportunities for alternative employment opened for minority women. Household workers themselves had provoked many of these changes through their daily acts of individual defiance. Yet prior to the 1960s, organized efforts to reform domestic work, largely led by middle-class white reformers, had been sporadic. Local organizations of household employees—inspired by the civil rights and poor people's movements—had begun forming in the late 1960s. In the 1970s, for the first time, a national movement organized primarily by household workers arose.

Dorothy Bolden, a veteran community and civil-rights activist who had started cleaning houses in 1935 at the age of twelve, founded a domestic-workers organization in Atlanta in 1968. Its aim was to improve working conditions and build "respect for the women in this low-income field of labor." . . .

By the early 1970s, the majority joined in a loose national movement headed by the National Council of Household Employees (NCHE). The NCHE, formed in 1965 under the auspices of the Women's Bureau, grew out of the long-standing commitment of labor feminists like former Women's Bureau director Esther Peterson to revalue household labor. By 1968 the NCHE had secured funding from the Department of Labor for a series of eight pilot projects to "upgrade household employment standards"; by 1970, they had funding from the Ford Foundation. Initially, the NCHE focused on training household employees and on fostering minority contractors in the private household-services sector. Many thought this approach would give minority entrepreneurship a boost, expand the availability of household services, and benefit domestic workers whose terms of employment would be set formally through a contracting agency. In the early 1970s, under the leadership of Edith Sloan, a young African-American woman with legal training as well as experience as a domestic worker, the NCHE redefined itself as an advocacy organization promoting the interests of female domestic workers first and foremost. Instead of fostering small businesses, which usually were owned by minority men, the NCHE puts its energy into building a national movement of household workers.

The household-worker movement differed in many respects from that of flight attendants and clericals. In part, this divergence reflected differences among the women activists themselves: Household workers were older, and much more likely to be women of color and single heads of household. Further, household workers worked alone in private homes supervised almost wholly by women, and the norms governing these highly privatized encounters were rooted as much in racial and class prejudices as in gender. Hence, the movement relied upon different tactics than did the others, and it drew its inspiration more from traditions of race and class justice than from gender. Indeed, rather than attack the gender status quo, at times the household-worker movement used traditional gender values to justify their assaults upon the oppressive norms under which they worked.

Nevertheless, all three movements had remarkably similar goals. Like flight attendants and clericals, household workers sought to upgrade and professionalize their occupation. They wanted their skills as cooks, care-takers, and cleaners recognized. They sought dignity and respect for their person as well as concrete economic benefits. And at the heart of the movement was the effort to transform the nature of interpersonal relations at work.

Household workers, however, were much further from achieving these goals in the 1960s and early 1970s than were flight attendants and clericals. Household workers were denied the basic statutory protections governing wages, hours, and working conditions afforded other employees. The average yearly income of household employees were below poverty level, and many domestics still worked from sunup to sundown. Moreover, despite the formal end of slavery some one hundred years earlier, the relationship between mistress and maid was often reminiscent of slavery. As a worker in the big house, the domestic still was seen as part of the white family, despite her own outside household. Her wages and hours were often arranged informally, and many household employees were expected to work long hours out of loyalty and love for the white family. . . .

Like clericals, household workers wanted their tasks and their compensation more formalized. "We want to be treated like an employee," explained one maid. "Everyone tells you're in the family and then they won't even give you a holiday." They wanted compensation in cash rather than in gifts of old clothes and food; they wanted their job to be defined as a set of discrete tasks that they themselves could manage. Like other service workers, they wanted occupational criteria that revolved around objective skills rather than the more subjective criteria of personality and the right attitude.

The "right attitude" for household workers differed from that expected of flight attendants and clericals. Domestics had to meet the psychosocial needs of female employers rather than those of male bosses or customers. Female bosses did not need sexually attractive subordinates; indeed, they preferred older, more matronly figures with whom one could develop intimacy. At the same time and in part due to this emotional connection, household employees were expected to reinforce the unequal power dynamic by displaying deference. Domestics became adept at "learning people," as one expressed it. They knew when to be invisible, when to be best friend and spiritual guide, and when childlike obedience was required.

The consequences of "misreading" one's employer or "sassin" could be severe. Maids who strayed from the familiar scripts found themselves without a job or worse. When Dorothy Bolden refused an order to wash dishes and walked out, her employer had her arrested for insubordination. "They said I was mental because I talked back. . . . I was in jail five days." She was only released after her uncle hired two psychiatrists who testified to her mental health.

Household workers wanted to be adults, to be treated with "the respect due any human being"; they objected to the "common use of first names, and uninvited familiarity by employers." They wanted to replace the oppressive one-way personalism with a relationship that was "a two-way street," one with "promptness, integrity, and courtesy" from both parties.

The dilemma for the reform movement was how to bring about these changes and push domestic work, "the last holdout against modernization," into the twentieth century. A range of answers emerged. Some groups, such as a statewide organization in Massachusetts, focused primarily on extending state protective statutes to household workers. Others, like the Detroit Household Workers Organization (HWO) and the Atlanta-based National Domestic Workers Union (NDWU), acted as a combination "lobby group, training program, placement service, and grievance committee."

Dorothy Bolden, head of the Atlanta-based NDWU, spent much of her time staffing the union's employment placement service, accepting requests from employers who would agree to abide by the union's wages and working conditions. She also leafleted maids at bus stops to spread the word about the new standards: fifteen dollars a day plus carfare. "After we set the price," she explained, "you had to teach these women how to ask for it. You had to learn how to communicate with the lady and tell her about the cost of living." In their career center program, the NDWU offered "human relations training on how to *handle* employee-employer relationships including 'rap' sessions with employer volunteers." The NDWU, like the Detroit HWO, sought to improve the bargaining power of individual women by fostering self-esteem, creating "an awareness of the value of their labor," and upgrading household workers' skills and marketability.

In 1970, Bolden initiated one of the NDWU's most successful projects, what she called "Maid's Honor Day." Maid's Honor Day quickly turned into a well-attended annual Atlanta affair with distinguished women speakers such as Mrs. Herman Talmadge, Mrs. Lillian Carter, and Mrs. Andrew Young. Yet as with National Secretaries Day, the affair and its rituals became contested terrain. This annual occasion and the rhetoric surrounding it clearly reveal the gulf between the new, less demeaning norms advocated by many household employees and the older paternalistic practices of white employers.

Bolden organized the event with the aim of recognizing "those who toil in the home without recognition" and honoring "outstanding women in the field of domestic labor for their professional skills, great common knowledge," and their ability to "mastermind two households." Despite Bolden's intentions, however, the annual affair became for many whites an occasion to reinforce their own expectations of loyalty, sacrifice, and self-abnegation from their maids. Atlanta's mayor established July 15, 1970, as "Maid's Day." . . .

Bolden herself and many of the other domestic workers who participated in this ritual also claimed for themselves the role of stand-in mother, spiritual advisor, and caretaker. Yet at the same time, they rejected the possessive and demeaning overtones in many of the employer accolades, and they used these well-worn maternal roles to challenge the status quo rather than reinforce it. As Patricia Collins argues, mothering is a source of power and self-esteem in the African-American community. Moreover, the point for Bolden was to honor the domestic work of these women in their own community as well as in the white family, a nuance almost completely lost on the white community.

Womanhood itself could also be a source of pride and a resource in resistance. As Bolden explained, "I was born poor, grew up poor, and I am still poor, but I am not going to bow down. I am still a woman." As was also true for the Memphis sanitation men who carried signs simply saying, "I Am a Man," for household workers, traditional gender ideology could be deployed to undercut racial and class domination.

But not everyone in the household-workers movement embraced Bolden's maternalist rhetoric. Neither did they see an emphasis on "self-sacrifice" and "love" as the best tactic for improving the lot of household workers. Indeed, for many, it was precisely the "'personal' aspect of the existing relationship" that had to be eliminated. Real change could only come through unionization, Edith Sloan of the NCHE asserted, or by imposing a third party—a contractor—between the employer and employee. Otherwise, she promised to loud cheers at the first national conference of domestic workers in 1971, "'Madam' is going to have to clean her own house and cook and serve her own meals because everyone is going to quit."

By the end of the 1970s, the NCHE and most of its affiliates were in decline, but the movement could claim some crucial victories. The lobbying of grassroots domestic workers combined with pressure from female legislators such as Shirley Chisholm, Yvonne Burke, and Patsy Mink forced the inclusion of domestic workers workers under the Fair Labor Standards Act provisions for the first time in 1974. A few states also added domestic workers to their minimum wage, unemployment insurance, and workers' compensation coverage. In addition, although wages for household employees remained unconscionably low, significant economic gains were made in some key regional labor markets. And, as Geraldine Roberts, long-time civil-rights and later household worker activist explained in 1977, "We thought that we needed them to make a living, but we learned that they needed us, that we were important."

Although changing the ideology surrounding the work and redefining its psychology at the "point of personal contact" proved formidable indeed, the nature of the employee-employer relationship continued to transform. While many private domestic jobs still involve the oppressive one-on-one personalism and deference of the past, household cleaning is increasingly done by teams of workers from agencies or by individual workers who contract on a fee-for-service basis. Moreover, many of the domestic functions once performed by individual women in the home have shifted into the commercial realm. African-American women in particular moved into these newly commercialized "domestic" jobs of hotel maid, home health care aide, janitor, day care and kitchen worker. And, during the late 1970s and 1980s, they and their coworkers built strong unions in many of these "public household" occupations. Indeed, some of the most important union breakthroughs in the 1980s occurred precisely in these sectors.

## Conclusion

How then are these movements to be characterized, and how do they expand our understandings of the history of work and collective action? Arguable, one could gather these stories under the broad rubric of a belated modernization. After all, like industrial workers of the 1930s and 1940s, they too wanted to do away with the feudal, paternalistic trappings of their work and to depersonalize employment relations. . . .

One might also put these movements in a class framework. For in many ways, women service workers in the 1970s sought to realize the familiar demands of organized workers. . . .

But neither of these frameworks captures the soul of these movements, the spirit that animated these women and sparked their rebellion. For fundamentally, these movements were about degendering women's jobs, about dismantling the gendered structures and norms around which these occupations had been created. In short, flight attendants, clericals and household workers sought escape from the gender constraints of their work. They wanted to be treated as human beings and as "real workers," not as sex objects, office wives, or "mammies." Women service workers subjected these age-old scripts to public scrutiny and brought them into the area of labor—management negotiation.

Race and class norms infuse women's jobs as well and intersect with gender expectations in complicated ways. Flight attendants, often young, white single women, faced heightened sexualization at work, but it was tempered by competing notions of flight attendants as respectable and potential marriage partners. Similarly, the elite of the clerical work force, secretaries and administrative assistants, also benefitted from being white and having some college education. In contrast, household workers, mainly poor women of color, had not such shields. Dismantling the "mammy" stereotype with its expectations of self-sacrifice and deference required an assault against multiple ideologies of domination. . . .

In the unions of the future just as in the scholarship of the present, the differences between men's and women's jobs and the differences in their reform ideologies and practices must be confronted. The old industrial vision of one big union based on class identity and class solidarity must give way to a new ideal, one in which psychological and cultural as well as economic issues are paramount, one in which control over one's emotional terrain is as central as control over one's mind and body. And, ultimately, this new ideal must recognize the multiple constructs of domination and the variety of collective movements that will arise in response.

## ⚓ *F U R T H E R   R E A D I N G*

Acker, Joan. *Doing Comparable Worth: Gender, Class, and Pay Equity* (1989).

Blum, Linda. *Between Feminism and Labor: The Significance of the Comparable Worth Movement* (1991).

Cobble, Dorothy Sue, ed. *Women and Unions: Forging a Partnership* (1993).

Crittenden, Ann. *The Price of Motherhood: Why the Most Important Job in the World Is Still the Least Valued* (2001).

Eisenberg, Susan. *We'll Call You If We Need You: Experiences of Women Working Construction* (1998).

Faludi, Susan. *Stiffed: The Betrayal of the American Man* (1999).

Freeman, Joshua. *Working-Class New York: Life and Labor Since World War II* (2000).

Garson, Barbara. *Electronic Sweatshop: How Computers Are Transforming the Office of the Future into the Factory of the Past* (1988).

Geoghegan, Thomas. *Which Side Are You On? Trying to Be for Labor When It's Flat on Its Back* (1992).

Halle, David. *America's Working Man: Work, Home, and Politics Among Blue-Collar Property Owners* (1984).

Hochschild, Arlie. *The Time Bind: When Work Becomes Home and Home Becomes Work* (1997).

Hochschild, Arlie, with Anne Machung. *The Second Shift* (1997).

Howe, Louise Kapp. *Pink Collar Workers: Inside the World of Women's Work* (1977).

Kingsolver, Barbara. *Holding the Line: Women in the Great Arizona Mine Strike of 1983* (1997).

Kuttner, Robert. *Revolt of the Haves: Taxpayers Revolts and the Politics of Austerity* (1980).

Levitt, Martin Jay. *Confessions of a Union Buster* (1993).

Linder, Marc. *Wars of Attrition: Vietnam, the Business Roundtable, and the Decline of Construction Unions* (1999).

Moody, Kim. *An Injury to All: The Decline of American Unionism* (1988).

Newman, Katherine. *Falling from Grace: Downward Mobility in the Age of Affluence* (1999).

Peters, Joan K. *When Mothers Work: Loving Our Children Without Sacrificing Our Selves* (1997).

Rieder, Jonathan. *Canarsie: The Jews and Italians of Brooklyn Against Liberalism* (1987).

Rollins, Judith. *Between Women: Domestics and Their Employers* (1985).

Sacks, Karen Brodkin. *Caring by the Hour: Women, Work, and Organization at Duke Medical Center* (1988).

Schor, Juliet. *The Overworked American: The Unexpected Decline of Leisure* (1993).

Stein, Judith. *Running Steel, Running America: Race, Economic Policy, and the Decline of Liberalism* (1998).

Sugrue, Thomas. *The Origins of the Urban Crisis: Race and Inequality in Postwar Detroit* (1996).

Vogel, Lise. *Mothers on the Job: Maternity Policy in the U.S. Workplace* (1991).

Williams, Joan. *Unbending Gender: Why Family and Work Conflict and What to Do About It* (2000).

Wilson, William Julius. *The Truly Disadvantaged: The Inner City, the Underclass, and Public Policy* (1990).

CHAPTER 14

# *Mobile Capital, Migrating Workers*

*For most American workers, as well as for the labor movement, the 1970s and 1980s ushered in an era of great difficulty. American capitalism stumbled at home, just as an increasingly global system of production exposed U.S. firms to a competitive world market in labor, capital, and new technology. The Vietnam War had sapped American strength, touched off a round of inflation, and given oil-producing countries the opportunity to jack up the prices of their vital commodity. Profits and productivity stagnated, corporate debt soared, and the stable industrial order established just after World War II began to crack. The U.S. government abandoned Keynesian efforts to sustain working-class incomes and fought the chronic inflation of the 1970s and early 1980s by boosting interest rates, thereby plunging the economy into two deep recessions that pushed unemployment to levels not seen since the 1930s.*

*Working-class living standards stagnated, and organized labor lost members and power in a downward spiral that slashed union membership as a proportion of the entire workforce—from 29 percent in 1973 to just above 16 percent in 1991. The losses were concentrated in the old, unionized core of the economy—what used to be called "basic" industry—where factory shutdowns devastated unions in the steel, garment, electrical products, and auto industries. But the losses were not limited to unions whose members made products subject to a new wave of international competition. The venerable construction trades dropped nearly a million dues payers, and the Teamsters, whose truck drivers, warehousemen, and food processing workers were largely immune to pressure from foreign producers, lost almost as many members.*

*Why this decline in union power? Historians and social scientists have not reached a consensus, in part because all their answers are so ideologically charged. Some have argued that contemporary workers, especially in service work or technically advanced industries, are uninterested in organizations based on the principle of social solidarity. An even more widespread argument, but also the most ahistorical, holds that trade unions are no longer necessary to ensure social justice on the job. The 1930s are over; managers are more enlightened; and most work, even that in factories, requires cooperation rather than conflict between labor and* capital. *Although such views are themselves part of the larger ideological assault against the contemporary union movement, they gain credibility to the extent that some unions themselves are bureaucratic institutions, unresponsive to the needs of their members and potential recruits.*

*But the most compelling explanation for the decline of the unions and for income stagnation has been a political one. Rising costs and steep foreign competition have forced U.S. employers to inaugurate a long-term offensive against the welfare state and the wage standards and working conditions that evolved when U.S. capitalism had a more expansive character. High wages and secure employment, the touchstones of the New Deal–era system of labor relations, suddenly came to seem counterproductive, divisive, and vaguely unpatriotic. Such standards seemed to make American manufacturing uncompetitive, while Keynesian programs of economic stimulation, whether through government tax policy or union wage advance, have worked best when the boundaries of the nation-state coincided with those of the market.*

*By the end of the twentieth century, the mobility of capital, the ease of communication, and the cheapness of transport had gone a long way toward obliterating the economic boundaries that divided one nation from another. In what economic nation are the hundreds of* Maquiladoras *(U.S.-owned factories) that crowd against Mexico's northern border? Or the ultramodern Indonesian shoe factories that export all their product to the United States and Europe? Despite much talk of a postindustrial society more workers stand on a factory assembly line today than at any other time in world history.*

*But if dollars, yen, and marks are free to roam the globe, workers are increasingly constrained. American workers have no incentive to follow their jobs to Mexico or Thailand. Instead, labor flows in the opposite direction. In the years since reform of the immigration laws in 1965, the United States has witnessed a surge of immigration quite as large as that which poured through Ellis Island a century ago. But when these immigrants arrive in the United States they find themselves something less than full-fledged citizens. Millions of the poor lack the proper documents (because they came illegally or overstayed their visas), while others have status as but temporary workers. And even for those who have taken the oath of allegiance to the U.S. Constitution, barriers of language, race, and culture shadow their capacity to take advantage of their political rights and economic opportunities.*

*What is the difference between "free trade," a phrase coined in the nineteenth century, and "globalization," popular in today's nomenclature? What accounts for a corporate decision to produce within the United States or outside of it? Why are union struggles in other nations important to American workers? Are immigrant workers more difficult to organize than native-born U.S. workers today than a century ago?*

## ✣ D O C U M E N T S

In Document 1, *New York Times* reporter Peter Kilborn finds that high levels of unemployment make it easy for employers to recruit strikebreakers during several of the most bitter labor-management conflicts of the 1980s. Morton Bahr of the Communications Workers of America (CWA) labels in Document 2 extensive computerization a threat to worker interests because of the ease with which employers can transfer work to distant, low-wage countries. In Document 3, reporter Laura McClure finds that contingent, temporary work grew rapidly during the 1980s and 1990s, even in relatively high wage, highly skilled occupations such as journalism and publishing. The life of a Thai immigrant worker, literally imprisoned within a notorious California sweatshop, is described in her own words in the interview that constitutes Document 4. Because employers have so often taken advantage of such undocumented immigrants, making their life miserable and organizing near impossible, the AFL-CIO has become a far stronger advocate of immigrant rights, as Document 5 demonstrates.

Finally, the massive, anti–World Trade Organization demonstrations of November 1999 made Seattle a synonym for a new social movement designed to challenge corporate power by linking together labor, environmentalist, and human rights concerns. Journalist Harold Meyerson salutes the new alliance of "Teamsters and Turtles" in Document 6, while in Document 7, *New York Times* columnist Thomas Friedman ridicules the Seattle demonstrations in a report that reflects the dominant neoliberal ideology.

## 1. Management's Weapon: Scab Labor, 1990

To keep operating in a strike, more and more companies have been deploying a weapon they long shunned—hiring permanent replacements for workers who are on the picket lines.

When 6,300 drivers for the Greyhound Corporation abandoned their buses . . . , management had 700 new recruits on hand to drive its fleet and 900 more in training. Thousands of new pilots, mechanics and flight attendants who have been assured careers with Eastern are keeping the airline aloft. And long after the end of the strikes in which they were hired, thousands of new workers remain on the job at the International Paper Company, the Boise Cascade Corporation, the Phelps Dodge Corporation and at Continental Airlines. . . .

Labor experts maintain that management's wide use of permanent replacements has upset the symmetry that has been a tradition of labor disputes. On the one hand, management has said it has a right to lock workers out at the risk of losing profits; on the other, labor has said it can withhold its services at the risk of losing income.

"The balance has shifted," said Mark A. de Bernando, director of the Labor Law Action Center at the United States Chamber of Commerce [in Washington]. "Labor's trump card in a dispute, the strike, is no longer trump."

Robert M. Baptiste, a Washington attorney for labor unions, said that in a strike "there was always a sense that people would eventually say, 'Enough, let's sit down and get serious.'" But he added, "Now, companies just want to get rid of unions."

One reason that companies now think that goal is possible is the lesson they drew from the illegal strike of 11,500 Federal air traffic controllers in August 1981, seven months into Ronald Reagan's first term as President. After the striking controllers defied a back-to-work order, Mr. Reagan dismissed them, filled their ranks with permanent replacements [, and] the union collapsed.

### "A Signal to Other Employers"

The government's success in keeping the air traffic system working impressed many unionized companies.

"Reagan made it respectable to bust unions," Mr. Baptiste said.

Gary Burtless, a labor economist at the Brookings Institution, said Mr. Reagan emboldened management to risk the strain to its business of taking on less experienced workers. "The fact that the President was able to keep the air traffic system going indicated that there was a lot more scope for replacing workers than people imagined," Mr. Burtless said. "If you can replace air traffic controllers you can certainly replace bus drivers."

The permanent replacements, often recruited from the ranks of the unemployed or from low-paid employees of other businesses, are a variation on the temporary substitutes vilified by trade unionists as "scabs" or "strikebreakers" but nevertheless regarded as a part of management's legitimate arsenal. Temporary replacements leave at the end of a strike, but permanent replacements are assured the strikers' jobs. After a strike, the law allows strikers first claim on their old jobs, but only if replacements vacate them.

### Risk of Permanent Replacements

Many companies still shun permanent replacements, in part because they run some risk in using them. Even if they decide they can get by without the expertise of skilled workers, companies must weigh the potential costs of incurring the wrath of workers who are not involved in the strike and of losing customers because of consumer doubts about the quality of the service provided by replacement workers.

This change in management's attitude has occurred along with a change in workers' loyalties, both to their unions and to their companies, which makes it harder for unions to sustain strikes and easier for management to persuade workers to move into the strikers' jobs.

Workers no longer think unions can deliver the gains in wages and benefits that made blue-collar members the world's best paid workers. For several years, union workers in private industry have been winning smaller wage increases than nonunion workers, and trade union membership as a part of the national work force has declined from 30 percent in the 1970s to 16.4 percent in 1989.

And for all that attention that recent strikes at companies like Greyhound, Eastern, the Pittston Coal Group Inc., Boeing and the Nynex Corporation have received, unions are increasingly wary of using their ultimate weapon, the strike, and risking both their members' jobs and the embarrassment of failing to win concessions from management. In the 1970s the Bureau of Labor Statistics recorded an average of 289 strikes a year involving 1,000 or more workers. In the last five years [1984–1989] the average was 52.

### The Seeds of Acrimony

Furthermore, some companies have found it easier than they expected to find replacement workers.

That is what happened in an especially vitriolic strike in 1987 and 1988 involving three International Paper mills in Jay, Me. The company proposed eliminating premium pay for work on Sundays and holidays, and the paper-workers union walked out. The company started bringing in permanent replacements just 13 days later, planting the seeds of acrimony that local officials say will persist for years.

"It's something you do only as a last resort," said James W. Gilliland, the company's director of employee relations. "It's not fun for anybody."

In Jay, he said, the company has reduced its work force from 1,250 to 1,062, and 80 percent of the employees are permanent replacements. They started at $9 to $10 an hour, about $4 less than the strikers, Mr. Gilliland said, and premium pay was abolished.

Once the company decided to proceed, Mr. Gilliland said it found a surprisingly large pool of candidates for the strikers' jobs despite the nation's relatively low unemployment rate.

"As more and more young people have entered the labor market, they have found fewer and fewer high-paying industrial jobs," he said. "So when an industrial company enters the market to hire permanent replacements, it has no trouble whatever."

## 2. A Unionist Blasts Overseas Office Work, 1987

For the past 15 years, we have been occupied with the very real problem of jobs leaving this country. In most cases, these are jobs like the making of a wrench, or making apparel, steel, autos. We have tried to deal with this problem through legislation as well as in collective bargaining. However, with the advent of new technology, such as satellite communication and computers, it is easier than ever for employers to move new technology and capital across borders.

One example of this is American Airlines, which historically used keypunch operators earning between $8 and $10 an hour to process the previous day's used tickets and handle the billing and record keeping. This is now done in Barbados for $2 an hour!

Each day an American Airline aircraft flies to Barbados and deposits the tickets which are keypunched at one-fourth or one-fifth the U.S. wage level, and then transmitted back to the United States via satellite in finished form.

Trammel Crow Company, the nation's largest real estate company, has established a series of data bases in the People's Republic of China. They train university students in the English language, not in reading and writing, but in the recognition of letters so they can keypunch them into the data base. Then, upon graduation, they are hired at a wage of a dollar a day!

When questioned, Trammel Crow said that it did not go to China for the dollar a day wage, but that the Chinese workers are more efficient because they cannot read and understand the English language, so they don't become engrossed in what they are punching.

Pier 1 Imports became the first American company to store its inventory records in China. Several hospitals followed, and now American hospitals are storing medical records in China.

The scope of this is endless.

---

From speech in possession of Eileen Boris, Women's Studies Program, University of California, Santa Barbara.

Anyone who has a business where record keeping is a vital part can store data anywhere in the globe through satellite transmission and a relatively simple computer with a printer. And it can retrieve it at will.

What is on the drawing board is even more frightening. There will be more intelligence stored from now until 2010, less than 25 years from now, than in the entire history of mankind.

That is mind-boggling and raises many questions: Who is going to control that intelligence? How do you retrieve it? How will it be used?

To point out the seriousness of the situation, two years ago, just prior to his retirement, the then chairman of the board of AT&T, speaking at the Aspen Institute, talked about the technology that they now have at the Bell Laboratory. They already have a computer, no larger than a cigar box, into which you can speak in any language to seek information that is stored anywhere in this world, or even in space, and the computer will seek it out, retrieve it, and give it back to you in the appropriate language.

What makes all of this technology frightening as well as exciting is that it was supposed to create a new type of service job that was going to somehow supplement, if not totally offset, the blue collar jobs that have been lost.

But the lesson it teaches us is that notwithstanding our particular occupations or job titles, that job, if not now, in the very near future, is going to be totally done in another country where wages are cheaper.

Therefore, it is important that we face these problems today and take charge of our own destiny, because no one else is going to do it.

## 3. Temp Blues, 1994

Lena is tired of being a temp. For a year now, she's been looking for a full-time job—no luck. Unemployment in New York City is high, and competition for jobs is intense. In the meantime, Lena has been paying the rent with temp jobs. And it hasn't been fun.

"I remember one day I registered at five different places," says Lena. "I felt like a migrant worker, just walking around the city, calling from phone booths. I went to the library to use the phone. Next to me I noticed another woman standing there with the want ads, and she was making phone calls, too. And then a security guard came over and tapped us both on the shoulder and told us to move on. It was one of the worse days of my life."

In the past year, Lena has worked for a bank, a pharmaceutical company, an advertising agency, and an insurance company. The insurance company was the worst.

"My desk was across from the elevator in a hallway," says Lena. "I was doing these idiot jobs, but it took some time to figure out which paper goes where, which form goes with what. It's insurance, so there are 5,000 forms, and I couldn't tell one from another. I was terrible at it. And my supervisor would yell at me. I was running to the bathroom and crying every day. And then people were talking to me like I was

"Working the Risk Shift," by Laura McClure, a freelance writer in Brooklyn, NY, *The Progressive* (February 1994), pp. 23–27. Reprinted by permission of Laura McClure, freelance writer, Brooklyn, NY.

going to be there forever. And I thought: Just hand me the nails for the coffin! But I was afraid to leave, because I was afraid there would be no more work."

That's the tricky thing about the temp agencies, Lena says. You're afraid to say no for fear they won't call again. You're afraid to leave a job even if you are miserable. "It feels like unless you play it their way, you don't get the work," she says. . . . Lena makes a good wage—$16 an hour. But she has no benefits, no health coverage. Here's how she describes her dream: "I would like a full-time job with benefits and good pay."

It doesn't sound like Lena is asking for that much, but the fact is, regular, old-fashioned, full-time jobs with benefits are becoming precious. After all, the number-one private employer in the United States is not General Motors or Boeing; it's Manpower, Inc., a temporary agency.

Temps, together with part-time workers, contractors, consultants, and free-lancers, now constitute 25 o 30 per cent of the civilian work fore, according to the National Planning Association. These workers are called "contingent" because of their tenuous, on-again, off-again relationship to employers. Insecurity is only one problem besetting contingent workers: Most go without health insurance, sick pay, and other benefits. And only a tiny percentage are unionized.

Contingent labor wasn't discovered in the 1990s, of course—part-time and temporary jobs have long been part of the economy. Temporary agencies got their start in the 1940s, and really became an economic force in the 1970s. But in the past decade, all types of contingent employment have surged. According to the National Association of Temporary Services, the annual payroll of the temporary work force jumped from $3.5 billion in 1981 to $14 billion in 1991.

In the course of our dismal economic "recovery" of the past two years, a significant percentage of the new jobs created were temporary or part-time. The Washington-based Economic Policy Institute found that 28 per cent were temp jobs, and 26 per cent were part-time. And many were taken by people who, like Lena, would rather be working full-time, permanently.

"This whole system—I hate it!" cries Dick Leonard, special projects director at the Oil, Chemical, and Atomic Workers Union. Leonard's union has seen rela-tively low-paid, nonunion contractors replacing thousands of union members over the years. "It's the worst form of wage slavery you can imagine. Labor has become more of a commodity than ever," he says. By turning to temporary or contract labor, companies often get away with rolling back benefit costs to zero, sidestepping union agreements, and skirting employment standards in general.

"I think it's all about deindustrialization," says Leonard. Only a minority of well-paying jobs are going to low-wage countries, he says, but that flow of jobs "is driving everything else down, it's setting a floor." Employers who don't want to risk moving businesses overseas "look for these other really cruel ways to increase productivity."

Some have described the turn to contingent labor as a breaking of the postwar social compact between management and unions. But as any old CIO organizer will tell you, that compact was a product not only of the growing postwar economy, but also of hard-fought battles by unions and social movements to force better benefits and standards. The crumbling of the compact today has everything to do with the withering power of unions and the prevailing power of the multinationals.

But even a robust labor movement might not be able to stop the ebb of full-time, full-benefit jobs, which may be the victims of new technology and the integration of the global economy. Even in Europe, where workers generally have stronger unions and more political clout, the temporary work force is growing. (England and Germany, which have larger temp markets than the United States, require temps to work through licensed agencies that provide full benefits. In most of Europe, part-time employees must receive at least pro-rated sick pay and other benefits.)

Business puts its own happy spin on the contingent-worker phenomenon. Employers gush about the new model they call the "virtual corporation." In this stripped down, "competitive" company, a core of well-paid managers and owners with good benefits contract with a variety of free-lancers or subcontractors to get the work done. Product designers, marketing experts, and low-paid, subcontracted production workers are easily hired and easily dispensed with. Even top-level managers can be shipped in as needed. Already, there is a temp agency that devotes itself entirely to finding "human-resource executives" for companies in need.

Workers should learn to cast themselves as free-lancing entrepreneurs, the business press advises. They need to stay constantly on top of new technology, ready to adapt to each new development and to market themselves appropriately.

"The revolution in the 1980s was toward just-in-time inventory," business consultant Nancy Hutchens told *The New York Times* recently. "The revolution of the 1990s is toward just-in-time employment. Companies will use people only as they need them." Both trends are made possible partly by computerization. Companies can now predict more precisely just how much inventory or labor they'll be needing. With just-in-time inventory, companies can avoid the cost of storing large stockpiles, relying instead on rapid, last-minute deliveries from suppliers. Just-in-time labor cuts the cost of labor overhead by bringing in just the workers the company needs, just when it needs them.

In a way, it's all about risk-shifting. With "just-in-time" labor, the company no longer advances salaries to workers in the hopes that their labor will prove profitable. All the risk is absorbed by workers, who can never be sure of their next dollar. In the oil and chemical industries, for instance, individual contractors and contracting companies move from employer to employer and from town to town, soaking up whatever work is available. Whenever a contractor doesn't meet with the employer's satisfaction, the employer can quickly cancel the contract.

"What happens is, the contractors feel very insecure," says unionist Leonard. "They know that you have to work, work fast, work hard, do what you're told, don't complain, certainly don't get banged up—or your ass is out of there. Don't report illnesses, don't report accidents."

The union has discovered that accident rates among contractors far exceed those of unionized workers. And accidents in these industries can endanger whole communities. The most dramatic illustration of the problem occurred on October 23, 1989, when an explosion rocked Phillips Petroleum Company's Houston chemical complex, killing twenty-three people. Leonard's union had long been concerned about poorly trained contractors at this and other plants. A Presidential commission later found the explosion happened as a result of a contractor error.

"Our system of labor relations depends on balancing the interests of workers and employers," argues Leonard. "The labor laws in this country are antique—they don't address this contracting-out system at all. It's totally legal for a company that uses nothing but outside contractors to go nonunion by simply canceling all its contracts and getting new ones—immediate firing of an entire work force for union-related reasons is legal under this system."

To some extent, the contingent work force is growing because the supply of people who want these jobs is expanding. People with kids—especially women—want jobs that give them greater flexibility. About 64 per cent of temps are women. And many more women than men work part-time—27 per cent of women, 11 per cent of men. However, in the past few years especially, the swelling of the part-time and temporary work force has been mostly among people who would rather be working full-time. . . . Even for those who choose part-time and temporary work to have time for their families, there's often an element of coercion. Because of dropping real wages, most families find they are forced to have two incomes. Many of the parents who "choose" part-time or temporary jobs might opt for being full-time parents in better economic times.

Still, plenty of workers are happy to hold part-time or temporary jobs. Ideally, temp agencies let workers choose just how much and when they want to work. The agency does the legwork of finding the jobs and setting the pay scale. . . . About a quarter of the agencies offer health coverage to temps who work a minimum number of hours per year. Only about a fifth of part-time workers receive health insurance through their employers. . . .

One worker who chose part-time work—despite the drawbacks—is Sally Ferraro, a credit analyst in Chicago. Ferraro knew she wanted a part-time job after her baby was born last February. She was glad to find work at a major mail-order house, checking credit applications three evenings a week. She takes care of the baby in the daytime, and her husband takes over in the evening. They rarely see each other.

Ferraro says her employer has shifted a large chunk of its work force from full-time to part-time in the past several years in an effort to save money. She thinks the part-timers—who are mostly women—get short shrift. "None of the part-time people get benefits, and a lot of times we don't get paid for holidays," says Ferraro. "Our wages are lower. In my opinion, they really abuse the part-time people." She says not getting health insurance is okay for her, because she's covered under her husband's plan. "But a lot of the women here are widows who are supplementing Social Security, and the lack of benefits is really hurting them."

Ferraro hates the working conditions. "We call it an electronic sweatshop," she says. "They've got us on a production schedule, and we're sitting in these little pods, and they don't allow us to talk to anybody. We can't go to the bathroom unless we get permission.

"All they care about it numbers. You have to get so many applications out per hour, and if you don't, then you don't have a job. You're supposed to do twenty an hour. I do twenty-six an hour, and I still haven't heard them say, 'Oh, that's wonderful.' What I keep hearing is 'Oh, now you can try for twenty-seven.' They monitor how many minutes you're on the computer, how many minutes you're off. You're always supposed to be on the computer.

"A lot of people have quit, a lot of people have gotten angry," she continues. "I think it's outdated management. They're not getting production because of loyalty, that's for sure."

Ferraro's experience at the mail-order house has changed her attitude about unions. "They do need a union there, believe it or not," she says. "I was never for a union before, but I am now, after seeing how they treat these older people and people in general. My husband is in a union, and I used to tease him that I thought the union was really off the wall. But now, after working here, I really understand why you'd want one."

The problem is that only a tiny number of contingent workers are unionized. Temps are not organized, and only 7 per cent of part-timers are union members. The United Food and Commercial Workers, which claims to be the largest union of part-timers, represents nearly 400,000 part-time grocery employees. The union has been able to establish minimum standards for these workers, including health benefits and a degree of job security.

"There have always been part-time workers in the grocery business," says UFCW staffer Greg Denier. "The move for employers to make more work part-time is motivated in part by a desire to avoid paying health benefits." Under the union's contracts with grocers, part-timers who work more than twelve or fourteen hours a week are paid at least pro-rated health benefits. And that, says Denier, takes some incentive away from employers to make jobs part-time. Still, he says, probably about 40 per cent of union grocery jobs are part-time. Wages range from $6 an hour for grocery-baggers to $16 an hour for unionized department managers.

Organizing a part-time work force and keeping it organized is a constant struggle, Denier says. The union long ago gave up using the National Labor Relations Board to organize new shops. The process was too long and cumbersome for organizing people in high-turnover jobs like part-time grocery work. And new organizing is constant, since stores go in and out of business, he says. To keep its membership even, the UFCW has to organize 100,000 new workers every year. . . .

Contingent employment is, by definition, insecure. Turnover is high and protections are few. Workers are often afraid to complain about or organize against poor conditions. And so employers get away with murder. . . .

Randa Cross, an airline employee in Los Angeles, knows how vulnerable contingent workers can be. Cross talked to me through a bad case of laryngitis, so anxious was she to tell her story. Although she's obviously sick, she is using up vacation days during her illness. "And I'm glad," she says, "because every time you're sick, they put it down as an 'occurrence.' And after so many occurrences, you get a letter of 'concern' in your file—like, your employment is in question."

Cross now works full-time, after a long and painful tenure as a temporary. "As a temporary, part-time person, I basically worked forty hours a week anyway. They just don't have to pay you the benefits. That's exactly what it is. Temporary part-timers is what they call it—TPTs. But they're really full-time permanent. We have people who have been TPTs for five or six years. We have one woman in our department who is a TPT who has been at the airline for twenty-five years." When you're part-time, says Cross, "you have to work harder because you have to prove yourself all the time. And you're getting paid less."

Cross's new job is at the reservations counter, which, she says, is "the worst department. Everyone hates it. But I went there because I needed the permanent, full-time work, because I'm a single mother with a kid." In her department, she says, "we have mandatory overtime. Everybody has to put their life on hold. Because they're trying to get back to profitability, they're working us to the bone."

But Cross says she's most concerned about the people still stuck in the TPT nether world. "The company recently told the TPTs that it would be light-years before there would be any permanent jobs for them. I hate to complain, but it really isn't right how they treat people. I really feel sorry for people—they're talented, they're hard workers." . . .

A similar pattern exists in such industries as publishing and the arts, where companies and institutions are shedding full-time workers in favor of free-lancers with no benefits.

Jon Crowe was happy doing desktop publishing for a performance hall in Brooklyn. It was a full-time, salaried job, and that was what he wanted. Then Crowe's supervisor got it into his head that he could save money by laying off Crowe and hiring him as a free-lancer for a limited number of hours. "What he really wanted was to hire mostly interns and kids right out of college whom he could pay less," Crowe says.

He did free-lance work for his old employer for a while. But he wanted full-time work. "I'm uncomfortable not knowing where I'm going next week," Crowe says. "Some people would prefer to be free-lancers and have the freedom. But I don't see it as much of a freedom. If I was offered a job, I'd have to take it, because I want to work. That's not freedom."

Many writers, photographers, and graphic artists like the flexibility and control of the creative process they have as free-lancers. But they suffer economically. Free-lance writers rarely clear $20,000 a year with writing jobs alone—even if they work from morning to night. That leaves little money to purchase health insurance. Free-lancers also often find they spend as much time tending to the business of free-lancing—finding the next job, billing, making proposals—as they do in creative work.

Earlier in this century, the shift to mass production gave rise to the organizing of millions of industrial workers. Now the trend is in the opposite direction, as the work force is broken down into units of one: the single free-lancer working at home. Free-lancers, who act as one-person entrepreneurs, often feel they are competing with other free-lancers for work—not an attitude conducive to organizing.

Nevertheless, the National Writers Union, which represents several thousand free-lancers around the country, has had some success. The union is trying to enforce better standards for free-lance writers with a "standard journalism contract" its members ask publishers to sign. The union represents writers in grievances against magazine and book publishers, and offers members a group health-insurance plan. . . . Other unions of free-lancers, including the American Federation of Musicians and the Graphic Arts Guild, have also helped to improve standards for their members, although organizing is a constant struggle.

Impact Visuals, a cooperative of progressive photojournalists, markets members' photos and serves as a place for members to socialize and share skills. It also fulfills some of the role of a union, since the cooperative seeks to set and maintain pay and other work standards.

Historically, many unions representing full-time workers have viewed free-lancers, temps, and part-timers essentially as scabs rather than as potential members to be organized. Few unions have been in a rush to sign up the country's growing ranks of contingent workers.

Of the many workers who are dragged kicking and screaming into the contingent work force, some manage to resist, even without a union to fight for them.

Employees at the Bank of America got some unwelcome news last year. After the bank merged with Security Pacific Corporation, it announced it would be cutting back branch employees to nineteen hours a week—and no more benefits. Workers at the bank were so outraged, they leaked the news to the *San Francisco Chronicle.*

Dick Delaney, an organizer for the Office and Professional Employees International Union, got in touch with the unorganized workers and later testified on their behalf before a Senate subcommittee. "I got calls from people who had worked for the bank for thirty years. People felt really degraded by this. And the little people who bank at BOA felt outraged too. At one little branch in a small town called San Leandro, more than $500,000 went out the door in a week—just people who were outraged that the Bank of America would do that to its employees."

Partly because of the pressure the workers themselves and bank clientele put on the bank, the company decided to shift its branch employees to contingent status more gradually, largely through attribution, according to Delaney. Still, he says, the end result will be severe. "They're going to end up with just the officers, a half dozen people, who will be full-time at the branch offices. By and large, the tellers will all be part-time without benefits." And this, he adds, is at a company that made $1.6 billion in profit per year.

## 4. Sweatshop Workers Speak Out, 1998

Employer recruitment of low-wage workers from abroad has reproduced conditions that most Americans thought long since abolished. When police raided a notorious El Monte, California, sweatshop in 1995, they found barbed wire, armed guards, and virtual slavery for scores of frightened women. This is one of their stories, as told in a 1998 interview with Smithsonian Institution historians.

*Interviewer:* Tell us your name and what kind of work you do.

*Praphapan Pongpid:* My name is Praphapan Pongpid, and I'm a garment worker. I sew with the single-needle machine, and I sew anything that is requested of me.

*IV:* What kind of clothes do you sew? Women's clothes? Children's?

*PP:* Mostly women.

*IV:* Have you done this kind of work for a long time?

*PP:* I've been a garment worker since living in Thailand, five years in Thailand, in El Monte and outside of El Monte another five years.

*IV:* Where do you come from in Thailand?

From "Interviews with Two Thai Workers," in Peter Liebhold and Harry R. Rubenstein, *Between a Rock and a Hard Place: A History of American Sweatshops, 1820–Present,* pp. 71–79. UCLA Asian American Studies Center and Simon Wiesenthal Center Museum of Tolerance, 1999.

*PP:* I'm from Chenglai, Thailand, and I worked in Bangkok, Thailand.

Where I'm from—Chenglai—my parents were rice farmers and we were always short of money and resources and funds, and that's why I had to migrate to Bangkok. To find money so that I could help my family and my parents out, but money was always hard to come by.

*IV:* How did you start in the clothing industry?

*PP:* When I migrated to Bangkok, my friend, whom I stayed with, referred me to a garment factory and was able to find a job and started working.

It was very hard at first, but I eventually learned how to use a sewing machine because I had no knowledge in any other areas. So this was it, I had to first try to work in the garment factory because I couldn't find any other work.

*IV:* How did you meet the recruiter for the El Monte shop in the United States?

*PP:* It was a friend, who was working with me in the same factory recommended me to this job prospect abroad in the United States. She mentioned that it was a good paying job and I didn't have to pay anything up front to get to the US but rather once I started working, I could pay off that debt.

*IV:* When you met this person, did he tell you what it was like, did he show you pictures?

*PP:* I met with the son of the family, Suni, who asked me if I was truly interested in coming abroad to work because it's a really good job, and well-paying, and I didn't have to put up any cost right now, but rather once I started working there, I could pay off my debt in the amount of 120,000 *bhat,* which is equivalent to $4,800. So I said, yeah, that seems like a good idea and so then I left.

*IV:* Did he tell you what it was like working in America?

*PP:* I was only told that I would have my weekends free. He was going to take me places once I was there, and I would go to many places and see many things.

*IV:* What kind of places?

*PP:* I was told that if there was time I would be able to go and see Universal Studios and Disneyland.

*IV:* Did you come with friends on the airplane?

*PP:* There were three of us who came on the plane. Once we arrived here we ended up living together.

We sat together on the plane, we talked to each other about this place we were going to, which we didn't know anything about, because we hardly had been given any kind of description of the place where we were going. So we were very excited but uncertain and were curious at the same time. We were also instructed not to talk to anyone at all, anyone who passed by, to ask any questions, any one—we were not allowed to say anything or talk to anyone.

*IV:* Who met you at the airport?

*PP:* When we arrived at the airport here, we waited for awhile before someone finally arrived to pick us up. It turned out to be one of the sons. He just tapped us on the shoulders. He had photos of us, what we looked like, and he tapped us on the shoulder. We realize this was the person we were supposed to go with. We went into this van and were taken directly to El Monte.

*IV:* When you came to this country was this what you expected?

*PP:* I never imagined America to be like that. As soon as we arrived in El Monte, we were taken to see Auntie Suni, and then she asked for all our paperwork and took everything from us, passports even though the passports had our photos but not our names.

After she took all of our passports and documents, she then took us to Unit E where all the new arrivals go first and gather there and so that's where we were taken to Unit E.

*IV:* Did she talk to you in Unit E and tell you what was going to happen?

*PP:* She instructed us not to talk to any of the other workers, in particular the workers who had been there for a while because she didn't want us to find out how they got there and whether they came to the U.S. in the same manner, whether their passports were also falsified.

*IV:* Did she show you where you were going to live?

*PP:* She showed us to our sleeping area, gave us our pillow and blanket, but we were to find our own piece of cloth to put on the floor to sleep on. We would have to make [a pad] ourselves and sleep on that on the floor. . . .

*IV:* When you were able to work, did someone show you the workplace?

*PP:* The employer would divide up the work between the workers, between the more difficult labor work and the work that was not as hard. I was familiar with sewing pockets onto the clothes, but I was made to do the hemming and the finishing on the clothing which is the very last step in the production of the clothing and that was the most difficult because by that point at the last stage, there was a rush to get that done and so that was very labor intensive.

*IV:* When you saw the place that you were going to be working, did it look like the place you worked in Thailand? Was it different?

*PP:* It was nothing like the work I experienced in Thailand. Here they would rush us to get the work done, rush us to get it done no matter what. If they needed it the next morning we had to work all night long to get it done the next morning. I was more familiar and used to a system where things were scheduled and I would know when to get certain work done by and time the work is needed done by, but here there were no standards, no such thing as a schedule, just on an as-needed basis. Whatever they demanded and we just needed to comply, and they wanted rush and we needed to fulfill that all the time.

*IV:* How did the employers treat you?

*PP:* I remember the daughter-in-law being very hard to us and always complained and always giving us orders to work faster. She also told us that we need to produce these clothes by the next morning, and we had to do what we can even if it means staying up all night to get those pieces of clothing by the next morning. The daughter-in-law was extremely harsh and rude and demanding.

*IV:* Did you work in any other factory which Aunti Suni owned besides El Monte?

*PP:* I was taken to work in the downtown shop by the same employers once when there was a rush to get the work done.

*IV:* What were the guards like?

*PP:* The guards kept us constantly under their surveillance. We were never allowed to step out of our unit, even outside within the compound. Anytime we ventured out, the guards would question why we're out there, what we're doing here, would remind us we didn't belong here.

*IV:* At night where you lived, could you look outside and see the neighborhood?

*PP:* The first year I arrived I was able to look right outside my window, but only see the area right immediately outside the window, but I couldn't really see far. But then, after people had escaped, they started boarding up the windows with plywood and maybe leaving, a small space for ventilation, for air to pass. Occasionally, when we had time we would stand on a chair or table to look outside that small window, but we rarely had time even to do that because we were constantly working. . . .

*IV:* Did you think you were able to escape?

*PP:* I had thought of escaping. I also thought of what I would do if I had escaped. I didn't know how to use the phone, I didn't know anyone, I couldn't speak the language, I didn't know how to use the bus, the transportation system. I didn't know what I would do if I were to escape and so I then just decided to endure, stay put and just accept my fate.

*IV:* What did you think when the police came?

*PP:* I was very nervous and excited at the same time, and frightened because I wasn't sure what was going to happen. But when I heard in Thai, "we're here to help you, we're here to help you," I felt reassured. Had it not been for someone saying that in Thai, then I wouldn't know what was going to happen, or what was going to become of me. I was sure something good was going to come of it.

*IV:* What happened after the police came?

*PP:* When the police first entered, they questioned Auntie Suni first and they kept asking her: do you know these men and women here? And she kept denying knowing of them, and she kept saying: "No I didn't know any of them, they just came here to have a good time," and the police asked each one of us, one at a time, if each of us know her. We told them exactly what we knew, "Yes, she's our employer, she's the main person here in charge." Even after we said this, they went back and asked her if she still denied knowing any of us. And then she told the police: "My name is Mali, not Suni, and I don't know any of these women."

*IV:* What did you think when they arrested her?

*PP:* I thought, finally now that she's been arrested, she may realize what it feels like to be restricted and held in prison. I was very content to see her being arrested. I hope that she realizes what she's put us through and finally she is getting rewarded for what she's done to us.

*IV:* What did you think of the companies that bought clothes from El Monte. Do you think they knew what was going on?

*PP:* The reality is I believe they did know where the clothing came from as they went to pick up those clothing. I believe they just ignored where it was coming from, and the conditions the clothing was being produced because it was being gotten so cheaply, and they were able to make so much money off of us, and off of those clothing and buying it so cheaply. That was all that mattered to them. That was the most important fact in all of this. They didn't care to know where the clothing was being produced, who was producing the clothing, in what conditions it was being produced under. It's like all they cared about was making as much profit, as much as possible, being able to keep as much profit as possible, being able to buy it cheaply. I do believe whether they want to admit or deny where the clothing came from, they have responsibility in our enslavement and what happened, and they should be held responsible.

*IV:* Do you plan to stay in the U.S. now?

*PP:* Since being let free from El Monte, I was able to experience the good side of America. Now I've come to see the good aspects of this country. I'd like to continue living here because I'm studying now and I'd like to learn English. They provide me an opportunity to study and I'd like to do this. I believe this country is truly a land of freedom and I've come to see that.

## 5. The AFL-CIO Defends Immigrant Workers, 2000

The AFL-CIO proudly stands on the side of immigrant workers. Throughout the history of this country, immigrants have played an important role in building our nation and its democratic institutions. New arrivals from every continent have contributed their energy, talent, and commitment to making the United States richer and stronger. Likewise, the American union movement has been enriched by the contributions and courage of immigrant workers. Newly arriving workers continue to make indispensable contributions to the strength and growth of our unions. These efforts have created new unions and strengthened and revived others, benefitting all workers, immigrant and native-born alike. It is increasingly clear that if the United States is to have an immigration system that really works, it must be simultaneously orderly, responsible and fair. The policies of both the AFL-CIO and our country must reflect those goals.

The United States is a nation of laws. This means that the federal government has the sovereign authority and constitutional responsibility to set and enforce limits on immigration. It also means that our government has the obligation to enact and enforce laws in ways that respect due process and civil liberties, safeguard public health and safety, and protect the rights and opportunities of workers.

The AFL-CIO believes the current system of immigration enforcement in the United States is broken and needs to be fixed. Our starting points are simple:

•    Undocumented workers and their families make enormous contributions to their communities and workplaces and should be provided permanent legal status through a new amnesty program.

•    Regulated legal immigration is better than unregulated illegal immigration.

•    Immigrant workers should have full workplace rights in order to protect their own interests as well as the labor rights of all American workers.

•    Labor and business should work together to design cooperative mechanisms that allow law-abiding employers to satisfy legitimate needs for new workers in a timely manner without compromising the rights and opportunities of workers already here.

•    Labor and business should cooperate to undertake expanded efforts to educate and train American workers in order to upgrade their skill levels in ways that enhance our shared economic prosperity.

•    Criminal penalties should be established to punish employers who recruit undocumented workers from abroad for the purpose of exploiting workers for economic gain.

From AFL-CIO, "Immigration," Executive Council Actions, February 16, 2000, New Orleans, LA.

Current efforts to improve immigration enforcement, while failing to stop the flow of undocumented people into the United States, have resulted in a system that causes discrimination and leaves unpunished unscrupulous employers who exploit undocumented workers, thus denying labor rights for *all* workers.

The combination of a poorly constructed and ineffectively enforced system that results in penalties for only a few of the employers who violate immigration laws has had especially detrimental impacts on efforts to organize and adequately represent workers. Unscrupulous employers have systematically used the I-9 process in their efforts to retaliate against workers who seek to join unions, improve their working conditions, and otherwise assert their rights.

Therefore, the AFL-CIO calls for replacing the current I-9 system as a tool of workplace immigration enforcement. We should substitute a system of immigration enforcement strategies that focuses on the criminalization of employer behavior, targeting those employers who recruit undocumented workers from abroad, either directly or indirectly. It should be supplemented with strong penalties against employer who abuse workers' immigration status to suppress their rights and labor protections. The federal government should aggressively investigate, and criminally prosecute, those employers who knowingly exploit a worker's undocumented status in order to prevent enforcement of workplace protection laws.

We strongly believe employer sanctions, as a nationwide policy applied to all workplaces, has failed and should be eliminated. It should be replaced with an alternative policy to reduce undocumented immigration and prevent employer abuse. Any new policy must meet the following principles: (1) it must seek to prevent employer discrimination against people who look or sound foreign; (2) it must allow workers to pursue legal remedies, including supporting a union, regardless or immigration status; and (3) it must avoid unfairly targeting immigrant workers of a particular nationality.

There is a long tradition in the United States of protecting those who risk their financial and physical well-being to come forward to report violations of laws that were enacted for the public good. Courageous undocumented workers who come forward to assert their rights should not be faced with deportation as a result of their actions. . . . Therefore the AFL-CIO calls for the enactment of whistleblower protections providing protected immigration status for undocumented workers who report violations of worker protection laws or cooperate with federal agencies during investigations of employment, labor and discrimination violations. Such workers should be accorded full remedies, including reinstatement and back pay. Further, undocumented workers who exercise their rights to organize and bargain collectively should also be provided protected immigration status.

Millions of hard-working people who make enormous contributions to their communities and workplace are denied basic human rights because of their undocumented status. Many of these men and women are the parents of children who are birthright U.S. citizens. The AFL-CIO supports a new amnesty program that would allow these members of local communities to adjust their status to permanent resident and become eligible for naturalization. . . .

Immediate steps should include legalization for three distinct groups of established residents: (1) approximately half-a-million Salvadorans, Guatemalans, Hondurans, and Haitians, who fled civil war and civil strife during the 1980s and early

1990s and were unfairly denied refugee status, and have lived under various forms of temporary legal status; (2) approximately 350,000 long-resident immigrants who were unfairly denied legalization due to illegal behavior by the INS during the amnesty program enacted in the late 1980s; and (3) approximately 10,000 Liberians who fled their homeland's brutal civil war and have lived in the United States for years under temporary legal status.

Guestworker programs too often are used to discriminate against U.S. workers, depress wages and distort labor markets. For these reasons, the AFL-CIO has long been troubled by the operation of such programs. The proliferation of guestworker programs has resulted in the creation of a class of easily exploited workers, who find themselves in a situation very similar to that faced by undocumented workers. The AFL-CIO renews our call for the halt to the expansion of guestworker programs. Moreover, these programs should be reformed to include more rigorous labor market tests and the involvement of labor unions in the labor certification process. All temporary guestworkers should be afforded the same workplace protections available to all workers.

## 6. The Battle in Seattle, 1999

The last time the World Trade Organization had a major meeting, it was in Singapore, and now we know why.

Singapore, of course, is the city-state that accords near-perfect freedom to banks and corporations while jailing political activists and caning messy tenants and people who chew gum in public. When WTO ministers gathered in Singapore in 1997, their businesses was unimpeded by any outside agitators. (Or, for that matter, any internal dissidents: Advocates for worker rights or environmental standards are not allowed into the deliberations that set the rules for global commerce.)

That Seattle wasn't going to be another Singapore was never in question. On Tuesday, though, Seattle wasn't even Seattle. It was more like Petrograd-for-a-Day. The TV news may be filled with replays of the day's violence, but that was just a small part of the Seattle revolution, and something that hundreds of demonstrators personally tried to stop. But like Petrograd circa 1917, Seattle in just the past 24 hours has had something for nearly every species of reformer and revolutionary. Here was economist Bob Kuttner, with a scholarly presentation to an upscale and decorous gathering on the perils of laissez-faire capitalism. Over there, Ralph Nader was giving a more spirited rendition of the same basic tune. On the waterfront, the entire port clanged shut, as the longshoremen welcomed the trade ministers to Seattle by closing off trade altogether. Down one boulevard paraded 100 uniformed airline pilots indignant about growing employer power; down another, 100 environmentalists decked out in turtle suits to dramatize the WTO's overturning of national endangered-species laws. Not to mention the thousands of students who trudged downtown from the University of Washington, the leaders of the American union movement who suddenly sounded like Gene Debs, and the nearly 20,000

From Harold Meyerson, "The Battle in Seattle," *LA Weekly,* December 3–9, 1999, pp. 6–9. Copyright © 2000, *LA Weekly* Media, Inc. All rights reserved. Reprinted by permission of Executive Editor, *The American Prospect* and Political Editor, *LA Weekly.*

workers who paraded around the outskirts of downtown while 20,000 other activists, most of them college-age, peaceably sat down in the middle of downtown
and kept the WTO from convening.

Most astonishing, there was the intermingling of all these disparate movements, generations, nations and lifestyles. There were the kids blocking the WTO
delegates, who parted like the Red Sea to make way for a group of Steelworkers,
identifiable by their blue-poncho rain gear as members of the most ubiquitous of the
protesting unions this week. There was Amparo Reyes, a single mother who puts in
a 74-hour week (for a lordly $69) at her local maquiladora, shouting "Long live the
Zapastistas!" at the official AFL-CIO rally. And amid Teamsters chanting "Hoffa!
Hoffa!" and baby-faced animal rightsters chanting "No violence! No violence!"
there was the sign that proclaimed, "Teamsters and Turtles—Together at Last!"

Team the Teamsters with the turtles, and what you get—what the world got in
Seattle on Tuesday—could well be an ideological turning point—or at least, an end
to the unchallenged dominance that right-wing economics has enjoyed for the past
two decades.

For 20 years now, the greatest achievements of the world's industrial democracies—the broadly shared prosperity created by unions and social insurance, the
attempts to restore and preserve clean air and water, the whole idea of leisure
time—have been eroded by the resurrection of laissez-faire economics on the global
level, even while living standards in much of the developing world have been held
in check by the coming of laissez faire. For 20 years, movements that knew how to
change national and state and local laws were paralyzed by this shift to the global.
At first, this new global terrain was a realm of practices, not laws; there was no
legislature to lobby or win over; there was just businesses without government—
Singapore writ large. National governments remained, but they were whipsawed
by multinational business just as state governments had been whipsawed by the
first national businesses—the railroads—100 years ago.

At which point, the global corporate and financial powers—preponderantly
American—made a serious mistake. Mere practices weren't enough for them; they
wanted some global codes. France was still blocking the exports of American food
out of some sentimental attachment to its farmers; nations of the former communist bloc were pirating American films without paying the studios; and investment houses wanted developing nations to make their banks and businesses keep a
clean set of books so they'd know what exactly they were buying. So five years
ago, the governments of the West obliged their major businesses by bundling all
their separate trade deals into one neat package and creating the WTO to make sure
that transnational investment would encounter no significant obstacles.

In short, without fully grasping exactly what they'd done, they created at least
the appearance of a legislature. Its mandate was limited to helping global capital,
and its members weren't chosen by election, but it had an office, held meetings,
and set rules. At long last, global capital had a street address.

And Tuesday, in one convulsive outburst that had been building for 20 years,
the movements shut it down. For just a day—but a day that already has altered the
ideological balance of our time.

Convulsive, in this instance, means neither violent nor unplanned. . . . [T]he civil
disobedience of the kids was both morally irreproachable and tactically brilliant.

Indeed, the free-spirit wing of the American Left was a lot better organized than the two other groups on the street—organized labor and the cops. The unions had to re-route their 20,000 marchers so they wouldn't plow into the downtown sit-down. That called for a midmarch U-turn—which half the unions executed while the other half wandered blindly into sit-down central. Roughly 100 briskly trotting and generally apprehensive parade marshals fanned out in search of their missing columns. As for the police, they were badly outnumbered until well after nightfall. Despite a full year of planning, police officials couldn't come up with a remotely accurate assessment of their needs.

The kids, by contrast, knew every street, every hotel, every plausible technique for linking arms to one another and the nearby lamppost. They managed to block off the Paramount Theater, where the opening session was supposed to take place. When I got there, the standoff was almost done—just a few delegate cars remained obstructed by the sit-downers, whose numbers had dwindled to around 30. Ten feet in front of them was a line of nine cops, in riot helmets and holding their nightsticks. . . .

The ghost of the '60s hung over the afternoon: There was a loud recording of Hendrix playing "The Star-Spangled Banner"; Tom Hayden walked up and down the street, the crowd chanted "The whole world's watching" when the police fired off tear gas. Gassing and pepper spray were the cops' preferred modes of attack on Tuesday, and the clouds wafted over the just and unjust alike. Young protesters complained to me of the police brutality. But at the risk of sounding like the most hackeneyed of grizzled elders, I am compelled to say: I was in Chicago in 1968, and I know a police riot, having been on the receiving end of one, when I see one. Seattle's finest were comparative pussycats. They made scarcely any arrests, and when an altercation threatened to get out of hand—when the black-clad self-proclaimed anarchists trashed display windows and stores—they resolutely refused to do anything that could have resulted in a serious injury to anyone. . . . In all the news coverage on Seattle TV Tuesday night, there was just one shot of a gun being pulled—not by a cop or a demonstrator, but by a WTO delegate frustrated by his inability to get to the hall. . . .

Mass opinion has always been dubious about free trade; that is one reason why the AFL-CIO was able to persuade House Democrats to kill the administration's proposal for a fast-track process to approve trade deals (that is, a process with no possibility of congressional amendment of the deal) in 1997. One recent University of Maryland poll shows 78 percent public support for the idea of making labor and environmental concerns a factor in all trade deals.

Elite opinion, however, has long viewed the case for free trade as axiomatic. Free trade made nations richer, which made them more democratic, except when it didn't (one of those pesky anomalies the theory hasn't fully explained away). But labor has already forced one key segment of the elite—the administration and its consulting ideologists at the Democratic Leadership Council—to alter its rhetorical position on trade. This week, everyone from Treasury Secretary Lawrence Summers to trade rep Charlene Barshevsky—has suddenly been talking up the virtues of a humane global-trade order. "We must pay more attention to labor issues," Summers wrote in Monday's *Financial Times,* casually jettisoning the beliefs of a lifetime. . . . The momentum for laissez-faire policies in domestic affairs has peaked. The war on the state waged by Reagan, Thatcher and Gingrich has been called off. Only at the level of world trade does the cult of laissez fare continue to hold sway, but the case is getting harder and harder to make. If increased wage equity and environmental safeguards are once again valid concerns in national affairs, it grows harder and harder to argue that they're mere sideshows to the transnational economy and society.

While elite opinion begins to waver, popular opinion has now gained a focus. At Monday night's march for debt forgiveness, at Tuesday's labor march, people came out of their shops and businesses to cheer the marchers on. While the trashing and gassing was proceeding apace on Tuesday afternoon, just three blocks away office workers laughed as a chorus sung mock Christmas carols with anti-WTO lyrics. There was anger at the inconveniences the marches caused, anger at the anarchists for sure. But on the whole, the protesters in Seattle were nobody's outside agitators. These were the kids at U Wash, the ladies from church, the guys at Boeing. It was Seattle that was marching this week. To the WTO, Singapore has never looked better.

## 7. Senseless in Seattle, 1999

Is there anything more ridiculous in the news today than the protests against the World Trade Organization in Seattle? I doubt it.

These anti-W.T.O. protesters—who are a Noah's ark of flat-earth advocates, protectionist trade unions and yuppies looking for their 1960's fix—are protesting against the wrong target with the wrong tools. Here's why:

What unites the anti-W.T.O. crowd is their realization that we now live in a world without walls. The cold-war system we just emerged from was built around division and walls; the globalization system that we are now in is built around integration and webs. In this new system, jobs, cultures, environmental problems and labor standards can much more easily flow back and forth.

The ridiculous thing about the protesters is that they find fault with this, and blame the W.T.O. The W.T.O. is not the cause of this world without walls, it's the effect. The more countries trade with one another, the more they need an institution to set the basic rules of trade, and that is all the W.T.O. does. "Rules are a substitute for walls—when you don't have walls you need more rules," notes the Council on Foreign Relations expert Michael Mandelbaum.

Because some countries try to use their own rules to erect new walls against trade, the W.T.O. adjudicates such cases. For instance, there was the famous "Flipper vs. GATTzilla" dispute. (The W.T.O. used to be known as GATT.) America has rules against catching tuna in nets that might also snare dolphins; other countries don't, and those other countries took the U.S. before a GATT tribunal and charged that our insistence on Flipper-free tuna was a trade barrier. The anti-W.T.O. protesters extrapolate from such narrow cases that the W.T.O. is going to become a Big Brother and tell us how to live generally. Nonsense.

What's crazy is that the protesters want the W.T.O. to become precisely what they accuse it of already being—a global government. They want it to set more rules—their rules, which would impose our labor and environmental standards on everyone else. I'm for such higher standards, and over time the W.T.O. may be a vehicle to enforce them, but it's not the main vehicle to achieve them. And they are certainly not going to be achieved by putting up new trade walls.

Every country and company that has improved its labor, legal and environmental standards has done so because of more global trade, more integration, more Internet—not less. These are the best tools we have for improving global governance.

Who is one of the top environmental advisers to DuPont today? Paul Gilding, the former head of Greenpeace! How could that be? A DuPont official told me that in the old days, if DuPont wanted to put a chemical factory in a city, it knew it just had to persuade the local neighbors. "Now we have six billion neighbors," said the DuPont official—meaning that DuPont knows that in a world without walls if it wants to put up a chemical plant in a country, every environmentalist is watching. And if that factory makes even a tiny spill those environmentalists will put it on the World Wide Web and soil DuPont's name from one end of the earth to the other.

I recently visited a Victoria's Secret garment factory in Sri Lanka that, in terms of conditions, I would let my own daughters work in. Why does it have such a high standard? Because anti-sweatshop activists have started to mobilize enough consumers to impress Victoria's Secret that if it doesn't get its shop standards up, consumers won't buy its goods. Sri Lanka is about to pass new copyright laws, which Sri Lanka software writers have been seeking for years to protect their own innovations. Why the new law now? Because Microsoft told Sri Lanka it wouldn't sell its products in a country with such weak intellectual property laws.

Hey, I want to save Flipper too. It's a question of how. If the protesters in Seattle stopped yapping, they would realize that they have been duped by knaves like Pat Buchanan—duped into thinking that power lies with the W.T.O. It doesn't. There's never going to be a global government to impose the rules the protesters want. But there can be better global governance—on the environment, intellectual property and labor. You achieve that not by adopting 1960's tactics in a Web-based world—not by blocking trade, choking globalization or getting the W.T.O. to put up more walls. That's a fool's errand.

You make a difference today by using globalization—by mobilizing the power of trade, the power of the Internet and the power of consumers to persuade, or embrace, global corporations and nations to upgrade their standards. You change the world when you get the big players to do the right things for the wrong reasons. But that takes hard work—coalition-building with companies and consumers, and follow-up. It's not as much fun as a circus in Seattle.

## ✤ E S S A Y S

In the first essay, labor journalist and activist, Kim Moody offers a historical analysis of the process of globalization. Moody argues, in Marxist fashion, that worldwide economic integration is driven less by the exchange of finished products and services than by corporate efforts to lower their production costs, including those that arise from the use of relatively high priced labor in the advanced industrial nations. In the second essay, Andrew Ross, a cultural historian at New York University, examines the underside of cyberspace, whose mobile workers and "virtual" workplaces have become synonyms for a global, postindustrial market. Like Moody, Ross finds that whatever the character of the technological innovations, the cost and quality of labor have become a competitive, political battleground. And in the third essay, activist-sociologist Grace Chang of Evergreen State College offers a revealing probe into the world of immigrant women workers, whose care-giving labor has made them indispensable in many hospitals, nursing homes, and private residences.

To what extend has the globalization of capital reshaped the agenda of the U.S. labor movement? Why, if the labor of foreign workers is so necessary, do some Americans resent their presence within the United States?

# A Certain Kind of Globalization

## KIM MOODY

Beginning in the 1980s . . . , the world experienced a crisis in employment. By 1996, the International Labor Office estimated that nearly a billion people were either unemployed or underemployed across the world. In the developed industrial world as a whole at least 34 million were out of work, with unemployment rates hovering chronically above 10% in many of these countries. Disguising deeper employment problems, particularly in the United States and Britain, where official rates were lower, was the rise of part-time and temporary employment in place of "steady work." In eastern Europe and the former Soviet Union, where governments were abandoning centralized planning for market-based economies and isolation from the world market for rapid integration, economic activity actually dropped, while unemployment climbed from almost zero a few years previously to above 10% across the region.

By the 1990s in the Third World, some 75 million people a year were being driven from their country of birth in the world's less prosperous nations in search of asylum and/or employment elsewhere. For those left behind in the less developed countries, high unemployment was compounded (some would say mitigated) by the growth of the informal sector, where millions eked out a living in their homes or in the streets of exploding urban conglomerations. Only a handful of small countries in Southeast Asia seemed to defy the trends, and even these faced the beginnings of recession and industrial restructuring by the mid-1990s.

Despite the promises and predictions of neoclassical economists and neoliberal politicians that deeper world economic integration and regulation by market forces would (eventually) bring prosperity as the world's resources were more efficiently allocated, the employment crisis grew as the process of globalization proceeded. The coming of recovery following the recession of the early 1990s did not bring relief to most countries, and it became clearer to millions that the so-called "efficiency" of the market or the competitiveness of business ran counter to the economic well-being of the vast majority. Partly a consequence of policy, partly of countless business decisions, partly of technology, and partly of the opaque forces of the market, this crisis in the provision of the means by which a

From Kim Moody, *Workers in a Lean World: Unions in the International Economy* (New York: Verso, 1997), pp. 41–50. Reprinted by permission of Verso.

majority of the world's people make a living deepened as international economic integration deepened.

The problem was that the world was not simply becoming more economically integrated, it was becoming more capitalist. As trade and investment barriers fell, government ownership and planning shrank, and private corporations became the major organizers of the world's economic activity, competition and its effects (such as workforce reduction) became more volatile. In terms of geographic reach, market penetration and regulation, and private ownership, the world has become more thoroughly subjected to the reign of a system in which the unending accumulation of capital is the object and profit the sole measure of success.

Globalization is a process, not a fact of life. The deepening of economic integration under capitalist terms is a reality, but its effects are very different in different parts of the world. Although deeply affected by this process, most world economic activity occurred within, not between, nations. The world remained a patchwork of national economies and economic regions tied together by those forces associated with the idea of globalization. The notion of a single seamless world economy was still far from a reality in the mid-1990s. What was real, however, was the universalizing of capitalism: operating both nationally in more places and internationally at various levels, always with profound results.

One result was the global jobs crisis, another was the following obscene fact reported by the United Nations:

> Today, the worth of the 358 richest people, the dollar billionaires, is equal to the combined income of the poorest 45% of the world's population 2.3 billion people.

This system has now become world-wide. At the most obvious geopolitical level, the collapse of the Communist regimes of eastern Europe and the Soviet Union at the end of the 1890s opened vast new territories to capitalist social relations and market functioning where only marginal trade with any borrowing from Western capitalism had existed for decades. This unprecedented transition had brought over 400 million people and some $1.5 trillion in gross domestic product into the world capitalist economy by 1994. If China and Vietnam are included, another 1.3 billion people and $538 billion have come more or less directly under the regime of capital and its world market. While few would mourn the passing of the dictatorships that dared to call themselves "socialist," the applause for the new market regimes has faded fast.

Somewhat less dramatic, but of at least equal significance, was the rise from the later 1970s onward, of neoliberalism: the policy of dismantling much of the national regulation of economic life throughout the already existing capitalist world in favor of market governance, a process euphemistically referred to as "reform" or "liberalization." A sign of this was the fact that of the 373 national legislative changes governing foreign investment during 1991–94 in countries surveyed by the United Nations, only 5 "were *not* in the direction of greater liberalization." Equally important was the accelerating elimination of publicly owned industry and services. Between 1988 and 1992, the world-wide sales of state-owned enterprises amounted to $185 billion, not including the $25 billion in privatizations in the former East Germany or an additional $106 billion in commitments to purchase state-owned assets. Then, of course, there were the multilateral trade agreements of the early 1990s that further opened the world market and restricted national regulation of trade and investment: the Maastricht Treaty, North American Free Trade Agreement, and the World Trade Organization, which supersedes and broadens the General Agreement on Tariffs and Trade.

## "All that is Solid Melts into Air"

Taken together, these changes in geographic scale, regulatory regime, and ownership patterns are unprecedented in the rapidity, scope, and depth to which the world has been subjected to the forces of capitalist accumulation and market regulation. Even before the collapse of Communism, economic geographers Michael Storper and Richard Walker styled the new economic world as "a mosaic of unevenness in a continuous state of flux." Peter Dicken, whose *Global Shift* is the virtual textbook on globalization, calls today "an era of *turbulence* and *volatility.*"

So rapid and disruptive has been this combined process on the transition of the countries of eastern Europe and the former Soviet Union from centrally (and bureaucratically) planned and and regulated economies to the new market-based capitalism that the World Bank chose to quote Karl Marx in the introduction to its 1996 *World Development Report,* which focuses on the transformation of the former Communist countries.

The quote, which comes from the *Communist Manifesto,* is worth noting because of what it says about the way in which the economic system the World Bank holds so dear actually spreads and the class that commands, the system acts. In somewhat fuller form it reads:

> The bourgeoisie cannot exist without constantly revolutionizing the instruments of production, and thereby the relations of production and with them the whole relations of society. . . . Constant revolutionizing of production, uninterrupted disturbance of all social conditions, everlasting uncertainty and agitation distinguish the bourgeois epoch from the earlier ones. All fixed, fast-frozen relations, with their train of ancient and venerable prejudices and opinions, are swept away, all new-formed ones become antiquated before they can ossify. All that is solid melts into air, all that is holy is profaned, and man is at last compelled to face with sober senses his real conditions of life and his relations with his kind.
>
> The need of a constantly expanding market for its products chases the bourgeoisie over the whole surface of the globe. It must nestle everywhere, settle everywhere, establish connections everywhere.

Though the language may seem old fashioned, the concepts are surprisingly up-to-the-moment in three important ways. First is the constant changing of the way goods and services are produced—the revolutionizing of the instruments of production. Certainly the alternation and adaption of mass production, Taylorism, and automation to lean production, team and "quality"-based work systems, and robotization and information-based technologies represents such a revolutionizing of the instruments of production—one that often seems to have no end itself.

Second is the disruption of social life. Here Marx was referring primarily to pre-capitalist societies, but it is evident that changes in production (downsizing, plant closings, contingent jobs, etc.) have reshaped the towns and cities we live in, the jobs we hold or lose, and the ways we relate to one another within and between nations. The unemployed and underemployed, the migrants and the homeless all stand as the symbols of the chain of social dislocation wrought by the race for profit and accumulation.

Finally, there is the concept of globalization itself. Writing in the middle of the nineteenth century, Marx saw the international spread of capitalism as inherent in the system and already well under way. Unlike much of the formal or academic discussion of globalization today, however, Marx did not see this as a process removed from human activity. The spread and constant renewal of capitalism has a human agent, the "bourgeoisie" or capitalist class. Increasingly organized today at its commanding heights in giant, transnational corporations, this class itself faces the dilemma of having the power to reshape the face of the earth through its thousands of daily decisions; while, at the same time, being subjected to the laws and tendencies of the political economy from which it so richly benefits. Indeed, much of what appears as irrational (short-sighted profit-taking, disregard for its traditional national consumer base, defiance of environmental limitations, etc.), is rooted in this contradiction.

The capitalist system is driven, as its neoliberal policy-makers and apologists never tire of telling us, by competition. But it is not the orderly and largely passive "perfect" competition envisioned in their theories—a competition always tending toward a peaceful equilibrium and an optimal allocation of resources. Rather, as economist Anwar Shaikh put it, "It is war, in which the big devour the small, and the strong happily crush the weak. The laws which competition executes in turn frequently execute many competitors. And the principal weapon of this warfare is the reduction of production costs. . . ." It should be underlined that the object of this warfare is the highest rate of return on investment possible.

Indeed, the competition itself is rooted in the increase of the size of the capital (usually organized as a corporation or company) through the realization of a profit. This accumulation process is unending. As economist Howard Botwinick puts it concisely:

> the relentless drive to expand capital value is necessarily accompanied by a growing struggle over market share. These two dynamics, accumulation and rivalry, are inextricably bound up with one another.

This relentless competition, in turn, means that far from quietly tending toward some equilibrium, capitalism is regulated by constant crises, some deep and long-lasting (like the Great Depression or the persistent crisis of profitability since World War Two), others brief but repetitive (as with business-cycle recessions like 1981–83 or 1990–93). Competition fuels crisis, among other ways, by driving firms to invest more and more to improve efficiency and reduce costs. Under these circumstances, the stock of capital (and the production materials it requires) tends to increase faster than the size of the profits generated by labor, even when, as recently, those profits grow quite dramatically. Thus, the ratio of profits to capital, the rate of return (profit) on this mounting investment, tends to fall.

The irony is that the amount of profits can grow and the size of the capitals (companies or corporations) become massive and the capitalists still face a falling rate of return. There is no crisis in the wealth amassed by those who command and own these businesses. Indeed, throughout the world the rich have been getting richer the more the rest of us are subjected to the socially disastrous results of their decisions—as the UN report on the world's billionaires reminds us.

As we shall see, in the US and increasingly elsewhere, an enormous intensification of work associated with downsizing and lean production has produced higher productivity in many industries, increasing the amount of profit produced by labor. But it is the rate of profit not just the amount of it, that matters in the world of business competition. It is as though a rising surf of profits is overwhelmed and buried beneath a tidal wave of accumulated capital.

Thus, the twin motors of competition (as in warfare) and crisis (particularly in the rate of profit) drive capital abroad in search of lower production costs that, it is hoped, will improve returns on investment. This is not simply a matter of optimal business choices in the search for what is best for the business, but also of what capital is fleeing (below-average rates of return on investment, high taxes, other businesses that have achieved lower costs or higher efficiency), on the one hand, and the real alternatives, on the other. The flight abroad, then, where costs are presumed to be lower, is one in search of above-average rates of profit, even where the gains are marginal. This is the age-old secret behind the global imperative of capitalism. Real capitalist competition is the root of both its crisis and its drive to globalization.

### Crisis and Integration: A Long View

The road to world-wide integration of economic activity . . . has been long and turbulent. In 1820, for example, trade accounted for only about 1% of world economic output. By 1913, however, it had grown to 8.7%. This growth had been marked by a series of crises and financial panics in the 1870s and 1890s, and in the early years of the new century. What was even newer about the period from 1870 through 1913, according to . . . . [a recent] study, "was a massive flow of foreign capital, particularly from the UK, which directed about half its savings abroad." Much of this went into railroads, which helped intensify international integration. It was this export of capital that both the British liberal J. A. Hobson and the Russian revolutionary V. I. Lenin saw as underlying the scramble for colonies that eventually pushed the European powers toward war in 1914.

Yet, by today's standards, the level of global integration was low. While some countries like Britain or Germany had high ratios of exports to domestic output (17.7% and 15.6% respectively in 1913) the US had only 3.7%, Russia 2.9%, and Japan 2.4%. By 1994, in comparison, exports accounted for about 17% of world output, almost twice the rate of 1913. For the US it was about 8%, while for (the new capitalist) Russia it was 14%, and for Japan it was 8.7%. Britain was up to 20%, while Germany sent 21% of its output abroad in 1994. Clearly, in trade terms the world is far more integrated today than when Lenin wrote *Imperialism,* with what now seems the ironic subtitle: *The Highest Stage of Capitalism.* Even the flow of capital abroad that impressed Hobson, Lenin, and others at that time was small compared with today's. The stock of capital (foreign direct investment—FDI) invested abroad in 1914 was $143 billion (roughly, in 1990 dollars) compared with $2,135 billion in 1993. By this definition, direct overseas investment (in the form of ownership) grew by fifteen times compared with a tenfold growth of world output in these eight decades, indicating that it was accumulation rather than trade that led the process.

This growth in integration, however, has been far from linear. The growing integration of the world economy from the early nineteenth through the early twentieth century was shattered by three decades of war and crisis from 1914 through 1945. Economic competition turned into military confrontation in 1914 and again in 1939. The Russian Revolution pulled the vast collection of nations that composed the Tsarist (and later Stalinist) empire out of the world market after 1917. The world market itself fragmented as the major powers (Britain, France, US, Japan) formed rival currency and trading blocs. Faced with wild accumulation in the US and stagnation in Europe, the world careened toward the Great Depression, fascism, and another world war. Probably at no time has capitalism had less support around the world than in the years between and just following the two world wars. At no time had the system plunged so many people into economic deprivation, political repression, and total warfare.

As Europe and Asia recovered from World War Two, the process of world economic integration resumed. World exports grew by ten times from 1950 to 1992 in real terms, doubling as a proportion of world output from 7% to almost 14%. The accumulated stock of FDI, the most important kind of overseas investment, increased by five times in real terms from 1960 through 1993, reaching a total value of $2.1 trillion. Never before had so much cross-border economic activity occurred.

The content of international economic activity also changed. Whereas prior to World War One most trade and foreign investment had been in primary agricultural and mining products or in improvements in transportation and communications, the driving force of the globalization process that began around 1950 was manufacturing. The proportion of manufactured products in total merchandise trade rose from 52 % in 1952 to 73% in 1988. As a 1989 GATT) General Agreement on Tariffs and Trade) report noted, "manufacturers have played the dominant role in increasing the share of world production traded internationally." Globalization was anything but a "post-industrial" process.

In the late 1980s, services began to surpass goods in total trade, but, as Peter Dicken points out in *Global Shift,* the largest portion of the growth in services came from business services such as telecommunications and financial and technical services related to industrial production and the distribution of its products. The pattern in foreign investment was predictably similar, since it was largely this investment . . . that created the trade in both goods and services. In other words, the alleged drive toward a post-industrial world was still pushed by industry itself.

The agent of economic integration has also changed in form. In the era up to 1914 most overseas investment was "portfolio" investment, where the investor owned less than 10% of the overseas operation and the investment was frequently speculative in nature, while direct investment was mainly in railroads and extractive primary industries like agriculture or mining. Prior to 1914, there were at most a few hundred genuine transnational corporations. Today there are about 40,000, and they invest in every conceivable type of goods and service production. Their assets in 1992 were $3.4 trillion, of which $1.3 trillion was outside their "home" country. The sales of their overseas affiliates alone amounted to $5.4 trillion by 1992, which exceeded world exports of goods and services of $4.9 trillion.

Indeed, the transnational corporations (TNCs) changed the shape and content of international integration. By the 1990s the TNCs dominated world trade and the "arm's length" trade between small nationally based producers envisioned in classical and neoclassic economic theory had all but disappeared. Trade was less and less between nations and more and more between or within capitalist corporations. The United Nations estimates that TNCs accounted for two-thirds of the value of all exports by 1993. Half of this, or one-third of total world trade, was intra-form trade; that is, cross-border transactions between affiliates of the same corporation. Intra-firm trade for US TNCs was 42.4% of the parent firms' exports and 63.8% of their foreign affiliates' exports trading within the channels of the same TNC. The overall proportion of intra-firm trade for Japanese corporations was about 50%, while that for British firms was as much as 80%.

Much of this "trade" is the basis of internationalized production, the newest and one of the most important aspects of today's globalization process. Indeed, the UN estimates that if all international transactions of TNCs are taken into account, including the huge overseas sales of foreign affiliates, by the early 1990s "only about one third of international transactions are not associated with international production."

What is clear is that today's world economic integration is both deeper than and different from either of the two major epochs (1870–1914 and 1914–45) that preceded it. Trade and foreign investment compose a greater part of the world's economic activity. TNC's sit astride both of these aspects of integration and themselves form the major active force for integration.

As massive as these TNCs are, however, they are not monopolists in the classic sense. For one thing, even as they grow in size and consume one another through mergers and buyouts they proliferate in numbers. By the early 1990s, there were some 37,000 TNCs with 170,000 foreign affiliates. By 1994, only a couple of years later, there were 40,000 TNCs with 250,000 overseas affiliates. Even by the conventional definition they are not monopolies in the context of the world market. In any case, this conventional "quantity" theory of competition misses the deeper point that the process of capitalist accumulation is what drives competition, regardless of the number of players. Far from being incompatible with competition, the growth in the size of business, their accumulation of capital, pushes them toward greater clashes with one another. Indeed, it is the constant clash of the TNCs, driven by their need to accumulate, that gives rise to the crisis that had driven globalization, in fits and starts, itself.

## Crisis and Expansion since 1950

The deepening of international economic integration since the end of World War Two had not been a smooth or linear process. . . . Prior to the 1990s, most conventional (neoclassical) analyses saw the rise of the TNC as a consequence of the continuous growth of trade. The argument went that increased world trade created a larger market, which was in turn an incentive for businesses to seek economies of scale through growth. The organization of production across borders, in this theory, is explained largely by the savings in international transaction costs (of doing business between different firms) to be had from bringing production under one corporate roof. While more up-to-date neoclassical analyses admit that in recent years, on the contrary, it is the growth of TNCs and their foreign investment that has spurred the growth in trade, their theoretical framework remains untouched.

What is argued here is that the process of international integration has been led by overseas investment (accumulation), much of it in internationalized production systems. This has created more and larger TNCs, which, in turn, have promoted increased trade. A huge portion of the vale of this trade, as high as 80% by one estimate, is in the capital and intermediate goods consumed by businesses in the production process. In other words, it is the accumulation process that has expanded the world market and deepened the globalization process. With the beginning of the crisis of accumulation, however, trade shows down, along with growth in general, but, in reaction to the falling rate of profit, foreign direct investments speeds up as capital seeks higher profits.

After a period of recovery from the devastation of the war in Europe and Asia the rate at which trade grew accelerated. In the years from 1950 through 1973, world trade grew by an average of 7% a year. With the coming of recessions in 1974, the early 1980s and again in the early 1990s, trade slowed by almost half, to an annual average of 3.7% from 1973 through 1992. . . . [Foreign direct investment], on the other hand, doubled from 1960 through 1973, and then from 1973 through 1993 grew by ten times. This race of foreign investment ahead of trade and national economic growth became spectacular in the second half of the 1980s (between the recessions of 1981–83 and 1990–93), when FDI grew at twice the rate of trade and four times that of world-wide gross national product. With the coming of economic recovery after the recession of the early 1990s, FDI again leaped forward. . . .

It is in the years since the 1950s and the phenomenon of intra-firm trade became significant as a result of the internationalization of production. While national accumulation slowed down, international accumulation accelerated and the so-called "global factory" was born. Capital was attempting to solve its accumulation (profit-rate) problem by expanding abroad in search of even marginal increases in the rate of return. The process of globalization accelerated and deepened—and with it the crisis in employment.

# Sweated Labor in Cyberspace

### ANDREW ROSS

A few years ago, *Suck,* the irreverent webzine in San Francisco *(http://www.suck. com)* that offers daily comments on the latest media buzz, cunningly revealed that the staff of *Wired* magazine occupied a floor in a building full of garment sweatshops. *Wired* had been the town crier of the information revolution and an obligating booster for the global chamber of commerce that lives or dies by the NASDAQ index. The sweatshops were a chronic outbreak of an old disease that had once been contained, not unlike tuberculosis itself, the historic scourge of the turn-of-the-century garment industry. Here we had geeky Generation X wordsmiths test-driving the latest software geewhizzery just fifteen feet above the traditional labors of greenhorn immigrant seamstresses. Suddenly, the century-long gulf between the postindustrial high-tech world, for which *Wired* is the most glittering advertisement,

From Andrew Ross, "Sweated Labor in Cyberspace," *New Labor Forum* (Spring/Summer, 1999), pp. 47–56. Reprinted by permission of the author.

and the pre-industrial no-tech world for which the sweatshop is the most sordid advertisement, appeared to have dissolved.

In San Francisco's "Multi-Media Gulch," where parcels of the new Internet industries are located, this kind of juxtaposition is not uncommon. The degree of the contrast between these two workplaces—however—between the nineteenth and the twenty-first century workplace—is much more pronounced in New York City, where the ragged strip of "Silicon Alley" cuts through areas of old industrial loft spaces that were once, and are again, home to the burgeoning sweatshop sector of the garment industry. Manhattan's downtown concentration of webshops—those much romanticized laboratories of the brave new technological future—shares much of the same urban space as the new sweatshops, where patterns of work for large portions of the immigrant population increasingly resemble those in the very early years of the century, before the first elements of industrial democracy were adopted into law.

As it happens, the comparison between these workplaces has its echoes in the earlier period. Then, the sweatshop with its primitive mode of production and the cutter's artisanal loft coexisted with semiautomated workplaces that would very soon industrialize with economies of scale under the pull of the Fordist factory. Today, the sewing machines foot pedal is still very much in business, although no longer competing with steampower, of course, but with the CPU, which, at the higher end of garment production, is used to govern computer-assisted design, ensuring fast turnaround and just-in-time supplies for the volatile seasonal trade in fashion lines. In fact, the sewing machine—the basic sweatshop technology—has barely changed in almost one hundred and fifty years, which affords it a rather unusual place in industrial history. The main reason for its long survival has to do with the physical limpness of fabric. There is a portion of garment production that cannot be fully automated and that requires human attention to sewing and stitching and assembly. With a cheap labor supply in abundance, developing countries often begin their industrialization process in textiles and apparel, because of the low capital investment in the labor-intensive end of production.

In many of the free-trade export zones of the developing world, workplaces for electronic assembly keep company with those for garment assembly. In addition, in the industrial sectors of many other countries, workers in chip manufacture, data processing, and digital programming experience many of the same debilitating barriers to fair labor standards as do garment workers. Yet there has been much less attention paid to these workplaces in the public mind and the media. The glamour of high technology carries a powerful mystique, and its preeminence in industry has eclipsed its capacity for the moral abhorrence necessary to rectify exploitation. Are there lessons from recent anti-sweatshop campaigns that can be applied to combat labor abuses in this other industry?

There are many reasons for the flourishing of garment sweatshops, both in the poor countries of the world and in the old metropolitan cores. These include regional and global free-trade agreements, the advent of subcontracting as a universal principle, the shift of power toward large retailers and away from manufacturers, the weakening of the labor movement and labor legislation, and, last but not least, the transnational reach of fashion itself, especially among youth. The international mass consumer wants the latest fashion posthaste, which necessitates turnaround and flexibility at levels that disrupt all stable norms of industrial competition.

. . . [I]t's fair to say that public awareness is the conditions of low-wage garment labor is relatively far advanced. The public at least recognizes the situation, even if we choose, for the most part, to ignore the fact that much of the clothing we wear is made illegally and under atrocious conditions. The anti-sweatshop movement of recent years has been immensely successful in penetrating the public domain of media space. Part of this success is due to the repugnance attached to the term "sweatshop," which commands a moral power, second only to "slavery," to rouse public opinion. A more significant factor, however, has been the elastic nature of the movement's coalition-building. The involvement of interfaith and human rights groups, students, and NGOs with workers had offered a stunningly effective model for transnational activism. These coalitions have demonstrated that organized labor cannot go it alone, and that there is no alternative, in the age of global economies, to this kind of activism.

Ultimately, of course, the endpoint must lie in an appreciable alteration of consumption. The challenge is in making an impact at the point of sale; that is, reforming consumer psychology to the point that criteria of style, quality, and affordability are affected by appeals to the advantages of paying a living wage. Surprisingly, we are further forward than anyone could have imagined just a few years ago.

The same cannot be said of the high technology industry. The gulf between the fashion catwalk and the garment sweatshop is nowhere near as great as the gulf between the high-investment glitz and megahertz wizardy at the top of the cyberspace chain, and the electronic sweatshops at the bottom. Why is this the case?

### Whiz Kids or Cyberdrudges?

Cyberspace, (for want of a better term to describe the virtual worked of digital communication and e-commerce) is not simply a libertarian medium for free expression and wealth accumulation. It is a labor-intensive workplace. Masses of people work in cyberspace, or work to make cyberspace possible, a fact that receives virtually no recognition from the so-called digerati like John Perry Barlow or Kevin Kelly, who edit and write for *Wired* magazine, let alone the pundits and managers who are employed to pump hot air into the great Internet stock bubble. Indeed, it's fair to say that most people have little real sense of the material labor that produces their computer technologies, nor are they very attentive to the industrial uses to which these technologies are put in the workplaces of the world. Like all other sectors of the economy, the high-tech industries have been penetrated by the low-wage revolution—affecting everyone from the janitors who service Silicon Valley in California to the part-time programmers and designers who service Silicon Alley in New York. Just as Silicon Valley once provided a pioneering model for flexible postindustrial employment, Silicon Alley may be poised to deliver an upgrade.

New York's new media sector has seen the biggest job growth of any urban industry in the metropolitan area for decades. Web design, programming, and marketing in this industry accounted for over 100,000 new jobs in the last three years. Yet these are entirely nonunionized workplaces, plagued by overwork, low wages, flexible contracts, and job insecurity. Over half of the jobs are filled by contract employees of perma-temps, with no benefits or paid vacations. Seventy hour weeks without overtime are a way of life for webshop workers, who are commonly signed up on the promise that their "sweat equity" will lead to a pot of stock proceeds at the end of the rainbow. For the majority, the stock plan that will deliver the big payoff never comes. Startups have a high failure rate, and those companies that merge with giants like America Online, Microsoft, and Sun generate fortunes for their investors and founding entrepreneurs but seldom create any returns for employees. Upgrades in software programs can put skilled workers out of a job overnight. The average salary for full-timers in Silicon Alley is about $37,000 per year, which is hardly a starvation wage, but is still well below salaries of old media industries, like advertising, at $71,000, and television broadcasting, at $85,000.

Silicon Alley is the face of the future, not because its whizz kids are designing a brave new wired world, but because its new industry is a prescient example of the kind of workplace that skilled technicians will increasingly confront. Its structures of capital financing and the sheer volatility of its labor landscape make the new media workforces notoriously difficult to organize. As many traditional labor unions have been slow to use websites and Internet technologies in their own organizing efforts, organizing is almost nonexistent in the Internet industries themselves. . . .

## Going Down the Chain

Many of the readers of this article probably want their computers to go faster, and yet most people who work with computers, or according to schedules set by computers, already want them to go slower. For those who view the personal computer as an artisanal tool of comparative advantage with which to compete in the field of skills, resources, and rewards, it makes sense to respond to the heady promise of velocification in all of its forms: the relentless boosting of chip clock speed, of magnification of storage density, of faster traffic on Internet backbones, of higher baud rate modems, of hyperefficient database searches, and of rapid data-transfer techniques.

For workers who are not masters of their own work environment, the speed controls of technology are routinely used to regulate their labor. These forms of regulation are well documented—widespread workplace monitoring and electronic surveillance, with keyboard quotas and other automated measures geared to time every operation, from the length of bathroom visits to the wasted productivity claimed by personal e-mail. Software is programmed to control and monitor task performance. Occupationally, this world stretches from the high-turnover burger flippers at McDonald's to the workers in offshore data-entry pools in Asia and the Caribbean (and, arguably, stretches even further to include front-office managers, who complain about their accountability to inflexible productivity schedules).

Low-skilled information processing, in particular, is characterized by musculoskeletal and psychological disorders, chronic stress and fatigue, and reproductive problems. Women occupy a huge majority of low-skilled offshore data-entry jobs, while men dominate the professional end of the scale. In general, advanced automation has allowed the global outsourcing of low wage labor, and the wholesale replacement of human decision making by expert systems and smart tools. Our processed world thrives on undereducation, undermotivation, and underpayment; and it appears to be primarily aimed at the control of workers, rather than at tapping their potential for efficiency, let alone their native ingenuity.

For most low-wage employees who work with computers, there is simply nothing to be gained from going faster; it is not in their interests to do so, and so their ingenuity on the job is devoted to ways of slowing down the work regime, beating the system, and sabotaging its automated schedules. The cumulative loss of productivity from computer downtime caused by worker sabotage on the job is one of the biggest of all corporate secrets. This point alone helps explain the "productivity paradox": that is has yet to be empirically proven that the introduction of information technology into workplaces boosts productivity.

If we go further down the chain of high-tech production, we find ourselves in the semiconductor workplaces, where the operating machinery of computers is manufactured in the least unionized of all goods-producing industries. While 56.2 percent of steel workers, 54.6 percent of automobile workers, 43.8 percent of telecommunications workers, and 23.7 percent of workers in durable goods manufacturing overall are unionized, only 2.7 percent of workers in electronics and computers equipment belong to unions. One of the world's fastest-growing industrial sectors, semiconductor factories (or "fabs") have mostly been concentrated in the United States, Western Europe, and Japan, but the passage of NAFTA and GATT has extended the mobility of the industry. Lower wages and weak environmental standards in Southeast Asia, Central America, and the Caribbean have drawn off much of the new investment. Even within the United States, it is the Southwest, with its sparse union activity and softer environmental and safety regulations, that has attracted many of the new fabs. The new destinations for "toxic flight" are Albuquerque, Phoenix, and Austin.

The hazards to workers and to the environment in the sterile, dustless "clean rooms" of these fabs (designed to protect silicon wafers, not workers) are already excessive and are likely to multiply with each new generation of components. Semiconductor manufacturing (which produces over 220 billion chips a year) uses more highly toxic gases (including lethal ones like arsine and phosphine) and chemicals than any other industry, its plants discharge tons of toxic pollutants into the air, and they use millions of gallons of water each day; there are more groundwater contamination and EPA Superfund sites in Silicon Valley than anywhere else in the United States. The ecological footprint of a single silicon chip is massive.

Despite the public perception of these plants as light manufacturing workplaces, microchip workers suffer industrial illness at three times the average for other manufacturing workers, and studies routinely find significantly increased miscarriage rates and birth defect rates among women working in chemical handling jobs. The more common and well-documented illnesses include breast, uterine and stomach cancer, leukemia, asthma, vision impairment, and carpal tunnel syndrome. In many of these jobs, workers are exposed to the hundreds of different chemicals and over 700 compounds that can go into the production of a single work station, most of which is destined for technological obsolescence in a couple of years— 12 million computers are disposed of annually, which amounts to 300,000 tons of electronic trash that is difficult to recycle. Very little occupational health research exists that analyses the impact on the human body of combining several of these compounds, and research on reproductive hazards, in particular, has been seen as a women's issue and is therefore underfunded and underreported.

Increasingly, the "dirtier" processes of high-tech production are located in lower income communities with large immigrant populations in the United States, or are dispersed throughout the developing countries, augmenting existing patterns of environmental and economic injustice. With them will go modular industries like the printed circuit board sector and other electronic assembly operations, where immigrant workers, employed at rock-bottom wages, with even less benefits than workers in the clean rooms, use solders and solvents that are almost as toxic as those handled by chip workers. Large United States and Japanese companies are steadily relocating their fabrication lines to Thailand, Vietnam, Malaysia, Indonesia, Mexico, Panama, Costa Rica, and Brazil. In ten to fifteen years, the geography of high-tech global production may increasingly resemble that of the garment industry.

Fabrication flight is accelerated at the least sign of an organizing drive with teeth. Nonetheless, groups like the Silicon Valley Toxics Coalition (see *http://www. svtc.org*) have played a leading role in coordinating semiconductor activism, formulating the Silicon Principles, and petitioning companies like Intel, GTE, and Motorola to establish a code of conduct to protect the health, safety, and human rights of workers in their factories, and of communities where the factories are located. Through the Campaign for Responsible Technology, an international network is now being formed to create links with local labor, environmental, and human rights groups around the world. Much of the groundwork for this was laid at a European work hazards convention in the Netherlands in March 1998, which brought together activists with the common goal of holding companies to codes of conduct through the acceptance of independent workplace monitoring. Clearly, some kind of local accounting is needed, since transnational companies tend to export hazards to countries where labor is least organized and where media and government whistleblowing is least likely.

## Sullying the Name

The model for such a campaign already exists in the anti-sweatshop movement. Struggles for a workable code of conduct that respects worker safety, union rights, and a living wage already have a proven record of success—and failures. One of the more successful tactics has been to tarnish a company's name with high-profile media exposure. The integrity of a company's brand name is all-important, and such vulnerability is amply reflected in management's skittishness about sour publicity. A company must keep its brand name clean, because it is often the only thing that distinguishes its product from that of its market competitors. If that name is sullied it does not matter whether the company has access to the very cheapest labor pool in the world—all is lost.

The most recent round of anti-sweatshop campaigning has involved the integrity of some of the more prominent United States varsity names in a $2.5 billion sector of the garment industry. In the winter of 1998–99, college presidents were asked to review and sign a code of conduct governing the labor conditions under which licensed articles, bearing their college's name, are manufactured. This code of conduct had been prepared by the Collegiate Licensing Company (CLC) and was loosely based on the set of regulatory provisions drawn up by the Apparel Industry Partnership (AIP), a task force of garment companies, organized labor, and human rights and religious groups convened by the Clinton administration in 1996. At that point, virtually all of the labor, religious, and human rights groups had withdrawn from the AIP, in the understanding that its provisions were unenforceable. It is now widely accepted that the AIP agreement is virtually consistent with current industry policies and will not have any appreciable impact on the exploitative practices associated with those policies. The CLC code ran into student opposition for much the same reason, relating specifically to two points:

1. [A]bsence of a "disclosure" provision, whereby garment companies would be required to disclose the locations of factories where their products are manufactured or assembled. Without such disclosure, it is impossible to monitor the working conditions at these factories;

2. [A]bsence of a provision guaranteeing a living wage, as opposed to a minimum wage. In most countries, including the United States, the minimum wage does not ensure subsistence levels of living for working families and is therefore a subpoverty wage.

The national mobilization of students, through United Students Against Sweatshops, resulted in major concessions on both of these points. At many campuses, students secured agreements similar to an initial settlement reached with the Duke University administration. Under such agreements, colleges would pull out of the CLC if full disclosure of factories did not occur within twelve months. They are also committed to funding interim studies on the criteria for a living wage in countries around the world. Plainly attentive to the need to keep their names "sweat-free," college presidents were pulled into the bargaining pit, while the media coverage of student sit-ins and mass rallies expanded public consciousness of the issues. The campaign reaffirmed what was rapidly becoming common sense—no one wants the name of their company or institution mentioned in the same paragraph as that of Nike.

Will the same strategies work in high-tech industries? There is no reason why the brand names of AT&T, Phillips, Intel, IBM, Hewlett Packard, Toshiba, Samsung, and Fugitsu cannot by publicity shamed in the same way as those of Nike, The Gap, Guess, Phillips Van Heusen, and Disney have been. Name recognition of such companies has long been a fixture of the mass market and is increasingly a mark of distinction on the advertising landscape. Above all, it is important not to underestimate public outrage. The public is far from apathetic; public concern has been inflamed by revelations about labor abuses in the industrialized and non-industrialized world, where workers are physically, sexually, and economically abused to save ten cents on the cost of a pricey item of clothing. Consumption of high-tech goods, unlike clothing, is not yet a daily necessity, but the rate of market penetration in the last twenty years has been phenomenal. It will not be too long before high-tech household items are as disposable, and subject to the same volatile seasonal turnover, as fashion goods. At that point, the high-tech market will be fully within the orbit of consumer politics, on the scale of boycott threats.

In concluding, perhaps it is worth reviewing why so little attention is paid to high-tech labor issues in the flood of commentary directed at cyberspace. One reason certainly is the lack of any tradition of organized labor in these industries. The fight against the garment sweatshop was a milestone in trade union history and gave rise to the first accords on industrial democracy. The recent campaigns have also been on the leading edge of the resurgent labor movement, at least in the United States. Nothing comparable exists in the high-tech workplaces of the new information order. They have emerged in a climate intrinsically hostile to the principles of trade unionism. Indeed, high-tech industry lobbyists have been zealous leaders in efforts to undermine the existing protections of labor legislation.

A second reason has to do with ideology of the "clean machine." In the public mind, the computer is still viewed as the product of magic, not industry. It is as if computers fall from the skies; they work in ways that are entirely beyond our understanding. The fact that we can repair our cars but not our computers does not help. As a result, the process of manufacturing is obscured and mystified.

A third reason is related to the special treatment afforded to microelectronics by state managers, who are aware of the industry's strategic importance to the national economy. Currently, nations assess their competitive standing in world trade by the growth of their advanced technology sectors, and so government's regulatory eye often looks the other way when abuses and hazards proliferate.

Lastly, there is the utopian rhetoric employed by the intellectuals and pundits of cyberspace. Choose any one of the bestselling books that extol the praises of the new frontier of virtual life[;] chances are that there will be no mention of the crippling workplace injuries sustained in the manufacturing of the new clean machines, nor any recognition of the cruel outsourcing economies that export low-wage labor to piecework contractors, whether local or far-flung. There is a complete and utter disconnection between the public discourse of the new media whizz kids, intellectuals, and entrepreneurs, and any awareness of high-tech workplace hazards. As long as we separate the world of ideas and high-tech buzz from the testimony and experience of the workplace, people simply will not make connections between the two.

The success of anti-sweatshop garment organizing have come as a surprise to many seasoned activists, long accustomed to being shut out of the media, to dealing with the often stony indifference of the public, and to watching the cruel march of corporate armies across the killing fields of labor. In the case of information technology, the time is ripe for capitalizing on the climate for such successes. Perhaps we can exercise a little foresight and anticipate the public appetite for responding to such abuses. The history of the Internet should remind us that nothing is impossible, and what was unimaginable just a few days ago is a fact of life today.

# The Nanny Visa

## GRACE CHANG

The notion that immigrants can be treated as expendable commodities, to be used then expelled from the country or simply from any public concern, has guided immigration law and labor practice throughout US history. This view can be traced back to at least 1911, when the Dillingham Immigration Commission reported on the particular advantages of using Mexican laborers: "While they are not easily assimilated, this is of no very great importance as long as most of them return to their native land. In the case of the Mexican, he is less desirable as a citizen than

From Grace Chang, *Disposable Domestics: Immigrant Women Workers in the Global Economy* (Boston: South End Press, 2000), pp. 93–95, 97–116. Reprinted by permission of South End Press.

as a laborer." One will find this attitude to be thriving today in any work site where there are immigrant women, although it may be couched in more covert rhetoric. The tale of Filipina/o workers at Casa San Miguel, a nursing home in suburban Concord, California, illustrates this all too well.

Most of the workers identify the unfair termination of sixty-five-year-old Natie Llever as the beginning of the struggle. Llever had been working at Casa San Miguel as a Certified Nursing Assistant (CNA) when she injured her back while trying to move a patient in December 1991. When she reported to work three months later, she was told by the director of nursing, Esther Van Buren, to quit her job. In other words, she had been terminated. According to Llever, Van Buren said: "You can no longer do this job because of your age. You are a sickly woman, and we want a young and strong worker for this job." Ben Medina, a coworker, said that the Filipina/o workers "hearts began to burn" when Llever was fired, and they knew they had to find a way to challenge this unfair treatment. They began organizing to unionize the staff, 87 percent of whom were Filipina/o.

Demonstrating outside the facility before the union election in September 1992, workers marched and shouted *"Makibaka"* ("Let's fight" in Tagalog) and *"Huwag Matakot"* ("Don't get scared"), flying in the face of one of their employers' most egregious practices, an English-only policy. Workers active in the union reported that, once they realized their intention to form a union, their employers stepped up selective enforcement of the English-only policy against Filipina/os, along with "extreme verbal and mental abuse."

Reports of these worker abuses prompted Filipina/o community and religious leaders in the Bay Area to form the Citizens' Commission for Justice at Casa San Miguel. In public hearings before the Commission in December 1992, several workers, including those charging unfair termination, testified about workplace abuses they endured at the hands of their employers, Lenore and Moshe Shenker. Ben Medina reported that the Shankers had wrongfully fired or suspended all of the strongest union leaders and had openly made racial slurs and threats. For example in a meeting in July 1992, Moshe Shenker screamed at the Filipina/o workers, "If you don't understand English, just bow your heads and go back to your country. I'll call the police and send you back to the Philippines. You Filipinos are dumb-headed." Medina pointed out that all of the Filipina/o workers were citizens or permanent residents, with only one exception. . . .

The workers testified that they were terminated ostensibly for violating the English-only policy, although they understood clearly that these were trumped-up charges to cover the real intent, to intimidate and harass leadership in the union movement. One CNA, Caridad Gusman, said she was reprimanded for addressing an older CNA in Tagalog using a title of respect, "Auntie Love." On another occasion, she was reprimanded by her supervisor, Thelma Smith, when a nurse asked her name one day and she responded, "Caridad." . . .

Although the workers voted to join SEIU Local 250 as early as September 25, 1992, the Shenkers refused to negotiate with the union. The Shenkers carried their resistance to great lengths, appealing the election and thus delaying negotiations for years. The National Labor Relations Board rejected the Shenkers' objections and certified the union on April 8, 1994. Meanwhile, Local 250 filed charges against Casa San Miguel with the Equal Employment Opportunity Commission (EEOC) on

January 31, 1994, claiming that the employers "deliberately and intentionally discriminated against individuals . . . because of their national origin of the Philippines or because of their Filipino ancestry." The union also filed charges of age discrimination on behalf of Natie Llever, 62, and Bienvendio Mercado, 65. Finally, the complainants charged that Casa San Miguel's English-only rule violated their rights under California Code Section 12940 by creating a hostile environment for some workers because of their national origin.

According to EEOC guidelines, a rule requiring employees to speak only English on the job violates the 1964 Civil Rights Act unless the employer can show that this is "necessary for conducting business." If the employer believes that an English-only rule is "critical for business purposes," then the employer is responsible for informing employees when they must speak English and the consequences for not doing so. Otherwise, any "negative employment decision" based on breaking an English-only policy will be considered evidence of discrimination. The guidelines state that prohibiting workers from speaking their main language can create "an atmosphere of inferiority, isolation, and intimidation based on national origin." . . .

. . . In many cases, like Casa San Miguel, the point of English-only policies is not exclusively social control but also—and in some cases, primarily—labor control. The goal is not actually to encourage or even force people to assimilate, learn English, or become "American," but to make the assertion that immigrants or people of color are unassimilable, incapable, or unwilling to learn English or become "American," and thereby to exclude them from workplaces or society once they have served their purpose. As in the case of Casa San Miguel, English-only rules serve as a covert tool for ejecting immigrant speakers of a particular language out of a work site, rather than infusing "American" culture into the site or the workers. . . .

This view of immigrants as unassimilable seems to diverge from the rationale behind the "Americanization" programs of the 1910s that 1920s, which operated on the assumption that immigrants could and should be assimilated and that immigrant women could play key roles in either the cultural maintenance or transformation of their communities. While these ideologies appear to contradict each other, they can be seen as two sides of the same coin. The early 20th-century programs and contemporary practices share much the same goals: capturing immigrant women's labor separate from their human needs or cultural attributes. Indeed, in the case of the Americanization programs, immigrant women were targeted as potential agents to aid in the destruction of their traditional immigrant cultures. Through working in the homes of their American employers, immigrant women were to shed their own "backward" cultures and learn the values and habits of good American homemakers and "worker-machines." Furthermore, they were deputized with the task of guiding their children to adopt these new ways in preparation for their service roles in the new industrial order. . . .

## Alien-ated Labor

Identifying immigrant women either as unassimilable or as agents of assimilation into American society serves the same purpose: to capture their low-wage or unpaid labors as worker-machines without human needs or rights. Employers attempt to justify this extraction by constructing immigrant women as unable to absorb

"American" culture and unable to contribute value to "American" society, beyond destroying their own cultures. The contemporary rhetoric, de-emphasizing or ignoring immigrant women's potential roles as cultural transformers, may reflect only the "modern" preference of employers for exploiting immigrant women's productive functions over their reproductive services. Or, as Maria Mies observes in *Patriarchy and Accumulation on a World Scale,* First World efforts to increase the productivity of Third World women through education, on the one hand, and their knowledge and willingness to practice contraception, on the other, are "part and parcel of the same strategy to integrate poor women's supposedly underutilized productivity into the global accumulation process."

Similarly, June Nash explains that the practice of distributing birth-control pills to women workers at the checkout clock in *maquiladoras* reflects the multinational corporations' multiple goals of "intensifying the appropriation of surplus and accelerating the pace of capital accumulation—but in such a way as to destroy the reproduction of society." In other words, global capital prefers to exploit women as producers, rather than reproducers, and can accomplish this through a variety of tactics, including outlawing or otherwise preventing women of color and immigrant women's cultural and biological reproduction. Increasing immigrant women's production while limiting their reproduction facilitates utilizing immigrant women as expendable workers by ensuring that they will not bear more unwanted consumers or expand a population that has needs.

Several scholars have analyzed the systematic use of people of color and immigrants as expendable workers or as a reserve labor army in the United States. Robert Blauner's theory of internal colonialism, developed in *Racial Oppression in America,* proposes that the state channels people of color into a colonized labor force within the United States by restricting their physical and social mobility and political participation. Elaborating on this model in *Race and Class in the Southwest,* Mario Barrera observes that immigration policies allowing for the "recruitment" or importation of foreign laborers are coupled with policies denying these laborers the rights of citizen workers, thus rendering them more easily exploitable. In *Inside the State: The Bracero Program, Immigration and the INS,* Kitty Calavita proposes that the state formulates immigration policy not only to accommodate capital's demands for cheap labor, but to fulfill its own agenda. Calavita says that the state seeks to maximize the utility of immigrants as laborers while minimizing its own costs and responsibilities associated with maintaining a surplus labor army of immigrants.

. . . A number of examples of migrant contract-labor programs in recent US history illustrate how the state fulfills this agenda, maintaining a reserve labor force of immigrants without having to provide citizen-worker rights or benefits. The Bracero program involved hundreds of thousands of Mexican, primarily male, migrant workers imported to labor in agriculture in the American Southwest in the 1940s through 1960s. While the conventional wisdom is that contract labor programs are a thing of the past, such programs are not merely a phenomenon of distant history, as many people may think. Furthermore, efforts to resurrect something closely resembling the Bracero program are underway in a number of industries. . . . [Proposals have been] made to bring in female migrants as domestic, child-care, or elderly-care workers under a special, temporary worker visa called the "nanny visa."

## The Bracero Program: An Army of "Arm-Men"

. . . [T]he Bracero program is one of the best examples of systematic, government-sanctioned exploitation of migrant laborers. The program was instituted in response to wartime demands for labor by Southwestern agricultural employers. Although it was originally conceived of as a temporary measure, it allowed for the importation of hundreds of thousands of Mexican men each year from 1942 to 1964. "Bracero" translates roughly as "farm hand" (from "brazo," Spanish for arm) and literally as "arm-man." Calavita suggests that this term reflects "the function these braceros were to play in the American economy, supplying a pair of arms and imposing few obligations on the host society as human beings."

While certain guidelines were established in an agreement with the Mexican government to give braceros basic protections, these were rarely enforced. Braceros tried in vain to report poor conditions to Mexican consuls in the United States. Among the most common complaints were substandard food and housing, inadequate wages, harsh working conditions, and insufficient work during the contract period. It was a common practice of growers to over-contract or apply for more braceros than they anticipated needing, or to keep braceros unemployed for portions of a day or even for weeks at a time because of bad weather or a late harvest. Some employers maneuvered a system much like debt bondage, charging braceros for room and board during these off-periods and deducting these expenses from future wages. Testifying to the subhuman treatment of these men, one Border Patrol memo from Arizona reported that braceros were "fumigated prior to their departure to the United States . . . by spraying them [with] airplanes, much in the same manner as agricultural fields are sprayed." Once they arrived in the United States and were contracted to certain growers, braceros were obligated to stay on these farms, rather than migrating to the cities for work, until they were to be returned to Mexico at the end of their contract periods. . . . One immigration official told . . . [a] President[ial] Commission: "The contract worker is tied down to one employer [and] is not a free agent to leave whenever he desires and seek more lucrative employment elsewhere."

The wage-setting process was also maneuvered to the advantage of growers. Theoretically, the Bureau of Employment Security (BES), under the Department of Labor, was responsible for certifying that domestic labor had been sought at "prevailing wages," but the BES merely took the growers' lead. Growers offered employment to domestic laborers at a certain wage and, when they had no takers, could then contract braceros at the wage found unacceptable by domestic workers. Although technically growers were eligible for braceros only if there was a labor shortage, they could set wages low enough so that domestic workers would not apply and thus create the necessary preconditions. . . .

Despite its origins as a "temporary" measure, the Bracero program operated officially or otherwise for more than two decades to import an uninterrupted supply of close to 5 million workers in total. Many scholars agree that the Bracero program had two enduring consequences after its termination in 1964. First, it was a major stimulus for illegal migration from Mexico to the United States during and subsequent to the program. Second, as Barrera says, it "established a type of worker who was clearly set off as a Mexican national only temporarily in the United States."

More broadly, it set the precedent for the temporary or "guestworker" programs used extensively by US employers to secure cheap contract labor.

The nonimmigrant, temporary visa is understood by scholars to be a legacy of the Bracero era. Now a staple of US immigration practice, it can be issued once the Department of Labor certifies that there is a shortage of domestic (that is, citizen or resident) workers in any given industry. Those entering under this type of visa are conferred nonimmigrant status and are presumed to be residing temporarily in the United States to work, not intending to remain. Much like braceros, guestworkers are seen as offering the advantages of being tied to one employer or sector of the economy and imposing few costs to the "host" society.

Guestworkers have probably been used most often in the agricultural sector, where the concept originated. For example, three provisions were included in the Immigration Reform and Control Act (IRCA) of 1986 as concessions to agribusiness, which protested that they would suffer a shortage of workers. First, undocumented workers who had worked for 90 days in agriculture between May 1985 and May 1986 could be given temporary legal-resident status as special agricultural workers (SAWs). If the SAW pool dropped below sufficient numbers, additional workers could be admitted as replenishment agricultural workers (RAWs). Finally, if growers were unable to find legal resident or citizen workers, they could apply for temporary workers under H-2A visas.

In 1986, Pete Wilson, then a US senator, was instrumental in pushing for these provisions to be included in IRCA, over objections by some House Democrats that temporary workers would most likely be subject to exploitation. Many critics have since observed that these programs, like Bracero program, stimulate or exacerbate "illegal" immigration. Yet growers continue to lobby vigorously with their friends in Washington for such programs. . . . [Shortly] after the passage of Proposition 187, [a 1994 initiative penalizing undocumented immigrants], California growers clamored in Congress for a guestworker program that would bring people from Mexico and elsewhere to work in the United States temporarily as field hands. Ironically, then-Governor Pete Wilson, the self-proclaimed champion of eradicating the "illegal immigration problem," endorsed the proposals.

Some critics pointed to the history of the Bracero program. Others pointed out that growers already could avail themselves of H-2A visas for temporary workers. But most growers rely on the ready supply of undocumented workers and cannot be bothered with the red tape of the H-2A program or its requirements to provide workers with free housing, transportation, and higher wages. Growers seek, an ultimately convenient, super-exploitable labor pool. As Don Villarejo, director of the California Institute for Rural Studies in Davis, said, "What growers are interested in is a 1-800-SEND-A-WORKER program." With great regularity, proposals are raised in Congress to make guestworker programs even more favorable to growers. Recent proposals would provide for guestworkers to be imported during peak harvest season on two- or three-month visas, tied to particular employers, with no option to apply for legal immigrant status. Wages would be set at the "prevailing wage," rather than the "adverse effect wage," the rate required under current provisions to prevent wage depression caused by guestworker importation. The employers will be able to set wages according to results of their own prevailing wage studies. Moreover, 25 percent of the guestworkers' wage would be withheld in a trust fund until the workers leave the country.

A number of protective measures for guestworkers and employer obligations would be wiped out under such proposals. While current provisions require the Department of Labor to certify that there is a shortage of domestic workers in the region, this would not be required under the proposed programs. Employers would not be required to provide housing or transportation from the workers' country of origin. Nor would they be required to provide at least 75 percent of seasonal work or pay its equivalent, as is now guaranteed under H-2A provisions. As Mark Schacht, deputy director of California Rural Legal Assistance (CRLA) Foundation, said: "If the employer fires you for any reason, you're out of status on your visa and you're subject to deportation. Every guestworker that come into this country knows the employer has that power over them." . . .

## The "Nanny Visa"

In 1953, a group of women in El Paso, Texas, organized the Association for Legalized Domestics. Contrary to what its name suggested, this group of Anglo women were housewives calling for a program to facilitate hiring Mexican women to work for them as maids. The association proposed that potential workers could be screened for age, health problems, and criminal records. Employees were to earn a minimum wage of $15 a week and were to be given room, board, and one and a half days off on weekends. A group of Chicana women working as maids in El Paso organized to try to block these efforts. They protested that the housewives merely wanted to import Mexicana women to work for lower wages, while local workers were readily available but demanded higher wages. Ultimately, the association's efforts to enlist government support in obtaining cheap "household help" was frustrated when the Department of Justice rejected the proposal.

Forty years later, proposals with much the same goals as those of the El Paso housewives' association emerged in the wake of the Zoë Baird controversy. When Baird lost the nomination for US attorney general because she had employed two "illegal aliens" as a baby-sitter and a driver, she attempted to defend herself, claiming: "I was forced into this dilemma to care for my child. . . . In my hope to find appropriate child care for my son, I gave too little emphasis to what was described to me as a technical violation of the law."

Apparently, this did garner the sympathies of many people. While some condemned Baird for what was seen as a flagrant violation of the law and a white-collar crime, other flocked to her defense. Many argued that what she did should not be considered a crime, that the law should be changed to make it easier (and legal) for working women or two-career couples to do what she had done. Writing for the *New York Times,* Deborah Sontag reported: "Many say, at the least, that household employers should be exempt, or that household workers should get a special visa." Sontage quoted sociologist Philip Kasnitz: "A law that forces thousands of illegal immigrants and middle-class families to engage in criminal activity desperately needs to be reformed." Soon after the Baird controversy began to quiet down, proposals began to be circulated to allow private household employers to legally hire those who might otherwise be "illegal" immigrant workers. . . .

Responses to the Baird controversy indicate that neither heightened "awareness" nor fear of the law have influenced household employers to change their practices or attitudes about the use of immigrant workers, undocumented or otherwise.

One woman explained that she would continue to flout the law, employing an un-documented Peruvian as a housekeeper: "After Zoë Baird, my husband and I dis-cussed whether it was now an issue for us, and decided that neither of us will ever run for office." Another woman, seeking specifically to hire an "illegal" immigrant, said: "I want someone who cannot leave the country, who doesn't know anyone in New York, who basically does not have a life. I want someone who is completely dependent on me and loyal to my family." These comments should give us pause before considering home-care worker visa proposals relying on the good graces or ethics of household employers to uphold their employees' rights.

The experience to date with nonimmigrant, temporary worker visas in sectors besides agriculture has been just as bad as in the agricultural sector. For example, in response to the claim that trained nurses were in short supply, hospitals were allowed to bring in skilled nurses through H-1 visas under the Nursing Relief Act of 1989. Many Filipinas entered the United States under the H-1 visa classification in the late 1980s and early 1990s. Cathleen Yasuda of the Asian Pacific American Labor Alliance says that during this period, many schools were set up in the Philippines designed just for the export of women to be H-1 nurses in the United States. She adds that H-1 nurses typically work six or seven days a week, 12 hours a day, often for two employers. Maria Griffith-Cañas, lead organizer in Local 250's campaign at Casa San Miguel, reports that in 1995 she found 18 H-1 nurses from the Philippines living in the basement of Golden Cross nursing home in Santa Cruz. They were woken up at any time to go on duty and were paid what amounted to $1 an hour after various "fees" were deducted. The union succeeded in having the operation shut down, and Griffith-Cañas pleaded with Philippines President Ramos to take measures to ensure that Filipina migrants would be informed of their rights as H-1 workers.

## Duty-Free Employers

When US employers lobby for access to cheap immigrant laborers yet at the same time call for an end to the "illegal" immigration problem, it poses quite a contra-diction. Illegality lies not with the immigrants who do the most scorned work for a pittance; the true crimes are perpetrated by exploitative employers of undocumented workers and by the government, which facilitates these abuses.

Several immigration scholars have proposed that illegal immigration is not merely tolerated but actively encouraged by the US government. Much historical evidence suggests that the INS and Border Patrol function to regulate the flow of immigration to ensure a reserve army of labor. For example, immigration officials reported in 1950 that farmers would complain to the Commissioner of Immigration during cotton-picking time to create some pretense for an investigation to disrupt border patrol work. During harvest season, Border Patrol officials and growers traditionally had an implicit agreement that efforts to round-up or deport illegal immigrants would be eased. Kitty Calavita documents that lax border enforcement during harvests "seems to have been the official policy through much of the 1940s and early 1950s." . . .

. . . Calavita points to an unofficial policy after 1954 that braceros would not be regarded as prospective immigrants, or that immigrant visas were not to be granted to Mexican farmworkers. This potentially controversial policy was adopted in a secret meeting between top State Department and INS officials. Calavita says that the policy was designed to preserve the vulnerability of Mexican agricultural workers inherent in their bracero status. This policy provides another good example of how the state acts to render immigrant workers more easily exploitable and simultaneously limits its own ethical and financial responsibility to these workers.

In the contemporary period, this pattern of state complicity continues. The federal government persists in creating a militarized border by pouring money into increasing Border Patrol efforts, using high-technology equipment and building high-security fences and steel walls at border cities. Moreover, while employer sanctions were instituted ostensibly to reduce the employment and abuses of undocumented workers, they have actually functioned to facilitate these abuses by making all immigrant workers more vulnerable to retaliation for organizing. Many other provisions in current immigrant law enabling employers to avoid prosecution or penalties for employing undocumented workers suggest that this may be the real goal of such laws—to enable immigration agencies to secure the cooperation of employers without imposing penalties, just as in the Bracero era.

The 1992 Federal Commission on Agricultural Workers found a number of provisions exempting farmers from providing their workers with overtime pay, housing with toilets, unemployment insurance, workers' compensation, or the right to organize. The commission recommended that this system of "agricultural protectionism" would have to be tackled to control "illegal" immigration. Expanding on this observation, one might say that the illegal and abusive practices of employers of undocumented and other vulnerable immigrant workers will not be remedied until "employer protectionism" is ended.

In March 1995, New York State Senator Frank Padavan introduced a five-bill package prohibiting the use of the state funds for health, education, and welfare for undocumented immigrants. Padavan said that the legislation was drafted "in the spirit of California's Proposition 187." Clearly, US lawmakers will continue to attempt to "have it both ways"—that is, to have an endless supply of immigrants as cheap laborers without having to provide basic rights and protections for them as workers and human beings. . . . None of these measures suggest that we punish exploitative employers or require them to share the "costs" of the immigrant labor they rely on by providing decent wages or benefits. Instead, they propose that we punish immigrant women and children by denying them critical nutrition, medical care, and schooling.

### "Caring Till It Hurts"

Immigrant women workers may battle internalized forces, as well. Dominant US ideology identifies women as care takers and women of color/Third World women . . . as servants to nurture and clean up after First World elites. This may reinforce roles often defined for immigrant women in their home countries as dutiful daughters, mothers, and wives, raised in cultures emphasizing respect for elders and the protection of children. Explains Maria Griffith-Cañas, who emigrated from El Salvador and worked in convalescent homes for many years before she began organizing home- and health-care workers in SEIU Local 250: "You see minorities as the ones tending because our cultures say that we care for elders."

The workers she organizes now in nursing homes around the East Bay tell of grueling work conditions at the same time that they express great emotional attachment to and concern for their patients. A typical day shift begins at 7:30 a.m. and ends at 3:30 p.m., with a half-hour lunch break, and usually entails tending to six or seven patients each for two or three hours, including waking, bathing, toileting or "diapering," dressing, and seating them in wheelchairs for lunch by 11 a.m., then returning them to bed. Many have done this work as CNAs for years, earning from $5.39 per hour as a starting wage to a maximum of $7 per hour, earned by one woman who had worked in the industry for nine years.

Many of the workers are somewhat elderly themselves, and are tested by the physically demanding nature of the work. A report by SEIU, "Caring Till It Hurts," documents that nursing-home workers are also at great risk of assaults by patients suffering some form of dementia and of injuries from lifting and moving patients, particularly when there is understaffing and outmoded equipment. In response to these high injury rates, employers have introduced an insidious invention in nursing homes around the country called "safety bingo." Whenever a week passes without staff reporting an injury, they draw a bingo number. If an injury is reported, everyone has to throw their bingo card out and start over. The grand prize is a color television. A poster announcing "safety bingo" was posted prominently in the lunchroom of a Santa Cruz facility I visited in 1998. I witnessed one associate administrator congratulating the shop steward there: "You're tough, Reina. What has it been, eight or nine years since you have called in sick?" . . .

Even amidst their employers' assaults on them, many of the workers at Casa San Miguel could not bring themselves to leave their patients. Ireno Llever recalled that worker morale was so low after Shenker's "dumb-headed" remark that "We wanted to resign but . . . we just couldn't leave the residents." Ultimately, of course, they were fired. The statement of Ben Medina, one of the Casa San Miguel workers, captures well the beliefs that may motivate many immigrants—men and women—who work as care-takers. Medina represented the group of aggrieved workers in introducing the testimony before the Citizens' Commission for Justice at Casa San Miguel:

> Our main duty as health-care workers is to give our utmost and sincere service to the residents. We are to love and respect them because we know the residents are not there by choice, and they need our care, love, and attention. For this, the residents pay our wages, which we, in turn, use to feed our families. This career we have chosen—to take care of the elderly—comes naturally to us, as we Filipinos believe and practice respect and dignity to our elders. This is part of our culture that we will always practice and are proud of.

Cathleen Yasuda, a longtime union leader in the health-care industry, encountered similar beliefs, citing them as one obstacle in organizing RNs and CNAs. Yasuda noted that health-care professional are often "caregivers" (in the popular usage of the term) and "codependent." Standing up for themselves is "something they won't do if it's at the possible risk of the patients." Only recently have people begun to see that hospitals are corporations concerned with profit and not with care, she explained. Thus, her new organizing tactic is to market their campaigns as an issue of quality of patient care. Nurses "will go out on the streets for that, then they begin to see that better wages and conditions will attract better nurses."

My aim here is not to suggest that immigrant women are in need of feminist consciousness-raising or politicization, but to suggest that immigrant women's culturally inscribed values and identities may play into the hands of employers eager to capture these women's "labors of love" for themselves, their dependents, and clients. Thus, employers are able to exploit immigrant women's beliefs and roles that may be deeply engrained. When these ideologies are formalized in government policy and employer practice, immigrant women are doomed to become disposable workers. . . .

While the proposals for a home-care worker visa . . . did not gain momentum, similar policy proposals will undoubtedly arise again. When they do, it will be crucial that provisions are made to ensure fair wages and conditions for household workers and some means of holding employers accountable to these standards. Without these, immigrant women are in danger of becoming the new "braceras"—a pair of arms to rock the cradle or scrub the floors for their employers, then go home tired and empty-handed to their own children.

## ✣ F U R T H E R   R E A D I N G

Barber, Benjamin. *Jihad vs. McWorld: How Globalism and Tribalism Are Re-Shaping the World* (1996).

Bensman, David, and Roberta Lynch. *Rusted Dreams: Hard Times in a Steel Community* (1988).

Bluestone, Barry, and Bennett Harrison. *The Great U-Turn: Corporate Restructuring and the Polarizing of America* (1988).

Bonacich, Edna, and Richard P. Appelbaum. *Behind the Label: Inequality in the Los Angeles Apparel Industry* (2000).

Bowles, Samuel, David Gordon, and Thomas Weisskopf. *Beyond the Waste Land* (1982).

Chang, Grace. *Disposable Domestics: Immigrant Women Workers in the Global Economy* (2000).

Christensen, Kathleen. *Women and Home-Based Work: The Unspoken Contract* (1988).

Cowie, Jefferson. *Capital Moves: RCA's Seventy-Year Quest for Cheap Labor* (1999).

Frank, Dana. *Buy American: The Untold Story of Economic Nationalism* (2000).

Freeman, Richard, and James L. Medoff. *What Do Unions Do?* (1984).

Galbraith, James K. *Created Unequal: The Crisis in American Pay* (1998).

Garson, Barbara. *The Electronic Sweatshop* (1988).

Goldfield, Michael. *The Decline of Organized Labor in the United States* (1987).

Gordon, David. *Fat and Mean: The Corporate Squeeze of Working American and the Myth of Managerial "Downsizing"* (1996).

Holland, Max. *When the Machine Stopped: A Cautionary Tale from Industrial America* (1990).

Hondagneu-Sotelo, Pierrette. *Doméstica: Immigrant Workers Cleaning and Caring in the Shadows of Affluence* (2001).

Kingsolver, Barbara. *Holding the Line: Women in the Great Arizona Mine Strike of 1983* (1989).

Kochan, Thomas, Robert Mckersie, and Harry Katz. *The Transformation of American Industrial Relations* (1986).

Louie, Miriam C. Y. *Sweatshop Warriors* (2001).

Lamphere, Louise, et al., eds. *Newcomers in the Workplace: Immigrants and the Restructuring of the U.S. Economy* (1994).

McCall, Leslie. *Complex Inequality: Gender, Class and Race in the New Economy* (2001).

Milkman, Ruth. *Farewell to the Factory: Auto Workers in the Late Twentieth Century* (1997).

Moody, Kim. *Workers in a Lean World: Unions in the International Economy* (1997).

Nelson, Margaret K., and Joan Smith. *Working Hard and Making Do: Surviving in Small Town America* (1999).

Noble, David. *Forces of Production* (1984).

Parker, Mike, and Jane Slaughter. *Choosing Sides: Unions and the Team Concept* (1988).

Perusek, Glenn, and Kent Worcester. *Trade Union Politics: American Unions and Economic Change, 1960s–1990s* (1995).

Piore, Michael, and Charles Sabel. *The Second Industrial Divide: Possibilities for Prosperity* (1984).

Ross, Andrew, ed. *No Sweat: Fashion, Free Trade, and the Rights of Garment Workers* (1997).

Serrin, William. *Homestead: The Glory and Tragedy of an American Steel Town* (1999).

Shaiken, Harley. *Work Transformed: Automation and Labor in the Computer Age* (1985).

Vanderbilt, Tom. *The Sneaker Book: Anatomy of an Industry and an Icon* (1998).

Zuboff, Shoshana. *In the Age of the Smart Machine: The Future of Work and Power* (1988).

CHAPTER
15

# *New Labor, New Century*

*" 'Organized Labor.' Say those words, and your heart sinks. I am a labor lawyer, and my heart sinks. Dumb, stupid, organized labor; this is my cause."*

*Thus did Thomas Geoghegan assert the despair and the commitment that were the dual themes of his 1991 memoir, a battle-scarred account of the contemporary industrial scene during a Chicago winter that chilled union hearts like the winter wind off Lake Michigan. The title of his book said it all:* Which Side Are You On? Trying to Be for Labor When It's Flat on Its Back.

*The union movement lost strikes and members during the 1980s and early 1990s, but its greatest defeat came in the realm of ideas, energy, and hope. The AFL-CIO was hardly monolithic, and there were thousands of dedicated, imaginative activists within its ranks, many militants who fought against leadership complacency. But at the very top, this steamship of an organization seemed adrift. Lane Kirkland, who had succeeded George Meany as AFL-CIO president in 1980, did sponsor two huge "Solidarity Day" mobilizations on the Washington, D.C., mall, but after the end of the Cold War, the defeat of President Bill Clinton's health reform, and the Republican capture of Congress in 1994, his cautious, conservative leadership collapsed.*

*In a rare internal union challenge, Kirkland was ousted from the AFL-CIO presidency in 1995 and replaced by an insurgent slate lead by John Sweeney, who had almost doubled the size of the Service Employees International Union during his fifteen-year presidency. This revolt was half palace coup, half nascent social movement. Sweeney was no radical, but he did recognize that unless the AFL-CIO began to organize millions of new workers, the labor movement would soon wither away. Sweeney represented a wing of the trade union leadership—largely composed of the old industrial unions and those institutions organizing service and government workers—whose most clear-sighted elements had come to understand that the labor movement's capacity to defend itself required that the unions once again demonstrate their willingness to play a disruptive, insurgent role in society.*

*The Sweeny record has been a mixed one. Despite much rhetoric about and a real increase in the resources devoted to organizing, the proportion of all American workers who belong to unions has continued to decline. At the beginning of the twenty-first century, less than one in ten private sector workers are unionists, although the proportion of public employees enrolled in a labor organization stands nearly four times higher. But this failure has been counterbalanced by a genuine revitalization that has made the unions a far more potent force in American life. For the first time in two generations, the trade unions stand on the left side of American political culture. The old iron curtain that once divided official labor from many of the social movements spawned during the 1960s and the decades thereafter has begun to rust away. Many unions recruit organizers from the college campuses, ally themselves with feminists and civil rights activists, and combine traditional forms of organizing with civil disobedience and community mobilization. They have become more active and more potent in the political arena.*

*In the 1930s the union movement tripled in size. What would it take to do the same thing in the early years of the twenty-first century? What institutions and ideas stand in opposition; what social and cultural forces might provide the launching pad for such growth?*

## ⚜ D O C U M E N T S

In Document 1, John Sweeney's 1995 acceptance speech, the new AFL-CIO president outlines an ambitious organizing campaign for American labor. But organizing is a grassroots affair, as both Harvard University secretaries and California janitors can attest. In Document 2, Harvard unionists project their hope for a democratic, participatory workplace; and in Document 3, a Service Employees International Union organizer describes a successful, tactically innovative "rolling strike" in northern California. Likewise, Document 4 demonstrates that the union victory over the United Parcel Service in 1997 was a product of rank-and-file power and mobilization. Labor's new vigor soon generated a backlash, as discussed in Document 5, a Republican attack on the trade union capacity to use membership dues on behalf of labor-friendly candidates during recent election campaigns.

# 1. John Sweeney's Victory Speech Before the AFL-CIO, 1995

Brothers and sisters, in just six months we've changed the labor movement. Now we're going to change America. (Applause)

At this historic moment, I'm filled with gratitude, humility and hope. To those who supported us and fought for us and made history at this convention, I thank you; and I will honor you by implementing the changes that you have mandated. . . .

To my teammates who represent the new American workforce, Richard Trumka and Linda Chavez-Thompson, you are two of the best things that ever happened to the trade union movement.

And we owe you a great deal for our success.

I've spent a lifetime in this labor movement, and all along life's journey I've tried not to forget where I came from. This movement gives all of us something rare and wonderful. We have the chance to even the odds for people who give the world an honest day's work but don't have power over their own lives.

I thank God every day that I have the chance to do work that I love. I'm a lucky man, but this movement and this moment isn't about me or Rich or Linda or the members of this united Executive Council. This movement is about all of you and the working people that we have met along the way.

Excerpt from *1995 Convention Proceedings,* 21st Constitutional Convention, October 23–26, 1995, New York City (Washington, D.C.: AFL-CIO, 1995), pp. 309–312.

People like Machinist Bill Damaron, who joined us for our kickoff and shouted in a voice cracking with desperation, "Workers like me have been on the losing end too long."

Or janitor Maria Herrara, who described through an interpreter the futility of trying to raise a family on $5 an hour.

For the sake of Bill and Maria and hundreds of thousands of American workers like them, we begin today to build a new AFL-CIO that will be a movement of, by and for working Americans.

To the more than 13 million workers we represent and to millions more who are not represented, our commitment is firm and clear. When you struggle for justice, you will not struggle alone. Our problem is your stagnant wages. America needs a raise.

The solution is a bigger, stronger labor movement. The problem is American companies that export jobs instead of products. The solution is a union movement that fights for American workers as well as American values. The problem is that we all want to do our jobs better, but our employers too often care only about the bottom line. The solution is a union movement that fights for quality in the products we make and the services we provide. We're going to make sure that everyone knows that "union made" is another way of saying "world class."

The problem is the decline of democracy in America. We all know that the power of big money is shouting down the voices of workers and their families. The solution is all of us working together in a labor movement where we all can raise our voices from our workplaces in Washington.

Finally, the problem is that America is coming apart. We're fracturing along the lines of race, ethnicity and income. The solution is American workers coming together as never before, because this movement is for everyone, women and men, black and white, Asian-Pacific-American and Latino, white collar and blue collar and new collar.

Our unions are all that stand between America and shrinking paychecks, disappearing jobs, vanishing health care, increasing inequality and more racism, rancor and resentment.

Rich, Linda and I ran on a powerful and detailed plan for reviving American labor, and with your help we're going to put it into action.

But I'm here to tell you that the most important thing we can do starting right now, today, is to organize every working woman and man who needs a better deal and a new voice. As long as we speak for scarcely one-sixth of the workforce, we will never be able to win what we deserve at the bargaining table or in the legislative process. That is why we're going to pour resources into organizing at a pace and a scale that is unprecedented—and to offer our hands and open our ranks to workers from the Rust Belt to the Sun Belt. We're going to spread the union message from coast to coast and border to border; from clothing workers to manufacturing workers and from health care to high tech to hard hat. If anyone denies American workers their constitutional right to freedom of association, we will use old-fashioned mass demonstrations as well as sophisticated corporate campaigns to make worker rights the civil rights issue of the 1990s.

We're going to spend whatever it takes, work as hard as it takes and stick with it as long as it takes to help American workers win the right to speak for themselves in strong unions. That is what we mean by a New Voice for American workers. And we mean more than just changing the leadership of our labor federation at the top. We mean building a strong new movement from the ground up.

And as we win higher wages, better benefits and more dignity and opportunity for more workers, other workers will benefit, our current members and our future members alike.

For too long, we've been caught in a downward spiral of defeat and retreat where some lose their jobs, others give back benefits and everyone becomes less secure. We've learned the hard way that an injury to one is an injury to all. We're going to start proving that a victory for one is a victory for all.

To our employers, we say, if you are wise, labor's victories can be your victories. With decent paychecks, we can buy your products and your services. We prefer cooperation to confrontation, but we are prepared for both.

To our nation's leaders, we say, American labor is a proud part of the American community. To every officeholder in America, we say, when you do the right thing, we will be the best friends that you've ever had. But when you do the wrong thing, we will be the first in line with our criticism and last in line with our money and our people. (Standing ovation)

Next year, we're determined to go from a union summer to an American autumn. It is then that we will re-elect a president and elect a Democratic Congress committed to the people who work hard and play by the rules. To the new leadership of this movement, Linda, Rich and I say we have a mandate and a mission, and they are to fight and to win in organizing campaigns, contract struggles, political and legislative fights and the battle to shape public opinion. Together, we can meet the awesome challenges that we face.

My sisters and brothers, if you will invest your passion, your energy and your commitment, Rich, Linda and I can live up to our commitment, together with the elected members of our Executive Council, to revitalize the labor movement at every level and to our pledge to continue to change its face to represent the faces of all American workers.

Together, we can write a proud new chapter, not just in labor history, but in American history. Together, we can create a strong, new voice for American workers. And with your help, we will be heard.

## 2. Harvard Union Clerical and Technical Workers State Their Principles, 1988

Our organizing effort is founded on several simple but important principles:

First, we believe that with intelligence, good faith and creativity, differences can be overcome, rather than just covered over. Reasonable people or groups often disagree. But through cooperation and communication, they can resolve disputes and eliminate long-standing problems. Together, they can achieve things that neither could alone. But to do so, each group must have a voice. They must speak as equals, and listen with mutual respect.

From Harvard Union Clerical and Technical Workers, "Working Together," 1988, in HUCTW "We Believe in Ourselves" handout in possession of the authors.

Second, we believe in self-representation. We are building our union for this reason, and not out of anger or negativity. Responsible, self-respecting adults should represent themselves in important matters affecting their work lives. Now we are ready to participate as equals in making those decisions. We are sure that no Harvard administrator or professor would ever abdicate a right to participate in decision making, and we can no longer afford to give up that right ourselves.

Third, we believe in the mission of the university. We value our role in its educational and research work. We appreciate our relationships with Harvard's faculty, students and administrators. But too often our knowledge and expertise are overlooked, rather than treated as resources for overcoming some of Harvard's managerial problems. One example is an annual turnover rate which rivals that of many fast food employers. Working together, the union and the university can improve this situation.

Fourth, we believe that a worker is a worker regardless of her sex. Harvard's support staff is 83% women. Whether male or female, we are all hurt by the subtle effects of discrimination against women in the workplace. Now that women have permanently entered the work force in significant numbers, everyone must work together to remove economic and social barriers to their success. Pay equity must be a reality, and not merely a rhetorical flourish. Child care, parental leave and job flexibility have to be addressed seriously and comprehensively. Harvard cannot dismiss these problems of working women by claiming that such issues can only be solved on a national level.

Fifth, we believe that dedication and loyalty must be honored. Long-term employees must be dealt with as fairly as they have dealt with the university through many years of service. Tragically, "job reorganization" is often an euphemism for age discrimination. A flexible but meaningful career advancement plan would redress a salary structure that often pays new employees a salary comparable to the wages paid those with two or three decades of service. The pension plan must be dramatically overhauled. Long-term Harvard employees should be treated as an especially valuable resource, bringing continuity and perspective to a workplace that is often chaotic.

## 3. Queremos Justicia! We Want Justice! 1996

*In this article for a labor newsletter, Marcy Rein, communications coordinator for Service Employees International Union [SEIU] Local 1877 during a strike by janitors in northern California, describes the "rolling strike" strategy used to win higher wages for the union's membership.*

"In the beginning the [janitorial] contractors said, 'I'm the boss, you do what I say,'" recalls Reyna Alferez of Service Employees Local 1877's bargaining committee. Softly she continues, "I told them, 'You pay a little to us and you take a lot from us. You have Volvos and BMW's. Who makes the money to buy them?'"

From Marcy Rein, "Aggressive Tactics Help Janitors Clean Up on Contract," *Labor Notes*, September 1996.

"The employers said we're paying just a little because those people are just minority people. We got mad, and we understood that when we want something, we have to fight for it."

And fight they did. Local 1877 blindsided the contractors with a month-long rolling strike in June. The bosses never knew where trouble would visit next or how long it would stay. . . .

Local 1877 represents 5,000 janitors in four Northern California counties: Alameda, Contra Costa, San Mateo, and Santa Clara. More than 80 percent are Latino, most of the rest are African American and Asian. Under the old contract, two-thirds earned less than the federal poverty wage—$7.28 per hour for a family of four.

The janitors work for building maintenance companies, which in turn are hired by commercial real estate, high-tech, and other firms. Many of them are household names like Hewlett-Packard, Chevron and AT&T. On the pit end of the income gap, they typify the new workforce in Silicon Valley where nearly 40 percent of the jobs are subcontracted.

Justice for Janitors [the SEIU campaign] rolled into the Valley in 1991 with an organizing drive at . . . the contractor serving Apple Computer. Over the next five years, Local 1877 organized three-fourths of the janitors in the area. . . .

Four months of strike preparation began in February with the selection of bargaining committee members and worksite organizers. These members were charged with informing and mobilizing others in their buildings.

At a special convention . . . , some 700 janitors set their contract goals: one master agreement, wages above poverty level, family health insurance, and protections for immigrant workers.

Then they hit the streets, demonstrating at work, marching on San Jose Airport, and doing civil disobedience in Oakland and Palo Alto. Each action sent the same emphatic message: "Queremos justicia! We want justice!"

Meanwhile bargaining was getting nowhere. . . . A few people were fired. Two got anonymous death threats, accompanied by warnings to "stop that shift with the union."

Faced with this intimidation and a pitiful contract offer, members voted June 1 to strike.

Local 1877 organizers decided on the "rolling strike" to maximize disruption for the contractors—making it harder to hire permanent replacements—and minimize hardship for members who, living paycheck to paycheck, couldn't weather a continuous strike.

In the first week, workers struck in a different county each night, taking out three to five work sites. But in the second week the strike overran the organizers' careful plans. Workers hit in every county every night, walking out and staying out. Altogether about 70 sites were struck. . . .

Strike committees ran the strike day by day in many places. "Good people came forward who'd never done anything like strike before" said Eugenia Gutierrez, a contract enforcement rep in Oakland. "And mostly it was women who took leadership."

As in other . . . campaigns, community and labor supporters bolstered the strike. Teamsters, communications workers, and construction workers honored picket lines. . . .

Supporters joined the public actions that whirled on at a pace of two to three a week, marching and leafleting, holding a trash-in and a candlelight vigil. They helped take the janitors' case to the public and to the contractors' client companies—and built up a $40,000 strike fund.

After four weeks, the contractors gave in to most of the union's demands.

The new master contract, approved 6-1, brings all members above the current poverty wage. Annual increases average four percent. Members on the bottom of the scale get 5.5 percent, and everyone stays ahead of inflation. . . .

## 4. Big Win at UPS! 1997

The Teamsters' strike at United Parcel Service may go a long way towards bringing the American labor movement new life.

For nearly 20 years, unions have enduring a string of highly visible defeats. For over a dozen years, labor leaders and outside consultants alike have encouraged unions to shed adversarial relations in favor of labor-management cooperation. More recently, pundits have concluded that unions are no longer needed or relevant.

Now the Teamsters have stood up and said: "Oh yeah?" The spirit and solidarity the UPS Teamsters showed would not have been possible without the decades-long struggle to democratize the Teamsters. Now the democracy that was built has flowered in a most visible, and for UPSers a tangible, way.

The union captured the public's imagination and won overwhelming public support by putting the part-time issue at the top of its agenda. In doing so, it put the issue of part-time, contingent, and temporary work on the national agenda from coast to coast. In a library in Alameda County, California, part-time clericals who want full-time work to support their families are comparing themselves to UPSers. In Detroit, a contingent hospice nurse working full time without any job security thinks the same thing.

### The Settlement

The tentative agreement is a near-total victory for the union. It bears no resemblance to the company's "last, best, and final offer." It is close to the terms of the Teamster proposal that was on the table when the strike began. UPS agreed to create 10,000 new full-time jobs by combining existing part-time positions. Before the strike, the company had offered to create only 200 such jobs per year, or a total of only 1,000 over the five-year contract. These new full-time positions are in addition to an estimated 10,000 or more full-time jobs that will open up as a result of attrition and expansion. The contract requires that five out of every six full-time job openings go to current part-timers; that's up from four out of every five in the last contract.

The Teamsters defeated UPS' attempt to pull out of the union's multi-employer pension plans. The company wanted to set up its own pension plan for UPS workers only, promising that it could pay higher pensions than the Teamsters plans do. Instead, the Teamsters won increased contributions to the multi-employer plans. The union expects that higher contribution levels will allow these plans to offer benefits equal to or better than those UPS promised. . . .

---

From Jim West, "Big Win at UPS! Strike Puts Part-Timers on National Agenda," *Labor Notes,* September 1996.

The newly-created full-time jobs will start at $15 and go up to $17.50 by the end of the contract. Current part-timers will get $4.10 more over five years—that's a 50 percent increase for some; 40 percent for most. There's a small increase in the starting wage for newly-hired part-timers. They'll get $8.50 to start—up from $8.00. Their pay will increase to $10.75 after four years on the job. . . .

### How They Did It

Over and over, Teamster President Ron Carey told his members that the strike would be won on the picket line—not at the bargaining table. The members' solidarity, and the full-timers' willingness to fight for the part-timers, gave the strike its power.

The victory is also the payoff to the 20-year struggle to bring democracy to the Teamsters. When Teamsters for a Democratic Union began organizing, there was little membership involvement in the bargaining process and the union liked it that way.

In 1984, Teamster President Jackie Presser negotiated a UPS contract in secret. When local union officials showed up for the beginning of negotiations, they were told negotiations were over. In 1987, Presser ordered the UPS contract approved even though a majority had voted against it.

The whole reform process—whether it was TDU members campaigning to reject a contract or to change their local's bylaws—got members involved in the union. This accelerated when Ron Carey—president of a large UPS local in New York—won the union's first-ever democratic election for top officers in 1991.

Many of these activists were elected to lead their locals; others were shop-floor leaders who could mobilize the members even when the official leadership was reluctant. This network was key to winning this year's contract battle.

The union leadership did its part to keep the network involved. For at least nine months before the contract expired, the international organized for the campaign. They hired rank and file activists from UPS centers as coordinators; mapped out an extensive one-on-one communications network; surveyed members on the issues; published flyers; prodded locals to hold before-work rallies; and put some rank and filers on the national bargaining committee. International officers and staff traveled to local meetings around the country; some attended the TDU convention last fall.

Not all of these plans came off perfectly, but the message was clear among the ranks that "something big is happening." Some locals, such as 174 in Seattle, picketed their workplaces before contract expiration, carrying signs reading, "Just Practicing."

In a sharp contrast to standard union practice, the Teamsters kept members informed about the union's goals and the process of negotiations. Once a week during the strike, the union set up a phone network; all local unions were asked to hold meetings at that time so that members could listen to live reports.

### Public Support

Another key to victory was choosing the right issues. Fighting for full-time jobs that can support a family resonated with workers throughout the country, many of whom have similar problems. "People realize that unless something is done, the American Dream is going to be just a memory for our children and grandchildren," Carey said.

The public support buoyed the strikers' spirits and made it harder for President Clinton to intervene with a Taft-Hartley injunction. Striking package car drivers in many cities helped build support by visiting their customers to explain the strike. Some took family members or part-timers along. Although customers were inconvenienced by the strike, they were overwhelmingly supportive.

The strikers were also helped by a relatively low unemployment rate. Even before the strike, UPS was having a hard time hiring enough part-time workers; it would have been difficult to hire replacement workers quickly enough to avoid doing enormous damage to its business.

Solidarity from UPS pilots was another factor. In the midst of their own contract talks, the pilots honored Teamster picket lines and refused to fly. The Teamsters promised to return the favor if the pilots strike, as they have threatened to do later this year.

### Company Unprepared

UPS seemed to be unprepared for the kind of strike the Teamsters wages. And it must have totally misjudged how the workers and the union would handle the strike.

The company apparently thought that divisions between the Carey reformers and old guard forces loyal to Jimmy Hoffa Jr. would sap the union's unity. Old guard local leaders had refused to join a 1994 strike Carey called after UPS increased its package weight limit from 70 to 150 pounds. In 1994, the old guard stood behind the fig leaf that the strike was illegal. And since Carey had called that strike quickly, there had been little advance preparation.

Hoffa narrowly lost to Carey in last fall's election, and had since campaigned strenuously for a new election, based on the Carey campaign's fundraising irregularities, UPS apparently thought this meant Carey would be a weak strike leader, that Hoffa's old guard allies would stir up trouble to undermine Carey, and that the lack of a strike fund would send the rank and file running for their brown uniforms after a few days.

It was a hell of a misjudgment. The union had done its work. It had prepared the membership. It had chosen the right issues. And UPS workers are Carey's strongest supporters in the union. Only a handful of members scabbed. Even where local officials may have wanted to undermine the strike for partisan purposes, it would have been political suicide.

## 5. Republican Kellyanne Fitzpatrick Promotes California's Proposition 226 as "Paycheck Protection," 1998

The most important thing the Republican Party can do in '98 will occur far from Washington, D.C. and long before November. On June 2, voters in California will be faced with a singularly critical decision: whether to pass Proposition 226, the Campaign Reform Initiative ("CRI").

From Kellyanne Fitzpatrick, "Paycheck Protection," *Campaigns & Elections,* Vol. 19 (May 1998), pp. 60–61.

CRI would require labor unions to secure members' express, written permission each year before spending their dues money for political activity. If passed, CRI could take effect immediately, thereby stopping the shameless shakedown of hard-working teachers, miners and carpenters by union bosses who pay themselves six-figure salaries and use workers' money to fund political candidates and causes traditionally opposed by rank-and-file members—everything from quotas and preferences to legalization of illicit drugs to higher taxes.

Pundits who proclaimed campaign finance reform dead this year ought to turn a watchful eye toward the West, where Golden State voters are poised to send the Democratic machine a decisive message.

Called "paycheck protection" by its proponents, it's a solidly popular idea. . . . At its heart, the "paycheck protection" measure is about this nation's most cherished and enduring values, namely choice, freedom and fairness. Businessman and tireless activist Pat Rooney, who spent $2 million fighting discrimination against blacks in the Illinois insurance agent testing program, is Chairman of the Initiative in California. To Mr. Rooney, the issue is simple: "No employer and no union should have the ability to take any worker's money and use it for political purposes without that worker's consent."

Who would disagree?

The usual suspects, of course. Union bosses and their friends in high places, including Al Gore and Bill Clinton, whose re-election effort in '96 was funded in part off the backs of union men and women, oppose the initiative. In so doing, they have trotted out the same tired lexicon of "racist," "sexist," "extreme" and "right-wing" that seems to seep into every policy question where they are out-of-step with majority opinion. Ironically, and arrogantly, most of the funding for the opposition is coming from the unions themselves, as fat-cat bosses force working men and women to pony up the cash to defeat Prop 226—a practice that would be outlawed were the initiative to pass!

These opponents of the measure are scrambling like ants around a sugar cube. The AFL-CIO recently pledged to spend $13 million to defeat the initiative. In '96, the unions hurled every last penny, scare tactic and lie to regain control of the House for the Democrats. They fell short of their goal.

Most significant, though, is the opposition the union heads face within their own ranks. The California Teachers' Association's own internal polling discovered that fully 70 percent of their membership support 226. With two-thirds of union workers supportive of the initiative, and 35–40 percent of them voting Republican, the game may be up for union bosses who have been taking food out of the mouths of union babies without first asking their moms and dads.

"I feel they are extorting money from me," a union worker at Disneyland in Anaheim told Nation's Business recently. "They use my dues to campaign against politicians I support and vote for."

The raw power and rank paternalism of the union bosses in this regard is demonstrable. "There are only two groups in this country who can pick your pocket legally and without your permission: the IRS and the AFL-CIO," observes Grover Norquist, President of Americans for Tax Reform.

Polls show that only about one in five union workers are even aware that the Supreme Court has recognized their right to a refund on dues used for political activity.

In this way, the campaign for Prop 226 in California helps to expose the untoward conduct of union heads and educate the rank-and-file as to their rights.

⚶ *E S S A Y S*

In the first essay, journalist Harold Meyerson discusses why the rise of a new leadership to the very top of the AFL-CIO may be more than just a "palace coup." Organizational inertia and the political defeat of the old Meany-Kirkland leadership opened the door to a successful insurgency that soon put the AFL-CIO clearly on the left side of American politics and culture for the first time in half a century. But can different faces at the top have an impact on labor at the grassroots? In the second essay, New York University historian Robin D. G. Kelley explores the new social and demographic forces at work in urban America, where the unions face some of their greatest challenges and most significant opportunities. He argues that organized labor will flourish when its meaning and purpose become virtually synonymous with the impulses that have motivated progressives in the African American community and among the wave of Latinos and other new immigrants who have transformed the metropolitan face of the United States. Finally, in the third essay, labor educator Gordon Lafer argues that the movement to unionize graduate teaching assistants is important, not only for the well-being of these young people but because their success is part of a larger defense of academic freedom and humanistic education against corporate and market influence in so many universities.

Since John Sweeney became president of the AFL-CIO in 1995, the proportion of all U.S. workers enrolled in unions has continued a slow decline. Why then are Meyerson, Kelley, Lafer, and so many others optimistic about the fate of the labor movement in the United States?

# A New AFL-CIO

### HAROLD MEYERSON

"Does a movement ever get a second chance?" critic Irving Howe once asked of socialism after Stalin—a question that can surely be applied to the union movement in the time of John Sweeney. For forty years, labor had watched—at first, with arrogant indifference, later, with stunned helplessness—as economic and political changes eroded its ability to secure middle-class living standards for American workers. For the first twenty years after the AFL-CIO's 1995 merger, its attitude toward its strength had best been expressed by Federation president George Meany's airy assertion, when asked if he was worried about the growing number of unorganized workers, that "the organized fellow is the fellow who counts." Over the subsequent twenty years, labor—at least, everyone but Meany's successor as Federation president, Lane Kirkland—slowly came to realize that it was growing relentlessly smaller as a percentage of the workforce, and was unable to provide the kind of income and

From Harold Meyerson, "A Second Chance: The New AFL-CIO and the Prospective Revival of American Labor," in Jo-Ann Mort, ed., *Not Your Father's Union Movement: Inside the AFL-CIO* (New York: Verso, 1998), pp. 1–6, 8–23, 25–26. Reprinted by permission of Verso.

benefits to its members that it had offered in its heyday. Labor lamented its weakness in the face of a dysfunctional labor law and implacably hostile employers.

The question of whether labor can come back bears on more than the future of American unions. The waning of American labor is a prime factor in the rising levels of income polarization in the United States over the past quarter-century; in the relative stagnation of wages in the midst of soaring profits; in the attack on both government- and employer-provided health and retirement benefits and the rise of for-profit health-maintenance organizations; and in the growth of temporary, part-time and contingent jobs. The renaissance of American unions could alter these trends. It could also create an important new force for regulating the global economy to ensure a more equitable distribution of wealth—much as the union movement of the 1930s and 1940s played a key role in regulating the national economy to the same end. These are all causes that the AFL-CIO under Sweeney's leadership has taken up—already, in some instances, to considerable effect. But they are causes in which Sweeney and Co. know they cannot ultimately prevail unless and until union membership takes a quantum leap upwards.

If the Sweeney regime has delivered in many particulars, it has yet to increase labor's numbers. As a result, Republicans have sharpened their attacks, before the pendulum swings too far. . . .

It was, appropriately enough, the dismal performance of the Federation's political program in the 1994 elections that led to the insurgency against the *ancién regime* at the AFL-CIO—the first such insurgency in the 109-year history of the organization and its predecessors.

For, even as the rate of unionization had toppled and wages had stagnated while profits soared, there remained as labor's last line of defense the Democratic-controlled House of Representatives. So long as the Democrats held the House, pro-union committee chairmen would bottle up whatever union-busting brainstorms and bludgeoning of the welfare state bubbled forth from Newt Gingrich and other Hill Republicans. In November of 1994, though, forty years of Democratic rule in the House came to an abrupt end. In a little under a year, forty years of old-guard rule in labor's house met a similar fate.

The presidents of two of the Federation's four million-member unions, Gerald McEntee of the American Federation of State, County & Municipal Employees (AFSCME) and John J. Sweeney of the Service Employees International Union (SEIU), began the revolt. Historically, AFSCME and SEIU were among the relative handful of Federation unions with large-scale and highly effective political action programs of their own: as public sector unions (AFSCME almost entirely so, SEIU about half), they had a more direct stake than other Federation members in the outcomes of elections. And historically, like other politically active internationals, they had grown accustomed to bypassing the Federation's own political programs when necessary. The problem wasn't simply that the Federation's programs were too modest and too top-down to make a difference. For decades, the Federation had also tended to steer clear of campaign alliances with community, civil rights and feminist groups, while unions like AFSCME and SEIU characteristically viewed such constituencies as natural allies on matters of ideology and indispensable partners in assembling effective coalitions.

It wasn't just a critique of past Federation programs that set McEntee and Sweeney into action, however; it was also a presentiment that the current leadership would be unable to impede the Gingrich juggernaut. Shortly after the election, AFSCME and SEIU set up a multi-union coalition with a range of non-labor progressive organizations to plot strategies and to coordinate resources over the next two years. It was a direct challenge to the AFL-CIO hierarchy at 16th Street. "We don't trust you to mount the right kind of program," Sweeney and McEntee seemed to be telling Lane Kirkland and his operatives. . . .

To say that McEntee and Sweeney had strayed onto terra incognita would be to understate. No one had ever campaigned against a sitting president of the AFL-CIO. By all statistical measures, in fact, it seemed the single safest job in America. Since the American Federation of Labor had been founded by Samuel Gompers in 1886, the AFL and then the merged AFL-CIO had had just five presidents in its 109-year history—four, if you don't count the guy who held the office for one year during the middle of Gomper's thirty-seven-year tenure. During this time, there were twenty presidents of the United States and nine popes. The House of Labor was not to be rushed to judgment.

AFL-CIO presidents are elected by the presidents of all member AFL-CIO unions, each casting a ballot weighted to the size of his or her international (the president of the Teamsters cast 1.4 million votes, and so on down the line). Thus the Federation president was also protected by a most exquisite expression of working-class solidarity: an injury to one union president is an injury to all union presidents. Deposing Lane Kirkland meant he would have to be bumped by his peers, at the Federation's upcoming convention slated for October in New York. . . .

Over the past four decades, the Federation had gone from viewing organizing as unnecessary to viewing organizing as impossible. The Federation was gripped by a Brezhnevian torpor, and that attitude permeated the entire movement. The one comprehensive research project that sought to deduce just what percentage of union resources were devoted to organizing measured all union activity in California in the mid-1980s, and concluded it was roughly 2 percent. Despite the union's decline, Kirkland bewilderingly insisted that the union movement was still the powerhouse of yore, and that the cries of alarm rising from unionist and their friends amounted to unjustified hand-wringing that only served to give aid and comfort to labor's enemies (or "labor's afflicters," as Kirkland put it).

While not directly responsible for labor's neglect of organizing, the Federation had a clear responsibility for marshaling labor's political forces, and here, it had failed dismally as well. Mobilizing any sizable number of union members to pressure Congress or to swing elections was plainly beyond its capacities. Politics had come to consist of donating money to Democratic pols, who often waged campaigns devoid of issues of concern to unions. Even when it came to lobbying Capitol Hill, lobbyists for internationals complained that the Federation had failed to build a consensus for a clear legislative program in the 1993–1994 session, which proved a factor in the chaos that dissolved the session. . . .

Above all, the Federation under Kirkland was accused of having no public presence, no private planning capacity, and no energy whatever. Labor leaders were distressed that Kirkland had let Ross Perot, the eccentric nationalist billionaire, become the leading voice against the North American Free Trade Agreement (NAFTA).

"They're convinced we can't organize and they've devoted no resources to figuring out what we can do," one senior official for a leading international said in the week that the revolt broke out into the open. "The Right has a number of well-funded think tanks. We have the Economic Policy Institute, and that's all." Nor did labor fare any better with mass opinion than it did in shaping elite opinion. One 1994 poll conducted by the Peter Hart firm for the AFL-CIO showed that while the public said it would favor workers over management in disputes by a 52 to 17 percent margin, it would favor unions over management by a mere 38 to 30 percent margin. The word that most commonly arose in discussing unions in the focus groups was "dinosaur."

Finally, there was the enigmatic figure of Kirkland himself. A onetime foreign policy expert who had been a speechwriter for Adlai Stevenson during the 1952 campaign, he had succeeded the eighty-five-year-old George Meany as Federation president just six weeks before Meany's death in 1979 (after serving as the Federation's secretary-treasurer). In an increasingly media-driven age, Kirkland had a profound aversion to talk shows or interviews, as well as unconcealed contempt for the press. . . .

Discontent with the permanent government at 16th Street had long been a feature of intra-labor politics, but for years it had been confined to a distinct wing of the labor movement. In the late 1970s, opposition on the AFL-CIO executive council (comprised chiefly of the presidents of the larger AFL-CIO internationals) to Meany's and then Kirkland's policies was largely confined to three presidents: Doug Fraser of the United Auto Workers (UAW), Jerry Wurf (AFSCME), and William Winpisinger of the International Association of Machinists and Aerospace Workers (IAM). Each set up his own liberal alliances to circumvent more conservative Federation policies (Fraser established the Progressive Alliance, Wurf the Coalition of American Public Employees, Winpisinger the Citizen-Labor Energy Coalition). Each reached out to social movements that had arisen in the 1960s, an effort both to rebuild American liberalism after the rifts of the Vietnam War and to bring new blood to the unions themselves. Each lined up in intra-Democratic Party battles with their new coalition partners against more traditional cold war, Southern, and anti-reformer coalitions anchored by the AFL-CIO. All were influenced by Michael Harrington, the democratic socialist leader who sought to be a bridge between the insurgents of the 1960s and the institutions of the 1930s, and who was in turn viewed as an apostate by the more right-wing social democrats who staffed key Federation positions under both Meany and Kirkland.

During the 1970s and 1980s, other internationals that were not part of this well-defined AFL-CIO opposition caucus nonetheless began to deviate from Federation practice, if not yet from theory. The Amalgamated Clothing & Textile Workers, the Communications Workers, and the SEIU were among the few unions that persisted in organizing campaigns, and thus in hiring younger activists sympathetic to newer social movements. In the early 1990s, under the leadership of the dynamic young Richard Trumka, the United Mineworkers waged one of the very few successful strikes of the Reagan-Bush years at the Pittston, Virginia mines, from which Trumka emerged as a tribune for those union activists critical of the Federation's lethargy and timidity.

At some of these unions, a culture devoted to more militant organizing and more aggressive political action had emerged by the 1990s. Occasionally, officials of these internationals were able to persuade the Federation to embrace one of their programs, most notably the Organizing Institute, an in-house academy that trained students and rank-and-filers in the ABCs of organizing. But no clear opposition bloc developed until after the electoral debacle of 1994.

By the time the AFL-CIO executive council repaired to its winter meeting in Bal Harbour, Florida, in February, 1995, there were already three key groups of insurgent unions. The first consisted of the manufacturing unions, many of which had the most long-standing arguments with the Federation old guard; these included the UAW, the IAM, the Steelworkers, and the Mine Workers. The second comprised the two million-member public sector unions, AFSCME, and SEIU. The third was the new-model Teamsters. There, in 1991, a federally-mandated, and supervised election had elevated veteran dissident leader Ron Carey to the Teamster presidency. Carey had moved aggressively against the corrupt old guard within his union, and surrounded himself with a number of left-leaning reform activists. All three of these groups were thoroughly discontented with Kirkland's entire regime, and together they constituted over forty percent of the Federation's membership.

Yet this insurgency was not ideologically based. The revolt would not have broken out even among the most diehard anti-Kirkland unions had the Democrats maintained their hold on Congress. Nor would the revolt have succeeded without the backing of a number of historically centrist unions, from the building trades and elsewhere, whose leaders simply saw no future for American labor without a complete shift in direction at the top. The original sin of Kirklandism, finally, wasn't ideology; it was narcolepsy. While unions had declined, the Federation slept. McEntee and Sweeney had sounded a wake-up call.

No one on the executive council could remember the procedure for reviewing the performance of the Federation's president because there was no procedure. So when the council met at Bal Harbour in February of 1995, the members finally decided to close the doors and proceed around the table, letting every member have his say. By several accounts, it took five increasingly bitter hours to get around the table. When it was done, not just the three anti-Kirkland clusters were on record wishing Kirkland to go, but also some key building trades internationals: the Carpenters, Operating Engineers, Laborers, Painters, and Sheet Metal Workers. The president of the last of the Federation's four million-member internationals to be heard from, the United Food & Commercial Workers, expressed major misgivings about Kirkland's tenure. Unions whose strength amounted to nearly half the Federation members were clearly in the "Lane-Must-Go" camp, while Kirkland's defenders accounted for little more than a quarter of Federation membership. The rest of the unions perched uneasily on the fence. The insurgents were leaving Bal Harbour with a near-majority of support. And without a candidate.

There was, to be sure, a candidate who had broad support within the coalition and among the fence-sitters—only he didn't want to run against Kirkland. The reluctant candidate was Tom Donahue, the then-sixty-seven-year-old Federation secretary-treasurer who was widely acknowledged as one of the most articulate and talented leaders in the movement. Donahue had gone to work for New York's building service local in the 1950s and become one of the Federation's brightest lights under Meany—so bright that Kirkland had elevated him to the position of secretary-treasurer when he became president in 1979.

Over the years, without really rocking the Federation boat, Donahue had worked diligently to undo the groundless complacency that Kirkland seemed determined to perpetuate in every Federation policy. Donahue convened and chaired committees that issued bleak reports about labor's future. After McEntee and Sweeney and other member presidents had begun the Organizing Institute, Donahue brought the institute under the Federation's wing fighting the hide-bound and threatened Federation functionaries who sought to have it killed. And, though it was not widely realized even within labor's topmost circles, relations between Kirkland and Donahue had been chilly for years.

But Donahue would not run against the man who sponsored his rise. And there, with its candidate flatly unavailable, the insurgency paused. But it did not flounder.

For McEntee, Sweeney, and their associates had realized that victory was in their grasp, and that they could now do something that was unthinkable even two months earlier: run a public campaign for control of the AFL-CIO that raised all the questions about strategy and vision that union activists had been discussing privately for years. The insurgents began drawing up a platform and settling on a slate.

McEntee had been to that point the most visible leader of the revolt, but much of what made McEntee so implacable a foe of Kirkland—his indifference to peer group pressure, his abrasiveness, his arrogance—also made him unelectable among his fellow presidents. Mineworker President Richard Trumka was supported by some progressives as a canny strategist and dynamic speaker, but at forty-six he was widely thought to be too young and too militant to win the kind of support it would take to defeat Kirkland. Inevitably, then, the insurgents turned to Sweeney.

At first glance, John J. Sweeney seemed the most improbable of revolutionists. Portly, bald, placid in demeanor, with a voice off the sidewalks of New York, the then-sixty-one-year-old Sweeney looked like one of the Fifth-Avenue doormen he had represented at SEIU's building service local in New York. But Sweeney, in fact, had had a brilliant career as a union leader. In his fifteen year tenure at the helm of SEIU, it had grown from 625,000 to 1.1 million members—partly through mergers, but also through innovative organizing drives among public employees, health care workers, and big-city janitors. SEIU's Justice for Janitors campaign had succeeded in organizing workers whom conventional wisdom said were unorganizable— service sector workers, many of them immigrants, spread out over many worksites and different shifts, employed by contractors often based in other cities. Building coalitions with a range of community and religious organizations and re-introducing such militant tactics as sit-downs and bridge-blocking into the arsenal or organizing, the SEIU managed to organize tens of thousands of janitors around the country. At the same time, Sweeney presided over the difficult transformation of SEIU's leadership from the typical assemblage of middle-aged white men to a much more racially and sexually diverse corps of leaders.

What stood out above all else, though, was the near-doubling of SEIU's size during Sweeney's presidency. And the fact that, while most unions were spending virtually nothing on organizing and had no notion of how to grow, the SEIU under Sweeney was spending a third of its budget on getting new members and had a strategic plan for expansion.

By mid-spring, the insurgents had settled on a slate of Sweeney-for-President and Trumka-for-Secretary-Treasurer. In no small part to dramatize their commitment to racial and gender diversity (particularly since polling showed non-whites and women far more favorably disposed to unions than their white male counterparts), they rounded out the slate with Linda Chavez-Thompson as candidate for the new position of Executive Vice-President, which the upcoming convention would have to create. Chavez-Thompson, a Mexican-American born to cotton sharecropper parents in Lubbock, Texas, had been active in organizing public sector workers in right-to-work Texas, as an AFSCME vice president. . . .

Like all campaigns, the "New Voice" insurgency came complete with a slogan—"America Needs a Raise"—and a program. The slogan itself defined the campaign as something novel in labor politics: it clearly suggested a strategic mission for the labor movement, tapped into pre-existing public concern about rising inequality and working-class poverty, indicated a target population for union organizing, and sought to recapture a moral clarity that the movement had been lacking for decades. The slogan was accompanied by a program that called for devoting a third of the Federation's resources to organizing, for establishing an organizing department within the AFL-CIO that would help unions coordinate and target their efforts, for creating an independent political action program based on mobilizing members, and for a host of other reforms. Both the slogan and the program were designed to excite broad public interest and the intense interest of union activists, which they certainly did.

In the weeks immediately preceding the announcement of the slate, Kirkland realized that he could not prevail at October's convention. Belatedly, he informed Donahue of his decision, and Donahue tried at the last moment to forestall Sweeney's announcement—only to find that a solid coalition of unions had already settled on its candidates and its program. Kirkland announced his resignation shortly after the "New Voice" challenge was unveiled in June, and Donahue became interim president of the Federation, elevating CWA official Barbara Easterling to the position of secretary-treasurer. Donahue also became the candidate of the unions, such as the American Federation of Teachers, that had up until that point struck with Kirkland, as well as of other unions, like the UFCW, that had been critical of Kirkland but unwilling to align themselves with the "New Voice" forces.

In short, Donahue was in an extremely difficult position. Like Sweeney, he promised wholesale change and a quantum leap in organizing; unlike Sweeney, he presided over the ancient regime and needed its backing to hold onto his office. "He should be firing one hundred people here, and he knows who they are," said one disgruntled Federation official during the brief summer of Donahue's presidency. "But he won't—he's not a confrontational kind of guy." At most, Donahue promised a remixing of old guard and new, while the unions in the New Voice coalition were already envisioning a labor movement moving in directions the old guard wouldn't abide. . . .

By the time of the AFL-CIO convention in late October, Donahue's only hope was to pry away Sweeney's supporters in the building trades and other more traditional unions. He had one success—Doug McCarron, the new president of the Carpenters, did switch his union to Donahue's column, a shift chiefly prompted by the Byzantine politics of the building trades. The other unions held in their commitments, and Sweeney and Trumka were elected by a 56 to 44 percent margin over Donahue and Easterling. Donahue's supporters then agreed to elect Chavez-Thompson by acclamation, and both sides agreed on a common slate for an expanded executive council, which grew from thirty-five to fifty-four members. The new council was nearly 30 percent female and minority, and included such leaders as Bill Lucy, AFSCME's secretary-treasurer and the longtime president of the Coalition of Black Trade Unionists, whom Kirkland had kept from executive council membership, and Arturo Rodriguez, president of the United Farm Workers, whose founder, the late Cesar Chavez, had also been kept off the council.

Once in office, Sweeney, Trumka, and Chavez-Thompson maintained the same kind of travel schedules they had kept while campaigning. During their tenure, the Federation has held scores of regional conferences on organizing, political action, constituency groups activities, and the like, which the three constitutional officers frequently attend. All three also travelled to the sites of notable organizing drives and strikes. . . . Meany and Kirkland saw themselves primarily as bureaucratic leaders, behind-the-scenes operators for a movement that didn't require their public encouragement. Sweeney conducts his share of closed-door negotiations, too, but he also sees himself as a movement leader, whose presence symbolizes a commitment that can encourage and materially help organizers and workers embroiled in a conflict, students pondering a commitment to labor, and liberals trying to reconstruct a progressive coalition.

At the AFL-CIO's 1997 convention in Pittsburgh, Sweeney was preceded to the podium by a parade of one hundred activists from organizing drives around the country, a number of which Sweeney had visited. The display, which would have been unimaginable at any previous AFL-CIO convention, was a testament to how much labor had changed in the first two years of the Sweeney presidency—and how far it still had to ensure its survival. Clearly, there was more organizing going on than in decades. But many of the workers onstage came from drives that had yet to succeed, like the Farmworkers' campaign to organize strawberry workers in Watsonville. Most of the organizing was still confined to about a dozen unions—and even if all this organizing were successful, it would be barely sufficient to arrest the decline in the unionized share of the workforce.

The Federation had begun shifting resources to organizing almost immediately after Sweeney took office. . . . But it is at the level of the individual internationals that organizing is still either undertaken or sloughed off. A number of unions have increased their organizing budgets and staffs over the past two years, and some have won notable victories: the Teamsters at Continental Airlines, the CWA at US Air, the Laborers among New York asbestos workers, the Farmworkers in the San Joaquin Valley. The Hotel and Restaurant Employees have continued their success in organizing Las Vegas hotel workers, 45,000 of whom now work under contract in Vegas hotels. But precious few major corporations have gone union during Sweeney's tenure.

The union that is setting the pace in converting to an organizing structure is Sweeney's own Service Employees. Under the leadership of Andy Stern, formerly the union's organizing director who succeeded Sweeney as president in 1996, SEIU is currently putting 47 percent of its resources into organizing. . . . In the winter of 1998, the international had over 200 organizers on staff, while another 200 organizers worked for various SEIU locals.

This transformation has been anything but easy. In order to hire so many organizers, seven of SEIU's headquarter departments had to be closed down. At the local level, the shift of staff into organizing requires that the elected and volunteer member leaders, the shop stewards, handle the grievance processing and other member services that traditionally have been performed by staff. Elected leaders of some locals have been called upon to help other locals draft contracts. The international devotes considerable resources to helping their member locals make these kinds of transitions. "We don't know the best way to shift resources," Stern admits. "We don't know the best way to rebuild the steward system. But we have to get people in motion. You have to row before you can steer."

Nor had finding so many organizers been a simple chore. With community organizing in decline, the union has hired many off-campus organizers. It has also encountered what Stern calls the "missing generation" problem: with so few veteran organizers in the labor movement, the number of people with the experience to head a local's organizing program is woefully small. . . .

While Sweeney's emphasis on organizing is roundly applauded, the organizing programs themselves are not without their critics. The Organizing Institute's emphasis on recruiting students, which is now also common practice at SEIU and other internationals, has been questioned by other organizers who favor recruiting from within the union membership (though a number of these organizers themselves entered the movement as students). Even the critics concede, though, that by emphasizing unions' role in securing social justice and by targeting campuses with programs like Union Summer, the Federation has tapped into a new generation of activists who might otherwise never have considered working for unions.

Other critics complain, though quietly, that under Sweeney, the Federation has disproportionately prioritized low-wage workers and is relying too heavily on the rhetoric and symbols of the left in their organizing drives. Defenders of the Sweeney approach argue that polling shows that non-white and female workers—disproportionately to be found in low-wage jobs, and often connected to communities where the legacy of the civil rights movement still persists—are far more receptive to unionization than their white and male counterparts. . . .

For now at least, Sweeney's critics are not willing to make a major issue of their criticisms of that strategy. "During Kirkland's presidency, we were intellectually convinced—because of the law, because of the economy—that organizing was impossible," one staffer close to Kirkland said. "The people around Sweeney believe they can organize. And because of that, they just may."

Sweeney's commitment to transform the Federation's political program was second only to his commitment to rebuild organizing. The "New Voice" campaign called for a shift in emphasis away from donating money to candidates and toward waging labor-run campaigns on behalf of candidates and causes the movement prioritized. It called for cultivating thousands of labor candidates and tens of thousands of labor volunteers. . . .

Union political action campaigns were most successful in those places where the perestroika of American labor reached down to the local level. Just a few months after Sweeney became AFL-CIO president, for instance, a new generation of more activist leaders took control of both the California and Los Angeles labor Federations; and California, at least, saw a near-total transformation of its political programs in the 1996 vote. Within clusters of congressional and legislative districts targeted by national, state, and local federations, thousands of volunteers flooded the districts in the campaign's closing weeks. On election day, Democrats carried a range of California districts they had not won in decades, returning the Legislative to Democratic control. In all of these districts, labor made the difference.

These were also disproportionately districts with large immigrant and/or Latino populations—the district that Loretta Sanchez took from Bob Dornan among them. In California and throughout the nation, Latinos have been moving both to the polls and to the Democrats in angry response to the Republicans' support for anti-immigrant provisions in the federal welfare bill and California's Proposition 187. By and large, it has been labor—through its naturalization and get-out-the-vote programs—that has translated that anger into clout at the polls. Much as CIO organizers reached out to the second wave of immigrants in the industrial Midwest during the 1936 elections, the new union organizers—many of them involved in organizing immigrants at their worksites—are bringing the third wave of immigrants to the polls today in cities across America. . . .

The AFL-CIO's political program made all the difference. Labor had shown itself . . . to be the indispensable force in Democratic House races. . . . Individual international had become more active, too. One hundred seventy thousand members of the Steelworkers sent off letters to their congressional representatives. "We couldn't have done this," one steelworker official commented, "when we were at the height of our power forty years ago." . . .

Many . . . organizers were sent to California in the spring of 1998 to coordinate what many experts viewed as campaign doomed to defeat: the effort to turn back Proposition 226, the initiative that required unions to obtain the annual signed permission from members in order to spend dues money for political purposes. The measure would have had a chilling effect on union political programs: in Washington, the one state where an analogous measure has been enacted, union political spending has been more than halved, and the legislature and congressional delegation has gone from Scoop Jackson-Democrat to Christian right-Republican. With Democratic fortunes in California district elections heavily dependent on unions' ability to contribute money and volunteer time, an even greater political shift was forecast if, as expected, 226 passed. Indeed, 226's sponsors, most especially Grover Norquist, director of Americans for Tax Reform and a key lieutenant of Newt Gingrich, backed the measure chiefly because they felt it would enable Republicans to retake the state legislature and to hold the statehouse—thereby producing a GOP-friendly congressional reapportionment after the year 2000 census. In short, the paychecks that this so-called "paycheck-protection" measure were most intended to protect were those of the Republican majority staffers on Capitol Hill.

On its face, the initiative sounded all but unarguable: who would oppose getting members' consent for spending their money? In fact, unions engaged the individual-rights argument—though when they did, they pointed out that under the Supreme Court's Beck decision, members already had the right to withhold dues, and that the turnover rate among local union leadership was high enough to suggest that discontent with union leadership does not go unregistered. Instead, unions chiefly focused on the aggregate effect that 226 would have, and on the agendas of its backers. The measure, they argued, mandated a shift in class power in California, for it was only unions that were required to obtain such permission; corporations, for instance, did not have to obtain shareholder permission to make political donations.

While Norquist and his allies have complained that the unions ducked a discussion of the issues that 226 raised, in fact labor's campaign, which addressed the effects of erasing unions from California's political landscape, was entirely on point. Union-sponsored advertising highlighted such issues as the increased privatization of education, the continued export of jobs, and the reduction in the pressure for HMO reform—all predictable consequences of 226's enactment. The advertisements were just one part of a massive campaign the AFL-CIO threw together in a few short months. . . . Nearly sixty union staffers coordinated an effort which saw tens of thousands of AFL-CIO members walk more than 5,000 precincts, phone 650,000 union households, and hold meetings in more than 18,000 worksites. It was the most massive political mobilization the movement had mounted since 1958. And, confounding the predictions of virtually every pundit, it succeeded: a measure that had over 70 percent support in February polling went down to defeat in June by a 46 to 54 percent margin.

The unions' efforts among their own members were particularly critical. In the February polling, 67 percent of union household voters supported the measure. On election day, 64 percent of union household voters opposed it, as did 71 percent of AFL-CIO union members, and 81 percent of AFL-CIO members familiar with their union's position. Perhaps most impressive—indeed, astonishing—was the finding of one exit poll that fully 35 percent of primary voters came from union households. In a state where the rate of unionization is just 17 percent, labor's mobilization of its own members was key to the measurer's defeat. Perhaps just as impressive, Latinos opposed 226 by a 75 to 25 percent margin—a reflection of unions' increased focus on Latino workers, and a confirmation of an overall organizing strategy that increasingly targets heavily Latino workforces.

By forcing labor to spend so much time and energy on defeating 226, Norquist and Co. did succeed in delaying labor from imposing its agenda on the broader 1998 campaign: such themes as opposing the privatization of Social Security or demeaning HMO reform were still largely unvoiced at summer's outset. Despite that, the campaign against 226 had raised the level of mobilization among union members to a forty-year high, and union leaders were hopeful that they could maintain that activism for the fall campaign. The "No-on-226" campaign may have produced a defensive victory, but it was nonetheless labor's greatest victory not just of the Sweeney years but of the several preceding decades. . . .

What may be the greatest, albeit unheralded, success of John Sweeney's AFL-CIO is a new direction for contemporary liberalism. At a time when liberalism was largely stalled in the cul-de-sac of identity politics, and when support for other long-standing liberal causes was clearly collapsing, Sweeney's emphasis on issues of wage and income equity placed economic inequality at the center of modern progressivism.

Sweeney's insistence that "America needs a raise" did more than just place a new emphasis on low-wage workers whom labor would seek to organize. It also tapped into a vast public uneasiness at the Dickensian polarities of the new American economy. Even as welfare and affirmative action programs were being repealed, labor-liberal coalitions won a string of victories in campaigns to raise the minimum wage, to establish "living wage" guarantees for municipal workers, to support low-wage part-timers at UPS, and to defeat fast-track trade authority.

Labor's much-maligned position on trade, in fact, also tapped into American's anxiety about the long-term consequences of globalization, and offered liberals a nuanced and politically sustainable approach to this increasingly critical issue. Though attacked by both Republicans and New Democrats for espousing "protectionist" trade policies, Sweeney actually advanced a vision of a global mixed economy or social democracy. "If this global economy cannot be made to work for working people," Sweeney warned the annual gathering of megacapitalists at Davos, Switzerland, in 1977, "it will reap a reaction that may make the twentieth century seem tranquil by comparison."

Ironically, the fact that U.S. workers have been vulnerable for at least two decades to the kinds of corporate flight that their European counterparts are only now experiencing has meant that the American labor movement has taken the point in pushing for minimum labor and human rights standards on the global level. At the Singapore conference that established the World Trade Organization, the AFL-CIO was the leading advocate for enforceable standards. On an ongoing basis, the Federation's international department meets with unions from other nations toward the goal of formulating realistic social charters.

Freed from the strictures of a cold war foreign policy that saw the Federation align itself with every union that claimed an anti-communist pedigree, the AFL-CIO is now reaching out to a range of independent unions, "to develop cross-border organizing and bargaining strategies," as Sweeney said in a 1997 Mexico City address. Newly independent unions in Mexico have received Federation support for their struggles to organize in the maquiladoras. And in the 1997 bargaining by a dozen U.S.-based unions (coordinated by Trumka) with that most global of corporations, General Electric, the U.S. unions brought representatives from Brazil and elsewhere with GE contracts of their own to join them at the bargaining table.

The Federation's newly redirected global activism comes at a time when governments and unions throughout the world have yet to evolve a minimally effective response to the transnationalization of both corporations and investment. European workers retain the kind of wages and benefits that American workers have given up over the past two decades, though their hold grows steadily weaker as Europe-based corporations increasingly invest abroad. America, of course, has little trouble creating jobs, though many pay low wages and most offer fewer benefits than was the norm a generation ago. Europe has a growing unemployment problem, but it is Americans who place bars on their windows and gates around their homes. Neither model can be judged a success from the standpoint of working people; the Federation has recognized that a supranational model is required to address these problems, though the particulars of that model will take many years to develop.

While it is plainly too early to pass judgment on the efforts of the new AFL-CIO to rebuild the American labor movement, there can be little doubt that labor does not have an abundance of time. In 1997, the rate of private sector unionization slipped into single digits for the first time since before the New Deal. How long a de-unionized private sector workforce will be willing to support a unionized public sector workforce is a question that the movement would rather not confront, but it will have to unless the private sector organizing now getting underway results in significant victories.

What the new AFL-CIO has imparted to that movement is a new sense of urgency—and possibility. "John Sweeney has forced unions to confront whether they'll just be grave-diggers, or have a role in the new millennium," one senior official of a leading international commented in early 1998. "We're still wrestling with moving resources into organizing, and it's not easy. Still, I see people struggling with the right questions—and that's something labor hasn't seen in decades."

# How the New Working Class Can Transform Urban America

## ROBIN D. G. KELLEY

The purpose of this [reading] is not to propose a utopian movement that does not yet exist. On the contrary, the following is a survey of movements in existence right now that are trying to develop a visionary strategy for change. I will examine labor or labor-based movements that have reached beyond workplace concerns to encompass the broader community and make issues of culture, race, gender, and sexuality fundamental to their agenda. These movements have pushed working-class politics beyond a defensive posture, beyond acceptance of the principle that profit, competition, and productivity are more important for both labor and capital than social justice. They are not perfect, nor are they all "mass movements" in terms of membership and resources, but together they represent the possible future of the labor movement and the future of the city.

### Making of the New Urban Working Class

. . . [T]he pervasive imagery of the "underclass" makes the very idea of a contempo-rary urban working class seem obsolete. Instead of hardworking urban residents, many of whom are Latino, Asian-Pacific Islanders, West Indian immigrants, and U.S.-born African Americans, the dominant image of the "ghetto" is of idle black men drinking forty-ounce bottles of malt liquor and young black women "with dis-tended bellies, their youthful faces belying the fact that they are often close to deliv-ering their second or third child." . . . [W]hite leftists nostalgic for the days before identity politics allegedly undermined the "class struggle" often have trouble seeing beyond the ruddy-faced hard hats or European immigrant factory workers who populate social history's images of the American working class. The ghetto is the last place to find American workers.

If you are looking for the American working class today, however, you will do just as well to look in hospitals and universities as in the sooty industrial suburbs and smokestack districts of days past. In Bethlehem, Pennsylvania, for example, once a stronghold of the steel industry, nursing homes have become the fastest growing source of employment, and the unions that set out to organize these workers have outgrown the steelworkers' union by leaps and bounds. The new working class is also concentrated in food processing, food services, and various retail establishments. In the world of manufacturing, sweatshops are making a huge comeback, particularly in the garment industry and electronics assembling plants, and home-work (telephone sales, for example) is growing. These workers are more likely to be brown and female than the old blue-collar white boys we are so accustomed to seeing in popular culture. While white male membership dropped from 55.8 percent in 1986 to 49.7 percent in 1995, women now make up 37 percent of organized labor's membership—a higher percentage than at any time in the U.S. labor movement's history. Between 1976 and 1988, while the nation's overall labor force grew by 26 percent, the percentage of black workers rose by 38 percent, Asian American workers by 103 percent, and Latinos by 110 percent. According to the 1980 census, approximately one out of every three "Spanish origin persons" and three out of every five Asians in the United States were born in other countries.

Organizing the new immigrant labor force is perhaps the fundamental chal-lenge facing the labor movement. For one, a substantial proportion of immigrant workers is employed by small ethnic firms with little tolerance for labor unions. Besides obvious language and cultural barriers, union leaders are trying to tackle the herculean task of organizing thousands of tiny, independent, sometimes tran-sient firms. Immigrants are also less represented in public sector jobs, which tend to have a much higher percentage of unionized employees. (Indeed, the heavy concentration of native-born black people in public sector jobs partly explains why African Americans have such a high unionization rate.) The most obvious barrier to organizing immigrant workers, however, has been discriminatory immigration policy. Even before Proposition 187 got on the ballot, the 1986 Immigration Reform and Control Act imposed legal sanctions against employers of "aliens" without proper documents. Thus, even when unions were willing to organize undocumented workers, fear of deportation kept many workers from joining the labor movement.

Unions are also partly to blame for the state of labor organizing among immi-grant workers. Until recently, union leaders too often assumed that Latino and Asian workers were unorganizable or difficult to organize—arguments that have been made about women and African American workers in the past. . . . [T]he American labor movement has a long and tragic history of xenophobia, racism, and anti-immigrant sentiment. Therefore, even when union organizers were willing to approach undocumented workers, they often operated on the assumption that immigrants were easily manipulated by employers, willing to undercut prevailing wages, or were "target workers" whose goal was to make enough money to return to their place of origin.

The changing face of labor and the task of organizing workers of color turned out to be one of the most important issues in the bid for leadership of the AFL-CIO in 1995. In many ways, the victory of John Sweeney (president), Richard Trumka (secretary-treasurer), and Linda Chavez-Thompson (executive vice-president)—the triumvirate that defeated the established old guard of Tom Donahue, heir apparent to Lane Kirkland and George Meany—depended to a large degree on their position vis-à-vis the so-called minority workers. As Sweeney himself put it, "The secret to our success, and the greatest potential for organizing, is among women, people of color, and young workers." It was not Sweeney's liberal good heartedness that put the issue of women and workers of color on the agenda. Rather, it was the rank and file itself, particularly members of the public employees' unions, that for so long had been in the forefront of the battle to diversify the AFL-CIO and force it to recognize the pivotal role black, Latino, Asian-Pacific, and women workers irrespective of race and ethnicity, will play in the coming struggles. John Sturdivan, president of the American Federation of Government Employees and member of the AFL-CIO executive council, consistently challenged his colleagues to reach out to the most subordinate sectors of the working class. "As I tell my colleagues on the executive council," he explained, "if you can't promote diversity because it's the right thing to do, then look at the work force and recognize that you have to do it if you want to survive."

Very early into their respective campaigns, however, neither Donahue nor Sweeney reached out to black workers. As William Burrus, executive vice president of the American Postal Workers Union explained, "Decisions were made that Donahue and Sweeney would be the candidates . . . and those decisions were made without including us. Now, after the fact, they are reaching out to hear our views." The Coalition of Black Trade Unionists (CBTU), along with several other key black union leaders, approached the candidates about diversifying the leadership of the union but remained skeptical of Sweeney and Donahue. CBTU leader William Lucy believed that, had black labor's position been fully represented in the upper echelons of the AFL-CIO before, some of the union's recent battles, such as their fight against the North American Free Trade Agreement, might have been more successful, or at least might have been posed more sharply. In Lucy's view, NAFTA was a civil rights issue as well as a labor issue, since the agreement enables corporate interests to abandon urban communities where African Americans in particular were dependent on employment.

After the historic election of Sweeney, Trumka, and Chavez-Thompson, the pressures on the AFL-CIO to diversity did not cease. At the first convention held three months after the elections, a coalition made up of the CBTU, the A. Philip Randolph Institute, the Asian-Pacific American Labor Alliance, the Labor Council for Latin American Advancement, and the Coalition of Labor Union Women came together and called for an expansion of the executive council to include more women and people of color. As a result, they gained some modest successes: the executive council was expanded and by the close of the convention included six women, nine African Americans, one Latino and one Asian American.

As dramatic as these changes in national leadership might appear, they reflect several decades of grassroots, rank-and-file efforts on the part of workers of color to re-orient unions toward issues of social justice, racism, sexism, and cultural difference within their ranks. Indeed, one of the most significant labor-based social justice movements emerged out of the Service Employees International Union (SEIU), the union headed by John J. Sweeney before he took over the leadership of the AFL-CIO. Launched in 1985, Justice for Janitors sought to build a mass movement to win union recognition and to address the needs of a workforce made up primarily of people of color, mainly immigrants. As Sweeney explained, "The strategy of Justice for Janitors was to build a mass movement, with workers making clear that they wanted union representation and winning 'voluntary recognition' from employers. The campaign addressed the special needs of an immigrant workforce, largely from Latin America. In many cities, the janitors' cause became a civil rights movement—and a cultural crusade." Throughout the mid- to late 1980s, Justice for Janitors waged several successful "crusades" in Pittsburgh, Denver, San Diego, Los Angeles, and Washington, D.C. With support from Latino leaders and local church officials, for example, their Denver campaign yielded a sudden growth in unionization among janitors and wage increases of about ninety cents an hour.

From its inception, Justice for Janitors has been deeply committed to antiracism and mass mobilization through community-based organizing and civil disobedience. Heirs of the sit-down strikers of the 1930s and the Civil Rights movement of the 1950s and 1960s, they have waged militant, highly visible campaigns in major cities throughout the country. In Los Angeles, for example, Justice for Janitors is largely responsible for the dramatic increase in unionized custodial employees, particularly among workers contracted out by big firms to clean high-rise buildings. The percentage of janitors belonging to unions rose from 10 percent of the workforce in 1987 to 90 percent in 1995. Their success certainly did not come easily. Indeed, the turning point in their campaign began around 1990, when two hundred janitors struck International Service Systems (ISS), a Danish-owned company. A mass march in Century City, California, in support of the strikers generated enormous publicity after police viciously attacked the demonstrators. Overall, more than sixty people were hospitalized, including a pregnant woman who was beaten so severely she miscarried. An outpouring of sympathy for the strikers turned the tables, enabling them to win a contract with ISS covering some 2,500 janitors in Southern California.

. . . [I]n April 1995 Justice for Janitors (SEIU Local 399) won a major victory over seven leading Los Angeles janitorial contractors. Their threat of a strike and mass civil disobedience persuaded the contractors and the Building Owners' Management Association to agree to practically all of the union's demands. Among other things, they won a uniform minimum wage rate of $6.80, to be implemented within five years in all buildings covered by the contract. It was a significant victory because many of the incoming janitors were making as little as $4.25 an hour. Moreover, the purpose of the agreement was to bring the lowest-paid workers closer to a living wage rather than to achieve an across-the-board percentage increase for all janitors. Higher-paid workers had to sacrifice a bit, but most agreed that a unified wage base would strengthen the union movement and thus put workers in a stronger position to bargain at a later date. Justice for Janitors also defeated a management proposal that would have forced workers to pay 25 percent of their health care premiums. Instead they successfully negotiated for a fully paid family health care plan for each member, to be phased in over five years.

Justice for Janitors succeeded precisely because it was able to build links to community leaders, to forge an alliance with black and Latino organizations, churches, and progressive activists from all over the city. They built a powerful mass movement that went beyond the downtown luxury office buildings and the SEIU Local 399 headquarters into the streets and boardrooms. Their challenge is all the more remarkable when we consider the fact that Proposition 187, a California initiative denying basic rights to immigrants, had only recently been passed.

After all, the SEIU in Los Angeles was primarily a union of immigrant workers—workers at whom Proposition 187 was directed. (I should add that Local 399 and Local 660 of the SEIU, the latter under the leadership of Gilbert Cedillo, waged a militant fight against Proposition 187). Yet, what neither the contractors nor the conservative lawmakers nor many ordinary immigrant bashers realized was that, as L.A. activists Eric Mann put it, "Many of those workers began as militants in the shops and streets of El Salvador, Guatemala and Mexico. Their fight for a fair contract in Los Angeles was an 'in your face' answer to the immigrant-bashers of both political parties."

In Washington, D.C., Justice for Janitors led the struggle of Local 82 of the SEIU in its fight against U.S. Service Industries (USSI)—a private janitorial company that used nonunion labor to clean downtown office buildings. But because they conceived of themselves as a social movement, they did not stop with the protection of union jobs. In March 1995, Justice for Janitors organized several demonstrations in the district that led to over 200 arrests. Blocking traffic and engaging in other forms of civil disobedience, the protesters demanded an end to tax breaks to real estate developers as well as cutbacks in social programs for the poor. As union spokesperson Manny Pastreich put it, "This isn't just about 5,000 janitors; it's about issues that concern all D.C. residents—what's happening to their schools, their streets, their neighborhoods." Many people who participated in the March demonstrations came from all over the country, and not all were janitors. Greg Ceci, a longshoreman from Baltimore, saw the struggle as a general revitalization of the labor movement and a recognition, finally, that the unions need to lead a larger fight for social justice. "We need to reach out to the workers who have been ignored by mainstream unions. We need to fight back, and I want to be a part of it."

Indeed, D.C.'s Justice for Janitors is made up precisely of workers who have been ignored—poor women of color. Black and Latino women make up the majority of its membership, hold key leadership positions, and have put their bodies on the line for the SEIU as well the larger cause of social justice. Twenty-four-year-old Dania Herring is an example of Justice for Janitors' new leadership cadre. A mother of four and resident of one of the poorest neighborhoods in the southeast section of the District, whose husband (at the time of the demonstrations) was an unemployed bricklayer, Herring had quit her job to become a full-time organizer for Local 82 and Justice for Janitors. Yet, these women were so militant that members of Washington's District Council dismissed them as "hooligans." "Essentially, they use anarchy as a means of organizing workers," stated African American councilman Harold Brazil. "And they do that under the mantle of justice—for janitors—or whoever else they want to organize."

In the end, their challenge to the city and to USSI paid off. In December 1995, the National Labor Relations Board (NLRB) concluded that USSI had "a history of pervasive illegal conduct" by threatening, interrogating, and firing employees they deemed unacceptable, especially those committed to union organizing. African American workers, in particular, had suffered most from the wave of firings, in part because USSI, like other employers, believed immigrant workers were more malleable and less committed to unionization because of their tenuous status as residents. The pattern was clear to Amy Parker, a janitor who had worked under USSI for three years. "Before USSI got the contract to clean my building, there were 18 African-Americans. Now, I am the only one." After three steady years cleaning the same building, she earned only $5.50 an hour. The NLRB's decision against USSI, therefore, was a substantial victory for Local 82 of the SEIU. It meant that USSI could no longer discriminate against the union and it generated at least a modicum of recognition for Justice for Janitors. . . .

The most dynamic unions are also turning increasingly to community-based organizing. In situations like Los Angeles, where Latino and Asian American garment workers are spread across many small plants and shops, organizing shop by shop would prove costly and time-consuming. The Union of Needletrades, Industrial and Textile Employees (UNITE) adopted a community-based strategy that has been quite successful. In the predominantly Latino community near MacArthur Park (downtown Los Angeles), UNITE runs a "justice center" that provides language and citizenship classes, as well as a support network to help workers resolve workplace disputes. By maintaining a major presence in these neighborhoods, providing services and working with neighborhood groups, organizers not only helped build the union but gained a better understanding of the community, its culture, and its leadership base. . . .

### The Proletariat Goes to College

When we think of the contemporary labor movement, we often evoke images of overcrowded fly-by-night sweatshops, declining primary industries, huge retail conglomerates (i.e., K-Mart, Wal-Mart, and all the other multinational "marts" dotting the suburban/urban landscape). Many of my own colleagues in the groves of academe, for example, have always looked elsewhere for the working class rather than in our own campus cafes and hallways. The janitors, groundskeepers, cafeteria workers, and clerical workers are pretty much invisible on college campuses—at least until they raise their voices for better working conditions, dignity, and justice. The recent wave of campuswide strikes at places like Yale University and Barnard College, made even more pronounced by the struggles of graduate student teachers for union representation, compelled many observers to pay more attention to universities as sites of labor exploitation and corporatization. Of course, these battles were not the first time workers on college campuses fought back, but for many labor activists these recent struggles certainly highlighted the changing character and position of the American working class.

Universities (as well as hospitals) stand among the largest and fastest growing sectors of the service economy. Universities, after all, employ a vast army of clerical workers, food service workers, janitors, and other employees whose job it is to maintain the physical plant, not to mention full- and part-time faculty and researchers. In 1991, for instance, colleges and universities directly employed 2,662,085 workers—a figure that does not include employees who work for other firms contracted out by universities and colleges.

Public and private universities, like the rest of corporate America, are also undergoing major restructuring. Administrators claim that cutbacks in governmental and private support, compounded by political attacks on university affirmative action policies and multicultural curriculums, have created a major financial crisis.

The past decade has witnessed massive downsizing in staff and even faculty while enrollments have remained steady or increased. These circumstances translate into layoffs, wage freezes, speed-ups, and the increased use of part-time and temporary labor without benefits or union protection. . . .

Clearly, the university is as much a part of the "real world" as Citibank and AT&T. Institutions of higher learning are by no means above exploitation or resistance, and the rules of the game are determined by the flow of capital. Thus unions are critical for defending university employees from corporate downsizing—a lesson few full-time faculty want to acknowledge. Beyond the obvious issues facing low-wage service workers at universities, few of my colleagues recognize that they are about to be caught in the crisis themselves, especially with the elimination of tenure just around the corner, the hiring of casual labor to teach undergrads, and the reliance on academic stardom as the first wedge in the creation of a two-tiered faculty. The only way to overturn these developments is by challenging the universities we work for and the administrators who carry out these corporate downsizing policies. We have to decide whose side we are on and realize that our base of support has already been established by the very black and brown workers who clean our offices, and to whom most faculty do not even speak.

But the question of unionization is not just a pragmatic issue. What kind of unions should university employees build, especially if their work brings them in contract with students? What should be the relationship between low-wage workers, faculty, students, and the larger community? After all, despite the resemblance universities are not exactly banks or investments firms. They have historically been places where alternatives to exploitation and oppression have been discussed and imagined in an institutional setting. They have been the sites of historic movements for social change precisely because the ostensible function of the university is to interrogate knowledge, society, and history. Students and some faculty at City College of New York participated directly in the labor and unemployed movement of the 1930s; African American students at Fisk University and North Carolina Agricultural and Technical College helped launch the Civil Rights movement; the Free Speech and subsequent student movement got its start partly at the University of California at Berkeley. And even when important social movements emerged out of factory settings, such as the Dodge Revolutionary Union Movement in Detroit, students at Wayne State University played a key role.

Not surprisingly, unions that operate in the universities have not only been at the forefront of labor conflicts on campuses, but have also on occasion articulated a larger vision of social justice. Two important examples . . . took place almost three decades ago at Duke University and the University of North Carolina (UNC) at Chapel Hill. Because the struggles at Duke and UNC were as much a product of the Black Revolution in the South as the horrible working conditions of dining hall and maintenance workers, strikers made demands that extended far beyond basic bread-and-butter issues. On April 8, 1968, just four days after the assassination of Dr. King, students and faculty organized a massive sit-in in the quadrangle in front of Duke Chapel to demand $1.60 an hour minimum for nonacademic employees—primarily maintenance workers and food service employees organized in Local 77 of the American Federation of State, County, and Municipal Employees (AFSCME). They also demanded that Duke University president Douglas Knight form a grievance committee consisting of faculty, students, and employees; that he resign from the all-white Hope Valley Country Club; and that he sign a petition in support of open housing for African Americans. Despite militant opposition from workers and students, Duke University proved more powerful. When the food and maintenance workers finally returned to work, their union was in shambles.

In Chapel Hill, black food service workers at the University of North Carolina walked off their jobs in November 1969. It was the second strike that year—the first ending in success with the University paying $180,000 in back overtime. And their success depended on support from black students and faculty. The second UNC strike is remarkably similar to the struggles being waged by Yale's locals of the Federation of University Employees, in that they, too, were fighting the practice of subcontracting out work to firms that hire cheap nonunion labor. In Chapel Hill, the food service workers, members of AFSCME, fought the university's decision to contract out the running of dining halls by Saga Food Service. Saga had pretty much ignored the earlier contract between the university and strikers, and had apparently fired ten workers for alleged union membership. They also cut back UNC's staff from 147 to 100, despite protestations from workers. It turned out to be an extremely violent strike, with sixteen arrests and six people injured—most of whom were students in solidarity with striking workers.

Both of these strikes anticipated the current situation university workers are facing, and they both point to the need to think critically about the unique opportunities universities offer as sites of working-class struggle. First, during the last quarter-century, at least, subcontracting has been part of a larger corporate strategy to reduce wages and benefits and to bring in casualized, temporary, nonunion labor. Of course, this general trend mirrors the rest of the corporate world, but within a university it also serves to take the administration off the hook by rendering even more invisible the exploitation of labor at the university. University officials work hard to project an image of their campuses as places of free exchange and intellectual inquiry. That universities are often the biggest exploiters of labor, not to mention the biggest landlords in some cities, is a fact their public relations people try to bury.

Second, the low-wage workforce at most major universities and colleges really reflects the American working class in general, and the renewed labor movement in particular. Workers of color, especially women, were at the forefront of the struggles at Duke and UNC in the late 1960s. . . . Despite the fact that these workers tend to have relatively high union participation rates, they are nevertheless among the poorest paid and most exploited workers on campus. Indeed, Yale officials could justify such draconian policies toward dining hall and custodial workers precisely because these kinds of jobs have historically been associated with black labor (domestic servants, janitors, and the like). Racism and sexism largely explain the disparity in wages, as well as the labeling of these jobs as unskilled. Clearly there is skill involved, but definitions of skill are raced, sexed, and historically determined. Hence, any union fighting for the rights of low-wage service workers, in the university or elsewhere, must make the struggle against racism and sexism fundamental.

Finally, the role of students and faculty in all of these strikes offers key lessons for future labor conflicts on college campuses. At both Duke and UNC, student and faculty support was pivotal. During the UNC strike, for example, student groups mobilized African American students from all over the state of North Carolina to descend on campus to observe "Black Monday" when the university failed to reach a settlement. Fear of unrest forced Chapel Hill Mayor Howard Lee to withdraw police from campus and compelled university officials to negotiate a settlement between the union and the Saga Food Service. Students helped organize workers, joined picket lines, and incorporated tactics developed in the Civil Rights movement. . . .

Unions at the universities and elsewhere need to adopt a broad vision of social justice if they are to succeed. They cannot be business-as-usual unions. They need to embrace a far-reaching civil rights agenda and the struggle against class-based racism in addition to the basic bread-and-butter issues. One sparkling example of a campus union that embraces such a broad-reaching, antiracist agenda is the Campaign to Organize Graduate Students (COGS) at the University of Iowa. An affiliate of the United Electrical Workers (UE), COGS insisted that the university administration agree to a "no discrimination" clause in their contract. Such a clause, consistent with the University of Iowa's own human rights policy, would enable graduate student employees to use a union grievance procedure to deal with workplace discrimination. When the administration refused, COGS activists decided to protest the university's position by disrupting a highly publicized campus lecture by visiting historian Taylor Branch, author of a Pulitzer Prize–winning biography of Dr. Martin Luther King, Jr., to honor King's birthday in January 1997. A group of about forty students marched into the auditorium ten minutes before Branch's talk carrying signs and leaflets that read "Respect the Memory: Support the No Discrimination Clause," and singing "This Little Light of Mine." Their presence won support of the crowd and revealed to many observers that discrimination was not a thing of the past. While the demonstration was a success, behind the scenes UE staff persons and their allies in COGS tried to block the event, arguing that it would upset delicate contract negotiations. Whereas the "veteran" labor organizers believed that basic "bread-and-butter" issues should take precedence over antiracism and antisexism, COGS activists such as John Scott, David Colman, Margaret Loose, and Paul Young recognized how inseparable these issues are. Fortunately, the militant wing of COGs prevailed, proving that it is possible to build a dynamic labor movement without subordinating race or gender. As COGS leader and veteran black radical John Scott put it in a moving speech to his fellow graduate students, never in his twenty-six years of movement work had he ever been involved with a predominantly white union willing to risk contract negotiations in support of racial justice. Perhaps a new day is on the horizon.

Movements like these contain the seeds of a new political vision. A new vision is something progressives and labor organizers are sorely lacking, especially when it comes to dealing with the problems of a predominantly nonwhite urban working class relegated to low-wage service work, part-time work, or outright joblessness. Ironically, universities might ultimately be the source of a new radical vision, but instead of looking to the classroom and its attendant culture wars, we should pay more attention to the cafeteria.

# Graduate Student Unions Fight
# the Corporate University

## GORDON LAFER

[In 2001], graduate students at New York University made history when they won recognition for the first graduate student union at a private university. To accomplish this feat, students had to overcome the political and legal opposition of virtually every elite school in the country. In a series of hearings before the National Labor Relations Board, arguments opposing the union were voiced not only by NYU's own administration but by those of Yale, Princeton, Columbia University, the Massachusetts Institute of Technology, Stanford, John Hopkins, Boston University, the American Association of Universities, the American Council on Education, and the Council on Graduate Schools. In a series of landmark rulings, the Labor Board rejected the arguments of these scions of higher education and opened the door to a new wave of organizing on the nation's campuses.

The fact that the entire organizational leadership of elite higher eduction mobilized against the NYU union indicates what was at stake in this fight. In fact, though, the NYU decision was only one of several . . . decisions that have marked a sea [of] change in academic labor relations. . . . [Labor board] officials in California, Illinois, and Pennsylvania have issued rulings similar to that in the NYU case, invalidating the claims made by administrators for the past two decades. These rulings have helped to spur an unprecedented boom in graduate student organizing. Within three months of the NYU union's winning recognition, unions were voted in by lopsided margins at both Temple University and Michigan State University, a majority of graduate students at Columbia and Brown petitioned the NLRB for an election, and new organizing drives were announced at Penn State and the University of Pennsylvania. These activities come on the heels of what is already a fast-growing movement. Since 1995, the number of graduate student unions in the country has grown from ten to twenty-seven, and an estimated 20 percent of all graduate employees are now covered by union contracts—a level comparable to the most highly organized states in the country and 50 percent above the national norm.

## The Economic Function of Graduate Students
## in the Corporate University

Although the legal decisions have been important, the recent boom in organizing activity is primarily a reaction to dynamics within the university itself. The traditional ideal of college education pictures a setting that is specifically outside the rat race—an opportunity to explore ideas, make friendships, and develop a sense of one's self in ways that are not possible amid the dog-eat-dog pressures of commercial life. However, for the past thirty years, universities have moved progressively away from this community-of-scholars model, fashioning themselves instead in the image of private corporations. Rather than pursuing the romantic vision of the classroom as

From Gordon Lafer, "Graduate Student Unions Fight the Corporate University," *Dissent* (Fall 2001), pp. 63–70.

an encounter between seasoned scholars and eager young minds, administrators across the country have radically shifted teaching duties away from regular faculty and onto the shoulders of graduate students and adjunct instructors. The economic logic of this strategy is simple to grasp: in 1999, an average full professor earned $71,000 per year, while graduate student teachers earned between $5,000 and $20,000. Not surprisingly, the number of tenure-track faculty was cut by 10 percent between 1975 and 1995—a period during which overall enrollment was expanding significantly—while the number of graduate teaching assistants increased by nearly 40 percent. Nationally, it is estimated that between 50 percent and 70 percent of all teaching hours are now performed by graduate students and other contingent teachers; an undergraduate signing up for an introductory English class has less than a one-in-four chance of being taught by a tenure-track professor. And in both natural science and humanities departments, graduate students are responsible for 90 percent of the grading. As administrators have been increasingly driven by bottom-line considerations, graduate students have become an indispensable ingredient in the financial calculations of every major university.

Moreover, graduate students appear likely to play an even more central role in what are emerging as the critical growth markets for American universities: corporate research in the natural sciences and distance learning in the humanities and social sciences. Across the country, administrators are competing to cement corporate partnerships supporting jointly funded science research. Beyond the immediate value of funding, universities have been accelerating efforts to capture the intellectual property rights that emerge from this research, with many schools pioneering in-house venture-capital offices to support for-profit startups based on the results of laboratory research. The potential earnings from pharmaceutical, technology, and biotech patents represent a major new profit center for university managers and have led many schools to market their science departments aggressively to potential private sector partners.

For the university, these joint ventures are valuable sources of revenue to complement or replace federal science funding, along with the lure of future profits on a scale never before contemplated. For pharmaceutical giants, they are a much cheaper alternative to in-house research. Outside the confines of the nation's campuses, it is impossible to get highly educated scientists to do rigorous work for sixty hours a week at $20,000 per year; this is the unbeatable deal that universities offer their corporate partners. This win-win solution, however, relies critically on the availability of thousands of graduate students who are simultaneously among the nation's most highly trained and most poorly paid technology workers.

In the humanities and social science departments, the key emerging market is distance learning. Administrators across the country are racing each other to establish online courses that will be sold to a variety of market niches: working adults who can afford tuition but are unable to attend on-campus classes, individuals in rural communities who are willing to pay for a more marketable degree than that provided by the local community college, and wealthy foreigners who may be eager to pay a premium for an American degree. Administrators have rushed headlong into this emerging market. In 1998, NYU itself made history when it became the first university in the country to establish a for-profit subsidiary devoted to capturing the distance-learning market. If graduate assistants are instrumental to the delivery of large lecture classes on campus, their importance will be multiplied when popular courses are marketed to tens of thousands of students around the globe. Although distance learning may suggest a fully automated education, it is unlikely that tuition-paying students will settle for it. As the market gets more competitive, wealthy consumers in Beijing or Bangalore will look for online chat-classrooms, e-mail "office hours," and detailed feedback on term papers.

Indeed, as universities look to identify market winners, most faculty are likely to be squeezed out of the virtual university. In the beginning stages, thousands of professors may be asked to convert their current courses into online offerings. Ultimately, however, the logic of distance learning means that universities will look to standardize their educational products by patenting the lectures and course materials of name faculty who will serve as "content providers"; thus, students in Hong Kong may sign up for the "Henry Kissinger Lectures in Post-War Diplomacy" or similar name-brand courses. Clearly, the big names will have little or no contact with students; their time is too expensive. The profit strategy of these new ventures, then, relies explicitly on an army of graduate students and adjuncts to monitor online discussions, critique papers, answer questions, and get to know individual students' work well enough to write the obligatory letters of recommendation. Similar applications are now being developed for science departments as well; thus MIT recently announced an ambitous effort, developed in collaboration with Microsoft Research, to create online science labs that would allow physics and engineering students to participate in laboratory instruction from remote portals. Here too, it is likely that graduate students will play a critical role in the creation of the for-profit market for online laboratory training.

But the same dynamics that make graduate students such a good buy while they are in school make them increasingly unemployable after they complete their degrees, leading a coalition of national faculty associations to bemoan "the vanishing traditional faculty member." The wholesale substitution of casual teachers for tenure-track positions has marked the decimation of the academic job market. At Yale, it was estimated that the use of graduate teachers produced a savings of over $5 million per year and allowed administrators to eliminate nearly two hundred junior faculty positions at that school alone. . . . In the natural sciences, the turn to commercially sponsored research has likewise encouraged a more corporate structure in which a limited number of principal investigators oversee a large staff of graduate students and postdoctoral fellows. As a result, the number of faculty positions has decreased while the time one is expected to apprentice in the purgatory between graduate school and a junior faculty slot has lengthened, with Ph.D.'s in the biological sciences now spending an average of four years in low-wage postdoctoral "fellowships." Even at the nation's top schools, the share of life sciences Ph.D.s who go on to permanent research jobs in either academia or industry has fallen from 87 percent in 1973 to 56 percent in 1995. The Commission on Life Sciences warns that "many graduate students entered life science training with the expectation that they would become like their mentors: they would be able to establish laboratories in which they would pursue research based on their own scientific ideas. The reality that now faces many of them seems very different."

Finally, even those ultimately lucky enough to land tenure-track positions find that they are still not inhabiting the lives of their mentors. While other professional salaries have soared over the past three decades, downsizing has enabled university administrators to cut faculty pay, despite significant growth in the higher education market. At the end of the century, average salaries for tenured faculty were approximately 5 percent lower than they were in 1970. This, then, is the contradiction that lies at the heart of the corporatization process: the very dynamics that make graduate students so useful to the business mission of the university are also destroying the academic careers that are supposed to justify the long haul of earning a Ph.D.

In the 1980 National Labor Relations Board Yeshiva University case that largely banned faculty unions at private universities, Justice William Brennan's dissent warned of the dangers of leaving academia a union-free environment. Removing the possibility of faculty organizing, he predicted, "threatens to eliminate much of the administration's incentive to resolve its disputes . . . through open discussion and mutual agreement . . . [and] removes whatever deterrent value [labor law] may offer against unreasonable administrative conduct." Twenty years later, it appears that graduate education has fallen victim, in part, to just this unchecked administrative power feared by Brennan. Given a free hand to unilaterally mold the university to their own liking, administrators have produced a system that—while financially successful—has undercut much of what used to stand at the heart of academic life.

## Anti-unionism and "Academic Freedom"

For twenty years, administrators across the country have relied on a common set of arguments to oppose granting their graduate students the same rights afforded secretaries and librarians: that graduate teachers and researchers are "students, not employees," that the tasks they carry out are "training, not work," and that unionization would destroy the collegiality of campus relations. These arguments, carefully honed by anti-union lawyers, were all decisively rejected by the Labor Board. The single most counter-intuitive argument launched against unionization is the proposition that unions threaten academic freedom. NYU asserted that all working conditions of teachers—including salary and workload—were "educational policy" issues that could not be subject to collective bargaining without undermining fundamental freedoms. The Labor Board roundly rebuffed this argument. The university already negotiates over terms of employment with individual graduate students, the board noted, as individuals are free to reject teaching positions if they deem the salary inadequate. Thus, NYU's real concern was to avoid negotiating terms of employment collectively rather than individually, presumably based on the fear that collective bargaining would prove more expensive. But this has nothing to do with academic freedom and, on the contrary, amounts to a direct refutation of the very purpose of federal labor law—to provide workers the ability to negotiate on a more even footing with their employers. The administration's argument, the Labor Board concluded, "runs directly contrary to the express purposes of the [National Labor Relations] Act." . . .

Indeed, all the arguments about academic freedom ring hollow for a simple reason: this problem has already been solved. Administrators often talk as if the prospect of academic bargaining is a new problem, fraught with unknown procedures and unpredictable pitfalls. In fact, the correct response to this worry is: been there, done that. Both graduate student unions and faculty unions have been conducting negotiations for decades; in all this time, there has never been a suggestion that academic freedom was compromised. "After nearly 30 years of experience with bargaining units of faculty members," the Labor Board concluded, "we are confident" that issues of academic versus employment considerations can be easily resolved.

Nevertheless, there is a meaningful—and disturbing—conception of "academic freedom" that animates administrators' opposition to unionization. It is telling that both NYU and Columbia administrators have pointed to charges that the Labor Board filed against Yale faculty in the wake of that school's 1996 graduate teachers' strike as evidence of the propensity of unions to chill academic freedom. In the case in question, Yale faculty and administrators threatened strike participants with being banned from future teaching assignments; suggested that participants could be kicked out of graduate school; and adopted a policy allowing faculty advisers to write negative letters of recommendation on the basis of strike participation. These reprisals led the federal government to file charges against Yale administrators and faculty and to resolutions of censure against the school from the Modern Language Association, the American History Association, and the American Association of University Professors (AAUP). Ultimately, the government dropped most of its charges based on a technicality regarding the particular form of this strike—withholding undergraduate grades at the conclusion of the fall semester—even though such threats would clearly be illegal in the context of a normal teaching strike. The Labor Board agreed to a settlement on the remaining charges that required Yale to post prominent notices outside the graduate school administration offices promising that in the future no employee would be subject to threats for participation in union activities.

Given that there is no question the threats voiced during the grade strike would be prima facie illegal in a normal strike action, it is curious that administrators have chosen to uphold these reprisals as the hallmark of academic freedom. For most of the academic community, academic freedom consists precisely in the protection against such threats. Nevertheless, Columbia administrators now cite the Yale case as an instance of unions threatening a hallowed right of academic freedom. Similarly, Yale provost Alison Richard charges that applying the Labor Board's standard of behavior to faculty—that is, banning the use of "threats" or promises" to turn graduate students against the union—would undermine the fundamental nature of higher education. "These restrictions on what could be legally discussed with an employee,'" Richard insists, "would strike at the freedom of expression central to the whole conception of the university as an intellectual community." In the minds of campus administrators, then, the principle of "academic freedom" has been reformulated along frighteningly Orwellian lines. The revised principle seems to boil down to the right of administrators to threaten those lower down the academic food chain. This debate over contrasting visions of academic freedom points, at the deepest levels, to what is at stake in campus organizing campaigns. Beyond the immediate economic issues of wages and benefits, this is a fight over the extent to which universities will be democratized. The romantic vision of the medieval university run by its scholars is long gone. But the difference between a democratized and corporatized university remains more critical than ever as universities face the future.

## Faculty: Caught in the Crossfire?

The second front of the graduate unionization struggle is the administrators' war for the hearts and minds of campus faculty. Graduate student unions have repeatedly insisted that their conflict is solely with the central administration. Faculty have, in fact, found unions easy to work with. In a comprehensive survey of faculty at universities with established graduate student unions, 95 percent of faculty stated that graduate student collective bargaining did not inhibit the free exchange of ideas between faculty and graduate students; an overwhelming majority reported similarly that graduate student unions had not created an adversarial relationship, and that the union had not inhibited their ability to advise or mentor their own students. Administrators, though, have adopted a conscious strategy of placing faculty at the fulcrum of union conflicts. Thus, one school's recommendation to fellow administrators was to stock the university's negotiating committee with a majority of faculty members—even though they would have no final say over university positions. By forcing graduate students to negotiate with those who hold the most immediate power over their coursework, grades, and ultimate career prospects, administrators seek to gain an edge in intimidating graduate employees into substandard settlements. Faculty are encouraged to play this role, in part, by administration suggestions that unions threaten the freedoms of faculty themselves. In fact, faculty may find that the biggest threat to academic freedom comes from above. Administrators' anti-unionism has too often led them to impose the equivalent of an academic state of emergency, in which the normal protections of faculty and graduate students are suspended, with everything subject to the single goal of beating back organizing efforts. Increasingly, these anti-union campaigns have threatened the liberties of faculty as well as graduate students. Earlier this year, for instance, the dean at the State University of New York at Buffalo removed Professor Barbara Bono from her position as chair of the English department after she refused to sign a letter threatening striking graduate student teachers with being banned from future employment. Professor Bono explained, "I was not going to turn to threatening my students." One might view this as a noble defense of the mentoring relationship. In the eyes of the administration, however, department chairs are delinquent in their duties if they refuse to be part of the anti-union machinery. Thus, Dean Charles Stiger explained that he removed Professor Bono because "she expressed considerable sympathy for the students' situation and didn't see that forceful action was required." . . .

Just as administrators may have feared, the success of graduate student unions have spurred increased organizing among other academic employees, including both adjunct and tenure-track faculty. Ironically, in the private sector, the same corporate ethos that has redefined the university may serve to reinstate the Labor Board's recognition of faculty as employees rather than managers, restoring the right to private university professors to organize. The Yeshiva decision drastically restricted faculty organizing on the basis that, in the model of medieval scholarly communities, faculty hold primary decision-making authority and therefore are themselves managerial employees with no right to organize. "If there were a single group comprising the essential heart of management," Yeshiva's lawyers insisted, "it would be the faculty." If this description of faculty-run universities was dated.in 1980, it has become utterly untenable twenty years later. As the president of NYU's AAUP chapter notes, "today it's undeniable that universities . . . are modeled not on medieval guilds, governed by their members, but on modern corporations." . . . While the Yeshiva ruling remains in effect until challenged at the Supreme Court level, the recent reasoning of the Labor Board suggests that—with the dramatic changes in university governance over the past twenty years—faculty on more and more campuses may be defined as not fitting the fact—pattern outlined in Yeshiva. At some point, a new faculty union will force this principle to be reheard in federal court; and when this happens, the administrators who have remade the university in the decades since faculty were cut out of collective bargaining will be hard-pressed to keep a straight face while suggesting that faculty still run the place.

### Where Do We Go From Here?

. . . [T]here is every sign that the recent boom in graduate student unionization will continue. . . . While an outright reversal of the NYU precedent is unlikely, some administrators have pinned their hopes on an ambitious effort to re-disguise graduate employment as training. On the final day of NYU's forty-two-day hearing before the Labor Board, the school's attorneys rushed into evidence a plan to make over the funding mechanism for graduate education as a whole. Under the new scheme, most graduate students will receive a fixed stipend for five years and will be required to teach several times in order to obtain their degree. Since teaching will then be an educational degree requirement, and graduate students will receive the same "stipend" during semesters when they teach as when they do not, the university argued that this plan would legally convert graduate teachers back into "students" and their work back into "training." The Labor Board rejected this late-minute maneuver; but similar efforts lie at the heart of current anti-union strategies at Yale, Columbia, and elsewhere.

Administrators face an uphill battle, because the reality of graduate student teaching loads makes it hard to conceal their work through the magic of newly invented degree requirements. For instance, the Labor Board's ruling was partly predicated on the fact that "the number of TA positions available is tied to undergraduate enrollment, not graduate enrollment." In order to disguise the work of graduate teachers as part of their own educational training, administrators must concoct elaborate rationales for "training" assignments that happen to match up perfectly with undergraduate teaching needs. . . .

It is unclear what the chances of such a project are. The Internal Revenue Service, the Immigration and Naturalization Service, and federal financial aid offices all have regulations based on the assumption that graduate teachers are employees; and it is unlikely that administrator's re-labeling projects will convince them not to deduct payroll taxes. Moreover, the amount of work done by graduate students is simply too great and too varied to be disguised out of existence. The bottom line, in the Labor Board's words, is that "the undergraduate students at NYU, qua customers, pay for the services they receive, which are provided to a large degree by the graduate assistants. . . . If the services were not provided by the graduate assistants, they would be provided by instructors who may be statutory employees."

Thus, unless universities actually reverse the trends of the past three decades, dramatically cutting graduate teaching and boosting tenure-track hires, administrators appear to be stuck. And with all the creative strategies at their disposal, the one thing universities cannot do is decrease their reliance on graduate labor. The fact that administrators have responded to the NYU ruling not by finally honoring the democratic rights of their own graduate employees, but by devoting their primary energy to a transparently Orwellian scheme whose sole purpose is to disempower the very people the university is charged with mentoring, is a testament to administrators' desperation to maintain corporate control. We have moved very far from the model of the university as a community of scholars.

Finally, there is an on-the-ground reality to the new unions that will not be changed even if the law is reinterpreted. At NYU and Columbia, national union representatives warn that "once teachers have gotten organized, we will never go away. We have made a commitment—these people are part of our union—and law or no law we will stick with it to make sure there is a fair contract for graduate teachers." Perhaps the most prescient advice comes from leaders of the California state legislature. When University of California administrators refused to bargain with their graduate student union, the leaders of the state Assembly and Senate warned them that, all legalities aside, their strategy had plainly backfired: after a fifteen-year campaign to defeat unionization, "huge sums of state money have been spent . . . to circumvent recognition . . . [but] the movement has grown stronger and deeper."

## ✦ *F U R T H E R    R E A D I N G*

Bronfenbrenner, Kate, et al., eds. *Organizing to Win: New Research on Union Strategies* (1998).

Davis, Mike. *Magical Urbanism: Latinos Reinvent the U.S. City* (2001).

Fraser, Jill Andresky. *White Collar Sweatshop: The Deterioration of Work and Its Rewards in Corporate America* (2001).

Gottschalk, Marie. *The Shadow Welfare State: Labor, Business, and the Politics of Health Care in the United States* (2001).

Juravich, Tom, and Kate Bronfenbrenner. *Ravenswood: The Steelworkers' Victory and the Revival of American Labor* (1999).

Klein, Naomi. *No Logo: Taking Aim at the Brand Bullies* (1999).

Lynd, Staughton, and Alice Lynd, ed. *The New Rank and File* (2000).

Milkman, Ruth, ed. *Organizing Immigrants: The Challenge for Unions in Contemporary California* (2000).

Mort, Jo-Ann. *Not Your Father's Union Movement: Inside the AFL-CIO* (1998).

Nissin, Bruce, ed. *Unions and Workplace Reorganization* (1997).

———, ed. *Which Direction for Organized Labor? Essays on Organizing, Outreach, and Internal Transformations* (1999).

Tillman, Ray, and Michael Cummings, eds. *The Transformation of U.S. Unions: Voices, Visions, and Strategies from the Grassroots* (1999).

Zweig, Michael. *The Working Class Majority: America's Best Kept Secret* (2000).

# American Labor;
# A Statistical Portrait

---

**Figure 1    U.S. Work Stoppages Involving 1,000 Workers or More, 1947–2000**

---

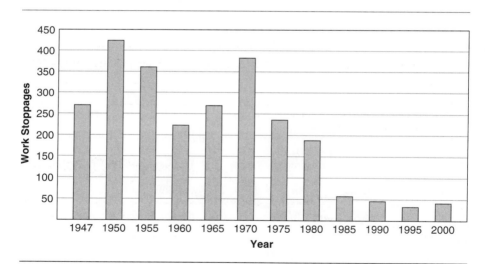

Bureau of Labor Statistics press release, 2000.

**Figure 2   Trade Union Membership as a Proportion of All U.S. Workers, 1930–2000**

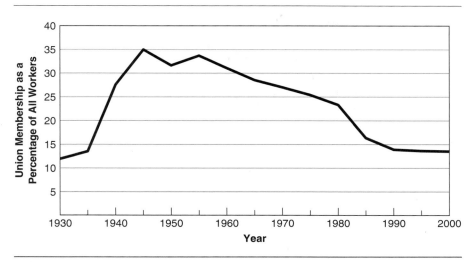

U.S. Bureau of the Census, *Historical Statistics of the United States, Colonial Times to 1970* (Washington, D.C.: Government Printing Office, 1975), p. 178; Bureau of Labor Statistics Press Releases, 1990, 2001.

**Figure 3   Percentage of Women in the U.S. Labor Force by Marital Status, 1947–1997**

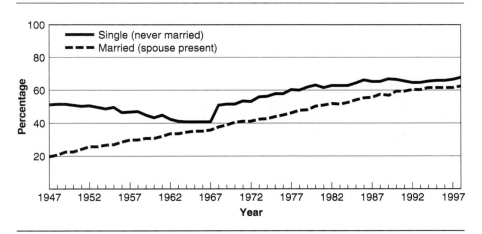

Data for 1947–1966 include women fourteen years old and older. Beginning in 1967, all data refer to women ages sixteen and older. Single teenagers not in the labor force may be in school.
U.S. Department of Labor, Bureau of Labor Statistics.

**Figure 4     Earnings Differences Between U.S. Women and Men, 1951–1999**

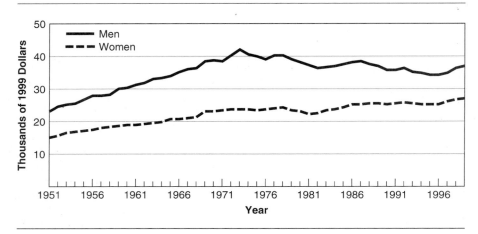

U.S. Census Bureau, March Supplement to the Current Population Survey. Median annual earnings for full-time, year-round workers, age fifteen or more.

**Figure 5     Employment Rates Grouped by Race and Sex, 1975, 1990, and 1996**

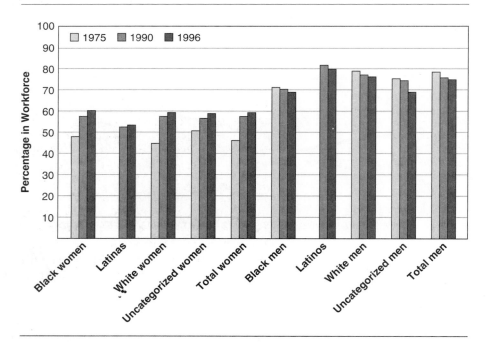

Bureau of Labor Statistics.